(6a)

647
668

PURCHASING AND MATERIALS MANAGEMENT
Text and Cases

McGRAW-HILL SERIES IN MANAGEMENT

Keith Davis and Fred Luthans, Consulting Editors

McGRAW-HILL SERIES IN MARKETING

Consulting Editor
Charles Schewe
University of Massachusetts

PURCHASING AND MATERIALS MANAGEMENT

Text and Cases

Third Edition

Lamar Lee, Jr.
Stanford University
Retired

Donald W. Dobler
College of Business
Colorado State University

McGRAW-HILL BOOK COMPANY
New York St. Louis San Francisco Auckland Bogotá Düsseldorf
Johannesburg London Madrid Mexico Montreal
New Delhi Panama Paris São Paulo Singapore Sydney Tokyo Toronto

PURCHASING AND MATERIALS MANAGEMENT
Text and Cases

Copyright © 1977, 1971, 1965 by McGraw-Hill, Inc. All rights
reserved. Printed in the United States of America. No part of this
publication may be reproduced, stored in a retrieval system, or
transmitted, in any form or by any means, electronic, mechanical,
photocopying, recording, or otherwise, without the prior written
permission of the publisher.

7890 DODO 83210

This book was set in Times Roman by Black Dot, Inc. The editors
were William J. Kane and Michael Weber; the cover was designed by
John Hite; the production supervisor was Angela Kardovich.
R. R. Donnelley & Sons Company was printer and binder.

Library of Congress Cataloging in Publication Data

Lee, Lamar.
    Purchasing and materials management.

    (McGraw-Hill series in marketing)
    (McGraw-Hill Series in Management)
    Bibliography: p.
    Includes indexes.
    1. Industrial procurement. 2. Purchasing.
3. Materials management. I. Dobler, Donald W., joint
author. II. Title.
HD52.5.L4   1977   658.7   76-20611
ISBN 0-07-037027-3

Contents

Preface

This book discusses the management of materials and the control of material costs in a business enterprise. It emphasizes purchasing as a primary materials activity; however, it also explicitly integrates the purchasing activity with all other materials activities. Further, the book views the purchasing and materials function in the context of a total business operation; it consistently relates this function to relevant activities in the engineering, production, marketing, and finance functions, as well as to the business as a whole.

In recent years, the purchasing and materials function has undergone a complete reevaluation by business management. Materials management is sometimes described as "the last gold mine" for business managers. Indeed, it is among the last of the specialized business functions to be centralized and given the responsibility and the authority for making major contributions to profits. Yet progress in this area of business management is just beginning.

In most business operations today, the cost of materials is the last remaining cost that is truly variable—all other major costs are either fixed or tend to be semifixed. Hence, a reduction in the cost of materials per se clearly offers an unusual opportunity for profit improvement. When one considers that materials cost in a typical manufacturing firm represents approximately 50 percent of total cost, the opportunity for profit improvement in the materials area is virtually impossible to match in any other area of business operation.

To date, only the most progressive manufacturing firms realize that materials availability, engineering/purchasing specifications, fabrication cost, and distribution cost are all factors which impinge on total materials cost. These progressive firms also realize that all materials cost factors must be coordinated and controlled by a systems-oriented materials management department if total materials cost is to be optimized. Regrettably, most manufacturers still have to learn the two basic materials lessons that the nation's large, successful retailers learned over forty years ago: (1) buying well is as important as selling well, and (2) even the most capable sales effort cannot compensate for poor purchasing specifications.

Fundamental economic reasons such as those noted above, coupled with business' growing recognition of the superiority of the systems approach to management made possible by continuing advances in electronic data processing, are what essentially guarantee continued development and utilization of materials management in American business and industry.

This book is written primarily for college students preparing for careers in business. Its use, however, is not limited to students with career interests in the purchasing and materials management field. Indeed, it will be extremely useful to students with career interests in any functional area of business. To achieve optimum performance in their own areas, all functional managers should understand the general concepts and problems in purchasing and managing materials.

The book is also written as a general reference for people already in business. Without reducing its academic soundness, the book is designed to serve as a useful working tool for the business practitioner.

Purchasing and Materials Management: Text and Cases is an adaptable text. It provides a sound and complete basic introduction to the purchasing and materials function. For the sophisticated reader, the book also offers advanced discussions and cases. Consequently, it should be a useful text for a basic course in the community college or the four-year undergraduate curriculum. It should also be appropriate for a more advanced course in the M.B.A. curriculum or in industrial training programs for government and industrial buyers. Undergraduate schools offering a course in purchasing may choose to cover only part of the book. For this reason, the book is designed so that the specialized activities covered in Chapters 16, 17, 18, 23, 27, and 28 may be omitted if time does not permit covering the complete book. Also, Chapters 14, 15, 19, and 25 may be covered briefly to present only general concepts, rather than treating these topics in depth. For schools that include the subject of purchasing and materials management as part of a course in production or marketing or industrial engineering, the first fifteen chapters of the text will provide the beginning student with an introduction to the basic concepts of purchasing and materials management. In graduate school courses or industrial courses, it is suggested that the complete text be used and that all topics and cases be covered as thoroughly as time allows.

The authors are aware of the growing participation of women in areas formerly occupied primarily by men, and they have attempted to make the text reflect this. Occasionally, however, the pronoun "he" and words such as "manpower" have been used where it would be awkward to avoid them. The authors hope that readers will understand that these traditional usages refer to persons of both sexes.

In developing this text, the authors have drawn freely on the research and experience of scholars and business executives who have studied the subject. A heavy debt is owed and acknowledged to these myriad contributors to knowledge in the field of purchasing and materials management. In developing an original statement of concepts, the contributions of these individuals have been blended with the personal managerial and research experience of the authors. The original concepts have been revised in the second and third editions to accommodate the suggestions of hundreds of students and scores of teachers who have generously given the authors the benefit of their constructive criticism. Gratitude is also acknowledged to the many friends and colleagues of the authors at the Graduate School of Business, Stanford University, and at the College of Business, Colorado State University, who so unselfishly shared their knowledge and time by reviewing various parts of the text.

The cases for this book have been drawn from many sources. The authors are indebted to International Business Machines, Westinghouse Electric, the Connecticut Purchasing Agents' Association, McGraw-Hill, Inc., and Harbridge House for making many of their cases available.

The authors are indebted to so many persons that individual acknowledgment is impossible. However, they wish particularly to thank David E. Reeves and O. Richard Blanton, who read much of the original manuscript and who also offered many helpful structural suggestions. The assistance of reviewers Kenneth E. Mast of the University of Akron, John B. Kline of the University of Colorado, Boulder, and Mildred Golden Pryor of East Texas University is gratefully appreciated. The authors also wish to thank David L. Belden, Alf E. Brandin, and Theodore J. Kreps for their contributions to the third edition of this book, which has been revised and updated in its entirety.

In connection with the third edition, a very special debt of gratitude is owed to Peggy Lee. Her understanding and help in the preparation of the manuscript made a difficult task distinctly easier, as did the assistance of Carol Robinson and Kathy Dobler. We sincerely thank them all.

Lamar Lee, Jr.
Donald W. Dobler

PURCHASING AND MATERIALS MANAGEMENT
Text and Cases

Part One

The Functions of Purchasing and Materials Management

Purchasing's Role in Business

There are two basic types of purchasing in the business world: purchasing for resale and purchasing for consumption or conversion. Purchasing for resale is performed by merchants and speculators. From the beginning of time, purchasing for resale has been the prime responsiblity of merchants. The quest for goods to sell was the motivating force that led to the discovery of the New World and the riches of the Indies. Ancient merchants spent some of their time dealing with sales problems, but they devoted by far the largest portion of it to the search for suitable purchases of new and desirable materials.

The basic problem of the merchant has not changed. Following the techniques of their predecessors, today's merchants ascertain what consumers want, buy it at a price to which they can add a profitable markup, and sell it to the consumers' satisfaction as to quality and service. For example, if a merchant decides his customers want washcloths when in fact they want sponges, his purchase will be a failure, regardless of any other consideration.

Today's merchants serve as the executive heads of trading firms. Additionally, they serve as the department heads in most merchandising houses, including department stores and mail-order houses. Every department within a merchandising house is normally a profit-centered unit. The buyers who head the units are completely responsible for the operation of their departments,

3

including profits and losses. They must decide whether their customers want washcloths or sponges. They must buy what is wanted at a price which will permit resale at a profit.

Purchasing managers buying for consumption or conversion are faced with different problems. The decision of "washcloths or sponges" is still one of their problems, but it is *not* the paramount problem. *Industrial buyers* (the designation for those who buy for consumption or conversion) have other important problems. They participate in determining what products their company should make, what components or parts of these products the company should manufacture, and what components or parts should be purchased from outside suppliers. They correlate their purchasing actions with sales forecasts and production schedules. They select suppliers from whom purchases can be made on a continuing and mutually profitable basis. For optimum results, they integrate the efforts of their departments with those of the other departments of the firm.

This book is concerned primarily with industrial buyers and how they contribute to the managerial decisions and to the profits of their firms. However, many of their basic problems, such as inventory control, buying at the right price, and negotiation, are problems that also confront the merchandise buyer. It should be noted that institutional buyers (college, hospital, etc.) and government buyers (city, county, state, and federal) are included in the definition of industrial buyer.

PURCHASING'S PLACE IN BUSINESS

What is purchasing's place in business management? Why is it important? To answer these questions, a quick panoramic view of the purchasing function will be sketched from three viewpoints: Purchasing will be viewed first as a function of business, next as one of the basic elements required to accomplish productive work, and finally in terms of the department responsible for outside manufacturing.

Purchasing as a Function of Business

Purchasing is one of the basic functions common to all types of business enterprise. These functions are basic because no business can operate without them. All businesses are administered or managed by coordinating and integrating these six functions:[1]

1 *Creation,* the idea or design function
2 *Finance,* the capital acquisition and financial records function
3 *Personnel,* the human resources and labor relations function

[1]Some authorities now include a seventh, research.

    4 *Purchasing,* the buying of required equipment, materials, and services

    5 *Conversion,* the changing of materials to economic goods

    6 *Distribution,* the selling or marketing of goods produced

The design engineering department, the finance or controller's department, the personnel or industrial relations department, the purchasing department, the production department, and the sales or marketing department are the common industrial titles of the organizations responsible for performing these functions. In nonindustiral enterprises, some of these basic functions may be identified by different names.

Depending on a company's size, these basic functions may be supervised by a single manager or by individual managers for each function. Regardless of how they are supervised, they are performed by someone in any business. Some small firms, for example, do not have a purchasing department; nevertheless, the purchasing function must still be performed. Sometimes it is performed by the president; at other times it is performed by an executive who administers several basic functions, including purchasing.

By its very nature, then, purchasing is a basic and integral part of business management. Why is this fact important? For a business to be successful, all its individual parts must be successful. It is impossible for any organization to achieve its full potential without a successful purchasing activity. The success of a business enterprise depends every bit as much on the purchasing executive as it does on the executives who administer the other functions of business.

This is not to imply that all purchasing departments are of equal importance to the success of their companies. They are not; their importance varies widely. The importance of any individual business function within a specific organization is dependent on a number of factors. Among these factors are the type of business, its goals, its economic circumstances, and how the enterprise operates to achieve these goals. In some situations purchasing can function in a perfunctory manner without jeopardizing a company's profits. These situations, however, are exceptional. Similar exceptions to functional importance can be found in sales, finance, or any other function of business. For example, in a firm selling a highly advanced technical product, the sales department usually does not have weighty responsibilities. Engineering excellence does more than efficient selling techniques to market the product. On the other hand, marketing a highly competitive standard product requires selling ability of the highest order. In such companies, the sales department has a position of major importance.

Purchased Materials as an Element of Productive Work

The basic goal of any industrial activity is the development and manufacture of products that can be marketed at a profit. This goal is accomplished by the appropriate blending of what many management authorities call the *five M's:*

machines, men, materials, money, and management. Materials today are the lifeblood of industry. No industrial organization can operate without them. They must be available at the proper time, in the proper quantity, at the proper place, and at the proper price. Failure of any of these responsibilities concerning materials adds to company costs and decreases company profits just as surely as do outmoded production methods, inefficient personnel, and ineffective selling.

Materials have not always been so vital. During the nation's industrial development, the relative importance of the five M's has continually shifted. In the management sense, materials became important around 1900. Before then they were rightfully taken for granted, as they presented no significant problem in either availability or cost. The place of the purchasing function in business can be seen more clearly after exploring the reasons for the shift in the relative importance of the five M's.

During the first hundred years of our industrial system, productivity increased very little. The availability of manpower and horsepower exceeded machine power almost one hundredfold. This relationship started to change around 1850. Between 1850 and 1950 an unbelievable increase in productivity took place. In 1850, productive power was divided as follows: 2 percent machine power and 98 percent horsepower and manpower. By 1900, this division of power became approximately equal. In 1950, the 1850 power relationship was reversed: 98 percent machine power and 2 percent horsepower and manpower (see Figure 1-1).

Because manpower was the first source of productive power, the initial industrial emphasis was on men. As machines became more productive, the emphasis shifted toward them. As new products, specialized labor, and

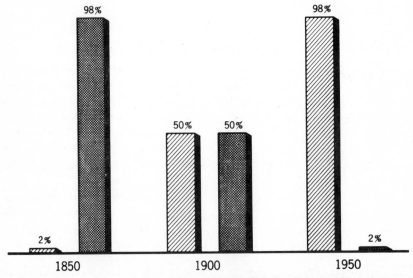

Figure 1-1   Power source relationships, 1850 to 1950. The light-shaded columns represent machine power, and the dark-shaded columns represent horsepower and manpower.

materials distribution became more complex, emphasis shifted toward scientific management. Still later, as both the complexity of materials and the volume of production skyrocketed, materials became a much larger element of cost. Emphasis naturally shifted to this aspect of the five M's.

Before 1900, both the industrial machines and the items they produced were relatively simple. The manufacturing process was uncomplicated and slow. Materials and components of production were simple, readily available, and cheap. Distribution was restricted to a limited area. In fact, a prerequisite to production for almost one hundred years was location of the plant close to plentiful and cheap materials. This prerequisite in turn limited the area of distribution, or the market. Within these constraints, labor costs represented the major portion of production expense.

The introduction of better machines, coupled with scientific management to develop and utilize more sophisticated man-machine systems, made possible the factory system, which in turn sparked many industrial changes. Inventions such as the steam turbine, the electric motor, and automatic controls changed the entire complex of manufacturing. Gradually, materials became more complex, labor became more specialized, and mechanization increased. These changes inevitably led to specialization in manufacturing and to longer production runs.

As the volume of production increased, *unit* labor costs decreased. The reduction of unit labor costs increased the relative cost and importance of materials in the manufacturing process. *Percentagewise, labor costs went down while material costs went up.* This change in the value of materials relative to total production costs continues today. For example, in 1945 materials represented approximately 40 percent of the manufacturer's total cost to produce an airplane. In 1955 the materials proportion of total cost increased to around 50 percent. Today it is over 60 percent.

Purchasing as the Manager for Outside Manufacturing

The materials that go into a typical company product originate from two sources. The company's manufacturing department is the first source. This department converts raw materials into fabricated parts. The company's purchasing department is the second source. This department not only purchases raw materials, which the production department converts into fabricated parts, but it also purchases finished fabricated parts. The parts made by the production department are combined in assembly with the parts bought by the purchasing department to form the company's final products.[2]

The percentage of component parts being purchased externally is constantly increasing compared with the percentage being manufactured internally. The trend toward specialization within our system inherently brings about such a situation. The increasing specialization of labor, the increasing complex-

---

[2]The capably managed Du Pont Company was among the first to recognize the importance of whether a company should make something itself or let its purchasing department buy it. See Ernest Dale, *The Great Organizers*, McGraw-Hill Book Company, New York, 1960, p. 53.

ity of new materials, and the increasing cost of high-volume specialty machines all tend to cause more buying and less making. Not even the largest manufacturing concerns have sufficiently high volume requirements to compete with specialty manufacturers in all fields. For example, RCA, one of the nation's largest manufacturers of electronic equipment, buys nearly all its capacitors and resistors. This purchasing action is taken not because RCA cannot make these components, but because it can buy them more cheaply from a specialty supplier.

The trend in manufacturing is toward the development of three distinct types of factories. The first type does not make finished end products; it is equipped with costly high-volume specialty machines and produces fabricated parts in large quantities at low unit cost. These parts are sold to numerous factories of the second and third types. The second type of factory, like the first type, does not make finished end products; it makes subassemblies. The required parts for the subassemblies come from factories of the first type, or from the parts it makes, or from a combination of both. The third type of factory makes finished end products. As economic circumstances dictate, it assembles the finished product from a combination of the parts it makes (usually parts that are peculiar to its product) and the standard parts or subassemblies it buys from factories of the first and second types.

In the multiple-type factory system of today, any company generally uses two distinct sources of supply: *inside* manufacture and *outside* manufacture. The production department is responsible for inside manufacture. Included in this responsibility is the authority to schedule production in economical quantities, and to do so far enough in advance to have materials available when needed.

The purchasing department, on the other hand, has the responsibility and authority to schedule outside production. Purchasing executives have the same managerial interests concerning their outside production as production executives have concerning their internal production. Both must schedule accurately. Production executives are interested in low unit costs and high quality. Purchasing executives are interested in keeping their suppliers' costs down and in reducing special tooling costs. In addition, they are interested in maintaining scheduled deliveries and good quality control to assure meeting production schedules and to reduce the cost of inspection.

THE PURCHASING FUNCTION

Purchasing Function versus Purchasing Department

From the preceding panoramic view of the purchasing function, it is clear that purchasing is an integral and essential part of business management. All the functions of business must mesh into a unified whole if management is to fulfill its basic responsibility of optimizing company profits. Each function of business must share in this responsibility.

There is a fundamental distinction, however, between the purchasing function and the purchasing department. They are not necessarily the same. The purchasing function is a basic business function which is common to all types of business enterprise. The purchasing department is an organizational unit of a firm whose duties include some part or all of the purchasing function. This distinction between "function" and "department" is not always appreciated or understood by top management. The purchasing function is usually performed most economically and efficiently by a specialized, centralized purchasing department, directed by a skilled purchasing manager. However, the purchasing function does not have to be performed in such a manner. In theory it can be performed, and in practice it sometimes is performed, by any number of different company executives or departments.

Some managers view the purchasing department primarily as a clerical department, and assign the department primarily clerical duties. In such cases, the major management responsibilities of the purchasing function, including negotiation of the firm's major contracts, are usually performed by the chief executive himself, or by other members of his or her staff. In this textbook, to preclude making continuous exceptions and qualifications, it is assumed that the major portion of the purchasing function is assigned to the purchasing department. Therefore, unless otherwise noted, when the purchasing department is referred to in this textbook it also means the purchasing function.

Profit-making Potential

How can purchasing increase company profits? The average purchasing department is responsible for spending over half of every dollar its company receives as income from sales and other sources. More dollars are spent for purchases of materials and services than for all other expense items combined, including expenses for wages, taxes, dividends, and depreciation. Figure 1-2 shows the percentage distribution of the sales dollar in the 100 largest United States manufacturing firms.[3] An earlier study of small companies reveals similar percentages.[4]

The fact that the purchasing department is responsible for the expenditure of over half of most companies' dollars highlights the profit-making possibilities of the purchasing function. Every dollar saved in purchasing is a new dollar of profit. An additional dollar of income from sales, however, is not a new dollar of profit; applicable expenses must be deducted from the sales dollar to determine the remaining profit.

A typical situation illustrates the profit-making potential of purchasing. The ABC Manufacturing Company has a sales volume of approximately $80 million. Materials costs, for ease of illustration, will be calculated at 50 percent ($40 million). At a 10 percent (before taxes) profit margin, a 25 percent increase in sales ($20 million) could be equaled profitwise by a 5 percent saving in purchasing. Either of these two actions results in a $2 million increase in profit

---

[3]*Business Week,* Jan. 13, 1975, p. 63.
[4]Donald W. Dobler, "A Study of Materials Management and Its Problems in Small Manufacturing Businesses," Stanford University, Stanford, Calif., 1960, p. 5.

($20 million $\times$ 0.10 = $2 million; $40 million $\times$ 0.05 = $2 million). The firm's profit and loss statement reflects profit dollars resulting from reduced costs as well as those resulting from increased sales. Profit is the difference between income and outgo. Progressive managers strive to increase profit both by increasing the income and reducing the outgo. At lower profit margins, to produce the $2 million increase in profit, increases in sales volumes must be even higher than the $20 million figure of the preceding example. (See Table 1-1.)

The cost of materials can vary as much as 10 to 15 percent, depending on the skill with which the purchasing function is organized and operated. It is for this reason that there are usually more opportunities available for reducing purchasing costs 5 percent than there are for increasing sales volume 25 percent. Also, additional profit from purchasing savings can normally be made without any kind of increase in expense. If an increase is required, it is usually for only one person to do analytical work. On the other hand, additional profit from increased sales volume normally entails both increases in expenses and increases in the risk of capital. Additional expenses are incurred for such things as an expanded sales force, a larger advertising budget, additional plant capacity, overtime production pay, or some combination of these factors. Each factor involves an increased risk of capital. Additional profits from sales, therefore, entail increased capital risk and increased management effort. Additional profits from purchasing normally entail only increased management effort. Occasionally, they require a slight increase in management expense as well.

In a study made for the guidance of company presidents, the American Management Association has quantitatively evaluated the profit value of an effective centralized purchasing department.[5] A key section of the study asks the presidents a series of searching questions. Three of the key questions asked are: do you realize that 20 to 30 percent of your profits can come from savings generated in your purchasing department? Do you know that 2 percent of your

[5]Samuel C. Farmer, "A Look at Purchasing Through the President's Eye," American Management Association Bull. 33, 1963. This study was initially prepared by the Presidents' Professional Association, an affiliate of the American Management Association.

Table 1-1   Sales Increases Required to Produce $2 Million Additional Profit

At a gross profit margin of	A purchasing saving of $2 million produces the same profit as a sales increase of
10%	$ 20,000,000
8%	25,000,000
5%	40,000,000
3%	66,666,667
2%	100,000,000

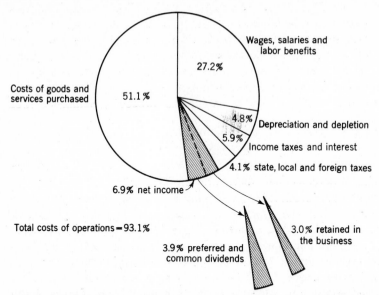

Figure 1-2   Percentage distribution of the sales dollar in the 100 largest United States manufacturing concerns in 1974.

firm's annual purchasing expenditures should be set as a target for purchasing's yearly profit contribution? Do you know that your purchasing organization can and should return between 300 and 500 percent of its own operating cost in profits to your company?

The essence of all these questions is that large savings are possible from an efficient, centralized purchasing department. The president should assure himself that his or her firm is achieving these savings. This can be done by measuring purchasing savings against a general standard of performance, such as one of those suggested by the questions in the preceding paragraph.

Objectives of Purchasing

What are the objectives and responsibilities of the purchasing department? The classical definition of purchasing's objectives is to buy materials and services of the right quality, in the right quantity, at the right price, from the right source, and at the right time. One or more chapters later in the text are devoted to each of these "rights." For the present overview of the purchasing function, objectives will be described in general management terms. In these terms, there are eight basic objectives of purchasing:

1   To support company operations with an uninterrupted flow of materials and services.
2   To buy competitively and wisely. (This includes two distinct considerations. To buy competitively involves keeping abreast of the forces of

supply and demand that regulate prices and availability of materials. To buy wisely involves a constant search for better values that yield the best combination of price, quality, and service. A buyer who pays more for copper than a competitor is not buying competitively. A buyer who purchases silver when copper could perform the function just as well is not buying wisely. It is the combination of competitive buying and wise buying that contributes most to maximizing a company's profits.)

3   To keep inventory investment losses (due to deterioration, obsolescence, and theft) at a practical minimum.

4   To develop reliable alternate sources of supply. (This is often one of the most difficult objectives to accomplish, particularly if other departments of the firm think purchasing is paying too high a price for one of those sources.)

5   To develop good, continuing vendor relationships. (Good vendor relationships are invaluable. Under such relationships the myriad problems that inevitably arise between buyer and seller are readily solved. Vendors naturally direct their research, give advance information on new products and prices, and give better service to their permanent customers.)

6   To achieve maximum integration with the other departments of the firm. (This requires understanding the needs of the other departments so that these needs can be translated into materials support action. These actions will vary from firm to firm; however, they normally require the purchasing department to support another department in one of its major responsibilities. The most common areas of support are in developing favorable reciprocity agreements, effective standardization programs, forecasts of future prices and general business conditions, economic make-or-buy decisions, and a repository of information and knowledge from suppliers regarding new materials, processes, and prices.)

7   To train and develop highly competent personnel who are motivated to make the firm as well as their department succeed. (Such personnel, in addition to fulfilling the responsibilities of the purchasing department, also serve as a reservoir of talent from which future executives of the firm can be selected.)

8   To develop policies and procedures which permit accomplishment of the preceding seven objectives at the lowest reasonable operating cost. (It is not reasonable to deny an increase of $1 for additional payroll if this expense can increase earnings by $1.01 through better achievement of departmental objectives.)

These objectives apply in principle to all categories of industrial buying activities: manufacturing concerns, governmental units, universities, hospitals, and all other types of activities that do not buy for resale. A nonprofit activity, of course, cannot seek "to maximize its profits." It can, however, seek to maximize the benefits the organization receives from its appropriated or endowed dollar. To obtain the greatest value from each dollar the purchasing department spends is a principle common to all types of purchasing activities.

Under the first purchasing objective (uninterrupted materials flow), for example, a manufacturing concern seeks to support its production schedule. The United States Navy seeks to support its ships, its aircraft, and its bases. A hospital seeks to support its patients. The principles underlying the first objective of purchasing apply with equal force to all types of organizations. It is the same with the other seven objectives; they apply to all types of industrial buying. The principles are also equally applicable to all sizes of industrial operations, large and small. There are many situations where a slight change in the phraseology of a specific objective would be required to make it fit a particular company. The fact remains, however, that only the words change; the principles remain the same.

RELATIONS WITH OTHER DEPARTMENTS

A purchasing department is the center of a large part of a company's business activity. By its very nature, purchasing has continuing relationships with all other departments in the firm as well as with the firm's suppliers. Purchasing operations cut across all departmental lines. Purchasing and other departments (production, engineering, sales, and finance) often view common problems differently. This is a normal and healthy situation—provided the departmental opinions are held objectively.

Purchasing and Engineering

Purchasing, engineering, and production have many mutual problems. Design engineering, like production, greatly influences the amount of time purchasing has to handle a procurement job. Engineering is usually responsible for preparing the technical specifications for a company's products and the materials that go into them. To exercise this responsibility effectively, engineering must have the constant help of purchasing and production. The prices paid for production materials and the costs to fabricate them are inextricably related to their specifications. Similarly, specifications can be written in a manner that reduces or enlarges the number of firms willing to supply specific items. If profits are to be maximized, the materials specified by engineering must be both economical to procure and economical to fabricate, and they should normally be available from more than one efficient, low-cost producer.

Purchasing and engineering occasionally differ in their concepts of materials problems. This is understandable. Engineers naturally tend to design conservatively. Their specifications provide amply for quality, safety, and performance. By training, the engineer may be inclined to seek the "ideal" design, material, or equipment without complete regard for cost or timing. The buyer, on the other hand, often wants to lower the engineer's performance and safety margins and work to minimum standards. Is a conservative design with a safety factor of 5 necessary if a lighter design with a safety factor of 3 will do the job? Why use costly chrome plate if brushed aluminum is adequate? Clearly, such conflicting departmental interests cannot always be resolved easily. The answers to the problems involved are seldom clearly either all white or all black. Mutual understanding and a willingness to give and take are required from both sides if mutually satisfactory solutions are to be reached.

Purchasing and Production

The purchasing-production relationship begins when the production department transmits its manufacturing schedule to the purchasing department. Purchasing subsequently translates this schedule into a procurement schedule. Purchase timing is often a cardinal difficulty in making this translation. When production does not allow purchasing sufficient time to purchase wisely, many needless expenses inevitably creep into the final costs of a company's products. When purchasing is not given sufficient time to develop competition, premium prices are certain to be paid for materials. Costly *special production runs* and *premium transportation* costs are two additional factors that frequently result from inadequate purchasing lead time.[6]

The most serious result possible from insufficient procurement lead time is a production shutdown. In the process type of production (chemical, cement, paint, flour, etc.), equipment either runs at full capacity or it does not run at all. Consequently, material shortages in these industries can be catastrophic, resulting in complete production stoppage. Losses resulting from material shortages in nonprocess industries are not always so disastrous or apparent. Production shutdown in a metal fabricating shop, for example, can be piecemeal. The indirect costs of such shortages, consequently, are often hidden in production costs. One or two machines from a large battery of perhaps fifty can be shut down as a routine operation. Conventional accounting records fail to reveal the financial impact of this kind of slow profit-draining inefficiency.

Coordination between purchasing and production pays off in many ways. For example, a more expensive alternative material that will save the company money can on occasion be selected. This sounds like a paradox. "Pay more and save more"—how can this happen? Savings in manufacturing and assembling costs can exceed the increased purchasing costs. In the normal manufacturing operations of casting, forging, machining, grinding, stamping, cutting, and cleaning, some materials are much more economical to work with than others. The government is saving thousands of dollars by using bronze instead of steel extrusions in aircraft elevator and rudder counterweights. Bronze costs more than steel, but savings in machining time more than offset the increase in material cost. In this case, not only is the direct cost reduced, but as an added benefit skilled machinists and expensive machine tools are freed to do other high-priority work.

---

[6]It is purchasing's responsibility to keep production informed concerning what lead times are for all categories of production materials.

The severe consequences of a production stoppage cause many production managers to advocate an excessively large inventory of production materials. Again, this is understandable. In order for them to reach their main manufacturing objective of low unit costs, they must keep the production line operating. A large inventory is a logical safeguard to prevent possible production stoppages resulting from materials shortages.

Purchasing shares in the production manager's desire to keep the production line operating. In fact, to do so is purchasing's first objective. In addition to keeping the production line operating, however, purchasing has the correlative objective of accomplishing the task with the minimum reasonable capital investment in inventory. The capital cost of carrying inventory is high. For example, the average cost for metalworking firms is approximately 25 percent of the inventory's average value. Reconciling these two conflicting company objectives (one calling for a higher inventory than the other) requires capable, informed, and understanding department heads. Although chief executives themselves must occasionally resolve the issue, it should normally be resolved by the department heads.

The above are just a few of many operating situations that illustrate the continuing and coordinative nature of the purchasing and production relationship.

Purchasing and Sales

All companies recognize the direct relationship between sales and profits. In their enthusiasm to increase sales, however, many companies overlook the leaks in profit that can occur when the sales function is not properly meshed with the purchasing and production functions.

The purchasing-production-sales cycle has its genesis in a sales forecast. Most sales forecasts include two important parts: (1) an estimate of sales based on what has happened in the past to a company's products, territories, and markets and (2) an adjustment of this estimate to reflect changes the company expects in its future sales. The changes include alterations in the marketing program and shifts in economic and competitive conditions. The sales forecast is the basis for the production schedule, which in turn is the basis for the purchasing schedule. The sales forecast also influences a firm's capital equipment budget, as well as its advertising campaigns and other sales activities.

Prompt communication to production and purchasing of changes in the sales forecast will permit these departments to change their schedules as painlessly and as economically as possible. Changes in the production schedules should be communicated immediately to sales. This action will permit sales to alter its distribution schedule in a manner that will not alienate customers. Purchasing must immediately transmit to sales information about rises in material prices. This action will permit sales to evaluate the effect of price rises in price estimates given for future sales quotations, on current selling prices, and on plans for future product lines.

Purchasing and sales must wisely blend their interests in the delicate area of reciprocity (buying from customers). If satisfactory legal reciprocal arrangements are to be negotiated, this course of action must be pursued with an understanding of the true costs of reciprocity. Buying from friends can be good business, but not when such action is at the expense of company profits or product quality. In a zest for increased sales, a company can lose sight of the fact that increased sales do not always result in increased profits. Sometimes increased sales result in *decreased* profits if they simultaneously require an increase in purchasing costs.

A purchasing department can be of major help to its sales department by serving as its practical sales laboratory. A firm's purchasing department is the target for many other manufacturers' sales departments. Purchasing's files are replete with sales literature, sales policies, and sales promotion methods of a broad range of manufacturers and distributors. Buyers are aware of the personal selling methods that salesmen have used most effectively on them. They are equally aware of sales practices that fail or irritate them. Therefore, a company's buyers can be an excellent source of information for developing and refining the company's own sales policies and procedures.

Purchasing and Finance

Purchasing's relationship with finance is different from its relationships with production, engineering, and sales. The difference stems from the fact that cost determinations cannot be hidden in the purchasing-finance relationship as they often can in the other relationships. The importance of good financial planning is highlighted by the fact that poor financial planning is the major single cause of business failure. Among the basic data needed by an organization for proper planning of its working-capital and cash-flow positions are accurate sales forecasts and accurate purchasing schedules. It is just as important for purchasing to inform finance of changes in its schedule as it is to inform production and sales of these changes.

There are many economic factors that periodically bring about favorable and completely unexpected buying opportunities. A supplier, for example, may momentarily have excess capacity because of the cancellation of a large order. During the period that this condition exists, the supplier may sell his products at prices designed to recover only out-of-pocket costs.[7] This may be done because it is in the long-term interest of the firm not to reduce its labor force. The potential income from such unexpected buying opportunities must be weighed against the potential income from other alternative uses of the company's capital. Acquiring new equipment, adding to plant facilities, and increasing sales and promotional efforts are some of the alternative uses of

---

[7]A manufacturing concern can be thought of as having two sets of costs: out-of-pocket costs and all other costs. Out-of-pocket costs include direct costs paid for making a specific product. They do not include rent of the factory, taxes, insurance, etc., all of which must be paid whether or not a specific product is made.

capital that a company must consider. Usually, the alternative offering the greatest income in the long run should be selected, since no firm has enough capital to satisfy all requirements.

Regardless of the price advantage obtainable, the right time to buy from the standpoint of basic economics is not always the right time to buy from the standpoint of the company's treasury. If the purchasing department places orders to take advantage of unusually low prices without consulting the finance department, the company could find itself paying for these purchases with funds needed for other purposes. On the other hand, if the finance department does not strive diligently to make funds available for such favorable buying opportunities, the company may have to pay higher prices later for the same material.

FOR DISCUSSION

1-1 Describe the two types of purchasing in the business world. Discuss the differences between the two. Have you had any experience with either? Explain how your experience relates to the discussion in this chapter.

1-2 "Purchasing is more important in an industrial firm today than it was one hundred years ago." Discuss.

1-3 What challenges does knowlege of the potential of good purchasing offer you? How can this purchasing course help you?

1-4 Do you think it would be easier for a company to increase its profits by increasing the efficiency of purchasing, or by increasing sales? Explain.

1-5 How can efficient purchasing generate savings? How great are the possible savings?

1-6 What do you think are the attributes required of an efficient purchasing executive? Explain.

1-7 Economists frequently make the statement that labor costs make up the bulk of industrial expenditures today. Does this contradict the view taken in this chapter? Discuss.

1-8 Discuss the problems involved in purchasing-production relationships.

1-9 How can increased purchasing costs sometimes result in greater profits for a company? Is it possible to "pay more and save more"? Explain.

1-10 Explain how sales and purchasing can help each other by establishing a good relationship.

1-11 "The responsibilities of a firm's purchasing function and its purchasing department are not always the same." Explain.

CASES FOR CHAPTER 1

Picking a Buyer—What Really Counts? page 642
Heathe Company, page 622

The Role of Materials
Management in Business

To complete the overview started in Chapter 1, this chapter discusses the book's second major topic heading—materials management. The chapter also investigates the relationships among the concepts of materials management, physical distribution management, and logistics management.

CONSOLIDATION OF MATERIALS ACTIVITIES

From the concluding discussion in the first chapter, some readers may have sensed a need for coordination and perhaps integration of materials activities. In most industrial firms, a need for such action does exist. During the past ten years many firms have made considerable progress toward the accomplishment of this objective, but much work still remains to be done. The concepts of "materials management," "physical distribution management," and "logistics management" are the primary materials organizational tools—tools which have been used in the past and will be used increasingly in the future to achieve closer coordination and control of a firm's various materials activities.

Most authorities do not agree entirely on which functional activities should be included in any of these three integrating types of organizations. Fortunately, this difference of opinion is of little consequence to the reader. This book is concerned primarily with basic concepts, and only minimally with minor differences of opinion about details of application. Although such differences exist with respect to the precise form of the organization structures, theoreticians and practitioners agree unanimously that consolidating and centralizing the management of materials activities reduces materials costs.

The paramount objective of all three types of organizations (materials management, physical distribution management, and logistics management) is to reduce materials costs—more precisely, the *total costs* associated with the acquisition and management of materials. Each of these three forms of organization seeks to answer the question: how can material costs best be identified and measured, and through an integration of related operations be controlled and reduced?

Generally speaking, a firm can attain effective control over its costs only when it is analyzed and controlled as a total operating unit (a total system). Uncoordinated cost reductions can be misleading, because cost reductions made in one area frequently appear as increased costs in another area(s). For example, purchasing costs can be reduced by buying in larger quantities and passing increased carrying costs along to inventories. Or inventories can be reduced to the bone, passing additional costs along to (1) production, in the form of manufacturing delays and/or possible downtimes, and (2) purchasing, in the form of higher ordering costs, additional receiving activities, payments, etc. Similarly, reduced transportation costs resulting from the use of slower methods of transport can be passed along as increased inventory costs and possible production delays. Packaging costs can be reduced by passing the costs along to materials handling and customer claims.

Industrial firms generally acknowledge two salient facts regarding total materials costs. First, for an average firm, materials costs represent over one-half of its total operating expense. Materials costs, therefore, are a prime area for cost reduction. Second, to reduce materials costs (or any other cost) to the lowest practical level, a firm must be analyzed and controlled from a total systems point of view.

The following overview of the major kinds of organizational units in the materials field highlights the organizational changes which have been, or could be, made to reduce materials costs.

TYPES OF MATERIALS ORGANIZATIONS

Purchasing

What specific activities are performed by a typical purchasing department? A series of studies conducted by one of the authors in 186 firms reveals the following assignments of responsibilities to the purchasing departments in these firms (see top of page 20).

"Buying," as used in the listing below, includes activities such as interviewing salesmen, negotiating with vendors, analyzing bids and making awards, selecting suppliers, issuing purchase orders, making adjustments with suppliers, and keeping appropriate records. A review of the complete list of activities studied makes it clear that the *primary* responsibilities of a purchasing department involve buying, value analysis, and purchasing research. Many· purchasing departments, however, also include activities such as inventory control, stores, receiving, subcontracting, and traffic. Consequently, when one

Activity	Number of purch. depts. responsible	Percentage of purch. depts. responsible
Buying	186	100
Value analysis	139	75
Purchasing research	131	70
Inventory control	96	52
Auditing invoices	82	44
Stores	79	42
Standardization	63	34
Receiving	51	27
Traffic	48	26
Subcontracting	28	15

encounters the term "purchasing department" the name alone does not reveal precisely what operations are involved. The observer can be sure, however, that among firms of the same size, departments which include all the activities listed above have more responsible and higher-paid personnel than departments which include only a minimum number of those activities.

Procurement

Procurement is a term originated by the Armed Forces to define one of several supply functions involved in logistics. In the broadest sense, the Armed Forces define "procurement" as including the whole process whereby all classes of resources (people, materials, facilities, and services) required by the Armed Forces are obtained.

Although the term "procurement" originated in military organizations, it has for many years also been adopted and used by American industry. It is even included in the title of a well-known textbook. In scope, procurement's industrial meaning parallels its military meaning. In both settings, procurement encompasses a wider range of supply activities than does purchasing alone.

Materials Management

Materials management, as practiced in business today, can be defined as a confederacy of traditional materials activities bound by a common idea—the idea of an integrated management approach to planning, acquisition, conversion, flow, and distribution of *production materials* from the raw-material state to the finished-product state.

The materials management concept advocates the assignment of all major activities which contribute to materials' cost to a single materials management department. This includes the primary responsibilities which are generally found in the purchasing department, plus all other major procurement responsibilities, including inventory management, traffic, receiving, warehousing, surplus and salvage, and frequently production planning and control. Some companies also include customer service, scheduling, shipping, materials handling, and physical distribution in their definition of materials management.[1]

The *specific form* of materials organization most appropriate for one company may not be the best form for another company. A brief discussion of two materials activities will illustrate why the unique nature of a specific firm's operating activities influences its form of materials organization so heavily. Assume that a plant purchases all the parts, components, and subassemblies for the product it manufactures. In this situation, if production were uniform, the production planning schedule and the purchasing schedule would be similar or identical. Consequently, for this firm to achieve optimal material and cost control, production control should realistically be included in the materials management department. Assume now that a plant manufactures all the parts, components, and subassemblies that are used in turning out its product. In this situation, there may be very little similarity between the production planning and purchasing schedules. Therefore, in this firm, a strong case could be made for locating production control within the production department.

In practice, the theoretical extremes discussed above seldom exist. For most firms, the production planning and purchasing schedules overlap significantly. Unfortunately, this frequently produces a continuing source of conflict. One of the paramount advantages of materials management is that it forces coordination between purchasing and production control. Purchasing and production control are both responsible for the on-time delivery of production materials. Division of this authority between two different operating units inevitably leads to conflict. When materials do not arrive on time, production control is seldom satisfied to work through the purchasing department. Frequently, production control personnel proceed to expedite the materials directly with the supplier. Since the expediting of purchased materials and negotiation with suppliers are basic purchasing responsibilities, conflict ensues. Such conflict is resolved much more easily when production control and purchasing report to a single boss—the materials manager.

As with purchasing and production control, substantial benefits also accrue when inventory management, value analysis, receiving, stores, and surplus and salvage are placed in a materials management department. (Each of these activities and its role in the materials system is discussed in a separate chapter later in the book.)

Probably the single greatest benefit a firm receives from having a materials manager is that this manager thinks as the president and other top vice presidents do—that is, in terms of the firm as a whole. Managers of individual materials functions, such as purchasing, inventory, and traffic, usually are compelled to think more narrowly in terms of the unique responsibilities associated with their specific functions. Consider a typical situation. Produc-

---

[1]It is interesting to note that the United States Navy assigned all the first-named materials activities and a good many of the second to its supply corps for materials management well over a hundred years ago.

tion and purchasing traditionally reach a tacit agreement on a higher level of inventories than a good materials manager would normally sanction. High inventories protect production from manufacturing delays and purchasing from production pressures. If top management complains of high inventories, production and purchasing blame each other for the condition. One large firm, with sales exceeding $1 billion, recently reduced inventories over 25 percent after creating a materials management organization and appointing an experienced top management person as its new vice president for materials. Many other firms have experienced similar results.

Examples of Materials Management Implementation

Business Week recently allocated its entire Management section to a report on materials management progress. The report opens with a covering statement that adoption of the materials management concept is progressing rapidly.[2] Du Pont's vice president for Energy and Materials states: "The Du Pont Energy and Materials Department buys all materials worldwide and plans for a long-term procurement of energy, conducts exploration for minerals and petroleum, plans development of alternative energy sources, and recommends investments in mineral resources, where necessary, to assure adequate supplies." This statement is noteworthy because it points up the practical importance of a new materials management problem—that of planning for *future* supplies. During an era of recurring shortages of basic materials, an increasing number of firms are confronted with this perplexing and growing problem.

Vice-presidents for materials of other large, well-managed industrial firms, including Gillette Company, Champion International, Rockwell International, Scott Paper Company, GTE Sylvania, and Xerox, report similar materials problems. Gillette Company, where 90 percent of the cost of a typical product is in materials, reports that its materials management functions now include coordination with research personnel on the development of substitute materials as well as purchasing, inventory control, warehousing, and shipping. Champion International Corporation's materials staff reports that it has been given authority to recommend transfers of supplies from one plant to another, and to help decide when new plants will be built. The Scott Paper Company's vice president for Procurement and Transportation reports that his department is emphasizing planning for future supplies of raw materials.

The *Business Week* report makes it clear that top management and materials management personnel are focusing attention sharply on materials costs. The report also leaves no doubt that reliable long-term supply of materials is an increasingly important materials management problem *and responsibility*.

Each firm is unique in terms of its orientation, its internal operations, its

[2]Management Section, *Business Week,* Jan. 13, 1975, pp. 62–63.

external operating environment, and its specific problems. Consequently, as noted earlier, the best materials management organization for one company might not be the best for another. Specific details of the organizational arrangement should be tailored to meet the unique needs of each firm. One large, multiplant firm uses the following criteria as an organizational guide for its large operating divisions. A divisional materials management department is recommended when a division has the following characteristics: large outside procurements, varied production processes involving differing cycle times, and dynamic marketing problems. If the conditions for establishing a materials management department exist, and one is formed, departmental activities are grouped around three basic functions:

- Planning and control
- Purchasing, including value analysis
- Physical distribution

The planning and control functions are inventory control and production planning and scheduling. Purchasing functions are buying, subcontracting, value analysis, and expediting. Distribution functions are receiving, packaging, shipping, transportation, and warehousing.

Physical Distribution Management

Physical distribution management is related to marketing in a manner similar to the way materials management is related to production. Advocates of the physical distribution type organization traditionally refer to it as "the other half of marketing." This view divides marketing into two parts: conventional marketing (market research, product development, sales promotion, advertising, and selling), and physical distribution. To people holding this view, physical distribution consists of the following minimum functions:

Sales order processing
Traffic and transportation
Production control
Inventory control
Materials handling
Sales planning

It can also include additional functions such as customer service and technical service.

Many of these materials functions are clearly the same functions claimed by materials management. For the most part, however, the functions are concerned with different materials and are performed at different points in time with respect to the materials system (cycle). For example, the inventories controlled by materials management are production inventories; the inventories controlled by physical distribution management are finished goods inventories. The warehouses controlled by physical distribution are primarily finished goods warehouses, field warehouses, or distribution centers; those controlled by materials management are the raw materials and production stores warehouses. On the other hand, traffic and production control frequently constitute points of contention between physical distribution management advocates and materials management advocates. In the case of both functions, each organizational group can lay legitimate claim to them. The optimum location for traffic and production control will vary from one company to another, depending on specific operating and organizational factors within each firm.

Logistics Management

Logistics management is a combination of materials management and physical distribution management. Based on the preceding discussions of these two concepts, it is clear that a number of similarities exist. Not only are the activities involved in both concepts part of the same overall materials system, many of the skills required to perform the respective operating activities are also very similar. The same skills and knowledge required to control production inventories are also those used to control finished goods inventories. Similarly the materials management and physical distribution skills used in traffic, materials planning, and materials handling are identical skills. Although physical distribution is the final stage of the marketing process, the training and orientation of physical distribution personnel is much more akin to that of materials management personnel. These factors have combined to produce the logistics management concept.

Historically, these similarities and relationships were first recognized by military officers, and the organizational concept of logistics was initially developed in the Armed Forces. The concept has gradually worked its way into European and American industry. In industry today, logistics management includes all of the functions of both materials management and physical distribution management. In the broadest sense, logistics management views a firm as a single operating system; it seeks to minimize total costs associated with the acquisition and handling of materials from the inception of materials requirements to the final delivery of finished products to their users.

SYNTHESIS

Throughout the chapter three systems management concepts have been explored—materials management, physical distribution management, and logistics management. Although most practitioners and theorists currently do not agree on all the functional and operating details associated with each of these systems, general agreement does exist with respect to the fundamental concepts themselves. Figure 2-1 relates these concepts to a firm's materials system and reflects generally the major areas of agreement.

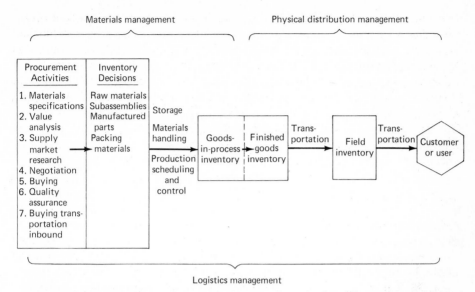

Figure 2-1 Systems management concepts imposed on the flow of materials and related activities in a firm's materials system.

The discussion thus far has focused heavily on the advantages accruing from centralizing the management of materials activities. The presentation would be incomplete, however, without recognizing that consolidation of the activities and managing them centrally also produces some disadvantages. While coordination among the materials activities in general is greatly improved, coordination and communication between some materials activities and the production and sales departments typically is somewhat diminished. This frequently necessitates the development of additional formal reports and some increase in related paperwork and attendant problems. These matters are discussed in detail in Chapter 22. It is sufficient at this point simply to say that in most companies the advantages gained from consolidating and controlling materials activities far outweigh the disadvantages. Clearly billions of dollars are lost by United States industry year after year because of poor overall control of materials activities.

Despite proven benefits from visible "track records" of some companies, American industry generally has been slow to consolidate and control its materials activities. Why? There are several reasons. Reduced profits stemming from sales declines and increased production (and other "direct") costs are immediately reflected in a firm's profit and loss statement. On the other hand, losses from poor materials management are *not seen directly* in the firm's cost accounting records or its profit and loss statement. This does not make them any less real than the more visible losses. However, because they are not seen, there is less immediate incentive to control them. Another cluster of reasons stems from the disposition of people to resist change. A major organizational change upsets time-honored, "comfortable" operating patterns and procedures. Likewise, professional jealousies and vested interests of various managerial groups frequently generate overwhelming resistance to change. Such resistance is frequently augmented by the fact that a shortage of fully qualified materials managers exists.

Despite these obstacles, the tide has definitely turned. The new concepts associated with the management of materials are now being adopted in various forms at an accelerating rate. Several professional associations, which previously rejected the materials management concept, now support it. Increasing research is being conducted in the materials management field, and a number of colleges and universities now offer comprehensive courses in the field. Widespread use of computer-based information and control systems by business firms is serving as an operational catalyst. Management is being forced to rethink the design and the significance of the interrelationships of most of a firm's operating functions. Computer-based systems in the production and sales areas, in fact, require more closely coordinated operation of production planning, inventory control, purchasing, warehousing, receiving, and accounting. Thus, the trend is toward *system optimization* rather than suboptimization of the efforts of individual operating units in the firm.

Dr. Dean Ammer, a noted authority in the materials management field, estimates that the materials management concept is now utilized to some extent in over 70 percent of all American industrial firms. Additionally, he finds that materials management is nearly as common among small firms as among large ones.[3] By comparing Dr. Ammer's 70 percent figure with a corresponding 3 percent figure reported in a 1967 study, the progress made during the past decade toward implementing this concept is readily apparent.[4]

FOR DISCUSSION

2-1   Discuss the benefits that can result when materials activities are integrated.

2-2   "Generally speaking, a firm can attain effective control over the bulk of its costs only when it is analyzed and controlled as a total operating unit." Do you agree with this statement? Discuss.

2-3   When the term "purchasing department" is heard, what scope of activities do you envision? What range of activities could you envision?

2-4   Discuss the important differences between purchasing and procurement.

2-5   Define and discuss the significance of the materials management concept.

2-6   What are the important differences between materials management and physical distribution management? Could these two organizational units realistically be combined into one organizational unit?

[3]*Guide to Purchasing,* National Association of Purchasing Management, New York, 1974, p. 3.6.22.

[4]G. V. Schultz, "The Real Low-Down on Materials Management," *Factory,* December 1967, pp. 49–58.

2-7 The *Business Week* materials management report discussed in this chapter identified two trends. Discuss them.

2-8 What has accelerated industry's recent trend toward materials management? Explain fully.

2-9 Explain why materials management losses are not readily visible and sales and production losses are.

2-10 What do you believe would be the major operational problems of a materials manager? Explain.

CASES FOR CHAPTER 2

Northeastern Equipment Company, page 634

Part Two

Fundamentals of Purchasing and Materials Management

Chapter 3

Quality

> **KEY CONCEPTS**
>
> What is quality?
> Determination of quality
>   Management responsibility
>   Availability; new sources
>   Substitutes; seller's suggestions
>   Standardization; cost considerations
> How quality is described
>   Market grade; brand name
>   Commercial standards
>   Specifications—physical;
>   blueprints; performance; material and method of manufacture
>   Samples
> Methods used in practice

The dictionary defines *quality* as "fitness; merit; excellence." This is the definition most people have in mind when they think of quality. The rolls Royce is taken for granted to be a quality automobile. The diamond is accepted without question to be a quality gem. People believe generally that "high quality" is something desirable in itself.

In industrial and institutional purchasing, quality has an entirely different meaning. Here quality is related to *suitability* and *cost* (not price),[1] rather than to intrisic excellence. The best quality is that which can be purchased at the lowest cost to fulfill the need or satisfy the intended function for which the material is being purchased.

Quality has no meaning in purchasing except as it is related to function and ultimate cost. A few examples will clarify this point. It would be unnecessarily costly to print the pages of this book on the high-quality parchment used for college diplomas. Because of its high price, it would be needlessly wasteful to use silver as an electrical conductor, even though its conductivity is approximately 9 percent higher than that of copper. The high cost of labor for painting would make an attempt to save money on the price of the paint foolish without

---

[1]Price is only one element of cost, as is discussed later in this chapter.

considering its lasting qualities. To use the finest unblemished walnut lumber to make packing boxes would serve no purpose except to increase costs unnecessarily.

When high-pressure turbines were first installed on ships, some misguided shipowners attempted to save money by using the same quality of lubricating oil as was used for the old low-pressure turbines. Steam from the new high-pressure system condensed in the bearings of the turbines, and this in turn contaminated the lubricating oil. The contaminated oil pitted the turbines' bearings, and expensive repairs followed. Not until the shipowners started using a more effective, and more costly, lubricating oil did these unnecessary repairs cease.

There is nothing wrong with seeking lower prices. All experienced buyers rightly do this. It is wrong, however, to put price out of its proper sequence. In buying for our personal needs, we generally start our buying considerations with price. We decide how much money we can allocate for a new television set, a new automobile, or a new deepfreeze. We then seek the highest quality we can buy for this amount of money. In industrial purchasing the sequence is reversed. Quality comes first; price comes second. Stated a little differently, in industrial purchasing quality determines price.

Purchasing executives are in an excellent position to contribute to that portion of their company's profits that originates in the area of quality. Why? Because they can bring to bear three important types of knowledge: their knowledge of *the materials they buy*, their knowledge of *markets and economic trends*, and their knowledge of *reliable sources of supply*. With this background they can analyze the designer's material requirements. They can report the market availability of those materials, their price, their possible substitutes, and the reliable vendors who can supply the required materials when needed at competitive prices. If a firm does not conduct such an analysis, it sacrifices profits by failing to utilize purchasing's full capability to assist in determining the optimum quality.

Three major considerations are involved in assuring a purchase of the right quality: (1) how to determine it, (2) how to define it, and (3) how to control it. This chapter discusses the first two considerations. The control of quality is discussed in Chapter 9.

HOW QUALITY IS DETERMINED

Quality is determined by balancing two major considerations: (1) the technical consideration of *suitability* and (2) the economic consideration of *price* and *availability*.

The design engineering department has the basic responsibility for determining the technical quality of materials to be used in production. Engineering works closely with production and sales in this determination. The using department is normally responsible for the suitability determination of materials not used in production. The office manager, for example, is responsible for determining the quality of typewriters, calculators, and other office machines. The maintenance engineer is responsible for determining the quality of the tools, greases, and oils to be used in maintaining the plant.

The purchasing department is responsible for the second major consideration in quality determination—the economic consideration of quality. After the technical decision of quality has been made, purchasing must determine whether the materials selected can actually be purchased on a continuing and competitive basis.

Management Responsibility

In the area of quality, most progressive companies give the purchasing department a major management responsibility along with its economic responsibility. This management responsibility is the right to challenge the quality requirements on all requisitions received in the purchasing department. The right to *challenge* is not the right to *change*. To challenge means to request reconsideration of the technical decisions for economic reasons. For example, a buyer recently challenged a requisition for 500,000 pounds of crystals of a specified chemical. Engineering agreed that the same chemical in the form of flakes rather than crystals could be used. The company saves $50,000 annually from this change. The ultimate right to determine quality, including the right to change, rightly rests with the department responsible for the performance or the use of the material (i.e., the engineering or using department).[2] The fact that purchasing has the responsibility to challenge quality tends to keep all departments alert to their responsibilities in determining the "right quality."

Material Availability

Given enough time and a willingness to pay a high enough price, practically any material could be manufactured to any specification and made available for use. Business, however, cannot operate under such a criterion of material availability and remain competitive. A more practical standard of availability is: "Can the material be purchased in a timely manner, from alternate sources of supply, on a continuing basis, and at a competitive price?" If not, the technical quality determination should be challenged.

To resolve problems of material availability, the purchasing and requisitioning departments should work together closely. In cases of conflict, two basic ways are available to mesh a firm's requirements with marketplace availability. First, the technical requirements of the originating departments can be modified to conform with what the market can realistically supply.

---

[2]It should be noted that the purchasing departments of a large number of companies are given the technical as well as the economic responsibility for many nontechnical materials in common use, such as office supplies, janitorial supplies, etc. (principally stores materials).

Second, if the modification of technical requirements turns out to be impractical, it may be profitable to develop a new source of supply.

As world and domestic production continue to increase, large companies are becoming increasingly concerned over the availability of their principal raw materials. Many firms now project their materials requirements for ten years ahead. Their purchasing departments attempt to correlate their materials needs with future availability and price, just as their marketing and production departments try to correlate future production capacities with future sales.

New Sources

Both government and big business routinely develop new sources of supply. These big buyers, by underwriting the production of new suppliers during the developmental stage, and by giving them long-range contracts, are able to persuade new suppliers to produce the new materials they need. The government, for example, completely underwrites costs in many missile plants, providing all facilities required during the life of a project.

Large industrial companies operating plants in newly developing industrial areas frequently underwrite new local sources of supply. Generally, the subsidy is only for the early stages of production, while the new supplier is developing his capabilities. Thereafter, the supplier's production costs are expected to be competitive with those of more distant vendors. The long-run cost saving comes through reduced transportation costs. This method of achieving materials availability by developing new sources of supply is increasing. The increase is a result of rapidly developing technology and a general marketing policy of decentralizing production plants to distant areas of consumption and low labor costs.

Substitutes

Two broad types of material substitutes are possible: substitutes of *existing products* and substitutes of *newly developed products.* Both types of substitution can be immensely profitable. For example, purchasing might suggest that spruce be substituted for yellow pine as crating material. Initial costs of these two types of lumber are comparable, but spruce is over 20 percent lighter than yellow pine, and will therefore generate savings in shipping costs. A large electrical company anticipates savings of roughly $220,000 annually from making such a change in crating materials.

The rate of new product development is increasing sharply. Over half the sales of many American companies today result from products that did not exist ten years ago. This single fact illustrates clearly why materials substitution represents an outstanding possibility for savings. An electronics buyer recently challenged a requisition for machined metal knobs used in large numbers on the instruments his company manufactures. He recommended using newly developed molded plastic knobs at a savings of 85 percent per knob. Engineering accepted the recommendation. The total savings in this case were roughly $8,000 per year. This dollar total may not be overly impressive, but the cumulative effect of such possibilities for savings should excite the imagination of any profit-conscious business executive.

Seller Suggestions

Suppliers can help their customers determine the right quality. Sellers of complicated, high-cost technical products, materials, or parts can be particularly helpful. For example, a supplier can frequently recommend minor changes in design tolerances that do not reduce the desired quality, but materially reduce his production costs, thus making it possible for him to sell at lower prices. Sellers can present for the consideration of a buyer the experiences of other customers who have already experienced production and procurement problems similar to his. Such suggestions often lead to important savings.

A supplier can frequently recommend changes in either his own or the buyer's production processes that will permit blending both processes into a more suitably integrated whole. The seller's production line, in a very realistic sense, is an adjunct of the buyer's production line. To have it operating as such, under coordinated direction, is an important purchasing objective. As the manager of outside production, the purchasing executive is a natural liaison for bringing about an integrated buyer-seller production effort.

To gain the greatest benefit from seller cooperation, many progressive companies hold annual seller-buyer symposiums. At these meetings all of the buyer's firm's principal parts and finished products are displayed for seller analysis. The meetings are held primarily to generate a mutual interest in developing the right quality and to seek ways of integrating the production efforts of buyer and seller. The ultimate in purchasing profit results when mutual understanding and interest exist between buyer and seller, and when this mutuality is implemented by the closest possible teamwork. In such circumstances, a supplier is highly stimulated to work for the buyer. He will think in terms of improving his customer's competitive position, rather than in terms of just filling his orders. The seller knows that in the long run the action resulting from such creative thinking will help him as much as it helps his customer.

Standardization

Standardization is discussed in the next chapter. It is mentioned here only to emphasize its relationship to total materials costs. The more highly standardized a firm's materials requirements are, the greater is the probability that materials will be readily available at reasonable prices. For this reason, all requests for nonstandard materials should be challenged by purchasing. The need justifying the higher prices, and the reduced availability, of nonstandard materials should always be verified, never assumed.

Cost Considerations

Price is only one element of total *cost;* it is the first cost payment in a series of payments. Transportation is another important cost payment. In many industries, transportation costs exceed 10 percent of total material costs; in others they exceed 40 percent. Receiving, delivery, and materials handling are also factors included in the cost of materials. Additionally, incremental costs arising from the use of certain materials in manufacturing operations must be included as a cost factor. Some materials are easier to work than others. Easy-to-work materials permit increased machine speeds and feeds; thus they save personnel and machine hours and reduce costs. Even though their initial prices may be higher, materials requiring fewer fabrication operations or having superior lasting qualities can also result in lower ultimate costs. For capital items, cost includes the cost of installation, operation, repair, manitenance, and depreciation.

Cost considerations should influence the technical and economic considerations of quality either individually or collectively. Unfortunately, in terms of cost, considerations concerning technical suitability are seldom accorded the same thorough analyses given economic considerations. Regrettably, profits are needlessly lost as a result of this neglect.

Value engineering/analysis is probably the greatest cost-saving technique used in industry today. Millions of dollars are saved annually from such analysis. Value engineering/analysis focuses on the cost side of the quality problem. It seeks to achieve the proper relationship among price, cost, and value received. It constantly strives to reduce cost by better integrating the technical and economic factors of quality. Figure 3-1 illustrates the important concept of value engineering/analysis. This subject is discussed fully in Chapter 13.

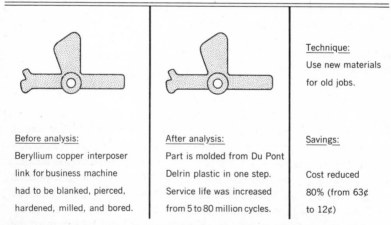

Technique:

Use new materials

for old jobs.

Before analysis:

Beryllium copper interposer

link for business machine

had to be blanked, pierced,

hardened, milled, and bored.

After analysis:

Part is molded from Du Pont

Delrin plastic in one step.

Service life was increased

from 5 to 80 million cycles.

Savings:

Cost reduced

80% (from 63¢

to 12¢)

Figure 3-1 An example of value analysis *(Courtesy of Sperry Rand Corp., Remington Rand Division, South Norwalk, Conn.)*

HOW QUALITY IS DESCRIBED

After the right quality has been determined, it must be described in such a way that the seller can understand and supply it. This is not as easy to accomplish as might be assumed. Industrial buying is not comparable to personal buying. If one wants to buy a rug, for example, one can examine the rugs in stock at various stores. One can see the colors, the patterns, and the weaves. One can tell the sales clerk where and how the rug is expected to be used, and one can ask and answer questions. The physical surroundings of the area of use and what the traffic pattern will be can be described. From such personal discussion, a good choice can usually be made. Compare this method of buying with one in which a buyer must describe in writing all the characteristics the seller should know about the item desired. In industrial purchasing, purchases are regularly made from suppliers thousands of miles away. These distant suppliers must determine buyers' wishes from a piece of paper—the purchase order. Personal discussions and references to floor samples are missing. Under these circumstances, quality description is much more difficult. Also, the description must be precisely understandable to all competing sellers, not just to one seller.

Quality descriptions perform three main purposes: (1) they make it possible to describe items on purchase orders, (2) they let the vendor know exactly what the buyer wants, and (3) they permit inspection by specified measurement or test which can verify that the material received is in fact the material described on the purchase order.

Quality is usually described on purchase orders by the following methods:

1 Market grades
2 Brand or trade names
3 Commercial standards
4 Chemical or physical specifications
5 Performance specifications
6 Material and method-of-manufacture specifications
7 Blueprints (engineering drawings)
8 Samples
9 Qualified products list
10 Combination of above

Market Grades

Grading is a method of determining the quality of commodities. A grade is determined by comparing a specific commodity with standards previously agreed upon. Grading is generally limited to natural products such as lumber, wheat, hides, cotton, tobacco, food products, etc. The value of grades as a description of quality depends on the accuracy with which the grades can be established and the ease with which they can be recognized upon inspection. There are, for example, thirteen grades of cotton, each of which must be determined from an examination of individual samples. Trade associations, commodity exchanges, and government agencies all expend great effort in establishing and policing usable grades.

In buying graded commodities, industrial buyers often use personal inspection as a part of their buying technique. Just as individuals select by inspection the shoes, dresses, and shirts they buy, so the industrial buyer selects by inspection some of the commodities he buys in primary markets. There can be a significant difference between the upper and lower grade limits of many commodities. The difference is so great in some commodities that materials near the lower limit of the grade may be unacceptable. Hence, inspection is critically important in buying many materials by market grade. Brewers and millers, for example, usually inspect all the grains they buy. Inspection is necessary if they are to obtain raw materials of the quality needed to produce a finished product of consistent quality.

Beef is an excellent illustration of the wide quality spread that can exist within a grade. Normally, 700-pound steers dressed and graded as "U.S. Prime" have a spread of roughly 40 pounds in fat content between the beef at the top of the grade and beef at the bottom of the grade. Such a wide spread may be a minor consideration to the purchaser of a one-pound steak. However, to the industrial feeder buying millions of pounds of beef, the difference can be thousands or hundreds of thousands of dollars.

Brand or Trade Names

When a manufacturer develops and markets a new product, he must decide whether or not to brand it. Branding or differentiating a product is generally done to gain repeat sales, protect the product against substitutes, maintain price stability, and simplify sales promotion.[3] The primary reason most manufacturers brand their products is to obtain repeat sales. Consumers develop a preference for brands. Therefore, branded products can generally be sold at higher prices than unbranded products of similar quality. A brand represents the manufacturer's pledge that the quality of the brand will be consistent from one purchase to the next. A buyer can be certain that a reputable manufacturer will strive to keep this pledge. Violation of the pledge carries the severest penalty possible—consumer rejection of the manufacturer's product.

Brand-name products are among the simplest to describe on a purchase order. Thus, they save purchasing time and reduce purchasing expense. Inspection expense is also low for branded products. The only inspection required is sight verification of the brand labels. The brand is the quality ordered. The higher prices usually paid for name brands are thus offset to some extent by reduced description and inspection costs.

A supplier's success in maintaining a consistent quality level is greatest in those situations where production and quality control are under the supplier's

---

[3]Manufacturers also produce merchandise for wholesalers and retailers who market it under their own private brands. In such arrangements the manufacturer is relieved of marketing and promotional responsibilities.

supervision. If a supplier buys an item from several manufacturers (each exercising his own quality control), the quality variation in all probability will be larger than if the supplier made the item himself or bought it from a single source. For this reason, it is important for buyers to know who is responsible for the production and quality control of all branded products they buy. In situations where tight quality control is essential, multiple sources of production should be avoided if possible.

The statement is often made that when a buyer purchases by brand name he eliminates competition by limiting himself to a single source of supply. If a buyer had to limit his purchases to a single brand from a single source, this would represent a major disadvantage of purchasing by brand name. In fact, however, there are very few situations in which only one brand is acceptable for a given purpose. A profitable market for any item, by the very nature of the free enterprise system, attracts many manufacturers to make this item. Competition, therefore, is available by brands just as it is by other types of quality descriptions. In addition, the same branded product may be available from different wholesalers or jobbers who are willing to compete on price and service to get a buyer's order.

Competition among brands is usually attained by specifying "brand A or equal" on the bid forms. What does "or equal" mean? This question has generated many arguments. Realistically, it means materials that are of equal quality and are capable of performing the function intended. Equal quality means similar quality of materials and similar quality of workmanship. Comparing the quality of materials is relatively easy, but comparing the quality of workmanship is particularly difficult. Here such nebulous considerations as precision of production, fit and matching of adjacent parts, types of finish, and shades of color must be resolved. The key "or equal" consideration is "Can the 'equal' perform the function for which the specified brand is desired?" If it cannot, it certainly is not equal; if it can, it is equal.

One practical way of resolving the "or equal" problem is to let the requisitioning department decide what is equal. This is best done before bids are solicited. All brands alleged by their manufacturers to be equal to the brand designated are reviewed by the requisitioning department. Only the companies whose products are accepted by the requisition department as equal are offered an invitation to bid. This technique helps avoid wounded or hostile feelings among vendors. It also permits requisitioning departments to make more objective decisions, because under these conditions the influences of price differentials and vendor pressures are at a minimum.

In some situations, purchasing by brand name can be made more effective by including in the purchasing description additional references or limitations. For example, if the buyer suspects that other materials can perform the desired function, reference in the description should give prospective suppliers the opportunity to offer such other materials for consideration. When limitations concerning physical, functional, and other characteristics of the materials to be purchased are essential to the buyer's needs, they should be clearly set forth in the brand name description. For example, in many purchases of equipment, interchangeability of repair parts is essential. When this is the case, this limitation should be spelled out in the brand name description.

Quality and psychological factors bear heavily on when to purchase by brand names. The psychological reactions that can stem from brand substitutions are almost unbelievable. The faith that some mechanics develop in certain brands of tools, and the equally blind faith some maintenance personnel develop in certain brands of cleaners, plus their unyielding resistance to change and unwillingness to try new products, almost defy reason. To make changes in brands under such circumstances can sometimes be detrimental, regardless of the economics involved.

For small quantities, brand buying is excellent. The primary disadvantage of purchasing by brands is higher prices. Many categories of branded items sell at such high price levels that they are economically prohibitive for a firm which buys in large quantities. Antiseptics and cleaning compounds are common examples of such items. For these, another type of quality description is preferable. When purchased by specifications, savings often exceed 50 percent. In recent years, buying drugs by generic name rather than by brand has resulted in spectacular savings for many hospitals; savings up to 70 percent are not uncommon.

Commercial Standards

Recurring needs for the same materials have led industry and government to develop commercial standards for these materials. A commercial standard is nothing more than a complete quality description of the item standardized. The description includes the quality of materials and the quality of workmanship that should be used in manufacturing the item. It also includes a method for testing both materials and workmanship. Commercial standards are a cornerstone of the mass production system; therefore, they are important to efficient purchasing and to our standard of living in the United States.

All nuts, bolts, pipes, and electrical items that are made to standard specifications can be expected to fit all standard applications, regardless of who manufactured the item. Materials ordered by standardized specification leave no doubt on the part of either the buyer or the seller as to what is required. Standard specifications have been prepared for many goods in commercial trade. National trade associations, national engineering societies, the federal government, and national testing societies all contribute to the development of standard specifications and standard methods of testing. Commercial standards are applicable to raw materials, fabricating materials, individual parts, and subassemblies.

Purchase by commercial standards is somewhat similar to purchase by brand name. In both methods, the description of what is wanted can be set forth accurately and easily. With the exception of proprietary products, most widely used items are standard in nature; hence, they are highly competitive and readily available at reasonable prices. There are many users of standard products; therefore, manufacturers who make them can safely schedule long, low-cost production runs for inventory. They do not need specific sales commitments before production. They know that when needed the materials will be ordered under these standard specifications.

Inspection is more expensive for materials purchased by commercial standards than for materials purchased by brand. Commercially standard products require periodic checking in addition to sight identification to assure buyers that they are getting the quality specified.

Commercially standard items should be used whenever possible. They contribute greatly to the simplification of design, purchasing procedures, inventory management, and cost reduction. Copies of standard specifications can be obtained from a number of government, trade association, and testing association sources. In fact, the easiest way to get a particular specification is to ask a manufacturer to provide a copy of the standard specification of the material or product that he recommends for the buyer's intended need.

Chemical or Physical Specifications

Not all items and materials used in industry are covered by standard specifications or brands. For many items, therefore, a large number of buyers prepare their own specifications. By so doing, these buyers broaden their field of competition. All manufacturers capable of making the item described in the buyer's specifications are potential suppliers.

By preparing its own specifications, a company can often avoid the premium prices of brands and the sole-source problems of patented, copyrighted, and proprietary products. When preparing its own specifications, a company should attempt to make them as close to industry standards as possible. If any special dimensions, tolerances, or features are required, every effort should be made to attain these "specials" by making them additions or alterations to standard parts. This action will save time and money.

Describing quality by chemical or physical specifications entails some risk. For example, if a buyer tells a paint manufacturer the exact chemical specifications of the paint she wants to buy, she then assumes complete responsibility for the paint's performance. If the paint fades in the first month, it is the buyer's responsibility. If a buyer tells a metal fabricator the exact dimensions he wants in a part, the buyer assumes all responsibility for the part's fitting or functioning. Should it develop that a part, to fit and function properly, must be $26^1/_{16}$ inches long, rather than 26 inches as specified in the purchase order, the responsibility for failure is solely that of the buyer.

A large company purchased 25,000 padlocks using the physical specifications its engineering department had laboriously prepared. In due time the padlocks arrived, passed inspection, and were put in the storeroom. A short time later it was discovered that the locks had one major shortcoming—*any key would open any lock.* The company sued the manufacturer for recovery of the purchase price. The court ruled that the supplier had fully performed the contract in accordance with its terms, and the buyer lost the case. In accordance with the law, the supplier had delivered the quality specified. There was nothing in the specifications requiring each padlock to be opened by its own unique key; the specifications had required only that each padlock be opened by a 2-inch bronze key. This requirement was met. It cost this company $13,000 to learn the practical dangers of a poorly prepared specification.

The cost of inspection can be high to assure compliance with company-prepared specifications. The very nature of the materials purchased under this method of description tends to require special inspection.

Performance Specifications

A performance specification, in theory, is the perfect method of describing quality. Instead of describing an item in terms of its physical or chemical properties, performance specifications describe in words what the item is to do. This type of description is used extensively in buying highly technical military and space products. For example, the product wanted could be a missile capable of being launched from a submarine with a designated speed, range, and accuracy. Or it could be a telemetering system capable of tracking and reporting missiles or satellites during their flight. Vendors are told only the performance that is required. They are not told how the product should be manufactured or what materials should be used in its manufacture.

Performance specifications are not limited to such complex items as spacecraft. Electronics and aircraft companies frequently use this purchasing method to buy such common materials as wire. The specifications for wire could require it to withstand a temperature of 2500°F, have a designated resistance to abrasion, and have a given conductivity capability. No mention would be made in the specification of the material of which the wire is to be made or covered to give it the required characteristics. Manufacturers are free to make these choices as they see fit.

Industry uses performance specifications extensively with considerable success in buying expensive, complicated machines and machine tools. Today more machines are replaced because of technological obsolescence than because of physical deterioration. Therefore, in buying a new machine, a firm should make every effort to obtain the ultimate in technological advancement. This can best be done by using performance specifications. It must be pointed out, however, that purchasing by performance specifications can be expensive. To reduce and control the expense, buyers should write descriptions as explicitly as possible. Also, the product being purchased should be sectionalized into the greatest practical number of distinct components, and sellers should be required to quote on each component. This practice helps solve the difficult problem of comparing sellers' prices, by allowing comparison of individual components.

There are two primary advantages of describing quality by performance specifications: ease of preparation and assurance of obtaining the precise performance desired. The performance specification is not difficult to prepare. For complex products, it is by far the easiest type of specification to write. It assures performance, and if the seller is competent, it assures inclusion of all applicable new developments.

Potential disadvantages of performance specifications include inappropriate use, poor supplier selection, and pricing. Because performance specifications are so easy to prepare, indifferent buyers often apply them inappropriately. They use them to avoid the effort of preparing more suitable and less costly descriptions. Proper supplier selection is essential when performance specifications are used. *In fact, the ability to select capable and honest suppliers is prerequisite to the proper use of performance specifications.* Because the supplier assumes the entire responsibility for making the product, quality is entirely in his hands. If he is not capable, he cannot apply the most advanced technical and manufacturing knowledge. If he is not honest, materials and workmanship may be inferior. When using performance specifications, buyers must solicit wide competition among a number of capable sellers. This is their fundamental safeguard. Capable sellers will ensure quality. Competition among them will ensure reasonable prices.

Material and Method-of-Manufacture Specifications

This type of description is at the opposite end of the description spectrum from performance specifications. When this method is used, the vendor is instructed precisely as to the specific materials to be used and how they are to be processed. Full responsibility for product performance is assumed by the purchasing company. Buyers assume that for the item being purchased under these specifications their own organization has the latest knowledge concerning materials, techniques, and manufacturing methods. In this case, therefore, buyers see no reason to pay another company for this knowledge.

Material and method-of-manufacture specifications are used primarily by the armed services and the Atomic Energy Commission. A modified version of these specifications, however, is at times used by industry. Large buyers of paint, for example, frequently request manufacturers of a standard paint to add or delete certain chemicals when producing paint for them. Large steel buyers make the same type of request when purchasing specific steels. Chemical and drug buyers, for reasons of health and safety, sometimes approach full use of the material and method-of-manufacture method of describing quality. Also, these specifications can sometimes be used most appropriately in those situations where technically sophisticated buyers in large companies deal with small suppliers having limited research and development staffs. Normally, however, this technique is little used in industry because it puts such great responsibility on the buyer. It can deny his company the latest advancements in both technical development and manufacturing processes. Specifications of this type are expensive to prepare and expensive to inspect for compliance.

There are two important advantages of this method of description. The widest competition is possible; thus good pricing is assured. Since the product is nonstandard, the antidiscriminatory provisions of the Robinson-Patman Act pose no barrier to obtaining outstanding pricing and service.

Blueprints

Blueprints (engineering drawings) are often used in conjunction with one of the other methods of quality description. Where precise dimensional limits are required, blueprints are the most accurate method of describing what is wanted. Despite their potential for accuracy, exceptional care must be exercised in using blueprints. Ambiguity at times can be an expensive cause of difficulty in this method of description. All dimensions, therefore, should be completely covered, and the descriptive instructions should be explicitly clear.

Blueprints are used extensively in describing quality for construction projects and for mechanical parts (cast, forged, and machined). There are four principal advantages in using a blueprint for description: it is accurate and precise; it is the most practical way of describing mechanical parts and tools requiring extremely close tolerances; it permits wide competition (what is wanted can easily be made known to a wide range of vendors); and it clearly establishes the standards for inspection.

The primary disadvantage of blueprints involves cost. Because blueprints have a limited scope of application, they are expensive to produce. The high cost of preparing blueprints must usually be absorbed by relatively few purchase orders.

Samples

Samples have been called the lazy person's method of describing quality. When samples are used, the buyer does not have to look for an equal brand, pick a standard specification, or describe the performance wanted. Samples are neither the cheapest nor the most satisfactory method of purchase. Usually the money saved in description costs is substantially exceeded by the money spent for inspection costs. It is usually difficult to determine by inspection that the product delivered is in fact the same as the sample. Quality of materials and quality of workmanship are generally exceedingly difficult to determine from routine inspection. Therefore, in many cases, the quality that will be accepted or rejected becomes a matter of subjective judgment.

Samples generally should be used only if other methods of description are not feasible. Color, printing, and grading are three broad areas in which other methods of description are not feasible. A precise shade of green, for example, is difficult to describe without a sample. Proposed lithographic work is best judged by the vendor's proofs. Establishing grades for commodities such as wheat, corn, and cotton by samples has proved to be the best method for establishing quality for these products.

Qualified Products

In some situations, it is necessary in advance of purchase to determine whether a product can meet specifications. These situations normally exist when: (1) it takes too long a time to conduct the normal postpurchase inspections and tests that are required to insure quality compliance (the federal government and some large industrial companies have defined too long a time as a period exceeding 30 days); (2) inspection to ensure compliance with the quality aspects of the specifications requires special testing equipment that is not commonly or immediately available; and (3) the purchase involves materials concerned with safety equipment, life survival equipment, research equipment, or materials described by performance specifications.

When advance qualification is indicated, suppliers are prequalified by a thorough review and test of the entire process by which they ensure compliance with their specifications. After qualification, the products of the approved suppliers are placed on what is called a Qualified Products List (QPL). On the QPL, approved products are described by trade name, model number, part number, place of manufacture, and similar identifying data.

Combination of Methods

Many products cannot adequately be described by a single method of description. In such cases, a combination of two or more methods should be used. For example, in describing the quality desired for a space vehicle, performance specifications could be used to describe numerous overall characteristics of the vehicle, such as its ability to withstand certain temperatures, to perform certain predetermined maneuvers in space at precise time sequences, and to stay in space for a specific period of time. Physical specifications could be used for describing the vehicle's television cameras and other instruments it will be required to carry. Chemical specifications could be used to describe the vehicle's paint. Lastly, a sample could be used to show the color of this paint.

Few products are as complex as space vehicles; nevertheless, an increasing number of industrial products require two or more methods of quality descriptions. For instance, something as commonplace as office drapes could require chemical specifications to describe the cloth and fireproofing desired, physical specifications to describe the dimensions desired, and samples to describe the colors desired.

METHODS USED IN PRACTICE

A recent survey[4] of 168 typical industrial companies indicates that quality in these companies is presently being described as follows (figures indicate percentages of total items purchased):

[4]An unpublished survey made by one of the authors at the Graduate School of Business, Stanford University, August 1973.

Brand name*	27
Commercial standards	25
Specifications	31
Combination	7
All other methods	10
	100

*Ninety-three percent of the purchasing executives buying brands stated they were able to get competition when purchasing by this method. Competition came from competitive brands accepted as equal and competitive sources selling the same brand.

Regardless of the method(s) used to describe quality, only the minimum quality needed for the product to perform the function intended should be specified. Over-specifying and including restrictive features in quality descriptions can cause delays and increase costs to the buyer. In the actual contract, the section including quality descriptions should also include all applicable warranties.

FOR DISCUSSION

3-1   What does *quality* mean in purchasing? What does it mean to the layman? What does it mean to you? Why is the meaning of this one word so important?

3-2   What is the difference between *cost* and *price?* Which is the more important in purchasing? Why?

3-3   Name a product for which the main material needed in manufacture should be the best that is obtainable. Explain.

3-4   Name a product for which the main material needed in manufacture can be of a very low quality. Explain.

3-5   Why is it said that "quality determines price"?

3-6   Does the purchasing department have the right to change the quality of the material requisitioned? What management responsibility does the purchasing department have regarding quality? How must this responsibility be exercised?

3-7   As a purchasing executive, what would you do to make a supplier feel more like an extension of your own manufacturing facilities? Discuss.

3-8   What is *value analysis?* Why is it important? Take any item from your daily life (e.g., a lead pencil, an automobile part) and find a better way to perform its same function at lower cost.

3-9   Why is description difficult? Why is it important? Discuss.

3-10   Describe to a seller 3,000 miles away an order for 50 seats for a new classroom at your college. To the same seller describe an order for 25 gallons of paint to match the color presently used in your school classroom. To the same seller describe an order for enough new light fixtures to give twice the candlepower readings of your present light fixtures.

3-11   Explain why Qualified Product Lists are sometimes necessary.

CASES FOR CHAPTER 3

Acme Wire Products Company, page 581
The Flanistor Problem, page 614
Harvey Company, page 621
Smithson Company, page 658

Specifications and Standardization

Proper specifications and standardization can contribute significantly to a firm's profitability. Surprisingly, the potential of these important concepts, though fundamental, is exploited by only the most progressively managed firms. Why are proper specifications so important? If they are so important, why does not management always insist on the ultimate in both specifications and standardization? These are the questions discussed in this chapter.

SPECIFICATIONS

Specifications are detailed descriptions of the materials, parts, and components used in making a product. They are the verbal and quantitative descriptions of a product's design. Because they are used extensively by engineering, production, and purchasing, optimum specifications help maximize the performance of all these departments.

When specifications are fixed, the final design of the product to be sold is also fixed. When final design is fixed, the product's competitive stance and profit potential are also fixed. Hence, developing proper specifications is an important management task. The task is difficult because it involves many variables, including the problem of conflicting human sensitivities. Many departments are capable of contributing to design; however, they frequently have conflicting views. Before the optimum in design can be achieved, major conflicting views must be reconciled. For example, to gain a competitive advantage, the *sales* department normally desires features in the product that are nonstandard and unique. *Engineering* sometimes desires features of design excellence that contribute little to sales potential, and may complicate the manufacturing process. *Production,* to achieve its goal of low unit costs, favors materials that are easy to work and designs which result in the smallest possible number of items in the production line. Such natural departmental differences regarding design problems can be resolved only by perceptive and skillful management.

Reduced costs lead to increased profits. Attempts to reduce labor costs directly normally result in strong counterpressures. Labor unions and individual workers are innately suspicious of attempts to save money by reducing labor costs. Hence, when an attempt is made to reduce these costs, regardless of its wisdom, labor troubles often follow. Cost reduction in the design area may also generate opposition, but such opposition generally is much less severe. Consequently, by imaginative and creative thinking, costs in this area typically can be reduced more easily than in any other area of industrial management. This is why the design area is an extremely fruitful field for management cooperation and coordination among engineering, production, and purchasing.

Basic Importance of Specifications

Some managers start measuring materials costs at the point where requisitions are submitted to the purchasing department. In reality, however, many materials costs are firmly engineered into a product's specifications during the design stage, long before requisitions are submitted to the purchasing department. If materials costs are really to be controlled, this is the point at which control must be initiated. The design stage is the first (and sometimes the only) point at which many costs can be reduced and controlled. If costs can be, but are not, reduced at this point, it is possible that they will be *built into the product* permanently and will be forever hidden in the firm's cost accounting records. They will not show up on the firm's profit and loss statement as a loss; rather, they will continue as an unnecessary and undetected profit drain.

Purchasing and inventory control have long been primary materials target areas for cost reduction. More correctly, the *complete materials cycle* should be a single target area for materials cost examination. This means that cost investigations should start at the beginning of the cycle—the design engineering phase. If this is not done, the use of many superior materials and suppliers may be denied to the buyer because of shortcomings in the design itself. In this event, even the most skilled purchasing executive can do little to effect important savings that would otherwise be readily available to a buyer's firm.

The case of a large typewriter manufacturer faced with intense competition is an excellent illustration of such a situation. By achieving a close working relationship between the firm's engineering department and its purchasing department during the design phase, a new machine was developed with 554 fewer parts in the carriage-return and tabulator mechanism; the motor was reduced in size by 50 percent, yet increased in capacity over the old one; twenty-one parts in each type-bar mechanism were reduced to five parts in each. These reductions would not have been possible without interdepartmental cooperation at the *beginning* of the design stage of the new machine.

As will be discussed in Chapter 13, "Value Analysis/Engineering," all is not lost if changes are not made at the design stage. Because markets, materials, and methods are constantly changing, a second look to modify, simplify, or improve specifications will always be necessary, justified, and profitable. However, it is at the time of *original design* that the greatest dollar savings from both specifications and standardization are possible. Remember the cost-sales relationship discussed in Chapter 1: to make up a 1 percent increase in costs (because of overspecification), a sales increase of 10 percent or more is required.

Preparing specifications for a product involves four distinct major considerations:

1 Design considerations of function
2 Sales considerations of consumer acceptance
3 Manufacturing considerations of economical production
4 Procurement considerations of markets, materials availability, and prices

As pointed out, it is not uncommon for these considerations to conflict with one another. Consequently, all departments concerned must cooperate, and top management must provide the encouragement and direction that will motivate the departments to seek a *company* solution rather than departmental solutions. A design capable of solving the functional problem perfectly might very well present difficult production problems of machining or fabricating. A design could function well and be easy to produce, but present insoluble problems of materials procurement and pricing. It happens with surprising frequency that a product design is functionally good, production is economical, and procurement is effective—but the consumer does not want to buy the product! A few years ago one of the large automobile manufacturers built a car that was superbly engineered and very economical to operate. These were the two qualities the manufacturer thought the consumer wanted most. This turned out to be an erroneous assumption. Because the car lacked some of the style features of its competitors, it did not sell well, and the manufacturer lost almost half its previous share of the total automobile market.

Conflicts of departmental interest are seldom as grave as the extremes just cited. Although aggressive department managers will disagree occasionally, compromises can usually be worked out when the various aspects of the problem are understood and the organizational mechanism for resolution of these problems has been established. Unfortunately, it appears that either industry in general does not understand the problem fully, or its solution suffers from limited direction from top management.

How Balanced Specifications Are Developed

Purchasing's interest regarding specifications preparation is frequently not recognized. Consequently, design engineers and industrial engineers too often resolve between themselves all four of the major considerations of specifications preparation, without consulting purchasing or the other concerned departments. This is regrettable because the professional engineer seldom has either the required experience or adequate information with which to resolve the procurement considerations of specifications. In their attempts to do so, a frequent result is the development of stringent specifications that do not provide sufficient latitude to develop effective competition. This can indeed be a costly practice for design engineers to pursue.

As discussed in Chapter 3, when specifications conflicts arise, final authority for the decision should rest with the department having responsibility for the product's performance. This is usually the design engineering department. This is not a justifiable reason, however, for engineering unnecessarily to subordinate the design considerations of manufacturing, procurement, and sales. From a company viewpoint, the right specifications are those that blend the requirements of all departments. Only such specifications can satisfy the goals of top management—i.e., increased sales, decreased costs, and the added corporate security which ensues from an increasingly strong competitive position.

To develop specifications that properly balance product quality characteristics and product cost, management must coordinate the firm's business and technical skills. Traditionally three approaches are used to accomplish this purpose: (1) the formal committee approach, (2) the informal approach, and (3) the purchasing coordinator approach.

The *formal committee* approach recognizes that a good specification is a compromise of basic objectives. A specifications review committee, therefore, is established, with representatives (as appropriate) from design engineering, production engineering, purchasing, sales, production (including production control), quality control, and standards. When a new product design is proposed, all members of the committee receive copies of all drawings, bills of materials, and specifications. No design becomes final until it is approved by the committee. One electronics firm estimates that it saves over $500,000 annually by using a purchasing-engineering team to evaluate new specifications in this way.

The *informal* approach emphasizes the concept of a buyer's responsibility to challenge material requests. At the same time, top management urges designers to request advice from buyers and work with them on all items that may involve commercial considerations. The emphasis at all times is placed on person-to-person communication and cooperation between individual buyers and designers. Using this approach, a company-oriented, cost-conscious attitude is developed at the grass-roots level throughout the organization.

The _purchasing coordinator_ approach entails creating one or more positions in the purchasing department for individuals to serve in a troubleshooting, liaison capacity with the design department. Typically, the purchasing coordinator spends most of his time in the engineering department reviewing design work just as soon as it comes off the drawing boards. He searches for potential commercial problems in an attempt to forestall them before they become serious. The purchasing coordinator approach is the most highly structured, as well as the most expensive, of the three approaches to purchasing-engineering coordination. It is also the most effective. It should therefore be used whenever coordination problems stemming from the technical nature of a firm's product or from its size justify the cost.

The reader should not infer from this discussion of specifications development any intent to derogate the work of the design engineer. There is none whatsoever. Often, for reasons of organization or tradition, the design engineer is _required_ to make decisions alone that could better be made in collaboration with others. Nevertheless, there is little doubt concerning the millions of dollars lost annually through the adoption of unnecessarily stringent specifications at the design stage. James L. Lundy, a national authority in the field of industrial management, was among the first to emphasize this source of industrial inefficiency. Twenty years ago, Lundy stated emphatically, "There is no telling how many millions of dollars have been wasted as a result of unsound tolerance specifications and the unnecessary work created."[1] The General Services Administration (purchasing department for the federal government) states that by exercising extreme care in specifications development, it is achieving a saving of roughly $70,000 for each new specification developed.[2]

Writing the Specifications

After the design of the product has been determined, the next step is to reduce the specifications to writing. This procedure requires great care. The specifications must be written in a manner that serves the rightful needs of many departments of the organization. Certainly, clear specifications are essential to good purchasing. For satisfactory performance, not only purchasing but also manufacturing, production control, sales, inspection, stores, and engineering are dependent on good specifications.

To meet the needs of all departments, a specification must satisfy the following requirements:

[1]James L. Lundy, *Effective Industrial Management,* Macmillan, New York, 1957, pp. 141–142.
[2]George W. Ritter, GSA, Sixteenth National Conference on Standards, San Francisco, Feb. 14–16, 1966, in "Government Posture in National Standardization," *Magazine of Standards,* April 1966. Restated 1975.

1 Engineering and sales requirements of, for example, physical characteristics, chemical properties, and dimensions
2 Purchasing and manufacturing requirements of availability and worka-
bility of materials
3 Inspection's responsibility to test materials for compliance with the
specifications
4 Stores' ability to receive, store, and issue the material
5 Production control's requirement to schedule the material economically and manufacturing's requirement to fabricate it without resorting to
costly methods
6 Purchasing's ability to procure material without difficulty and with
adequate competition from reliable sources of supply
7 Production control's and purchasing's ability to substitute materials
when such action becomes necessary
8 The company's requirements of suitable quality at the lowest overall
cost
9 The company's (engineering, purchasing, inspection, production control, manufacturing, and storing) requirement to use commercial and
industrial standard material whenever possible, and to establish company standards in all other cases where nonstandard material is used
repetitively

Procurement Importance of the Specification

One of the basic requirements of a good specification is to satisfy the
procurement consideration of markets, materials availability, and price. The
specification must also be clear enough for both buyer and seller to be
absolutely certain they are considering the same thing. Clarity in written
expression is not always easy to achieve. One company recently lost $35,000 on
a closed-circuit television installation because its written specifications misled
the supplier into believing that a more expensive installation than the buyer
really wanted was specified.

In addition to achieving clarity, care must be taken to ensure that
specifications are not written around a specific product, so as to limit
competition. A fire chief recently wrote into the specifications for a new fire
truck the requirement that the truck's 12-cylinder engine be produced by the
manufacturer of the truck. This completely restricted the competition, since
only one manufacturer of fire engines manufactured 12-cylinder engines in his
own plant. Had the fire chief specified what he wanted in terms of performance
characteristics, such as speed and acceleration, competition would have been
plentiful. This example typifies one of industry's most common forms of
specifications abuse, i.e., slanting specifications to one manufacturer's product,
thus reducing or precluding competition. In this particular case, fortunately, the
situation had a happy ending; the purchasing department challenged the
specifications, and the fire chief agreed to rewite them in a form permitting
maximum competition.

As discussed previously, specifying unreasonable tolerances is another common specification difficulty. Unnecessary precision pyramids costs! It costs more to make materials to close tolerances, it costs more to inspect them, and more rejects are certain. The best method of avoiding such unnecessary costs is to adhere to the most economical method of manufacture while using standard specifications wherever possible. For example, in procuring 1,000 drive pulleys for use in vacuum-sweeper motors, the first decision would be to determine whether the pulleys could be manufactured satisfactorily by a casting process. Although this method dictates the use of looser tolerances, in large volumes its unit cost is considerably lower then that of a second alternative, machining the pulley from bar stock. The second decision would be to select an industrial standard for the part, regardless of the method of manufacture used. This decision leads directly to a consideration of standardization.

STANDARDIZATION

Standardization Defined

In business practice, the concept of standardization is applied in two different areas. The first is concerned with the standardization of things—their size, shape, color, physical properties, chemical properties, performance characteristics, etc. The present chapter investigates this usage of the standardization concept, which is frequently called "industrial standardization." The second application deals with the managerial aspects of business activity—standardizing such things as operating practices, procedures, and systems. This type of standardization, frequently termed "managerial standardization," is discussed in the chapters that deal with managing purchasing and materials activities (Chapters 19 to 26).

Although minor differences are found in practice, industrial standardization can be defined as the process of establishing agreement upon uniform identifications for various characteristics of quality, design, performance, quantity, service, etc. A uniform identification that is agreed upon is called a standard.

Two historical incidents illustrate the importance of standardization. Eli Whitney is best known to most Americans for his invention of the cotton gin, but his contribution to the development of "standardization" was an even greater accomplishment. The cotton gin is an important machine, but standardization is the *prerequisite* to mass production. Mass production, in turn, has made it possible for the United States to produce over 30 percent of the world's goods with only 6 percent of the world's population.

Whitney's intense interest in standardization started in 1801 as he fell behind on his contract delivery schedule to finish 10,000 muskets to the United States government. Because these muskets were urgently needed to protect the nation from both hostile Indians and aggressive foreign powers, Whitney was summoned to Washington by Thomas Jefferson to explain his delay. The explanation is a little-known but extremely important landmark in American history. Whitney took with him to Washington a box containing the parts of ten muskets. On a table before his congressional interrogators, he separated these parts into piles of stocks, barrels, triggers, firing hammers, and so on. He asked a congressman to pick a part from each pile. These parts Whitney then assembled into a finished musket, repeating the process until all ten muskets had been assembled.

After this demonstration, it was easy for Whitney to explain his contract position. Rather than furnishing a proportional number of guns each month, as an artisan gunsmith would have done after individually making the parts for each gun and then assembling each gun in turn, Whitney had been working to design machine tools with which he could mass-produce parts which were interchangeable with each other. He had standardized the parts. When his machine tools were completed, he was able to produce the 10,000 muskets called for in his contract in the same time that an artisan gunsmith could have produced only a few muskets. This effort gave birth to the techniques of mass production, subsequently revolutionizing the concept and value of human labor in the western world.

Eli Whitney, inspired primarily by his inability to meet his contract commitment for guns by the artisan method, not only solved America's immediate need for arms, but also started the nation on the road to world industrial supremacy. Whitney had perceived that making standardized parts on specialized machines would accomplish two important things. First, it would greatly increase national production, and second, it would greatly reduce the need for skilled labor. The country urgently needed both benefits. The shortage of skilled labor was preventing any sizable industrial growth, and the need for production of all types was overwhelming.

The burning of Baltimore's business district to the ground in 1904, probably more than any other single incident, illustrates the need for standards in urban living. Like the battle that was lost for the lack of a horseshoe nail, Baltimore was lost for the lack of standard fire-hose coupling. Washington, New York, and Philadelphia all responded to Baltimore's cry for help. When their equipment arrived in Baltimore, however, it just stood by helplessly. There was no way to connect the different-sized hose couplings.

The Broad Implications of Standardization

There are three basic systems of production: job-shop production, line or mass production, and process production. The systems themselves can represent degrees of industrial progress. This is not to imply that in all cases progress lies in advancing from the job-shop to the process system of production. Each of these systems has its own applications and benefits. Whenever feasible, however, production should progress from a less technologically sophisticated to a more technologically sophisticated system. Management must be ever alert to the great gains that can accrue when production can be so organized that it can move to a more sophisticated system.

This concept of advancement is well understood in industry, although it is not always equally well applied. Less well understood is the fact that production systems are heavily influenced by standardization. Eli Whitney introduced mass production in the United States, Henry Ford made it universal. Ford, however, misinterpreted one important relationship of standardization to mass production. He thought he was acting correctly when he stated "the customer can have any color car he wants as long as it is black." Ford visualized mass production to mean a standard product produced from an assembly line. Actually, he missed the full implication of mass production. More correctly, mass production is the production of many diverse products, assembled from standardized parts which themselves have been mass-produced.

A West Coast manufacturer who yearly produces only a few hundred machines for picking apples, harvesting beans, and picking tomatoes comes closer to the concept of true mass production than did Henry Ford. This manufacturer, although he produces only a few machines of a given type, designs his specialized machines from standardized parts which are mass-produced. The design engineers of this company are fully aware that their job entails more than designing specific machines that can perform functions that will make farming more efficient. For this company's unique machines to sell at prices customers can pay, they *must* be designed from standard parts and assemblies that are themselves mass-produced.

Billions of dollars have been saved by companies through standardization. A survey by the American National Standards Institute lists the following examples:[3]

- A maker of business machines spends about $90,000 a year on standards work. It estimates annual savings at $500,000.
- A manufacturer of electronic equipment spends $24,000 annually on standards to save $125,000.
- A division of a major lubricating-equipment maker believes it saves $3.50 for every $1.00 spent on standards work.
- Two major standards projects of a certain manufacturing concern are tank design and minimum piping. Total savings equal $500,000.
- An engineering firm saves $25,000 per year, mostly on engineering and drafting time, through standards. The cost is $2,000.

Sperry Rand Corporation cites the following examples:

1 Standardization on a time-delay relay saves $20,000 a year.
2 Revision of electron tube specifications results in savings estimated to be $150,000 annually.

[3]"Does Standardization Pay Off?" *Iron Age*, Nov. 27, 1968, p. 26.

3 Issuance of a riveting standard yields a minimum annual saving of
$25,000.
4 Development of a low-cost microwave plumbing finish saves about
$50,000 each year.

How Standardization Reduces Costs

The use of standards permits a firm to purchase fewer items, in larger
quantities, and at lower prices. If fewer items are purchased, fewer items are
processed and stocked. Processing fewer items lowers purchasing, receiving,
inspection, and payment costs. Stocking fewer items makes controlling inventories easier and less costly. Consequently, the purchase of standardized
materials saves money three ways: lower prices, lower processing costs, and
lower inventory costs. Additionally, because sellers routinely stock standard
items in their inventories, deliveries can be made quickly from stock, thus
permitting a buyer to maintain lower stock levels and achieve still another
important saving.

Contrariwise, the use of nonstandard items, commonly referred to as
"specials," assures a firm of higher total acquisition and carrying costs. The
reasons for higher costs are the reverse of those given above. Additionally,
because for specials there is an absence of manufacturing experience, the use
of nonstandard items can result in problems of unknown quality, uncertain
delivery schedules, and lack of uniformity.

Clearly, many benefits accrue to the firm and its purchasing department
that maximize the use of standard items.

Awakening Interest in Standardization

The current trend toward standardization is evidenced by its increasing
recognition among industry, government, and consumer groups. The many
standards recently imposed by the Environmental Protection Agency throughout industry have sensitized industry to the need for voluntary standardization.
In consonance with the rapid rate at which science and technology are
advancing, it is especially important that standards be established as new
products are developed. Standardization after the fact is becoming increasingly
expensive and difficult to administer.

Interestingly, the government has started imposing standardization requirements in connection with its major purchases. Joint Military Specification
No. 81398 requires prime military contractors to develop standardization
programs for systems and major items of hardware purchased. Under this
specification, prime contractors must also stipulate to the government their
procedures for imposing adequate standardization requirements on their
subcontractors. Incentive awards are given to those contractors who use the
smallest feasible number of different components in a system design and who

select the maximum feasible number from those already standardized in the military supply system.

Kinds and Sources of Industrial Standards

There are two basic kinds of materials standards: industry or national standards, and company standards. It seems likely that there will soon be three, with international standards coming into increased usage. If a design or maintenance engineer cannot adapt a national standard for his purpose, his next best choice is to develop a company standard. If the part being manufactured is truly a nonrepetitive "special," then no standard is required.

Where can one get standard specifications? Specifications for items that have been standardized can be obtained from organizations that have developed them, such as those listed below:

> National Bureau of Standards
> American National Standards Institute
> American Society for Testing and Materials
> Underwriters' Laboratories
> Society of Automotive Engineers
> Society of Mechanical Engineers
> American Institute of Electrical Engineers
> Federal Bureau of Specifications
> National Lumber Manufacturers' Association

A catalog of United States standards, international recommendations, and other related information is published annually and distributed without charge by the American National Standards Institute (ANSI). This is a federation of more than a hundred nationally recognized organizations, trade associations, and technical societies, or groups of such organizations. Any one of its members can gain ANSI assistance in developing any standard it desires. Recommendations for establishing a standard can be made at any time. If, after appropriate research and debate, ANSI approves the recommended standard, it will be adopted as a United States standard.

Simplification

Simplification, a corollary of standardization, is another term for which recognized authorities have several definitions. Most frequently, it means reducing the number of standard items utilized in product design and carried in a company's inventory. For example, one large company used twenty-seven different kinds of standard lubricating greases in the maintenance of its machinery. Analysis showed that the same standard grease could be used for several difficult applications and that a total of only six kinds of grease were needed. Similar analysis showed that the number of standard bearings and fasteners used in maintenance and production could be reduced by half. Reductions of this scope are commonplace. Here are some typical examples:

- A large electrical manufacturer reduced its number of standard washers from 1,350 to 150 varieties.
- Another large company is saving $150,000 yearly from simplifying its standard typewriter desks, formerly purchased at prices ranging from $30 to $290.
- Still another company is saving $167,000 yearly from standardizing the paper towels used throughout its multiplant operations.
- The United States Navy is saving several million dollars yearly from simplifying its stock of ball bearings.

Simplification indeed results in big savings. The preceding examples illustrate that simplification can yield far greater savings than initially appears possible. Simplification savings result primarily from reduced inventory investment, more competitive prices (because of greater unit volume), greater quantity discounts, and reduced clerical and handling costs (because fewer different items have to be recorded, controlled, received, inspected, and delivered).

Some authorities consider simplification an integral part of standardization, not a corollary of it. These individuals visualize the simplification process as taking place primarily at the design level, rather than at the stocking level. They think in terms of simplifying (or reducing) the number of related items that are approved as standards in the first place.

Organizing a Standardization Program

A company can organize its standardization program in various ways. Because so many departments are affected by standards decisions, however, a committee effort is by far the most commonly used approach. At a minimum, a standards committee normally is made up of representatives from engineering, purchasing, production, marketing, and transportation. This committee typically is charged with the responsibility of obtaining input from all user departments, reconciling differences between departments, and making the final standards decisions. Theoretically, a member from any department could serve as head of the committee. In companies where nationally standard materials ("industry standards") and MRO items form a large portion of the company's total purchases, purchasing is particularly well qualified to head the committee. In companies that manufacture highly differentiated technical products assembled from parts made to "company standards," engineering is particularly well qualified to head the committee.

The form of organization used, or who heads it, is not of major importance. What is important is that a firm utilizes an effective standards program and attains the substantial benefits that standardization affords. Regardless of the organization employed, the purchasing department occupies a focal point in the process. It is only in purchasing that duplicate requests for identical (or nearly identical) materials, overlapping requests, and "special buy" requests from *all* departments become visible. Hence, no program for standardization can be optimally successful unless purchasing is assigned a major role in the program.

International Standards

Standardization plays an important and growing role in international trade. The American National Standards Institute (ANSI) represents the interests of the United States' voluntary standards system in programs carried out by non-treaty organizations, such as the International Organization for Standardization (ISO), the International Electrotechnical Commission (IEC), and the Pan American Standards Commission (COPANT). ISO and IEC are the most important of over fifteen active international voluntary standards organizations. ANSI is a participating member in more than 800 international technical committees, subcommittees, and working groups. ANSI also holds the secretariat for a number of critically important committees. For example, it holds the post of secretariat for the ISO committee on plastics standardization. This group developed a standard glossary of technical terms and characteristics in French, English, German, and Russian. Producers and buyers of plastics in the world market now have a common reference point for doing business. This kind of progress eases the problems faced by American purchasing managers who buy abroad. Further progress in developing international standards will produce similar benefits for purchasing managers in all industrialized countries.

Apathy on the part of some United States industries is still a major stumbling block in attaining more international agreements. The American "superiority complex" coupled with reluctance to give up so-called "trade secrets" are cited most frequently by authorities as the primary barriers to obtaining the cooperation of U.S. industry. Interestingly, the Soviet Union appears to be more open and more active than the United States in negotiations for international standards.

At one time, ANSI believed that adoption of the metric system, formally called the International System of Units (SI),[4] by United States industry was just about a dead issue. This, however, is no longer the case; ANSI now considers adoption of the metric system inevitable since the United States is the world's only major industrialized nonmetric country.

It is generally agreed that conversion to the metric system will increase United States exports by a minimum of $800 million annually.[5] Indisputably,

---

[4]The International System of Units (SI) was defined and given official status by the Eleventh General Conference of Weights and Measures in 1960. A complete listing of SI units of weights and measures is presented in detail in the National Bureau of Standards Special Publication 330, 1974 edition.

[5]National Bureau of Standards, Special Bulletin 330, 1974 edition.

bringing the United States' system of measurements in line with those of other countries will make U.S. exports more acceptable abroad. The stumbling block to speedy conversion is cost, the apathy of some industries, and lack of congressional direction. Actually, the cost is unknown, but it has been estimated to be as high as $20 billion.

Regardless of cost and the lack of congressional direction, there is considerable evidence that the country nevertheless is adopting the metric system. The National Association of Purchasing Management estimates that 19 percent of the United States Gross National Product is metric and that 35 percent of the *"Fortune 500"* companies have firm metric plans which are being implemented.[6] In many aspects of its business and personal life, America has already "gone metric." Daily the shutters of thousands of 8-, 16-, and 35-millimeter cameras click across the American scene. Work is done daily in hundreds of repair shops on thousands of foreign automobiles manufactured in metric countries. The Ford Motor Company currently produces automobiles with metric engines. United States pharmaceutical companies went metric over fifteen years ago. The electronics industry has used the metric system since 1954. The State of Ohio uses both kilometers and miles on its road signs; at least nine other states have adopted the same practice.

In late December 1975, the United States Congress passed and the President signed a bill for the nation's voluntary conversion to the metric system. Despite the fact that the Metric Conversion Act provides only for voluntary action, it is proving to be an unexpectedly strong conversion stimulant. Because of the Act and the Planning Board it established, interested persons and associations now have a focal point around which they are rallying and exchanging implementing plans and ideas.

CONCLUSION

Specifications and standardization play important roles in the search for the right quality. Proper specifications assist in resolving the functional conflicts of design, sales, manufacturing, and procurement. Many companies do not yet appreciate *fully* the concepts embraced in standardization and its corollary, simplification. Nevertheless, the philosophies underlying these concepts have played an important part in bringing the United States to its present position of industrial might and prosperity. It seems likely that these philosophies will play a still more important part in the future. They seem to be the only realistic answer to the lower labor costs of some foreign competitors. By further standardizing its component parts, its processes, and its operations, United States industry can refine and streamline the system that propelled it to the fore as an industrial power. Such refinement should permit the production of

[6]National Association of Purchasing Management Monthly Bulletin, June 1974.

additional lines of low-cost, high-quality, differentiated products that would be difficult to match competitively.

FOR DISCUSSION

4-1   What are specifications?

4-2   Why are good specifications so important to profit?

4-3   What are the three possible ways to increase profit? Do good specifications bear on any of these ways? Explain.

4-4   Why should the purchasing department participate in product development?

4-5   How can high costs be built into a product? What products can you name that appear to have high costs built into them? What products can you name that appear to have been designed for minimum cost?

4-6   Why are good specifications difficult to write?

4-7   Try writing a specification for an ordinary lead pencil.

4-8   How can tight tolerances unnecessarily increase the price of an item?

4-9   Is it correct to say that standardization was the key to the industrial revolution? Explain.

4-10   Examples have been given in this chapter of savings through standardization. How are these savings achieved?

4-11   Do you believe that there will be a trend toward greater use of international standards in the United States? What do you believe will hinder wider adoption of these standards in this country?

4-12   Why are standardization and simplification "part of the same package"?

4-13   Do you think that the world is heading toward greater use of worldwide standards? Explain.

4-14   Hospital costs are high and rising. Do you believe that these costs could be reduced in most hospitals by a simplification program? Explain.

CASES FOR CHAPTER 4

Sources of Supply

Suppliers, like manufacturers, have no choice as far as industrial progress is concerned—either they keep pace with the times, or they fall by the wayside. Buyers doing business with suppliers who fall behind jeopardize the future of their own firms. Consequently, capable buyers must continually initiate three important supplier-oriented actions: they must (1) reward satisfactory suppliers, (2) eliminate unsatisfactory suppliers, and (3) develop new suppliers.

Every industrial enterprise has two primary sources of supply—the firm itself, and outside suppliers. Management *creates* the internal source by a capital investment in personnel, machines, materials, and management. It *purchases* the services of the external source as a supplement to its own internal capabilities. Both sources influence a company's success. The first decision to be made in selecting a source of supply is whether the source should be the company itself or an outside supplier. This important decision, the *make-or-buy decision,* is discussed in Chapter 15. The second decision, the subject of this chapter, concerns *external* supply sources.

THE IMPORTANCE OF GOOD SUPPLIERS

Source Selection, a Major Responsibility

Selecting capable suppliers is one of a purchasing manager's most important responsibilities. If the right supplier is selected, then competitive pricing, reliable quality, on-time delivery, good technical service, and other goals of good purchasing are more likely to be achieved than if only a mediocre supplier were selected. After a competent supplier is selected, however, the buyer still has work to do! A supplier must be *motivated, assisted,* and periodically *evaluated.*

Supplier Relations

Business has long recognized that *customer goodwill* is a valuable asset. In fact, customer goodwill has legal recognition, and it is carried as an asset on many company balance sheets. Business is just beginning to realize that *supplier goodwill* is also an important company asset. A company develops customer goodwill by selling an acceptable product at a fair price, along with good service and the customers' interests in mind. It develops supplier goodwill by being open, impartial, and scrupulously fair in all of its dealings with its suppliers.

A company's purchasing department should motivate its suppliers to participate in a mutually profitable buyer-seller relationship. To create such motivation fully, it is essential that both buyer and seller completely understand the mutual advantage of a *continuing relationship.* A continuing relationship permits the seller to learn the intricacies of the buyer's operations, and vice versa. The seller learns about the buyer's business problems—his manufacturing, inventory, receiving, and overall operational problems. As the relationship develops, the supplier typically can reduce his direct selling effort; consequently, he can afford to direct additional effort to the study of mutual problems that may reduce prices. The end result of good supplier relations is a "meshing" of the operations of both companies. The seller's production line in reality becomes an extension of the buyer's production line.

Regardless of the managerial skills of a buyer, he will periodically encounter difficulties from which only a friendly supplier can extricate him. Even the best sales and production forecasts are vulnerable to error. Emergencies of many types continually arise in business. For example, unexpected increases in sales cause material shortages. Unforeseeable declines in sales and plant breakdowns cause material excesses. As a result of unexpected material shortages and excesses, some orders have to be canceled, others spread out, and still others increased or accelerated. Purchasing departments must have suppliers motivated by goodwill to cooperate with them in such emergencies; otherwise, additional costs will needlessly be incurred.

Supplier relations impinge directly on a company's public relations objectives. Many individuals and organizations form their image of a company almost entirely from their contact with its purchasing department. It is important that a company's image be a favorable one, because the nature of its image can influence both its profits and its future. A purchasing department, therefore, should strive to maintain good relations with all who call at its offices either in person or by telephone. Sales people are usually realistic. They realize that not every salesman or saleswoman can get every order. Nonetheless, when a salesman fails to get an order, particularly one on which he has worked unusually hard, he naturally feels disappointed. He will, however, bear no ill will toward a purchasing department that has developed a reputation for fairness to all vendors. Such a reputation is a valuable asset. Although a reputation for fairness does not appear on the balance sheet, it has real capital value—a value which is particularly enhanced during periods of short supply.

A salesman's time is money; to waste it is to reduce his income. Therefore, when a salesman calls, he should not be kept waiting longer than a few minutes. If it is apparent that a buyer cannot quickly see a calling salesman, the buyer should notify him of this fact immediately. If possible, as a matter of common courtesy, he should notify the salesman in person.

How are good suppliers identified? Where do buyers begin to search to find the suppliers who can serve their company best? What problems must be solved before the search for a specific supplier begins?

FACTORS IN SUPPLIER SELECTION

A buyer must consider many factors in selecting sources of supply. This section of the chapter investigates two primary areas of concern— characteristics of the supplying markets, and acceptable ethical practices in these markets. These are the areas most buyers consider before getting down to more specific factors of supplier selection.

Assurance of Supply

Reliability of supply is becoming increasingly important to both buyers and suppliers. Hence, suppliers who suffer recurring shortages themselves must be used with great care, regardless of their other desirable capabilities. Suppliers who have assured, long-term sources for their raw materials and component parts should be favored and developed. Recurring worldwide scarcities of materials seem certain to make assurance of supply a continuing problem that will become even more important with the passage of time.

Size of Supplier

Some purchasing authorities theorize that the size of an order should correlate with the size of the supplier receiving the order. For example, a small annual volume of perhaps $5,000 would be placed with a small company. A large annual volume, say $150,000 or more, would be placed with a large company. By following this procedure, the buyer is assured of always being an important account to his supplier; yet he will not overload any single supplier. For example, a large West Coast research company spends a small number of dollars each year on rubber stamps. It places its orders for rubber stamps with a small local company. This same company spends over $2.5 million yearly on scientific apparatus. Most of this business is placed with the largest supplier of such equipment in the West. This concept suggests that if a company's annual usage for a particular item is small, its order could be "lost in the shuffle" by a very large supplier. For the smaller supplier, this same order would be much more important, thus assuring the motivation required to ensure better service for the buying company. Conversely, if the annual usage were a very large quantity, a small supplier would not be able to service properly such a large account.

The concept of correlating the size of an order with the size of a supplier is valid; however, it does not always answer the question of what size supplier should be used. A small supplier frequently will work exceedingly hard to perform a very large order superbly, and large suppliers, on occasion, are very interested in developing small accounts.

For example, one very large East Coast corporation places all orders for its cutting tools with a very small distirbutor. This buyer is the largest single customer of the distributor, accounting for roughly 10 percent of the supplier's total sales. The benefits to the buyer in this arrangement are manifold. His company receives outstanding service and outstanding technical advice. The distributor's vice-president personally services this account. He constantly recommends ways of reducing costs and improving performance.

Had this same order for cutting tools been placed with a large firm, the account would probably have been serviced by a salesman or saleswoman of average ability. This individual would not have been able to make the same on-the-spot decisions or give the same analytical suggestions for economy as the vice-president of the smaller company. Thus, under some circumstances, it is possible for the technical assistance of a smaller company to be of higher quality than that of a larger company.[1] Theoretically, a large company can service a large order better than a small company. To compete in such circumstances, therefore, small companies must be highly motivated. Desire for prestige and potential expansion are frequently the factors that provide such motivation.

The same East Coast corporation that buys its cutting tools from a small company buys all its basic raw materials from the largest supplier in the industry. The buyer believes that for these materials, using the largest supplier in the industry is essential. Only the large supplier can maintain the dollar volume of inventory the buyer feels necessary to assure uninterrupted production. Moreover, only the large supplier can assure continuity of supply; in this age of scarcity, the buyer considers this capability mandatory.

Judgment must be blended with theory in selecting a supplier of the right size. There are potential dangers in placing large orders with a small firm that constitute a high percentage of the firm's total production. In such situations,

---

[1]Of course it is possible for the salesman to outperform the vice-president—not on-the-spot, but by having daily access to a superior technical staff.

the small supplier can become dependent on the buying company for its very survival. This, in turn, can place strong moral restraints on the buyer, whose actions can determine whether the small company prospers or fails. What happens if, as a result of technological advances, or a host of other possible reasons, the small vendor falls behind competitively. What happens to the small supplier if the buyer is forced to change suppliers to assure the competitive survival of his own company? A buyer should avoid the creation of such problems in the first place. It is normally unwise to place orders with a supplier that are so large that they consistently tie up a large percentage of his total productive capacity.

Number of Suppliers

Should one supplier be used, or two, or more than two? The argument for placing all a firm's business with one supplier is that in times of shortage, knowing all the buyer's eggs are in one basket, this supplier will take better care of his special customer. Also, a single supplier can provide the best pricing because of an assured and continual sales volume. The argument is also advanced that if a company uses two or three suppliers, it will be protected in times of shortage by having alternate sources of supply. Very large companies buy in such large volume that they can receive excellent pricing and service from two or more suppliers. For example, Sears, Roebuck and Company has sometimes used as many as three manufacturers for its Coldspot refrigerator, which it buys in huge quantities.

Certainly, if a single supplier's plant is closed because of a strike, a fire, or any other reason, its customers will be caught without material. When the General Motors Hydra-Matic Division plant burned to the ground, automobile production was halted on all cars utilizing the Hydra-Matic transmission. It took considerable time before the Oldsmobile and Cadillac Divisions of General Motors were able to secure enough Dynaflow transmissions from Buick to meet their needs pending rebuilding of the Hydra-Matic plant.

Similarly, during a glass strike, all automobile companies using glass from single sources of supply were forced to discontinue the use of tinted glass in their automobiles. One major corporation was forced to close its entire assembly line for lack of glass, tinted or clear. An independent automobile manufacturer, however, had been consistently buying some of its glass from a Canadian source as well as from its traditional United States source. When the strike occurred at its traditional source, it merely ordered larger quantities of glass from its Canadian supplier. Although the Canadian source could not supply tinted glass, it could supply enough clear glass to keep production lines operating. Thus, at no time was this company forced to close down its assembly lines. The airframe industry, on the other hand, has found that where high tooling costs are necessary, it is neither feasible nor possible to make use of more than one supplier. However, if high tooling costs are not involved, most buyers prefer at least two suppliers for high-volume items.

The number of suppliers to use is always a problem. One practical solution is to use two suppliers for a material category which has an annual dollar volume of, for example, $100,000 or more. Two contracts could be placed on a 70 percent to 30 percent basis. Such a distribution gives the supplier with the larger part of the business the required profit and incentive to perform any extra services the buyer may need, such as warehousing, special deliveries, and inventory and usage analysis. At the same time, the small supplier has enough business to want more. Hence, he is competitively motivated to keep nipping at the heels of the larger supplier. Active competition is thus used to stimulate both suppliers to vigorous performance. If the supplier with the larger portion of the business does not perform to the buyer's expectations, the distribution can be adjusted to give more business to the company with the smaller share.

Developing Sources of Supply

In some cases a buyer is not able to *select* but must *create* a satisfactory supplier. If existing suppliers cannot satisfy a company's needs, a logical alternative is to create a supplier that can. A large food company that used refrigeration equipment in its processes found only two refrigeration repair suppliers in its area. Neither was competitive as to price, and neither was fully qualified technically. To improve the situation, the company's purchasing manager approached a highly regarded local plumbing contractor with a view toward establishing a third refrigeration repair company. The plumbing contractor saw the potential opportunities available, and with the financial aid of the food company established a modern refrigeration repair unit as a division of his company. This division is now supplying the buyer very satisfactorily. Interestingly, and as is usually the case in such situations, the original two companies have become fully qualified technically, and they now compete intensely for a part of the total business—and prices have dropped 15 percent!

Occasionally, a buyer's company must create its own separate subsidiary corporation in order to have a reliable source of supply. The necessity for such action, for example, has occurred frequently in the machine-shop area of the rapidly growing electronics industry.

In the preceding examples, buyers developed new sources because they *needed* them. Supplier development can involve much more than this. An innovative buyer may deliberately develop a new supply source, not because he needs it, but because he knows that doing so will improve his firm's purchasing efficiency. If necessary, the buyer may even provide the prospective new supplier with the financial, technical, and managerial help that is needed to enable the new source to achieve efficient production. Three unremitting forces spur this type of purchasing action: (1) rapidly changing technology, which continuously creates a need for new specialty suppliers, (2) expanding international trade, which brings large multinational companies to the doorstep of virtually every country in the world, and (3) an ever-increasing scarcity of raw materials.

Technology is changing so fast that 40 percent of the products which are sold in the United States today did not exist ten years ago. This rapid change inevitably results in sources of supply getting out of balance, as far as a buyer's specific requirements are concerned. One alternative buyers can take to correct this imbalance is to develop new sources of supply.

For years, to assure continuity of supply, manufacturers have integrated vertically, sometimes by acquiring their suppliers. For example, the Ford Motor Company owns one of the largest steel mills in the United States. Many other companies similarly control some of their suppliers. Hence, supplier development is not a new concept.[2] What is new is the increasing importance and urgency of obtaining reliable sources of supply. The world's population explosion, its shrinking resources, and the formation of cartels (such as the OPEC bloc) have all combined to intensify the necessity of new source development.

Buying Locally

In some situations, community relations dictate that the purchasing department make maximum use of local sources. Public relations problems in some communities require a wider use of local sources than could be justified solely by economic factors. One large hospital in a city of approximately 500,000 people, for example, has found that it must purchase at least half its materials requirements within the community; otherwise, local businessmen will not support the fund-raising campaigns needed by the hospital to obtain its required operating money.

Local buying can frequently be justified solely on an economic basis. A local supplier can often furnish smaller quantities of materials at lower prices than could be obtained from distant sources. Local suppliers can also maintain and finance a balanced inventory of materials for repetitive local users. Working with local vendors and encouraging them to be capable suppliers is a part of progressive purchasing.

The question of when to buy locally involves two basic considerations. First, large dollar purchases should be placed at sources as close to the manufacturer as possible to obtain optimum prices and discounts. Second, small and medium dollar purchases should be placed with local sources when price differentials are small or when such action is necessary to keep materials physically available in the immediate area.

Most buyers prefer to patronize local sources whenever such action is prudent. A recent Stanford University research study indicates that approxi-

---

[2]There are legal restrictions regarding the owning of suppliers which will be discussed in subsequent chapters. The essence of the legal restriction is that under the Sherman and Clayton Antitrust Acts, firms can be punished that attempt to monopolize, to substantially lessen competition, or to create unfair methods of competition.

mately three-fourths of the 152 buyers surveyed prefer to buy from local sources whenever possible. Many of these buyers indicate they are willing to pay slightly higher prices to gain the advantages of better service and immediate availability of materials offered by some local suppliers.

Local suppliers can often be made more effective if buyers from different firms coordinate their requirements. For example, a large number of oil companies actively drill for oil and gas in the area around Bakersfield, California. It is costly to shut down a producing well. Until a few years ago, to minimize such occurrences, each drilling company carried its own inventory of expensive valves, pumps, and similar critical production components. At that time, buyers from each oil company involved met to discuss the possibilities of eliminating this costly, duplicate expense. They concluded that if the local suppliers would carry reasonable levels of the expensive items of inventory now carried by each oil company, and if the suppliers would guarantee around-the-clock delivery of these items in case of emergency, everyone could benefit economically. The suppliers were most willing to render this kind of service for a reasonable profit. Now, instead of each oil company carrying, for example, a $12,000 valve that it may never use, the selected supplier carries one of these valves which is available to all companies. The price for the valve is slightly higher than when it was carried in the storeroom for each company. However, savings from reduced valve inventories and from reduced valve obsolescence have reduced total costs for all companies to a fraction of their former level. Thus, this arrangement results in a worthwhile gain for both the oil companies and the local suppliers.

Local buying has the following advantages:

1 Closer cooperation between buyer and seller is possible because of close geographical proximity.
2 Delivery dates are more certain as transportation is only a minor factor in delivery.
3 Lower prices can result from consolidated transportation and insurance charges. The local supplier, in effect, brings in many local buyers' orders in the same shipment.
4 Shorter lead times can frequently permit reductions in inventory. In effect, the seller carries the buyer's inventory.
5 Rush orders are likely to be filled faster.
6 Disputes are usually more easily resolved.
7 Implied social responsibilities to the community are fulfilled.

National buying has the following advantages:

1 National sources, as a result of the economies of scale, can in some situations be more efficient and offer higher quality or better service at a lower price.
2 National companies can often provide superior technical assistance.
3 Large national companies have greater production capacity and therefore greater production flexibility to handle fluctuating demands.

4 Shortages are less likely with national companies because of their broader markets.

Buyers should give careful consideration to both the advantages and disadvantages of buying locally and buying nationally. Provided that applicable economic and technical considerations can justify the selection of local sources, it is the policy of most companies to buy locally.

Buying Internationally

The possibility of buying from foreign sources is a situation confronting a growing number of buyers today. A survey in *Purchasing* magazine reports that roughly 45 percent of all buyers now buy some materials from foreign sources. This compares with only 21 percent reported in a similar survey twenty-one months earlier.[3]

International purchasing is increasing and becoming easier and more profitable. It should become still easier as additional sources of information become available. For example, one of the easiest ways to purchase internationally, and at the same time deal in U.S. dollars, is to purchase through an importer, rather than buying directly from an overseas supplier. The number of importers is growing rapidly; a directory listing over 700 importers is now available from the American Importers Association in New York City.

Whether international purchasing will continue to increase in profitability and convenience is a question that hinges on many unknowns. For example: Will international trade agreements increase or decrease? Will tariffs go up or down? Will political stability permit industrial progress? Will advancing technology and technological breakthroughs increase foreign production? Will government controls reduce trade, as has happened in Canada? What effect will currency exchange rates and restraints have on future prices? What will be the long-term effect of the high price of oil? Will transportation costs continue to rise?

At the moment, increasing international trade seems highly probable. Over 100 nations are presently negotiating in Geneva, Switzerland, to reduce international trade barriers. Before this book is published, the President, who already has the authority to do so, will in all likelihood proclaim duty-free treatment for developing nations. Because of these facts, many foreign suppliers will increasingly consider the United States a long-term market, and more and more American companies will make foreign purchases.

Foreign buying policies vary greatly among individual companies. For example, one large electronics company has a policy of buying domestically even when overseas prices may be substantially lower, everything else (mainly quality) being equal. This company buys overseas only when the technical specifications and quality offered in foreign products (which are rapidly increasing in number) are much higher than those offered in similar domestic

[3]Somerly Dowst, "Nearly Half of Buyers Dealing Overseas," *Purchasing*, May 6, 1975, p. 55.

products. On the other hand, a large medical center with numerous national research contracts has a policy of buying all its scientific instruments overseas, even though lead time for these instruments normally exceeds one year. A large Detroit buyer of steel cites "antiquated methods of allocation" of domestic mills in times of shortages as his reason for buying steel from both Western Europe and Japan.

The strong forces at work throughout the world influencing foreign trade indicate that no company can long sustain an inflexible policy of no overseas buying. The economic progress of the underdeveloped countries, the opening up of Russia and China for trade, and steadily declining international tariffs all combine to present an ever-increasing number of foreign buying opportunities.

Manufacturer or Distributor

In choosing between a manufacturer and a distributor, the buyer's considerations should focus largely on methods of buying and distribution services, rather than on nearness of the materials source. The arguments which favor buying through a distributor are too often confused with the distributor's location. The real consideration is not his location, but the *functions he performs*.

In the steel industry, distributors pay the same price for steel as any other buyer. They buy in carload lots or larger, and sell in small lots to users whose operating circumstances do not justify carload purchases. The steel distributor realizes a profit from the operation because it is customary, even at the factory, to sell large lots (on a per-ton basis) at lower prices than small lots. If buyers wish to purchase steel directly from the mill and bypass the distributor, they are perfectly free to do so. When they do so, however, they usually forgo certain special services that a competent distributor is equipped to offer. The distributor is usually able to give immediate delivery on steel of all sizes and shapes, which means he maintains cutting and shaping tools and skilled personnel to operate them. He is able to deliver quantities in less-than-carload lots, which means he must carry a large inventory. The buyer has immediate access to large stocks, and inventory carrying costs are shifted from the buyer's company to the distributor. Some distributors offer "trade credit" to buyers by postponing billing to more favorable future dates. This benefit can be extremely valuable to small new companies.

The question of whether to use a distributor takes another form when the materials ordered are to be shipped directly to the user by the manufacturer (known as a drop shipment). The distributor in this situation does not handle the materials physically; he only acts as a broker.[4] Under such circumstances, a buyer could be strongly motivated to buy directly from the manufacturer if the manufacturer will let him. The answer to the manufacturer-distributor question

[4]Manufacturer's representatives, who usually deal only in technical items, also effect deliveries by drop shipments, and they act as brokers. Manufacturer's "reps" aid a buyer by being able to furnish him complementary product lines from a single source.

centers on the fact that the *functions* of distribution cannot be eliminated. The buyer needs these functions, and he should pay for them once, but not twice. Either the distributor or the manufacturer must perform such distribution functions as carrying the inventory, giving technical service, and extending credit. The buyer must decide for each individual buying situation how he can best purchase these functions, if the manufacturer gives him this choice.

A buyer should be aware that distributors stock many different manufacturers' products. Hence, ordering from a distributor can significantly reduce the total number of orders a buyer must place to fill his materials requirements. If there were no distributors, orders for production and maintenance, repair, and operating (MRO) requirements would have to be placed directly with each different manufacturer. This would vastly increase the number of orders placed. The fact that many distributors carry the products of hundreds of manufacturers illustrates the potential size of the increase. Every additional order in turn creates an additional receiving, inspection, and invoice operation.

As a final check on the decision to choose between a distributor and a manufacturer, the buyer should ask the question, "Can my company perform the services of distribution at a lower cost than it can buy these same services from a distributor?"

Miscellaneous Considerations

By the very nature of business, wherein managers move upward from functional to general management positions, almost all companies tend to have a specific functional orientation or bias. Thus, there are companies with a marketing orientation, a production orientation, a financial orientation, an engineering orientation, and so forth. Buyers should determine the management orientation of their potential suppliers so that they can select those suppliers whose management characteristics blend best with the requirements of their own companies.

By considering only routine factors of supplier evaluation, a buyer might end up selecting the efficient suppliers who are also the major suppliers to his major competitors. This could create an extremely dangerous situation, since the vagaries of business are certain to produce periodic shortages of supply. During such crises, economic pressures most assuredly will cause a seller to favor his major customers at the expense of his minor customers.

In selecting suppliers, buyers should consider the seller's general "product mix." Does it fit in with the product mix of the buyer's own company? How do the supply curves of the seller match the demand curves of the buyer? Would a long-term relationship provide economic gain for both?

Occasionally, a buyer must choose between a supplier with an average company and a superior sales force and a supplier with an excellent company and an average sales force. This choice can sometimes be difficult. Waldo L. Nelson, Purchasing Manager of General Mills, advises that sales-oriented companies such as General Mills, to whom meeting production and delivery schedules is vitally important, invariably choose the company with the superior sales force.

Conflicts of Interest

In selecting suppliers, buyers must be aware of conflicts of interest. A conflict of interest exists when buyers must divide their loyalty between the firm which employs them and another firm. In purchasing, this situation usually occurs when a buyer is a principal stockholder in a supplier's firm, and when he or she makes purchases from close friends and relatives. Conflicts of interest are discussed more fully in Chapter 20. The subject is introduced here solely to remind the reader that it can be a consideration of supplier selection.

Ethical Considerations

Buyers should keep themselves as free as is humanly possible from unethical influences in their choice of suppliers. It is very difficult to maintain complete objectivity in this matter, for it is only human to desire to favor one's friends. On occasion, friends can make unusually good suppliers. They will normally respond to emergency needs more readily than suppliers without a strong tie of personal friendship. On the other hand, buyers tend not to discipline and reprimand poorly performing friends to the same degree as they do other suppliers.

"Gifts" from suppliers which are intended to influence buying decisions have no place in a professional purchasing department. In most states commercial bribery is a criminal offense. Lunches with salesmen are not customarily considered gifts for the purpose of influencing decisions. Tradiationally, they are judged to be a means of providing more time for the buyer and seller to discuss business problems. Beyond this point, the issue of undue influence may be raised. It is for this reason that many companies prohibit their buyers from accepting any gift beyond a simple meal. Regarding meals, firms should provide expense accounts for members of their purchasing departments. This permits buyers to reciprocate with salesmen in paying for lunches, thus eliminating in this area any suspicion of undue influence.

Dishonest Suppliers

Dishonest sellers exist in the industrial world just as they do in the consumer world. This may surprise some readers, for it is logical to assume that dishonest suppliers would not tackle experienced industrial buyers, but they do. Dishonest suppliers, therefore, can be a problem in source selection. A recurring technique used by dishonest suppliers is to contact a buyer by telephone, usually stating that the buyer has been referred to them by a top corporate executive—commonly one who cannot be contacted quickly, or who is located in another city. A typical story centers upon an unfortunate person, frequently a poor widow, who must liquidate the family stationery business immediately. The entire inventory of office supplies is offered at very low prices. If the buyer takes the offer, and many do, the result is always the same: poor quality, high prices, and late delivery. How many buyers take such offers? Several recent studies indicate that from 12 to 15 percent of buyers, at one time or another, have been swindled by dishonest suppliers. It's caveat emptor, without a doubt—even in the industrial world!

A buyer's best protection against dishonest suppliers is the practice of thorough and prudent vendor investigation before becoming seriously involved. This type of professional purchasing performance, blended with a liberal dose of common sense, should keep buyers on safe ground in most cases.

What can buyers do if they are swindled by a dishonest seller? In most cases they have little legal recourse, from a practical standpoint, but they should attempt to expose such sellers. They should contact the nearest better business bureau and the postal inspector if mail solicitation is involved. They should also inform the district attorney and the local purchasing association. Dishonest sellers cannot operate in the light of publicity. The reluctance of victims to admit that they have been swindled is one of a dishonest seller's greatest protections.

Reciprocity and Trade Relations

When buyers give preference to suppliers who are also customers, they are engaging in a practice known as "reciprocity." The related practice of "trade relations" is more difficult to define. Trade relations executives define it as a management function which deals with the complex logistic intelligence factors of quality, service, and price.

Most observers, however, continue to wonder whether trade relations is not simply reciprocity masquerading in new dress. Reciprocal purchase-sales agreements are undeniably at the heart of most trade relations agreements. Most government agencies, particularly the Federal Trade Commission, view the two terms as being synonymous. For some years, both concepts have been under constant scrutiny by the Antitrust Divison of the Justice Department. The line between the two concepts, as well as that between reciprocal actions which are legal and those that are illegal, is frequently very thin.

The following cases clearly illustrate illegal practices. One of the nation's largest shippers was convicted for illegal reciprocity as a result of threatening to withdraw business from a large railroad, if the railroad did not use a braking system manufactured by a subsidiary of the large shipper. Another large company was convicted of unlawful reciprocal dealing under its announced policy of "I will buy from you if you buy from me." Under this policy, by means of its economic power the company forced other companies to purchase its products at higher than market prices under the threat of losing the firm's high dollar business. In contrast to these actions, it is entirely legal to buy from one's customers at fair market prices, without economic threat, and *without intent to restrict competition.*

Practical Pros and Cons of Reciprocity Most buyers disapprove of the practice of reciprocity even when legal, because it usually constrains purchasing's opportunity to increase profits by reducing the cost of materials. Those opposed to reciprocity cite the following dangers:

1 False markets can be created with companies that may later change their minds or fall behind technically.
2 Reciprocity does not follow sound principles of buying and selling on the fundamental criteria of quality, price, and service.
3 Companies may relax their competitive efforts in technical and production areas as a result of reduced competition. Consequently, purchasing costs may be higher.
4 Sales departments may develop a false sense of security, resulting in deterioration of a firm's selling effort.
5 New customers may be hard to find because of preestablished relationships with competitors.
6 Company reputations may be impaired because of bad publicity resulting from reciprocity. Sellers of new, advanced products and processes will not waste their time with companies known to be tied up with reciprocal agreements.
7 Conspiracy and restraint-of-trade situations can develop, with their attendant legal dangers.

Consequently, most United States firms proclaim a reciprocity policy similar to this one: "When important factors such as quality, service, and price are equal, we prefer to buy from our customers."[5] Buyers find, however, that combinations of quality, service, and price are seldom *exactly* equal. If quality and price are equal, then the supplier would be selected solely on the basis of service. Service is seldom equal except for standard off-the-shelf items because, as was discussed earlier, in the majority of cases it is a supplier's capabilities which are being purchased, not commodities. To test the validity of this conclusion, readers should ask themselves the following type of questions and also should consider how many times they believe the answers would be the same for different suppliers:

- Does the supplier have an effective value analysis program for his products?
- To what extent will the supplier provide engineering and design assistance?
- To what extent does the supplier have a service-shop organization that is available to me?

[5]Some firms use such vague phrases as "buy from customers when doing so will contribute to the greatest economic good of the firm."

- Are repair parts available locally? On short notice? Will the supplier make available reserve production facilities to meet my emergency demands?
- To what extent will the supplier plan shipments to minimize my inventory?
- To what extent will the supplier help me cut acquisition costs such as qualifying visits, telephone calls, spoilage and waste, and customers' complaints?

The proponents of reciprocity contend that it is simply good business. They believe that if a buyer buys from a friend, both the buyer and the friend will profit in the long run. They maintain that service is better from suppliers who are also customers. They argue that reciprocity is a legitimate way to expand a company's markets. For example, a battery manufacturer states that it only makes good sense to buy the brand of automobile that uses his company's batteries.

Companies manufacturing high-volume, highly competitive, standardized products are more susceptible to reciprocal pressures than companies manufacturing highly differentiated products. This is only logical. As a consequence, industries typically more receptive to reciprocal pressures are, for example, the transportation, petroleum, steel, and cement industries.[6] Industries less responsive to reciprocal pressures include those concerned with electronic data processing, electronics, and defense.

If a firm engages in reciprocal dealings, careful records of sales, procurement and materials costs, and related profit must be maintained to ensure that in the case of each reciprocal agreement, the resultant long-range sales advantages in terms of profit actually equal or exceed possible purchasing losses. (Remember that, on the average, it takes approximately $1,500 of increased sales to generate the same profit that would be produced by a $100 cost saving in purchasing or elsewhere in the organization.)

In the final analysis, reciprocity is neither a sales problem nor a purchasing problem; rather, it is a *management problem.* If management belives that it can expand its markets *permanently* and add to the firm's profits *legally* by reciprocity, then this is the decision management should make. Conversely, if management believes profits will be increased by buying without the constraints of reciprocity, then that is the policy management should adopt.

SOURCES OF SUPPLIER INFORMATION

Although some buyers rely on memory and experience for knowledge of sources of supply, competent buyers more correctly rely on the department's own records, published material, and personal contacts. Sources of information

---

[6]As might be suspected, the firms in these industries tend to have the largest and most active trade relations departments.

concerning supplers are plentiful. The following information sources should prove helpful to a buyer in preparing a list of potential suppliers.

Supplier Purchasing Information File

Purchasing departments should keep supplier information files on past and present suppliers which includes: the name of each supplier, a list of materials he can supply, his delivery history, his quality rejection record, his overall desirability as a supplier, and general information concerning his plant and management. In addition to a departmental file, buyers usually maintain a personal supplier file for their own use. Supplier information files are important because many purchasing operations are repetitive; hence, it would be poor management indeed if buyers spent time repeatedly recapturing information which was once available to them but had been needlessly lost.

Supplier Catalogs

Catalogs are a commonly used source of supplier information. Many purchasing departments maintain a catalog room, where users can examine the catalogs to try to locate the material they need. The catalogs are also used by the purchasing department's buyers to determine potential sources of supply and, on occasion, to estimate prices.

Large companies frequently value their catalog library sufficiently to employ a full-time librarian for indexing the catalogs and keeping them up to date. Without an adequate indexing system, use of manufacturers' and jobbers' catalogs can be excessively time-consuming. Catalogs are likely to cover a wide range of items; however, the buyer is usually interested in just a single item. Therefore, a usable catalog should not only contain information about the material desired, but it should also be *specific, definite,* and *easily understandable.* In addition to catalogs, purchasing libraries traditionally include a commodity file, a supplier name file, appropriate trade publications, and purchasing textbooks.

Trade Registers and Directories

Thomas' Register of American Manufacturers and *MacRae's Bluebook* are typical of several widely known trade registers and directories. These registers contain information on the addresses, number of branches, and affiliations of all leading manufacturers. Financial standings of firms are also frequently given. The registers are indexed by commodity, manufacturer, and trade name or trademark description of the item.

Trade Journals

Trade journals are another excellent source for obtaining information about possible suppliers. Advertisements in trade journals are often a buyer's first contact with vendors and their products. In the field of purchasing, the magazines *Purchasing* and *Purchasing World* are perhaps the best known and most widely read trade journals. Both contain purchasing, general management, and economic information that is valuable to all buyers and all purchasing managers. Specialized trade journals are available for more specific information about specific industries. For example, a buyer in the aircraft industry would routinely read *Aviation Week;* a buyer in the steel industry would routinely read *Iron Age.*

The "Yellow Pages"

Another commonly known directory is the classified "yellow pages" section of telephone directories. This source of information is of limited value to many industrial buyers because most of the listings are local companies. The size and capability of companies are also difficult to determine, as management and financial data are normally not included in the advertisements. The yellow pages do, however, have the virtue of being well indexed. Also, they can serve as a useful starting point if other sources have proved fruitless, and if local sources are desired.

Filing of Mailing Pieces

Many mail advertisements are worth saving. These should be given a file number and indexed by the name and number of each publication. When buyers seek a new source, they can then refer to the index and review the appropriate brochures and booklets.

Some purchasing departments ask prospective suppliers to complete a simple form giving basic information about themselves and their products. This information, which includes company name, address, officers, local representatives, and principal products, is kept in a set of loose-leaf notebooks. The buyer, by referring to these standardized forms, gains immediate, current information about new sources.

Sales Personnel

Sales personnel are excellent sources of information for possible sources of supply. Not only are they usually well informed about the capabilities and features of their own products, but they are also familiar with similar and competitive products as well. By the very nature of their specialized knowledge, sales people can often suggest new applications for their products which will eliminate the search for new suppliers. From calling on many companies, salesmen and saleswomen learn much about many products and services. All of this information is available to the alert, receptive buyer. This is an additional reason why sales personnel should always be treated courteously and given ample time to make their sales presentations. To deny them this opportunity is to risk the loss of valuable information, including information concerning new and reliable sources of supply.

Trade Exhibits

Regional and national trade shows are still another way in which buyers learn about possible sources of supply. The use of exhibits as a means of sales presentation is greatly increasing. They provide an excellent opportunity for buyers to see various new products and modifications of old products. They also offer buyers an opportunity to compare similar products of different manufacturers. Regional trade exhibits are sponsored periodically by manufacturers, distributors, and trade organizations. For example, a large distributor of scientific apparatus and glassware holds an annual trade exhibit in major cities throughout the country. Electronics distributors hold similar trade exhibits. Invitations to attend these exhibits are sent to all interested purchasing and technical personnel in the area. Although buyers must often find time to visit trade exhibits after working hours, doing so is usually worthwhile. Exhibits offer a buyer an excellent opportunity to expand his or her knowledge of new products, new vendors, and new ideas.

Company Personnel

Personnel in other departments of a firm can often provide helpful information about potential suppliers. Through their association in professional organizations, civic associations, or social groups, these employees often learn about outstanding suppliers. Scientific and research personnel who use sophisticated materials or services always have many valuable suggestions to make on possible sources of supply. From their trade exhibits and their discussions with associates, technical personnel learn much about new products, new methods, and new manufacturers.

Other Purchasing Departments

Purchasing departments in other companies are most helpful sources of information concerning suppliers with whom they deal. Information exchanged among purchasing departments can be mutually beneficial for all participating companies; therefore, this source of information should be actively developed.

Local purchasing associations, such as the local chapters of the National Association of Purchasing Management, the Canadian Association of Purchasing Agents, and the National Institute of Government Purchasing, publish a list of their members. The lists are indexed in two ways: alphabetically by name of each member and alphabetically by name of the member's company. One of the basic objectives of a purchasing association is that its members help each other in every possible way. Accordingly, members usually will do everything possible to help fellow members locate and evaluate new sources of supply.

However, they will not, and they should not, exchange pricing information. This would be unethical and self-defeating.

International Sources

A high percentage of buyers now use international sources. Therefore, information concerning foreign markets and companies is needed—and it is available from an increasing number of sources. Some typical sources are the following: The United States Department of Commerce, 1615 H Street, N.W., Washington, D.C., 20010; foreign commercial attachés, who are located in foreign embassies and consulates in the United States; American commercial attachés, who are located in United States embassies and consulates abroad; *Trade Directories of the World,* Croner Publications, Inc., 21105 Jamaica Ave., Queens Village, N.Y. 11428; New York Chamber of Commerce and Industry, 99 Church Street, New York, N.Y. 10007; *Handbook of International Purchasing,* by Paul H. Combs, Cahners Books, 88 Franklin Street, Boston, Mass. 02110; and the International Federation of Purchasing and Materials Management, York House, Westminister Bridge Road, London SE1 7UT, England.

EVALUATING A POTENTIAL SUPPLIER

Upon completing a list of all potential suppliers, a buyer's next step is to evaluate each of these suppliers individually. By the process of elimination, a selected *list of vendors* is developed with whom the buyer may desire to negotiate or solicit bids. The vendor list should be comprehensive enough to bring to bear every type of competition desired, including:

1 Price competition, resulting from pinpointing the lowest-cost producers or distributors
2 Technological competition, resulting from pinpointing potential suppliers who excel in good ideas, engineering planning, design, materials, and production techniques
3 Service competition, resulting from pinpointing those suppliers who are especially anxious to get contracts and who, to get them, will add "plus" values over and above functional value (quality) and price

What kind of company makes the best supplier? It would be difficult to improve upon the definition given by Wilbur England of Harvard University:[7]

A good supplier is one who is at all times honest and fair in his dealings with the customers, his own employees, and himself; who has adequate plant facilities, and know-how so as to be able to provide materials which meet the purchaser's

[7]Wilbur B. England, *Procurement Principles and Cases,* 5th ed., Richard D. Irwin, Homewood, Ill., 1967, p. 405.

specifications, in the quantities required, and at the time promised; whose financial position is sound; whose prices are reasonable both to the buyer and to himself; whose management policies are progressive; who is alert to the need for continued improvement in both his products and his manufacturing processes; and who realizes that, in the last analysis, his own interests are best served when he best serves his customers.

Type of Evaluation Needed

The type of evaluation required to determine supplier capability varies with the nature, complexity, and dollar value of the purchase to be made. It also varies with the buyer's knowledge of the firms being considered for the order. For many uncomplicated, low-dollar-value purchases, and examination of the information already available in the purchasing department (such as the supplier information file, catalogs, and brochures) is sufficient. For complex, high-dollar-value purchases, additional evaluation steps are necessary. These steps can include visits to the plants of carefully selected vendors, followed, as necessary, by even more detailed analyses of the most promising vendors' financial, managerial, and service capabilities. For an extremely difficult purchase, a vendor evaluation conference can be held at the buyer's plant. From the conference discussion of the purchase, it is usually easy to identify which vendors understand the complexities of the purchase and which do not. By eliminating those who do not, the search for the right supplier is further narrowed.

Plant Visits

To obtain first-hand information about the adequacy of a vendor's manufacturing facilities and technical know-how, a buyer should visit the vendor's plant. (The word "buyer" is used here in the broadest sense to mean the *buying company*.) Depending on the importance of the visit, the company may send representatives from only purchasing and engineering; or it may also include some combination of representation from finance, production, quality control, and industrial relations; occasionally top management may also participate in the visit and its evaluation.

Visits to plants, which should be made only after the choice of vendors has been narrowed to just a few, are made for many reasons other than observing the vendor's production line. It must also be determined whether the vendor is both capable and motivated to meet his contractual obligations. To make this determination properly requires an overall appraisal. Among the factors to be appraised are: the adequacy of equipment, production control, quality control, and cost control; the competence of the technical and managerial staffs; the morale of personnel in general; the quantity of back orders; the willingness of the plant to handle the buyer's orders and work cooperatively with his company; and the quality of the key materials management activities.

When observing equipment, buyers should determine whether the equipment is modern and up to date. Also, they should attempt to get answers to questions such as: Are the production rates adequate? Are machines in good operating condition? Will machines consistently hold the required tolerances? The buyer should look for special adaptations of equipment; these give a clue to the ingenuity of management. The first impression of a vendor's plant is generally received through observing the housekeeping of the plant itself. Is it clean and well organized? Are the machines clean? Are the tools, equipment, and benches kept orderly and accessible? Is the plant a fire hazard? Good housekeeping is an indication of efficiency. It is reasonable to expect that a firm having pride in its facilities will have pride in its workmanship and products.

While touring the plant, a buyer should evaluate production methods and efficiencies. Are there production bottlenecks? Is material moving freely from storage to production areas? Are production control and scheduling properly organized to allow promised delivery dates to be kept? Is there reserve production capacity? On what basis is it available, overtime or regular time? Is there a competent maintenance force? Is quality properly controlled from receipt of raw materials to shipment of finished goods? Are inventories of both raw materials and finished goods adequate?

The attitudes of employees are important. In the long run, production results depend more on people than they do on the physical plant. Do the employees seem to work harmoniously with one another and also with their supervisors? Are they interested in improving the product they are making? Is enthusiasm shown by employees and supervisors?

Financial Condition

Preliminary investigation of a vendor's financial condition can often eliminate the expense of further investigation. Investigation of financial statements and credit ratings can reveal whether a vendor is clearly incapable of performing satisfactorily. Financial stability is essential for suppliers to assure continuity of supply and reliability of product quality. Imagine the difficulty of getting (1) a financially unsound supplier to work overtime to meet a promised delivery date, (2) a supplier who does not have sufficient working capital to settle an expensive claim, or (3) a financially weak supplier who underbid to maintain quality.

Financial information can aid buyers in ways other than informing them of a supplier's capability to perform a contract. Financially strong firms are usually, although not always, managerially strong also; hence they generally make good suppliers. Analysis of balance sheets and profit and loss statements can benefit buyers in many ways. For example, when a firm's financial condition starts to regress, a buyer should either search for a new supplier, or reduce the size of the orders given to the distressed firm. When profit margins fluctuate upward, a buyer knows that it may be possible to obtain price reductions—if he has the purchasing skills and economic leverage to get them.

When profit margins fall, a buyer knows that price rises are probable. In this case, the supplier is becoming less efficient, or he is losing sales and working at lower percentages of capacity. In either case, price rises are probable, and they are certain if demand for the product is relatively inelastic.

Buyers are not expected to be trained financial analysts. However, competent buyers should be able to interpret financial reports and make intelligent comparisons from them. The financial information buyers routinely need is found in corporate annual reports, Moody's Industrials, Dun and Bradstreet (D & B) Reports, and occasional consultations with a supplier's banker.

Management

Normally, a buyer's first contact with a vendor is the vendor's salesman or saleswoman. A *properly trained* salesman knows his product thoroughly, understands the buyer's requirements, gives useful suggestions to the buyer, commits his company to specific delivery promises, and follows through on all orders placed with him. This type of salesman reflects the fact that the vendor's firm is directed and managed by responsible and enterprising men. A well-managed firm seldom experiences the instability that results from continual labor problems, and it strives continuously to reduce its costs. Such a company can be a good supplier.

When a buyer purchases an off-the-shelf item which a supplier has manufactured using his own design and tools, to a certain extent the buyer is buying a product. However, when a buyer purchases a high-dollar-value item made to his own unique specifications and special design, for which he may or may not furnish special, high-cost tooling, then he is buying far more than just a supplier's product. In this case, *he is buying the supplier's total technical and managerial capability.* Technical competence in itself does not assure that a firm will be a good supplier. Good business management must be blended with technical competence to ensure that a firm has the ability to be a *good source of supply* in the full sense of the term.

Service

Service is a term that varies in meaning, depending on the nature of the product being purchased. Good service always means delivering on time, treating special orders specially, filling back orders promptly, and informing buyers in advance of impending price changes or developing shortages. In specific situations, it may mean exceptional postsale service, such as stocking spare parts in inventory for immediate delivery. It might also mean extending suitable credit arrangements, or warranting the purchased item's quality and performance to a degree beyond that normally required. In the aggregate, good service means that a supplier will take every reasonable action to ensure the smooth flow of purchased materials between the seller and the buyer.

What kinds of companies can give buyers the best service? Service is usually measured by a supplier's ability to comply with promised delivery dates, specifications, and technical assistance. How do forward-looking companies feel about the service they expect from their suppliers? A leading valve manufacturer has said, "We want a supplier to do more than simply quote prices from an engineering drawing. We want him to know the parts intimately so that he can use his specialized knowledge of processing and alternative materials to help us cut costs. We make it quite clear to him that cost-saving ideas can win a contract."

A large manufacturing company states its position this way: "We feel our approach in recognizing our specialty suppliers' expert knowledge and letting them work with responsible people in our organization has paid off handsomely. We have effectively expanded our purchasing knowledge and gained experience that might have taken years with another approach."

An electrical company holds the following view concerning specialty suppliers: "Common sense should tell us that they know more about the design and building of their products than we do. So it's only natural for us to draw on their skill and experience in coming up with a better end product of our own."

POST-SELECTION PROBLEMS

Assistance to Suppliers

Once an order or a contract is awarded, the relationship between the buyer and the seller legally becomes a contractual one. Unfortunately, with the passage of time, this situation frequently produces buyer complacency. Too often buyers feel that consummating a contract with a carefully selected supplier ends their major responsibility, at least for the time being. Such buyers feel that the supplier is legally bound to perform and that using departments will inform the buyer whenever a supplier fails in this obligation.

Truly professional buyers view the situation quite differently. These buyers feel a strong obligation to help a newly selected supplier succeed. They also realize that contracts do not assure deliveries when materials are not readily available. Further, they realize that during periods of increasing materials shortages, supply assurance is an important goal of supplier relations which must be developed.

To progressive buyers, nothing short of *supplier success* is *buyer success*. To help assure such success, effective buyers will make available to a new supplier the research, management, and technical services of their own companies. They will instruct new suppliers on the buying company's methods of operation, its special problems, and its known areas of weakness. This information enables a new supplier to contribute its knowledge and skills to help solve the buying firm's problems. For other than off-the-shelf items, both buyer and seller realize that total company capabilities are involved, not just commodities.

If a new supplier's contract contains complex technical requirements, the purchasing professional frequently arranges for a post-award conference. Such conferences are held at the buyer's plant, shortly after the contract is signed, to clarify all questionable points. The technical personnel of both companies typically dominate the discussions of such conferences.

In total, progressive buyers not only search for progressive, capable suppliers, but after finding them take all reasonable steps to support them. Progressive companies realize that it is in their self-interest to develop competent suppliers who will be motivated to continue doing business with them over the long term.

Supplier Performance Ratings

After sources of supply are selected, their performance must be evaluated. Evaluation provides the buyer with objective information to use in subsequent negotiations and in making future source selections.

In its excellent research study, "Evaluation of Supplier Performance," the National Association of Purchasing Management investigates three evaluation plans. Each of these plans is reviewed briefly in the following pages. They are the categorical plan, the weighted-point plan, and the cost-ratio plan.

Categorical Plan   Under this plan, personnel from various divisions maintain informal evaluation records. Individuals involved traditionally include personnel from purchasing, engineering, quality control, inspection, and receiving. For each major supplier, each person prepares a list of performance factors which are important to him. At a monthly meeting, each major supplier is evaluated against each evaluator's list of factors. Each supplier is then assigned an overall group evaluation, usually expressed in simple categorical terms, such as "preferred," "neutral," or "unsatisfactory."

This simple qualitative plan is easy to administer and has been reported by many firms to be very effective.

The Weighted-Point Plan   Under this plan, the performance factors to be evaluated (often only quality, service, and price) are given "weights." For example, in one circumstance, quality might be weighted 25, service 25, and price 50. In another, quality would be raised to 50, and price reduced to 25. The weights selected in any specific situation represent buyer *judgments* about the relative importance of the respective factors.

After performance factors have been selected and weighted, a specific procedure must be developed for measuring *actual supplier performance* on each individual factor. Supplier performance on each factor must be expressed in quantitative terms. To determine a supplier's overall rating, each factor weight is multiplied by the supplier's corresponding performance number; these products (for each factor) are then totaled to get the supplier's final rating for the time period in question. The following hypothetical case illustrates the procedure.

Assume that the purchasing department has decided to weight and measure performance as follows:

Weight	Factor	Measurement formula
50	Quality performance	$= 100\% -$ percentage of rejects
25	Service performance	$= 100\% - 7\%$ for each failure
25	Price performance	$= \dfrac{\text{Lowest price offered}}{\text{Price actually paid}}$

Assume further that Supplier A performed as follows during the past month. Five percent of its items were rejected for quality reasons; three unsatisfactory split shipments were received; and A's price was $100/unit, compared with the lowest offer of $90/unit. Table 5-1 summarizes the total performance evaluation calculation for Supplier A.

This procedure can be used to evaluate any number of different suppliers whose performance is particularly important during a given operating period. The performance of competing suppliers can then be compared quantitatively and subsequent negotiating strategies developed accordingly. The user should always remember that valid comparisons of two or more suppliers' performances require that the same factors, weights, and measurement formulas be used consistently for all suppliers.

In contrast to the categorical plan, which is largely subjective, the weighted-point plan has the advantage of being somewhat more objective. The exercise of subjective judgment is constrained more tightly in the assignment of factor weights and the development of the factor measurement formulas. The plan is extremely flexible, since it can accommodate any number of evaluation factors that are important in any specific case. Also, the plan can be used in conjunction with the categorical plan if buyers wish to include important subjective matters in the final evaluation of their suppliers.

Cost-Ratio Plan   This plan evaluates supplier performance by using the various tools of "standard cost" analysis that business people traditionally use in evaluating a wide variety of business operations. When using this plan, the buying firm's costs uniquely associated with quality, delivery, and service are

Table 5-1   Illustrative Application of the Weighted-Point Plan

Supplier "A" monthly performance evaluation

Factor	Weight	Actual performance	Performance evaluation	
Quality	50	5% rejects	$50 \times (1.00 - .05)$	$= 47.50$
Service	25	3 failures	$25 \times [1.00 - (.07 \times 3)]$	$= 19.75$
Price	25	$100	$25 \times \dfrac{\$90}{\$100}$	$= 22.50$
			Overall evaluation:	89.75

determined for each supplier. Each of these costs is then converted to a "cost ratio" which expresses the cost as a percent of total purchases for each supplier. These three individual cost ratios are then totaled for each supplier, producing the supplier's overall cost ratio. For purposes of analysis, the supplier's bid price is then adjusted by applying his overall cost ratio. The "adjusted price" for each supplier is then compared with the adjusted price for every other supplier when the buyer conducts the overall evaluation of suppliers. For example, assume that for one supplier the quality cost ratio is 2 percent, the delivery cost ratio is 2 percent, the service cost ratio is − 1 percent, and the bid price $72.25. The sum of all cost ratios is 3 percent; hence, the "adjusted price" for this supplier is [72.25 + (.03 × 72.25)] = $74.42. This is the price used for evaluation purposes vis-á-vis other suppliers.

Although the cost-ratio plan is used by a number of large progressive firms, on the whole it is not widely used in American industry. Operationally speaking, it is a complex plan. It requires a specially designed, companywide, computerized cost-accounting system to generate the precise cost data needed for effective operation. Consequently, the majority of purchasing departments employing a quantitative type of evaluation rely on the simpler but effective weighted-point plan—typically modified specifically to meet their own unique circumstances.

For these reasons, the cost-ratio plan is not discussed in detail in this book. Nevertheless, it is an excellent plan that has the ability to provide the most precise evaluation data of the three plans discussed. For firms using sophisticated, computerized information systems, the cost of designing and implementing the cost-ratio plan typically is repaid many times by savings produced for more precise analysis of vendor performance.

All three of the plans discussed—categorical, weighted-point, and cost-ratio—involve varying degrees of subjectivity and guesswork. The mathematical treatment of data in two of the plans often tends to obscure the fact that the results are no more accurate than the assumptions on which the quantitative data are based. In the final analysis, therefore, supplier evaluation must represent a combined appraisal of facts, quantitative computations, and value judgments. It simply cannot be achieved effectively by mechanical formulas alone.

CONCLUSION

An industrial company has two ways of obtaining material—production orders and purchase orders. In the average company, purchase orders represent a larger dollar value than production orders. The importance of what is purchased with production orders seems to be innately understood in industry. Conversely, the importance of what is purchased from suppliers, and the importance of suppliers to the buyer's firm, are more difficult to see. Undoubtedly, this is because some companies incorrectly visualize their suppliers as sellers of only specific *commodities,* rather than as sellers of engineering, production, financial, purchasing, materials management, product application, and industrial relations *capabilities.*

Although most suppliers sell more than just commodities or hardware, some do not. It is important to note, though, that suppliers of "off-the-shelf" commodities now receive the smaller portion of the average industrial company's purchasing dollar (approximately 20 percent[8]). The larger portion goes to buy materials purchased to buyer-furnished specifications that are unique, or nearly so. Hence, industrial buyers are purchasers primarily of a supplier's total technical and managerial capabilities—not commodities. Until top management clearly recognizes the distinction between buying supplier capabilities and buying off-the-shelf commodities, materials management functions cannot be handled in the most profitable way.

For a manufacturing firm to be completely successful in today's competitive environment, it must analyze, coordinate, and, in part, direct the technical and managerial capabilities of its suppliers. It must do these things for the identical reasons that it does them with its in-house capabilities. A buyer's objective should be to develop suppliers who complement the buying firm's own technical, managerial, and marketing capabilities. Buyers also should seek out and, if necessary, develop promising new suppliers—particularly those whose own long-term supply is secure.

Maximum purchasing efficiency results only when buyer and seller integrate their total materials management efforts, including the interflow of data and communications. To achieve this end, the first step is selection of competent, motivated suppliers. What is the ultimate payoff for companies that successfully select and develop good suppliers, and then integrate their joint materials management efforts? It is the accomplishment of the total procurement cycle in the shortest possible time, with a high level of efficiency, and with the minimum investment and risk to both buyer and seller. This is a payoff that is well worth the effort required to attain it.

FOR DISCUSSION

5-1   Discuss the qualifications that a good supplier should possess. Do some
            buyers require supplier qualifications others do not? Discuss.
5-2   Compare customer goodwill with supplier goodwill.

---

[8]To the authors' knowledge, there are no research studies which precisely verify the exact dollar division between off-the-shelf items and made-to-order items. However, the authors find the 20 percent figure realistic because (1) it is the figure most frequently used by authorities in the field, (2) it correlates closely with the verified, typical A-B-C distribution of industrial inventories (see Chapter 10), and (3) it correlates closely with what is readily observable in the item breakdown of the products of the nation's largest companies, such as GE, GM, and RCA (which by dollar value produce the bulk of United States industrial goods). A television picture tube, for example, costs more than all the other components of the set combined, the cabinets used by various television manufacturers are produced to different company specifications, etc.

5-3 Should large companies buy from large companies and small companies buy from small companies? Discuss.

5-4 Much of the time, buyers are not buying a specific commodity, but something else. Discuss what they are usually buying.

5-5 Explain your concept of supplier development. How much aid do you believe should be extended to new suppliers?

5-6 Discuss how dishonest suppliers operate in industrial purchasing. Do you have recommendations to stop them?

5-7 Do you believe that overall reciprocity is good or bad for the American economy? Explain. Would your answer be the same for an individual company? Explain.

5-8 Should buyers pay a premium price for material from a local source? Evaluate the pros and cons for using local sources.

5-9 Discuss the future possibilities of buying from foreign suppliers. How do you think purchasing executives should prepare themselves for international buying? Discuss.

5-10 Discuss the factors to be considered in making a choice between buying from a distributor and buying from a manufacturer.

5-11 Assume your company is making an advanced communications device to be used on Mars. If you were inspecting a potential supplier of transmitters to be used in this product, what would you look for? Discuss. Whom would you want on your inspection team to help you with the inspection? Why?

5-12 On a plant inspection, would you review the purchasing or materials management department of the company you are inspecting? Explain.

5-13 How important is a supplier's financial information to a buyer? Explain.

5-14 Define and discuss your concept of service.

5-15 If you were a purchasing executive and your boss asked you to give business to a specific firm, how would you handle the situation? (You know this firm is slow in deliveries and is partly owned by your boss.)

5-16 Discuss the three plans for supplier evaluation. Which plan do you prefer? Why?

Chapter 6

Pricing Theory

P 651

KEY CONCEPTS
General economic considerations
Competition
Fair profit
Methods of pricing
Published prices
Competitive bidding
Two-step bidding
Negotiation
Price analysis
Cost analysis
Costs and competition
Discounts

Whether in periods of inflation, or price stability, or recession, obtaining materials at the right price can literally mean the difference between a firm's success or failure. Hence, the right price is of prime importance to every organization, profit or nonprofit. Professional buyers interpret the right price to mean a price that is fair and reasonable to both the buyer and seller. Unfortunately, no single set of pricing principles or criteria exist for calculating precisely what constitutes a "fair and reasonable price." The right price for one vendor is not necessarily the right price for all other vendors, at either the same or at different points in time. To determine the right price, for any specific purchase, a number of constantly changing variables and relationships must be evaluated. This evaluation must be made in consonance with the total circumstances surrounding a specific purchase at a specific point in time. The most important of these circumstances, both theoretical and empirical, will be discussed in this chapter.

GENERAL ECONOMIC CONSIDERATIONS

Conditions of Competition

Economists of the classical school speak of a competitive scale that includes three distinct kinds of competition: pure, monopolistic, and imperfect. At one end of the scale is *pure (or perfect) competition.* Under conditions of pure competition, the forces of supply and demand alone, not the actions of either buyers or sellers, determine prices.[1]

At the other end of the competitive scale is *monopoly*. Under condititions of monopoly, one seller controls the entire supply of a particular commodity, and thus is free to maximize his profits by regulating output and forcing a supply-demand relationship that is most favorable to him.

The competitive area between the extremes of pure competition and monopoly is called *imperfect competition*. Imperfect competition takes two forms: (1) markets characterized by few sellers, and (2) those in which many sellers operate. When there are just a few sellers an *oligopoly* is said to exist. The automobile, steel, and television industries are examples of oligopolies. Generally, oligopolistic firms produce relatively few different products.

In contrast to oligopolies, the second form of imperfect competition exists where many sellers produce many products. This form of competition does not have a distinctive name. Most of the products sold in this market are differentiated (distinguished by a specific difference), although some are not. Sellers, however, spend much money and effort to persuade buyers that their products are different. This is the market in which the majority of the products made in the United States are traded.

In practice, the three categories of competition are not mutually exclusive; actually, they overlap considerably. When one considers both the buying and selling sides of the total market, it is apparent that the number of market arrangements between individual buyers and sellers is very large indeed.

It is frequently suggested that oligopolists conspire and act together as monopolists to thwart price competition. The facts, however, indicate that price conspiracies among oligopolists are not the normal order of business. Although the United States Justice Department does uncover a few conspiracies every year, any buyer who has purchased in oligopolistic markets knows that price competition can be intense.[2] Chevrolet strives intensely to outsell Ford, and vice versa. This is not to say that oligopolistic industries do not periodically exercise monopolistic tendencies to their own advantage. They do. For example, in times of recession, it requires only a basic knowledge of economics, not a conspiracy, for oligopolies to lower production rates and thus direct a balance of the forces of supply and demand in their favor.[3] Conse-

---

[1]Pure competition exists only under the following circumstances:
The market contains a large number of buyers and sellers of approximately equal importance.
The products traded are homogeneous (a buyer would not desire one particular seller's product over any other's).
The buyers and sellers always have full knowledge of the market.
The buyers always act rationally, and sellers are free to enter and to leave the market at will.
[2]"Price Fixing Crackdown Underway," *Business Week*, June 1, 1975, p. 45.
[3]It should be noted that oligopolistic industries frequently hold firmly to their prices for long periods and appear noncompetitive. This appearance may be deceptive, however, because frequently in order to gain a competitive advantage without notice, they shift their competitive efforts to other areas, such as service. Sellers may agree to perform such additional services as carrying customers' inventories, extending the payment time of their bills, or absorbing their freight charges. Such indirect price reductions are not advertised. Consequently, the amount of service a firm is able to obtain usually correlates directly with the perception and skill of its purchasing personnel.

quently, the competent industrial buyer must learn to operate within the practices of oligopolistic industries.

Most firms and industries operating in the marketing areas of imperfect competition are not oligopolistic. Millions of people, working in thousands of factories, produce hundreds of thousands of products substantially without governmental, or any other, outside direction. The firms that make up this market exercise considerable control over their prices, and price conspiracies in this market are extremely rare.[4]

Most Prices Are Subject to Adjustment

It is because most firms are free, within broad limits, to adjust their prices at will that competent buyers can obtain better prices in direct proportion to their ability to analyze pricing problems. Prices can be negotiated very little with firms in the markets of pure competition and monopoly. They can be negotiated a great deal with firms operating in the markets of imperfect competition. The question then is, what proportion of the nation's total market falls within the area of imperfect competition? What percentage of a buyer's total purchases are subject to price flexibility?

Studies made by Theodore J. Kreps, Graduate School of Business, Stanford University, show the nation's economy to be approximately 70 percent free.[5] The results of similar studies by other authorities support Dr. Kreps's conclusion.[6] Buyers in most purchasing situations, therefore, have considerable latitude for negotiating prices with their suppliers. At the same time, however, every buyer should guard against the inducement of *illegal* price concessions. Buying personnel must understand the operation of federal and state restraint of trade laws. (See Chapters 7 and 25.)

Big Business Means Variable Margin Pricing

Despite all the publicity given to small business, the United States is essentially a nation of big business. It is the economies of bigness (or scale) that have given Americans an abundance of automobiles, television sets, washing machines, refrigerators, skyscrapers, and many other such products shared by few other nations on earth. It has been conservatively estimated that less than 15 percent of the nation's firms produce almost 80 percent of its total manufacturing output.

In order to smooth out irregular production levels and to gain competitive advantages, bigness encourages industrial firms to sell a *line* of products, rather than just a single product. Very few firms attempt to earn the same profit

---

[4]"Price Fixing Crackdown Underway," p. 45.

[5]T. J. Kreps, "An Evaluation of Antitrust Policy," Joint Committee Print, 86th Cong., Study Paper no. 22, Government Printing Office, 1960, p. 42. Reconfirmed 1973.

[6]Studies by such outstanding economists as Paul Samuelson of M.I.T., George Stigler of Chicago, Warren Nutter of Virginia, and Clair Wilcox of Swarthmore have reached conclusions similar to those of Dr. Kreps.

margin on each product in the line. Most firms price their products to generate a satisfactory profit return on their whole line, not on each product in the line. Such a variable-margin pricing policy permits maximum competition on individual products. The profits from the efficiently produced and "successfully priced" items are used to offset the losses or the lower profit margins of the inefficiently produced items needed to complete the product line.

An understanding of the theory of variable-margin pricing is essential if buyers are to obtain the right price. Because it is usually advantageous to them, sellers routinely use average profit margins for pricing many orders. In some cases, this practice results in prices that sophisticated buyers realize are too high—particularly when low-cost, efficiently produced items are being purchased. Invariably when average margins are used, prices considerably above fair prices result for large, long-term purchases such as annual contracts. When dealing with large, multiproduct firms utilizing this pricing concept, a buyer must also know which of the items purchased are high-margin and which are low-margin items. This fact is learned by noting the differences in volumes, manufacturing skills, and costs of the various producers.

The following case illustrates the preceding discussion. A large, high-technology research firm successfully negotiated a $1.8 million annual contract for medical and scientific supplies. At the outset, the seller proposed that the contract be priced at cost plus the firm's annual gross profit margin of 19 percent. The buyer responded that 19 percent was an average figure that did not relate to this specific contract. He further pointed out that the product mix being purchased was heavily weighted with the seller's low-cost items, for which a 19 percent profit margin was outrageous. After several hours of negotiation, the contract was priced at cost plus a 6 percent profit margin. Had the buyer not understood the concept of variable-margin pricing, and not known which items the seller produced efficiently, this contract would have cost his company an additional $200,000.

Fair Profit

There are no precise formulas which can be used to help form a positive judgment concerning the right price (of which profit is one component: price = cost ± profit). There are, however, certain basic concepts of pricing on which scholars and practitioners do agree. One objective of sound purchasing is to achieve good supplier relations. This objective implies that the price must be high enough to keep the supplier in business. The price must also include a profit sufficiently high to encourage him to accept the business in the first place, and, second, to motivate him to deliver the product on time. What profit does it take to get these two desired results? On what basis should it be calculated?

Were profit calculated on a percentage-of-cost basis, the high-cost, inefficient producer would receive the higher profit. To make matters even worse under the cost concept of pricing, producers who succeeded in lowering their costs by attaining greater efficiency would be "rewarded" by a reduction in profit. For example, if an efficient producer has costs of $1,000 and a fair profit is agreed to be 10 percent of cost, his profit would be $100. If an inefficient producer has costs of $1,500, his profit on the same basis would be $150. If by better techniques the efficient producer should lower his costs to $800, his reward would be a $20 loss in profit—from $100 to $80. Obviously, the concept of determining a fair profit as a fixed percentage of cost is unrealistic.

A second basis on which profit might be determined is its relationship to the capital investment required to produce the profit. Profit might be calculated as a percentage of capital investment. However, under this system, it would still be possible for the inefficient producer to receive the greater reward. For example, suppose firm A makes a capital investment of $2 million to produce product X. Firm B, on the other hand, invests only $1 million in its plant to produce product X successfully. From the buyer's point of view, there is no reason whatsoever why firm A, simply because of its greater investment, should receive a higher profit on product X than firm B. Firm B, in fact, is utilizing its investment more efficiently. Profit calculated as a fixed percentage of a firm's capital investment is thus not a satisfactory method for a buyer to use in determining a fair profit.

In a competitive economy, the major incentive for more efficient production is greater profit. A fair profit in our society, therefore, cannot be determined as a fixed percentage figure. Rather, it is a flexible figure that should be higher for the more efficient producer than it is for the less efficient producer. Low-cost producers can price lower than their competitors, while simultaneously enjoying higher profits. One of a buyer's greatest challenges, consequently, is constantly to seek out the efficient, low-cost producer.

Considerations other than production efficiency also rightly influence the relative size of profits. Six of the most important of these considerations are:

1 Profit is the basic reward for risk taking, as well as the reward for efficiency; therefore, higher profits justifiably accompany extraordinary risks, whatever form they take. For example, great financial risk always accompanies the production of new products. For this reason, a higher profit for new products is often necessary to induce a seller to take the risk of producing them.

2 A higher dollar profit per unit of product purchased on small special orders is generally justified over that allowed on larger orders. The justification stems from the fact that the producer incurs a fixed amount of setup and administrative expense, regardless of the size of the order. Consequently, the cost of production for each unit is greater on small orders than on large orders. Since producers incur this cost at the request of the buyer, they usually demand a proportionately higher absolute profit before accepting an order which forces them to use their facilities in a less efficient manner than they might otherwise do.

3 Rapid technological advancement creates a continuing nationwide shortage of technical talent. The cost in dollars and time of training

highly technical personnel frequently makes it necessary to pay a higher profit on jobs requiring highly skilled people.

4   In the space age, technical reliability can be a factor of overriding importance. A higher profit is generally conceded as justified for a firm which repeatedly turns out superbly reliable technical products than for one producing less reliable products. Good quality control, efficiency in controlling costs, on-time delivery, and technical assistance that has resulted in better production or design simplification all merit profit consideration.

5   On occasion, because of various *temporary* unfavorable supply-demand factors (e.g., excessive inventories, a shortage of capital, a cancellation of large orders), a firm may be forced to sell its products "at a loss" in order to recover quickly a portion of its invested capital or to keep its production facilities in operation.

6   A company that manufactures a product according to the design and specifications of another company is not entitled to the same percentage of profit as a company which incurs the risk of manufacturing to its own design. In the first instance, the manufacturing company is assured of a sale without marketing expense or risk of any kind, provided only that it fulfills the terms of the contract. In the second instance, the manufacturing company is without assurance that its product can be sold profitably, if at all, in a competitive market.

In summary, there is no single answer to the question, "What is a fair profit?" In a competitive free-enterprise society, profit is generally implied to mean the reward over costs that a firm receives for the measure of efficiency it attains and the degree of risk it assumes. From a purchasing viewpoint, profit provides two basic incentives. First, it induces the seller to take the order. Second, it induces him to perform as efficiently as possible, to deliver on time, and to provide all reasonable services associated with the order. Except in those temporary cases where a firm is willing to sell at a "loss," the profit is too low if it does not create these two incentives for the seller.

HOW TO OBTAIN THE RIGHT PRICE

Methods of Pricing

There are three basic methods by which a buyer can seek to arrive at the right price: published price lists, competitive bidding, and negotiation.

Published Price Lists   Published price lists in the form of daily quotations exist for standard commodities traded on the various commodity exchanges throughout the world. Price lists also exist for most standard items of "hardware" and office supplies carried by typical firms in their inventories.[7]

[7]Hardware in this usage includes all standard manufactured items of inventory. Most firms carry an inventory of common-use items, such as fasteners, hand tools, lubricants, and fabricated parts used in their industry—electronic parts for electronics firms, electrical parts for electrical firms, etc.

Usually price lists show different prices for varying quantities. Quite often a seller who has a particular commodity in inventory will sell at a price lower than the price quoted for the commodity on the exchange. The same kind of situation exists for several million standard manufactured items carried in sellers' inventories throughout the country. The prices shown on a seller's price list are *asking prices.* They may or may not be the actual *selling prices.*

Competitive Bidding   Competitive bidding is a widely discussed form of purchasing. Most of the discussion in newspaper and magazine articles centers on government (local, state, and federal) purchasing. Many well-meaning but grossly misinformed citizens have been led to believe that competitive bidding is an assured technique for the wise expenditure of public funds. Such is not always the case. Competitve bidding is but one of the three methods by which price can be determined. It is nothing else. It is not a panacea or an infallible technique that assures the honest purchase of quality products at rock-bottom prices!

When competitive bidding is used by private industry, requests for bids are usually sent to three to eight vendors, depending on the dollar size of the purchase. Requests for bids ask vendors to quote the price at which they will perform in accordance with the terms and conditions of the order or contract, should they be the successful bidder. Governmental purchasers generally are not able to restrict the number of bidders to only eight. Rather, all vendors desiring to bid are permitted to do so (for large purchases, the numbers are literally in the hundreds). Under competitive bidding, industrial buyers generally, *but not always,* give the order to the lowest bidder. By law, government buyers are routinely required to give the order to the lowest bidder, provided the lowest bidder is deemed qualified to perform the contract.

The proper use of competitive bidding, as the best method of pricing available to a buyer, is dictated by five criteria. When all five criteria prevail, competitive bidding *assures* the buyer of obtaining the lowest possible price. The criteria are:

1   The dollar value of the specific purchase is large enough to justify the expense, to both buyer and seller, that accompanies this method of purchase. Excluding informal telephone bids, $300 to $500 seems to be the reasonable low dollar average now used by industry for this type of purchasing. Government agencies vary their lows from $10 to $2,500.
2   The specifications of the item or service to be purchased are explicitly clear to both buyer and seller. In addition, the seller knows from actual previous experience, or can estimate accurately from similar past experience, the cost of producing the item or rendering the service.
3   The market consists of an adequate number of sellers.
4   The sellers comprising the market actively want the contract and are therefore willing to price competitively to get it. In our highly technical society, it frequently happens that criteria 1, 2, and 3 prevail, yet there is no real competition because the sellers are not anxious to bid. Huge backlogs of work in some sellers' plants may prevent competition.

Under such circumstances, additional orders would entail overtime operation and its attendant problems of scheduling difficulties and premium wage payment. Under such circumstances, if bids are made at all, they are at prices that include all manner of contingencies.

5 The time available is sufficient for using this method of purchasing. Vendors competing for large contracts must be allowed time to obtain and evaluate bids from their subcontractors before they can calculate their best price. Bidders must also have time to perform the necessary price analysis required within their own organization, and assure themselves of reliable sources of materials. The time required for preparing, mailing, opening, and evaluating bids is usually considerably longer than those unfamiliar with this system of pricing would expect. Thirty days is not an uncommon time.

The competitive bidding system itself, when all the prerequisite criteria prevail, perfectly evaluates the many pricing factors bearing on the purchase being made. These factors include such determinants as vendor production efficiency, willingness of the seller to price this particular contract at a low-profit level, the financial effect on the seller of shortages of capital or excesses of inventories, errors in the seller's sales forecast, and competitive conditions in general.

Because the proper uses of competitive bidding appear to be widely misunderstood, this system of pricing is frequently abused by both industry and government. Government officials, because of political pressures from their constituents, tend to force the overuse of competitive bidding on their purchasing departments. The reason for such behavior is easily understood. By stressing the applicability of competitive bidding as the best method of pricing, and by allowing all constituents the opportunity to compete, regardless of their qualifications, politicians can avoid disputes with their constituents. Conversely, industrial purchasing managers tend to underuse competive bidding. When it is used, too often industrial buyers hold steadfastly to the unsound premise that purchasing judgment is not required when competitive bidding is used. In fact, planning the preliminaries correctly for competitive bidding takes purchasing judgment of the highest order.

If the preliminary planning of tight specifications, proper selection of competing vendors, correct quantities, precise delivery schedules, adequate time for placing bids, and general economic analysis is done correctly, selecting the successful bidder after the bids are evaluated is generally routine. Except in unusual circumstances, the low bidder should receive the contract. An invitation to bid implies that the contract will be given to the lowest bidder. Purchasing judgment and analytical planning should normally be exercised *before* competitive bids are requested, not after the bids are in.

The general belief that *adequate competition* is the best way of obtaining the right price is correct. However, the belief that competitive bidding per se assures adequate competition is wrong. Competitive bidding assures adequate competition and the right price *only* when the mandatory five criteria for this method of pricing prevail. Too often industry and government alike err in using competitive bidding to buy highly technical products with vague specifications. This practice inevitably leads to faulty cost estimates and price padding. The price padding that attends such cases is not the result of the method of price determination. Rather, it is the result of the poor purchasing judgment of the buyer, who is guilty of incorrectly using a good and effective purchasing tool.

It must be remembered that sellers will bid on any product or service buyers ask them to bid on. It is not the seller's responsibility to tell a buyer that he is using the wrong method of pricing. However, if sellers do not have cost information, do not understand the specifications fully, or already have large backlogs, they will include in their bid prices contingencies for labor costs, material costs, and all other possible costs they can think of. For example, if a vendor is not sure how many hours it will take to complete a job (because he has not previously done a similar job), in order to protect himself he will base his bid on the greatest number of hours he estimates the job could take. Sellers are not at fault in accepting high competitive bid profits when buyers are naive enough to use an incorrect method of price determination. Caveat emptor! To buy wisely is the buyer's responsibility. Competitive bidding improperly used is not buying wisely. Competitive bidding properly used is an excellent method of obtaining a fair price. Generally speaking, this method of pricing is most applicable to highly standardized products and services that are widely used and produced abundantly for stock by many manufacturers.

Two-Step Bidding   On occasion, the government and a number of large, technically oriented firms use a modified type of competitive bidding called "two-step bidding." This method of pricing is used in situations where inadequate specifications preclude the initial use of regular competitive bidding. In the first step, bids are requested only for technical proposals, without any prices. Bidders are requested to set forth in their proposals technical details describing how they would produce the required materials, products, or services. After these bids are evaluated, and it is determined which proposals are technically satisfactory, the second step follows. In the second step, requests for bid are sent only to those sellers who in the first step submitted acceptable technical proposals. These sellers now compete for the business on a price basis, as they would in any routine, competitive-bidding situation.

Negotiation   Negotiation should be used in all situations where any one of the five mandatory criteria for competitive bidding does not prevail. When the time is too short, the dollar value of the order is too low, the number of bidders is inadequate, their willingness to compete is lacking, or the specifications are vague, the buyer has no choice but to negotiate. By use of individual skills coupled with research findings, the buyer must attempt to answer properly the questions that lead to an intelligent source selection decision—the important questions that the competitive-bidding technique answers automatically.

Use of the negotiation technique does not preclude competition or competitive bidding. In fact, negotiation as a method of price determination seeks and exploits competition just as vigorously as does competitive bidding. In negotiation, however, competition, is sought on a less formal basis and generally includes the areas of quality, quantity, and service, *as well as the area of price.* When adequate price competition does not exist, a fair price should be determined by first analyzing costs, profit, and price, and then by negotiating.

Negotiation is particularly useful, though not always fully successful, in dealing with sellers who are a sole source of supply, or with sellers controlling multiple sources that behave in a monopolistic manner. In cases where costs are not reliably determinable in advance, as in most research contracts and many contracts for items that have never been made before, there is no sound alternative to negotiation.

By far the major percentage of industrial buying (in dollar value) is done by negotiation. Contrary to popular belief, the same situation exists in military procurement (roughly 85 percent). On the other hand, nonmilitary departments of the federal government and most agencies of state and local governments currently buy almost exclusively by competitive bidding. In any given purchasing situation, where competing sellers are all qualified to perform the contract and where the five prerequisites for competitive bidding exist, the forces of competition are more likely to determine the right price than is the most skilled negotiator.

PRICE ANALYSIS

Some form of price or cost analysis is required for every purchase. The method and scope of analysis required are dictated by the dollar amount and circumstances attending each specific purchase. Generally speaking, cost analysis (to be discussed later) is used in connection with negotiated purchasing, and price analysis is used in connection with competitive-bid purchasing. Additionally, it is not uncommon for price analysis to be used to support cost analysis.

Price analysis is defined as the examination of a seller's price without examination and evaluation of the separate elements of the cost and profit making up the price.

Price analysis typically starts with a comprehensive comparison of the prices submitted in a specific competitive-bid purchase. Next, the bid prices of this specific purchase are compared with prices the buyer previously paid for the same or a similar item. It must be remembered, however, that prices are dependent on many factors, such as delivery schedules, order quantities, manufacturing costs, labor rates, and general economic conditions, all of which can vary with time. Price comparisons with earlier purchases, therefore, become less valid as the bid prices become more widely separated in time. During the periods of the comparisons, it is highly probable that labor rates will have changed; it is even more likely that for highly technical items productivity will have increased, and therefore manufacturing time will be less. Because of these factors, direct price comparisons can be less valid than they may at first appear. It is for this reason that a properly used competitive bid may be the best standard a buyer can hope to use for direct comparison of prices.

Even cursory bid comparisons can reveal very important information. For example, comparison will readily show if the prices of any bids are out of line. If all bids are out of line, high or low, it is apparent that exactly what the buyer wants to purchase is not clearly understood by the competing sellers. If just one bid is unrealistically low compared with all other bids, the buyer knows that further investigation of this bid is required. It must be determined whether the low bidder has miscalculated his costs, misinterpreted the contract requirements, or made some other serious mistake, or whether he actually has competitive superiority over the other bidders. One type of price comparison sometimes available to a buyer is a certified statement from the seller guaranteeing that the buyer's price is no less favorable than the seller is giving similar customers. A buyer has nothing to lose by requesting such a statement.

For really important purchases, buyers develop their own estimates of prices. When neither competitive bids nor company estimates are available, the buyer can often fall back on rule-of-thumb methods of estimating to arrive at a basis for price comparison. Even though these methods lack precision, rough estimates of price can be extremely useful. Buyers are therefore well advised to search for and develop price evaluation guides, such as dollars per pound, per square foot, per gallon, or per horsepower. Such rough guides are surprisingly reliable in uncovering grossly unreasonable prices. Even the most intricate and expensive scientific instruments and machines, as well as standard machines, routinely conform to an unbelievably reliable, empirically derived pound-per-dollar scale of value.

Practical Methods of Estimating Price *START*

Competent buyers correctly rely heavily on pricing and economic theory to determine the right price. Of necessity, they must also be able to use the practices of their trade. Successful pricing usually depends, as do most successful business actions, on a correct combination of both art and science.

In practice, one of the first things buyers must do to assure good pricing is acquire a thorough knowledge of the materials they buy. Such knowledge is absolutely essential. Buyers who purchase transistors must know about the different properties of transistors, how they function, and how they are used in different applications. They must also have a *practical* knowledge of transistor manufacture. Buyers who purchase carpets must know the detailed differences among wool, cotton, and the various synthetics. They must have a *practical* knowledge of each kind of carpet. They must know which carpet material is best for a specific use, how carpets are best cleaned, best repaired, etc. Only after buyers gain knowledge of the materials they purchase can they develop a feeling for the proper price range for these materials. With such practical knowledge, buyers can recognize instantly prices that are out of line.

When a buyer purchases material for the first time, he or she must look to reliable sources for practical help. Assume that paper is the product being purchased. Paper pricing is characterized by published price lists, which do not necessarily reflect the actual prices other buyers are paying for paper. However, as a guide it is possible to look at the General Services Administration (GSA)[8] paper contracts. These contracts show the GSA prices which historically are at or near bottom prices. Interestingly, a large banking corporation used the GSA catalog as a practical negotiating tool to reduce its paper prices by a substantial percentage. In addition to GSA catalog, publications such as *The Wall Street Journal, National Association of Purchasing Management Monthly Bulletin, Purchasing World, Purchasing,* and *Consumer Reports* often contain valuable pricing information.

COST ANALYSIS

Cost analysis is generally defined as "a review and an evaluation of a seller's actual or anticipated cost data." The evaluation phase involves the application of experience, knowledge, and judgment to these data in an attempt to project reasonable estimated contract costs. In turn, these estimated costs serve as the basis for buyer/seller negotiation to arrive at mutually agreeable contract prices. Cost analysis, in effect, is a substitute method of assuring the buyer that the seller considers all of the estimating methods, assumptions, and efficiencies that would be considered in competitive bidding.

Cost analysis starts with the buyer including requests for cost breakdowns along with requests for quotation. This is the proper time to make such a request, not after negotiations have started. Made at this time, vendors cannot complain that making this breakdown is an extra burden, since they must make such an analysis to prepare their bids. A simple procedure used by a number of progressive firms for obtaining cost breakdowns is to include the following statement with their request for quotations: "The buyer will not consider any quotation not accompanied by a cost breakdown." Not all vendors readily provide cost-of-production information; however, the number refusing to do so for nonstandard items is becoming progressively smaller.

The purpose of analyzing cost is to arrive at a price that both buyer and seller can accept as reasonable. The buyer can make estimates of his own; or, with the help of his engineering department, he can analyze the estimates submitted by the seller; or he can do both. To analyze a seller's costs, a buyer must understand the nature of each of the various costs a manufacturer incurs. He must know the difference between variable, semivariable, and fixed costs. *A*

---

[8]The General Services Administration buys this commodity for most agencies and departments of the federal government.

lack of appreciation of how these types of costs influence prices probably is the basic reason why many purchasing departments fail to exploit price negotiation to its fullest potential.

― *Variable costs* are those incurred by a seller as a result of his performing a specific contract. They are called variable because they vary directly with the production quantity of a particular product. Variable costs include direct labor wages, the cost of materials, and a small number of overhead costs which the supplier incurs in filling an order. For example, if a specific cutting tool costs $10 and lasts for 100 cuttings, each cut represents a variable cost of 10 cents. If three cuts were required in machining a specific item, the variable cost for cutting would be 30 cents. Thus, variable costs represent money sellers can keep if they do not perform a specific contract, and money they must pay if they do perform it.

➤ *Fixed costs* are costs sellers must pay simply because they are in business. They are a function of time and are not influenced by the volume of production. For example, if the lathe that held the cutting tool in the preceding example depreciates at the rate of $25 a month, this is a fixed cost. The seller has this $25 expense every month, whether or not any cuttings are made in a particular month. Fixed costs generally represent either money the seller has already spent for buildings and equipment or money he will have to spend in the future for such unavoidable things as taxes and rent, regardless of his plant's volume of production.

Generally, it is not possible to classify clearly all production costs as being either completely fixed or completely variable. Many others, called *semivaria-* ✝ *ble costs,* fall somewhere between these extremes. Costs such as maintenance, utilities, and postage are partly variable and partly fixed. Each is like a fixed cost, because its total cannot be tied directly to a particular unit of production. Yet, it is possible to sort out specific elements in each of these costs that are fixed as soon as the plant begins to operate. When the fixed portion is removed, the remaining elements frequently do vary rather closely in proportion to the production volume. For example, if a plant is producing an average of 5,000 items a month, it might have an average light bill of $175 a month. Should the number of units produced be increased to 8,000, the light bill might increase by $25 to $200. The $25 increase is not proportional to the production increase, because a certain segment of the light bill is fixed whether any production occurs or not. Above this fixed segment, however, light costs do vary in a fairly consistent relationship with production volume. This concept will become clearer when fixed and variable costs are discussed in the section on break-even analysis.

✚*Total costs* are calculated by adding the variable, fixed, and semivariable costs. As the volume of production increases, total costs increase. However, the cost to produce *each unit* of product decreases. This is because the fixed costs do not increase; rather, they are simply spread over a larger number of units of product. Suppose, for example, that a single-product firm has the following cost structure:

Variable costs, per unit	$ 2.25
Fixed costs, per month	1,200.00
Semivariable costs	
Fixed portion, per month	450.00
Variable portion, per unit	0.30

Under these circumstances, we can use Table 6-1 to show how unit costs change as volume changes. To understand fully the intricacies of the volume-cost-profit relationship it is essential to understand these three types of cost. Because it is difficult to allocate costs specifically as fixed, variable, and semivariable, accountants generally classify them as *direct costs* and *overhead costs*.

Direct costs accrue from the unit being produced. The three major direct costs are direct labor, direct materials, and purchased parts. Returning to the illustration of the cutting tool, if a contractor pays the worker 15 cents for making the three cuts required for each item, direct labor costs is 15 cents. If the value of the piece of metal being cut is 85 cents, total direct costs are $1.00. Direct costs are always 100 percent variable.

Overhead costs are all the other costs required to produce a firm's products and operate the business. These costs do not result directly from the production of a specific unit. Overhead costs can be variable, fixed, or semivariable. Executive salaries and property taxes are examples of fixed overhead costs. These costs are the same regardless of the number of units produced. Therefore, it cannot be said that any particular unit is responsible for these fixed costs. Utilities are an example of semivariable overhead costs. Cutting oil is an example of a completely variable overhead cost. If no cutting were done, no fluid would be used; thus the cost is variable.

The Significance of Cost Analysis

Because costs are such an important part of price determination in a large number of negotiated purchases, skilled buyers should possess a detailed knowledge of costing theory. Standard cost accounting and economics textbooks are good references for study.

Table 6-1 Volume-Unit-Cost Relationships

Monthly production units	Variable costs	Fixed costs	Semivariable costs Fixed	Semivariable costs Variable	Total cost	Unit cost
500	$1,125	$1,200	$450	$150	$2,925	$5.85
1,000	2,250	1,200	450	300	4,200	4.20
1,500	3,375	1,200	450	450	5,475	3.65
2,000	4,500	1,200	450	600	6,750	3.375
2,500	5,625	1,200	450	750	8,025	3.21

	Situation 1	Situation 2
Material	$ 2.00	$ 2.00
Direct labor	8.00	6.00
Fixed overhead at 150 percent of direct labor	12.00	9.00
Direct cost	$22.00	$17.00
General and administrative overhead at 10 percent of direct cost	2.20	1.70
Total cost	24.20	18.70
Profit at 10 percent of total cost	2.42	1.87
Price	$26.62	$20.57

Except in industries with heavy fixed capital investments, direct costs are normally the major portion of total costs. As such, they generally serve as the basis on which sellers allocate their overhead costs. The astute buyer, therefore, must carefully investigate a seller's direct costs, for a tiny reduction here (because they are relatively large) is worth more to the buyer price-wise than a major reduction in the percentage of profit (which is relatively small). A 25 percent reduction in the $8 direct-labor cost of situation 1 to the $6 direct-labor cost of situation 2 results in a $6.05 ($26.62 − $20.57) reduction in price (see table above). A 25 percent reduction in profit would result in only a 60-cent reduction in price ($0.25 × $2.42 = $0.60).

The need for cost analysis depends on a number of factors. The most important single factor is the result of price analysis. If price analysis indicates that the price is reasonable, there may be no need for cost analysis. On the other hand, if price analysis indicates that the price may be wrong, the price must be examined by cost analysis. This analysis should bring to light any invalidity in the pricing structure, and subsequent negotiation should seek to eliminate it.

In considering costs, the buyer should always be conscious of the fact that they vary widely among manufacturing firms. Some firms are high-cost producers; others are low-cost producers. Many elements affect the costs of individual firms, and also the cost of individual products within a given firm. Some of the most important elements affecting costs are:

- The capabilities of management
- The efficiency of labor
- Amount and quality of subcontracting
- Plant capacity and continuity of output
- Composition of overhead costs
- Price of materials and wages of labor

Each of these factors changes with respect to both product and time. For these reasons, a specific firm can be a high-cost producer for one item and a low-cost producer for another. Similarly, the firm can be a low-cost producer one year and a high-cost producer another year. These circumstances make it extremely important for a buyer to obtain competition among suppliers. Competition is the sure route to locating the desired low-cost producer.

The Capabilities of Management   The skill with which management plans, organizes, staffs, coordinates, and controls all the personnel and equipment at its disposal determines the efficiency of the firm. Managements utilize the resources available to them with substantially different degrees of efficiency. This is one basic reason why searching out the correct supplier (and price) is so profitable for astute buyers.

The Efficiency of Labor   Anyone who has visited a number of different firms surely has noticed the differences in attitudes and skills that exist among various labor forces. Some are cooperative, take great pride in their work, have high morale, and produce efficiently, while others do not. The skill with which management exercises its responsibilities contributes greatly to these differences between efficient and inefficient labor forces.

The Amount and Quality of Subcontracting   When a contract has been awarded to a supplier (the prime contractor), the supplier frequently subcontracts some of the production work required to complete the job. The supplier's subcontracting decisions are important to a buyer because they may involve a large percentage of prime contract money. The first decision a prime contractor must make regarding subcontracts is what specific items he should make and what specific items he should buy (subcontract). Should the prime contractor decide to buy some of those items which he can more efficiently make, and vice versa, the buyer suffers financially. Even if the prime contractor makes the correct "make" decision, he still is responsible for selecting those subcontractors which are needed for the "buy" items.

Subcontractor prices and performance directly influence the prices the buyer pays the prime contractor. Hence, the prime's skills in both making and administering his subcontracts are of great importance to the buyer. For this reason, buyers must assure themselves that their major suppliers have effective purchasing and subcontracting capabilities of their own.

Plant Capacity and Continuity of Output   A plant's overhead costs are directly influenced by its size. A plant can get too large for efficient production and, as a result, lose its competitive ability. On the other hand, plants with high capital investments, or those manufacturing products on a mass-production basis, can be too small to attain the most efficient production levels. A buyer must be alert to detect seller firms whose operations are adversely affected by size. The greater the uniformity of production, the greater is management's opportunity to plan production efficiently. Known quantities of production provide the opportunity for devising the most efficient man and machine setups, for studying job and procedure design, for acquiring or designing special tools and equipment, and for learning by experience. These are some of

Table 6-2 How Production Volume Affects Fixed Costs, Variable Costs, and Profit

Production quantity	Selling price	Sales revenue	Fixed costs	Variable costs	Total cost	Total profit	Profit per unit of added production
0	$20	$ 0	$4,000	$ 0	$4,000	−$4,000	$15
100	20	2,000	4,000	500	4,500	− 2,500	15
200	20	4,000	4,000	1,000	5,000	− 1,000	15
300	20	6,000	4,000	1,500	5,500	+ 500	15
400	20	8,000	4,000	2,000	6,000	+ 2,000	15
500	20	10,000	4,000	2,500	6,500	+ 3,500	15
600	20	12,000	4,000	3,000	7,000	+ 5,000	14
700*	20	14,000	4,000	3,600	7,600	+ 6,400	12
800*	20	16,000	4,000	4,400	8,400	+ 7,600	10
900*	20	18,000	4,000	5,400	9,400	+ 8,600	

*Plant begins to strain capacity and administrative capabilities. The result is less efficient operation, i.e., overtime is required, less experienced workers are utilized, scheduling and handling of materials becomes less efficient, and variable costs per unit rise. Consequently, although profit continues to increase beyond a production quantity of 600, it increases at a decreasing rate.

the reasons long-term contracts can be mutually advantageous to buyer and seller alike.

Plant output is clearly one of the controlling elements in the cost/profit picture. Table 6-2 illustrates this concept numerically. Note how volume affects profit when variable costs change because of inefficient use of facilities beyond optimum plant capacity. Note also that, while total profit continues to increase as production output increases, *beyond a certain output profit increases at a decreasing rate.* This relationship is a most important one for buyers to keep in mind.

Production volume can also affect profit if overhead costs are largely fixed. Assume that a company forecasts sales of $10 million for the year. These sales are broken down into costs of $6 million for materials, $1.5 million for labor, $1.5 million for fixed costs, and profits of $1 million.[9] Suppose a buyer makes a $200,000 contract with this company. After negotiation, a price is agreed upon that will give the seller his expected 10 percent gross profit. The contract represents 2 percent of the seller's estimated sales and profit. To the seller, the contract on his books looks as follows:

Direct costs:
  Material $120,000 (2 percent of $6 million)
  Labor   30,000 (2 percent of $1.5 million)
  Overhead cost   30,000 (2 percent of $1.5 million)
    Total Cost $180,000
  Profit   20,000 (2 percent of $1 million)
  Total sale $200,000

[9]In this case, for simplicity of illustration, the semivariable costs are divided between the fixed and variable costs.

Assume now that the seller completes the contract according to its terms and that his direct and overhead costs are exactly as he estimated them. He may or may not have made his $20,000 estimated profit. His profit on the contract depends not only on the contract itself, but also on his business obtained from other sources. If total sales, in fact, equaled the $10 million forecast, the profit from this order would be $20,000 as estimated. If total sales were higher than expected, then the seller's profit would also be higher than expected. Just how much higher depends on the total sales volume actually achieved. Table 6-3 shows a few of many possible outcomes.

This example clearly illustrates that profits forecast at the time of purchase (unless the buyer is taking the entire plant's production) are really only *estimates;* they cannot be precise figures. Hence, cost estimates alone are often an unsatisfactory basis on which a buyer should negotiate price. The buyer must also make an effort to forecast sales as well as costs over the production period of his contract. In the end, cost and profit figures depend on factors over which neither the buyer nor the seller has complete control. Hence, a buyer should not attempt to guarantee sellers a percentage of profit, nor should a seller be expected to reduce his contract price should his volume exceed his forecast. Variations of profits from projected figures are to be expected. The many uncertainties in the data used for forecasting volume suggest that the type of contract selected should be the one that best allows for these uncertainties.

TARGET COSTS

Target costs independently developed by a firm's own purchasing department can be a valuable pricing aid. In fact in many purchasing situations, a buyer

Table 6-3　The Influence of Overhead Costs on Profits at Various Levels of Output (Figures Rounded to Nearest Tenth)

Sales	Overhead, percent*	Under- or over absorption of overhead	Resulting profit from contract	Profit rate
$ 8,000,000	18.8	−$7,600+	$12,400	6.2
9,000,000	16.7	− 3,400	16,600	8.3
▶ 10,000,000	15.0	0	20,000	10.0
11,000,000	13.6	2,800	22,800	11.4
12,000,000	12.5	5,000	25,000	12.5

*Remember the assumption that total overhead costs were accurately forecast as $1.5 million at a sales level of $10 million. If sales drop to $8 million, overhead as a percentage of sales would rise to 18.75 percent (1,500,000/8,000,000 = 0.1875).

†Overhead on our $200,000 order, at the $8 million level of sales, would be $200,000 × 0.188 = $37,600. We estimated it to be $30,000, so it was under-absorbed by $7,600.

must possess target costs to be able to conduct intelligent price and cost analysis. Consequently, progressive purchasing departments have, on either a formal or an informal basis, a purchasing analysis section. This section generally performs three basic functions:

- Analyzes trends and determines prices of raw materials
- Analyzes production costs of purchased parts and subassemblies
- Helps in determining the price of purchased parts and subassemblies manufactured within the firm for assembly into the firm's products

A practical application of the first type of analysis for raw materials would be to analyze the price of the ingredients which make up paint. By analyzing the actual cost of the pigments (lead, titanium, gypsum, etc.) and the vehicles (drying oils, resin, thinner, etc.) going into the paint, and then adding to the cost of these ingredients the estimated cost of production and overhead, the analyst can calculate an estimated or target price toward which the buyer can negotiate.

For the second type of analysis, purchased parts and subassemblies can be subjected to the same type of practical analysis. An engineer in the price analysis section can estimate for each manufactured part the cost of materials, labor, and overhead. All these, added together, give a target cost toward which the buyer can negotiate. (Experienced buyers with a thorough knowledge of the materials they purchase and the markets in which they purchase them can make surprisingly accurate estimates of cost when specialized analytical assistance is not available.)

By appropriately combining the two types of analysis, much information can be acquired about the firm's own product costs. This information can be used within the firm to arrive at sound make-or-buy decisions and to improve production scheduling and techniques.

Buyers are constantly subjected to sellers' attempts to convince them that the seller's product is *distinctive* and should not be bought on such a mundane basis as price. This situation is not surprising. Truly distinctive products, such as Polaroid's cameras and Xerox's copying machines, usually enjoy relatively high profit margins (25 to 35 percent net is not uncommon for long time periods). Where products are more competitive, profit margins are relatively low (typically 4 to 6 percent net). Informed buyers are well aware of these realities, and with experience they can easily cope with them. To pay high profit margins for truly distinctive products can be good buying. However, to pay high profit margins for competitive products is poor buying, and such practice reflects a lack of fundamental purchasing analysis.

COSTS AND COMPETITION

Up to this point, much has been said about *costs,* because of their great importance. In the long run, a firm must recover its costs or go out of business. In the long run, for any given item, the price is roughly equal to the cost of the least efficient producer who is able to remain in business. In the short run, however, prices in the free, competitive segment of the economy (which Kreps estimated as roughly 70 percent of the whole) are determined primarily by competition, that is, by supply and demand, and not by costs.

There are basic differences between the kinds of products marketed in various segments of the economy. Some products in the competitive segment are what economists call *undifferentiated* products. Other products in the competitive segment of the economy are *differentiated.* In some cases the products are intrinsically different, and in others, manufacturers are successful in making their products appear different from those of their competitors. Even though a product cannot be made different in substance, producers can still get premium prices if they can persuade buyers *to think* that their products are superior. It is to accomplish such a purpose that some producers spend huge sums of money on sales personnel and advertising. In the jargon of the economists, "They attempt to make the demand curve for the products of their firm somewhat inelastic." If their efforts are successful, they can charge higher prices for their products. On the other hand, if their efforts are defeated by the counter efforts of competitors, as is frequently the case, price competition comparable to that in pure competition can result. Grocers, for example, are well acquainted with this economic fact.

For both differentiated and undifferentiated products, producers compete on quality and service as well as price. The consumer market is more susceptible to producers' advertising claims than the industrial market; therefore, the major portion of advertising effort is directed toward the consumer market. Nonetheless, industrial buyers must be aware of advertising and sales tactics and be very careful that they determine quality from an analysis of facts, not from unsupported claims.

From a buyer's point of view, competition is the mainspring of good pricing. As pointed out previously, most producers do not have the same real costs of production. Even when their costs are the same, however, their competitive positions can be quite different. Hence, their prices can also be quite different. Consider the following example. Assume that a buyer is ready to purchase 10,000 specially designed cutting tools for his plant. He sends the specifications to five companies for quotations. All five respond. For the sake of simplicity, assume that direct costs in these five companies are identical. Assume further that each company uses the same pricing-estimating formula; overhead is figured as 150 percent of direct labor, and profit is calculated as 10 percent of total cost. Each company could then lay out its figures as follows:

Cost of material	$12,000	
Cost of direct labor	3,000	
Cost of overhead*	4,500	(150 percent of direct labor)
Total cost	$19,500	
Profit	1,950	(10 percent of total cost)
Price	$21,450	

*To simplify the example, assume all overhead is classified as fixed.

Even with all the controlling figures fixed, the companies more than likely would not quote the same price, the reason being that *cost-of-production and profit formulas are only two of the factors a seller considers in determining price.* In the end, it is the factors stemming from competition that determine the exact price each firm will quote. That is, when faced with competition, the price quoted by any specific firm is governed largely by its need for business and by what it thinks its competitors will quote.

Who is responsible for final determination of the price to be quoted? Generally, it is the chief marketing executive; in some cases, it is the president of the company. Pricing is one of the most important management decisions a firm must make. As an objective, a firm tends to seek the highest price that is compatible with its long-range goals. What is the possible price range for the order in the preceding example? The out-of-pocket (variable) costs to the firm for this order are $12,000 for material and $3,000 for direct labor, a total of $15,000. This is the lowest price any company could accept under any circumstances. The highest price is $21,450, based on the assumption that a profit in excess of 10 percent is not in the long-range interest of the firm.

What could cause one of the firms to consider a price of $17,000? Keen competition among suppliers could. On the other hand, keen competition among buyers could drive the price higher. This is why competition, as a leveler, is such a dominant factor in pricing. If the firm had been unable to obtain a satisfactory volume of other business, it would gladly take this order for a price of $17,000. As a result of the order, the $15,000 out-of-pocket costs would be covered, the experienced work force could be kept working, and a $2,000 contribution could be made to overhead. Remember that fixed overhead continues whether the firm receives this order or not. In the *long run,* a firm must recover all costs or go out of business, for in the long run, plant and machinery must be maintained, modernized, and replaced. In the *short run,* however, it is generally better for a firm to recover variable costs and some portion of overhead, rather than undergo a decline in business. This would not be true, of course, if such additional business would affect the pricing of other orders the firm has already filled or is going to fill.

Business in good times is not routinely done at out-of-pocket prices. A more usual situation would be for each of the five firms to quote prices above the total cost figure of $19,500. How much above this figure each would bid would depend on the specific economic circumstances applicable to each firm. Firms hungry for business would bid just slightly above the total cost figure of $19,500. Those with large backlogs and growing lists of steady customers (and therefore not in need of new business in the short run) would bid a larger profit margin (perhaps 12 percent). Sellers can be expected to evaluate competitive situations differently, depending on how much they want or need the business. Therefore, even with the simplifying assumption of identical costs, it is reasonable to expect bids in this situation to range from approximately $19,700 (1 percent profit) to $21,840 (12 percent profit). Prices close to out-of-pocket costs could be offered were the seller attempting to obtain a desirable, prestigious account, or if he desired to gain experience in a situation wherein additional large orders are expected to follow.

A seller must recover *all* costs from all products sold plus a little more if a profit is to be made. However, *each* product in the line does not have to make a profit, and all accounts do not have to yield the same profit margin. Bearing these thoughts in mind, the principal cost/competition implications of pricing can be summarized as follows: Sound pricing policy dictates that sellers, in accordance with their interpretation of the prevailing competitive forces, quote prices that are high enough to include (1) all variable costs, and (2) the maximum possible contribution toward fixed costs and profits.

Similarly, sound pricing policy dictates that, for any given purchase, buyers should use their knowledge of products, markets, costs, and competitive conditions to estimate the price range at which the seller can reasonably be expected to do business. Finally, with this knowledge, a knowledge of the value of the buyer's own account on a continuing basis, and a knowledge of the value of this specific order, the buyer with the application of all relevant purchasing principles and techniques should attempt to purchase at prices as close as possible to the bottom of the estimated price range.

DISCOUNTS

Discounts are frequently considered to be a routine, prosaic part of pricing. Perceptive buyers, however, recognize that this is not always the case. As will be illustrated in the discussion to follow, discounts can sometimes succeed as a technique for reducing prices, after all other techniques have failed. The four most commonly used kinds of discounts are: trade discounts, quantity discounts, seasonal discounts, and cash discounts.

Trade Discounts

These discounts are reductions from list price allowed various classes of buyers and distributors to compensate them for performing certain marketing functions for the original seller (the manufacturer) of the product. Trade discounts are frequently structured as a sequence of individual discounts (e.g., 25, 10, and 5 percent), and in such cases they are called *series discounts*. Use of series discounts facilitates pricing among distributors who perform different selling functions for a manufacturer. Those who perform all functions (warehousing, advertising, credit, delivery, etc.) get all three discounts; those who perform only a part of the distribution functions get only one or two of the discounts in the series. If the retail price of an item with such discounts is $100, the full discounted price is calculated as follows: 25 percent of $100 = $25; 10 percent of ($100 − $25) = $7.50; 5 percent of ($100 − $25 − $7.50) = $3.38. The price to be paid, then, is $100 − $25 − $7.50 − $3.38 = $64.12.

An industrial buyer who purchases through distributors must, as a result of the very nature of series trade discounts, be certain that he is buying from the right distributor (i.e., the distributor obtaining the most discounts). The general guidance rule is for a buyer to get as close to the manufacturer as possible. For example, a large buyer should not normally purchase his paper requirements from a janitorial supply house, which usually does not obtain all discounts in the series for paper. If his account is sufficiently large, the buyer should go to a paper distributor, who normally does obtain all discounts in the series and who, therefore, can at the same profit margin offer the buyer lower prices.

Quantity Discounts

These price reductions are given to a buyer for purchasing increasingly larger quantities of materials. They are normally offered under one of three purchasing arrangements:

1 For purchasing a specific quantity of items at one time
2 For purchasing a specified dollar total of any number of different items at one time
3 For purchasing a specified dollar total of any number of items over an agreed-upon time period

The third type of quantity discount is called a *cumulative discount.* The period of accumulation can be a month, a quarter, or more commonly a year. For large-dollar-value, repetitive purchases, buyers should always seek this type of discount. Also, because unplanned increases in business occur with regular frequency, buyers should include in all quantity discount contracts a condition that if the total purchases made under the contract exceed the estimated quantities, then an additional discount shall be allowed for all such excesses.

Seasonal Discounts

These are by far the least important of the industrial discounts. Because of the seasonal nature of some products (primarily consumer products), their producers offer discounts for purchases made in the off season.

Cash Discounts

In many industries, sellers traditionally offer price reductions for the prompt payment of bills. When such discounts are given, they are offered as a percentage of the net invoice price. When suppliers extend credit, they cannot avoid certain attendant costs, including the cost of tied-up capital, the cost of operating a credit department, and the cost of some "bad debt" losses. Most sellers can reduce these costs by dealing on a short-term payment basis, and they are therefore willing to pass on part of the savings to the buyer in the form of a cash discount.

Buyers should be aware of the importance of negotiating the highest possible cash discount. The most commonly used discount in practice is 2 percent 10 days, net 30 days. In industries where prompt payment is particularly important, cash discounts as high as 8 percent have been allowed. A cash discount of 2/10, net 30 means that a discount of 2 percent can be taken if the invoice is paid within 10 days, while the full amount must be remitted if payment is made between 10 and 30 days after receipt of the invoice.

A 2 percent discount, viewed casually, does not appear to represent much money. Actually, it is the equivalent of a 36.5 percent annual interest rate. Because the bill must be paid in 30 days, and the discount can be taken up to the tenth day, a buyer not taking the discount is paying 2 percent of the dollar amount of the invoice to use the cash involved for 20 days. In a 365-day year, there are 18.25 twenty-day periods (365/20 = 18.25). A 2/10 discount, therefore, translates into an annual discount rate of 36.5 percent (2 percent times 18.25). If a firm does not have sufficient cash on hand to take cash discounts, the possibility of borrowing the needed money should be investigated. Under normal conditions, paying 9 percent for capital that returns 36.5 percent is good business. Capable buyers understand the time value of money. In some situations, generous cash discounts can be obtained either for prepayment or for 48-hour payment.

Various other types of cash discounts are in use. One other common type is the end-of-month (EOM) dating system. This system of cash discounting permits the buyer to take a designated percentage discount if payment is made within a specified number of days after the end of the month in which the order is shipped. If materials are shipped on October 16 under 2/10 EOM terms, a 2 percent discount can be taken at any time until November 10.

Lower prices, in the form of higher cash discounts, are an ever-present avenue of price reduction which buyers should never fail to explore. Frequently, sellers who will not consider reducing the prices of their products will consider allowing higher cash discounts—which accomplishes the identical result for the buyer. For example, a major petroleum company recently was able to gain a 6 percent price reduction on the purchase of a complex testing machine—a machine the manufacturer had never before sold below its standard $44,000 selling price. The $2,640 price reduction was achieved by the buyer offering to pay one-half of the purchase price one week in advance of the machine's delivery to his company's testing laboratory.

FOR DISCUSSION

6-1   Why is it important for a buyer to recognize the difference between pure competition, imperfect competition, and monopoly? Which kind of competition do industrial buyers encounter most often? With which type can a buyer deal most effectively? Explain.

6-2   What control do large industrial firms have over their selling prices? Explain.

6-3 Why do prices usually move upward more freely than they move downward?

6-4 Discuss why competitive bidding does not always produce the lowest price. If buyers compete vigorously, does this improve the situation? If sellers compete vigorously, does this improve the situation?

6-5 Explain the difference between price analysis and cost analysis.

6-6 Discuss the potential merits and problems of two-step bidding.

6-7 Why is there a tendency for government agencies to overuse competitive bidding and industry to underuse competitive bidding?

6-8 Why is it important for a buyer to know the difference between fixed costs and variable costs?

6-9 Why do product costs vary from company to company for an identical product?

6-10 Is pricing usually based on competition or on costs? Why?

6-11 When would a company not want to quote on a firm fixed-price basis? Explain.

6-12 What products can you name that command a premium price because of an alleged differentiation? Is the differentiation real or imagined? How can it be measured?

6-13 Discuss the significance of the various price discounts a buyer may encounter.

6-14 The list price of a particular type of conveyor belt is $4.87 per running foot when purchased in quantities of 1,000 feet or more. When purchased in quantities of less than 1,000 feet, the list price is $5.32 per running foot.

    a. Buyer A's firm receives a trade discount of 25-10-5; it also receives a cash discount of 2/10, net 30. Buyer A places an order for 1,050 feet of belt. What price does he pay for the order?

    b. Buyer B's firm receives a trade discount of 25-10, and a cash discount of 2/10 EOM, net 30 EOM. Buyer B places an order for 895 feet of belt. What price does he pay for the order?

CASES FOR CHAPTER 6

Contract and Pricing Practices

TYPES OF CONTRACTS
AND THEIR PRICING SIGNIFICANCE

In the quest for fair and reasonable prices, one of the major aids available to a buyer is a wide variety of contract types. The type of contract selected for any given purchase directly affects its pricing. In determining the best type of contract to use, therefore, the buyer must consider all available contract types and the factors influencing the use of each. The most important factors that influence contract type selection are:

- The intensity of competition among vendors
- The vendor's cost and production experience in manufacturing identical or similar items
- The availability, accuracy, and reliability of pricing data
- The extent of the business risk involved

Were it always possible to purchase on a fixed-price basis, selection of contract type would be no problem. In a rapidly changing economic and technological world, however, purchasing many items on a fixed-price basis is costly and wasteful. Generally speaking, the type of contract increases in complexity with the increase in complexity of the item being purchased. Industry and government use two *basic* types of contracts: fixed-price contracts and cost-type contracts.

I Fixed price
   A Firm fixed price
   B Fixed price with escalation
   C Fixed price with redetermination
      1 Maximum price
      2 Flexible price
   D Fixed-price incentive
   E Firm fixed-price level of effort
II Cost type
   F Cost plus a percentage of cost
   G Cost plus fixed fee
   H Cost plus incentive fee
   I Cost without fee
   J Cost sharing
   K Time and materials
   L Letter contracts

Fixed-Price Contracts

Firm Fixed Price   This type of contract is the one most preferred by all buyers. It is simply an agreement for the buyer to pay a specificied price to the seller when the latter delivers what was purchased. If a fair and reasonable price can be determined, either by competition or by adequate price or cost analysis, a firm fixed-price contract should always be used. It has many advantages. It requires minimum administration; it gives the seller the maximum incentive to produce efficiently; and all financial risks are borne entirely by the seller.

Fixed Price with Escalation   For a contract involving a long period of production and a large amount of money ($100,000 or more), sellers usually prefer not to quote a firm fixed price because of the risks associated with the possibility of inflation. If forced to make such a quotation, particularly in periods of increasing inflation, sellers will include in their price contingencies for increases in the cost of labor and materials. These contingencies may not actually materialize. Hence, to avoid paying for something not received, the buyer should use an escalator clause. Esclalation provides for either an upward or downward change in price as a result of changes in either material prices or labor rates.[1] The escalation clause should be as simple as possible, and

---

[1]Upward adjustments are normally limited to 10 percent, or are tied directly to reliable and timely price indexes.

adjustments should normally be made in accordance with the prescribed movements of well-known, regularly published indexes. The two indexes most commonly used are the Bureau of Labor Statistics' Wholesale Price Index (for materials) and the Wage and Increase Series by Standard Industrial Classification (for labor). Many other government and commercial indexes, however, are also used for escalation purposes. It should be noted that price adjustments of this type apply only to out-of-pocket costs of labor and material, not to overhead and profit.

Fixed Price with Redetermination   Redetermination as a means of pricing is different in concept from escalation. In contracts with escalation, the *amounts* of labor and material required to complete the contract are known, but the *wages* of labor and the *prices* of material are unknown. In cases involving price redetermination, the amounts of labor and material (and in some cases their prices also) are initially unknown, but they can become known with limited production experience.

Because of labor and material unknowns, a firm fixed-price contract initially would be impractical; however, enough is known so that a temporary estimated fixed price can be agreed to. The buyer generally believes the agreed-upon price is too high, and he expects it ultimately to be lowered when it is reviewed later. In the meantime, he is protected from unknown raises. This is why the contract is classified as a fixed-price type; the price cannot go higher than the temporary price. After an agreed-upon percentage of work has been performed under the contract, the unknowns are translated to knowns. At this time, the costs incurred to date are analyzed, future costs are estimated, and a fixed price is determined for the remainder of the contract. This new price may or may not be the same as the original temporary price. It may or may not apply to the items already produced, depending on the terms agreed to. Learning experiences, expected future volume, expected increases in efficiency, and similar factors relating to future production are all considered in arriving at the firm price.

The earlier in the life of a contract that price redetermination can be made, the more effective this type of contract is (30 percent completion is typically a satisfactory redetermination point). *Maximum price redetermination* provides that prices can only be adjusted *downward* at the time of redetermination. *Flexible price redetermination* means price adjustments can be made *upward or downward;* however, an upward limit of 10 percent is usually imposed.

Fixed-Price Incentive   This is a variation of the redeterminable type of pricing. It is complicated in that it provides for a target price, a ceiling price, and a variable profit formula, depending on the type of contract for which it is used. This contract is generally used when a reasonable target price can be established, but exact pricing is impossible.

The contract works like this: suppose both buyer and seller agree that $990 is a reasonable price at which to sell item A. This price was calculated roughly as follows: cost $900, profit $90, total price $990. The buyer intends to purchase large numbers of item A; consequently, he wants to be sure the seller has the maximum incentive to produce efficiently. They agree that every dollar by which the seller reduces his costs below $900 will be shared equally by buyer and seller. For example, if the costs are reduced to $800, the price will be $800 + $50 + $90 = $940. Both buyer and seller "saved" $50 because of increased efficiency and the cost reduction of $100. At the upper limit, it was agreed that if costs equaled or exceeded the ceiling figure of $1,100, the seller would receive no profit and the maximum price to the buyer would be $1,100, regardless of the seller's costs. All costs between $900 and $1,000 reduce the seller's profit by 50 percent of these costs, just as they increase it by 50 percent below $900 (see Table 7-1). All costs between $1,000 and $1,100 reduce the seller's profit from $40 to $0 proportionally.

This type of contract initially was used almost exclusively by the Department of Defense for the purchase of complex weapon systems of large dollar value and involving lengthy development time. It is now used routinely by industry.[2] The incentive type of contract still has greatest application in the purchase of high-cost, long-production-time items, such as airplanes, ships, and complex machinery. Its use is increasing in construction contracts for high-cost office and factory buildings. Also, it is now used occasionally for purchasing lower-value technical and construction products.

Firm Fixed-Price Level of Effort   This type of contract is used primarily for research and development work. It is used when the work cannot be precisely described in advance, but the level of effort required to accomplish it

[2]A modification of this basic contract type is now emerging, with the incentive fee based on some combination of dollar cost and system performance. In the modified contract type, the contractor also agrees to meet certain quantified performance standards (such as specified range and accuracy in a missile system) as well as meeting cost goals. If performance is above standard, the contractor's fee is increased; if the performance is below standard, the fee is reduced. This combination of performance and incentive can also be used in cost-plus-incentive-fee contract. The new contract type is not a departure from the basic incentive concept; rather it is a refinement of it.

Table 7-1   Profits and Savings from Cost-Incentive Contract

Seller's cost per unit	Profit per unit	Price per unit
$1,200	−$100	$1,100
1,100	0	1,100 (ceiling price)
1,000	+ 40	1,040
900	90	990 (target price)
800	140	940
700	190	890

can be both described and agreed to by the buyer and seller. Under this type of contract, the seller is obligated to a specified level of effort, for an agreed-upon time, and for an agreed-upon fixed price.

Cost-Type Contracts

Cost-type contracts are used only when it is impossible to contract on any type of fixed-price basis. The distinctive difference between a fixed-price and a cost-type contract is that *under cost pricing, the buyer assumes almost all the financial risks.* Generally, sellers do not have to achieve any performance results to be paid. They are guaranteed reimbursement for all their allowable costs, up to a predetermined figure. Beyond this point, they will do no additional work unless the buyer agrees to provide more money. Also, sellers are usually guaranteed a fee in addition to their costs. Therefore, under a cost contract a seller has no effective incentive to keep costs, and thus prices, down. This is a clear disadvantage to a buyer. Another disadvantage of cost-type contracts is that they are very expensive to administer. All costs that are allowable must be agreed upon in advance, and they subsequently must be audited. For this to be possible, the seller must have an accounting system that can separate the costs applicable to a specific cost contract. Despite advance agreement on what costs are allowable, intensive arguments routinely develop between buyer and seller over the validity of certain cost inclusions.

What often seems to be a justifiable item of cost to the seller may not seem to be one to the buyer. For example, a reasonable percentage of research expense for scientists' and engineers' salaries may be considered an entirely proper expense by the seller, even though these particular people did not work directly on the buyer's product. The buyer may have different feelings about including this type of cost as an expense against his contract. His feeling could be particularly strong if he had provided the seller with extensive research and development information of his own concerning what he wanted done and how he wanted it done.

Cost Plus Percentage of Cost   Although used by the federal government extensively during World War I, this is the most undesirable of all types of contracts. Today it is outlawed for use by the federal government. Despite the obvious fallacy of the concept "the higher the cost the greater the profit," this type of contract is still used in private industry, especially in the construction industry.

Cost Plus Fixed Fee   This contract type provides that the seller shall be paid for all allowable costs up to a stated amount, plus a fixed fee. The fixed fee is usually a percentage of the estimated cost. For example, if the estimated cost to perform the contract is $2,000 and a 10 percent profit fee is agreed upon, the fee is $200; the fee remains fixed at $200 even if the cost rises to $3,000 or more, or if it is held to $1,000. This contract type is used primarily in research projects and exploratory studies where the level of effort required to achieve success, if it can be achieved at all, is unknown.

Cost Plus Incentive Fee   This is a variation of the fixed-price incentive contract. The buyer and seller agree beforehand on a tentative fee based on the estimated costs, and they establish target costs. If the seller can reduce his costs below target costs, both he and the buyer share in the reduction. Under this type of contract, a seller can lose all or part of his fee, but all his costs must be paid by the buyer.[3] This type of contract is used in development work where successful results are reasonably certain. Target costs are not exact, but they are considered close enough to provide a basis on which management efficiencies can be rewarded with incentive fees.

Cost Without Fee   Nonprofit institutions, such as universities, usually do research work for both government and industry without the objective of making a profit. Such research is done under cost-type contracts without a fee. Because universities do much of the nation's pure research, as distinguished from applied research done by industry, a growing number of contracts of this type are being used. Naturally, the universities recover all overhead costs which, in most cases, include remuneration for faculty, staff, and graduate students for their work on such contracts.

Cost Sharing   In some situations, a company doing research under a cost type of contract stands to benefit if the product developed can be used in its own product line. Under such circumstances, the buyer and seller agree on what they consider to be a fair basis to share the costs (most often it is 50:50).

Time and Materials   In certain types of contracts, such as those calling for repairs to certain machinery, the precise work to be done cannot be predicted in advance. For instance, it cannot be known exactly what must be done to a malfunctioning pump until it is opened and examined. Perhaps it will need only a new gasket to put it in good working order. On the other hand, its impeller could require a major job of balancing and realignment. One method of pricing this type of work is the *time and materials contract,* in which the parties agree on a fixed rate per labor hour that includes overhead and profit, with materials supplied at cost.

[3]The Defense Department and a few private firms use an offshoot of this contract type, called a cost plus award fee contract (CPAF). The fee under such a contract consists of two parts: a fixed amount, which does not vary with contract performance, and an award amount, a sum in addition to the fixed amount. The award amount is intended to be sufficient to provide motivation for excellence in contract performance in areas such as quality, timeliness, ingenuity, and cost effectiveness. The amount of the award fee is based on a subjective evaluation by the buyer of the seller's performance, judged in the light of the criteria set forth in the contract.

Suppose a mechanic working on a ship's pump is paid $15 per hour. Assume also that overhead is calculated as 100 percent of labor cost and profit is set at 10 percent of total cost. A billing rate for this mechanic for one hour would be calculated as follows:

Direct labor cost, per hour	$15
Overhead at 100 percent of labor	15
Total cost	$30
Profit at 10 percent of total cost	3
Billing rate, per hour	$33

If it took the mechanic two days (16 hours) to repair the pump, using $160 worth of material, the job price would be $688 (16 × 33 + $160).[4] Profit should be paid only on costs. Sellers have been known to compute profits on taxes and fees.

A variant of the time-and-materials type of contract is called a "labor hour contract." In this type of contract, materials are not supplied by the seller; otherwise costs are agreed to as in time and materials contracts.

Letter Contracts   Letter contracts are used in those situations (which should be rare) wherein an urgency makes it imperative that work start on a complex project immediately. Examples of situations justifying the use of letter contracts are unplanned purchases of complex, capital items, or the immediate need for a relatively inexpensive item which is delaying completion of an expensive, major project. Letter contracts are preliminary contractual authorizations under which the seller can commence work immediately. He can prepare drawings, obtain required materials, and start actual production. Under letter contracts, the seller is reimbursed for his costs up to a specified amount. Letter contracts should be converted to definite contracts at the earliest possible dates.

Recapitulation of Contract Considerations

Because there is such a wide choice of contract types, a buyer must exercise considerable care in selecting the best one for a particular use. If a bid or a quoted price is reasonable, this will help the buyer decide to use a firm fixed-price contract. On the other hand, if the fairness of the price is in doubt, a fixed-price contract could entail excessive expense to the buyer and would be a poor choice. If price uncertainty stems from unstable labor or market conditions, escalation may be a solution. If it is due to a potential improvement in

---

[4]The alert reader will observe that this is really a cost plus percentage of cost contract. If the mechanic is the best worker in the yard, he might complete the job in 10 hours ($30 profit to his employer). If he is the worst worker, he could take 20 hours, and his employer would receive $60 in profit. Obviously, buyers must exercise close control over this type of contract to be sure that inefficient or wasteful methods are not used.

production effort, an incentive contract may be the best answer. Thus, the many factors which affect procurement costs can themselves guide the buyer in his or her selection of the best type of contract for a given purchasing situation.

The specific nature of the supplies or services to be purchased also can frequently point up advantages of one contract type over another. The more complex or developmental the purchased item, the greater the risks and difficulties in using a fixed-price contract. Any uncertainty in design affects a seller's ability to estimate costs, as does a lack of cost experience with a new item. The details of any given purchase will themselves indicate the magnitude of the price uncertainties involved. A full understanding of these uncertainties will permit buyers to allocate the risks more equitably between their firm and a supplier's firm by the proper choice of contract type.

Timing of the procurement is quite frequently a controlling factor in selection of contract type. Allowing sellers only a short time to prepare their bids can reduce the reliability of the cost estimates and increase prices. A short delivery period usually rules out the effective use of incentive contracts. On the other hand, a long contract period allows time to generate and apply cost-reducing efficiencies, an ideal situation for an incentive contract. The facts of each procurement must be considered individually in determining the contract type the buyer should use.

Business practices in specific industries can frequently provide additional clues as to the best choice of contract type. The construction industry, for example, traditionally accepts a wider range of competitive fixed-price jobs than the aerospace industry. The lumber industry accepts prices established by open auctions. Architects and engineers normally will not enter into price competition with one another for architectural or engineering services; neither will management consulting firms compete with each other on price. Business factors such as these help determine the best contract type in a great many purchasing situations.

The scope and intensity of competition can definitely influence the type of contract to use. If competition is intense and the prices bid or quoted are close, then the buyer can justifiably feel that the prices are fair and reasonable and use a fixed-price contract. On the other hand, if competition is not adequate, the buyer should have doubts concerning the fairness of prices, and without other evidence favor a cost-type contract.

The buyer's experience with his own company's requirements and with its traditional suppliers provides him with further guides as to the best type of contract to use. The basic background of the markets in which he buys is a critical consideration against which all his procurements must be analyzed. This kind of knowledge frequently indicates which type of contract is best for specific types of purchases.

In short, the buyer's basic preference for a firm fixed-price contract is just the starting point for his analysis of alternative contract choices. As he considers all available contract types, he must weigh his preference for fixed prices against the risks involved, the time available, the degree of competition involved, his experience with the industry involved, the apparent soundness of the offered price, the technical and developmental state of the item being purchased, and all the other technical and economic information that affects the purchase transaction. Determination of the best contract type for a given situation requires a careful analysis of all the factors relevant to that situation.

PRACTICAL FACTORS INFLUENCING CONTRACT TYPES

Times of Delivery and Dollar Values Affect Prices

Regardless of the type of contract used, the dollar value of the materials or services being purchased and their delivery schedules greatly influence contract prices. Because of the economies of scale, large quantity buyers generally purchase their high-dollar-value materials, such as production materials, under long-term contracts. One-year contracts are typical. Contracts made for longer than one year are normally limited to situations involving large start-up costs, substantial investments in capital equipment, or major expenses in connection with assembling and training specialized personnel. Under these conditions, multi-year contracts are desirable. They preclude duplicate yearly start-up costs and duplicate costs in connection with phasing out one group of employees and training another. Lower prices are the natural result.

In addition to the direct price benefits which accrue from the economies of scale, long-term contracts provide the buyer other benefits. For example, under such contracts, the seller is assured of a large volume of business; hence, he may inventory part of this business. Consequently, the buyer can reduce his inventory accordingly. When the seller knows the buyer's delivery schedule well in advance, he can frequently reduce his distribution costs as well as his production costs. Some of this saving is passed along to the buyer. In times of scarcity, the buyer is assured of a reliable source of supply, as well as the best possible protection against unjustified price increases. Because long-term contracts are only negotiated once a year, the buyer is freed for other productive work such as purchasing research, value analysis, and administration. To equalize his workload, the sophisticated buyer schedules his major contracts to fall due at equal intervals throughout the year.

Most production materials are purchased with firm fixed-price or fixed price with escalation–type contracts. However, cost contracts with a predetermined profit rate are not uncommon, and fixed price with redetermination contracts are used occasionally.

Some of the contracts that buyers commonly use to cope with varying quantities and varying delivery schedules are discussed below.

Definite Delivery–Type Contracts   When the production schedules for the entire period of a contract are known, definite quantites for delivery on definite dates can be ordered. A contract with these provisions is called a "definite delivery–type contract." This is the ideal type of contract.

Indefinite Delivery–Type Contracts   In some cases, production schedules cannot be planned; hence, the quantities of materials required and their times of use, or both, could be unknown. Materials and services for the support of such operations must be contracted for on an indefinite delivery schedule. There are three basic types of indefinite delivery contracts. In their order of preference for the best pricing, they are (1) definite quantity contracts, (2) requirements contracts, and (3) indefinite quantity contracts.

Definite Quantity Contracts   These provide for the purchase of definite quantities of materials or services—whose time of use is unknown. The contract, therefore, provides that instructions regarding delivery schedules shall be given later. Because the quantities are known, very favorable prices are possible for this type of contract.

Requirements Contracts   These provide, during the contract period, for the purchase from a single supplier of *all* of a buyer's requirements for materials or services for a designated operation or activity. Requirements contracts are typically used in applications such as the support of a firm's automotive repair shop, with parts being purchased from a specific parts dealer.

Indefinite Quantity Contracts   These provide, during an agreed-upon period of time, for the delivery of a specific category of materials or services. Quantities and delivery dates are indefinite, but the buyer is committed to purchase between designated high and low quantity limits.

The indefinite quantities associated with both indefinite quantity contracts and requirements contracts preclude optimum pricing. However, the contracts represent a total volume of business that—although indefinite—is large enough for vendors to want and to price competitively to get.

Systems Contracts

Although the words "systems" and "contracts" both have a variety of definitions in business today, in purchasing parlance the term "systems contracts" has a very specific meaning. In its basic form, a systems contract is a contract that authorizes designated employees of the buyer, using a predetermined release system, to place orders directly with the supplier for specified materials during a given contract period. *The contract is finalized after an attempt has been made to integrate as many buyer-seller materials management functions as possible.* For example, careful analysis usually makes it possible to reduce the combined inventories of the buyer and the seller. Frequently, the same release form used by the buyer to order materials can also be used by the seller for stock-picking and delivery of materials, etc. While systems contracts, blanket orders, and indefinite quantity contracts have certain common features, it is this *integration* of buyer-seller operations that clearly distinguishes systems contracts from these and other types of contracts.

Systems contracts are referred to by some writers as "stockless purchasing." This definition stems from the fact that if this method of contracting were used to the ultimate, a buyer's company would not have to maintain any inventories at all. Not everyone agrees that systems contracting should be stockless purchasing. Most people do agree, however, that one principal objective of systems contracting is to reduce the buyer's inventories to a level as low as is consistent with assured continuity of supply. There is general agreement, too, that order releases under systems contracts should usually be made by personnel from the using department. Most authorities likewise agree that maintenance, repair, and operating (MRO) materials are the categories of materials best suited for purchase using systems contracts.

The following example illustrates a typical application of this method of contracting. A large United States firm that has production operations in five Latin American countries uses and maintains field inventories of thousands of individual repair parts and components. These materials are used to support a wide variety of activities which use many types of heavy equipment. For example, to operate several railroad systems there are locomotives, many types of cars, stations, roundhouses, and shops. To operate numerous large agribusinesses, there are various types of tractors, heavy-duty trucks, many large pumps, power plant equipment, and every imaginable kind of production equipment. All of this equipment requires supply support. Before systems contracts were used, stores inventories were the principal supply support used to keep all equipment operational. Most purchases of needed parts and components were made in the New Orleans market. Emergency items were purchased for direct delivery to users; all other purchases were made for delivery to various stores inventories.

In total, the company had twenty-eight categories of support materials, each of which was reviewed jointly by the firm's executives and their counterparts in vendors' organizations that were capable of supplying the company's requirements for each material category. During these review conferences, both groups explored each other's major operating problems and found that through a planned, cooperative effort mutual benefits could be achieved. Subsequently, systems contracts proposals were solicited and received. Five systems contracts were negotiated from the initial proposals, and additional contracts were negotiated from later proposals.

Competition was excellent for these contracts. This was not the case, however, until the decision to use systems contracts was made, after the joint conferences were held, and the estimated yearly usage for each material category was disclosed to the potential suppliers. The sellers were surprised at the total dollar amounts. Because each seller had been getting only a part of the total quantity, no one seller could know what the total dollar value was. In return for being given the company's total annual business for one category of materials, sellers agreed to keep on hand for immediate shipment those items in the company's inventory which showed active usage in the past year. Without giving a supplier all of the company's yearly business for a category of material, getting such an agreement would not have been possible.

In the final analysis, the company saved well over 20 percent in material costs on all contracts. Additionally, the large inventory stocks which yearly had cost the company 25 percent of the average inventory dollar value were no longer necessary.

Under these systems contracts, order releases were made almost entirely by individual production and stores units. Many were made by teletype. Paperwork was reduced, billing was simplified, equipment downtime for lack of repair parts was greatly reduced, and to the present time suppliers continue to make profit-improving suggestions (they have been assured that such action will favorably influence the selection of next year's suppliers). In addition to the above benefits, total dollar savings for the first year exceeded a quarter of a million dollars. The largest savings came from inventory reductions.

PRICING TOOLS

Break-even Analysis

Break-even analysis is a planning tool frequently used by top management. When conducted in a detailed manner with precise cost data, break-even analysis helps management make intelligent decisions about proposed changes in the firm's product mix, about the pricing of individual products, and about the purchase of new production equipment.

Break-even analysis can also be used as an analytical tool by buyers in a purchasing department. In this situation, however, it is used very differently from the way it is used in the management planning situation. A buyer's analysis of the break-even phenomenon focuses not on his own firm's products and costs, but on his suppliers' products, costs, and production volume. By constructing and analyzing a supplier's break-even chart, a buyer can sometimes uncover clues to the timing of future price changes. At the same time, he can obtain a more complete understanding of why a supplier prices the way he does.

What is a firm's break-even point? It is exactly what the term implies—the dividing point between profit and loss. It is the volume of sales during a particular year which produces enough revenue just to cover total expenses. The existence of fixed costs prevents most firms from operating profitably at a low percentage of capacity. These costs, spread over only a small number of units at low production rates, make unit costs very high. Consider a firm which incurs millions of dollars of fixed overhead. If it produces and sells only one unit, that unit of product costs millions of dollars in fixed costs alone. The more units that are produced, the lower the cost per unit, and the more closely unit cost approaches unit selling price. At the break-even point, the *average* unit cost of all units produced exactly equals the average unit selling price. Beyond this point, the sales revenue generated by one unit of product is greater than its *total* cost of production; hence, each sale produces a profit.

How can a buyer construct a supplier's break-even chart? The following six steps illustrate the procedure (the results are shown graphically in Figure 7-1).

- Scale on graph paper the range of operating capacity from 0 to 100 percent on the horizontal scale. On the vertical scale, place the firm's actual and potential sales.
- Take the total sales ($10 million, Figure 7-1) from the firm's latest financial statement (Table 7-2), and plot the value at the firm's normal operating rate for the period covered by the statement (70 percent in this example).
- Draw a line from 0 in the lower left-hand corner to the sales figure just plotted, and extend it to the limit of the chart (see Figure 7-1). This line gives a rough sales volume measured for every operating rate up to full production capacity.
- Take the fixed costs—rent, depreciation, interest charges, taxes, etc.—which remain the same no matter what the operating rate is, locate the dollar sum of fixed costs on the vertical axis, and draw a line horizontally across the chart.
- Take the total cost figure ($9 million) from the firm's financial statement (Table 7-2), and position it above the same operating rate (70 percent) as used for the total sales figure.

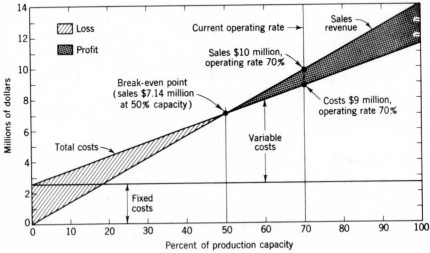

Figure 7-1 How to figure a firm's break-even point. (*Note:* For ease in illustrating the break even point concept, the example shown has purposely been oversimplified. The sales and cost lines have been shown as straight lines when in reality they are normally curved. See any current basic economics text for a more complete explanation of marginal cost analysis.)

- Connect that point with the beginning of the fixed-cost line (at 0 capacity, since fixed costs are total costs at that point), and extend the line to the limit of the chart (see Figure 7-1). This line gives a rough indication of costs for every operating rate.

The break-even point is the point at which the total-cost line intersects the total sales line. To the right of that point, the vertical distance between the two lines represents profit (sales revenue in excess of costs). To the left of the point, losses are represented in a similar manner (costs in excess of sales revenue). The percentage of capacity at which the firm must operate to avoid loss (50 percent in this example) can be read directly below the break-even point.

Not all costs fall into the fixed and variable categories. Some are semivariable (such as overtime costs resulting from increased use of maintenance personnel). For simplicity, in this example semivariable costs have been allocated among the fixed and variable groupings in Table 7-2.

If the analyst is interested only in the sales value, and not the operating rate at the break-even point, this can be computed quickly without constructing the chart. The statement shows that variable costs are $6.5 million for sales of $10 million. Therefore, 65 percent of every sales dollar goes for variable expenses. This means that 35 percent of sales contributes to fixed costs and net profit. If there is no net profit—as is the case at the break-even point—then the full 35 percent of sales just covers fixed costs. If fixed costs equal 35 percent of break-even sales value, then

$$\$2.5 \text{ million fixed costs} = 0.35 \text{ sales at break-even point}$$

$$\text{Sales at break-even point} = \$2.5 \text{ million}/0.35 = \$7.14 \text{ million}$$

A check of the break-even chart verifies that $7.14 million in sales must be made for the firm to break even.

If a buyer can approximate a supplier's break-even chart, he can determine

**Table 7-2 Selected Figures from Company
Financial Reports (in Millions of Dollars)**

	Fixed	Variable	
Total sales			$10.0
Total costs			9.0
Direct labor		$2.0	
Direct materials		3.0	
Factory overhead	$1.0	0.5	
Sales	0.6	0.9	
General administrative	0.9	0.1	
	$2.5	$6.5	
Net profit (before taxes)			$ 1.0

the approximate production rate (in percentage of capacity) that the supplier must average during the year to attain a particular profit goal. Then, by periodically observing the supplier's actual production levels, he can evaluate the success of the supplier's efforts and attempt to ascertain what influence they may have on future pricing actions. Thus a buyer knows that when a supplier's operating rate is close to the break-even rate and is declining, there is considerable pressure to increase sales revenue. If the supplier's product demand is elastic, the buyer might well expect a future price reduction (as the supplier attempts to increase revenue by boosting sales). If the supplier's product demand is relatively inelastic, a price increase may be in the offing (as the supplier attempts to increase revenue on low-volume sales by increasing selling price). Such information clearly aids the buyer in developing his negotiating or buying strategy. When he observes a supplier operating well above his break-even rate of production and steadily increasing, a buyer may well be able to negotiate more advantageous prices. The success of his negotiations, however, is conditioned significantly by the total demand situation in the industry.

Break-even analysis finds its most effective use when a buyer deals with companies in a process industry or with companies making one product or a small number of products. The reason for this is clear; an enterprising buyer can usually obtain adequate cost and sales data from published sources to approximate a supplier's break-even chart *in the aggregate* (on a companywide basis). Seldom, however, can he obtain such information broken down accurately by major product lines for a multiproduct company. Generally speaking, the more closely a break-even analysis relates to the product line being purchased, the more sensitive a tool it is in the hands of a buyer. Hence, it is considerably more effective in dealing with single-product companies than with multiproduct or multiplant giants.

One final note of caution is needed. The results of break-even analysis are no more reliable than the accuracy of the data used in the analysis. Since the cost information available to most people outside the supplier's firm does not include meaningful details of its origin, the break-even chart constructed by a buyer is at best a rough approximation. Consequently, it should not be considered a precision tool, but rather a general guide in determining buying and negotiating strategy.

The Learning Curve

The *learning curve* (sometimes called the *improvement curve*) can be defined as an *empirical* relationship between the number of units produced and the number of labor hours required to produce them. Production managers can use this relationship in scheduling production and in determining manpower requirements for a particular product over a given time period. Buyers can use the relationship to analyze the effects of production and management "learning" on a supplier's unit cost of production.

The learning curve has been used for many years, primarily for more sophisticated buying situations in the aircraft and missile industries. Recently, its use has spread to other industries. Winfred B. Hirchmann, in discussing this subject for the *Harvard Business Review,* states, "No matter what products you manufacture or what type of operation you manage, there is a good possibility you can profit from the learning curve."[5]

In purchasing, the learning curve is probably most useful in across-the-table negotiations, as a starting point for pricing a new item. In addition to providing "buyer's insurance" against overcharging, the learning curve is also used effectively by both government and commercial buyers in developing (1) target costs for new products, (2) make-or-buy information, (3) delivery schedules, and (4) progress payments to vendors.

Target Costs If a new product that is custom made to unique specifications is ordered, what should be paid for the first item? The 50th item? The 500th item? Obviously costs should decline—but by how much. Analysis of the learning curve provides an answer. Using the learning curve, cost reductions and estimated prices can be obtained merely by reading figures from a chart. The learning curve is an invaluable aid in establishing an initial supplier-buyer basis for arriving at a fair schedule of prices for future orders.

If the learning curve technique is new to an industry, it can provoke initial supplier hostility. Since the learning curve implies steadily falling prices, many vendors at first tend to look upon it as an old club (in modern dress) for beating down prices. However, once suppliers grasp the concept behind this pricing approach—and are convinced that it is fair and impartial—they are usually quite eager to cooperate.

The learning curve is a quantitative model of commonsense observation that the unit cost of a new product decreases as more units of the product are made. The manufacturer, through the repetitive production process, learns how to make the product at lower cost. For example, the more times a worker repeats a complicated operation, the more efficient he or she becomes, both in speed and skill. This, in turn, means progressively lower unit labor costs. It also means lower costs in other ways. Familiarity with an operation results in fewer rejects and reworks, better scheduling, possible improvements in tooling, fewer engineering changes, and more efficient management control.

Suppose a buyer knows that it took a vendor 100 hours of labor to turn out the first unit of a new product, as indicated on Figure 7-3 (see page 132). The vendor reports that the second unit took 80 hours to make, so the average labor requirement for the two items is 180/2 = 90 hours per unit. The production report for the first four units is summarized in Table 7-3.

Observe that the labor requirement dropped to 74 hours for the third unit and to 70 hours for the fourth unit. Column 4 shows that the *average* number of

[5]Winfred B. Hirchmann, "Profit from the Learning Curve," *Harvard Business Review,* January-February 1964, p. 125.

Table 7-3   Ninety Percent Learning Curve Data

Unit produced	Labor hours required	Cumulative labor hours required	Average labor hours required per unit
1st	100	100	100.0
2nd	80	180	90.0
3rd	74	254	84.7
4th	70	324	81.0

labor hours required for the first four units was 81 hours per unit. Investigation of the learning rate shows the following relationships:

- As production doubled from one to two units, the *average* labor hours required per unit dropped from 100 to 90, a reduction of 10 percent.
- As production doubled from two to four units, the *average* labor hours required per unit dropped from 90 to 81, a reduction of 10 percent.

Figure 7-2 indicates that the same learning rate continues as production of the new item increases. If eight units were made, the vendor would have learned to make them at an average of approximately 73 hours per unit for all units to date. If sixteen units were produced, the average number of labor hours required would be about 66. Each time production doubles the average labor requirement for all units declines by 10 percent, as a result of the composite learning process. Thus the product is said to have a 90 percent learning rate, or a 90 percent learning curve.[6] The basic point revealed by the learning curve is that *a specific and constant percentage reduction in the average direct labor hours required per unit results each time the number of units produced is doubled.* It is an established fact that specific learning rates occur with reasonable regularity for similar groups of products in many different industries.

Studies made in the aircraft, electronics, and small electromechanical subassembly fields indicate that learning rates of 75 to 95 percent are typical.[7] However, learning curves can vary anywhere within the practical limits of 50 to 100 percent. Moreover, from a practical point of view, as more units are produced the effect of a constant learning rate on unit costs gradually diminishes. After several thousand units, the absolute reduction in cost from

[6]The discussion and charts throughout this section are based on the "average hours" learning curve phenomenon. Learning curves can also be plotted in terms of actual labor hours per last unit produced. Some firms find that their production processes exhibit a more constant learning rate when expressed in these terms. A majority of firms, however, find the "average hours" learning curve most applicable to their processes.

[7]The cost-of materials curve also improves with time, for the same reasons as the cost-of-labor curve. As better methods are developed and as employees become more familiar with the work being done, the spoilage and scrap rates of materials decrease. Materials learning curves average roughly 95 percent, with a range of approximately 90 percent to just below 100 percent.

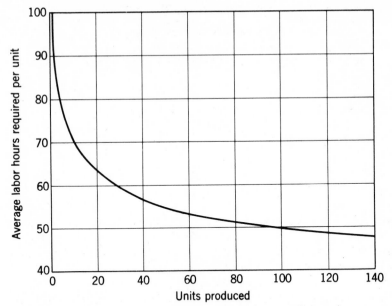

Figure 7-2 Ninety percent learning curve plotted on regular graph paper.

learning becomes negligible. Note in Figure 7-2 how the curve flattens out as the number of units produced increases. This is why learning curve analysis is of greatest value for new products.[8]

Most analysts prefer to plot the data for learning curves on log-log paper, as in Figure 7-3. The logarithmic scales on both the horizontal and vertical axes convert the curve of Figure 7-4 into a straight line. The straight line is easier to read, and it also simplifies forecasting, since a constant learning rate always appears as a straight line on log-log coordinates. To verify the fact that both charts represent the same thing, look at the number of hours needed to produce 100 units in Figures 7-2 and 7-3; both figures indicate about 50 hours per unit.

In addition to determining the critical direct-labor component of price, the learning curve also has the following purchasing applications:

Make-or-Buy Decisions A comparison of separate learning curves for both a buyer's firm and his supplier's firm can help the buyer decide whether to make or buy a specific part, particularly when his own plant is operating well below capacity. Projections on the learning curves will tell the buyer whether he or the supplier will have lower *average costs* for the number of units needed.

---

[8]Different types of labor generate different percentages of learning. Assembly-type labor generates the most rapid improvement and fabrication-type labor the least. Fabrication labor has a lower learning rate, because the speed of jobs dependent on this type of labor is governed more by the capability of the equipment than the skill of the operator. The operator's learning in this case is confined to setup and maintenance times. In some situations, therefore, when a precise analysis is desired, a learning curve should be developed for each category of labor.

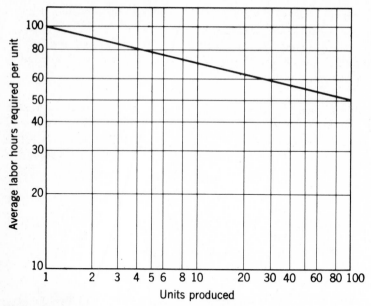

Figure 7-3 The 90 percent learning curve of Figure 7-2 plotted on log-log paper.

Estimating Delivery Times Since the learning curve can be used to forecast labor time required, it is possible to estimate how many units a vendor can turn out over a specified time with a given labor force. This information can be extremely helpful to the buyer in scheduling deliveries, in planning his own firm's production, and in identifying suppliers who obviously cannot meet desired delivery schedules.

Supplier Progress Payments Since the learning curve reflects changing labor costs, it provides a basis for figuring a supplier's financial commitment on any given number of units. This information is important because suppliers often operate in the red during the initial part of a production run, until learning can reduce costs below the average price. Buyers can minimize supplier hardship by using the learning curve to break down an order into two or more production lots—each with successively lower average prices—and then set up progress payments based on the supplier's costs.

Application of Learning Curves

The *misapplication* of learning curves is a pitfall buyers must guard against. Before applying a learning curve to a particular item, a buyer must be certain that production processes do in fact exhibit continuing learning at a reasonably constant rate. Many production operations do not possess such properties. Gross errors can be made if a learning curve is misapplied in such situations. In using learning curves, buyers must be alert to the following problems.

Nonuniform Learning Rates   Learning curve analysis, as discussed here, is predicated on the assumption that the production process in question exhibits learning at a reasonably constant rate. Direct labor data from such a process plot in a straight line on a log-log grid. If a straight line cannot be fitted to the data reasonably well, the technique should not be used.

Low-Labor-Content Items   Continued learning occurs to the greatest extent for products involving a high percentage of labor in their production. The learning opportunity is particularly high in complex assembly work. On the other hand, if most work on a new item involves machine time, where output tends to be determined by machine capacity, there is little opportunity for continued learning.

Small Payoffs   Obtaining historical cost data to construct a learning curve entails much time and effort, particularly when a supplier uses a standard cost accounting system. Therefore, learning curve analysis is worthwhile only if the amount of money saved is substantial.

Incorrect Learning Rates   Learning varies from industry to industry, plant to plant, product to product, and part to part. Applying one rate just because someone in the industry has used it can give misleading results. Intelligent use of learning curves demands that learning rates be determined as accurately as possible from comparable past experience.

Established Items   If a vendor has made the item for someone else before, a buyer should not use the learning curve even if the product is nonstandard and new for him. Because most of the learning has already been done on previous work, any additional cost reduction may well be negligible.

Misleading Data   Not all cost savings stem from learning. The economies of large-scale production may reduce costs, but this can hardly be described as learning.

Estimated Prices   Buyers who apply the learning curve to *estimated* price data deceive themselves. Application of the learning curve to incorrect data only multiplies the initial error. Under pressure from the government to use competitive budding in all situations and also to use the modern tools of purchasing whenever possible, government prime contractors and subcontractors not infrequently get themselves into this kind of situation.

An Example of Learning Curve Application   The following simplified example shows a basic application of the learning curve concept in contract pricing:

The ABC Corporation has purchased 50 pieces of a specially designed electronic component at $2,000 per unit. Of the $2,000 selling price, $1,000 represents direct labor. An audit of production costs for the first 50 units established that the operation is subject to an **80 percent** learning curve. What should ABC pay for the purchase of 350 more units?

1 Using log-log paper, plot 50 units (on the horizontal axis) against $1,000 direct labor cost on the vertical axis (see Figure 7-4).
2 Double the number of units to 100 on the horizontal axis and plot against a labor cost of $800 (80 percent as high as the original $1,000 cost).
3 Draw a straight line through the two cost points. The line represents an 80 percent learning curve, constructed on the basis of labor cost data for the first 50 units of production.
4 Locate 400 units on the horizontal axis (the total expected production of 50 original units plus 350 new ones). Read from the curve the labor cost of $510. This is the average expected labor cost per unit for the total production of 400 units.
5 To find the labor cost for 400 units, multiply 400 × $510, the direct labor cost per unit. The total is $204,000.
6 Subtract the labor paid in the original order to determine the labor cost of the new order of 350 units. Hence, subtract $50,000 (50 × $1,000) from $204,000. The answer is $154.000, the labor cost which should be paid for the new order of 350 units: $154,000/350 units = $440 per unit labor cost, as compared with the original $1,000 per unit.
7 Now determine the cost for materials, overhead, and profit on the 350 units. Add this figure to the labor cost determined in step 6 to obtain the total price ABC should pay for the additional 350 units.

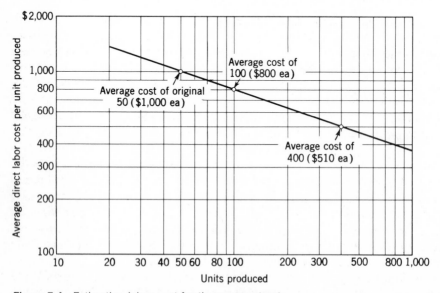

Figure 7-4 Estimating labor cost for the new contract.

LEGAL IMPLICATIONS OF PRICING

Laws Influencing Prices

Pricing cannot always be decided solely on the basis of economic considerations. Legislation and court decisions, both federal and state, sometimes influence pricing.

Sherman Antitrust Act   This act, passed by Congress in 1890, stands as the first legislative attempt to prohibit business monopolies in the United States. The law is short, but its provisions are far-reaching. It prohibits contracts, conspiracies, or combinations which act in restraint of trade or attempt to monopolize any part of interstate trade. As a result of the act, business firms cannot lawfully make price agreements that restrain trade except where they are exempted or where they do not affect interstate commerce.

Clayton Act   The Clayton Act was passed in 1914 to extend and supplement the Sherman Antitrust Act. It prohibits price discrimination between different buyers where the effect is substantially to lessen competition or tend to create a monopoly in any line of business. Hence, the main purpose of this act is to prevent monopoly by outlawing discriminations in pricing. It outlaws interlocking directorates, certain intercorporate stockholding, and some asset acquisitions (defined in a 1951 amendment). Organized labor refers to this act as its Magna Charta, for it states that labor is not subject to the nation's antitrust laws, since it is not an article of commerce. Court decisions since the 1920s, however, have served to modify this exemption somewhat.

Federal Trade Commission Act   This act, passed in 1914, was enacted to enforce the Clayton and Sherman Acts. Enforcement is vested in a five-man Federal Trade Commission (FTC). The FTC is given the power to issue cease and desist orders against parties not playing the competitive game fairly, as set forth in the acts and their subsequent interpretation by the courts. If the Commission's cease and desist orders are not obeyed, the courts will be appealed to for enforcement. Misleading price advertising is one of the major practices classified as unfair by the FTC.

Robinson-Patman Act   The Robinson-Patman Act further expands the Clayton Act, making it unlawful for sellers to (1) discriminate in price between buyers of like grade and quality materials where the consequence of so doing tends to create a monopoly or to injure, destroy, or prevent competition, (2) offer brokerage fees to buyers except for services actually rendered to the seller, and (3) pay for advertising and similar services unless they are made available on proportionally equal terms to all buyers.

The first provision of this act is of special interest to purchasing executives and buyers. Under this provision, a firm is allowed to sell a *given product* to different buyers at *different prices* only when the price difference is justified by differences in the seller's costs of production and distribution. This means that quantity discounts must be offered equally to all buyers. In addition, price reductions for larger purchase quantities must not only be the same for all buyers, but must also be directly traceable to economies arising from production and distribution of the item in larger quantities. This means, for example, that if a vendor saves $1 per unit by packaging and shipping in quantities of 100, it is unlawful for him to reduce the selling price for lots of 100 by $1.10 per unit. *Of prime interest to buyers is the fact that the act makes the buyer as guilty for knowingly accepting unfair discounts as it does the seller for offering them.*

In addition to permitting price differentials because of savings that result from quantity, the act permits selling at reduced prices in order to dispose of deteriorating perishable goods, to dispose of seasonable goods, and to meet in good faith an equally low price of a competitor. This provision of the law "to meet an equally low price of a competitor" is obviously of great importance to buyers. It gives all companies flexibility to reduce prices when competitors do so.

If charged with violation of the act, the burden of proof of nonviolation rests with the person charged. Generally speaking, this is the seller. It is his responsibility to demonstrate that the lower prices he offers for large quantities stem from cost savings that are equal to or exceed his reduction in prices. It is possible, however, for a buyer to be charged with violation. The buyer's violation would result from the fact that he used his economic buying power, in violation of the act, to force the seller into illegal price concessions. For instance, a large buyer might threaten to withdraw his account if price concessions were not made.

What can buyers do when they think a seller is giving better pricing to a competitor in violation of the Robinson-Patman Act? They have at least four alternative courses of action. They may report the facts to the United States Department of Justice, either directly or via the United States district attorney in their area; report the facts to the Federal Trade Commission; initiate a private lawsuit; or discuss the apparent violation with the vendor.

The fourth alternative is always the best initial course of action. By discussing the matter with the vendor, certain unpleasantness and possible expense can be avoided. The vendor may have an entirely logical explanation for his pricing policy, or he may have made an honest mistake which he would quite willingly correct. If the vendor's explanation turns out to be unsatisfactory, then the first or second alternatives can be initiated. Because of the expense involved, the third alternative should be an action of last resort.

Unfair Trade Practices Acts These acts, generally applicable to the wholesale and retail sales of all consumer items, have been passed in twenty-eight states, primarily to prohibit the sale of goods below "cost." Cost is most often defined as invoice cost plus a percentage, varying from 4 to 12 percent in the twenty-eight states. Many reasons, particularly the difficulty of determining costs, make it almost impossible to enforce these laws. As a consequence, these acts are of minor importance today to industrial buyers, although they are of considerable importance in some areas of retailing.

Davis-Bacon Act   This act was passed in 1931. In essence, the act provides that the Secretary of Labor must set minimum pay rates, at the level of prevailing wages in the immediate area, for government construction contracts over $2,000. Construction is defined to mean construction, alterations, or repair (including painting and decorating) of public buildings or public works of the United States. Hence, before contractors can bid on a government contract, they are told precisely what dollar rates they must pay their employees.

This law, like the fair trade laws, is a present-day anachronism. It forces the payment of construction wages as high as $100 per day when workers otherwise would willingly and fairly accept less. A recent public survey provides many interesting examples of such situations.[9] Consider one: "In Chittendon County, Vermont, roofers make $4 per hour. There is not a single union roofer in the county. Nevertheless, the Labor Department imposed on local contractors bidding for public housing jobs a $9.25 an hour minimum, a wage prevalent in union-dominated Albany, New York, 125 miles away." In total, the study estimates that Davis-Bacon is costing United States taxpayers $1.5 billion annually.

This act, similar to many others, is one that started with a worthy purpose, but with changing circumstances strayed considerably from that purpose. When passed during the Great Depression, Davis-Bacon was enacted to prevent well-financed itinerant contractors from successfully bidding on and winning government contracts, then transporting low-wage workers from distant points to displace local workers. Clearly, this was not what the act accomplished in the Vermont roofing wage example.

The Defense Production Act and Government Price Control   The Defense Production Act, passed on September 8, 1950, gives the President the power to take steps to stabilize prices. The next day the Economic Stabilization Agency was established, and shortly thereafter the Office of Price Stabilization (OPS) was created. In 1951, the Capehart and Herlong amendment to the Defense Production Act was passed. During national emergencies, the OPS can issue price ceiling regulations. Direct government control over prices of consumer and industrial goods is a measure which, until 1971, had been resorted to only under pressure of war, when the demand for most products greatly exceeded the available supply.

To stem the rising tide of inflation, on August 15, 1971 the President issued Executive Order 11615 which froze all prices, rents, and wages for a period of

[9]"Your Move on Inflation, Mr. President," Charles Stevenson, *Reader's Digest*, April 1975, pp. 157–162.

90 days. This freeze (ceiling) continued in various forms for approximately two years. Most observers believe that this price-control measure was largely ineffective in achieving its objectives and that similar governmental control efforts are not likely to develop in the near future.

Items Purchased to Individual Specifications

The Robinson-Patman Act does not outlaw price reductions; it merely outlaws discriminatory and preferential prices. Sellers can legally offer lower prices to meet legitimate competition. They can also reduce prices by offering lower quality and by affecting cost savings which they can pass on to the buyer.

By means of value analysis, buyers can review specifications for all parts and materials used in their products. Such an analysis can bring to light many situations allowing deviation from the seller's present specifications. These changes in turn permit the negotiation of lower prices.

Most industrial firms purchase at least three distinct kinds of items: standard commercial, or off-the-shelf items; items produced to a vendor's design for a buyer's specific application; and items and services produced only to the buyer's design. The third category represents a special situation; it is in this area that buyers can really test their abilities.

When buying to unique specifications, to a large degree the buyer *is* the market for these purchases. In such circumstances, there are no human laws or economic laws that directly dictate specific prices to either the buyer or the seller. The price finally agreed upon depends as much on the skill of the negotiators as on competitive market or supply-demand considerations. Buying to unique specifications is, without doubt, an effective method of avoiding legal pricing restrictions. In technically advanced industries, like the electronics industry, stringent performance and reliability requirements often leave no alternative to the buyers but to develop their own specifications. In these instances, prices are usually determined by direct negotiation using both cost analysis and price analysis techniques. Where performance and reliability requirements can be met by standard items, however, it is questionable whether the development of a special item merely to secure freedom from pricing laws is economically justifiable. The special item must be one required in unusually large quantities in order to bring its price below that for a standard item mass-produced on specialized equipment.

SYNTHESIS

Determining a fair and reasonable price, and negotiating to get it, requires a very high degree of skill and judgment, because *most prices are derived from estimates and judgments, not precise facts.* Because a supplier cannot precisely forecast his sales and production volumes, he is unable to calculate his costs precisely. Hence, he is unable to calculate the precise price he needs to maximize profit and is thus forced to rely on his business judgment. Judgments of costs, profits, and prices are always subject to analysis and negotiation.

The free market itself plays a dominant role in pricing. When business is booming, manufacturers can generally increase their prices. Sales go up, and during such times there is little even the most skillful buyer can do to gain price concessions. On the other hand, when the market weakens or turns downward, circumstances change radically. Now the supplier, for survival reasons, must review his costs and be willing to make price concessions. If necessary, the concessions can drop the price all the way down to out-of-pocket costs.

Sophisticated buyers have a comprehensive knowledge of how cost, production, sales, competitive relationships, and legal restrictions influence a supplier's pricing in both booms and recessions. They also have knowledge of negotiating principles, make-or-buy analysis, techniques of group ordering, and selection of the best type of contract. With this knowledge, competent buyers are in a very strong position to use, without abuse, their firm's total buying power. In most industrial purchasing situations, vendors do not cast the only votes in price determination. Capable buyers also cast votes. For these reasons, prices can often be influenced as much by purchasing skill as by the impersonal supply and demand forces of the marketplace.

FOR DISCUSSION

7-1   Explain the principal differences between fixed-price contracts and cost-type contracts.

7-2   Why are escalation clauses used in contracts?

7-3   Explain the difference between escalation and redetermination clauses. Under what circumstances are each used?

7-4   Name the three basic types of indefinite delivery contracts, and discuss the distinguishing characteristics of a requirements contract.

7-5   Discuss systems contracts, pointing out specifically how this type of contract is different from others used to purchase repetitively used items.

7-6   Why is it important for a purchasing executive to understand how to calculate a vendor's break-even point?

7-7   Explain the concept underlying the learning curve. In what circumstances can it be used most effectively?

7-8   Explain the purpose of the Sherman Antitrust Act, the Clayton Act, and the Federal Trade Commission Act.

7-9   What is the purpose of the Robinson-Patman Act? Explain how buyers could be guilty of improper conduct under this act.

7-10 Many firms purchase thousands of items made to their own specifications. Do you believe this is done to develop differentiated products for competitive reasons, or to avoid the provisions of the Robinson-Patman Act? Explain.

CASES FOR CHAPTER 7

Negotiation

Negotiation is one of the most important as well as one of the most interesting elements of purchasing and materials management. Because negotiation is complex and costly, it is used primarily for high dollar value purchases. However, high dollar value per se does not dictate using negotiated purchasing. For high dollar purchases, where the five criteria which dictate competitive bidding prevail, competitive bidding is the preferred method of purchase; when this is not the case, negotiation is the appropriate method.

Negotiation involves rigorous study and training for those who would truly master it. Russian negotiators, for example, are trained for three years at the Institute of Foreign Trade in Moscow before they enter into their first actual contract negotiations.[1]

NEGOTIATION DEFINED

In industry, and at most levels of government, the term "negotiation" causes misunderstandings. In industry, negotiation is sometimes confused with "haggling" and "price chiseling." In government, negotiation is frequently visua-

[1]"The Type and Tactics of Moscow's Traders," *Business Week*, October 21, 1972, p. 70.

lized as a nefarious means of avoiding competitive bidding and of awarding large contracts surreptitiously to favored suppliers.

Webster defines negotiation broadly as "conferring, discussing, or bargaining to reach agreement in business transactions." To be fully effective in purchasing, negotiation must be utilized in its broadest context, i.e., as a decision-making process. In this context, negotiation is a process of planning, reviewing, and analyzing used by a buyer and a seller to reach acceptable agreements or compromises. These agreements and compromises include all aspects of the business transaction, not just price.

Negotiations differ from a ball game or a war. In those activities, only one side can win; the other side must lose. In successful negotiations, both sides win something. Although both sides win, the "winnings" are seldom equally divided. Invariably, one side wins more than the other. This is as it should be in business—superior business skills merit superior rewards.

OBJECTIVES OF NEGOTIATION

Five major objectives are common to all negotiations:

1 To obtain a fair and reasonable price for the quality specified
2 To get the supplier to perform the contract on time
3 To exert some control over the manner in which the contract is performed
4 To persuade the supplier to give maximum cooperation to the buyer's company
5 To develop a sound and continuing relationship with competent suppliers

Fair and Reasonable Price

Negotiation may be used alone or in conjunction with competitive bidding to determine price. When used alone, it should be preceded by cost or price analysis. When competitive bidding is used in conjunction with negotiation, the buyer first attempts to get a reasonable number of competitive bids. He then negotiates with the two or three sellers who submit the best bids. It is important for buyers to negotiate only with sellers who consistently submit attractive (usually close to their best) offers initially. Otherwise, sellers will routinely bid prices higher than they are actually willing to accept; they will speculate that negotiations may be concluded before they are forced to make their best offer.

Delivery Schedules

Inability to meet delivery schedules is the single greatest supplier failure encountered in purchasing operations. This failure results primarily from (1) requisitioners not submitting their purchase requests early enough to allow for necessary purchasing and manufacturing lead times, and (2) buyers failing to plan this part of the negotiations properly. Because unrealistic delivery schedules reduce competition and increase prices, it is important that buyers negotiate delivery schedules which suppliers can actually and economically meet.

Buyers should know with certainty that a supplier's plant is not overloaded to the point that his production is running behind schedule. Despite having gained such knowledge, some buyers continue to place orders with suppliers who constantly fall behind on their scheduled production dates. This common and unwise practice assures delays in deliveries, under both present and future contracts. A supplier with a large backlog of orders is simply unable to schedule or expedite orders with the precision of a supplier who has available production capacity.

Supplier Performance

Deficiencies in supplier performance can seriously affect, and in some cases completely disrupt, the operations of the buyer's company. For this reason, on important contracts the buyer should negotiate for controls which will help assure compliance with the quality, quantity, delivery, and service terms of the contract. Controls sometimes are useful in areas such as man-hours of effort, levels of scientific talent, special test equipment requirements, and the amount and type of work to be subcontracted.

Supplier Cooperation

Supplier cooperation is best obtained by a policy of rewarding those suppliers who perform well with additional future orders. In addition to subsequent orders, however, good suppliers also expect courtesy, pleasant working relations, and cooperation from their customers—cooperation begets cooperation.

Continuing Supplier Relationships

When negotiating with suppliers, a buyer should recognize that current actions usually constitute only a part of a continuing relationship. Negotiating conditions which permit buyers to take unfair advantage of sellers invariably with time change to conditions which allow sellers to "hold up" buyers. For this reason, the buyer must realize that any advantage not honestly won will in all likelihood be recovered by the supplier at a later date—probably with interest. Thus, as a matter of self-interest, buyers must maintain a proper balance between their concern for a supplier's immediate performance, on the one hand, and their interest in the supplier's long-run performance on the other.

In summary, the objectives of negotiation require investigation (with the supplier) of every area of negotiable concern—considering both short-term and long-term performance. The buyer's major analytical tools for negotiating prices were discussed in the preceding chapter; i.e., price, cost, break-even, learning-curve, and cost-volume-profit analysis. Additional negotiating tools, as well as the development of strategy and tactics for negotiation, are discussed throughout this chapter.

WHEN TO NEGOTIATE

Negotiation is the appropriate method of purchasing when competitive bidding is impractical. Some of the most common circumstances dictating the use of negotiation are:

1 When any of the five prerequisite criteria for competitive bidding are missing (see pages 97–98 for a complete discussion of these criteria).

2 When many variable factors bear not only on price, but also on quality and service. (Many high dollar value industrial and governmental contracts fall into this category.)

3 When a buyer is contracting for a portion of the seller's production capacity, rather than for a product the seller has designed and manufactured. (In such cases, the buyer has designed the product to be manufactured, and as an entrepreneur, he assumes all risks concerning the product's quality and salability. In buying production capacity, the buyer's objective is to attain not only production capability, but also such control over it as may be needed to perfect the product and the production process. This type of control can be achieved only by negotiation and the voluntary cooperation of suppliers.)

4 When the business risks involved cannot be accurately predetermined. (When buyers ask for competitive bids under these circumstances, and unfortunately they frequently do, losses inevitably result. As a matter of self-protection, suppliers include in their bid prices every possible contingency factor. This is a normal procedure prudent business executives employ to reduce the risk of incurring potentially large losses. In practice, all of the perceived contingencies usually do not actually occur. Hence, the buyer pays unnecessarily for potential risks that do not materialize.)

5 When tooling and setup costs represent a large percentage of total costs. (For many contracts, the supplier must buy or make many costly jigs, dies, fixtures, molds, special test equipment, gauges, etc. Because of their special nature, these jigs and fixtures are primarily limited in use to the buyer's contract. The division of special tooling costs between a buyer and a seller is subject to negotiation. This negotiation includes a thorough analysis of future buyer or seller use of the tools, the length and dollar amount of the contract, the type of contract to be used, etc.)

6 When a long period of time is required to produce the items purchased. (Under these circumstances, suitable economic price adjustment clauses must be negotiated. Also opportunities for various improvements may develop—for example, new manufacturing methods, new packag-

ing possibilities, substitute materials, new plant layouts, and new tools. Negotiation permits an examination and evaluation of all these potential improvements. Competitive bidding does not. What supplier, for example, would modify his plant layout to achieve increased efficiency, without assurance of sufficient long-term business to cover the cost involved and assurance of a reasonable profit for his effort?)

7 When production is interrupted frequently because of numerous change orders. (This is a common situation in fields of fast-changing technology. Contracts in these fields must provide for frequent change orders, otherwise the product being purchased could be obsolete before completion of production. The ways in which expensive changes in drawings, designs, and specifications are to be handled and paid for are subjects for mutual agreement arrived at through negotiation.)

8 When a thorough analysis is required to solve difficult make-or-buy decisions. (Precisely what a seller is going to make and what he is going to subcontract should be decided by negotiation. When free to make his own decision, the seller often makes the easiest decision for himself in terms of production scheduling. This may well be the most costly decision for the buyer in terms of price.)

9 When the products of a specific supplier are desired to the exclusion of others. (In this case, competition is totally lacking. Terms and prices, therefore, must be negotiated to prevent unreasonable dictation by the seller.)

In all nine of these cases, negotiation is essential; and, in each case, quality and service are as important as price.

BUYER'S ROLE IN NEGOTIATION

Depending on the purchase being made, a buyer plays one of two distinct roles in negotiation. In the first role, he or she is the company's sole negotiator. In the second, the buyer heads a team of specialists who collectively negotiate for their company.

Buyer Acting Alone

For recurring purchases of standard items, regardless of their dollar amounts, the buyer invariably acts alone. Typically, for this type of purchase, a negotiation conference is held in the buyer's office with the supplier's sales manager (the seller's sole negotiator). These two persons in turn negotiate all the important terms and conditions of the contract.

A buyer's "solo negotiations" are not limited to periodic formal negotiating sessions. Rather, such negotiations continue on a daily basis with both current suppliers and visiting vendors who wish to be suppliers. Consider several typical examples. A supplier calls on the telephone and informs the buyer that prices are to be raised 20 percent within 60 days. The buyer responds with the thought that production in his company's plant is slack and that a price rise as high as 20 percent could well trigger a "make" decision, in lieu of what is now a "buy" decision. The buyer is negotiating!

A seller's value analyst discovers a substantially cheaper method of manufacturing one of the buyer's products. However, there is one drawback; an expensive new machine is required for the job. The supplier's salesman informs the buyer of the discovery. The buyer and his engineer study the concept; it is a good one. The buyer contacts the salesman to thank him for bringing the new idea to his attention. At the same time, the buyer explains that his company is financially unable at this particular time to invest in the required new machine. Further, he conjectures that if the salesman's company were to agree to purchase the machine, then the buyer without doubt could get his company to reconsider the rejected long-term contract the seller proposed last year. Informal, unplanned negotiations are being conducted!

A saleswoman calls, and the buyer says, "I have been thinking about your contract with us. Under the contract, our purchases now total roughly $25,000 per year, primarily for valves. But your company also manufactures a number of fittings that we use. If these fittings were combined with the purchase of the valves, what benefits would your company be able to grant us?" Another informal negotiation is under way.

The preceding year a buyer purchased $150,000 worth of liquid oxygen in individual cylinders from a single supplier. Because of its high dollar value, the buyer began to analyze oxygen usage requirements thoroughly. In doing so, he discovered an interesting fact. By installing a bulk storage tank at the buyer's plant (at a cost of $80,000) and having his stores personnel deliver the required liquid oxygen to the shops, $30,000 per year could be saved. When the supplier's salesman called, he was informed of the buyer's study and was given the buyer's worksheets for his review and study. Negotiations were under way, and the price of liquid oxygen would soon be reduced.

These examples are just a few typical illustrations of how buyers negotiate continually on an individual basis. The potential number of situations involving individual negotiations is almost limitless. The combined analytical abilities of buyers and sellers, coupled with their motivation to reduce mutual costs and improve service, establish any limits that exist.

Buyer Acting as Leader of a Team

The complexity of a purchasing contract correlates directly with the complexity of the item being purchased. For high-value, complex contracts (such as those developed for the purchase of high-technology products, capital equipment, and research and development work), the buyer typically is no longer qualified to act as a *sole* negotiator. The buyer's role, therefore, shifts from that of negotiator to that of the leader of a negotiating team. The team is constituted in consonance with the complexity and importance of the purchase to be made. It traditionally consists of a combination of specialists from fields such as design engineering, cost analysis and estimating, finance, price analysis, production, traffic, purchasing, and law.

In the team approach to negotiation, the purchasing manager traditionally serves as the leader of the team (called the negotiator). In this capacity he or she functions as the coordinator of the heterogeneous group of different specialists, who can be expected to view similar matters differently. As head of the team, the negotiator must weld it into an integrated whole. By careful planning, he must draw on the specialized knowledge of each team member and combine this specialized knowledge with his own. Thus, he develops a sound, unified approach to uncover, analyze, and resolve (from a company wide point of view) all the problems applicable to the contract being negotiated.

THE NEGOTIATION PROCESS

In the broadest sense, negotiation begins with the origin of a firm's requirements for specific materials or services. As discussed in Chapter 4, the ultimate in purchasing value is possible only if design, production, procurement, and sales are able to reconcile their differing views with respect to materials specifications. Buyers must always think in terms of total cost and total value, not in terms of price alone. Actual two-party negotiation begins with a buyer's requests for proposals from potential suppliers. It develops as the negotiator carefully evaluates these proposals and prepares for discussion of the important issues that may arise in the impending negotiation conference. The negotiation process ends with the resolution of all issues that actually do arise during the negotiation conference.

A negotiator's most important single responsibility in preparing for negotiations is to appraise his own strengths and weaknesses accurately in relation to the seller's strengths and weaknesses. The ability with which the negotiator executes this responsibility in large measure influences the actual course and outcome of the negotiations. Only as a result of an accurate appraisal of relative bargaining strengths can the negotiator skillfully demand the right things at the right time and concede the right things at the right time. *Timing* in negotiation is often as important as substance.

The Seller's Bargaining Strengths

The seller's bargaining strength usually depends on three basic factors: how badly the seller wants the contract, how certain he or she feels of getting it, and how much time is available to reach agreement on suitable terms.

Seller's Desire for the Contract The buyer should encounter no difficulty in determining how urgently a seller wants a contract. The frequency with which his salesman calls and general market conditions are positive indicators of seller interest. Sellers' annual profit and loss statements, as well as miscellaneous reports concerning backlog, volume of operations, and trends, are valuable sources of information about individual sellers. Publications such as the Department of Commerce "Economic Indicators," *The Federal Reserve Bulletin,* industrial trade papers, and local newspapers provide a wealth of basic information about potential suppliers' industries in general.

The less a seller needs or wants a contract, the stronger his bargaining position becomes. The presence of an industry boom, for example, places him in a strong position. On the other hand, when a seller finds himself in a general recession or in an industry plagued with excess capacity, his bargaining position is decidedly weakened.

Seller Certainty of Getting Contract   If a seller learns that his prices are lower than his competitor's, or if he learns from engineering or production personnel that he is a preferred source of supply for technical reasons, or if he is a sole source, he natually concludes that his chances of getting the contract are next to certain. In these circumstances, he may become most difficult to deal with during negotiations. In extreme situations, he may be unwilling to make any concessions whatever. When this happens, the negotiator sometimes has only one alternative—to accept the supplier's terms.

When trapped by such circumstances, a negotiator can threaten delay to search for other sources. Such threats are likely to be ineffective, unless the seller knows that alternate sources are actually available and interested in the business. An alternative threat which may be effective when patents are not involved is the threat to manufacture the needed item in the buyer's plant. When made realistically (the supplier believes the buyer has the technical capability, determination and open capacity to make the product), this threat usually gains concessions.

A firm's negotiating position is always strengthened when the company has a clear policy that permits only its purchasing department to discuss pricing, timing, and other contractual terms with sellers. Most prenegotiation information leaks that give sellers a feeling of confidence about getting a contract occur in the technical departments of a firm. Such leaks can be extremely costly, and because they are often undetected by general management, they can be a continuing source of profit loss.

Time Available for Negotiation   Short lead times drastically reduce the buyer's negotiating strength. Conversely, they significantly increase the seller's bargaining strength. Once a supplier knows that a buyer has a tight deadline, it becomes an easy matter for him to "drag his feet" and then negotiate terms favorable to himself at the last minute when the buyer is under severe pressure to consummate the contract.

The Buyer's Bargaining Strengths

The buyer's bargaining strength usually depends on three basic factors: the extent of competition present among potential suppliers, the adequacy of cost or price analysis, and the thoroughness with which he or she has prepared for negotiation.

The Extent of Competition   The presence of supplier competition always strengthens a buyer's negotiating position. Competition is always keenest when a number of competent sellers eagerly desire the order. General economic conditions, among other factors, also have a substantial bearing on the extent to which a firm really wants to compete. A firm's shop load, its inventory position, and its back-order position, for example, are additional factors that bear heavily on the everchanging competitive climate.

When necessary, a buyer can increase competition by developing new suppliers; buying suppliers' companies; making items in-house rather than buying them; providing tools, money, and management to competent but financially weak vendors; and, above all, hiring highly skilled negotiators.

The Adequacy of Cost or Price Analysis   A comprehensive knowledge of the principles of cost analysis and price analysis is one of the basic responsibilities of a negotiator. When an initial contract is awarded for a portion of a supplier's production capacity rather then for a finished product, cost analysis becomes vital. In this situation, the negotiator is not prepared to explore with the supplier the reasonableness of his proposals until after the completion of a comprehensive analysis of all applicable costs. Cost analysis in such purchases, in a very real sense, becomes a substitute for direct competition. For follow-on contracts of this type, and for contracts for common commercial items, price analysis is usually sufficient to assure the buyer that prices are reasonable. In the aggregate, the greater the amount of available cost, price, and financial data, the greater are the buyer's chances for successful negotiation.

The Thoroughness of Buyer Preparation

Knowledge is power. The more knowledge the negotiator acquires about the theory and practice of negotiation, the seller's negotiating position, and the product being purchased, the stronger his or her own negotiating stance will be. A negotiator without a thorough knowledge of the product being purchased (how it is used, its alternative methods of manufacture, what products can be substituted for it, what are the company's future requirements for the product, etc.) is greatly handicapped. A negotiator is similarly handicapped if he has not studied and analyzed every detail of the supplier's proposal. Whenever feasible, *before requesting bids,* the negotiator should develop an estimate of the price and value levels for the items being purchased. Knowledge of current economic conditions in the market for the product in question is also an essential element of preparation.

Prior to the main negotiating session, the negotiator must evaluate all relevant data and carefully assess his own and his supplier's strengths and weaknesses. From this assessment, he develops not only a basic strategy of operation, but also specific negotiating tactics. Alert suppliers readily recognize negotiators who are not prepared. They gladly accept the real and psychological bargaining advantage that comes to them from lack of buyer preparation.

Planning for Negotiation

The outcome of contract negotiations hinges on relative buyer-seller power, negotiating skills, and how both perceive the logic of the impending negotiations. Each of these controlling factors of negotiation can be influenced by adroit advanced planning. This is why proper planning is without question the most important step in successful negotiations.

The first step in planning for negotiation is the same as the first step for any type of business planning—to establish objectives. Negotiation objectives must be specific. General objectives such as "lower than previous prices," "good delivery," or "satisfactory technical assistance" are inadequate. For each term and condition to be negotiated, the negotiator must develop three specific positions: (1) an objective position, (2) a minimum position, and (3) a maximum position. The minimum position is developed on the premise that every required seller action will turn out satisfactorily and with minimum cost. The maximum position is developed on the premise that every required seller action will turn out unsatisfactorily and with maximum cost. The objective position is the negotiator's best estimate of what he or she expects the seller's actual costs to be.

In developing concrete objectives, actual dates are established for delivery schedules, actual numerical ranges for quality acceptance, and actual dollar levels for applicable elements of cost. The major elements of cost traditionally negotiated (and for which objective, maximum, and minimum positions are developed) include quantity of labor, labor wages, quantity of materials, prices of materials, factory overhead, engineering expense, tooling expense, general and administrative expense, and profit. In addition to determining his or her own position for each major element of cost, the buyer must appraise what he believes to be the objective, maximum, and minimum positions of the seller. Determining the seller's maximum position is easy; it is the offer made in his proposal.

Reaching Negotiation Objectives

Typically, the two opposing positions appear as shown in Figure 8-1. The seller's positions are generally all higher than the corresponding positions of the buyer. The closer the two objectives are initially, the easier will be the negotiations. As negotiations proceed, the seller tends to make concessions from his maximum position toward his objective. At the same time, the buyer reduces his demands, moving from his minimum position toward his objective.[2] Usually, little difficulty arises during this preliminary skirmish. This is not to

---

[2]If the negotiator believes there is a possiblity of actually achieving his minimum position, he should open with a position below this point—provided such a position can be logically supported.

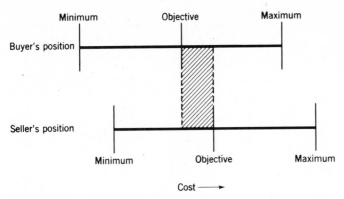

 "Essence" or "heart" of negotiation

Figure 8-1 Typical bargaining positions of the buyer and the seller. (*From Paul R. McDonald,* Government Prime Contracts and Subcontracts, *Procurement Associates, Glendora, Calif., 1975, pp. F-1–18.*

say that this part of the negotiation process is easy or that it does not take time. Normally, vigorous testing is required to convince each party that the other is actually at his objective. Each party, of course, by bluffing attempts to convince the other that he has arrived at his objective before he actually has.

As each party reaches his objective, negotiation becomes difficult. The distance between the buyer's objective and the supplier's objective can well be called the "essence" or "heart" of the negotiation (see Figure 8-1). Any concession made by either party from the position of his objective will appear unreasonable to him, based on his previous analysis of the facts. Changes in position, therefore, must now be the result of either logical persuasion and negotiating skills (entailing further investigation, analysis, and reassessment of the facts) or the pressure of brute economic strength.

It is in the area of objective persuasion that the skillful negotiator stands out. He makes progress by uncovering new facts and additional areas of negotiation that permit the supplier to reduce his demands. For example, an analysis of the supplier's manufacturing operations might reveal that if lead time were increased by only one week, the job could be done with fewer machines making longer production runs. This change could substantially reduce the supplier's setup and scheduling costs, thus permitting a price reduction. Additional lead time might be made available by a slight modification in the buyer's production schedule. The cost of making this change could well be much less than the seller's savings from the longer production runs. Thus both parties would profit from the change. It is this type of situation that the competent negotiator constantly seeks to discover and exploit in his attempt to close the gap between the seller's objective and his own. Such situations have the highly desirable effect of benefiting each party at no expense to the other party.

In some sole-source negotiations, the seller's objective is to maximize his position at the expense of the buyer. In these situations, a continuing relationship is of no interest to the seller; therefore, he uses his bargaining strength to maximize price, rather than to achieve a mutaully advantageous contract that will lead to continued business. The buyer who senses such a situation should start negotiations by attacking the reasonableness of the seller's cost breakdown, using his own prepared cost estimates as the basis for his contentions. In the absence of competition this is a buyer's most logical and most effective plan of action. If the supplier refuses to divulge his cost data, the negotiator has only two available courses of action, both admittedly weak. He can appeal to the seller's reason, pointing out the long-run implications of his actions, or he can attempt to fight force with force by threatening to use substitutes, to redesign the product and manufacture it himself, etc. When faced with this type of problem, the negotiator must do his best to bring the supplier's price as close to his own objective as possible. In the short run, he usually pays the seller's price. In the long run, he works toward the development of competing sources and substitute products.

If a seller's negotiation objective is to resolve issues as quickly as possible, employing logical analysis rather than economic bargaining power, it is sometimes reasonable for the buyer to start negotiations by proposing his actual objective as the counter-offer to the seller's proposal. In fact, in industrial situations where continuing relationships are the rule, each successive negotiation brings the objectives of both parties ever closer together. Under these conditions, buyers and sellers need develop only their objective positions; there is no need for maximum and minimum positions.

NEGOTIATING FOR PRICE

Historically, price is the most difficult of all the contract terms to be negotiated. Because of both its high relative importance and its complexity, negotiation for price will be used as an example to illustrate what is involved in negotiating all the terms of a contract. If the reader understands what is involved in negotiating price, he or she can easily visualize what is involved in negotiating the less complex terms of a contract.

When negotiating price, the negotiator must concurrently consider the type of contract to be used. Contract type and the negotiation of price are directly related; hence, they must be considered together.

To assure buying at favorable prices, buyers strive to develop the greatest practical amount of competition. Conversely, to assure selling at favorable prices, sellers strive to restrict the number of suppliers. Whenever it is possible, therefore, the initial step for a buyer seeking successful negotiation is to get an adequate number of bids or proposals from among those vendors who are genuinely interested in competing for the contract.[3] In negotiated purchasing,

[3]The term "bids" is traditionally used in competitive bid purchases. Consequently, bids used in negotiated purchases are sometimes referred to as proposals, to clearly identify the buy as a negotiated purchase.

requests for proposals usually request not only total price, but also a complete breakdown of all attendant costs.

For every negotiated purchase, either price analysis or cost analysis, or both, is required. Which analysis is best to use and the extent of the analysis required are determined by the facts bearing on each specific purchase being negotiated. Generally speaking, price analysis is used for lower dollar value contracts and cost analysis for higher dollar value contracts. A discussion of the applicable uses of both price and cost negotiation follows.

Price Analysis Negotiation

Price analysis negotiation (commonly referred to as price negotiation) is the most commonly used form of price negotiation. Some proponents of cost negotiation disparage price negotiation, referring to it as "unsophisticated" and "emotional." In the many cases where price negotiations are undertaken in an unprofessional manner, such criticism is fully justified. Banging on the table and shouting "I want lower prices" or "I can get it cheaper from B" is certainly not professional price negotiation.

On the other hand, in many specific cases where pricing data are developed and utilized with professional skill, price negotiation can be just as advantageous as cost negotiation, or more so. Compared with cost negotiation, price negotiation has three distinct advantages: (1) negotiation time is shorter, (2) support of technical specialists is seldom needed, and (3) pricing data are relatively easily acquired.

The traditional sources from which buyers get pricing data are federal government publications, purchasing trade publications (NAMP's *Monthly Bulletin* is outstanding), and business journals. Competing vendors are also excellent sources of pricing data. They can provide the buyer with price lists, catalogs, numerous special pricing data, and formal price quotations. From these competing vendor data, the buyer can readily determine two very important facts: (1) the nature of the market (competitive or noncompetitive) and (2) the extent of vendor interest in this particular purchase.

Price Comparison   Determination of market competitiveness and vendor interest is typically a negotiator's first step in price analysis. His second step is to examine in detail the absolute and relative differences existing among the various prices quoted by the competing vendors. From this examination, a buyer detects that differences in prices among vendors exist, but he does not learn the causes of these differences. His search for causes begins in the purchasing department's supplier information file.

The bid prices of the competing vendors are compared with past prices of similar purchases from the supplier information file. The causes of all significant variations are pinpointed and analyzed. Adjustments are made for differences in factors such as specifications, quantities ordered, times of deliveries, changes which have taken place in the general levels of business activity and prices, and changes which have resulted from learning experience. After these adjustments are made, the negotiator (sometimes with the help of an engineering estimator or a price analyst) determines whether or not the prices offered are reasonable. From this determination, the negotiator decides on the target price he will use for his negotiating position.

Trend Comparisons   Historical prices paid for purchases of similar quantities can be analyzed to disclose helpful price trend information. For example, if prices have been increasing, it is reasonable to expect that the seller will attempt to maintain a similar pattern of increase. Hence, by carefully analyzing the reasons for all increases, the negotiator can structure his bargaining position on the basis of any invalidities he uncovers.

Similarly, the negotiator can analyze decreasing prices to determine whether the price decrease is too little or too much. If he determines it is too much, he must then determine whether the trend is creating, or is likely to create, quality or service problems in contract performance. If it is too little, he must then determine whether the benefits of improved production processes are being proportionally reflected in the lower bid prices.

Even a level price trend offers opportunities for price analysis. For example, the negotiator may ask whether level prices are justified, considering the many manufacturing improvements which have been made. Did the supplier charge too much initially? Has the supplier's competitive position in the industry changed? If the negotiator's analysis indicates that costs have fallen because of reductions in the supplier's prices of materials or because of improvements in his production processes, his negotiating position is then clear. He negotiates for pro-rata reductions reflecting these changes.

Cost Analysis Negotiation

As previously stated, price analysis negotiation is more commonly used than cost analysis negotiation. However, cost analysis negotiation (commonly referred to as cost negotiation) is steadily growing in use. It has been used successfully for decades in large firms such as General Electric and IBM, and in recent years it has been employed increasingly in small and medium-size firms.

In cost negotiations, each applicable cost element is negotiated individually, i.e., design engineering cost, tooling cost, direct materials cost, labor hours, labor rates, subcontracting, overhead cost, other direct costs, profit, and so on. One cost element—direct labor cost—will be discussed as an example to illustrate how all applicable costs are negotiated.

Direct labor cost is defined as the labor cost directly traceable to the creation of a firm's products. Unfortunately, agreement does not exist concerning the precise and universal classification of charges properly included as a part of this cost. All companies are free to develop their own individual accounting practices; hence, whether any specific element of cost is classified as direct or indirect can be an entirely arbitrary company decision. For example, in some firms, the labor costs of materials handling and quality control are classified as direct labor costs; in others, they are classified as indirect labor costs. Consequently, negotiators can make no assumptions regarding how labor costs are classified and charged. Rather, they must study and analyze the accounting practices of each supplier or bidder whose costs are being negotiated.

For most negotiated contracts, direct labor cost is not only the most difficult of all costs to analyze and to negotiate, but it is also the most important. It is the most important because in purchasing high-cost, high-technology capital products that are nonstandard or manufactured in small quantities (the very type of purchases that are negotiated), labor and overhead costs combined traditionally represent the largest element of total product cost.

In most accounting systems, overhead costs are expressed as a percentage of direct labor cost. The paramount importance of this fact to buyers can be pinpointed by an example. Assume a product's selling price is $715. This price is determined as follows: $150 of direct materials, 25 hours of direct labor at $8 per hour, overhead of 150 percent of direct labor, and profit at 10 percent of total manufacturing cost. Assume further that the buyer, as a result of skillful cost analysis and negotiation, is able to negotiate a reduction of 20 percent in direct labor cost. If direct labor cost is reduced 20 percent from 25 hours to 20 hours, the price of the product will be reduced from $715 to $605 (see Table 8-1).

Because of its multiplier effect, reduction in direct labor cost frequently yields the largest possible price reduction. In the preceding illustration, a 20 percent reduction in direct labor cost results in a price reduction of $110 ($715 − $605). A 20 percent reduction in materials cost would result in a price reduction of just $30 (20 percent × $150). A 20 percent reduction in profit would result in a price reduction of only $13 (20 percent × $65).

Direct labor cost is divided into two parts: the absolute number of hours worked, and the applicable hourly wage rate.

Establishing the validity of wage rates is generally easy. Quoted rates can be checked against those of comparable industries, the buyer's own company, and the current wage rates published by government agencies and trade

Table 8-1 Quoted and Negotiated Costs Compared

Cost element	Quoted cost	Negotiated cost
Material	$150	$150
Labor	200	160
Overhead	300	240
Profit	65	55
Total	$715	$605

associations. However, establishing the fact that the correct type of labor is assigned to each individual job is not so easy. Careless suppliers can unnecessarily run wage rates up rapidly by assigning jobs to higher-skilled individuals than are actually required. Hence, negotiators must assure themselves that sellers match workers' abilities with job requirements.

Determining the absolute number of hours needed to perform a contract can also be difficult. Absolute numbers of work hours are related to methods of manufacturing, the kinds of tooling used, and the accuracy of a seller's estimating and accounting methods. In buying standard commercial products, past pricing history and industry standard times can often be combined to determine reasonably accurate estimates of direct labor cost. However, in buying products not previously manufactured, such readily usable "tools" are not available.

For such products, the buyer's cost analyst typically estimates production hours by using one or a combination of the following methods: (1) the development and use of synthetic time standards, (2) the development of estimates from simulated time and motion studies,[4] (3) the use of learning-curve analysis, and (4) the comparison of present requirements with similar previous requirements. (From an analysis of the differences in these requirements, some analysts can estimate the labor hours of the new requirements with surprising efficiency.)

For products not previously manufactured, sellers generally develop their quotations (estimates) using one of the three methods: (1) by totaling the standard times used in the manufacture of similar items, (2) by employing detailed time and motion studies, and (3) by bidding a ball-park estimate, suitably padded for protection against unforeseen contingencies.

Regardless of the method used by the seller in making his estimate for direct labor cost, it is apparent that ample opportunity will always exist for buyer analysis, comparison with his own estimate, and negotiation of existing differences. It is *equally* apparent that a thoroughly well-prepared negotiator has a marked advantage over an unprepared opponent.

TECHNIQUES OF NEGOTIATION

Negotiation techniques (tactics) are the negotiator's working tools. The negotiator uses them to achieve his or her strategic goals. In the hands of a skillful negotiator, these tools are very powerful weapons. In the hands of a novice, they can be dangerous booby traps. Competent negotiators, therefore, spend a great deal of time studying and perfecting the use of these techniques. There

---

[4]The buyer's manufacturing engineering department frequently simulates some of the supplier's more important production operations and conducts time studies on them. Data based on such simulations, combined with data developed by the use of synthetic standards, can sometimes provide the buyer with surprisingly accurate labor hour estimates.

are so many negotiating techniques that all cannot be discussed in the following sections of this chapter. However, those selected for discussion are typical examples that have been proved sound in practice as well as theory.

Organizing The Issues

All negotiations center on specific issues. One of the difficult tasks of negotiation is to define fully the important issues which are to be included on the agenda, and then to be sure that the discussion is confined to these issues. Traditionally, though not always, the seller first presents the issues as he sees them, then the buyer presents the issues as they appear to him. The issues on which there is agreement are disposed of immediately. Those remaining become the issues of the negotiation.

Most authorities feel that the issues should be discussed in the order of their probable ease of solution. With this priority system, an atmosphere of cooperation can develop that may facilitate solving the more difficult issues. Other authorities, however, believe that first one party and then the other party should present an issue until all issues are solved.

The objective of negotiation is agreement. Once either party adopts the position of "take it or leave it," negotiations break down. Even though agreement is the fundamental goal of negotiation, negotiations occasionally end without agreement. In the short run, reaching no agreement is sometimes better than reaching an unsatisfactory agreement. Generally speaking, however, experienced negotiators seldom let negotiations break down completely. They do not intentionally maneuver or let their opponents maneuver themselves into "take it or leave it" or "walkout" situations. However, this is not always true of international negotiations. The Russians seem to enjoy "brinkmanship." It is not uncommon for an American in Moscow to be told the deal is off when he will not accept a Russian proposal. When arriving at the airport for the trip home, he receives a pleading message requesting that negotiations be resumed.[5]

Learn from Labor Unions

Much can be learned from the labor unions about the techniques of successful negotiation. Through experience and research, some unions have developed negotiating skills of the highest degree. Unions stress the importance of thorough planning and preliminary negotiation meetings. At these meetings, the union's objectives are clearly defined. Then in mock sessions, through practice and experimentation, experience is gained in achieving the desired objectives. Union objectives are classified and ranked in order of importance—some are classified as vital, some as wanted most, others as less important, etc. A labor

[5]"The Style and Tactics of Moscow's Traders," *Business Week,* Oct. 21, 1972, p. 70.

negotiator would never make the mistake of entering a negotiating arena without being fully prepared to utilize both the traditional and the psychological techniques of negotiation.

Be Sure of Opponent's Authority

Before starting negotiations, a buyer should be absolutely certain that the seller's representatives have full legal power to conclude the contract and sign for the seller's firm. If doubt exists, verification of authority should be obtained from the appropriate official in the seller's firm. Many naive buyers have revealed their negotiating plans, only to discover that the supplier's representative had no power to bind his company, but rather was required to send the proposed contract to the home office for approval.

Negotiate on Home Grounds

If at all possible, the buyer should hold the negotiations at the offices of his own company. Aside from the strong psychological advantage of being on one's home grounds, in many cases there is a real informational advantage to be gained. The availability of additional legal and other corporate counsel, as well as access to company records, can at times provide a substantial negotiating advantage. Finally, there may be a degree of physical advantage as well; traveling, living in noisy hotels, and eating in restaurants can reduce a person's mental alertness.

Concessions and Compromises

A competent buyer determines as early as possible in negotiations which of the concessions that he is prepared to make are of greatest importance to the seller. By holding off in these areas, while making minor compromises in other areas, he retains the assurance of making substantial gains later in the session. Once he makes the concessions most important to his adversary, he loses most of his bargaining power. An experienced negotiator is never the first to make an absolute demand for what is important to him. The party maneuvered into making such a demand is frequently the one who has to make the first major concession.

Keep the Initiative

The buyer should strive never to lose the initiative which he automatically obtains when he receives the supplier's proposal. There is a good deal of truth in the old proverb that "a good offense is the best defense." The buyer should constantly "carry the game" to the supplier; he should keep the supplier on the defensive by confronting him with point after point, making him continually justify his position. For example, if the supplier states the cost of materials in dollars, the buyer should ask him to justify the figures with a bill of materials, appropriate scrap rates, and a full explanation of the manufacturing processes to be used. The more the buyer "bores in" and the more pressure he maintains, the better will be his bargaining position. If the supplier's position seems sound, the buyer can offer a counterproposal. In either case, the buyer has the initiative, and he should work hard to retain it.

Use Diversions

On the human side of negotiations, the buyer who knows the seller personally, or has carefully studied his personal behavior patterns (as he should), has an advantage. When tempers start to get out of hand, as they occasionally do, the experienced negotiator quickly diverts attention away from the issue at hand. At such times a joke, an anecdote, or a coffee break can be an effective means of easing tensions. This type of diversion is usually more easily accomplished when the participants know what situations are most irritating to the other.

Questions Are Highly Important

The wise use of questions is the most important single technique in negotiation. By properly timing and phrasing his questions, the negotiator can control the progress and trend of negotiation. With a perceptive question he can forcefully, yet tactfully, attack the supplier's position. Similarly, he can effectively defend his own position by asking the seller to evaluate certain carefully chosen data he (the buyer) has developed.

The technique of answering questions properly is as important as the technique of asking them properly. The successful negotiator knows when to answer, when not to answer, when to answer clearly, and when to answer vaguely. Not all questions require an answer. Many questions are asked for which the seller knows there is no answer; therefore, he does not really expect a reply.

The correct answer to questions in negotiation is not governed by the same criteria governing the correct answer to questions in most other situations. For negotiation questions, the correct answer is the answer that furthers either the negotiator's short-term tactics or his long-range strategy. Labor leaders and politicians are experts at asking and answering questions. Their questions and their answers are made to correlate with their strategic plans (strike platforms, party platforms, etc.). To an uninformed observer it often appears that the answers given by politicians and labor leaders do not relate to the questions that they are asked. These observations are only partially correct. When answering questions, politicians and labor leaders tell their listeners what they want them to know about their platforms, whether or not it fully answers the questions they are asked.

Successful negotiators realize that negotiation sessions are not like the classroom, where precise answers earn high marks. In negotiation, the purpose of questions and answers is not to illustrate to the seller how smart the negotiator is. Rather, it is to ferret out the seller's objectives, and to learn as much as possible about how he intends to maneuver to achieve them. For this purpose, precise answers are sometimes the wrong answers. The correct degree of precision is dictated by the particular circumstances of each negotiation.

Positive Statements

As with sophisticated questions, perceptively used positive statements can favorably influence the course of negotiations. For example, assume a buyer knows that certain questions will evoke an emotional reaction from the seller. The questions are asked, and an opportunity is created for the proper use of a positive statement. A competent negotiator would say something like this: "I see your point, and I understand how you feel about this matter. Your posititon is well taken." Contrast the effect of this type of positive response with that of an emotional, negative response in which the buyer tells the seller that he is "dead wrong." When a buyer tells a seller that he understands the seller's viewpoint, and that he considers it reasonable, even though he does not agree with it, the seller is certain to consider the buyer's viewpoint more objectively.

Machiavelli, in *The Prince*, gave the world some unusually sage advice concerning the use and misuse of positive statements: "I hold it to be proof of great prudence for men to abstain from threats and insulting words toward anyone, for neither . . . diminishes the strength of the enemy; but the one makes him more cautious, and the other increases his hatred of you, and makes him more perservering in his efforts to injure you."[6]

Be a Good Listener

Generally speaking, salesmen and saleswomen thoroughly enjoy talking. Consequently buyers should let them talk and talk. While talking, salesmen very often talk themselves into concessions that a buyer could never gain by negotiation. Listening, per se, recognizes a basic need of a seller. Additionally, listening carefully to a seller's choice of words, phrases, and tone of voice, while at the same time observing his gestures and other uses of body language can be rewarding. From observing such actions, a buyer can gain many clues to a seller's negotiating position.

Be Considerate of Sellers

A small number of negotiation experts contend that negotiations are best won by negotiators who are as brutal and as arbitrary as possible. Although some evidence supports this viewpoint, it is definitely a minority viewpoint.

[6]Niccolo Machiavelli, *The Prince*, Great Books of the Western World, Encyclopedia Britannica, 1952, vol. 23.

Unquestionably, there are some purchasing situations in which a merciless frontal assault can be a proper and successful negotiating technique. However, for the vast majority of firms, i.e., those who seek profitable, continuing relationships with the seller, a more considerate and reasoned technique is recommended. Buyers lose no negotiating advantages whatsoever by being fully considerate of sellers personally, by letting them save face, and by reasonably satisfying their emotional needs.

Never Give Anything Away

As a matter of strategy, a successful negotiator periodically lets the seller maneuver him into accepting one of his proposals. This does not mean that the negotiator gives something away. He never "gives anything away." He always expects to get a concession in exchange. Contrariwise, he does not feel obligated to match every concession made by the seller. Consequently, in the exchange process, the successful negotiator makes fewer concessions than his less successful adversary. By a continuation of this exchange process, a position close to the objectives of both parties is usually reached. Mutual concessions benefit both parties, and a contract so negotiated is *mutually* advantageous; but it is not *equally* advantageous.

Benefits Are Not Divided Equally

A common misunderstanding exists in some purchasing circles that successful negotiation implies an equally advantageous agreement. While both buyer and seller benefit from a well-negotiated contract, the benefits are seldom divided 50:50. Probably 60 to 70 percent of the benefits of a typical contract negotiation normally go to the more skillful negotiator, leaving about 30 to 40 percent for his less-skilled adversary.

CHARACTERISTICS OF A SUCCESSFUL NEGOTIATOR

The characteristics of a successful negotiator should now be clear. He or she is a skillful individual, with broad business experience. He possesses a good working knowledge of all of the primary functions of business. He knows how to use the tools of management—accounting, human relations, economics, business law, and quantitative methods. He is knowledgeable about the techniques of negotiation and the products he buys. He is able to lead conferences and to integrate specialists into a smoothly functioning team. In addition to being educated and experienced, the successful negotiator also excels in good judgment. It is good judgment that causes him to attach the correct degree of importance to each of the factors bearing on important problems. Combining his skills, knowledge, and judgment, he develops superior tactical and strategic plans. Also, he considers problems from the viewpoint of the company as a whole, not from the viewpoint of a functional manager.

Fully successful negotiators share two common attributes: (1) all habitually enter negotiations with higher negotiating goals than their adversaries, and generally they achieve them; (2) all already are included, or are destined to quickly become included, among a firm's most highly valued and highly paid professionals.

FOR DISCUSSION

8-1   Define "negotiation" as it is used in purchasing. How it is distinguished from "horse trading" and "war"?

8-2   Discuss some of the principal situations in which competitive bidding is impractical and negotiation, therefore, is mandatory.

8-3   Discuss the two roles a buyer plays in negotiation. Explain why both roles are necessary.

8-4   The determination of a fair and reasonable price is a paramount objective of negotiation. What precisely do the words "fair" and "reasonable" mean, as used here?

8-5   Discuss the advantages of using price analysis negotiation rather than cost analysis negotiation.

8-6   Why is thorough planning for negotiations so important? Explain.

8-7   Discuss the three factors which influence a buyer's negotiating strengths and weaknesses. Also, discuss the three factors which influence a seller's strengths and weaknesses.

8-8   Assume that, as a buyer, you have received bids from two good suppliers applicable to a contract to be negotiated in two weeks. The contract is for a year's supply of a complex, high-priced machined part used in one of the products your firm manufactures. List, and briefly explain, the things you would do in preparation for negotiating this contract.

8-9   In the process of negotiations, after both sides reach their negotiation objectives, progress becomes difficult. How are such difficulties resolved?

8-10   An experienced negotiator attempts as early as possible to determine what issues are critically important to the seller. After obtaining this information, how does the buyer use it?

8-11   Which two techniques of negotiation seem most important to you? Explain fully.

8-12   Negotiators traditionally encounter difficulty in analyzing a seller's direct labor costs. Explain.

8-13   What difficulties, if any, do you believe a negotiator could encounter in analyzing a seller's direct materials costs?

8-14   Judgment is said to be the key integrating ingredient in a negotiator's composite abilities. Exactly what is judgment, as used in this context?

8-15   Why do some negotiators consistently get substantially more than half of the benefits from all negotiations in which they participate?

CASES FOR CHAPTER 8

Quality Assurance
and Reliability

A firm's quality assurance program has always been an important element in the determination of its competitive position in the marketplace. In the final analysis, top management is interested in producing and selling profitably a product that reliably performs a specific function. Consequently, it must be vitally concerned with the *total cost* of product quality—a factor influenced by engineering design, production methods, *and* the performance of external suppliers.

During an era of projected worldwide energy and materials shortages, the quality assurance function additionally assumes a more macroscopic role of increasing importance—nationally and internationally. The conservation of natural resources and the energy required to turn them into *usable* finished products is, in the aggregate, directly influenced by the efficiency of the materials procurement and manufacturing activities of a vast network of interrelated individual firms. The efficiency with which these firms interact in utilizing natural resources in their conversion processes (to satisfy each other's needs) clearly affects the usage rate of the resources. The related roles of purchasing and quality assurance in this overall function are examined in this chapter.

PURCHASING'S ROLE IN QUALITY ASSURANCE

The designer alone cannot impart quality to a product, nor can the inspector inspect quality into a product; rather, quality must be *built into* a product. It is the responsibility of the purchasing department to ensure that suppliers possess the ability, the motivation, and adequate information to produce efficiently materials and components of the desired quality. In fulfilling this responsibility, purchasing can exert positive control over the quality and attendant costs of incoming material.

Generally speaking, four factors determine the long-run quality level of a firm's incoming materials:

1   Creation of complete and proper specifications for quality require-
    ments
2   Selection of suppliers having the technical and production capabilities
    to do an adequate quality/cost job
3   Development of a realistic understanding with suppliers of quality
    requirements and creation of the motivation to perform accordingly
4   Measurement of suppliers' quality/cost performance and exercise of
    appropriate control

Purchasing should be directly involved in the first three factors and should play a supporting role in the fourth.

Material Specifications

In an earlier chapter it was pointed out that a sound material specification represents a compromise of three different points of view: (1) design considerations, (2) production considerations, and (3) commercial considerations. When dealing with the commercial considerations, purchasing personnel should make the following investigations with respect to quality:

- Study the quality requirements.
- Investigate their reasonableness, relative to cost.
- Determine whether the desired quality can be built into the material by
  existing suppliers.
- Ensure that specifications are written in a manner that permits competi-
  tion among potential suppliers.
- Ensure that quality requirements are completely and unambiguously
  stated in the specifications.

In the case of some materials and components, such investigations are relatively simple. With others, they can become extremely complex, at times involving highly technical considerations. For example, in one of its divisions the Boeing Company employs a highly structured specification review program in which the individual buyer plays a major role. To assist the buyer with complex technical problems, Boeing has established in the purchasing (materiél) department a group of technically trained specialists who serve in the staff capacity of "reliability (quality) engineers." When technical quality problems are involved, a person from this group works with the buyer in reviewing the specifications. Their objective is to determine the reasonableness and feasibility of quality requirements. The authority to change a specification, however, remains with the *design engineer.* The buyer and the reliability engineer serve in a coordinating capacity, calling to the design engineer's attention potential quality problems arising from commercial factors.[1]

Selection of Suppliers

Most firms can minimize their quality problems with incoming materials simply by doing a good job of selecting vendors in the first place.

Product Testing   One practical approach used in determining a vendor's quality capabilities is to test his product before purchasing it. The quality of the majority of materials purchased by most manufacturing firms can be effectively determined by "engineering tests" or by "use tests." Often such tests can be conducted by the buying firm. In cases where this is not practical, commercial testing agencies can be engaged to do the job.

The object of product testing is twofold: (1) to determine that a potential supplier's quality level is commensurate with the buyer's quality needs and (2) where feasible, to compare quality levels of several different suppliers. This permits the development of a list of acceptable suppliers, for whom the buyer can individually relate quality to cost for comparative purposes.

Since in a large number of companies elaborate testing facilities cannot be justified, numerous purchasing agents turn to their own operating departments for the performance of use tests. It is not uncommon, for example, for a purchasing agent to test several brands of tires on his firm's vehicles during the course of regular operations. Although still feasible, use testing of most *production* parts and components is difficult because tests cannot be conducted until the buyer's finished product is sold to the ultimate customer. In many cases, though, the buyer's sales force is in close enough touch with its customers to receive feedback data on operating performance. This is particularly true where the buyer's firm registers and maintains historical records for each of its individual finished products. In such cases, unknown to the customer, various kinds of use tests can be conducted to compare the performance of different vendors' components.

By whatever method use tests are conducted, the purchasing department usually needs the cooperation of personnel from other departments in setting up and actually conducting the tests. Consequently, the buyer, more often than

[1]R. T. Dewey, Boeing Company, Seattle, Wash., "The Role of the Buyer in Reliability," *Product Reliability and the Buyer's Role,* National Association of Purchasing Agents' Convention, June 5, 1963, pp. 3–4.

not, functions in the role of an organizer and an administrator in coordinating the efforts of others.

A word of caution is appropriate, however, for the practitioner unskilled in using the experimental method. If results of tests are to be compared and evaluated, the results must be obtained through well-designed experiments that permit *valid* comparison. For example, mileage data on two sets of tires, each taken from a different truck, are not comparable if the two trucks were operated under substantially different conditions.

Unfortunately, in conducting many use tests without the benefit of controlled laboratory conditions, it is difficult to generate truly comparable test data. For this reason, the simple notion of comparability may be difficult to apply precisely in practice. Nevertheless, the buyer who conducts use tests must take care not to attempt a comparison of noncomparable data. Furthermore, interpretation of such test data at times requires a basic understanding of statistical inference. The informed buyer should strive to be as familiar with statistical methods as he is with accounting and legal principles. While he may have to call on a staff expert for statistical advice, he still needs a general understanding of statistics to recognize when his problem is one that requires statistical interpretation.

In those firms large enough to justify the existence of testing laboratories for their engineering and research work, the purchasing department finds an extra arm to support its quality assurance activity. Such laboratories take much of the experimental and interpretive burden off purchasing's shoulders. They are also usually equipped to conduct more precise and sophisticated tests with greater speed and ease than use testing allows. An example will illustrate the point. One of IBM's computer-manufacturing plants has an electronic testing laboratory used primarily for research and development work. The laboratory, however, also serves the purchasing department. Before new electronic components are purchased for assembly into IBM products, a sample of each new component is subjected to rigorous laboratory tests to determine whether its performance characteristics meet the company's quality specifications.

If a firm does not have its own engineering testing laboratory, it may find it profitable to employ a commercial testing laboratory. Numerous laboratories of this type are found throughout the country. In this connection, the U.S. Department of Commerce publishes a helpful directory of commercial testing services which indicates the locations and the types of tests conducted in each laboratory.

Proposal Analysis   A second point at which the purchasing department assesses the likelihood that a vendor will produce a product of acceptable quality is in the analysis of the potential supplier's bid. In their proposals bidders indicate, either directly or indirectly, how they intend to comply with the quality requirements of the job. One of the buyer's paramount responsibilities is to determine the acceptability of the bidder's intent with respect to quality. The buyer must be especially alert in detecting areas of misinterpretation or possible areas of overemphasis by the bidder that could result in excessive costs. In purchases where quality requirements are critical, the trend in industry today is to require bidders to state explicitly and in some detail precisely how they plan to achieve the specified quality level.

Capability Survey   For those bidders whose written proposals survive the buyer's analysis, the next step in evaluating quality capabilities is an on-site capability survey. Because of the time and expense involved, most companies conduct this survey only for their more important orders and for government contracts requiring it. In inspecting the bidder's facilities and records, and in talking with management and operating personnel, the buyer's investigating team attempts to ferret out answers to such questions as these:

1   What is the general attitude of operators and supervisors toward quality? Does the bidder employ a "zero defects" program or a similar "quality-mindedness" program that focuses attention on the attitudes and responsibilities assumed by each individual for high-quality work?[2]

2   What is the bidder's engineering experience and ability with respect to this type of work?
3   Is the bidder's production equipment capable of producing the quality of work required?
4   Exactly how is the bidder organized to control quality, and to what extent does the quality control organization receive management support?
5   What specific quality control programs and techniques does the bidder employ?
6   To what extent is the bidder financially responsible?

Consideration of these questions clearly points out that an effective survey cannot be conducted by a buyer alone; rather, the endeavor must be a team effort. Specialists from production, engineering, quality control, and finance or accounting are needed to give professional interpretation to the facts the survey uncovers. A major portion of the buyer's job in such an endeavor is to coordinate the efforts of these specialists and to make a composite evaluation of the bidder, considering the findings of all team members.

Positive Motivation of the Supplier

To this point we have primarily discussed ways in which a purchasing department can contribute to quality assurance *prior* to the placement of business with a particular supplier. The next logical consideration is: What can be done to ensure vendors' quality performance *after* they have been added to the supply chain?

Just as in eliciting performance from individuals, the problem of supplier

---

[2]For an interesting discussion of the individual's responsibility for quality, see Robert M. Smith's article entitled "Zero-Defects and You," *Management Services,* January–February, 1966, pp. 35–38.

motivation can be approached in several ways. First, buyers can attempt to secure satisfactory performance by providing adequate positive stimuli to motivate the supplier to perform. In other words, they try to induce the supplier to *want* to perform satisfactorily. Second, a buyer can attempt to secure satisfactory performance by regularly checking the supplier's performance and rejecting unsatisfactory work. This can be done most easily by using some type of inspection system. Most managers are sensitive to the human problems in business and recognize a clear-cut need for the use of both approaches. The discussion at this point centers on the motivation approach.

There are at least four major areas which should be effectively handled by purchasing personnel if a buyer wants to motivate the supplier to perform optimally. These areas are discussed in the following paragraphs.

Buyer-Supplier Relationship   "One likes to do business with friends." This commonsense adage contains a bit of sage advice for purchasing people. This is not to say that buyers should develop a close personal friendship with each of their suppliers; normally they should not. However, they should develop a friendly *business* relationship.

An individual buyer and his or her firm earn the respect of suppliers by pursuing sound, ethical business policies and by treating all supplers fairly and impartially. We all make mistakes on the job at times and encounter problems beyond our control. When a supplier occasionally finds himself in such a situation, the buyer who benefits in the long run is the one who goes out of his way to make such situations less painful (within reason) for the supplier. The shoe may well be on the other foot at some future date. The gist of these ideas is simply this. During the course of a buyer's daily activities, consciously or *unconsciously,* he creates a relationship between his firm and its suppliers. This relationship should be developed very carefully, bearing in mind its effect upon the supplier's motivation to do a qualtiy job. A supplier is certainly more prone to want to do a good quality job for a customer that he respects and that consistently gives him a "fair shake" than he is for a customer of the opposite character. It is always more pleasant to do business with a good business friend.

Mutual Understanding of Quality Problems   It has long been the policy of most progressive firms to encourage buyers, along with quality control, production, and engineering personnel, to visit suppliers' plants periodically. Such visits develop a more complete understanding of the details of suppliers' operations and the problems involved in producing materials to given quality levels. On the other side of the communications coin, many buyers periodically invite suppliers' representatives to visit their production operations. This permits the supplier to see exactly how his product is used, and it enables him to understand and appraise the buyer's needs more intelligently.

Establishing a mutual understanding of quality needs and problems in this manner lays the foundation for future quality improvements or cost reductions, or both.

Competition   The reader has probably seen a football or basketball team perform superbly while playing a top-ranked opponent. Yet during the next game against a mediocre opponent, the same team's performance is somewhat less than mediocre. The two performances of the same team, under *different competitive* conditions, were drastically different! Has a four-minute mile ever been run by someone who had no competition? No, and it probably never will be. It has been proved repeatedly that the element of competition, if not carried to extremes, acts as a catalyst that elicits better performance from an individual than would be the case without competition.

Business organizations are not individuals, and they function in environments quite different from those of athletic teams. Nevertheless, it is generally agreed that the element of competition has approximately the same effect in business as in cases of individuals. A vendor who is the sole source of supply for a buyer sooner or later tends to become complacent with respect to such captive business. He is busy concentrating his efforts on more wily customers yet to be won. This is just as true for performance with respect to quality as for any other measure of performance. While there are some advantages in dealing with a single supplier, for most items the buyer can mitigate incoming quality problems by consciously maintaining a healthy competition among suppliers.

Supplier Evaluation   A final means by which the purchasing department can positively motivate suppliers for quality performance is the use of a formal supplier evaluation program.

Although there are numerous versions of supplier evaluation programs in operation today, the more sophisticated plans possess two distinctive features with respect to quality. First, the suppler's quality performance is evaluated quantitatively monthly or quarterly. The most common quantitative measure of quality performance is the percentage of shipments accepted by the buyer's inspection department. In addition to this figure, the buyer may compute a second measurement which reflects miscellaneous costs incurred because of poor quality performance by the supplier. Examples of such costs are (1) manufacturing losses due to supplier quality errors, (2) cost of complaints and spoilage traceable to defective supplier material, (3) travel expenses incurred in visiting a supplier to remedy quality problems, (4) cost of paperwork, packing, handling, and return shipping for rejected material. To dramatize the situation, some companies post all suppliers' evaluation figures on a display board in the purchasing department lobby.

A second feature of the more sophisticated programs is a regularly scheduled review of quality performance with each vendor. This review, usually conducted in the buyer's office, involves a face-to-face discussion among the buyer, the supplier's representative, and any desired technical personnel. In sessions such as this, specific performance difficulties can be isolated and the groundwork laid for their future correction.

To underscore the company's intense interest in supplier performance, the Whirlpool Corporation holds individual buyers responsible for their suppliers' performance. As a regular part of each *buyer's* annual merit review, he is evaluated on the effectiveness with which his suppliers perform. Hence, each buyer has a direct personal interest in this phase of his job.[3]

If it effectively draws upon the services of quality control personnel, a purchasing department is in a position to organize, coordinate, and administer a quality evaluation program. Such a program, if conducted objectively and constructively, can stimulate suppliers very positively toward more satisfactory quality performance.

Inspection and Control

A second major approach to the control of quality, *after* a supplier has been selected, is physical inspection of the material. Inspection should be conducted on a regular basis for two compelling reasons. First, it provides a quantitative measurement of suppliers' quality performance; this is essential to the development of an effective supplier evaluation program. Second, it represents sound business practice.

No matter how good a supplier's production operation may be, shifts in process quality levels do occur. In the event that unacceptable products are produced and shipped, the buying firm usually wants to detect such defective material as early as possible. Additionally, there is always the possibility that a supplier may misinterpret an order or a specification. Finally, the occasional slipshod or dishonest supplier encountered may cut corners, jeopardizing the quality of his output. In all cases, it is less costly to detect defective material at the outset than after it has absorbed the additional costs of further manufacture and assembly.

The purchasing department's responsiblility for material is fulfilled only when acceptable material is in storage ready for production use—not before. For this reason, purchasing management should have at least an advisory voice in the establishment of the firm's inspection system and the policies which govern its operation. One method of achieving this end is to include the purchasing manager in a general management staff group which has responsibility for interfunctional coordination within the total plant operation.

The conduct and administration of the inspection operation is a highly specialized activity, quite apart from normal purchasing activities. As a result, the average buyer usually possesses only a meager understanding of the "hows" and "whys" of inspection operations. This is unfortunate, because in many instances a basic understanding of these things would permit a buyer to negotiate more intelligently certain cost elements of a contract. It is also unfortunate because it limits a buyer's ability to serve as a liaison between his or her firm and the supplier. To perform this job correctly with respect to quality, a buyer needs to understand the significance of what he is communicating.

[3]David B. Jenkins, Whirlpool Corporation, St. Joseph, Mich., "Reliability in the Appliance Industry: The Role of the Buyer in Achieving Reliability," *Product Reliability and the Buyer's Role,* National Association of Purchasing Agents' Convention, June 5, 1963, p. 6.

For these reasons, much of the remainder of this chapter is devoted to a discussion of inspection concepts and fundamentals. Although desirable, a detailed discussion of inspection instruments and techniques is not included because this is a technical field in itself. All buyers, however, will find it rewarding to become familiar with the basic characteristics and capabilities of the instruments and techniques used in inspecting the materials they buy. The ensuing discussion focuses on those conceptual matters of a managerial nature which buyers and their superiors should understand. The objective of the discussion is to provide the reader with an introduction to these concepts, not to treat them in depth.

INSPECTION CONCEPTS

To place the total discussion in proper operational context, a summary of the receiving and inspection procedure is included at the outset.

Receiving and Inspection Procedure

When a purchase is consummated, the receiving and inspection departments both receive copies of the order, which specifies the inspection the material is to receive. When a shipment arrives, receiving personnel check the material against the supplier's packing slip and against the purchase order to ensure that the firm has received and will be billed for the material ordered. The receiving clerk then inspects the material in a nontechnical manner (looking for shipping damage, etc.) to determine its general condition. Finally, a receiving report is prepared on which the results of the investigation are noted. In some cases, no further inspection is required. In others, a copy of the receiving report is forwarded to the inspection department, advising it that material on a given order has been placed in the "pending inspection" area and is ready for technical inspection.

The inspection department performs the specified technical inspection on a sample or on the entire lot, as appropriate, and prepares an inspection report indicating the results of the inspection. If the material fails to meet specifications, a more detailed report is usually completed describing the reasons for rejection. Rejected material, in some cases, is clearly useless to the buying firm, and the purchasing department immediately arranges for its disposition with the supplier. In other situations, the desirable course of action is less clear-cut. The purchaser often has three alternative courses of action:

1 Return the material to the supplier.
2 Keep some of the more acceptable material and return the rest.
3 Keep all the material and rework it to the point where it is acceptable.

Cases in the latter category are usually sent to a material review board to study and decide. The typical board is composed primarily of personnel from production, production control, quality control, and purchasing. After the board reaches a decision, the appropriate papers are sent to the buyer, who concludes final cost negotiations with the supplier.

Economics of Inspection

Whether incoming material requires anything beyond general receiving inspection depends in part on the way in which it is described on the purchase order. If the material is identified by brand name or by commercial grade, visual inspection by receiving personnel is usually adequate. Materials that are described by performance characteristics, by detailed specifications, or perhaps by sample may well require technical inspection also.

In the case of an item specified by performance characteristics, the inspection job is essentially one of testing the product under simulated or actual operating conditions. For materials requiring tests beyond the capability of the buyer's firm, arrangements can frequently be made to have a commercial testing laboratory perform the specified tests before shipment. In this situation, the testing company submits a certificate of test that accompanies the material.

Materials purchased to unique specifications invariably have many features that are subject to inspection. However, some features typically are more critical than others. Consequently, technical features are commonly classified as "critical," "major," and "minor." Inspection effort, in turn, is allocated in accordance with the criticalness of the feature to be inspected. Such decisions should be made by technical personnel prior to placement of the order, and the classification of defects should be included as part of the purchase specifications.

When Is Inspection Justified? The discussion to this point has implied that a sizable number of items purchased by industrial firms do require technical inspection. What criteria does a purchaser use in determining whether technical inspection is, in fact, justified? Fundamentally, the decision hinges on the practical economics of each specific situation. Two basic costs are involved:

1 Costs of inspection
2 Costs resulting from defective parts entering the production operation and/or reaching the customer

An attempt to minimize the sum of these two costs is the guiding criterion in arriving at the basic inspection decision. The decision is also influenced by another factor which affects both cost factors—the average percentage of defective product normally submitted in the supplier's shipments. (This factor is commonly called the supplier's "process average.")

The initial decision involves a choice between 100 percent inspection and no inspection. For purposes of illustration, assume that a manager is confronted with the following hypothetical situation:

- He buys widgets in lots of 1,000 every week *(N)*.
- The cost of inspecting a widget *(C$_I$)* = $0.20.
- If a widget failing to meet specifications enters the production operation, the average added production or sales cost to correct the situation *(C$_D$)* = $10.
- Records indicate that past shipments of widgets have typically contained approximately 3 percent defective units *(p)*.

A simple calculation indicates that in this case the least costly of the two alternatives is to perform 100 percent inspection:

Total cost = cost of inspection + cost resulting from defectives accepted

For 100 percent inspection,

$$Total\ cost = (N \times C_I) + cost\ from\ defectives\ accepted$$
$$= (1,000 \times 0.20) + 0$$
$$= \$200\ per\ lot$$

For no inspection,

$$Total\ cost = cost\ of\ inspection + (N \times p \times C_D)$$
$$= 0 + (1,000 \times 0.03 \times 10)$$
$$= \$300\ per\ lot$$

What would the decision be if the supplier's process average were 2 percent or 1 percent? Further investigation reveals that the manager can determine a break-even point, *in terms of the supplier's process average.* The break-even point exists at the process average where the total cost of not inspecting any of the incoming lots just equals the total cost of inspecting all incoming lots 100 percent.

The break-even point exists where:

$$Total\ cost\ _{0\%\ Insp.} = total\ cost\ _{100\%\ Insp.}$$
$$0 + (N \times p \times C_D) = (N \times C_I) + 0$$
$$p = \frac{N \times C_I}{N \times C_D} = \frac{C_I}{C_D}$$

Thus, when the supplier's process average equals the ratio C_I/C_D, unit cost of inspection divided by unit cost per defective, from a cost standpoint it makes no difference to the purchaser whether he inspects or not. When the process average is greater than C_I/C_D, it is least costly to inspect 100 percent; and when it is less than C_I/C_D, it is least costly to inspect none of the items.

So far we have not considered the possibility of sampling inspection.

Suppose that in a given situation no inspection appears to be the least costly alternative. This assumes that the supplier's process average is stable and will not vary appreciably from the p value used in the computation. In some actual production situations this may be a valid assumption; in others it may not. If the process average is subject to significant variation from time to time, some type of sampling inspection should be employed to detect shifts beyond an acceptable limit.

Suppose that in another situation 100 percent inspection is indicated. In the illustrative computations, it was assumed that no defective products would slip through the 100 percent inspection operation. Is this a realistic assumption? Very rarely. In most inspection activities involving human operation or judgment, experience indicates that 100 percent inspection usually detects only 80 to 95 percent of the defects present. Thus, the expenditure for 100 percent inspection does not yield the quality protection assumed in the initial calculations. Might not it be possible to obtain nearly the same degree of quality protection, and at the same time reduce the volume of inspection work, by using some type of sampling inspection? In most cases the answer is yes, and the protection against accepting defective items is obtained at a considerably reduced inspection cost.

In reality, then, the manager has three alternatives from which to choose: (1) no inspection, (2) 100 percent inspection, (3) some type of sampling inspection. Although conceptually more involved than the previous illustration, a similar total cost computation can be made for any statistical sampling inspection plan. This cost can then be compared with costs of the other alternatives, enabling the manager to determine the minimum-cost alternative.

Using the same basic approach in determining total cost, sampling plan cost calculations can be made using the following formula. Several additional factors required in the computation are:

n = size of sample to be inspected using a given sampling plan
Pa = statistical probability that a given sampling plan will accept a lot of material containing a given percentage of defective units.

Total cost of sampling plan [4] = cost of inspection + costs resulting from defectives accepted

$$= C_I \times \begin{bmatrix} \text{no. of sample units inspected,} \\ \text{plus no. of units inspected} \\ \text{in lots rejected by sampling} \\ \text{inspection} \end{bmatrix} + C_D \times \begin{bmatrix} \text{no. of defective} \\ \text{units accepted} \\ \text{by the samp-} \\ \text{ling plan} \end{bmatrix}$$

$$= C_I \times [n + (1 - Pa)(N - n)] + C_D \times [(N - n)\,(p)\,(Pa)]$$

---

[4]This formula is developed for the operating situation in which all rejected lots are subjected to 100 percent inspection in an attempt to locate and use all parts which do meet specifications.

It should be noted that the above formula is developed for the situation in which the supplier's process average, for practical purposes, does not vary greatly from p. This produces a sampling plan cost which is comparable with the previously developed costs for no inspection and 100 percent inspection. In the event that it is desirable to compare the costs of two sampling plans when p does vary considerably from time to time, this can be done by generalizing the formula to include the probability of occurrence of the various p values in question.

Sampling Inspection

In years gone by, many inspectors have undoubtedly attempted to ascertain the quality characteristics of a lot of material by examining a sample of the lot. Then, having considered the results of the sample in light of some arbitrary rule of thumb, they made a decision to accept or reject the entire lot. The difficulty in using this approach lies in the fact that no way exists to predict the soundness of the decision. Sampling, like throwing dice, involves chance. Predictability can be attained only by using the mathematics of probability in developing the sampling plan. Today, literally thousands of such plans are available for business and industrial use. The statistical acceptance-sampling plans currently available have been developed by professional mathematicians using the probability approach.

Conditions for the Use of Sampling   The use of a statistical acceptance-sampling plan is predicated on the existence of certain conditions in the operating situation:

1   Complete accuracy in locating defective parts not conforming to specifications must *not* be required. No sampling procedure can detect all defective parts. The quality objectives of acceptance-sampling inspection are to establish a control that assures an *acceptable* material quality level *over the long run.*

2   Individual items in each shipment must be arranged so that a random sample can be drawn without excessive expense. The statistician defines a random sample as one in which each item in the lot has an equally likely chance of being drawn.

3   The quality characteristic to be measured must be easily definable as being acceptable or unacceptable. Valid results depend obviously upon the inspector's ability to make consistent decisions from one unit to the next.

4   Finally, from the standpoint of cost, sampling inspection is most effective when lots of incoming material are reasonably large. The absolute size of a sample influences its effectiveness considerably more than does its relative size. For example, from a lot of 1,000 pieces a 10 percent sample of 100 pieces yields much more protection against accepting an excessive percentage of defectives than does a 10 percent sample of 10 pieces form a lot size of 100. Hence, the use of acceptance

sampling in obtaining a given degree of protection against defectives yields more attractive cost savings as the lot size increases.

Attributes and Variables   Acceptance sampling can be conducted on two different bases: (1) by attributes and (2) by variables. It is important that the reader distinguish clearly between these two concepts. If measurements of a particular quality characteristic are taken and recorded in terms of the units in which the actual measurements were made (e.g., inches, millimeters, degrees), quality is expressed by "variables." If, on the other hand, a particular quality characteristic is investigated and the record indicates only the number of pieces which met the specified value and the number of pieces that did not, quality is expressed by "attributes." Attributes inspection is an "either-or" proposition; an item is either acceptable or unacceptable. The great bulk of inspection done in industry today is conducted on the basis of attributes.

Attributes inspection can generally be conducted more quickly and less expensively than variables inspection. It is typically done using many different types of special "go, no-go" gauges. If, for example, a hole drilled in a piece of metal has a specified diameter of 1.00 inch ± 0.01 inch, this inspection can be made quickly and easily with a special plug gauge as shown in Figure 9-1. The inspector simply inserts the gauge in the hole. If the 0.990-inch-diameter member does not go into the hole, the hole is too small. If the 1.011-inch-diameter member goes into the hole, it is too large. The small member of the gauge should "go"; the larger member should "not go." Therefore, the inspector's instructions are to accept the piece if only the small member of the gauge goes, but to reject the piece if both members go or if neither member goes.

Published Standard Sampling Plans   Industry uses a wide variety of sampling plans. Two of the more commonly used sources are Dodge and

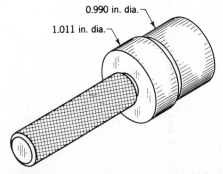

0.990 in. dia.
1.011 in. dia.

Figure 9-1   Go, no-go plug gauge used in attributes inspection.

Romig, *Sampling Inspection Tables—Single and Double Sampling,* John Wiley & Sons, Inc., New York, and Freeman, Friedman, Mosteller, and Wallis, *Sampling Inspection,* McGraw-Hill Book Company, New York.

The Dodge and Romig tables are designed specifically to minimize total sampling. All plans involve 100 percent inspection of rejected lots; such sampling plans commonly go under the name of acceptance/rectification plans. The Dodge and Romig publication includes single and double sampling plans indexed by LTPD and by AOQL.

Sampling Inspection, by Freeman et al., contains plans which are particularly useful in inspecting material coming from statistically controlled production processes. These plans tend to minimize "consumer's risk" by accepting most submitted lots whose quality level is in the acceptable range, and by rejecting a sizable percentage of incoming lots whose quality is below the acceptable range. The plans are based on the inspection/rejection idea; that is, rejected lots are returned to the supplier without further inspection. This publication includes single, double, and other multiple sampling plans indexed by AQL. An extended and modified version of these plans is available from the U.S. Government Printing Office under the title of *Military Standard— Sampling Procedures and Tables for Inspection by Attributes.*

SUPPLIERS AND THE INSPECTION PROGRAM

Communications Concerning Quality Measurement

It is extremely important that communications be clear and complete between buyer and seller concerning the quality measurements applied to incoming materials. A supplier whose shipments are to be subjected to sampling inspection should know it, because some shipments of satisfactory quality will be rejected by any sampling plan. No plan distinguishes perfectly between acceptable and unacceptable shipments. Users of sampling plans must be willing to tolerate the rejection of some acceptable shipments as well as the acceptance of some unsatisfactory shipments. The percentages of error associated with these two risks are governed by the design of the sampling plan and the number of units included in the sample.[5]

Agreement between buyer and seller therefore should be reached in advance concerning the disposition of rejected shipments. Should they be inspected 100 percent? If so, who pays the inspection costs? Should they be returned to the supplier? If so, who pays the transportation costs? Under stable operating conditions, such costs arising from the use of a given sampling plan can be estimated reasonably closely in advance, and a mutually satisfactory arrangement can be included as part of the purchase contract. A sampling plan is so intimately tied in with the supplier's production capabilities, as well as

[5]The probability of rejecting a supplier's satisfactory shipment is termed the "producer's risk." The probability of accepting an unsatisfactory shipment is called the "consumer's risk."

with the purchaser's quality needs, that from a total cost standpoint a strong case can be made for joint determination with the vendor of the sampling plans to be used. Cooperating closely with the vendor in this area can indeed be profitable, for the buyer should not forget that eventually *all* inspection costs are passed on to him. Astute purchasing managers, who are cognizant of the realities of inspection, can minimize endless costly disputes and, at the same time, initiate positive preventive action in developing sound vendor relations. As described so aptly by Victor Pooler of the Carrier Corporation, the *primary* job of the purchasing manager is *fire prevention,* not the repeated extinguishing of brush fires.

Inspection Cost Reduction

Because the purchaser ultimately bears the cost of all quality inspection, certain techniques are used by some companies to reduce total supplier-purchaser inspection costs. Several of these are discussed below.

In-Process Inspection   In an attempt to prevent quality errors before they actually occur, some large purchasers maintain a force of field inspectors. These personnel conduct in-process inspections in the supplier's plant at critical points in the manufacturing process. In some cases, field inspectors are actually headquartered in the supplier's plant. This is a rather common practice when the purchaser is the federal government, particularly if the purchase of military equipment is involved. This technique, more often than not, finds its widest application in situations where the material being purchased is costly and complex and/or requires a lengthy production cycle time.

Two formidable problems stand in the way of widespread use of this technique in private industry. The first, quite obviously, is cost. Not many companies have a volume of purchases sufficiently large to support a staff of field personnel trained in the different specialized areas of inspection work. Not surprisingly, the second problem concerns human relations difficulties that have a habit of cropping up frequently when an outsider looks too closely over a supplier's shoulder. This is not to say that such problems cannot be mitigated by wise administration. Nevertheless, many suppliers view the possibility of such problems as a distinct disadvantage of field inspection agreements.

Process Capability and Process Control   No production process can produce exactly identical parts time after time. Every process possesses some natural variability. If a process is properly adjusted and controlled, however, variability around the mean quality level is known and is statistically predictable.[6] Consequently, if the purchaser's desired range of quality is compatible with the normal quality range of the production process, under normal

---

[6]In statistical terms, this range of quality capability is defined as the "natural tolerance range" of the process.

operating conditions the supplier has little difficulty in providing the purchaser with a product of satisfactory quality. On the other hand, when the purchaser's required quality range is narrower than the capability range of the process, the supplier is bound to produce some unacceptable products.

To assist in controlling the quality levels of production processes, today many manufacturers utilize a relatively simple statistical technique known as "statistical process control." In practice, a process first must be stablized, or brought under control, at an economically satisfactory quality range. Then, by taking periodic samples of the product during operation and plotting the average quality of each sample on a statistical control chart, the manufacturer can detect operating changes which produce products outside the normally expected range of the process. By detecting such changes quickly, the manufacturer can correct the process before many defective products are made. Hence, the use of process control enables him to reduce the quantity of defective items produced. As a result, he also reduces the need for inspection of the finished items going to the purchaser.

Alert buyers recognize the direct economic relationship between their specified quality requirements and the producer's ability to perform consistently at the specified quality level. In the case of a nonstandard, high-value item, the capable buyer, prior to placing an order, determines (1) whether the supplier knows, in fact, what the normal quality range for his production process is, (2) if so, whether the desired range of quality is compatible with the supplier's normal quality range, and (3) if so, whether the supplier will maintain process control charts on the operation to assist in ensuring consistently satisfactory output. The following examples will clarify this idea.

In sketch *a* (Figure 9-2), assume that the buyer wants to purchase 100,000 metal shafts 1 inch in diameter, with a tolerance of ±0.005 inch. Assume further that the supplier has scientifically studied his process, stabilized it, and knows its capacity for this job to be 1 inch ±0.004. (This, in itself, indicates some production sophistication on the part of the supplier.) Examining sketch

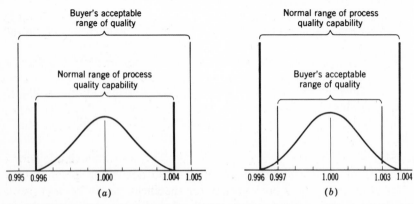

Figure 9-2 An illustrative comparison of quality requirements with process capability. (Process frequency distribution curves for shafts are shown.)

a, the buyer sees that as long as the supplier's process operates normally, every piece produced will fall within his acceptable range of quality. So far, so good. Occasionally, of course, the process will fail to operate normally because of such things as poor machine adjustment and dull cutting tools. Therefore, statistical process control could be used to detect the occurrence of such abnormalities and hence minimize the production of defective shafts. In this example, then, if the supplier knows how and is willing to apply statistical process control, this situation appears to represent a sound and economical purchase for the buyer.

Assume now that the buyer wants to purchase 100,000 shafts 1 inch in diameter, with a tolerance of ±0.003 inch. Examination of sketch *b* reveals that, dealing with the same supplier, the production process, under normal conditions, cannot entirely satisfy the buyer's requirement. It will produce a certain number of shafts with a diameter less than 0.997 inch, and a certain number larger than 1.003 inches. It is important that the buyer understand this situation. Someone (supplier or buyer) is going to have to pay for the production of the unusable shafts. In the long run, the chances are good that it will be the buyer, knowingly or unknowingly. Assuming that the buyer's requirements cannot be compromised, he is thus faced with two alternatives:

1   Negotiate with the supplier to determine whether the normal range of process capability can economically be narrowed to a point nearer the buyer's requirements.
2   Seek another supplier whose process can meet his requirements more economically.

In summary, capable buyers can reduce the costs of inspection and unsatisfactory products by working with their suppliers, sometimes utilizing their own quality control personnel, to accomplish two things:

1   A reasonable matching of the supplier's process capabilities with the buyer's quality requirements
2   An agreement that the supplier whenever practicable will employ statistical process control techniques at critical points in the operation

Supplier Certification   When a purchaser has dealt with a supplier for some time and has found him to be entirely honest and has determined that his product's quality is consistenly reliable, the question arises: Why should the purchaser duplicate the supplier's inspection work when the supplier does a capable and honest job? Many firms have answered this question with a positive policy of "supplier certification."

Certification agreements take many forms, ranging from a simple supplier's guarantee of quality to a formally negotiated document spelling out in detail the responsibilities of both parties for specifications, inspection procedures, reporting procedures, and so forth. Qualification requirements for certification should be rigorous. Before a supplier is certified, his output may well be subjected to periods of 100 percent inspection, and subsequently to trial periods of sampling inspection during which a high percent of all lots are required to pass. The supplier's quality control department and inspection procedures should be scrutinized. Generally, the purchaser's quality control personnel should work with the supplier in developing the inspection procedures to be used for final inspection.[7]

Once a supplier gains certification, most purchasers periodically check performance by using a reduced sampling inspection program, by reviewing the supplier's process control charts for critical manufacturing operations, by reviewing test reports from his laboratories, or by following other similar techniques. Generally speaking, firms that have tried certification programs have experienced favorable results with them. Inspection costs are typically reduced, while quality levels usually remain high. Most suppliers take pride in appearing on their customers' certification lists. They are also aware that good performance places them in a favored position to receive additional business.

FOR DISCUSSION

9-1 Discuss in reasonable detail the role which the purchasing department should play in a firm's overall quality assurance program.

9-2 Once an order has been negotiated and placed with a supplier, what interest does the purchasing department have in the quality level of the product the supplier delivers? Why?

[7]One firm that has successfully employed a supplier certification program for a number of years uses the following approach in qualifying suppliers for certification:

1 All incoming lots of material from the supplier are subjected to rigid sampling inspection for a period of six months (or until a minimum of seven lots have been received).

2 During this period, the supplier must receive an "Excellent" rating, based on the following empirically designed rating system:

$$R = 1,000 - \left(\frac{d}{N} + \frac{l}{L}\right) \times 500$$

where: R = quality rating
d = number of defective pieces found
N = number of pieces inspected
l = number of lots received containing defectives
L = number of lots inspected

Using this classification:

Excellent   = R of 990–1,000
Good   = R of 975–989
Satisfactory = R of 950–974
Poor   = R of 900–949
Undesirable = R of 0–899

3 After achieving an Excellent rating for six months, if additional qualitative investigations produce favorable results, the supplier qualifies for certification.

9-3   What is the purchasing department's interest in its firm's material specifications, as far as quality is concerned?

9-4   How do "use tests" differ from "engineering tests"? What role should the purchasing department play in the handling of use tests? What role should it play in the handling of engineering tests?

9-5   What specific precautions should be observed by the person conducting a use test?

9-6   What can a buyer tell about a vendor's quality capability from an analysis of the vendor's proposal for a particular job?

9-7   What is a capability survey? How is it conducted? What role does the purchasing department play in a capability survey?

9-8   A statement is made in the text to the effect that the buyer is responsible for positively motivating the supplier with respect to quality. What is meant by this statement? What specific courses of action might a buyer take in carrying out the responsibility implied in this statement?

9-9   Buyers frequently visit suppliers at their plants. Is there any reason why a buyer might ask a supplier's representative to visit him at his own plant (the buyer's plant)? Explain.

9-10   One large company feels so strongly that individual buyers should be responsible for the performance of their suppliers that, in the annual merit review for promotion, one of the points on which buyers are evaluated is the performance rating of their suppliers. Discuss the strengths and weaknesses of this policy.

9-11   Generally speaking, what should a top-notch buyer know about his or her firm's inspection department? How is this related to the actual buying job?

9-12   Explain the difference between receiving inspection and technical inspection. What generally determines whether an incoming material should be subjected to receiving inspection, technical inspection, or both?

9-13   "In reality, the purchaser usually seeks a practical balance between cost of quality and value of quality." What is your reaction to this statement?

9-14   Define the following terms:
a Costs of inspection
b Costs resulting from accepting defective parts
c Process average
Given the three factors noted above, develop a simple mathematical expression which indicates whether or not 100 percent inspection is justified. Assume now that you do not know the supplier's process average. Develop a simple mathematical expression which indicates at what process average the purchaser is indifferent to inspection (he does not care whether inspection is conducted or not).

9-15   What are the basic conditions which must exist before a purchaser can consider the use of sampling inspection in inspecting incoming materials? Discuss each condition in reasonable detail.

9-16   Distinguish between variables inspection and attributes inspection.

9-17   What courses of action might the buyer initiate to reduce the total cost
        of inspection? Discuss each.
9-18   "In the long run, all costs of inspection and all costs of producing
        unusable products are borne by the purchaser." Comment.
9-19   In a medium-sized automobile engine manufacturing plant, all person-
        nel associated with the inspection of incoming materials report to the
        manager of the purchasing department. Discuss possible strengths and
        weaknesses of this organizational arrangement.
9-20   Briefly discuss the concept of supplier certification. What possible
        dangers do you see in the use of this concept by a purchasing
        department?

CASES FOR CHAPTER 9

Inventory Management—I

The title of an article which appeared in *Business Week* several years ago—"Inventory Men Move Up"—might well set the stage for a discussion of inventory management. The past several decades have witnessed marked and steadily increasing changes in management disciplines. Numerous planning and control activities formerly performed in a routine manner by clerks have evolved into sophisticated functions with far-reaching effects on company profits. Inventory control, a vital element in the management of materials, is one of these functions. Business faces a continuing squeeze on profits. At the same time, development of analytical techniques and computer capability now permit more sophisticated analysis of inventory cost problems. These two phenomena have combined to transform inventory control into a critical function requiring professional managerial skills.

Several statistics clearly point up the current significance of the inventory control function. A study of corporate balance sheets shows that a firm's inventory commonly constitutes from 15 to 25 percent of its invested capital. This is a sizable segment of its investment, to say the least.

A second startling figure is uncovered when one ferrets out and totals the annual costs of carrying a given inventory. While the figure varies considerably from firm to firm, numerous studies made by consultants and by manufacturing firms reveal that a typical manufacturer incurs inventory carrying costs of from 17 to 24 percent of average inventory value. This means that a medium-sized firm pays in indirect costs approximately $200,000 per year merely for the convenience of having a million-dollar inventory in its warehouse. This figure is significantly greater than is apparent to the average businessman.

THE FUNCTION OF INVENTORIES

Inventories thus require high cost and investment commitments. It is understandable, then, why *some* businessmen view inventories and their attendant costs as a necessary evil. Such individuals, however, fail to make a fair analysis of the *total* situation. Before one looks unfavorably upon the size and costs of inventory, he must also assess carefully the benefits afforded his company by the existence of the inventory.

Generally speaking, inventories make possible smooth and efficient operation of a manufacturing organization by decoupling individual segments of the total operation. Purchased-part inventories permit activities of purchasing department personnel to be planned and conducted somewhat independently of shop production operations. By the same token, they allow flexibility for suppliers in planning, producing, and delivering an order for a given part.

Inventories of parts and components produced "in-house" decouple the many individual machines and production processes from various subassembly and assembly activities. This enables management to plan production runs in individual production areas in a manner which utilizes manpower and equipment considerably more efficiently than if all were tied directly to the final assembly line. Also, finished-goods inventories perform the function of decoupling the total production process from distribution demands, allowing on a broader scale the development of similar efficiencies of production. The results produced by these inventories should be good service to customers on stock items, lower direct production costs, lower materials-handling costs, and lower purchasing costs.

Thus, well-planned and effectively controlled inventories can contribute substantially to a firm's profit. The real problem is to determine the inventory level at which money invested in inventory produces a higher rate of return through these benefits than it would were it invested in some other phase of the business.

If this problem is viewed through the eyes of various operating department managers, an interesting situation appears. The *sales manager* tends to favor relatively large inventory stocks to assure rapid assembly and delivery of a wide range of product models. This capability can obviously be used as an effective sales tool. The *production manager* is inclined to go along with the sales manager, but for quite a different reason. He argues for high inventory levels because they allow more flexibility in his daily planning; unforeseen problems in producing a given component can be mitigated if he can easily transfer his productive efforts to another component for which the required raw materials inventory is on hand. Likewise, high inventory of the required items ensures against production shutdowns due to stock-outs, thus avoiding the incurrence of high production downtime costs.

The *financial officers* of the firm, on the other hand, argue convincingly in favor of low inventory levels. They point out that the company's need for funds usually exceeds availability and that reduced inventories free sorely needed working capital for other uses. They note also that total indirect inventory carrying costs drop proportionately with the inventory level. The *procurement officer* is the final participant; he is concerned with the size of individual orders. He favors a policy of placing fewer and larger purchase orders, which in turn usually increases the total inventory level. He points out that large-volume buying often results in reduced purchase prices, and that it also permits him to utilize buying personnel more efficiently and to effect more advance planning for major activities such as value analysis, vendor investigation, and so on.

Thus, it is clear that each departmental executive supports his position with quite legitimate justification. However, certain conflicts do exist between the objectives of the various departments. Concepts and techniques useful in analyzing this problem to arrive at sound policy decisions are the focal point of our investigation in the remainder of this chapter.

DEFINITION OF INVENTORIES

Although inventories are classified in many ways, the following classification proves convenient for use in further discussion of the topic:

1 *Production inventories:* raw materials, parts, and components which enter the firm's product in the production process. These may consist of two general types: (1) special items manufactured to company specifications, and (2) standard industrial items purchased "off the shelf."
2 *MRO inventories:* maintenance, repair, and operating supplies which are consumed in the production process but which do not become part of the product (e.g., lubricating oil, soap, machine repair parts).
3 *In-process inventories:* semifinished products found at various stages in the production operation.
4 *Finished-goods inventories:* completed products ready for shipment.

In most manufacturing companies, production and MRO inventories together represent the major segment of total inventory investment.

Let us now place the discussion in perspective. Inventory planning occurs at several levels in an organization and covers various time spans. Our concern in this and the next chapter focuses on the planning and control of production and MRO inventories in a short-run situation, involving weekly, monthly, and in some cases quarterly or yearly decisions. Hence, the discussion assumes that the longer-range activities of sales forecasting, product modification, and determination of manufacturing and assembly policy have for the moment been completed. Our investigation begins at this point in the planning cycle.

INVENTORY ANALYSIS

The inventory of a typical industrial firm comprises 10,000 to 50,000 different items. Initial planning and subsequent control of such an inventory is accomplished on the basis of knowledge about *each* of the individual items and the finished products of which each is a part. Consequently, the starting point for sound inventory management is the development of a complete inventory catalog, followed by a thorough ABC analysis.

Inventory Catalog

After all inventory items have been completely described, identified by manufacturer's part number, cross-indexed by user's identification number if necessary, and classified generically for indexing purposes, some form of inventory catalog should be prepared for use by all personnel. Careful preparation and maintenance of such a catalog pays two important dividends.

An inventory catalog serves, first, as a medium of communication. It enables personnel located in many different departments to perform their jobs more effectively. A design engineer, for example, may have a choice between using either of two standard parts in an experimental design; an inventory catalog quickly tells whether either part is carried in inventory and may immediately be available for use in the experimental work. Suppose the item in question is to be used in large quantities on the production line. If one of the alternative parts is a stock item and the other is not, the engineer knows immediately that procurement time and costs will probably be lower for the part which is already being purchased and used elsewhere in the plant.

As a further example, envision a mechanic who has just removed a faulty bearing from a major production machine which has broken down. Upon examination, he finds the manufacturer's name and part number stamped on the edge of the bearing. Unfortunately, though, the storeroom clerk cannot help him, because that particular bearing is not carried in stock. If the mechanic or his supervisor consults the inventory catalog, however, he may well find that a satisfactory substitute bearing, carried under another manufacturer's part number, is in stock. Proper cross indexing in the inventory catalog can advise users of common interchangeable parts, a typical situation with many MRO supplies.

A second significant benefit produced by an inventory catalog accrues to the inventory control operation itself. This benefit takes the form of more complete and correct records through the reduction of duplicate records for identical parts. A purchasing department often buys the same part from several different suppliers, under various manufacturers' part numbers. Unless control requirements dictate otherwise, identical parts from all suppliers should be consolidated on one inventory record. A simple situation? Perhaps, but one is amazed to find in highly reputable companies many similar cases in which two or more inventory records bear different numbers for the same part.

Such everyday occurrences obviously result in higher inventories and reduced operating flexibility. Similar situations sometimes occur even when the part is purchased from only one supplier. Changes in commercial nomenclature, in billing practices, or in office personnel frequently result in vendor documents which appear to describe two different items when in fact they cover the same part.

Use of an inventory catalog does not eliminate the possibility of undetected duplicate records, but if carefully developed and maintained, it significantly reduces such a possibility.

ABC Analysis

As soon as an inventory is reasonably well identified and described, it is imperative that the controlling manager recognize the dollar importance of each individual inventory item. This calls for a study of each item in terms of its price, usage (demand), and lead time, as well as specific procurement or technical problems. Without the information provided by such a study, controlling managers normally find themselves with a meager basis, at best, on which to allocate departmental effort and expense to tasks of controlling thousands of inventory items.

A study of several hundred medium-sized West Coast manufacturing firms conducted by the authors reveals the data illustrated in Figure 10-1. This figure shows that in the typical firm a small percentage of the total number of items carried in inventory constitutes the bulk of inventory investment. In the study cited, 10 percent of the inventory items account for approximately 75 percent of the investment, and only a quarter of the items make up approximately 90 percent of the total investment. The remaining 75 percent of the items constitute, roughly, only 10 percent of the inventory investment. While these figures vary somewhat from one firm to another, the magnitude of variation is not usually great. Several similar studies in large corporations have produced strikingly similar results, leading to what some firms call the 80-20 phenomenon (20 percent of the items account for 80 percent of total inventory investment).

Among different companies this type of analysis is known by several different names, *ABC analysis* being the most common. In practice, such an analysis can be made on the basis of either the average inventory investment in each item or the annual dollar usage of each item. The analysis is easy to conduct once inventory has been properly identified and usage records have been maintained for a complete operating cycle. All items are simply ranked in order of their average inventory investment (or dollar usage). The total of these values (average inventory investment or annual usage) for all inventory items is

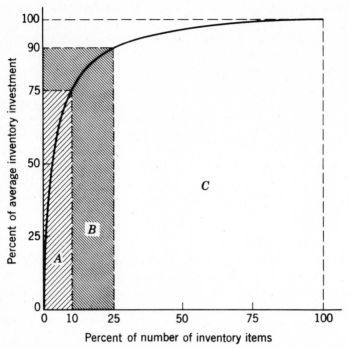

Figure 10-1   Graphic analysis of production and MRO inventories.

then computed. The value of each individual item is next expressed as a percentage of the total. By going down the list and successively cumulating the individual percentages for each item, one can determine which items make up the first 75 percent of inventory investment, the first 90 percent, and so on. If it is convenient to use the three arbitrary classifications noted above, they can be labeled *A, B,* and *C,* respectively, and each inventory item becomes an *A, B,* or *C* item.

The value of such an analysis to management is quite clear. It provides a sound basis on which to allocate funds and time of personnel with respect to the refinement of control over the individual inventory items. In this sense control may take several forms. It may be reflected in minimizing inventory investment, in minimizing indirect costs associated with inventory, in utilizing personnel effectively, or in assuring effective storage, handling, and delivering of material to production operations as scheduled. The concept clearly permeates a number of departmental operations—purchasing, production control, stores, and accounting, for example.

Management can use the information generated from such a study intuitively or formally. Some managers informally concentrate departmental efforts on the *A* and some of the *B* items. Others develop formal policies and procedures for handling *A, B,* and *C* items. One company, for example, has established the policy that all *A* items shall be reviewed and purchased every month, *B* items every one to six months, and *C* items every six to twelve months. Details of formal policies such as this, of course, are determined somewhat arbitrarily by management, based on knowledge and judgment concerning the unique features of each company's operating situation. It should be emphasized, however, that employment of ABC analysis greatly reduces the possibility of error in such judgements by clearly pointing up the specific items on which management can profitably concentrate its efforts.

In practice, a never-ending problem is that of adequately planning for handling the thousands of low-value *C* items. Even with good purchasing planning, because of the sheer number of *C* items, low-value nuisance purchases frequently require more time than should be allotted to them. Consequently, they reduce the amount of time available to purchasing personnel for value analysis, vendor investigation, and other creative work involving high-value *A* and *B* items. The "economic order quantity" concept, to be discussed later in the chapter, provides an insight into a partial solution to this problem for some items. It further suggests that although ABC analysis represents a good fundamental management tool, it does not, in its present form, permit precise consideration of all relevant factors which should enter this management decision. The relationship between ABC analysis and economic order quantity theory will be investigated shortly.

Dependent and Independent Demand

To do the job well, an inventory controller needs one additional bit of information about each of the items in inventory—is the demand (usage) for the item "dependent" or "independent"?

An item is said to exhibit *dependent demand* characteristics when its use is directly dependent on the scheduled production of a larger component or parent product, of which the item is a part. Hence, in a plant producing automobile engines the demand for engine block castings is a dependent demand; once the production schedule for a group of engines is established, the controller knows with certainty that one block will be required for each engine. Conversely, the demand for cutting oil used by the machines on the line cannot be calculated from the production schedule; thus, cutting oil is said to have an *independent demand.* Generally speaking, in an assembly or fabrication-type operation, most production inventory items will have a dependent demand, while MRO and similarly used items will have an independent demand.

Although the distinction seems relatively simple, it is important for the inventory manager to know whether an item exhibits a dependent or an independent demand. Certain inventory control systems function more effectively with one type of item than with the other. The importance of this distinction will be evident shortly when we consider operation of an MRP system.

TYPES OF INVENTORY CONTROL SYSTEMS

Generally speaking, three basic systems can be employed in controlling inventories: (1) the cyclical ordering system, (2) the fixed order quantity system, and (3) the material requirements planning system (MRP).

Cyclical Ordering System

The first is a *time*-based system which involves *scheduled periodic* reviews of the stock level of all inventory items. When the stock level of a given item is not sufficient to sustain the production operation until the next scheduled review, an order is placed replenishing the supply.[1] The frequency of reviews varies from firm to firm. It also varies among materials within the same firm, depending upon the importance of the material, specific production schedules, market conditions, and so forth. Order quantities likewise vary for different materials. For administrative convenience, however, each material's order quantity is usually chosen from a small number of predetermined coverage periods. (For example, all order quantities may represent operating coverage for two weeks, four weeks, eight weeks, or twelve weeks.)

Stock levels can be monitored by physical inspection, by a visual review of perpetual inventory cards, or by automatic computer surveillance. In operations where a small number of materials is involved, the simplest and most accurate method is a periodic physical count of the stock. Where this is not practical, as is the case with most firms of substantial size, a perpetual inventory record for each material can be maintained (manually or by computer) by posting receipts from invoices and disbursements form stores material requisitions. If this procedure is closely controlled, the inventory record for each material should at all times be in reasonably close agreement with the actual stock balance. Human errors inevitably creep into such a procedure, however, necessitating a physical stock count at least once or twice a year.

In practice, the cyclical ordering system is well suited for materials whose purchases must be planned months in advance because of established and infrequent production schedules maintained by the suppliers.[2] It also works well for materials which exhibit an irregular or seasonal usage and whose purchases must be planned in advance on the basis of sales estimates.

The system can, of course, be used for all materials in an inventory; used in this manner, however, it possesses three distinct disadvantages. First, it compels a periodic review of all items; this in itself makes the system somewhat inefficient. Because of differences in usage rates, many items may not have to be ordered until the succeeding review. Conversely, the usage of

---

[1] Anticipated usage during the period may be based on average historical usage data in a stable demand situation, or on specific calculation of requirements from known production schedules and product bills of material in either stable or unstable demand situations.

[2] Mill steel and glass typify such materials.

some items during the period may have increased to the point where they should have been ordered before the current review date. Consequently, this system must be augmented with a minimum balance figure which signals the need for an early reorder in the case of a sharp usage increase.

Second, and equally important, the system demands the establishment of rather inflexible order quantities in the interest of administrative efficiency. Theoretically, there exists an optimum economic order quantity for each item, depending upon its price structure, its rate of usage, and attendant internal costs. However, because all items must fit reasonably well into a limited number of ordering cycles under this system, actual order quantities may deviate substantially from the optimum. For a given material, the net effect frequently is an increase in the total inventory costs associated with that item.

Finally, the cyclical ordering system tends to peak the purchasing work load around the review dates. This disadvantage can be avoided to some extent by regulating the frequency of reviews. In practice, though, it is difficult indeed to smooth the load to the desired level.

Flow Control System   The "flow control" method of managing inventories represents a special variation of the cyclical system. This special method is applicable in continuous manufacturing operations which produce the same basic product in large quantities day after day. Most materials used in such an operation are purchased on term contracts and scheduled for daily or weekly delivery throughout the term. The production cycle is often a day or less in duration, and, in effect, material flows through the plant in continuous streams.

Inventory floats consequently can be kept quite low, thus requiring a minimum investment in production inventory. In such an operation, stores personnel daily review visually the level of all material stocks and report any imbalances to the purchasing or production control department. Changes in production schedules must be relayed immediately to buyers so that delivery schedules can be revised accordingly.

Fixed Order Quantity System

A second basic type of inventory control system—the fixed order quantity system—is based on the *order quantity* factor rather than on the time factor. The design of this system recognizes that each item possesses its own unique optimum order quantity, and, in practice, the system permits more effective utilization of this fact.

Operation of a fixed order quantity system requires for each inventory item:

1   The predetermination of a fixed quantity to be ordered each time the supply of the item is replenished. This determination typically is based on a consideration of price, rate of usage, and other pertinent production and administrative factors.

2   The predetermination of an order point, so that when the stock level on hand drops to the order point, the item is automatically "flagged" for reorder purposes. The order point is computed so that estimated usage of the item during the order lead time period will cause the actual stock level to fall to a planned minimum stock level by the time the new order is received. Receipt of the new order then increases the stock level to a planned maximum figure.

The automatic feature of the system is achieved most commonly by maintaining a perpetual inventory record for each item carried in stock. An inventory clerk, or a computer, continues to post all material issues until the balance of an item falls to its order point. At this time the clerk or the computer notifies the purchasing department. If the system operates correctly, purchasing replenishes the stock so that inventory levels for all items automatically remain between the planned minimum and maximum levels. The person responsible for inventories thus utilizes the management-by-exception principle in controlling them because no action is taken until action is required (i.e., until the order point is reached).

The major advantages claimed for the system are that (1) each material can be procured in the most economical quantity; (2) purchasing and inventory control personnel automatically devote attention to the items that need it *only when required;* and (3) positive control can easily be exerted to maintain total inventory investment at the desired level simply by manipulating the planned maximum and minimum values.

The system also possesses several severe limitations. It functions correctly only if each of the materials exhibits reasonably *stable usage and lead time.* When these factors change significantly, a new order quantity and a new order point must be determined if the system is to fulfill its objectives. Consequently, the system becomes extremely cumbersome to operate effectively when applied to materials with unstable usage patterns and lead times. As with any system using a perpetual inventory record, errors in posting and in the issuance of stores requisitions occasionally distort book balances and may lead to undetected material shortages.

Two-Bin System   A variation of the basic fixed order quantity system is found in the operation of the simple two-bin system. The distinguishing feature of this system is the absence of a perpetual inventory record. In practice, the stock is physically separated into two bins, or containers. The lower bin contains a quantity of stock equal to the order point figure. This, typically, is just enough stock (or slighly more) to last from the date a new order is placed until it is received in inventory. The upper bin contains a quantity of stock equal to the difference between the maximum and the order point figures. At the outset, stock is used from the upper bin; when this supply is depleted, it signals the clerk that the order point has been reached. At this point an order is placed, and material is used from the lower bin until the new stock is received. Upon receipt of the new order, the proper quantities of material are again placed in the two bins.

This method demonstrates very simply the fundamental concept which underlies the basic fixed order quantity system.

The two-bin method is widely used in handling low-value hardware and supplies whose usage is not recorded on a perpetual record. The major advantage of the method is the obvious reduction of clerical work. Issues do not have to be posted to determine the proper reorder time. Receipts, however, are usually posted to reveal significant changes in usage or lead time. A possible disadvantage of the system in some cases is the requirement of additional storage facilities and perhaps some practical difficulty in keeping the two stocks properly separated.

To generalize, it should be pointed out that none of the systems or their adaptations discussed so far are mutually exclusive. *Several or all of them may be used advantageously for different materials in a single firm.*

Material Requirements Planning (MRP) System

Widespread use of computer-based planning and control systems has greatly increased management's ability to analyze and manipulate large volumes of data to produce more timely and accurate information for decision-making purposes. In certain types of manufacturing firms, this data-handling revolution has spawned the development of a third type of production/inventory planning system. It is currently known as Material Requirements Planning, or MRP.

The MRP concept provides a very basic and different way of looking at the management of *production* inventories in an *intermittent* manufacturing operation. Fundamentally, MRP challenges the traditional concept that any significant level of production inventory need be carried prior to the time materials are actually required by the production operation. Once a firm's master production schedule has been established, and product bills of material have been finalized, it is possible to calculate precisely these production material needs for a given period of operation. The bill of material for a given finished product can be "exploded" and extended for the number of units to be produced to obtain that product's exact requirements for each component material or part. Since a given part typically is used in more than one finished product, requirements for that part in all products can be summed up to obtain the total requirements for the part during the operating period in question. Without a computer, this "explosion and aggregation" process is virtually impossible to do quickly and accurately in a firm producing many different products. With a properly programmed computer to process the huge volume of data, however, the task can be accomplished with relative ease.

In practice, the MRP approach calculates production material requirements weekly (based on production schedules that are updated weekly) several operating periods in advance of the actual need.[3] It then generates requisitions for each material to be delivered in the required quantity several days prior to the start of the manufacturing operation. In essence, the "pure" MRP approach attempts to eliminate (minimize) most inventory requirements and gear purchasing and production activities to the timing and quantity usage demands of the final product assembly schedule.

Consider for a moment, now, our prior discussion about the operation of a cyclical ordering system. When a given item is reviewed, how does this system determine whether an order should be placed and, if it should, what quantity should be ordered? Several methods can be used, but a commonly used method is identical to the "explosion and aggregation" method used in the MRP approach. The only difference lies in the timing of the order relative to the time that particular lot of material is required by production. The cyclical system calls for order delivery before the material is actually needed and maintains an inventory safety stock. Ideally, an MRP system times material delivery to coincide with production requirements and maintains no safety stock.[4]

Clearly, this major element in the MRP concept has evolved from experience with the cyclical ordering system. And more refined use of the computer has produced accurate and timely data that permit MRP to eliminate, or minimize, the need for safety stock inventory. A *cardinal difference* between the two systems, however, is the driving force which actuates the material acquisition cycle. In the case of the cyclical ordering system, it is the inventory control system itself that is designed to initiate the request for material. In an MRP operation the *master production schedule (as updated each week) is the force that directly intitiates and drives* subsequent activities of the purchasing and manufacturing functions. It is this fundamental difference which sets the MRP system apart from all other inventory control systems.

As implied earlier, the techniques of an MRP system are designed for use in certain specialized operating situations. The system can be used most advantageously under the following conditions:

1   When usage (demand) of the material is discontinuous or highly unstable during a firm's normal operating cycle. This situation is typified by an intermittent manufacturing or job-shop operation, as opposed to a continuous processing or mass production operation.

2   When demand for the material is *directly dependent* on the production of other specific inventory items or finished products. MRP can be thought of as primarily a component fabrication planning system, in which the demand for all parts (materials) is dependent on the demand

---

[3]Most MRP applications are designed to operate on a weekly cycle, although longer time periods may be used. Order lead time requirements will obviously vary for different materials and market conditions.

[4]In practice, the material obviously is delivered at least several days before it is actually required, so a small inventory does in fact exist on a continuing basis as long as that material is being used in current production runs. The size of the inventory depends on how far in advance of the need material is actually delivered.

(production schedule) for the parent product. Hence, most *production inventory* items meet this "dependent demand" requirement; MRO inventory items do not, because their demand is derived independently (and cannot be calculated) from the master production schedule.

3   When the purchasing department and its suppliers, as well as the firm's own manufacturing units, possess the flexibility to handle order placements or delivery releases on a weekly basis. Moreover, they must be able to respond effectively to sizable weekly changes in material demand requirements, without serious interference from such potential problems as unbalanced internal work loads or significant variation in supplier lead time requirements.

Further discussion of the MRP system's requirements and limitations will be more meaningful after we have explored the application and operation of the cyclical and fixed order quantity systems. This analysis follows in the next chapter.

DETERMINATION OF ORDER QUANTITY

When using a *cyclical ordering* system for a given material, the quantity of material which will be ordered when the next purchase is made is generally determined by three factors: the number of days between inventory reviews, the anticipated daily usage during the cycle period, and the quantity actually on hand at the time of the review. One of the often-stated objectives of this system is to maintain a relatively low investment in production inventory. It logically follows, then, that the order quantity will be the quantity required to cover only the ensuing period, with allowance for order lead time.

Obviously, smaller quantities than this cannot be ordered without precipitating a material shortage before the next review date. Although a larger quantity could be ordered, for administrative convenience it should represent an even two- or three-period supply. The issuance of an order covering one period plus a fraction of the next for many materials has a tendency to increase the average inventory level. It likewise complicates the review routine for the inventory controller. The rather inflexible cyclical ordering system, with its typical single-period order quantity, thus makes it difficult for the buyer consistently to take optimum advantage of quantity discounts, economical shipping quantity situations, and so forth. This same disadvantage is inherent in the tightly controlled *MRP system,* with its typical weekly review cycle.

When using a *fixed order quantity system* for a given material, the inventory controller can establish the order quantity at an infinite number of values, as long as the quantity is large enough to satisfy production requirements until the next shipment arrives. Practically speaking, the quantity can be set as large or as small as the controller wishes, because the quantity-based system will tell, for a given usage rate, at what stock level another order should be placed.

Although the fixed order quantity system offers unlimited flexibility in ordering materials, it still provides no criteria by which the inventory manager can determine the most advantageous order quantity for a given material. The following section investigates a concept which does offer practical assistance in this regard.

The Economic Order Quantity Concept

One guideline to determination of the most advantageous order quantity can come from an analysis of all incremental costs associated with order quantity. For practical purposes these costs can be grouped in two categories, (1) inventory carrying costs, and (2) inventory acquisition costs.

Cost Relationships   The carrying of materials in inventory is expensive. Several studies conducted a number of years ago indicate that the annual cost of carrying a production inventory averages approximately 25 percent of the value of the inventory.[5] Everet Welch, during his experience as a consultant, has found that annual carrying costs average somewhat over 20 percent of the inventory value, exhibiting a range of from 10 to 34 percent. Similar studies have replicated these results numerous times during the past several decades. Welch notes that five major elements comprise inventory carrying costs in the following manner:[6]

1	Interest charges on the investment	4 to 15%
2	Insurance costs	1 to 3%
3	Property taxes	1 to 3%
4	Storage costs	0 to 3%
5	Obsolescence and deterioration	4 to 10%
	Total carrying costs	10 to 34%

Let us briefly examine these carrying costs.

1 *Interest charges on the investment:* When a firm purchases $50,000 worth of a production material and keeps it in inventory, it simply has this much less cash to spend for other purposes. Since money invested in productive equipment or in external securities earns a return for the company, conceptually it is logical for the company to charge all money invested in inventory a rate of interest equal to that it could earn if invested in something else. This is the "opportunity cost" associated with inventory investment.

2 *Insurance costs:* Most firms insure their assets against possible loss

[5]L. P. Alford and J. R. Bangs (eds.), *Production Handbook*, The Ronald Press Company, New York, 1955, pp. 396–397.

[6]W. Everet Welch, *Tested Scientific Inventory Control*, Management Publishing Corporation, Greenwich, Conn., 1956, p. 64.

from fire or other forms of damage. An extra $50,000 worth of inventory represents an additional asset on which insurance premiums must be paid.

3   *Property taxes:* As with insurance, property taxes are levied on the assessed value of a firm's assets; the greater the inventory value, the greater the asset value, and consequently the higher is the firm's tax bill.

4   *Storage costs:* The warehouse in which a firm stores its inventory is depreciated a certain number of dollars per year over the length of its life. One may say, then, that the cost of warehouse space is a given number of dollars per cubic foot per year. And this cost conceptually can be charged against inventory occupying the space.

5   *Obsolescence and deterioration:* In most operations, a certain percentage of a given inventory stock spoils, is damaged, is pilfered, or eventually becomes obsolete. No matter how diligently warehouse managers guard against this occurrence, a certain amount always takes place. With new products being introduced at an increasing rate, the probability of obsolescence is increasing accordingly. Consequently, the larger the inventory, the greater is the absolute loss from this source.

Generally speaking, this group of carrying costs rises and falls nearly proportionately with the rise and fall of the inventory level. Furthermore, the inventory level is directly related to the quantity in which material is ordered. The larger the order quantity, the higher is the average inventory level during the period covered by the order. Hence, costs of carrying inventory vary nearly directly with the size of the order quantity. This relationship is illustrated by the *CC* curve in Figure 10-2.

Looking at inventory costs in another light, a different set of indirect material cost factors emerges. These factors all contribute to the cost of generating and processing an order and its related paper work. Examples of these costs are listed below and can be thought of as inventory acquisition costs.

1   A certain portion of wages and operating expenses for such departments as purchasing, production control, receiving, inspection, stores, and accounts payable

2   The cost of supplies such as forms for purchasing, production control, receiving and accounting, blueprints, envelopes, stationery, and so forth

3   The cost of services such as telephone, telegraph, and postage expended in procuring materials

When considering this group of acquisition costs, we observe that they behave quite differently from carrying costs. Acquisition costs are not related to inventory size per se, but rather they are a function of the number of orders placed during a given period of time.

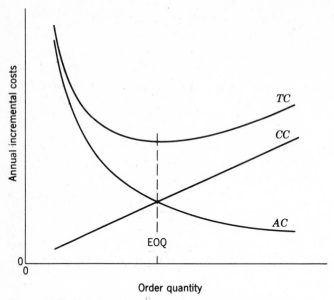

Figure 10-2   Relationship of indirect material costs to order quantity. (*AC* = incremental acquisition costs; *CC* = incremental carrying costs; *TC* = total incremental costs.)

One simplified example will illustrate the above point. Suppose a buyer in the purchasing department receives a requisition for a special fabricated part used in the manufacture of his firm's product. Assume further that the part has been purchased before and that price quotations from five or six shops are on file. The buyer first reviews the present inventory situation and probably checks with production control to see if any significant changes are anticipated in future production. He then reviews drawings and specifications of the part to refresh his memory regarding required tooling and other technical details of the purchase. Next, he reviews the quotations to determine why the order was placed with vendor A last time and to decide if vendor A should again receive the order; vendor performance data must also be reviewed. Finally, the buyer decides which vendor the order should be placed with; he telephones him to inquire about current shop loads and any other matters that have arisen during the investigation. It is entirely possible that a price negotiation session may also be called for.

In total, the buyer's investigation may require anywhere from an hour to several days. The total cost of the buyer's time to the company will be the same whether the purchase order is written for 20 parts or for 200 parts. And the next time the buyer purchases this part he will go through somewhat the same process, generating almost the same indirect cost for the company.

The bulk of inventory acquisition costs are indirect labor and overhead costs listed under item 1 above, generated in similar fashion in the various departments concerned either directly or indirectly with the material acquisition. The cost of supplies and services consumed in the placement and handling of an order varies directly with the number of orders placed; although costs are relatively small if measured on a per order basis, they add up to a significant figure over a year in a firm handling 30,000 to 50,000 different inventory items.

If a firm experiences a given annual usage of an item, the number of orders handled per year decreases as the order quantity increases, thus generating lower annual acquisition costs. Experiences of numerous firms show that this relationship is not linear, but that it follows the approximate contour of the *AC* curve in Figure 10-2.

Referring to Figure 10-2, observe that as the order quantity increases, carrying costs rise at the same time acquisition costs drop. Since the purchaser's primary concern is the *total* cost associated with inventory, he wants to know the specific order quantity at which the sum of these two costs is a minimum. The *TC* (total cost) curve can be drawn as a summation of the *AC* and *CC* functions. Examination of the *TC* curve reveals that *the lowest annual total cost occurs at the order quantity where inventory carrying costs equal acquisition costs.* This point, then, is the sought-after "economic order quantity."

Incremental Costs   Assume now that a firm is currently ordering an item in quantities of 50 units every month. A staff analyst makes a cost study of this item which culminates in an EOQ chart similar to Figure 10-2. Assume the chart indicates that the most economical ordering quantity is 500 units every ten months. It is said that "The proof of the pudding is in the eating." The relevant question, therefore, is: If this firm increases the order quantity for this item from 50 to 500, will it in fact reduce its acquisition costs more than it increases its carrying costs?

To answer this question, the method of computing acquisition costs must be analyzed carefully. At first glance it might appear that a quick study of the accounting records will yield the costs of operating the various departments involved with material acquisitions, as well as the costs of relevant supplies and services. By totaling these costs and dividing by the number of purchase orders issued during the period, inexperienced analysts may think they have determined the acquisition cost per order incurred by the firm. Historically speaking, perhaps they have. But is this figure useful in constructing the *AC* curve which is used in determing a material's most economical order quantity?

An acquisition cost figure determined in this way,

$$\text{Acquisition cost per order} = \frac{\Sigma \text{ annual department operating costs} + \text{ service and supply costs}}{\text{number of purchase orders issued per year}}$$

represents an average cost per order. But this cost figure does not reflect realistically the potential variability that total annual acquisition costs can be expected to exhibit when the number of purchase orders issued per year changes. Why? Because in making this acquisition cost determination, some fixed costs were included. The purchasing agent and some top-level staff people in the purchasing department will continue to draw the same salary (in the short and intermediate run) regardless of the number of purchase orders issued each year. If a sizable sum of such fixed costs is included in the acquisition cost figure, the resulting EOQ value is in reality fictitious. It is overstated because the fixed segment of the acquisition costs really does not decrease as the order quantity increases.

This brings us, then, to a definition of "incremental costs," the costs which are relevant in making an EOQ analysis. *Incremental costs are those costs which acutally change as a result of making a particular operating decision* (e.g., the decision to issue more purchase orders each year will increase the cost of P.O. forms and postage and will also increase payroll costs if a new buyer or clerical person has to be hired to handle the added workload). For a given period of time, incremental costs are the antithesis of fixed costs. Note that the vertical axis of Figure 10-2 is labeled "annual incremental costs." This means that all costs included in the acquisition cost curve, as well as the carrying cost curve, must be *incremental* costs; these costs *must in reality change as order quantity changes.*

In practice, how does an analyst determine the incremental acquisition cost per order? He can determine only an estimated value, and he begins just as he did in the prior example. After he has determined the total historical costs for a given period of operation, he estimates how much these costs could be reduced by issuing a smaller number of orders (say, an order reduction of 1,000 orders per year).[7] This figure can be determined only by making a careful analysis of the relevant activities and their time requirements. When the analyst has carefully estimated the savings resulting from potential work force reduction and reduced use of equipment and supplies, he then has sufficient data to make the cost determination. He has thus determined the total cost reduction resulting from the decision to reduce the number of purchase orders written by 1,000 per year. If he determined the total cost reduction to be $15,000 per year by issuing 1,000 fewer orders, it then appears that the incremental cost—the controllable short-run cost—is $15 per order ($15,000/1,000).

If the analysis is reasonably accurate, the analyst can then make the statement with some assurance that each additional purchase order issued above the new level will in reality cost the company approximately $15. It should be noted that in practice this $15 figure is well within the range of incremental acquisition costs that are experienced by a number of companies.

EOQ Computations   To this point the rationale of the economic order quantity concept has been developed. The discussion now turns to the

---

[7]He could also determine incremental acquisition costs by estimating how much the historical costs would be *increased* if a *larger* number of orders were issued during the same time period. Conceptually, this type of analysis is then conducted in a manner similar to the one described.

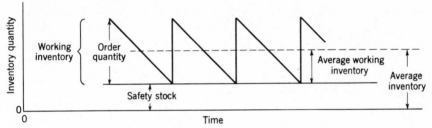

Figure 10-3 Ideal inventory movement pattern for a given material.

procedure used in making EOQ computations. The following terms and symbols will be used in these computations:

Q = order quantity for a given material

A = *incremental* acquisition cost per order for a given material, determined by a special cost study, as previously described

I = annual *incremental* inventory carrying cost (expressed as a percentage of average inventory value) for a given material, which can easily be computed using selected data from accounting records and from simple cost estimates for indirect expenses which actually vary with inventory size[8]

U = expected annual usage of the material

C = delivered unit cost of the material

Two additional concepts should also be discussed briefly: (1) average working inventory and (2) average inventory.

Although this topic will be developed in detail shortly, it should be noted here that the inventory of a given material conceptually is made up of two segments, namely, working inventory and safety stock. Figure 10-3 illustrates an ideal movement pattern for a material whose usage is constant day after day. *Theoretically,* safety stock is held for protection against emergencies, and is not used in production as long as daily usage and order lead time are completely predictable. Inasmuch as material consumption in the production operation reduces the inventory level slightly each day from the time one order is received until it is entirely consumed, for managerial purposes it is convenient to work with average inventory figures for the period of operation. The average inventory value for a given number of days can be computed just as any

[8]Before leaving the topic of incremental cost determination, one further word of clarification is in order. Investments in warehousing facilities and salaries of a certain minimum number of administrative and operative personnel represent short-run fixed costs which exist regardless of the size and the number of purchase orders issued. The only instances in which these costs would be considered as incremental are those in which such personnel and facilities are utilized to full capacity; and in the absence of the work occasioned by an additional purchase order, they could be utilized for other equally profitable activity. On these grounds, essentially those of economic opportunity cost, many small firms might make a case for considering the salary of a single purchasing specialist or the storage costs in an overloaded warehouse as incremental costs.

arithmetic average is computed. If we assume that daily usage is constant, however, the "average working inventory" figure becomes, simply, order quantity/2. The average total inventory, usually designated by the abbreviated term "average inventory," becomes (order quantity/2) + (safety stock). (If the reason for this is not clear, the reader should verify it by setting up a simple hypothetical problem and computing the averages both ways.)

With this background, then, computation of the order quantity producing the lowest total cost becomes a relatively easy task. The following example illustrates one approach.

A truck manufacturer uses 120,000 headlight assemblies per year in the production of a certain model truck. Daily production of this particular truck is reasonably stable throughout the year. The company's incremental acquisition cost is estimated to be $10 per order. Its incremental inventory carrying cost is 24 percent of the average inventory value per year. The delivered cost of each headlight assembly is $5. The company tries to maintain a safety stock of 100 lights.

Turning to Figure 10-2, our task is now to compute incremental carrying costs, incremental acquisition costs, and their total, at a series of different order quantities. To start, arbitrarily assume six order quantities listed in the left column of Table 10-1.

Table 10-1   Inventory Cost Computations for the Truck Manufacturer

Order quantity	Annual incremental costs		
	Carrying cost (CC = IQC/2)	Acquisition cost (AC = UA/Q)	Total cost (TC = CC + AC)
500	$ 300	$2,400	$2,700
1,000	600	1,200	1,800
1,500	900	800	1,700
2,000	1,200	600	1,800
2,500	1,500	480	1,980
3,000	1,800	400	2,200

Carrying costs are computed as $IQC/2$. Note that I is incremental carrying cost expressed as a percentage of average inventory value. $QC/2$ represents the dollar value of the average working inventory; this factor multiplied by I then yields the annual incremental dollar cost of carrying the working inventory. (Note that the cost of carrying safety stock has not been included. The analyst may include this cost if desired, but since the safety stock level is assumed to be the same regardless of the size of the order quantity, this cost is the same for all order quantities. Because the analyst will eventually compare total costs at different order quantities, and since the cost of carrying safety stock will appear as a constant in all alternatives being compared, it can be omitted without affecting the final decision.[9] Omission of this constant cost factor also simplifies calculations, as we shall see shortly.)

Acquisition costs are a function of the number of orders issued per year; number of orders issued per year can be expressed as U/Q. Multiplying this factor by A (incremental acquisition cost per order) yields the annual incremental dollar cost of acquiring the inventory.

Total annual incremental cost is then obtained by summing CC and AC. From this point an analyst can determine the economic order quantity in two ways. First, the computed data may be used to plot a curve similar to Figure 10-2 and to determine the EOQ by inspection of the graph. Second, the analyst may simply compare total cost figures in column 4. In this case the lowest total cost appears to correspond with an order quantity of 1,500 units. However, since CC and AC are not equal at 1,500 units, it appears that the EOQ point is produced by an order quantity which has not been investigated. Reviewing the CC and AC trends, it is apparent that the EOQ point lies between 1,500 and 1,000 units. Its location can be determined precisely by a further investigation of points within this range.

The reader has undoubtedly noted that direct material cost has not been included in this analysis. It is omitted for the same reason that safety stock carrying costs were omitted—often it is not an incremental cost because it does not vary with order quantity. In practice, however, the unit price for many materials actually does decrease in a steplike manner as the quantity ordered increases. When a quantity discount is available to a buyer, annual direct material cost may vary with the size of the order quantity—and hence becomes a relevant incremental cost factor that must be considered. In this case another column can be added to the table, and TC will then comprise CC, AC, and direct material cost. Differential shipping costs should be handled in the same way. (See page 212 for further discussion of the handling of quantity discounts.)

After computing the EOQ for a single material using this approach, one senses immediately the impracticality of the approach in a business operation. A minor refinement, however, can transform this basic idea into a formula which can be used quite practically, in several forms, in the everyday business situation.

Refer again to Figure 10-2. We have determined that a generalized mathematical expression for the carrying cost curve is $CC = IQC/2$. Similarly, a generalized expression for the acquisition cost is $AC = UA/Q$. Noting again that the low point on the total cost curve occurs at the point of intersection of the two elemental cost curves, the two above expressions can be equated and solved algebraically for Q:[10]

---

[9]At this point in the discussion we are viewing safety stock as a fixed quantity, independent of order quantity. If safety stock is viewed in the light of probability theory, it may well vary with order quantity. This concept is discussed in Chapter 11.

[10]A more straightforward mathematical solution is obtained by using differential calculus: (1) write the equation for the total cost curve; (2) differentiate the equation; (3) find the minimum value of the function by setting the derivative equal to 0 and solving for Q.

EOQ occurs when

$$CC = AC$$
$$\frac{IQC}{2} = \frac{UA}{Q}$$

Solving for Q,

$$IQ^2C = 2UA$$
$$Q^2 = \frac{2UA}{IC}$$

$$Q = \sqrt{\frac{2UA}{IC}}$$

This formula, then, is the fundamental mathematical representation of the EOQ concept. It can be modified to accommodate numerous special conditions, but in general practice it probably finds its most effective application in this form.

Returning momentarily to the example of the truck manufacturer, the exact EOQ computed with the formula is:

$$Q = \sqrt{\frac{2UA}{IC}}$$

$$= \sqrt{\frac{2 \times 120,000 \times 10}{0.24 \times 5}}$$

$$= 1,414.2, \text{ say } 1,414 \text{ lights}$$

This confirms the solution obtained by the initial approach, which indicated that the EOQ lay close to 1,500, within the range of 1,000 to 1,500 units.

FOR DISCUSSION

10-1   What function do inventories serve in a manufacturing concern? Some business executives view inventories as a "necessary evil." What is your reaction to this attitude?

10-2   What is ABC analysis? For what purpose do inventory managers use ABC analysis?

10-3   Discuss briefly the major features of the cyclical ordering system. What are the primary advantages and disadvantages of the cyclical ordering system?

10-4   Explain briefly how the fixed order quantity system operates. What are the major advantages and disadvantages of this system?

10-5   What is the flow control system? Under what conditions is the flow control system used? What are the advantages and disadvantages in using this system?

10-6 What is the primary objective of an MRP system? Explain briefly how an MRP system works.

10-7 What is the economic order quantity concept? Explain the basic ideas involved in this concept.

10-8 Can the economic order quantity approach be used just as easily with all three basic control systems (cyclical ordering system, fixed order quantity system, and MRP system)? Explain.

10-9 Explain what is meant by the terms "inventory carrying costs" and "inventory acquisition costs."

10-10 What is "opportunity cost," and why should it be included as an inventory carrying cost?

10-11 What is meant by "incremental costs?"

10-12 In what way are "incremental costs" used in determination of the most advantageous order quantity?

10-13 How does an inventory manager determine incremental acquisition cost per order?

10-14 In graphic or quantitative terms define the following:
a. Working inventory
b. Average working inventory
c. "Average inventory"
d. Safety stock

10-15 Derive mathematically the EOQ formula.

CASES FOR CHAPTER 10

The Inventory Octopus, page 624
The Controversial Freight Bill Case, page 609

Chapter 11

Inventory Management—II

KEY CONCEPTS

Application and limitations of EOQ
Order point and safety stock
   Basic computations
   The probability approach
Application of MRP
Responsibility for inventory control
Synthesis for application

APPLICATION OF THE ECONOMIC ORDER QUANTITY CONCEPT

From a business practitioner's point of view, the major problem with economic order quantity theory is one of practical application of the formula to a large number of items in an operating situation.

The first difficulty arises from the fact that all cost data required to compute factors A and I are not readily available in the accounting records of most firms. Thus, a certain amount of detailed cost investigation is initially required. It is important that each firm make an analysis of its own costs rather than electing to use a "typical" figure as an approximation. This is wise, if not essential, because the proportion of incremental cost included in each indirect cost factor varies significantly among different firms, depending upon a multitude of conditions within each firm.

The astute observer will note, however, that the total cost curve (see Figure 10-2) is usually relatively flat at its minimum value. Movement, of as much as 20 percent, along the order quantity axis in both directions from the EOQ point actually produces a fairly small increase in total incremental cost. So, while users strive for reasonable accuracy in a cost study, some error in development of the I and A factors can be tolerated without impairing the practical value of the resulting EOQ figures. This one feature makes EOQ analysis a very useful tool for the practical-minded business executive.

Fortunately, most firms find that they can use the same values for A and I factors for virtually all major materials. Because some materials do exhibit

significantly different cost-producing characteristics, however, a firm occasionally groups the inventory into several classes and determines a set of A and I
factors that are most realistic for each class. Once these factors are determined, factors C and U must be determined for each material; if adequate
purchasing and inventory records have been maintained, this information is
readily available. At this point, Q must be computed for each material. (If
certain materials exhibit markedly similar price and usage patterns, they may
also be grouped and a single Q can be computed for each group.)

During the early years of EOQ usage, manual calculation of the Q value
required considerable time and was a cumbersome process when dealing with a
large number of inventory items. Today, however, the actual computation of Q
can be cut to a matter of seconds through the use of one of several mechanical
aids or by means of a computer. Inasmuch as all factors in the formula except C
and U can be reduced to a mathematical constant after initial determination,
the formula itself can be translated into a three-scale nomograph. By locating
values for C and U on two of the scales and connecting these values with a
straight edge, Q can be read directly from the third scale. A variety of
applicable nomographs are available commercially, or they can be developed
easily by the user's own statisticians.

A similar timesaving procedure can be accomplished with the use of
various specially designed slide rules. Figure 11-1 illustrates a specialized

Figure 11-1 Economic order quantity calculator. *(Reproduced by permission from Dr.
Anton M. Groot and Anton Groot, Jr., inventory management consultants, Santa Ana,
Calif.)*

circular slide rule for calculating EOQs that is produced by Groot Inventory Management Consultants of Santa Ana, California. Both nomographs and slide rules can be used quite easily by clerical personnel after very little training. To make application even easier, some firms compute economic order quantities for numerous combinations of usage and cost values and then tabulate and index the predetermined values in such a manner that the inventory clerk need only refer to a printed sheet to determine the EOQ for a given item.

In firms utilizing computerized inventory control systems, EOQ calculation generally is accomplished automatically by the computer. The calculation can be programmed as a part of the computer's routine activity in generating information for each purchase order print-out. The analyst needs only to supply current values for factors $A, I, U,$ and C in the computer memory file for each material.

Quantity Discounts Situations frequently occur in practice where the delivered unit cost of a purchased material decreases significantly if a slightly larger quantity than the originally computed economic order quantity is purchased. (Remember that the computed EOQ does not take into consideration the cost of the material itself, except to the extent that it is reflected in the calculation of carrying costs.) Quantity discount schedules, freight rate schedules, and perhaps anticipated price rises may create such situations. These additional variables can also be included in the formula. But in so doing, the formula becomes rather complex, precluding effective use of some mechanical computation aids. Consequently, use of such a formula is often impracticable unless the user has access to a computer.

Using Q computed with the basic formula, however, such alternative quantity decisions can still be made quickly and accurately. By simply comparing annual material price savings, resulting from the purchase of the additional quantity, with the additional inventory carrying costs occasioned by the increased purchase, the most economical decision quickly becomes evident. With a limited amount of practice, a buyer can determine in a matter of seconds whether material price savings exceed carrying costs for the additional inventory.[1]

---

[1]To illustrate the technique, refer again to the truck manufacturer's EOQ purchase of headlights on page 208. Recall that $U = 120,000$ lights/year, $A = \$10$ per order, $I = 24$ per cent per year, and $C = \$5$ per light. Assume now that the supplier of headlights will sell at $C = \$4.90$ per light in quantities of 2,000 or more. Should the truck manufacturer buy in quantities of 1,414 or 2,000? First, calculate the annual material cost savings if purchases are made in quantities of 2,000:

$$\text{Material cost savings} = U \times \Delta C$$
$$= (120,000 \text{ lights/yr.}) \times (\$5.00 - \$4.90/\text{light})$$
$$= \$12,000 \text{ savings/year}$$

Next, calculate the annual added carrying costs if purchases are made in quantities of 2,000:

$$\text{Added carrying costs} = I \Delta Q C / 2$$
$$= (0.24/\text{yr.}) (2,000 - 1,414 \text{ lights}) (\$4.90/\text{light})/2$$
$$= \$345 \text{ added cost/year}$$

Hence, the truck manufacturer would save approximately $11,655 per year by buying in quantities of 2,000 rather than 1,414.

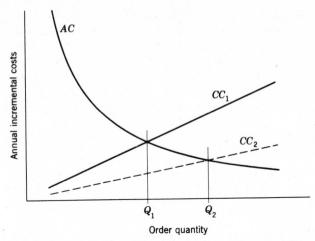

Figure 11-2 EOQ comparison for high- and low-cost items having the same annual usage.

EOQ and ABC Analysis Use of the economic order quantity approach in managing inventories not only tends to minimize indirect material costs, but from a control point of view it produces an equally important by-product. Application of the formula actually results in the placing of frequent orders for relatively small quantities of high-cost materials and less frequent orders for larger quantities of lower-cost materials.

Figure 11-2 illustrates this point. Assume that the solid curves AC and CC_1 on this EOQ graph were originally drawn for a relatively high-cost material whose annual usage is stable. Consider now a lower-cost material whose annual usage is the same in quantity and stability as the first material. If we assume that the two materials have approximately the same I factor (incremental carrying costs expressed as a percent of value), then the incremental carrying cost curve for the second material (dashed curve CC_2) will have a lesser slope and will be flatter than CC_1.[2] (Remember that $CC = IQC/2$.) If we assume also that the two materials have approximately the same A factor (incremental acquisition cost per order), then the two materials both have substantially the same AC curve.[2] (Remember that $AC = UA/Q$.) Consequently, as inspection of Figure 11-2 shows, CC_2 intersects AC farther to the right than does CC_1; thus, the economic order quantity for the low-cost material, Q_2, is considerably larger than the economic order quantity for the high-cost material, Q_1.

If we were to compare two identically priced materials, one having a high annual usage and the other having a low annual usage, a similar but less straightforward situation would be seen. Application of the EOQ concept results in the placing of more frequent orders for the high-usage material and less frequent orders for the low-usage material.

In both cases, this general situation permits all personnel involved with procurement and inventory management to devote less time to the infrequent

[2]In practice, these are both quite realistic assumptions.

acquisition of low-value items and compels them to devote a much greater percentage of their time and effort to a relatively small number of high-value items. Hence, it becomes evident that wide use of the EOQ concept automatically requires management to employ a version of the ABC approach to inventory control, whether it recognizes the fact formally or not.

Limitations of the Economic Order Quantity Approach To this point in the discussion nothing has been said about the shortcomings of the EOQ concept. They do exist. There are inventory control managers in practice who have experienced dismal results using the EOQ concept. More often than not, however, these experiences stem from an unwise application of the concept rather than from failure of the concept itself. It is therefore extremely important that the responsible manager understand clearly what EOQ can do and what it cannot do.

Examination of the economic order quantity formula, and the theory upon which it rests, reveals a major limitation of its application in practice. It is of little use in dealing with *materials whose prices or usage fluctuate radically,* or with *materials whose usage cannot be predicted* with a reasonable degree of accuracy. Under such conditions a figure which represents the correct order quantity today may not be valid tomorrow. Therefore, if the material in question is carried in inventory for a period of time which exceeds the period of stability of its economic order quantity, it becomes impossible for the formula to achieve its objectives. Likewise, if material is flow-controlled throughout the production operation, small inventories and the nature of this type of procurement operation render the formula inapplicable as far as direct usage is concerned.

Other Uses of the EOQ Concept A final word should be said about *general* usage of the EOQ concept. Our discussion has been set entirely in the purchasing environment. The EOQ concept quite logically has broader application as well.

A very common situation in which the concept is applicable is the determination of economic production lot sizes in a manufacturing operation. Consider the formula a moment ($Q = \sqrt{2UA/IC}$), and look at the individual factors in light of both the purchasing and the production operation. In converting the formula for production use, the annual usage and carrying cost factors are the same as they were in the purchasing application. The unit cost factor, however, is no longer delivered price, but consists of direct labor and material and production overhead costs. Production acquisition cost is similar to purchasing acquisition cost, except that production setup cost replaces the purchasing departmental cost.

Buyers may well consider (from the supplier's point of view) the formula in this form also when determining lot sizes on term-contract purchase orders going to various types of job-shop suppliers; a supplier's costs and subsequently his product price are obviously influenced by the size and frequency of such orders.

DETERMINATION OF ORDER POINT AND SAFETY STOCK

For many items, the quantity of safety stock carried significantly affects indirect material costs. This is true whether a cyclical ordering system or a fixed order quantity system is used. For purposes of explanation, the safety stock concept will be investigated in the context of a fixed order quantity system.

A production inventory, as previously noted, consists of two segments—working inventory and safety stock. Figure 11-3 illustrates an ideal inventory situation in which the usage rate for a given material is constant. Further, it assumes that material is always ordered at the proper order point and that the shipment arrives consistently in the same length of time. In practice, however, the two factors of usage and lead time seldom remain constant from month to month over a year's duration. This means that the low points of the saw-toothed inventory movement pattern in some cases will actually fall below the minimum level, and in others they will terminate above the minimum. A safety stock of material is therefore maintained as insurance against stock depletion when increased usage or unusually long delivery time causes the low point to fall below the minimum.

Fundamental Computations

The two-part question confronting management, then, is: How much safety stock should be carried as protection against a stock-out, and at precisely what inventory level should a new order for material be placed? The following example may be helpful in demonstrating a fundamental approach to answering this question.

> A typewriter manufacturer buys from a nearby foundry the base casting on which his machine is assembled. The foundry provides unusually good service and always makes delivery on the eighth day after it receives the order. The manufacturer uses typewriter bases at an average rate of 100 per day, but usage varies randomly from 80 to 120 bases per day.

Assume that the manager views the situation somewhat conservatively

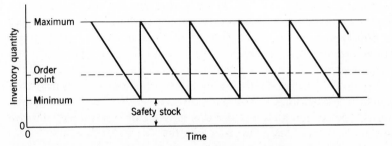

Figure 11-3 Ideal inventory movement pattern for a given material.

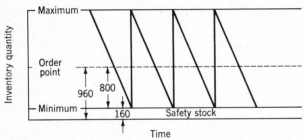

Figure 11-4 Typewriter base safety stock set to avoid stock-outs. Ideal inventory movement pattern is shown.

and decides he will set order point and safety stock values so that under present operating conditions he will not run out of stock. First he bases his order point computation on an average operating situation; he figures he will use 800 bases during the time his order is being produced and delivered.

> Average no. bases used during lead time = 100 per day × 8 days lead time = 800

Next he considers the situation from a pessimistic point of view, figuring that the maximum number of bases which could possibly be used during the lead time is 960.

> Maximum no. bases used during lead time = 120 × 8 = 960

He therefore concludes that if he does not choose to run out of stock, he should establish his order point at an inventory level of 960 units (the maximum lead time usage) and his safety stock level at 160 units (maximum lead time usage minus average lead time usage). These data are expressed in Figure 11-4.

Over a period of time this means that the low point of the inventory pattern sawtooth will occasionally fall to 0 as the new order arrives, and when usage is at its lightest, the low point of the sawtooth will be as high as 320 when the new order arrives [960 − (80 × 8) = 320]. Most of the time the low point of the sawtooth will fluctuate between these two extremes, with occurrences concentrated around the theoretical minimum value (safety stock) of 160. Figure 11-5 depicts this situation hypothetically.

In the example it was assumed that lead time was constant at 8 days. Assume now that the average lead time is 8 days, but that lead time varies randomly between 6 and 10 days. Assuming the manager still does not want to run out of stock, his computations under this new set of conditions will be as follows:

Average no. bases used during lead time = $100 \times 8 = 800$
Maximum no. bases used during lead time = $120 \times 10 = 1{,}200$
Minimum no. bases used during lead time = $80 \times 6 = 480$

Therefore:

Order point = maximum lead time usage
= 1,200 units
Safety stock = maximum lead time usage −

average lead time usage
= 1,200 − 800
= 400 units

$$\text{Range of low-point variation} = \begin{cases} \text{order point} - \text{minimum usage} \\ \qquad\qquad \text{to} \\ \text{order point} - \text{maximum usage} \end{cases}$$

= (1,200 − 480) to (1,200 − 1,200)
= 720 to 0

The Probability Approach[3]

To this point we have assumed that the manager does not want to run out of
stock. This may not always be the case. Even though a disruption of production
activities can be extremely costly, it is also costly to carry a large safety stock
which is used only on rare occasions. This situation produces a cost problem
which is analogous to that encountered in the discussion of order quantities.
Writing in the *Harvard Business Review,* consultant John Magee summarizes
the situation concisely.[4]

The objective is to arrive at a reasonable balance between the costs of [carrying]
the stock and the protection obtained against inventory exhaustion. Since exhaus-

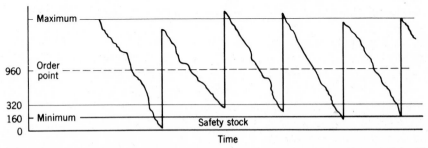

Figure 11-5 Typical inventory movement pattern for a reasonably stable material, with a
fixed order quantity.

[3]Some users refer to this concept as the "statistical order point" approach.
[4]John F. Magee, "Guides to Inventory Policy—II, Problems of Uncertainty," *Harvard
Business Review,* vol. 34, no. 2, p. 104, March–April, 1956.

tion becomes less likely as the safety inventory increases, each additional amount of safety inventory characteristically buys less protection. The return from increasing inventory balances therefore diminishes rapidly. So the question is: How much additional inventory as safety stock can be economically justified?

In some cases it may be most economical to carry a small safety stock and occasionally deplete that stock entirely. Management is concerned with a *total* cost made up of two elements: (1) inventory carrying cost for safety stock, and (2) costs resulting from a stock outage (arising from disrupted production activities and/or late deliveries). Theoretically, the ideal solution involves a minimization of the sum of these two costs. Several complex analytical approaches based on probability theory have been developed as guides for management in considering the problem. Without getting unduly involved in mathematics, the following example illustrates the basic concept underlying these approaches.

Returning the the example of the typewriter manufacturer, assume that he has compiled from his files certain historical usage data for typewriter base castings (see Table 11-1). Column 2 lists the number of eight-day work periods during the past year for which a given usage noted in column 1 occurred. This is a simple frequency distribution of casting usage during the average purchase lead time period. Column 3 simply expresses the values in column 2 as a percentage of 253, the total number of successive eight-day work periods in the year.

The last column represents a further refinement of the data, putting them in usable form. This column is a cumulative frequency distribution, showing the percentage of lead time periods during the past year for which the usage of typewriter bases exceeded any given usage figure in column 1. From the data in columns 1 and 4 the cumulative frequency curve in Figure 11-6 can be plotted.

Following the dashed lines, the cumulative frequency curve can be interpreted in this way. Approximately 44 percent of the time during the past year, the usage of typewriter bases exceeded 800 units per 8-day period.[5] Or, saying it inversely, approximately 56 percent of the time, usage of typewriter bases was less than 801 units per 8-day period.

How can an inventory manager use this curve in determining the order point for typewriter bases? Recall that in our first example (in which lead time was constant at 8 days), the manager decided he did not want to run out of stock, so he set the order point at 960 units, based on a maximum usage of 120 units per day. Examination of the cumulative frequency curve confirms that no

[5]Since the manufacturer has calculated his average usage to be 800 units per 8-day lead time period, one might wonder why 50 percent of the period usage values do not exceed 800 units and why 50 percent are not less than 800 units. The reason is that this is an average curve for a group of discrete values, not a curve of a continuous function. Hence, even though the mean and median period usage figures are 800 units, period usage exceeded 800 units only 44 percent of the time because during 26 periods out of the year usage was exactly 800 units.

lead time period usage has exceeded 960 units; therefore, the manager is safe in his assumption that there is no risk of a stock outage, assuming that conditions surrounding the production operation during the past year do not change.

Working under this same assumption, the manager might adopt a less conservative approach. If, for example, he knows that the costs incurred in the production and sales operations due to a stock outage are quite small, he may be willing to run out of stock several times a year if he can reduce safety stock and its attendant carrying costs by so doing. The cumulative frequency curve tells him that only 6.8 percent of the time last year did the lead time period usage exceed 880 units. Another way of interpreting this is to say that, assuming conditions do not change significantly, if the order point were computed on a maximum usage figure of 880 units per lead time period, in the long run approximately 6.8 percent of the orders placed would result in a stock-out. (Or in approximately 93.2 percent of the cases the manager would not run out of stock. In this case he would provide a "service level" of 93.2 percent to the production department.)

Table 11-1   The Typewriter Manufacturer's Usage Data for Typewriter Bases

Total usage, in units, during 8 successive work days	No. of 8-day periods when col. 1 usage was consumed	Percentage of total 8-day periods consuming col. 1 usage	Percentage of 8-day periods exceeding col. 1 usage
< 640	0	0.0	100.00
640	1	0.4	99.6
648	1	0.4	99.2
672	4	1.6	97.6
688	7	2.8	94.8
696	7	2.8	92.0
720	11	4.4	87.6
736	14	5.5	82.1
760	21	8.3	73.8
768	23	9.1	64.7
784	25	9.8	54.9
800	26	10.3	44.6
808	25	9.8	34.8
824	23	9.1	25.7
840	18	7.1	18.6
856	17	6.7	11.9
880	13	5.1	6.8
912	6	2.4	4.4
928	7	2.8	1.6
936	3	1.2	0.4
960	1	0.4	0.0
	253	100.0	

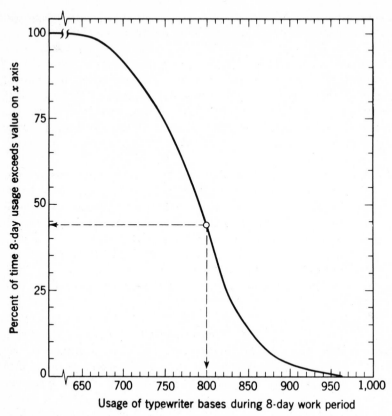

Figure 11-6 Cumulative frequency curve for the typewriter manufacturer's usage of bases.

Knowing the number of orders placed for bases each year, the manager can thus determine the average number of stock-outs to expect each year, over the long run. (The larger the number of orders placed during the year, the closer the number of stock-outs will approach the 6.8 percent figure.) If the manager knows the approximate costs resulting from a typewriter base stock-out, he can then compute the average annual stock-out cost incurred as a result of establishing the order point at 880 units rather than 960 units. Finally, this additional cost can be compared with the cost saving resulting from the reduced safety stock inventory and its lower attendant carrying costs.

The theory underlying the probability approach, then, implies that a manager should take a three-step approach in determining the order point for a given material carried in inventory:

1 Determine the total cost to the company of a stock-out.
2 Construct a cumulative frequency curve for material usage.
3 Set the order point at the lead time period usage figure which produces

a long-run percentage of stock-outs whose cost, when added to the cost of carrying safety stock, yields a minimum total annual cost.

In other words, the manager should be interested in minimizing the sum of safety-stock carrying costs and stock-out costs. In cases where the cost of stock-outs is extremely high relative to carrying costs, it may be least costly never to run out of stock. In other cases where stock-out costs are low relative to carrying costs, it will probably be most economical to carry a small safety stock and occasionally experience a stock-out.

The Problem of Lead Time Variation   To this point, the discussion has overlooked the possibility that lead time may also vary. In situations where lead time varies substantially from one order to the next, the problem of theoretical order point determination is compounded considerably. Under such conditions, usage during the lead time period is a function of two interacting probability distributions—the frequency distribution of material usage and the frequency distribution of purchase lead times. One method of handling this problem involves the generation of a distribution of lead time usage figures by means of simulation.

Using the simulation approach, an analyst begins by developing from historical records a frequency distribution of the material's daily usage and a frequency distribution of its purchasing lead time expressed in days. Using these two distributions, a third distribution of *material usage per lead time period* can be simulated either manually or by computer. First, a lead time figure is selected randomly from the lead time distribution. Next, daily usage figures are selected randomly from the usage distribution for each day of lead time specified by the randomly selected lead time figure. By totaling the selected daily usage figures, one composite usage figure that may occur during the lead time for some future order is simulated. This procedure can then be repeated for several years of simulated operation to generate a large distribution of usage per lead time period figures.

The validity of this simulation approach demands that daily material usage and individual order lead time requirements vary in an unrelated, random manner. If these conditions prevail, the simulated usage distribution should be representative of that expected during variable real-life lead time periods, over the long run. Once the lead time usage distribution has been generated, it can be converted to a cumulative frequency curve similar to that plotted in Figure 11-6. The cumulative frequency curve for lead time usage can then be used, as in the preceding example, to determine the reorder point value which yields the minimum sum for stock-out costs and safety stock carrying costs.

The Probability Approach in Practice

The concept underlying the probability approach—that of minimizing the sum of all costs associated with safety stock—is certainly logical and sound from a managerial point of view. In practice, however, few firms apply the concept in a formal manner for many production inventory items. A number of large corporations that once used it on a wide scale have subsequently abandoned the idea. There appear to be three major reasons why a majority of firms have not yet found it to be a practical operating tool:

1   The primary reason seems to be the inability of most large firms to determine an accurage stock-out cost. In a given plant the cost associated with a stock shortage of a given item often varies over an extremely wide range. It depends upon the duration of the shortage and a myriad of conditions in the shop which dictate the ease with which workers and facilities can be transferred to other jobs. In most manufacturing operations that are not highly automated, these conditions change from day to day.
2   The second reason is that a number of firms have found that for a majority of production inventory items the cost of a stock-out under most conditions far exceeds the cost of carrying the safety stock. Therefore they simply compute order point and safety stock values on the premise that they cannot afford to run out of stock.
3   A final reason—one that causes all business personnel to view quantitative analytical techniques with a skeptical eye—is the fact that a good deal of clerical and professional time is required to prepare and analyze historical data for each item before the theoretical determination can be made. Such work is currently much more time-consuming for the probability approach than is similar work required in implementing an EOQ system.

It is the authors' opinion that among those firms applying the probability approach to safety stock determination, most applications are of one of two types: (1) formal application of the technique to a very few highly unique and critical items, for which costs of thorough analyses can be justified; and (2) an informal and intuitive application of the concept to those inventory items that clearly produce low stock-out costs relative to their safety stock carrying charges. The concept, considered even in this manner, provides a service to the user by bringing to light the fallacy in carrying a fixed number of weeks' safety stock, or in carrying a safety stock equal to a given percentage of lead time requirements. It is apparent that such policies provide unequal degrees of protection for different items. Each additional unit of safety stock provides less protection, and the protection it does provide is a function of the variability of lead time, the variability of usage, and the size of the individual daily usage.

APPLICATION OF MRP

The bulk of Chapters 10 and 11 has dealt with basic inventory management concepts and their applications in traditional time-based and quantity-based control systems. On page 197 the rationale underlying the unique MRP system was introduced, but not explored in depth. Because MRP represents a major break with the traditional approaches, it is important to consider carefully not only its advantages, but also its limitations and its potential impact on operating policies and practices in purchasing, production support, and supplier organizations, as well as in the firm's own production operation.

Remember at the outset that, although an MRP system can be adapted for use with most inventory items in all types of firms, it is designed to function most effectively in *intermittent* manufacturing operations with *production* inventory items that exhibit *dependent demand* usage characteristics. Most MRP systems in use today are embodied in standard computer software packages developed by computer manufacturers themselves. This situation produces some constraints. Because standardized computer programs are used, modifications to accomodate unique operating situations in a given firm become major factors that must be considered thoroughly and built into the system at the time it is designed for use in that firm. Once the system is established, basic program changes cannot be made easily.

Use of an MRP system has some very fundamental and far-reaching implications for performance of the purchasing and related materials management activities. MRP, in its purest form, is a requirements-oriented system whose objective is to maintain virtually no inventory and to deliver materials to meet the timing requirements of the production schedule. Its major advantage, then, is that it tends to minimize inventory investment and carrying costs. In accomplishing this objective, however, it "gives up" some of the operating advantages provided by inventory buffer stocks. Absence of such buffer stocks mandates that the various operating units, including purchasing, must gear their daily activities more closely to the fluctuating demands of the master production schedule. In short, the system itself focuses on only one element of the total materials cost equation; it does not consider variable acquisition costs or the variability of the cost of purchased materials.

In the case of purchased items, both material and acquisition costs may well be expected to increase under MRP operation. Depending on the item, material and transportation costs frequently are influenced by order quantity, size of shipment, and the degree of flexibility of the delivery requirements imposed on suppliers. In the purchasing department itself, once MRP control is implemented, daily activities become tied more closely to fluctuating *short-term* production requirements. Clerical costs associated with the increased need for external transportation control, receiving, inspection, and accounting paperwork, as well as supplier expediting, obviously go up.

Consequently, if a manager wants to hold down material and acquisition costs, MRP is best suited for the control of purchased materials that exhibit the following characteristics.

1 Materials that can be purchased on long-term contracts or blanket orders and be released for frequent shipment in relatively small quantities

2 Raw materials or "standard" items for which lead time requirements are relatively short and seldom vary appreciably
3 Materials that can be purchased repetitively without requiring much creative purchasing analysis, or for which value analysis, purchasing research, and vendor studies have previously been completed

Proponents claim that to realize major benefits from an MRP system, nearly all production inventory items must be controlled by the system. For items made in the firm's own manufacturing facilities this view is valid. Determination of loading priorities and availability of capacity in the various production centers, for purposes of subsequent production scheduling, is obviously difficult if all demands on the centers are not channeled through the same control system. In the case of purchased items, however, the logic of the argument is less compelling. It appears to the authors that it is possible to use a combination of systems, controlling some items with MRP and others with a conventional quantity-based or time-based system. If tight control and low inventory levels are required for selected high-value items having one or more of the characteristics noted above, it appears that MRP control can be utilized in essentially the same way as a cyclical ordering system can be used. MRP application, of course, should be contingent on favorable results of a *total* cost study.

In the final analysis, desirability and usefulness of the MRP concept in controlling applicable production inventory items depend on a managerial assessment of trade-offs. More specifically, are anticipated savings from reduced inventory carrying costs greater than the potential increases in acquisition costs and operating problems that may be generated by use of the system? Answers to this question will vary from one operating situation to the next. Dr. Joseph Orlicky, an industry consultant with IBM, estimates that MRP had 150 users in 1971 and that by 1975 the number of firms committed to the concept had increased to approximately 700.[6] Although the total is still small when one looks at the whole of American industry, the growth rate is impressive.

RESPONSIBILITY FOR INVENTORY CONTROL

There should be little doubt at this point that the basic responsibility for inventory control lies with top management. The effects of poor inventory management, unfortunately, are not directly visible on the operating statement as a composite cost of inventory management. Nevertheless, in most companies these indirect costs, dispersed and hidden throughout the operating statement, can have a significant influence on profit. Top management should,

---

[6]Joseph Orlicky, *Material Requirements Planning*, McGraw-Hill Book Company, New York, 1975, p. ix.

for this reason, carefully formulate and periodically review the basic policies, plans, and forecasts which constitute the framework within which the daily inventory control operation functions.

In its everyday operational pattern, inventory control should be largely a clerical or computerized operation carried on within a carefully defined and controlled structural framework. This routinization of the daily operation often camouflages the importance of sound management in this area. And not infrequently, it creates a situation in which clerical personnel find themselves making decisions for which they are largely unqualified—decisions which should be made by an analytically oriented manager in a position to comprehend the total operating and cost pictures.

Organizationally speaking, the inventory control function historically has been assigned to either the purchasing department or the production control department, with slightly more firms placing it under the jurisdiction of purchasing. A production inventory is the reservoir which operationally connects these two departments. The production control group draws from the inventory reservoir in its daily routing and scheduling of all work through the manufacturing facilities. Inventory levels at any given time directly influence the effectiveness with which production control can do its job of utilizing production facilities and meeting sales delivery dates.

The purchasing department, on the other hand, feeds the inventory reservoir. Order quantities and resultant frequency of purchases, order points relative to lead time requirements, and the general efficiency with which the inventory control section is run are factors which greatly influence the effectiveness of the total purchasing operation. Prices paid for materials, work load planning, and the degree to which buyers have time to do a good creative job of purchasing are all affected by the inventory control operation.

Viewing the situation from a top management perspective, as it should be viewed, a strong case can be made for assigning inventory control to either purchasing or production control. Actually, the nature of a firm's production operation, its product, and the type of market in which it operates determine the relative weights given to advantages and disadvantages of both approaches in any particular company. An engineering-oriented company producing specialized technical products on a job-shop basis might well choose to emphasize production considerations at the slight expense of purchasing considerations as long as an analysis of total costs justifies such a decision; hence, inventory control may report to the production division. On the other hand, a mass producer of electric motors might well find itself in just the opposite situation and be compelled by relative cost considerations to integrate inventory control with purchasing.

An obvious consideration which is basic to the organization decision is the need for a high degree of coordination between the purchasing and production control departments relative to inventory control policy and operation. This is essential if management hopes to optimize results of the efforts of both groups. This dictate, when added to the fact that department managers occasionally fail to recognize fully the significance of costs outside their own departments, has led an increasing number of companies to adopt some form of the materials management organization. In the interest of coordination and cost control, many firms have organized most, if not all, activities concerned with materials into a single operating department headed by a materials manager. In well over half of the major United States firms today, purchasing and inventory control are included as components of a materials (or materials management) department. More than one-third of these companies also include production control in this same department. Since the topic of organization is discussed in a later chapter, it is sufficient at this point to observe that consolidation of purchasing, inventory control, and production control into a single operating unit offers tremendous operating advantages when viewed from the standpoint of inventory management.

SYNTHESIS

One of the underpinnings of mass-production-type manufacture in a typical American corporation is the concept of standardization of parts and components which are interchangeable among several products or among different models of the same product. In a given firm this generally results in the existence of a sizable inventory of production parts and components compared with a relatively small inventory of finished goods. A production inventory thus serves the function of decoupling the various production and service facilities from each other and from assembly operations. As a rule it is easier to expand and contract assembly operations with variations in sales demand than it is to expand and contract the operations buffered by inventories.

Each inventory item has its own characteristics in terms of cost, usage, unique production and sales features, and dozens of other qualities, which all have a bearing upon how it should be managed. Therefore, each inventory item should be analyzed separately, first determining the item's annual inventory investment and then appraising the stability of its usage. After completing the analysis the object is, of course, to group items with similar qualities and characteristics so a given group can be managed by using a particular inventory control system.

The manager first examines those items that might be controlled using the "flow control" approach, a specialized variation of the cyclical system. This approach produces extremely tight control because of its daily (or at least very frequent) reviews, and it also maintains inventory at a bare minimum. The types of materials to which it is most advantageously applied tend to be:

1   Critical high-value items that generally have very high rates of usage
2   Items that experience a reasonably stable rate of usage

3   Items with the above features that are used in short-cycle production operations

Some items do not possess the above characteristics to an extent permitting flow control, but because of their high values they do require unusually tight control. In such cases fairly low inventory levels can be maintained using the regular cyclical ordering system on a weekly (or very frequent) review basis. Such items are also good candidates for MRP system control.

The bulk of most firms' inventory items do not fit into the two preceding categories. Consequently, as many of these items as possible should be controlled by applying the fixed order quantity system, in an attempt to maximize utilization of personnel and possibly to take advantage of EOQ benefits. The essential characteristics of materials amenable to a fixed order quantity system are:

1   The item must experience a reasonably stable usage.
2   The item should have a lead time which does not exhibit radical variation.
3   The item must be acquired from a supplier who is able to accept irregularly timed and unscheduled orders.

Finally, if an item cannot be handled effectively using one of the preceding approaches, the remaining alternative is to control it with the basic cyclical system, using monthly or more lengthy review periods. Typical items which must be handled this way are:

1   Those exhibiting highly irregular usage and/or lead time
2   Items whose purchases must be scheduled in advance because of various conditions within the suppliers' operations
3   Perhaps items with volatile prices
4   Perhaps a group of items which are all purchased from the same supplier and can be ordered on one purchase order and shipped together

The use of an MRP system is, of course, an alternative to the last two approaches suggested. It functions most effectively when dealing with items characterized by unstable, dependent demand. In the case of items made in the buyer's own shops, use of MRP may be an "all or none" alternative, depending on the firm's ability to prioritize, schedule, and control shop orders if MRP is used in conjunction with another planning system. In the case of purchased items, MRP can be utilized in conjunction with one or both of the traditional inventory systems. It will do the best job of minimizing inventory levels and related investment, but it will also do the poorest job of facilitating effective utilization of purchasing personnel and systematic daily operation of the department.

As companies continue to implement computer control of inventories, one serious disadvantage of the cyclical ordering system becomes minimal. This is the disadvantage (in a manual system) of having to review many more items than those for which action is actually required. In a manual system this is costly. In a computerized system, despite the high cost of computer time, this inefficiency is minimized by the speed of the machine and the side benefits of various periodic management reports. Consequently, in a computer-controlled system numerous items having lead times and usages that are perhaps too variable for efficient fixed order quantity control can be more efficiently handled by a cyclical system.

In conclusion, when determining order quantities an astute manager attempts to apply the EOQ concept, wherever practical, to items exhibiting stable usage and stable unit costs. Likewise, as far as is practical, the progressive manager considers application of the concepts underlying the probability approach to determination of order points and safety stock. This is particularly true when considering critical high-value items.

CONCLUSION

It is becoming increasingly difficult for most companies to control inventories effectively. The reason for this stems from the fact that more and more components going into the typical company's products are being *purchased* as fabricated parts, rather than being fabricated from raw materials in the firm's shops. This means that the number of inventory accounts to be managed is constantly growing. Because of the increasingly technical nature of materials, the number of *dollars* invested in inventory is increasing at an even faster rate than the number of items. Computerization of the total inventory management system holds perhaps the major key to the minimization and effective solution of these growing problems.

Buying the optimal quantity can result only from a good inventory control system, which in turn is achieved only by wise reconciliation of the natural conflict of departmental objectives among a company's major departments. Failure to develop a system that balances these conflicting viewpoints can result in intensive interdepartmental strain. In fact, an inadequate inventory control plan (or the lack of such a plan) is one of the most common causes of departmental misunderstanding. It is not uncommon for departments continually to find fault with each other, when the true culprit is not any department, but inadequacy of the inventory control system itself. It is therefore imperative that management carefully study the ramifications of various approaches to specific inventory problems and adopt policies which in total satisfactorily balance its two major but conflicting objectives: (1) to tie up the minimum possible capital in inventory, and (2) to maintain an efficient continuity of operations in production and in the supporting departments.

FOR DISCUSSION

11-1   In determining a firm's incremental acquisition cost per purchase order, should the salary of the purchasing manager and the senior buyers be included? Explain.

11-2   How might quantity discounts be considered in making a practical EOQ computation in a going concern? Explain in detail.

11-3   Is ABC analysis compatible with the EOQ approach to order-quantity determination? Explain.

11-4   List and discuss the chief limitations of EOQ theory.

11-5   Discuss in some detail how an inventory manager determines the order point and the safety stock for a given material, assuming he does not want to run out of stock.

11-6   What are the basic ideas which underlie the probability approach to the determination of order point and safety stock values? Explain.

11-7   Explain how you would construct a cumulative frequency curve of lead time period usage of a given inventory item.

11-8   Explain further how the curve in question 11-7 might be used in the probability approach to determining order point and safety stock values for a given inventory item.

11-9   Discuss the major problems most firms encounter in using the probability approach to determine order points and safety stocks.

11-10 List and discuss the major advantages and disadvantages of an MRP system.

11-11 Under what conditions can an MRP system be utilized most effectively?

11-12 Who should be responsible for inventory control? Discuss this question from a top management point of view and also from the points of view of various interested operating departments.

11-13 Assume that you have just been hired to develop an inventory system for a company which in the past has given no attention to the management of inventories. Prepare an outline of the approach you would use in attempting to carry out this assignment. Discuss each of the points on your outline in some detail, indicating the information you would need, the problems you would expect to encounter, and any other pertinent factors management would be interested in when evaluating your approach to the problem.

CASES FOR CHAPTER 11

Chapter 12

Purchase Timing

KEY CONCEPTS

Stable and unstable markets
Effect of markets on timing
Policies for purchase timing
  Speculative buying
  Forward buying
  Hand-to-mouth buying
  Buying to current requirements
Timing and inventory management
Guides to business forecasting
  General economic conditions
  Specific markets
Buying practices in fluctuating markets
  Volume timing   ⎫
                     ⎬ Capitalize on market fluctuations
  Dollar budgeting   ⎭
  Time budgeting   ⎫
                     ⎬ Reduce market risk
  Hedging   ⎭

Stated in simplified form, the purchasing department's responsibility is to buy material of the right quality, from the right vendor, for the right price, at the right time, in the right quantity. When purchasing most materials, the last three responsibilities are closely interrelated. The time at which some purchases are made frequently determines the price paid; similarly, the quantity to be purchased at any given time is a direct function of anticipated future purchase timing. In this chapter, the timing of purchases and its effect upon the total materials operation will be investigated.

TIMING AND TYPES OF MARKETS

The importance of timing varies with the types of materials purchased. Or, stating it more precisely, it varies according to the type of market in which materials are purchased. Markets can be grouped into two general categories:

(1) markets in which the factors of supply and price are reasonably stable in the short run, and (2) markets in which supply and price fluctuate substantially, producing a highly unstable short-run situation.

Stable Markets

Materials purchased in stable markets are the multitude of standard, off-the-shelf industrial products, supplies, and hardware (e.g., standard electric motors, pumps, valves, bearings, chemicals, tools, nuts, bolts). In the long run, in a reasonably competitive economy, the general forces of supply and demand tend to determine the price levels at which these standard products will be sold. In conducting daily business, however, a buyer is more concerned with short-run market conditions. And, in the short run, prices of these materials are relatively insensitive to the general forces of supply and demand. In the short run, a buyer can usually do very little to influence suppliers' prices for these materials. An exception is the occasional situation in which a buyer's individual requirements are so great that, through some form of contractual arrangement, he is able to reduce the supplier's production or distribution costs. On this basis he may be able to negotiate with the buyer for a more favorable price.

Nonstandard components and materials, which constitute a substantial portion of most manufacturers' purchases, represent a special situation. Many nonstandard items are bought from numerous comparatively small machine shops, foundries, and similar job-shop producers. Consequently, the supply of these items adjusts fairly quickly to the general level of demand. As far as the buyer is concerned, the result in most cases is a reasonably stable supply situation. Because of the number and the flexibility of suppliers, the price a buyer pays for such materials is determined largely by the effect of his unique demand on the supplier's costs of production.

Unstable Markets

Unstable markets exhibiting substantial short-run fluctuation of the supply and price factors exist for numerous raw materials. Typical examples of such commodities are crude rubber, copper, tin, zinc, lead, scrap iron, burlap, wool, cotton, hides, wheat, flour, and vegetable oils. The supply of such raw materials, domestic and foreign, is frequently influenced by political forces, weather conditions, actions of speculators, and similar unpredictable factors. As a result, the short-run prices of such commodities may be extremely sensitive to the general forces of supply and demand.

In most cases, the market is supplied by a large number of producers, and the buying action is conducted by a large number of relatively small purchasers. This means that the actions of an *individual buyer* have little effect on the equilibrium price in the market. The market price of such commodities often varies substantially from week to week and month to month, as is indicated by recent price charts for several commodities shown in Figure 12-1.

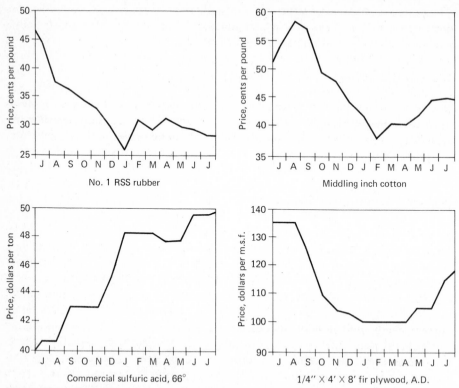

Figure 12-1 Illustration of commodity price movements for selected commodities.

Timing of Purchases

In considering the timing of purchases, buyers are primarily interested in assuring their firms an adequate supply of material and in acquiring the material at the best price consistent with quality and service requirements. As a general rule, timing is not a critical matter from either point of view when the purchase is made in a market which tends toward price stability. There are exceptions, of course. For example, a buyer always tries to anticipate general price increases arising from wage and other cost increases in his suppliers' industries. Likewise he keeps a close eye on the level of general demand for his suppliers' products. If general demand for a particular supplier's product increases sharply, a temporary shortage may develop until demand again tapers off, or until production capacity has increased to satisfy the increased level of demand.

Timing is a much more important matter when a purchase is made in a market which tends to be unstable. Careful observation and analysis of market conditions are essential if buyers hope to satisfy their objectives relative to supply and price. Although they cannot influence the *market price,* they can, by their timing of purchases, control to some extent the *price they pay.* In a highly competitive business, the results of their timing can significantly affect both the competitiveness and profitability of their firms' operation.

In recent years, demand for certain raw materials, and the products derived from them, has tended to increase more rapidly than supply. This phenomenon has frequently produced periodic shortages and an increase in the number of materials markets that are characterized by periodic instability. Expansion of multinational business activity and international purchasing, coupled with the volatility of some foreign political environments, has tended to compound the problem of market instability. Hence, the timing of purchases made in a growing number of these markets has become increasingly important—a situation which will likely continue into the foreseeable future.

POLICIES FOR PURCHASE TIMING

Somewhat apart from the discussion of inventory control decisions in Chapters 10 and 11, the purchasing executive must make a fundamental policy decision concerning the timing of purchases for certain major materials. Basically, he can choose one of two alternatives: (1) purchase according to current requirements, or (2) purchase according to market conditions. If he adopts the first policy, he bases his purchasing schedule strictly on the volume of his firm's current needs, and largely disregards the action of the market in which the purchase is made. This is the more conservative of the two alternatives, and is considered by many companies to be the soundest and when dealing in a market involving price risks. If the manager adopts the second policy, in addition to considering anticipated needs, he bases purchase timing decisions, in part, on the action of the market. In this case he may engage in three types of buying activity: (1) hand-to-mouth buying, (2) forward buying, and (3) speculative buying.

The length of time coverage (number of days' supply) afforded by each of these buying activities is the element which distinguishes one from the other. In business practice, there exists no clear-cut dividing line between these different types of buying. Variations in operating conditions, types of materials used, and lead time requirements among various plants cause purchasing executives to define them slightly differently. Each type of buying activity is discussed in the following sections.

Speculative Buying

Strictly speaking, a speculator is a person who buys an item at one price with the intention of profiting on the transaction by selling it at a higher price. A speculator adds no value to the purchased item and provides no service to customers, beyond that intrinsic in supplying the item itself. This type of purchasing activity has no place in the normal functions of an industrial purchasing department. If a firm wishes to engage in this type of speculation, such activity should be organized and administered apart from the normal purchasing activity.

A second type of speculative buying is conducted by some purchasing departments, and many authorities argue that it is a legitimate function of the purchasing office. This type of buying involves the purchase of material in excess of foreseeable requirements, in anticipation that a need will arise for the material and that the firm will profit by making the purchase at the current price. Opportunities for purchases of this kind arise when a market drops temporarily and the buying firm has sufficient working capital to finance the speculative investment.

Whether or not speculative activity of this kind should fall within the province of the purchasing department appears to depend upon the degree of risk involved. If the risk is substantial, the view taken here is that the activity should be conducted by a high-level staff group outside the purchasing department. As the risk decreases, the activity approaches a legitimate purchasing function. In any case, the final decision should rest with top management. A manufacturing concern is presumably in business to profit from the production and distribution services offered its customers, not from speculation in the materials market.

Forward Buying

Forward buying is the practice of buying materials in a quantity exceeding current requirements, but not beyond actual foreseeable requirements. The distinction between speculative buying and forward buying is that in the latter case, a definite production need for the material exists, while the former case it does not. Even so, the discriminating observer will recognize that most forward buying involves a certain element of speculation as far as price is concerned. While he may have a definite need for the material, the forward purchaser assumes a risk regarding future price fluctuations of the material. When he extends his coverage much beyond a year's requirements, in most industries the buyer has entered the realm of speculative buying. For some materials the time period is less than a year.

There are three major objectives which justify a policy of forward buying:

1 A significant portion of the forward buying done in unstable markets is designed to take advantage of what the buyer believes to be a favorable price situation. He merely attempts to fulfill his known needs at the "best price." Forward buying may also permit a buyer to purchase in quantities sufficiently large to receive volume freight rates which reduce unit costs.

2 Occasionally, when a material is purchased in an unstable market, the purchasing firm may find it advantageous to know material and production costs before beginning manufacturing operations in which the material will be used. Such would be the case when the finished goods are sold under a contract involving a predetermined price.

3 Forward buying reduces the risk of inadequate delivery in the event of

an impending material shortage, possible transportation difficulties, or the possibility of unreliable performance by a supplier.

A forward buying policy also possesses two undesirable features. The first disadvantage is the obvious price risk involved. Intelligent forward buying demands a thorough analysis of numerous market factors. This may be a difficult task. It should not be attempted by an unskilled analyst, nor should it be done in a cursory manner. A possible second disadvantage, which tends to offset possible gains, may appear in the form of added inventory carrying charges and the attendant tie-up of working capital. Any price advantage resulting from a forward purchase must be reduced by these costs to determine the real savings.

Hand-to-Mouth Buying

Hand-to-mouth buying is the practice of buying material to satisfy current operating requirements in quantities smaller than those normally considered economical. As the term indicates, the production operation literally exists on a *hand-to-mouth* supply of materials.

In the case of some high-value materials, it is difficult indeed to draw the line between a hand-to-mouth purchase and a purchase made to satisfy current operating requirements. In general, however, many firms consider a purchase quantity that provides from one to three months' coverage as one which normally satisfies current operating requirements. For purposes of discussion, this rather arbitrary definition will be used. Correspondingly, a hand-to-mouth purchase can then be defined as one which provides operating coverage from a bare minimum up to approximately three or four weeks.

There are three basic reasons for pursuing a hand-to-mouth buying policy:

1 If material is purchased in an unstable market, hand-to-mouth buying saves money when prices are dropping, because the buyer does not accumulate a high-priced inventory. Conversely, it loses money when the market is rising. But when conducted over the duration of the *entire* price cycle, hand-to-mouth buying permits purchasers to buy their total requirement at approximately the average market price for the cycle.
2 In the event that a firm plans an engineering design change which renders some materials obsolete, hand-to-mouth buying prevents inventory losses.
3 Occasionally, firms require additional cash for operating purposes; they may also be forced to reduce the indirect expenses of carrying inventory. These demands can be temporarily satisfied by reducing inventories and using hand-to-mouth buying.

Concomitant disadvantages of hand-to-mouth buying appear in two areas. First, the placement of numerous small orders is more costly in terms of buying and administrative expenses. Second, there is a danger of running out of stock if any one of the activities in the supply chain fails to perform exactly as scheduled.

A Fourth Course of Action

If a purchasing manager decides to follow a policy of buying certain commodities according to market conditions, *most* timing decisions will reflect either hand-to-mouth, forward, or speculative buying. Within this framework, the manager may, in some cases, also have a fourth alternative—that of *buying to current requirements.* The purchase of copper can be used as an illustration. Although copper is purchased primarily in a fluctuating market, during certain periods the price of copper remains fairly stable. During periods of fluctuation, the manager may decide to purchase copper using hand-to-mouth and forward buying techniques, according to his analysis of the market. During periods of relative price stability, however, the wisest course of action may be that of buying to current requirements.

Critique

Because of the many variables involved in any specific buying situation, there is no clear-cut definition of the dividing lines between the individual buying policies discussed. However, in order to place these policies in some concrete time perspective, they have been defined as shown in Figure 12-2.

Viewing the total industrial purchasing scene, buying to current requirements is the policy followed in buying a majority of most firms' important production materials. When dealing in unstable markets, however, the perceptive purchasing executive may employ one of the other policies. It is impossible to generalize about the wisdom of such action. Each case must be studied in detail in the light of its own individual peculiarities and of the validity of market forecasting data available. It is clear that such decisions must be made by an individual who is intimately familiar with the market in question, with general economic conditions, and with his or her own firm's probable needs. Moreover, since forecasting is a highly complex activity, the decision maker must either be skilled in forecasting or have competent personnel available to give assistance.

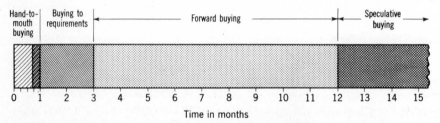

Figure 12-2   Buying policies in approximate relation to time.

TIMING AND BASIC APPROACHES TO INVENTORY MANAGEMENT

At this point, the critical reader is probably attempting to relate the current discussion of buying policies to the concepts of inventory management developed in Chapters 10 and 11.

Fixed Order Quantity System

When materials are controlled by a fixed order quantity system, they are ordered only when the inventory level reaches a predetermined order point. This establishes a general policy regarding the timing of these purchases. If the ABC or economic order quantity concepts are not applied, the order quantity is usually based on a "buying to current requirements" policy. In the event that either ABC or EOQ concepts are applied, it means that many items will be purchased according to current requirements, a sizable number will fall into the forward buying classification, and a few will probably extend into the extreme classifications of hand-to-mouth and speculative buying.

The important point to note is that virtually all materials controlled by a fixed order quantity system are materials purchased in reasonably stable markets. Their prices are extremely stable, supply and lead time requirements are stable, and, further, the buyer's demand for these materials is reasonably certain beyond the current operating period. Managers do not have to worry about cost variations resulting from erratic behavior of these *external* factors. They can therefore select an inventory control system which minimizes the variable *internal* cost factors, i.e., costs of acquiring materials, carrying inventory, and administration. *Thus, for materials purchased in stable markets, the inventory control system is usually established first. Buying policies are determined as a by-product of the inventory control system.*

In contrast with this situation, when materials are purchased in unstable markets, the manager must consider both sets of varying costs—one attributable to external factors and the other attributable to internal factors. As a rule, fluctuations in the external market produce considerably larger cost variations than changes in the internal cost factors. For this reason, *buying policy for materials purchased in unstable markets is usually geared directly to market considerations. The development of an inventory control system is then a by-product of the buying policy selected.* In most cases, some type of cyclical ordering system is used.

Cyclical Ordering System

A cyclical ordering system can be used in controlling materials that are purchased in stable as well as unstable markets. It can also be used for materials that exhibit both stable and unstable internal usage. Moreover, either the ABC concept or the economic order quantity concept can be imposed upon the cyclical system. In this system purchase timing is a function of two interacting factors: (1) length of review periods, and (2) order quantity. For materials whose market and usage are both reasonably stable, buying policy should be established on the basis of internal cost factors in the same manner already discussed in the preceding section for materials controlled under a fixed order quantity system.

For materials exhibiting either unstable usage or unstable market conditions, in most cases buying policy should be more heavily influenced by probable cost fluctuations arising from the variable *external* factors than from the internal factors.

MRP System

When materials are controlled by an MRP system, the system itself dictates hand-to-mouth delivery. The purchase commitment, however, may be made on either a hand-to-mouth or current requirements basis. An MRP system is most easily adapted to materials purchased in a stable market, in which case a purchase commitment made to cover current requirements represents the most appropriate timing policy. For materials purchased in an unstable market, timing policy should be most heavily influenced by cost fluctuations arising from the action of the market.

GUIDES TO BUSINESS FORECASTING

Every professional buyer should have a sound understanding of the significance and the operation of fundamental economic factors influencing the markets in which he deals. Rarely should a buyer without such an understanding employ any buying policy other than that of covering current requirements. Buyers who purchase in unstable markets must also understand the rudiments of business forecasting. The more highly developed their forecasting knowledge and skills, the greater are their chances of making wise buying decisions over the long run. Many large companies maintain a small staff of economists and statisticians whose duties include providing forecasting assistance to the purchasing department.

The purpose of this section is to highlight basic factors and approaches helpful in making an assessment of a market situation. To become familiar with the technical details involved in business forecasting, the reader should consult a standard textbook on the subject.[1]

General Economic Conditions

An assessment of general economic conditions represents the first step in a buyer's attempt to investigate a specific market. Generally speaking, buyers

[1]Two particularly useful references are W. A. Spurr and C. P. Bonini, *Statistical Analysis for Business Decisions,* Richard D. Irwin Inc., Homewood, Ill., 1967, chaps. 18–24; and E. C. Bratt, *Business Forecasting,* McGraw-Hill Book Company, New York, 1958.

can take two approaches: (1) consult professional forecasting services or (2) analyze published business statistics themselves.

A number of professional forecasting services issue regular publications to which a purchasing department can subscribe. Several well-known services are Babson's Statistical Organization and Moody's Investor's Service. Not infrequently, however, the professionals disagree. Consequently, to use these publications effectively one must become a critical reader. Analysis of the facts presented and of the reasoning underlying the forecast frequently will provide more insight into the total situation than will the forecast itself.

Inasmuch as most professional forecasters are not noted for their infallibility, buyers should temper the views of the professionals with their own analysis of available business statistics. Various business statistics are regularly published in numerous magazines and reports, some of which are listed below:

Name of publication	Frequency of publication	Publisher
The Survey of Current Business	Monthly (with weekly supplements)	U.S. Office of Business Economics
Federal Reserve Bulletin	Monthly	U.S. Board of Governors, Federal Reserve System
Dun's Statistical Review	Monthly	Dun & Bradstreet, Inc.
Economic Indicators	Monthly	U.S. Council of Economic Advisers
Barron's Magazine	Weekly	Dow Jones & Co.
Commercial and Financial Chronicle	Weekly	William B. Dana Co.
Business Week	Weekly	McGraw-Hill, Inc.
Wall Street Journal	Daily	Dow Jones & Co.

In addition to these sources, specialized data can often be found in various trade magazines (e.g., *Steel, Railway Age*). Of particular interest to the buyer are selected statistics published semimonthly in *Purchasing* magazine, monthly in *Purchasing World,* and monthly in *The Bulletin of the National Association of Purchasing Management.*[2]

Analysis of the various series of data found in the preceding publications is

[2]The National Association of Purchasing Management (NAPM) publishes monthly in its *Bulletin* a report of its Business Survey Committee. This report includes information on general business conditions, inventories, employment, and buying policy. The report has several distinctive characteristics. First, its information is current. It is prepared by the committee during the week of its publication. Second, it is factual. It represents the consensus of approximately 200 purchasing executives from a carefully selected cross section of American industry. Participating executives report prices they are actually paying, whereas economic services report prices producers and sellers report to them. For competitive reasons, these prices are sometimes reported as prices the producer would like to get, not what he is actually getting. (For example, in the summer of the 1958 recession, while many services reported prices were rising, the NAPM *Bulletin* correctly reported prices were falling.)

The NAPM *Bulletin* is not for sale, but is distributed free to members. The report of its Business Survey Committee, however, is published monthly in the *Wall Street Journal*.

not an easy task because of the many variable factors which influence each series. A good general approach, however, is to select a *group* of business indicators and study each of them individually in an attempt to determine probable activity in the near future, based on current and past activity.

After determining what significant movement is occurring in each of the individual indicators, the analyst then looks at them as a whole. If 80 percent of them indicate a strengthening of business, the probability of this indication's being correct is considerably greater than if it had come from an analysis of only one or two indicators.

In comparing the current activity of any indicator with its past activity, the analyst must be sure that all data have been adjusted for seasonal movements. Some indicators exhibit significant fluctuations during particular seasons of the year. Consequently, except when comparing current data with past data from the same season, comparisons should be made using seasonally adjusted data.

The forecaster's job is considerably easier if he can find business indicators which *lead* the activity he is attempting to forecast. It is not surprising that professional forecasters have studied numerous indicators, attempting to find those that lead general business activity and to determine their reliability. Among the indicators considered to be reasonably reliable are those listed in the accompanying tables.

Indicators which usually lead general business activity are:

Indicator	Source
New orders for durable goods	U.S. Department of Commerce
Commercial building contract awards	F. W. Dodge Corporation
Residential building contract awards	F. W. Dodge Corporation
Average hours worked per week in manufacturing industries	U.S. Bureau of Labor Statistics
Wholesale price index of 28 basic commodities	U.S. Bureau of Labor Statistics
Industrial common stock price index	Dow Jones & Co.
Number of business failures	Dun and Bradstreet, Inc.

Indicators whose activity tends to coincide with general business activity are:

Indicator	Source
Volume of freight-car loadings	Association of American Railroads
Bank debits outside New York City	Federal Reserve Board
Industrial production index	Federal Reserve Board
Unemployment	U.S. Department of Commerce
Corporate profits (quarterly)	U.S. Department of Commerce

Conditions in a Specific Market

Having obtained a feeling for general economic conditions, the buyer next investigates the *specific* market in which he or she is interested. Two approaches can be used: (1) obtain general market information from suppliers and trade literature; and (2) use statistical forecasting techniques.

Suppliers and Trade Literature   Buyers are as close to market activity as any business group. An alert buyer can learn much about conditions in a particular market simply by talking and listening to the suppliers with whom he comes in contact daily. If his contacts are widespread enough, they may provide information which is reasonably representative of the market as a whole.

Trade publications and suppliers' house organs are good sources of information for verifying possible trends which may be detected from discussion with salespeople and other supplier representatives. Information concerning operating problems, wage negotiations, and supply shortages may provide clues which indicate impending price advances or extended lead times. Likewise, information about technological production advancements, methods changes, plant expansions, and the installation of automated equipment may signal a basic capacity increase in the industry which will eventually result in a softening of the market.

No single piece of information is usually of much significance in predicting a market. When a buyer sifts and evaluates information from many sources, however, he is frequently in a position to make a reasonably well informed appraisal concerning future market action.

Statistical Forecasting   Correlation analysis and the analysis of cyclical data represent two statistical techniques commonly used in forecasting short-term movements in relatively unstable markets.

In using *correlation analysis,* the forecaster attempts to find several business indicators whose general pattern of activity correlates closely with the activity of the market to be forecast and also leads the activity of the market to be forecast. If adequate published indicators can be found, the forecaster is in a position to make a statement about future movement of the market in question, based on current movement of the leading indicators. For example, a buyer of major appliances (refrigerators, ranges, etc.) may find it helpful to analyze the residential building contract awards each month. If contract awards correlate closely with subsequent appliance sales, he has an indication of future activity in the appliance market. This information, coupled with a knowledge of industry capacity and inventory, provides an indication of future supply conditions and perhaps of future pricing policies.

As a rule, it is not an easy task to find series of data which lead the market in question and also move in a closely correlated pattern. However, if several leading indicators can be found that correlate even reasonably well, the forecaster has at least some quantitative evidence to use in making the evaluation. Because of the lack of precision found in most leading indicators, however, an analyst must use the correlation technique with the utmost care and judgment.

The *analysis of cyclical* data is a second statistical technique used to provide information helpful in predicting short-run activity in a specific market. The movement of a series of market data plotted over a ten- to fifteen-year period is usually composed of (1) variations caused by long-term secular trend movements, (2) variations stemming from shorter-term cyclical movements, (3) variations attributable to seasonal movements, and (4) minor variations arising from unpredictable irregular factors. The object of this technique is to isolate and study the cyclical movements. It is based on the premise that cyclical movements constitute the major short-run variable of interest to the buyer dealing in a particular market. The following approach is often used by forecasters:

1   Determine whether a seasonal pattern of activity exists in the market; if it does, seasonal indexes are computed. The seasonal influence is then removed by dividing the data by the appropriate index. The data at this point contain trend, cyclical, and irregular influences.
2   Next, the long-term secular trend is determined and removed. The data now contain cyclical and irregular influences.
3   An attempt may be made to eliminate irregular fluctuations if they can be logically analyzed in the light of known events which caused them. However, except for major irregularities, this is often a difficult and arbitrary procedure. At this point the data reflect cyclical and perhaps minor irregular influences and are usually in a form ready for analysis.
4   By drawing a curve through the refined data, the timing, amplitude, and general cyclical pattern of market activity are observable.
5   At this point the analyst has developed historical market data with which similarly adjusted current figures can be compared. The analyst can then attempt to assess the significance of current movements and predict to what extend the market will move up or down in the near future.

The Final Decision

In the course of his daily activities, a buyer concerned with forward buying continually accumulates statistical and qualitative information which he uses in modifying his current appraisal of general economic conditions. Similarly, he accumulates qualitative information helpful in developing a feel for the situation in the particular markets he patronizes. At the same time, he should be charting price and volume data for these markets so that he can periodically make a statistical analysis of each, based on what has happened in the past.

His final decision should be based on a composite evaluation of all the information he has gradually developed. On the one hand, he looks at data coming from statistical forecasts; these data largely reflect past conditions. On the other hand, he looks at qualitative data concerning both general economic conditions and conditions in a specific market; these data reflect, among other things, probable future events which will modify the supply-demand situation currently existing in a given market. He must then weigh this information in the light of his experience with individual suppliers and make his own assessment of subsequent availability and price movements during the time period in question. Because of the skill and time required to make a thorough market analysis, this approach is generally confined to key materials of large dollar value.

BUYING PRACTICES USED IN FLUCTUATING MARKETS

Two basic approaches can be employed when purchasing materials in an unstable market. The objective of the first approach is to reduce the average price paid for the material by using fluctuations of the market to purchasing advantage. The objective of the second approach, contrary to the first, is to reduce the financial risk resulting from market fluctuations.

Using Market Fluctuations to Advantage

By purchasing proportionately more of their material requirements during periods when market prices are below their average level, buyers can capitalize on the fluctuations of the market. Two techniques used in attempting to achieve this objective are (1) deliberate volume timing of purchases, and (2) dollar budgeting of purchases.

Deliberate Volume Timing of Purchases   This technique utilizes a forward buying policy when the market price cycle is on the upswing, and hand-to-mouth buying when the price cycle is on the downswing. The technique is illustrated in the following simplified example:

> Assume that a firm uses a material which is purchased in a market that exhibits small weekly price fluctuations and rather large price swings over a period of one to two years. Usage of the material is approximately 20,000 units per month.
>
> Figure 12-3 shows a smoothed market price curve for the material for a two-year period. Imposed on the curve are the purchases made during the period. Horizontal arrows near the base of the chart indicate the time coverage afforded by each purchase.

Examination of the buying pattern in the example shows that near the trough of the curve, in January, a four months' supply of 80,000 units is purchased. As prices continue to rise, similar purchases are made in May and

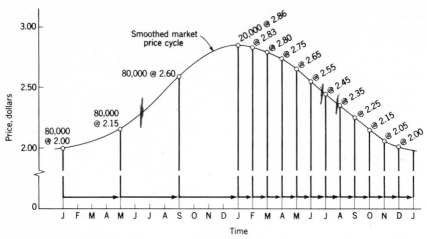

Figure 12-3 Illustration of the deliberate volume-timing technique of purchasing in a fluctuating market.

September. At the peak of the cycle the following January, a one-month supply of 20,000 units is purchased. During the period of price decline, similar monthly purchases are made for the next eleven months.

The net result of this purchasing pattern becomes clear upon further examination. During the period of rising prices three purchases are made. The average unit price for this purchased material is slightly above the May price and clearly below the average market price during the upswing. On the downswing, the average unit price for the material purchased is slightly above the average market price during the downswing. If purchase prices are averaged for the total cycle, then, the unit price paid is significantly below the average market price during the complete cycle. The computations shown in Table 12-1 verify this analysis.

Thus, the average price of purchases made during the upswing of the cycle is $0.22 per unit less than the average price of purchases made on the downswing. Considering the entire cycle, this method of buying yields a price saving of approximately $0.07 per unit, or 2.9 percent, over the average price which would have been paid had *all* purchases during the two-year period been made in quantities of one month's coverage.

Whether other purchases made using this technique yield greater or lesser savings depends upon the magnitude and duration of the price swing and upon timing of the specific purchases. In actuality, the buyer in the example probably would not have made three equal purchases on the upswing and twelve equal purchases on the downswing. Savings clearly would have been greater if purchases made below the average market price on the upswing had been larger and those made above the average market price had been somewhat smaller. But in practice, the difficult problem is that of estimating what the average market price will be and when the peak and the trough of the cycle will be

Table 12-1   Savings from Volume Timing of Purchases

Upswing purchase cost

Date	No. of units	Cost per unit	Total cost
Jan.	80,000	$2.00	$160,000
May	80,000	2.15	172,000
Sept.	80,000	2.60	208,000
	240,000		540,000

Average cost per unit = $540,000/240,000 = $2.25

Downswing purchase cost

Date	No. of units	Cost per unit	Total cost
Jan.	20,000	$2.86	$57,200
Feb.	20,000	2.83	56,600
Mar.	20,000	2.80	56,000
Apr.	20,000	2.75	55,000
May	20,000	2.65	53,000
June	20,000	2.55	51,000
July	20,000	2.45	49,000
Aug.	20,000	2.35	47,000
Sept.	20,000	2.25	45,000
Oct.	20,000	2.15	43,000
Nov.	20,000	2.05	41,000
Dec.	20,000	2.00	40,000
	240,000		593,800

Average cost per unit = $593,800/240,000 = $2.47

Total cycle

Average cost per unit, total cycle = $\dfrac{\$1,133,800}{480,000 \text{ units}}$ = $2.36

$$\text{Savings, total cycle} = \frac{\text{average market price} - \text{average price paid}}{\text{average market price}} \times 100$$

$$= \frac{2.43 - 2.36}{2.43} \times 100$$

$$= 2.9\%$$

reached. Consequently, the purchasing pattern for an actual purchase probably would be much less uniform as a result of the buyer's anticipation of these two critical factors.

The risk involved in using this technique should now be apparent. The less predictable the price movement, the greater the risk becomes. For this reason, the importance of accurate forecasting cannot be overemphasized.

Dollar Budgeting of Purchases   The dollar budgeting technique is similar in concept to the volume timing technique, but in practice it is operated somewhat differently. Dollar budgeting is also based on the idea of buying in large quantities when prices are low and reducing purchase quantities when prices rise. The objective is accomplished in an automatic manner by budgeting a constant number of dollars to be spent for a given material each operating period. The quantity to be purchased each operating period thus varies inversely with market price. (This technique is analogous to the "dollar-cost averaging" method of buying financial securities in the stock market.)

Using the same example as in the preceding section, Figure 12-4 shows a buying pattern determined by the dollar budgeting technique imposed on the same market price curve.

The quantity to be purchased each operating period is determined as follows:

1   First the buyer must estimate the average market price of the current price cycle based on previous forecasting investigations. In this example the average market price is predicted to be $2.50 per unit.
2   Next, the buyer computes approximate usage of the material for the duration of the price cycle. In the example, usage is estimated to be 20,000 units per month throughout the entire cycle.
3   From these data, the buyer computes the number of dollars to be spent each operating period. In this example, for convenience, it is assumed that purchases will be made on a quarterly basis. Thus, the quarterly expenditure for material will be 20,000 units per month $\times$ 3 $\times$ $2.50 per unit = $150,000.
4   As each purchase date arrives, the buyer computes the number of units to purchase as $150,000/current market price per unit. The following results are obtained:

Jan. $\dfrac{\$150,000}{\$2.00/\text{unit}} = 75,000$ units	Jan. $\dfrac{\$150,000}{\$2.86/\text{unit}} = 52,450$ units
Apr. $\dfrac{150,000}{2.09} = 71,770$	Apr. $\dfrac{150,000}{2.75} = 54,545$
July $\dfrac{150,000}{2.35} = 63,830$	July $\dfrac{150,000}{2.45} = 61,224$
Oct. $\dfrac{150,000}{2.70} = 55,550$	Oct. $\dfrac{150,000}{2.15} = 69,800$

Results of the order quantity calculations can be observed in Figure 12-4. During the first, second, third, seventh, and eighth periods, the purchase quantity exceeds period operating requirements, increasing inventory. During the fourth, fifth, and sixth periods, purchase coverage is less than requirements, causing a drain on accumulated inventory. Note also that total purchases over the duration of the cycle exceed operating requirements by 24,169 units. This is the result of overestimating average market price by several cents per unit. Had

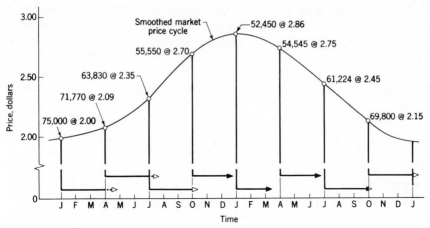

Figure 12-4 Illustration of the dollar-budgeting technique of purchasing in a fluctuating market.

this price been underestimated, total purchases would have been somewhat less than operating requirements.

Purchase Cost, Total Cycle

Date	No. of units	Cost per unit	Total cost	Date	No. of units	Cost per unit	Total cost
Jan.	75,000	$2.00	$150,000	Jan.	52,450	$2.86	$150,000
Apr.	71,770	2.09	150,000	Apr.	54,545	2.75	150,000
July	63,830	2.35	150,000	July	61,224	2.45	150,000
Oct.	55,550	2.70	150,000	Oct.	69,800	2.15	150,000
					504,169		$1,200,000

$$\text{Average cost per unit, total cycle} = \frac{\$1,200,000}{504,169 \text{ units}} = \$2.38$$

$$\text{Savings, total cycle} = \frac{2.43 - 2.38}{2.43} \times 100 = 2.1\%$$

In the example, the average unit price paid during the cycle duration is $0.05 less than average market price, yielding a saving of approximately 2.1 percent. Again, in actual practice, savings might be more or less, depending upon the contour of the price curve and, to some extent, upon the purchase period selected. A one-month period is probably more realistic for most materials.

Generally speaking, this technique is somewhat less practical than the volume timing technique. In the first place, effective use depends upon reasonably accurate estimation of the average market price; this is usually a difficult task if the cycle is erratic or lengthy. This factor introduces risk; not so much from the standpoint of price, however, as from the possibility of developing an over- or undersupply situation. Second, if cycle duration is lengthy, it may also be difficult to estimate future production requirements accurately.

Reducing Market Risk

Using a second and more conservative approach, a buyer may choose *not* to attempt to capitalize on the fluctuations of an unstable market. Markets for some materials behave so erratically that this is often the more prudent course of action. In these situations, a buyer is usually interested in minimizing the risk resulting from price fluctuations. Two techniques that may be used in attempting to accomplish this objective are (1) time budgeting of purchases, and (2) hedging.

Time Budgeting of Purchases   Using this technique buyers can frequently purchase a material over the long run at an average price very close to the average market price existing throughout the cycle. They do this by purchasing small quantities of material over short operating periods of equal length.

Consider again, for a moment, the preceding example of the volume-timing of purchases. Note that on the cycle downswing, 20,000 units of product were purchased every month until prices began to turn up. The result was that the average price paid was near, but somewhat above, the average market price during the downswing. Had the volume of each purchase been reduced to a two-week or a one-week or a single day's coverage, the average price paid would have moved successively closer to the average market price.

If a buyer also makes small equally spaced purchases on the cycle upswing, it will produce the same result, except that the average price paid will be somewhat under the average market price. Consequently, by employing this technique over the duration of the *entire* cycle, a buyer can be reasonably sure of paying an average price which is very close to the average market price. The smaller the purchases and the more frequently they are made, the closer the average price paid will be to the average market price. When purchases are small, this procedure affords good protection even if the price cycle behaves extremely irregularly. The disadvantages of this technique are the high costs of buying, administration, and materials handling, as well as the risk of possible stock-outs.

Hedging   Hedging is a second technique used to minimize the risk associated with fluctuating market prices. However, this technique can be used only in buying materials for which an organized commodity exchange exists.

An organized commodity exchange is a marketplace, usually located in a large city, where a particular commodity is bought and sold in substantial quantities. At many of the exchanges, both "cash" transactions and "futures" transactions take place. A cash transaction, as the words imply, involves a current exchange of cash for the physical commodity. A futures transaction involves a current purchase, at a quoted price, for which the physical commodity will be delivered at a specified date in the future. With the passage of time, the current cash price for a commodity and its futures price often fluctuate together, approximately paralleling one another.[3] It is the futures transaction that is essential in a hedging operation.

If the reader refers to the market section of the *Wall Street Journal,* or a similar financial publication, he will find a listing of the numerous commodity markets. Futures markets operate for many of these commodities, such as cotton, cocoa, coffee, sugar, hides, rubber, wool, and various metals, grains, and oils.

Hedging, for the industrial buyer, is a technique which can provide protection against market price declines during the period when his firm is processing a raw material preparatory to selling it in some form as a finished product. With this financial worry removed, the manufacturer is free to concentrate on normal production and sales activities.

For example, suppose a chocolate manufacturer has signed a contract to sell a large candy manufacturer ten carloads of refined chocolate syrup each month for the next year. The contract stipulates that chocolate syrup will be sold at a price based on the market price of raw cocoa *at the time of delivery of the chocolate syrup.* What happens to the chocolate manufacturer, then, if he buys raw cocoa at $0.26 per pound, and one month later, when he delivers the refined chocolate made from this cocoa, the market price for raw cocoa has fallen to $0.21 per pound? He has to sell the chocolate at a lower price than he had intended to when he purchased the cocoa. Consequently, his profit margin is reduced, or perhaps entirely eliminated. To protect himself against such an occurrence, the chocolate manufacturer might choose to engage in a hedging operation.

His hedge consists of the following market transactions:

1 First, he *buys raw cocoa* in the cash market. At the same time, he *sells a futures contract* in the futures market for the same quantity of raw cocoa, to be delivered shortly after he expects to sell the refined chocolate. (Note that he does not own any cocoa which he could deliver at this future date.)

2 At the time he *sells the refined chocolate,* he also *buys a futures contract for cocoa* to cover the futures contract he originally sold and would soon have to deliver.

---

[3]The most important single factor to the hedger is the difference between the cash price and the futures price, commonly called the "basis." In a completely competitive situation where supply and demand are in balance, the futures price would be expected to exceed the cash price by the total cost of carrying the commodity in storage until the future date. Because supply and demand typically do not remain in balance long for freemarket commodities, the difference between futures and cash prices is influenced considerably by the way buyers evaluate present and anticipated supply-demand conditions. This explains why futures prices exceed cash prices for some commodities at times, and why at other times cash prices exceed futures prices.

The protection offered by the hedge is based on the premise that should raw cocoa cash market prices drop during the manufacturing period (resulting in a reduced selling price for chocolate), futures prices will also drop proportionately. Thus, although the producer takes a loss by selling his chocolate at a reduced price, he makes an approximately equal profit by covering his futures contract at a similarly reduced price. Bear in mind that in this example the selling price of chocolate maintains a constant relationship to the purchase price of raw cocoa. An important prerequisite to the use of hedging requires that the purchaser's finished product be sold in a market where prices move approximately parallel to the prices of the purchased raw material. These concepts are illustrated numerically in the following simplified example. (See Figure 12-5.)

Cash activities

January 15:
  Cash market purchase of 100,000 pounds of raw cocoa at $0.26/pound
$$= 100{,}000 \times \$0.26 = \$26{,}000$$

January 15 to February 15:
  Purchaser incurs manufacturing costs (*including normal profit*) of $0.43/pound
$$= 100{,}000 \times \$0.43 = \$43{,}000$$

February 15:
  Sells refined chocolate (equivalent of 100,000 pounds of cocoa) to customer at $0.64/pound
$$= 100{,}000 \times \$0.64 = \$64{,}000$$

  Net gain on manufacturing activity:
$$= \$64{,}000 - (\$26{,}000 + 43{,}000) = -\$5{,}000$$

Futures market activities

January 15:
  Sells a March futures contract for 100,000 pounds of raw cocoa at $0.275/pound
$$= 100{,}000 \times \$0.275 = \$27{,}500$$

February 15:
  Buys a March futures contract for 100,000 pounds of raw cocoa at $0.225/pound
$$= 100{,}000 \times \$0.225 = \$22{,}500$$
  Net gain on activity in March futures cocoa market:
$$= \$27{,}500 - 22{,}500 = +\$5{,}000$$

Thus, while the chocolate manufacturer lost $5,000 on his manufacturing activity because of the drop in cocoa prices, he was able to offset this loss with a $5,000 gain by hedging in the futures market. Had the price of cocoa risen from January 15 to February 15, the situation would have been reversed. He would have shown an extra profit in his manufacturing operation because of the price increase, but he would have suffered a loss on his futures transaction;

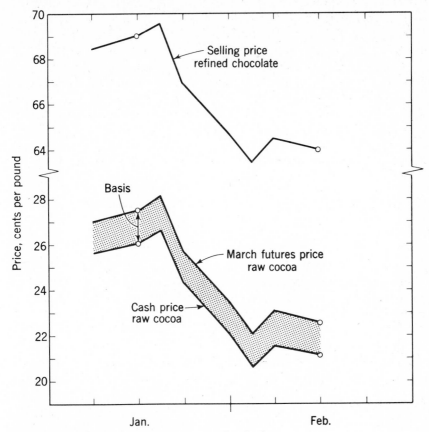

Figure 12-5 Simplified illustration of a perfect hedge.

thus he would still experience no net gain or loss as a result of fluctuating market prices.

The preceding case is a simplified example of a perfect hedge, which, to reiterate, is based on two assumptions:

1 The selling price of the buyer's finished product will move exactly parallel to the cash market price of his major raw material.
2 Futures prices will move exactly parallel to cash market prices.

In practice, these conditions exist only imperfectly. The degree of perfection found in the relationship depends largely upon specific market conditions and upon the characteristics of each specific seller's market. The hedger nearly always gains or loses some money on a hedging transaction because the spread between futures and cash prices and the spread between product selling price and material purchase price both vary with time. However, this by no means invalidates the technique. Provided the relationships show reasonable stability, hedging can in many cases provide good protection against the risk of *wide* price swings. To use hedging successfully, buyers must be skilled enough to estimate the magnitude of possible gain or loss through "basis" variation. Their decision to hedge (or not to hedge) rests on a comparison of this factor with an assessment of the probable magnitude and direction of cash market price fluctuations.

CONCLUSION

During the normal course of activity, the imaginative purchasing executive probably employs each of the various timing policies discussed (hand-to-mouth, forward buying, etc.). The art of properly blending these policies in applying them to the various materials is acquired only through experience as he gains familiarity with specific materials and markets.

When buying in unstable markets, the purchasing executive has an additional opportunity to enhance the profit-making character of his or her department. However, it is not possible to generalize concerning the wisdom of using such techniques as volume timing and dollar budgeting of purchases. The nature of a given market and its behavior under various economic conditions influence the decision in each specific situation. In some cases, use of these techniques is prudent and wholly within the province of a management-oriented purchasing organization. In other cases, it is not. If a purchasing department is to be utilized to its fullest potential, however, it must make every effort to engage in such activity when the calculated risk of doing so is within reasonable limits. All managerial activity involves the making of decisions based on calculated risks. There is no reason to exempt a capable purchasing organization from this sphere of managerial responsibility.

In this, as in all areas of management, performance should be measured and controlled. The basic control should consist of a dollar limitation which is placed on all forward buying activity. Additionally, a buyer's performance when employing any buying technique involving risk can be compared with three norms:

1 Ideal performance
2 The performance level which would have been attained had the activity been conducted in a manner minimizing risk—in this case, the average market price level
3 The performance level which would have been attained had the activity been conducted in any acceptable alternative manner

In few cases is the first criterion realistic. Either of the latter criteria appears to be a reasonable guide for a manager to use in assessing the effectiveness of individual buying personnel. Similarly, either criterion can be used to determine the effectiveness of buying efforts with respect to individual commodities.

FOR DISCUSSION

12-1   What is meant by the terms "stable market" and "unstable market"? List six materials that are purchased in each type of market. Explain why the price of rubber fluctuates substantially, while the price of steel in the short run fluctuates very little.

12-2   Discuss the significance of the timing of purchases. (Include a discussion of the factors which affect the timing of purchases.)

12-3   Should the purchasing department of a shoe manufacturer ever engage in speculative buying? Explain.

12-4   What are the major reasons for forward buying? Discuss each briefly.

12-5   Suppose you are a buyer responsible for purchasing cotton for a textile mill. How would you approach the problem of determining probable activity of the cotton market during the next twelve months? Explain.

12-6   What statistics are helpful in appraising general economic conditions? In what publications are these statistics available? What is meant by "seasonally adjusted" data?

12-7   Discuss several common statistical techniques used in forecasting market activity.

12-8   Explain how the deliberate volume timing purchasing technique works.

12-9   Explain how the dollar budgeting of purchases works.

12-10   Explain how the time budgeting of purchases works.

12-11   Explain how a hedging activity is conducted.

12-12   What are the objectives of each of the preceding purchasing techniques (those in questions 12–8 to 12–11), and under what conditions might each be used?

12-13   What are the advantages and the problems associated with each of the preceding purchasing techniques? Discuss.

12-14   What is the "basis"? Why is it important in a hedging operation?

12-15   In a commodity market, what is the maximum value a futures price will reach relative to its corresponding cash price? Explain.

CASES FOR CHAPTER 12

Too Much, Too Soon, page 663
Springer Manufacturing Company, page 659

Value
Analysis/Engineering

WHAT IS VALUE ANALYSIS?

In American industry today, the alchemist's dream of yesteryear—that of transforming base materials into gold—has in one sense become a reality. Although the end product is not gold per se, modern techniques of value analysis enable the astute materials manager to convert material specifications into substantial dollar savings.

A good tie clasp sells at prices from $5 to $10. What is the function of a tie clasp? It holds a fashionable tie against the wearer's shirt and keeps it out of such things as soup, fans, and machines. It is not necessary, however, to pay even $5 to obtain a device that will perform this function. A paper clip will do the job perfectly. Why, then, do men buy tie clasps? Because tie clasps are more attractive than paper clips. In other words, men buy tie clasps for the esthetic value they possess.

Generally speaking, most things possess two types of value—*esthetic* value and *functional* value. Hence, a buyer must first determine which value is more important in the item he is purchasing. In industry, the vast majority of materials and components are purchased for their functional value. For example, a user has little concern for the esthetic value of internal machine parts that are hidden from view. Industrial value analysis therefore focuses on *function.* The analyst attempts to dertemine how a specific function can be performed effectively at the lowest total cost.

During World War II many critical materials and components were difficult to obtain, and most manufacturers were required to specify numerous substitutions in their design and production activities. Harry Erlicher, then Vice-President of Purchasing for the General Electric Company, observed that many of the required substitutions during this period resulted not only in reduced costs but also in functional product improvement. Consequently, Mr. Erlicher assigned to L. D. Miles the task of developing a systematic approach to the investigation of the function/cost aspect of existing materials specifications. Mr. Miles not only met this challenge successfully, but subsequently pioneered the scientific procurement concept General Electric called "value analysis."

In 1954 the Navy Bureau of Ships adopted a modified version of General Electric's value analysis concept in an attempt to reduce the cost of ships and related equipment. In its application, the Navy directed its efforts primarily at cost avoidance during the initial engineering design stage and called the program "value engineering," even though it embodied the same concepts and techniques as GE's value analysis program. In an operational sense, however, the two terms typically are used synonymously in industry today—only the timing differs. Hence, throughout this book, the term value analysis is used for the most part, and carries the same general conceptual meaning as the term value engineering, except for the practical matter of timing.

The techniques of value analysis represent a potentially powerful set of tools which can be used by management in controlling material costs. The fundamental objective of all value analysis activities is the procurement (or manufacture) of materials representing the "best buy" in terms of the function to be performed. In this sense the idea is not new; it is synonymous with a longstanding objective of good purchasing. The unique feature of current value analysis programs, however, lies in the systematic and thorough approach used in attaining this objective. Only after widespread publicity of Miles's original work did a significant number of manufacturing concerns make a concerted and methodical effort to engineer unnecessary costs out of the parts used in their products.

Much of the current effort devoted to value analysis closely parallels the activity involved in the interdepartmental development of material specifications. The major differences are in the depth of the analysis and in the timing. Interdepartmental development of material specifications, like the Navy's value engineering application, focuses on new specifications developed at the engineering design stage. On the other hand, in most value analysis applications, management attempts to coordinate the talents of personnel in engineering, production, and purchasing in conducting a meticulous investigation which usually leads to improvement of *existing* rather than new specifications.

Although different companies stress different variations of the fundamental idea, two general conceptual tools appear basic to the operation of a value analysis program:

1   Design analysis of the required material
2   Cost analysis of the required material

Design Analysis

The design analysis procedure entails a methodical step-by-step study of all phases of the design of a given item in relation to the function it performs. The philosophy underlying this approach is not concerned with appraisal of any given part per se. Rather, the appraisal focuses on the function which the part, or the larger assembly containing the part, performs. This approach is designed to lead the analyst away from a traditional perspective which views a part as having certain accepted characteristics and configurations. Instead, it encourages the analyst to adopt a broader point of view and to consider whether the part performs the required function both as efficiently and as inexpensively as possible.

One technique many firms use in analyzing component parts of a subassembly is to dismantle, or "explode," the unit and mount each part adjacent to its mating part on a pegboard or a table. The idea is to demonstrate visually the functional relationships of the various parts. Each component can thus be studied as it relates to the performance of the complete unit, rather than as an isolated element. Analysis of each component in this fashion attempts to answer four specific questions:

1   Can any part be eliminated without impairing the operation of the complete unit?
2   Can the design of the part be simplified to reduce its basic cost?
3   Can the design of the part be changed to permit the use of simplified and less costly production methods?
4   Can less expensive but equally satisfactory materials be used in the part?

When viewed in this manner, from the standpoint of overall cost, possibilities for making component design simplifications are frequently more apparent than is possible under the original design conditions. This in no way reflects unfavorably on the work done by the design engineer. The discovery of such potential improvements is simply the product of an analysis with a substantially broader orientation than that possessed by the original designer. An organized value analysis study usually utilizes a number of individuals with different types of background experience and skill impossible to combine in the person of a single designer. Resulting design changes often permit the substitution of standardized production operations for more expensive operations requiring special setup work. In some cases, considering the volume of parts to be produced, an entirely different material or production process turns out to be more efficient than the one originally specified.

The specific manner in which a value analyst approaches the problem of design analysis is a highly creative matter which differs from one analyst to another. Each possesses unique analytical abilities and develops unique patterns of thought. Some companies, however, require analysts to follow several general approaches which are designed to stimulate and organize the analyst's efforts. Those commonly used are (1) the value analysis checklist, (2) the functional cost approach, (3) the use of brainstorming, and (4) the use of suppliers.

The Value Analysis Checklist Most companies develop some type of checklist to systematize the analyst's activity. Literally hundreds of questions and key ideas appear on these lists. Some of them are highly specialized for particular types of products. Illustrative of the more general questions is the following checklist suggested by the National Association of Purchasing Management.[1]

First, determine the *function* of the item, then determine:
1   Can the item be eliminated?
2   If the item is not standard, can a standard item be used?
3   If it is a standard item, does it completely fit the application or is it a misfit?
4   Does the item have greater capacity than required?
5   Can the weight be reduced?
6   Is there a similar item in inventory that could be substituted?
7   Are closer tolerances specified than are necessary?
8   Is unnecessary machining performed on the item?
9   Are unnecessarily fine finishes specified?
10 Is "commercial quality" specified? (Commercial quality is usually most economical.)
11 Can you make the item more cheaply in your plant? If you are making it now, can you buy it for less?
12 Is the item properly classified for shipping purposes to obtain lowest transportation rates?
13 Can cost of packaging be reduced?
14 Are suppliers being asked for suggestions to reduce cost?

In using this and similar checklists, the analyst evaluates the component under investigation with respect to each item on the checklist. When a question

---

[1] *Basic Steps in Value Analysis,* a pamphlet prepared under the chairmanship of Martin S. Erb by the Value-Analysis-Standardization Committee, Reading Association, National Association of Purchasing Management, New York, pp. 4–18.

is found to which the answer is not entirely satisfactory, this becomes a starting point for more detailed investigation. The checklist focuses the analyst's attention on those factors which past experience has proved to be potentially fruitful cost reduction areas.

The Functional Cost Approach   An additional question which appears on some checklists may be worded somthing like this: "What does it cost to perform the function done by this part?" or "Is the importance of the function to be performed commensurate with the cost of performing it?" The idea underlying such a question is extremely broad and actually constitutes a separate approach to value investigation.

As value analysts in a particular industry gain experience, they quickly establish benchmark costs for performing certain functions characteristically encountered in their industry. For example, it may cost approximately X cents to join two pieces of metal of given sizes if the joint is to perform under conditions of mild vibration. On the other hand, it may typically cost approximately Y cents to made the same joint if it must perform under conditions of excessive vibration. In another case, a manufacturer may find that on the average it costs Z dollars to circulate coolant through a totally enclosed motor of a given size, designed to operate under certain conditions.

The important point is this: After analyzing certain types of equipment day after day, good value analysts learn in a general way approximately what it costs to accomplish certain functions. As these kinds of data are accumulated, costs of particular functions appearing on new jobs can be compared with historical benchmarks. If the cost seems excessive, the analyst investigates further to determine the reason. The cost may well be justified due to differences between the new unit and past units on which benchmarks were based. If this does not appear to be the case, the analyst continues to search for a lower-cost method of performing the function.

One important feature of this approach is the idea of comparing current performance with typical past performance. A second and perhaps more important feature of the approach is the concept that the cost of performing a function must be reasonably proportionate to the value of the function itself.

The Use of Brainstorming   A third technique which is sometimes used in conjunction with either of the preceding approaches is called brainstorming.

Brainstorming is a process designed to stimulate creative thinking. A group of people meet for the purpose of generating ideas useful in solving a particular problem. Emphasis is placed on the "free-wheeling" generation of ideas, which are recorded as soon as they are made. During this period no one in the group evaluates any ideas, since the objective at this point is to develop spontaneous and positive ideas. The theory underlying this approach to problem solving recognizes that many ideas spontaneously generated are completely infeasible. However, the theory holds that these ideas act as springboards that trigger thoughts from others in the group that lead to different and often highly feasible ideas. Throughout a period of thirty to sixty minutes as many as several hundred ideas are sometimes recorded. If only several workable ideas emerge from the session, a good chance often exists that one or two can be developed into a satisfactory solution to the problem.

The possible use of this technique in generating basic ideas for solving value analysis problems should be apparent. Once the facts of a problem are thoroughly defined and understood, some companies call upon several representatives from the various interested departments to participate in a brainstorming session. After the session, the resulting ideas are analyzed for practical feasibility and for cost. The promising ideas are subsequently turned over to an analyst for further development.

Some leading practioners and teachers of value analysis advocate that this technique be used as an integral part of the total value analysis procedure.[2] Not every firm with a value analysis program, however, subscribes to wide use of the brainstorming technique. Some feel that in certain cases a greater number of practical ideas can frequently be generated with the expenditure of fewer man-hours by permitting analysts to work independently.

The Use of Suppliers   An increasing number of major manufacturing firms subscribe to the idea that the primary responsibility of the purchasing department is to manage "outside manufacturing"—that is, in a very general way to help plan and to coordinate the relevant manufacturing activities of the firm's suppliers. This fundamental concept implies the development of a continuing long-term relationship with major suppliers. Some buying firms view this situation as a "partnership venture" with the supplier.[3] Functioning in this type of environment, suppliers frequently prove to be extremely valuable assets in a firm's total value analysis effort. One firm, for example, found that a large portion of its value analysis savings came directly from suggestions of suppliers who had been asked to participate in its value analysis program.[4]

Perhaps this fact is not too surprising. After all, as a rule, a supplier knows more about his product and its potential capabilities than do most of his customers. His technical knowledge, combined with broad experience in applying his product to hundreds of operations, frequently qualifies him to participate in most firms' value analysis programs.

A supplier's assistance can be enlisted in two ways: (1) by informal participation, and (2) by participation in a supplier clinic. When using the informal approach, a firm usually has numerous high-priority value analysis

---

[2] For example, in his value analysis workshop conducted at the national conference of the National Association of Purchasing Agents, June 4, 1963, C. W. Doyle, Value Control Coordinator, General Dynamics Corporation, advocated this approach.

[3] The "partnership" concept was strongly recommended by Mr. Donald Lyons, Vice President for Purchasing, Johns Manville Corp., and by Mr. Robert Giczewski, Director of Purchasing for Western Electric Corp., during *Purchasing Forum—'75*, sponsored by the Purchasing Management Association of Denver at Colorado State University, July 21, 1975.

[4] D. W. Dobler, "A Study of Materials Management and Its Problems in Small Manufacturing Businesses," unpublished doctoral dissertation, Stanford University, Stanford, Calif., 1960, p. 128.

projects exhibited on display boards, with all parts completely identified and tagged as to current cost. The purchasing executive makes a point of inviting current and potential suppliers to study informally particular exhibits for the purpose of offering possible cost-reduction suggestions with respect to items each might furnish. If a supplier can provide a lower-cost item that performs satisfactorily, or if he suggests feasible design modifications which permit the use of a lower-cost item, he is rewarded with additional business.

A second approach entails the use of periodic, formally organized supplier clinics. A group of perhaps fifty technical and managerial representatives from suppliers' firms is invited to the purchaser's plant for a one- or two-day clinic. The sessions include an introduction to the purchaser's new products, general company plans and their effects upon suppliers, basic buying policies, and selected major value analysis problems. An important segment of the program is a tour of the buyer's production facilities. Here top-level supplier representatives have an opportunity to see how, where, and why their products are used by the purchaser. Additionally, suppliers can be requested to study specific value analysis exhibits, as is done in the informal approach.

It should be emphasized that solicitation of vendor assistance in a value analysis program is based on the premise that creative vendors will be compensated for their efforts by receiving additional business or by sharing in the cost savings they help generate. Most companies find either approach to supplier participation profitable. In the case of the supplier clinic, improved supplier relations frequently emerge as a bonus benefit.

Cost Analysis

Many manufacturers do not base the selling prices of their products entirely on costs. In some cases, the complexities of multiproduct cost accounting make it virtually impossible to determine the exact cost of producing and marketing a specific product. In other cases, firms may follow a variable-margin pricing policy, whereby the markup on certain types of products is greater than on others. Still other firms may follow the industry leader in establishing product prices.

Whatever the reason, the industrial buyer realizes that many of the prices he pays do not accurately reflect the cost of the product. Moreover, unless the buyer has great bargaining power and substantial knowledge of production costs, in some cases he may not know whether he is paying a fair price. In 1928, C. F. Hirshfeld, then Chief Engineer of the Detroit Edison Company, advocated the practice of cost analysis to assist the purchaser in this quandary.[5] The concept was subsequently adopted widely throughout the automobile industry. Elsewhere it received only sporadic support until the value analysis movement again spotlighted its potential value.

As currently practiced, cost analysis involves the investigation of a

[5]C. F. Hirshfeld, "Engineers in the Purchasing Department," *Mechanical Engineering,* vol. 50, no. 11, pp 848–849, November 1928.

supplier's probable costs of producing a given product. The analyst constructs estimated elemental costs for material, labor, manufacturing overhead, and general overhead. When totaled, these figures represent the theoretical total cost incurred by an efficient producer. An experienced analyst, with the use of wage data, material price lists, and various industry time standards, can determine a total theoretical cost which reasonably approximates the actual cost. To this figure is added a reasonable profit margin. Although the calculated price is not exact, it provides the buyer with a powerful negotiating tool. By using this calculated price as a target, the buyer can place the seller in a position of having to point out any errors in the development of the figure, or else justify his own quoted price with cost data.

Cost analysis is not a tool whose use is confined to value analysis activity. It finds its basic use in negotiating an original price. In recent years, however, it has become an extremely useful adjunct of value analysis, playing two major roles:

1   Cost analysis is conducted for currently purchased items whose costs appear excessive. In such cases, the information developed from cost analysis is used as a basis for further price negotiation with the supplier.
2   Cost analysis also serves as a means of locating high-cost parts which should be subjected to design analysis. During the course of a cost analysis, some high-cost elements are frequently isolated for the first time. Subsequent design analysis often leads to specification and production modifications and ultimately to reduced costs.

The Value Analysis Study

Let us take a moment at this point to draw together the foregoing discussions in a simple procedural model of the typical value analysis study. Although many companies have developed well-organized formal analysis programs, it should be obvious now that value analysis studies can be conducted formally by organized groups, or they can be conducted informally by individuals such as buyers, engineers, production personnel, etc. In either case, the *elements* of the study are the same. Obviously, the depth and breadth of the analysis are influenced by the size and composition of the team making the study. Figure 13-1 illustrates in simplified form the elements of the overall value analysis study.[6]

Examples of Value Analysis

The following examples partially illustrate the types of modifications and savings that value analysis can produce.

[6]This model is based on a discussion of the value engineering job plan in *Value Engineering*, prepared by the Value Engineering Department, Lockheed-Georgia Company, Lockheed Aircraft Corp., pp. 12–15.

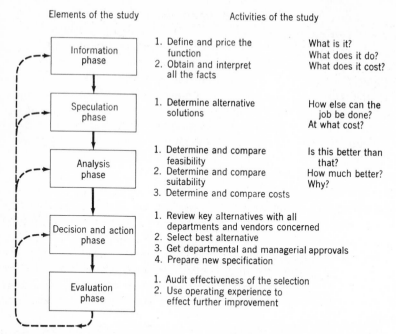

Figure 13-1   A generalized procedural model of the value analysis study.

Production Parts and Assemblies   Upon analyzing the components of a particular small motor, the value analyst for an electric motor manufacturer questioned the construction of the belt guard. The guard, shown in Figure 13-2, was a two-piece assembly made of expanded metal and sheet steel. The expanded metal was blanked to shape and then hand-welded to a metal frame which had also been blanked to shape. After studying the part and its functional requirements, the analyst recommended an equally suitable guard which could be completely produced from sheet metal in a single press-forming operation. The new guard was subsequently adopted and produced for approximately $3 less than the old one, a cost reduction of over 80 percent. Thus, a design change permitted less expensive material as well as less costly production methods to be used, producing an annual saving on this simple item of approximately $10,000.[7]

The part shown in Figure 13-3 illustrates how another very simple design change permitted the realization of a substantial saving in both material and production time. This part, which looks something like a bolt with a flat circular head, is a rotating machine part. The grooved stem must fit precisely with its adjacent parts. The manufacturer's engineers originally specified tolerances of very small dimensions for both the head and the stem. This design specification required that the part be made by maching it from large bar stock the size of the

[7]"General Electric's Program Still Sets the Pace," *Purchasing,* vol. 42, no. 5, p. 72, May 1957.

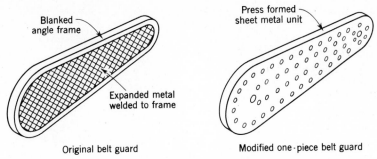

Figure 13-2   A belt guard before and after value analysis.

head. Consequently, a large amount of stock was wasted in the lengthy machining process. An investigation of the part's function revealed that the head tolerances could be loosened considerably without affecting the operation of the part. This meant that a less costly production method could be used. The part could now be produced by first cold-heading a piece of bar stock the size of the smaller stem, and then performing the required finishing machining operations. Cost of the added operation was more than offset by material and time savings.

Figure 13-4 shows how Walter Kidde & Company applied value analysis to a small, relatively simple assembly.[8] Note that cost savings were obtained using three different avenues of approach:

1   Elimination of the dual-mounting screw configuration and the left- and right-hand coupling reduced cost through design simplification.
2   Changing the cover from a brass stamping to molded plastic reduced cost through the use of less expensive material.
3   Substitution of a pulley machined from bar stock for the pulley machined from a casting further reduced cost through the use of less costly manufacturing methods.

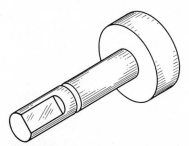

Figure 13-3   A value-analyzed machine part.

[8]Adapted from "Value Analysis in Action, II," *Purchasing*, vol. 54, no. 9, p. 52, May 6, 1963.

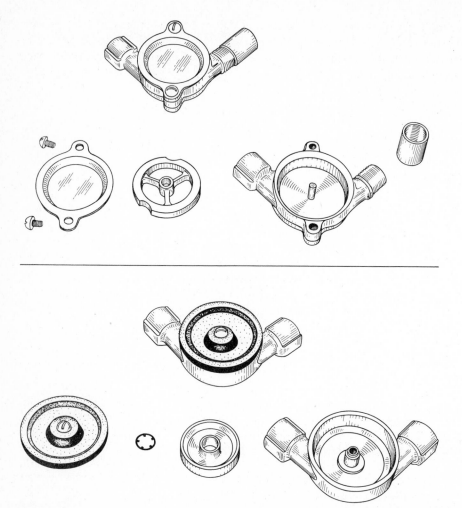

Figure 13-4   A value-analyzed assembly. After going through two cost-reduction studies, the assembly (used to direct steel cable through an angle-top) was value-analyzed with these results: Left- and right-hand coupling was eliminated (lower photo); cover was changed from brass stamping to plastic; special tapping operation was eliminated by using only one screw captive to cover (tapped hole was made concentric with body recess); pulley was made as screw machine piece rather than a machined casting, and made captive to body to ease field installation; only one assembly was used for two sizes of cable; specialty suppliers with high-speed equipment were used. Costs on unit dropped 60 percent; annual savings are $14,000. *(Reproduced with the permission of* Purchasing *magazine.)*

Additional examples of production parts which have been value-analyzed are shown in Figure 13-5.

Packaging   Some firms' products and production operations afford very little opportunity to value-analyze production parts. Consider, for example, a steel mill or a plant producing automobile batteries. Companies of this type use very few production parts. Moreover, the value analysis potential of those parts that are used is restricted because of technical constraints imposed by the requirements of the process or the finished product. Even so, it is amazing to

HOW VALUE ANALYSIS SLASHES COSTS

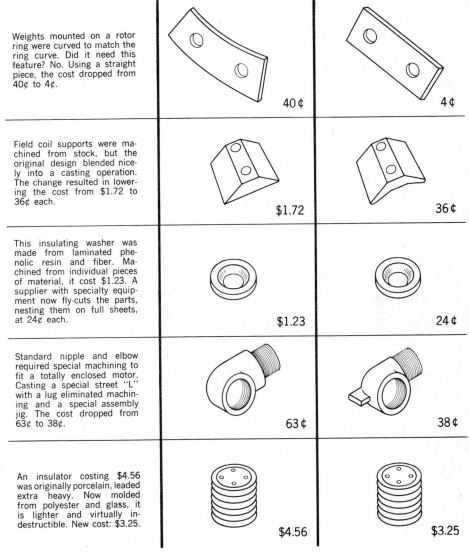

Weights mounted on a rotor ring were curved to match the ring curve. Did it need this feature? No. Using a straight piece, the cost dropped from 40¢ to 4¢.	40 ¢	4 ¢
Field coil supports were machined from stock, but the original design blended nicely into a casting operation. The change resulted in lowering the cost from $1.72 to 36¢ each.	$1.72	36 ¢
This insulating washer was made from laminated phenolic resin and fiber. Machined from individual pieces of material, it cost $1.23. A supplier with specialty equipment now fly-cuts the parts, nesting them on full sheets, at 24¢ each.	$1.23	24 ¢
Standard nipple and elbow required special machining to fit a totally enclosed motor. Casting a special street "L" with a lug eliminated machining and a special assembly jig. The cost dropped from 63¢ to 38¢.	63 ¢	38 ¢
An insulator costing $4.56 was originally porcelain, leaded extra heavy. Now molded from polyester and glass, it is lighter and virtually indestructible. New cost: $3.25.	$4.56	$3.25

Figure 13-5 Examples of value analysis producing spectacular cost reductions. *(Reproduced with the permission of* Business Management *magazine, formerly* Management Methods *magazine.)*

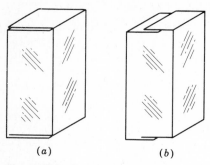

Figure 13-6 Box design before and after value analysis.

see how companies of this type locate problems *outside the production area* which lend themselves to value analysis. The general field of packaging appears to be an extremely fruitful area in many companies.

The nail-making department of one of the United States Steel Corporation's division plants provides a good example. This division originally shipped its nails to customers in wooden kegs. Value analysis of the packaging method produced a seven-part corrugated-cardboard box that did the job better than the keg and saved the firm over $500,000 per year. Subsequent analysis of the seven-part box resulted in the use of a two-part box which saved the company an additional $118,000 per year.[9]

A second very simple example occurred some years ago in a number of companies that packaged their products in light cardboard boxes (e.g., breakfast food, sugar, and soap producers). Originally, on the top and the bottom of the box the closure flaps completely overlapped each other, as in Figure 13-6a. When many firms analyzed the function the box performed, they found that the strength provided by a full overlap was not requied. Consequently, many redesigned their containers to provide only a partial overlap; as shown in Figure 13-6b. Such a simple modification as this in some cases reduced a firm's cardboard requirement by 5 percent, saving hundreds of thousands of dollars because of the large quantity of boxes used.

CONDITIONS CONDUCIVE TO VALUE ANALYSIS

A broad view of American industry reveals vast differences among its thousands of production operations and among the myriad of products manufactured. Because of these differences, value analysis holds considerably more cost-reduction potential for some firms than for others. Generally

[9]*Cost Reduction through Value Analysis: Conference Leader's Guide,* prepared by the Purchasing and Industrial Engineering Departments, Columbia-Geneva Steel Division of United States Steel Corporation, section on Shipping and Handling Applications.

speaking, the factors discussed in the following sections determine the usefulness of the value analysis concept to a particular company.

Design Analysis

Design analysis can be used to greatest advantage under the following conditions:

1   Design analysis is predicated on the assumption that material specifications can be changed. Therefore, the first condition of application requires that a firm's material specifications *not* be tied down rigidly by its products or processes. The greater the flexibility in the specifications, the greater is the potential value of this technique.

2   A design analysis program can be most easily supported when a firm produces, on a recurring basis, a large number of different products. Further, the probability of finding untapped cost-reduction areas is greater when each of these products is made up of a large number of complex components.

3   Greatest benefits accrue when a material is used in large quantities, either by virtue of a high rate of usage in one product or a lesser rate of usage in each of several products.

4   The opportunity to effect significant changes is greater when product designs have not been highly refined by similar analyses during earlier stages of development. Thus, if specifications are originally developed by the use of extensive interdepartmental participation, opportunities to produce savings through subsequent design analysis are reduced. Conversely, when a product design is modified frequently, opportunities for savings usually increase.

5   From the value analyst's point of view, a nonstandard industrial item presents more lucrative possibilities for design change than does a standard item whose design has been refined by its manufacturer.

6   The technique is most applicable to a product on which a single design change can be effected without altering the performance of a large number of other components of the product. In general, this favors mechanical designs as opposed to some electrical and thermodynamic designs in which all parts of the product are intricately interrelated.

7   The chance for profitable design change on a given product increases as the availability of alternative production materials increases.

Cost Analysis

When strong price competition exists among suppliers, competitive forces tend to keep prices in line with costs. Under these conditions, most suppliers have value-analyzed their own products, and cost analysis by the purchaser usually uncovers very few high-cost components. The buyer therefore finds cost analysis most effective when dealing with nonstandard materials or with standard materials whose markets do not exhibit rigid price structures. Likewise, greatest benefits accrue to the buyer when dealing in large quantities of materials.

ORGANIZATION AND ADMINISTRATION OF VALUE ANALYSIS

When a company decides to establish a value analysis program, it must initially answer two questions: (1) Who should be responsible for developing, leading, and controlling the program? (2) What devices should be used to facilitate communication and coordination among the various departments involved in the effort?

There are no "pat" answers to these questions. The more clearly top-level executives comprehend the total value analysis concept, the more clearly they realize that value analysis should really be everybody's business. In one sense, value analysis is a state of mind. Maximum potential can be realized from a value analysis program only if everyone in the plant is value-conscious, and then only if management properly taps these potential resouces. Consequently, while sound organization is essential to the success of a value analysis program, the total effects of organization per se are not as far-reaching as those stemming from the successful creation of value-conscious attitudes among employees.

It is not surprising, then, to find extreme variation among companies in respect to their value analysis organizations. Because of product and operational differences, each firm's need for value analysis differs. Consequently, each company may choose to emphasize certain aspects of value analysis and largely neglect others. This decision may, in turn, influence the subsequent decision concerning administrative policy. If a firm elects to concentrate on cost analysis, for example, there will probably be a strong inclination to center authority for the program in the purchasing department, because of purchasing's extensive role in this activity. On the other hand, if design analysis is the focal point of the program, the engineering department may logically play a more dominant role in its development and promotion.

Studies of current practice indicate that among firms with successful value analysis programs, three basic organizational approaches are most common: (1) the specialized staff approach, (2) the committee approach, and (3) the staff training approach.

Specialized Staff Approach

The most widely used type of value analysis program among large companies is one built around a group of highly trained value analysts who function in a staff capacity. In some situations the analysts constitute a separate staff agency reporting to a general management executive; occasionally, the group reports to a top-level engineering design manager. Most frequently, however, the value analysis staff is attached to the purchasing department.[10]

In some cases purchasing administration of the program can simply be traced to the fact that the purchasing department was largely responsible for the initiating value analysis. Aside from this, two important factors underscore the logic of such an arrangement. First, every buyer must be a value analyst in his or her own right. Formal value analysis is simply an intensified extension of the job every buyer should do when placing an order. Since the basic nature of the value analysis function ties closely with the purchasing function, a close organizational relationship for administrative purposes logically follows. Second, the purchasing department is normally the most cost-conscious department in a company as far as production materials and components are concerned. Its objectivity in evaluating the cost and performance of materials is usually unencumbered with the biases and goal conflicts which often hamper some departments that are totally performance-oriented. It should be noted that this factor also holds equal validity as a supporting argument for the independent status of value analysis; that is, assignment of the function directly to a general management executive.

In any case, in the specialized staff approach, most detailed analyses and recommendations are made by the staff analysts. This requires cooperation and assistance from buyers and design engineers. Any specification changes, however, are normally negotiated by the buyer and the engineer, based on the analyst's recommendations. While the manager of value analysis has no direct authority to enforce any staff recommendations, he does have a certain amount of indirect leverage. This leverage evolves from the fact that the recommendations are made by impartial and qualified analysts who are frequently also experienced engineers. Added to this is the fact that the value analysis staff usually enjoys a close relationship with higher management.

One medium-sized manufacturing plant which uses the specialized staff approach finds that a background in both purchasing *and* engineering or production is ideal for a value analyst. In this firm it takes a new analyst approximately six months to produce cost savings which exceed his salary. After approximately a year, however, the firm reports that the typical value analyst produces about five times his salary in savings annually.

The General Electric Company, where value analysis originated, continues to be one of the acknowledged leaders in the field. In describing the General Electric program, L. D. Miles states that GE has found the specialized staff approach to be the most successful method of operation.[11] Westinghouse Electric Corporation and the Ford Motor Company also conduct similarly designed programs. During the early years of its program's operation, in one year alone, Westinghouse effected savings totaling more than $7.5 million.[12]

[10]For a detailed study, see Stanley S. Miller, "How to Get the Most Out of Value Analysis," *Harvard Business Review*, vol. 33, no. 1, pp. 123–132, January–February 1955.

[11]"General Electric's Program Still Sets the Pace," *op. cit.*, pp. 71–73.

[12]A. H. Phelps, "Westinghouse Cost Reduction," *Purchasing*, vol. 30, no. 6, p. 108, June 1951.

The Committee Approach

A second approach used in both large and small firms involves committee administration of the value analysis program. The committee approach appears to be predominant among smaller firms.

A typical value analysis committee is usually composed of four to eight people, including senior representatives from such areas as production, engineering, purchasing, sales, and general management. The committee may be headed by a senior functional representative, frequently from purchasing or general management, or it may be headed by a full-time "value coordinator" assigned to the top management staff.

In most companies the suggestions for projects to be analyzed may come from any department. One firm requires each department head to submit ten potential value analysis projects to the committee every month. Another firm solicits suggestions from all employees, tying this activity into its broader employee suggestion system, which provides financial awards for those whose suggestions are developed into actual cost-saving operations.

However the suggestions are acquired, the value analysis committee then reviews them and selects the promising ones for detailed analysis. At this point, the committee approach often differs radically from the specialized staff approach. In many committee-administered programs the detailed value analysis work is conducted by operating personnel in the various interested departments. It is not uncommon for a project to be assigned jointly to a buyer, a design engineer, and a production supervisor. Analysis is done individually and jointly until the group is ready to submit the results of its study to the value analysis committee for review and decision.

Use of the committee approach does not prohibit the use of specialized value analysts. Many firms use the committee approach, however, because they consider it to be an ideal way to develop a team approach to value analysis. Consequently, they often prefer to involve as many operating personnel as possible in the detailed analytical work. The obvious bonus benefit accruing from such involvement is that each operating participant becomes a better value analyst, carrying this ability and attitude back to his daily work in design, production, or purchasing.

Thus, the committee acts as the authority and the coordinating medium for the total value analysis program. A potential weakness of this approach, so far as the total program is concerned, sometimes lies in a committee's inability to elicit support and cooperation. Consequently, for successful operation, a committee-oriented program must have a strong chairman and a clear-cut operating procedure which facilitates the enforcement of decisions.

The Staff Training Approach

The philosophy underlying the staff training approach to value analysis grows out of the same idea that leads some companies to involve operating personnel in detailed value analysis work. Companies subscribing to the staff training approach believe that value analysis yields maximum benefits only when it is practiced by all professional operating personnel. Consequently, this approach aims primarily at developing an understanding of the concept and a working knowledge of techniques among all professional personnel responsible for specifying, buying, and using production materials.

The value analysis organization in this case consists of a small staff group which reports to general management. The activities of this group focus on value analysis training. The group is responsible for developing a total value analysis training program and for conducting individual value analysis training sessions. In one company, forty training sessions, each one hour long, are conducted for small groups of all professional operating personnel. An individual's initial training experience is followed up every year or so with a short refresher session in which new techniques and ideas are demonstrated, discussed, and practiced.

Most companies adopting this approach have no staff groups of specialized value analysts. To achieve value analysis cost savings, they rely entirely upon a continuous training program and upon the individual application of this training by professional personnel in all departments.

To supplement the staff training approach and the committee approach, some companies publish a monthly "value analysis bulletin" which has the following goals:

1 To create a cost-conscious attitude on the part of employees and to develop a team spirit in the approach to value analysis.
2 To give examples of successful value analysis projects to employees so they can see "how to do it."
3 To give recognition to individuals who have submitted good ideas.

It is sometimes difficult to obtain employee acceptance of such a publication. If done successfully, however, it can produce outstanding results because it strikes at the heart of all cost-reduction-program goals—*individual* motivation.

Reporting Value Analysis

A company usually wants to determine the magnitude of the savings generated by each dollar it invests in its value analysis program. Such a control measure is clearly valuable to management. Most companies therefore develop a reasonably complete cost-reporting system, either as a part of or independent of the accounting system.

Some companies go even further. They tabulate and publish value analysis savings for each department and each individual. In this way, they attempt to promote the value analysis program and stimulate increased value analysis effort among personnel.

There is considerable disagreement, however, concerning the use of reporting systems which detail departmental or individual savings. While some firms find that publication of such data serves as an effective incentive for its individual employees, others voice contrary opinions. Those opposed maintain that in many cases the credit for a value analysis saving cannot clearly be given to one or even several individuals. They contend that many people usually contribute to the final solution. This view is supported by the fact that some firms have experienced employee dissatisfaction resulting from inequitable recognition and an occasional inflation of savings favoring certain analysts or departments. Nevertheless, it is generally agreed that some form of personal guidance and encouragement is helpful in motivating the individuals involved. This means that the reporting system must provide enough detail to apprise a supervisor of the general acceptability of each individual's value analysis performance.

Preproduction Purchase Analysis

As currently practiced in American industry, value analysis techniques find their greatest usage in programs designed to engineer unnecessary costs out of *existing* products. A growing number of applications are emerging, however, in companies that are concerned primarily with engineering unnecessary costs out of *new products* during the planning and engineering design stages. This latter application is frequently called preproduction purchase analysis or sometimes value engineering, reflecting the original use of the term by the Navy in 1954.

The concept of preproduction purchase analysis finds its widest use in companies that produce a limited number of units of a very expensive product and companies that mass-produce products requiring expensive tooling. In these types of companies, value analysis of an item already in production is often impractical because it is then too late to incorporate changes in the product economically. In manufacturing certain electronic instruments used in missile guidance systems, for example, the production run is often so short that it precludes the effective use of value analysis after production has been initiated. In fact, the Armed Services Procurement Regulations now stipulate that most major procurement contracts must be subjected to value analysis studies prior to initial production. A somewhat different situation that produces similar operating results is found in firms mass-producing major household appliances. For example, in manufacturing the housing panels on appliances such as refrigerators and ranges, once the design is fixed and the dies are purchased, it is normally too costly to change them, even though value analysis studies might subsequently disclose design inefficiencies.

Preproduction purchase analysis utilizes all the techniques of value analysis. In practice, it involves very close liaison work among the purchasing, production, and design engineering departments. This liaison is most frequently accomplished through the use of various purchasing and production coordinators who spend considerable time in the engineering department studying and analyzing engineering drawings as they come off the drafting boards. Once coordinators locate problem areas, value analysis techniques are employed to alleviate them.[13]

CONCLUSION

The value analysis concept possesses tremendous profit-making potential. However, if its potential is to be realized, those responsible for administration of the value analysis program must adopt a broad management viewpoint. This is essential because value analysis is a companywide activity whose purpose is to optimize returns to the *total* business operation.

In practice, the value analysis activity cuts across numerous functional lines of authority. For this reason, the activity must be organized and administered with care. Varying historical traditions and orientations in different firms may well point to different administrative approaches. In its most basic form, the administrative problem becomes one of *human relations and motivation* more than anything else. Management must not overlook the fact that in the long run it is the attitude of the participants that largely determines the degree of success achieved by any program. Value analysis concepts must be *understood, accepted,* and *practiced* by a majority of the various functional specialists involved in the program if such a program is to be fully effective.

FOR DISCUSSION

13-1   Discuss the basic objectives of value analysis.

13-2   What is cost analysis, and how is it used in a value analysis program?

13-3   What is design analysis, and how is it used in a value analysis program?

13-4   "Value analysis is more of a *human relations and motivation* problem than anything else." Discuss this statement.

13-5   Discuss the specific techniques used in design analysis.

13-6   Dismantle a desk stapler (or similar convenient object) and value-analyze it. Before starting, outline the total procedure to be followed, the records to be kept during the process, and the report to be submitted upon completion of the analysis. For all parts, estimate costs as closely as possible, using data in your library and data which may be available from local businesses.

13-7   Experiment with brainstorming by value-analyzing a multipart object in this way. Six people form one group and work jointly, using the

[13]For a complete discussion of this topic see D. W. Dobler, "How to Get Engineers and P.A.'s Together," *Purchasing,* vol. 55, no. 3, pp. 55–58, Aug. 12, 1963.

brainstorming technique, in value-analyzing the object. Six other individuals form a second group. Each of these persons will value-analyze the same object by himself. After finishing, these six individuals will meet and select the best of the individual solutions. Each group should prepare a report on its job. At a class meeting, the two groups will review their activities in detail and present their findings. The class will then compare and evaluate the two approaches. See question 13-6 for procedural details.

13-8   Why are suppliers sometimes helpful in value analysis programs? How can they be used? Does this use of suppliers in any way violate your concept of good business ethics?

13-9   Suppose you are the purchasing agent for a small manufacturing firm. How would you determine whether or not a value analysis program might pay off in your plant? Outline your investigation in step-by-step fashion, and discuss.

13-10   Referring to question 13-9, suppose you thought that value analysis would be profitable. Prepare a proposal to submit to the general manager attempting to convince him that the firm should establish a value analysis program. Detail the type of program you suggest, stating any assumptions you wish to make about the company and its products.

13-11   Discuss the advantages and the disadvantages, as you see them, of each of the organizational approaches used in implementing a value analysis program.

13-12   What, in your opinion, are the advantages of centering a value analysis program in the purchasing department? What are the disadvantages? Discuss.

13-13   What is preproduction purchase analysis? When is it most commonly used? Can any firm employ preproduction purchase analysis? Discuss.

CASES FOR CHAPTER 13

The Perils of Presumption, page 640
Harvey Company, page 621
The Wide, Wide World of Purchasing, page 668

Capital Equipment

The purchase of capital equipment differs substantially from the purchase of production materials and supplies. Such items as power generating equipment, machine tools, specialized production machinery, pumps, chemical processing equipment, conveyors and materials-handling trucks, and office furniture and fixtures are typical examples of capital equipment. For accounting purposes most firms classify these items as noncurrent assets (capitalize them) and depreciate them over the course of their economic lives.

SIGNIFICANT DIFFERENCES IN PROCUREMENT OF CAPITAL EQUIPMENT

Nonrecurring Purchases

The purchase of a particular piece of capital equipment typically occurs only once every five to twenty years. One buyer recently purchased a unique high-temperature electric furnace for use in his company's research and development laboratory. Since the furnace is used only periodically for experimental work, it is very likely that another purchase of this kind of equipment will not be made for the next twenty years.

On the other hand, a few industrial operations require the use of many identical machines in the production process. For example, in petroleum and chemical processing plants, the product is transported by pipeline throughout most of the production operation. This requires dozens, at times hundreds, of similar pumps which vary only in respect to size and minor details of construction. To keep capital expenditures at a fairly uniform level from year to year and to minimize maintenance costs, pumps are often replaced on a continuing basis, rather than all at once. Although it is relatively uncommon, this type of capital equipment purchase assumes some of the characteristics of conventional production purchasing.

A unique feature of many capital equipment purchases is the lead time requirement. While some types of capital equipment are standard off-the-shelf products, most are not. Much production machinery and prime moving equipment is built (at least in part) to operate under specific conditions peculiar to each purchaser's operation. Consequently, manufacturing lead time is usually a matter of months or years. The production of a large steam turbine, for example, may require negotiating and expediting work substantially different from that normally required in production purchasing.

Nature and Size of Expenditure

An expenditure of company funds for capital equipment is an "investment." If wisely purchased and efficiently operated, capital equipment generates profit for its owner. Because it exerts a direct influence on the costs of production, the selection of major capital equipment is a matter of significant concern to top management.

Although capital equipment prices cover a wide range, the purchase of most major equipment involves the expenditure of a substantial sum of money. The purchase price for a piece of equipment, however, is frequently overshadowed in importance by other elements of cost. Since a machine is often used for twenty years, total costs of operation and maintenance during its lifetime may far exceed its initial cost. Hence, the "ultimate" (or total life) cost of a machine, relative to its productivity, is the cost factor of primary importance. Estimating operating and maintenance costs which will be incurred in future years is not easy; frequently these costs vary from year to year. Consequently, discussions involving the choice among several alternative machines often center on the probable accuracy of specific cost estimates.

The timing of many capital purchases often presents a paradoxical situation. Typically, the general supply capabilities of capital equipment producers do not adjust quickly to changes in levels of demand. Thus, because capital equipment purchases are made infrequently and can often be postponed, producers of industrial capital goods frequently find themselves in a "feast or famine" type of business. When a purchaser's business is good, he needs additional production equipment to satisfy his customers' burgeoning sales demands. But because other purchasers are in the same situation, he also finds capital equipment prices rising in a market of short supply. Conversely, when his business is poor and he does not need additional production equipment, capital equipment is in plentiful supply, often at reduced prices.

Considerations in Source Selection

When purchasing capital equipment, selection of a supplier is governed largely by four general considerations: (1) operating characteristics of the equipment, (2) engineering features of the equipment, (3) total economic analysis, and (4) qualitative considerations.

Operating Characteristics This is by far the most influential factor in selecting the supplier for a particular production machine. Once the production and engineering departments clearly establish the function the equipment is to perform, design and operating capability are paramount in selecting the specific machine to be purchased.

Design and operating features for a given type of equipment can differ markedly among the machines available from different vendors. For this reason, the number of vendors willing to produce a machine capable of meeting every aspect of a purchaser's operating requirements is frequently limited. This, of course, is more likely to be the case for specialized equipment than for general-purpose equipment. Nevertheless, this is one reason why a purchasing department usually finds the latitude of its source selection activities considerably constrained in obtaining capital equipment as compared with buying production materials.

Engineering Features Closely related to the equipment's operating characteristics are its engineering features. These features must be compatible with the buyer's existing equipment, process, and plant layout; they must also be in accordance with standards established by state and federal regulatory agencies such as the Occupational Safety and Health Administration and the Environmental Protection Agency. For example, a few major considerations are the following:

1 Specific process capabilities: Is performance compatible with that of existing machines, thus minimizing process coordination problems? Will use of the new machine produce capacity imbalance problems?
2 Physical size and mounting dimensions: Will the machine fit into existing available space satisfactorily? Can it be tied into existing supporting structures without difficulty?
3 Flexibility: Can the equipment be moved and relocated without excessive difficulty?
4 Power requirements: Can existing power supplies be used?
5 Maintenance: Are lubrication fittings and adjusting mechanisms conve-

niently located? Is any special maintenance required that cannot be
handled by existing maintenance programs?

6 Safety features: Does the machine have any unsafe features? Does it
   meet OSHA standards, and is its general safety level comparable with
   that of existing equipment?

7 Pollution characteristics: Does the equipment perform in accordance
   with EPA requirements concerning pollution and contamination dis-
   charge levels?

The general question to be answered is: How does this piece of equipment
fit in with the existing operation? Will many costly modifications be involved in
adapting the equipment to the existing system?

Economic Analysis   After several acceptable machines have been found, a
thorough evaluation of their relative merits is undertaken. The task is a
complicated one. An analysis of each machine must be made, relating its
"ultimate" cost to its productivity. Several measures of profitability can be
used, the payback approach being the most common. However, one of several
more sophisticated discounted cash flow approaches, utilizing the "cost of
capital" concept, should also be used in conjunction with the payback
approach. Such techniques are discussed in a section to follow.

Before the total investigation proceeds too far, a formal proposal justifying the need for additional capital equipment should be prepared for top
management. Although the proposal must consist of more than an economic
analysis, a complete quantitative analysis showing potential profitability of
various courses of action should constitute a major section of such a proposal.

Qualitative Considerations   Certain qualitative factors concerning potential suppliers are important in making any purchase. However, not all the
factors important in selecting sources for production materials weigh as heavily
in selecting sources for capital equipment. Capital equipment purchases do not
normally require a continuing effort by the supplier. Neither does the supplier,
as a rule, become an integral participant in the purchaser's operation. These
conditions tend to dilute the significance of such qualitative factors as location
of the supplier's plant, his financial health, his willingness to render special
services or grant technical cooperation, and so on. These factors are still
meaningful because the purchaser may require installation assistance, replacement parts, and possibly a warranty adjustment. They are, however, considerably less critical than when a continuous stream of production materials is being
purchased. There are exceptions, of course—the purchase of electronic data
processing equipment is a good example.

Qualitative considerations the capital equipment buyer is most concerned
with are those indicating the vendor's ability to produce reliable equipment that
performs in accordance with specifications. This implies the definite need for
an assessment of the vendor's technical and production capabilities. As the

situtation demands, a good buyer uses various approaches in making such an assessment, including plant visits and technical discussions with the vendor's personnel. However, buyers should not overlook the simple technique of investigating a vendor's reputation among present customers. This is an invaluable source of information that is easy to tap.

In the main, qualitative considerations play a secondary role in the selection of a supplier for capital equipment. They are usually considered only in the final analysis, after the primary factors have been weighed. The qualitative factors are the straws that tip the balance one way or the other for the several vendors who rank high on combined technical and economic considerations.

Joint Selection of Equipment

It should now be clear that the final selection of capital equipment should be a joint undertaking by all departments having a legitimate interest in the decision. Because capital equipment represents a long-range investment, a general management executive frequently makes the final purchasing decision. This decision is based on recommendations from representatives of production, process engineering, plant engineering, finance, and purchasing, depanding on the circumstances of the purchase.

Because the production manager is responsible for the efficiency of the total production operation, his views logically carry a great deal of weight. As an additional consideration in the production area, Heinritz and Farrell suggest that the importance of the human element should not be overlooked. They point out that "the head of the department where the equipment is to be used and which is to be charged with expenditure and investment, has an important interest in the decision; the enthusiasm or reluctance of his acceptance may have a direct bearing on the efficiency of the equipment in actual use."[1] Consequently, the production manager may well choose to bring the appropriate foreman into the decision also. The technical contribution to be made by process engineering and plant engineering representatives is clearly an important one, for the reasons previously outlined.

The finance department has three primary interests in capital equipment purchases. First, this department usually administers the firm's capital budget; it is therefore concerned with the allocation of funds for the proposed purchase. If the budget contains a provision for such equipment, all is well; if not, a question arises concerning the priority of this purchase relative to others included in the budget. Second, the finance department has the responsibility of deciding how to finance such purchases. Is enough cash available? Can a long-term loan be negotiated? Might trade credit be used? Will it be necessary to raise the money through equity financing? For large purchases, the answers

---

[1] Stuart Heinritz and P. V. Farrell, *Purchasing Principles and Applications*, Prentice-Hall, Inc., Englewood Cliffs, N.J., 1965, p. 254.

to these questions bear heavily on the final decision. Third, the finance department is concerned with reviewing and evaluating the economic analysis of alternative machines. In some firms, the finance department makes these analyses. In others, they are made by engineering or purchasing. Regardless of which department makes the analysis, the finance department typically administers the total program in connection with its capital budgeting responsibility.

When the economic analysis has been completed, the purchasing department develops and evaluates the previously discussed qualitative factors relevant to this decision. After the supplier is selected, purchasing handles the negotiations and carries out the conventional purchasing responsibilities.

PROCEDURE FOR PURCHASING CAPITAL EQUIPMENT

The major differences between capital equipment purchasing and production purchasing have been pointed out. The entire procedure is now outlined briefly to illustrate how the differences fit into the overall scheme:

1   For more than 75 percent of the capital equipment purchases, recognition of the need arises in the using department. Typically, this is in the production department or in the general management area.
2   Rarely is the need for capital equipment absolute; it can usually be postponed until conditions for purchase become favorable. Although the initial inquiry may come to purchasing in the form of a requisition, more often than not the purpose at this point is only to obtain general information about the equipment in question, not to make an immediate purchase. The purchasing department consequently obtains general sales and operating literature together with approximate price and delivery information.
3   The using department studies the preliminary information obtained by the purchasing department and determines the feasibility of pursuing the matter further.
4   If the decision is affirmative, detailed specifications should be drawn up jointly by the using and engineering departments. Specifications should spell out unambiguously the required performance characteristics, desired operating features, and any unique design characteristics necessitated by the current situation.

   As a rule, the user wants to discuss various aspects of the equipment with manufacturers' representatives. A manufacturer's sales engineer can often provide valuable suggestions regarding application of his equipment in the user's unique situation. Moreover, in the case of complex applications, the sales engineer frequently offers to make an engineering study as a service to the buyer. Sellers in *some industries* customarily make preproposal technical studies as part of their regular sales efforts. Both parties realize that vendor participation is entirely voluntary and the expenses thereof are those normally encountered in stimulating sales. Selling prices in these industries are set so that the revenue from successful efforts covers those situations where prepoposal efforts do not result in eventual sales. In *other industries,* the cost of preproposal studies is *not* covered fully by the selling price.

The purchasing department, therefore, should always be cautious with respect to the acceptance of presale engineering work. The buyer natually wants all the assistance available. But in some cases presale engineering studies can entail excessive costs and place the buyer under obligation to the seller. The wise buyer avoids this kind of obligation. Before accepting a seller's offer for such a study, the buyer should find out how much money is involved and determine whether the offer is consistent with standard practice in the industry. If the costs exceed normal industry practice—yet the study is clearly worthwhile—the buyer should consider contracting and paying for the study itself. By separating the purchase of the study and the purchase of the machine, the buyer ensures against the incurrence of an unwise obligation.

5 When the investigation is complete and specifications are firm, the purchasing department formally requests proposals from the selected vendors. In the event that only one or two vendors can produce an acceptable machine, the buyer might very well choose to negotiate rather than bid the purchase.

6 An economic analysis of the various feasible alternatives is made at this point. The finance department typically makes the analysis, based on operating and technical information provided by the purchasing, engineering, and using departments.

7 The necessary facts are now ready for evaluation by the departments participating in the decision. In small companies, evaluation is frequently an informal affair; in large organizations, a formal committee meeting is the typical method of operation.

The end result of the evaluation should be the preparation of a written report justifying the recommendation that a certain machine be purchased. Included in the report should be a description of where and how the machine will be used, why it is required, and estimated figures for its utilization and its life. Also included should be cost data for the existing operation and for the several alternatives considered. Financial computations concerning the rate of return on investment (or other similar measures of profitability), together with any qualitative comments from the participants, should constitute the last section of the report.

8 The written report is submitted to top management for a decision.

PURCHASING'S ROLE IN CAPITAL EQUIPMENT PROCUREMENT

The purchasing department plays a distinctly different role in the acquisition of capital goods as compared with the acquisition of production materials. In the procurement of capital equipment, the purchasing department acts primarily in a service capacity as a gatherer of information, a contract administrator, and a purchasing consultant to top management.

Source of Information

No department is in a better position than purchasing to keep abreast of the general developments occurring in major equipment industries. Through daily contact with both salespeople and current trade literature, alert buyers pick up considerable information of value to production department managers. In a large company, one buyer may specialize solely in machinery and capital equipment purchasing. A good purchasing department makes a point of regularly relaying information concerning new developments in the capital equipment area to appropriate operating executives.

Once a requisition has been initiated, of course, it is purchasing's responsibility to locate potential suppliers and readily secure the information required by the user in making a preliminary analysis. Suppose the quality control manager, for example, wants to buy an expensive microscope. With his knowledge of the market, the capital equipment buyer can easily obtain the basic data needed for analysis. Moreover, with his vendor contacts, a good buyer should be able to arrange a display of major competitive models so that quality control personnel can test and compare them.

Liaison Service

During investigation of various manufacturers' equipment, an operating manager frequently finds it advantageous to discuss technical details with a machine manufacturer. A customary and sound practice is for the appropriate buyer to act as liaison in arranging meetings between potential suppliers and operating departments. As a rule, the capital equipment buyer should sit in on these meetings, or at least keep informed of significant developments. It is his responsibility to ensure that no premature commitments are made by line departments; likewise, he must at all times be aware of the current status of all negotiations if he is to function effectively in his buying capacity.

Specification Audit and Bids

When specifications are near completion and invitations for bids are to be issued, a good buyer should function in the role of an auditor. Although technical requirements predominate, the buyer should make every effort to see that specifications are written as functionally as possible. Most users hold biases for and against certain types of equipment. It is not unusual to find pilots who want to fly *only* Douglas airplanes, or printers who believe they obtain good work *only* on a Harris press, or machinists who believe *only* Cincinnati machine tools are accurate. Every effort should be made to exclude such personal biases from the specifications. The nature of many capital equipment requirements limits the number of possible suppliers in the first place. This number should not be further reduced by arbitrarily excluding certain types of equipment on the grounds of prejudice alone.

To function effectively as an auditor, the buyer should have participated in most of the technical discussions between the company's line personnel and the various manufacturers, and he *must* have a basic understanding of the significance of the technical problems involved. The buyer's job is still one of "challenging" questionable specification inclusions. His success in this endeavor, however, depends less on his technical knowledge than on his skill in understanding and dealing with people. In the realm of technical matters, he is at a disadvantage because he is dealing with professionals in this area. Therefore, his long-range approach should focus on an attempt to *gain the cooperation of technical managers.* He must *persuade them* that unbiased functional specifications serve the company's best interests.

Once specifications are completed, the buyer is responsible for securing bids from a reasonable number of qualified vendors.

Qualitative Analysis

Some vendors are more qualified than others. The degree of "qualification" should be considered by the committee in deciding which machine to buy. Purchasing normally gathers and analyzes such information for the committee. The buyer must first determine, perhaps with engineering assistance, the level of a vendor's *technical* and *production* capabilities. This is of utmost importance.

Second, the buyer must assess the vendor's *capability* and *willingness* to provide any engineering service required during the installation and start-up of the new equipment. This is an extremely important financial consideration when complex, expensive equipment such as steam turbines, numerically controlled machine tools, etc., is involved. Closely related to this factor is the necessity of training operators. What service is the vendor willing to provide in this area?

Another important consideration is the reliability of a vendor in standing behind his guarantees. Once the equipment is installed, unexpected problems beyond the purchaser's control sometimes add significantly to the total cost of a machine. Finally, what is the vendor's policy on providing replacement parts? When the purchased machine is superseded by a new model, what will be the availability of obsolete parts? The policy of one pump manufacturer, for example, is to produce a small stock of replacement parts for obsolete equipment once every six months. The semiannual production policy of this manufacturer, combined with his low inventory levels, forces some of his customers to carry unreasonably large stocks of major replacement parts. The other costly alternative for the customer is to risk occasional breakdowns, which might leave a machine out of service as long as three or four months, waiting for the next run of parts.

In practice, such considerations frequently play a *minor* role in the initial selection of equipment, only to assume *major* proportions at a later date. It is the purchasing department's responsibility to evaluate potential suppliers in light of these qualitative factors and to bring significant considerations of this kind before the evaluating group for adequate appraisal. After a machine is purchased, the wise buyer works closely with the maintenance department in keeping and interpreting historical records (part by part) of machine performance. Data of this kind are valuable in making similar future analyses.

Bid Tabulation and Economic Analysis

When bids are received, the buyer tabulates them and makes any adjustments necessary so that they can be interpreted on a comparable basis by the group responsible for the final recommendation.

As noted previously, the finance department frequently assumes responsibility for conducting the total profitability study, because administration and control of such activities is clearly related to the capital budgeting function. The view taken here, however, is that once management has selected the types of analysis to be used, the purchasing department might well perform the analysis with greater ease and effectiveness than the finance department. It is a logical extension of the purchasing department's bid analysis activities. As well as being familiar with bid complications, the buyer should also be familiar with some of the technical problems involved in estimates for maintenance and operating costs, through involvement in the preceding technical negotiations. Thus, *one* individual with a fairly complete understanding of the total cost situation could perhaps most effectively prepare, interpret, and present the complete package of price, cost, and profitability data for the group's consideration.

Negotiation, Purchase, and Follow-up

After top management has approved a purchase proposal, the buyer assumes his customary responsibility for negotiating the final price, terms, and delivery date for the machine. The purchase order should be written with particular care, specifying the responsibility of both parties in regard to equipment performance and postsale activities. Performance standards, inspection methods, and guarantee conditions should be clearly stated. Similarly, vendor responsibility for postsale services pertaining to installation, start-up, operator training, maintenance checks, and replacement parts should be clearly written so that there is no question about what is expected.

In the event that the purchase involves a lengthy manufacturing period, a special follow-up and expediting program should be developed. This may call for periodic plant visits and in-process inspection of the work. Responsibility for monitoring this activity often rests with the purchasing department.

Viewing the situation in total, purchasing's role in the acquisition of capital equipment assumes a considerably greater service orientation and a lesser decision-making orientation than is customary in the procurement of standard production materials.

TECHNIQUES OF ECONOMIC ANALYSIS

Texts dealing with management accounting, engineering economy, and finance investigate in minute theoretical detail various approaches to the economic analysis of capital investment alternatives. There are no "pat" answers to questions raised in this area, and noticeable differences of opinion exist among authorities in the field. Therefore, this section does not pursue a detailed investigation of the many approaches to economic analysis. Rather, it introduces the rationale and points out the strengths and weaknesses of several commonly used techniques. The approaches discussed are (1) payback analysis, (2) average rate of return analysis, and (3) time-adjusted rate of return analysis. The purchasing executive and his capital equipment buyers should understand the fundamentals of these techniques whether they are responsible for implementing them in practice or not.

Definition of Terms

In making an economic analysis of a potential capital equipment purchase, the object is to compare alternative proposals on the basis of profitability. The basic alternative against which others are compared is the existing operating situation. Consequently, the techniques discussed involve, in one way or another, a comparison of operating costs and earnings of potential purchases with operating costs and earnings of the existing situation. This comparison is then related to the required capital investment to determine a measure of profitability. Capital equipment purchases are generally made for purposes of expansion or equipment replacement. The basic analytical approach is the same in both cases, although more factors must be considered in the latter case. Therefore, to permit complete investigation, this discussion focuses on replacement purchases. In making cost comparisons, a number of terms are used. Among the most important are the following.

Net Investment (NI)   Net investment is defined as the out-of-pocket cost of the new machine. Basically, it is computed as the difference between the installed cost of the new machine and the realizable disposal value of the old machine which is replaced. In special situations, this figure should be adjusted to reflect any other incremental investment costs or benefits.

Annual Depreciation (AD)   Straight-line depreciation is assumed to simplify computations. It is computed in the conventional accounting manner, i.e., the selling price of the new machine less its estimated salvage value, divided by the length of life used for tax accounting purposes.

Annual Operating Savings (AOS)   Operation of the existing machine involves certain incremental costs such as power costs, operator's wages, material costs, maintenance costs, and so forth. Operation of the new machine involves a similar set of costs. If production rates of the two machines are equal, the *average annual difference* between these two sets of costs is defined as annual operating savings. Presumably, the new machine is more efficient and will incur a lower operating cost than the old machine. Notice that depreciation costs are excluded from this computation because they represent sunk costs, not incremental costs. The net savings figure resulting from this analysis includes all *incremental* costs of operation for both machines and represents a *real* saving which will result if the new machine is purchased.

Determination of cost data in practice may be quite difficult. Based on historical accounting data, average annual operating costs for the old machine can usually be determined with reasonable accuracy. Cost data for the new machine, however, are largely the product of engineering and production estimates. Therefore, depending upon the type of operation and machine involved, cost figures for the new machine may be open to question.

Effective Machine Life (EML)   Effective machine life is defined as the shortest estimated number of years that management believes the machine can be operated competitively. In some situations, effective machine life may be determined by the physical durability of the machine. In other cases, the machine may become noncompetitive because of technological obsolescence long before it wears out. In still other instances, a machine may become unusable before it wears out because of modified product designs or elimination of the product altogether. Whatever the reason that terminates its usefulness, effective machine life is management's best estimate of the number of years the machine can be utilized effectively in the business operation.

Annual Amortization (AA)   This factor is a *conceptual* capital recovery value. During a machine's effective life, management wants to recover from sale of the machine's products enough money to cover the net cost of the machine by the end of its effective life. Annual amortization, therefore, is defined as a conceptual *average* value that must be recovered each year during the machine's effective life to ensure that the machine will in fact pay for itself through its own productivity. Hence, annual amortization is computed as net investment divided by effective machine life.[2]

---

[2]As defined here, amortization differs from depreciation. (Note the specific differences by comparing the methods of calculation.) Hence, it is referred to as a *conceptual* element, as opposed to an actual cost defined by accounting theory. The amortization concept focuses on the assured recovery of all out-of-pocket expenditures associated with an equipment investment.

Payback Analysis

Although it has serious limitations, the payback approach is by far the most commonly used method of analysis in American business today. As its name indicates, the objective of payback analysis is to determine the number of years a machine requires to pay for itself from additional earnings generated by its increased level of operating efficiency.

Before considering the effect of income taxes on earnings produced by the new machine, its payback period can be computed in the following manner.[3]

$$\text{Payback}_{BT} = \frac{\text{net investment}}{\text{annual operating savings}} = \frac{NI}{AOS}$$

Because income taxes are a reality of business life, however, payback computed on an after-tax basis, is considerably more meaningful to most managers. To make this computation, annual operating savings must be expressed on an after-tax basis. One rationale utilized in making this conversion is as follows. Purchase of the new machine results in the generation of AOS that represent additional taxable income. At the same time, however, the new machine provides additional AD that is a tax-deductible operating expense. Hence, the net additional taxable income generated by the new machine is $AOS - AD$. The additional tax liability, then, can be calculated as $(AOS - AD) \times$ (tax rate). Consequently, annual operating savings on an after-tax basis can be expressed as $(AOS) - [(AOS - AD) \times$ (tax rate)]. This factor thus represents the average annual cash flow into the business resulting from the investment, after allowing for taxes. In simplified form, the after-tax payback equation becomes:

$$\text{Payback}_{AT} = \frac{NI}{(AOS) - [(AOS - AD) \times \text{(tax rate)}]}$$

Using the payback approach, two alternative replacement machines can be compared to determine which machine will pay for itself at the earliest date and thereafter produce a clear profit for the company. The primary advantage of the payback approach, other than its basic simplicity, is that it focuses attention on the *cash flow* aspect of a transaction. It shows management the rate at which cash will flow back into the business as a result of a specific capital equipment purchase decision. If rapid obsolescence of equipment is a definite possibility, or if liquidity is a primary corporate concern, the payback approach provides helpful data for evaluating a potential purchase of capital equipment.

On the other hand, the payback approach has three serious shortcomings:

---

[3]The subscript BT denotes "before taxes"; the subscript AT denotes "after taxes."

It should be noted that although this definition of payback is widely used in practice, other slightly different definitions are also in use.

1.   It does not reveal the *total profitability* of an investment. It is basically a break-even approach which fails to consider the investment's earning potential beyond the break-even point. Thus, comparing the profitability of a new-machine investment with other types of investment is difficult. Even comparing the ultimate profitability of two machines having different lives poses problems.

2.   Break-even analysis fails to consider the time value of money. Consequently, it fails to present a true comparative picture when evaluating several machines that have different lives or that produce uneven annual cash flows.

3.   Use of the payback concept requires the establishment of an *arbitrary* cutoff point as an acceptance criterion (e.g., a machine must pay for itself within three, or five, or seven years).

Average Rate of Return Analysis

Computation of the average annual rate of return an investment produces during its lifetime constitutes a second approach sometimes used in evaluating the profitability of alternative capital purchases.

A rate of return fundamentally relates the return from an investment to the value of the investment required to produce the return. Expressed simply as a percentage, this is:

$$\text{Rate of return} = \frac{\text{return}}{\text{investment}} \times 100$$

The average annual rate of return produced by a piece of production equipment can be computed by the following formula:

$$\text{Average annual rate of return}_{BT} = \frac{AOS - AA}{NI/2} \times 100$$

Expressed on an after-tax basis, this becomes:

$$\text{Average annual rate of return}_{AT} = \frac{(AOS) - [(AOS - AD) \times (\text{tax rate})] - (AA)}{NI/2} \times 100$$

Rates of return can be computed in numerous ways, and each has a different meaning. The logic of the preceding computations is as follows. Each year that a piece of capital equipment is operated it produces a certain return; to produce this return each year, a certain outlay of capital is required. Thus, using annual data, a rate of return could be computed for each individual year of the machine's life. Annual rates of return thus computed, however, would vary from year to year for any given machine, because each year the annual investment gets smaller. The business executive therefore may determine that a single *average* annual rate of return computed over the machine's entire life is a more useful figure for decision-making purposes. Consequently, the return in the preceding equations is calculated on the *average* annual basis, and the investment is also calculated as an *average* annual investment during the life of the machine.

The average annual return in the numerator of the equation is made up of two elements: (1) the average annual operating savings, or the average annual cash flow, from the investment, and (2) the annual amortization, or the amount of capital which must be recovered from the machine's earnings each year. The *average return* produced by the machine each year, then, is its cash flow less the amount of capital which must be recovered each year to eventually replace the machine.

The average annual investment in the denominator of the equation is one-half of the net investment, assuming that the machine returns capital to the business in equal annual increments during its life. The amount of capital tied up in the machine during its first year of ownership is the full net investment. As the machine returns capital to the business, each year a progressively smaller amount of the original investment is sunk in the machine, until at the end of the machine's life the capital investment becomes zero. If the investment decline from NI to zero occurs in a linear fashion, the *average* investment during each year of the equipment's life is then $NI/2$.[4]

The discussion to this point has implied (1) that the potential new machine provides equal annual returns throughout its life, and (2) that net investment required to obtain the machine is made in a lump sum at the time the machine is acquired. In practice, these assumptions may not always hold. Even so, the concept underlying the formula is still valid, although the formula must be modified to reflect actual conditions. When the assumptions are not valid, the simplest approach usually is to make computations for return (and/or investment) on an annual basis and then average the annual values before computing the rate of return.

Compared with payback analysis, the great value of using the average annual rate of return is that it provides an indication of profitability over the *total* life of the investment. As long as the investment serves out its estimated effective life, management has a reasonable idea what to expect beyond the break-even point.

Average annual rate of return analysis, however, also posseses one serious shortcoming. It, too, fails to consider the time value of money. It does not reveal the effect that timing of individual annual returns has upon the *true profitability* of the investment. In some cases the average annual rate of return approximates the true rate of return, and in other cases it does not.

When comparing average annual rates of return for two machines, one with an effective life of five years and the other with an effective life of fifteen years, the rates of return are misleading. The return for the fifteen-year machine is considerably overstated relative to that for the five-year machine. This happens because the average rate of return is computed in a manner which compares earnings to be received at future dates with an investment which is made today. The farther into the future earnings are projected in figuring average annual return, the smaller their current values are because of the time

---

[4]The arithmetical explanation of this computation is the same as that for the computation average working inventory discussed in Chapter 10.

factor involved. A dollar owned today can earn interest when invested; if the dollar is not received for fifteen year's, fifteen year's worth of compounded interest is lost. Thus, the *present value* of future earnings is less than the future value by the amount of interest the future earnings could earn if they were available today.

Therefore, the estimated savings during the last ten years of the fifteen-year machine's life are, in effect, smaller dollars than those used in computing the rate of return for the five-year machine. Consequently, if the rate of return for the fifteen-year machine were expressed on a basis comparable with that of the five-year machine, it would be substantially reduced.

When comparing alternative machines whose annual returns are reasonably uniform and whose estimated lives are approximately equal, average annual rate of return analysis provides a reasonably sound basis on which to make a purchasing decision. When investment lives are not the same, the method overstates the return of the longer-lived investments relative to the shorter-lived ones. Similarly, when either machine produces nonuniform annual returns, its average rate of return does not accurately reflect its true profitability. In many situations it is therefore preferable to use a more precise method which recognizes the time value of money.[5]

Time-adjusted Rate of Return Analysis

Various methods can be used to take into consideration the timing of returns, thus permitting direct comparison of the profitability of two machines having different lives, or the profitability of a single machine with a predetermined company standard of acceptance. Professor Robert Anthony of Harvard suggests the use of a very convenient and ingenious approach in which he uses present-value tables to determine directly a "time-adjusted return".[6]

The time-adjusted return is defined, in financial terminology, as the discount rate (interest rate) which equates the *present value* of the future flow of returns from an investment to the value of the investment. It works like this. The discounting procedure reduces a return's future value by the amount of interest earnable between the present date and the future date at which the return will be received. In other words, the future value of a return is reduced, or discounted, to its present value—the value of the return today. This is done for each return to be received at a future date from a given investment, and these present values are then totaled. The time-adjusted rate of return, then, is the specific discount rate which must be applied to the stream of returns to make the stream's *total present value* equal to the present value of the investment (which produces the stream in the first place).

[5]For further discussion of time-value concepts, see J. T. S. Porterfield, *Investment Decisions and Capital Costs*, Prentice-Hall, Inc., Englewood Cliffs, N.J., 1965, pp. 22–23.
[6]For a complete discussion of the approach see Robert N. Anthony, *Management Accounting*, Richard D. Irwin, Inc., Homewood, Ill., 1964, pp. 632–633.

Present-Value Tables A, B, and C The use of Professor Anthony's approach first requires an understanding of present-value Tables A, B, and C in the Appendix. Table A might be called a discount table, or a present-value table. Assuming a given discount or earning rate, the table shows the present value of $1 received at the end of a given number of years in the future. For example, the present value of $1 received five years from now, assuming an earning rate of 10 percent, is $0.621.[7]

Table B, which might be called a cumulative discount, or annuity, table, shows the present value of $1 received *each* year for a given number of years, assuming a given earning rate. For example, the total present value of $1 received each year for five years, assuming an earning rate of 10 percent, is $3.791.[8]

Examination of the formulas in footnotes 7 and 8 reveals that a value in Table B is the cumulative value of corresponding values in Table A. For example, if we assume an earning rate of 10 percent, Table A lists the following present value figures for $1 which is received in 1, 2, 3, 4, and 5 years:

Years hence	Present value
1	$0.909
2	0.826
3	0.751
4	0.683
5	0.621
	$3.790

Thus, the present value of $1 received each year for five years, at 10 percent, is $3.790. Compare this cumulative figure with the corresponding value in Table

[7]Values in this table are computed using the formula:

$$PV = \frac{FV_n}{(1 + i)^n}$$

where PV = present value of a payment to be received in the future
n = number of years in the future after which the payment will be received
i = applicable discount rate
FV_n = future value of the payment to be received at the end of the nth year

[8]Values in this table are computed using the following formula for the present value of a *stream* of future payments:

$$PV = \frac{FV_1}{(1 + i)^1} + \frac{FV_2}{(1 + i)^2} + \frac{FV_3}{(1 + i)^3} + \cdots + \frac{FV_n}{(1 + i)^n}$$

where PV = present value of a stream of future payments
n = number of years
i = applicable discount rate
FV_1 = future value of the payment to be made at the end of the first year
FV_2 = future value of the payment to be made at the end of the second year
FV_n = future value of the payment to be made at the end of the nth year

B. (The error of $0.001 is due to rounding the values in the table to the nearest thousandth of a dollar.) It is evident that Table B can be quite useful in determining the present value of a stream of equal annual savings produced by a piece of production equipment. The present value of a stream of future annual savings is the product of the appropriate Table B value (for $1) multiplied by the value of the annual average saving *(AOS)*.

Table C is quite similar to Table B. It shows the present value of $1 received *each year in twelve equal increments* for a given number of years, assuming a given earning rate. For example, the total present value of $1 received in twelve monthly increments every year for five years at an earning rate of 10 percent is $3.962. Note that this present value is higher than the corresponding figure of $3.791 in Table B. The reason for this is that in Table C the stream of payments is received on a monthly basis rather than on an annual basis as in Table B. Thus, the payments are available for reinvestment at an earlier date, ultimately producing a larger total sum to be discounted. Since in most businesses revenue from sales flows in on a monthly basis, Table C is somewhat more appropriate for practical use than is Table B.

Computational Procedure   Determination of the time-adjusted return using Professor Anthony's approach is quite simple. It requires only computation of the machine's payback period and use of Table C. Further analysis of the values in Tables B and C reveals that these values are in reality the same as payback values.[9] Consequently, once payback has been computed for a machine, the time-adjusted rate of return can be determined by referring to Table C. Enter the correct row in the table by locating the machine's *effective life* in the left column. Proceed across the table to the right until the machine's payback value equals a table value. When the payback value has been located in the table, the time-adjusted rate of return (the discount rate) is read at the top of this column. Interpolation is sometimes required to determine the exact rate of return value.

Illustrative Problem

The following simplified problem illustrates the techniques discussed and the computations involved. Assume that a firm must replace a piece of existing

---

[9] This fact is verified by the following computations.
Using Table C:
   Value in Table C $\times AOS = PV$ of total returns from investment
By definition, at the time-adjusted rate of return,
   PV of total returns from investment $= PV$ of investment $= NI$
Therefore,
   Value in Table C $\times AOS = NI$
or,   Value in Table C $= \dfrac{NI}{AOS}$

Also, Payback $= \dfrac{NI}{AOS}$
Therefore,
   Value in Table C = Payback

Table 14-1   Actual and Estimated Data

Item	Existing equipment	New machine #1	New machine #2
Total initial cost	$10,000	$10,000	$20,000
Equipment life for tax purposes, years	0	5	20
Estimated effective life, years	0	5	15
Undepreciated book value	0	—	—
Estimated salvage value at end of life	0	$1,500	$5,000
Average labor expense per year	$5,500	4,000	3,100
Average material expense per year	7,000	6,600	6,000
Average power expense per year	500	400	1,000
Average maintenance expense per year	1,500	1,000	500
Production capacity, units per hour	22	22	22

equipment and is considering the purchase of two different types of machines for the replacement. Data developed from accounting records and engineering estimates are shown in Table 14-1. Profitability computations are shown in Table 14-2.

A summary of the evaluation data substantiates several significant facts discussed previously (see Table 14-3). Notice that the payback figure fails to indicate relative profitability of the two machines. This could be dangerously misleading if a firm operated under the policy of rejecting all capital purchase requests that did not pay for themselves in five years. Notice also how, because of the time factor, the average annual rate of return overstates the profitability of the twenty-year machine compared with that of the five-year machine.

Critique

Computations involved in the three techniques discussed are reasonably straightforward and easy to perform. It must be emphasized, however, that the elements included in the basic factors of computation (effective life, incremental operating expenses, etc.) are much less easily determined and should be analyzed very carefully. The analysis must always include *all* factors which result in the incurrence of a real incremental cost or a real incremental gain due to making a particular decision. Several factors commonly encountered in practice are noted below.

If a new machine operates at an increased production rate, resultant incremental earnings must necessarily be included in the annual operating savings computation. In some instances, disposal of an existing machine may bring in more or less money than the value at which it is carried on the books, producing a capital gain or a capital loss. Taxes must be paid on the capital gain, and a tax benefit may accrue from the capital loss. These incremental figures should be considered in computing net investment. In still other cases, an existing machine may have a substantial book value when it is replaced with a new machine. In this instance a firm may forfeit a nontaxable depreciation allowance. In figuring the annual tax liability for the new machine for analytical

Table 14-2 Profitability Computations

Machine #1	Machine #2
$AOS = \$(5,500 + 7,000 + 500 + 1,500) - (4,000 + 6,600 + 400 + 1,000) = \$2,500$	$AOS = \$(5,500 + 7,000 + 500 + 1,500) - (3,100 + 6,000 + 1,000 + 500) = \$3,900$
$NI = \$10,000 - 0 = \$10,000$	$NI = \$20,000 - 0 = \$20,000$
$AD = \dfrac{\$10,000 - 1,500}{5} = \$1,700$	$AD = \dfrac{\$20,000 - 5,000}{20} = \$750$
$AA = \dfrac{\$10,000}{5} = \$2,000$	$AA = \dfrac{\$20,000}{15} = 1,333$
$Payback_{BT} = \dfrac{10,000}{2,500} = 4.0$ years	$Payback_{BT} = \dfrac{20,000}{3,900} = 5.1$ years
$Payback_{AT} = \dfrac{10,000}{(2,500) - [(2,500 - 1,700) \times (0.52)]} = 4.8$ years	$Payback_{AT} = \dfrac{20,000}{(3,900) - [(3,900 - 750) \times (0.52)]} = 8.8$ years
Av. annual rate of return$_{BT}$ $= \dfrac{2,500 - 2,000}{10,000/2} = 10\%$	Av. annual rate of return$_{BT}$ $= \dfrac{3,900 - 1,333}{20,000/2} = 25.7\%$
Av. annual rate of return$_{AT}$ $= \dfrac{(2,500) - [(2,500 - 1,700) \times (0.52)] - (2,000)}{10,000/2} = 1.7\%$	Av. annual rate of return$_{AT}$ $= \dfrac{(3,900) - [(3,900 - 750) \times (0.52)] - (1,333)}{20,000/2} = 9.3\%$
From Table C (see Appendix): Time-adjusted return$_{BT}$ = 9.5% Time-adjusted return$_{AT}$ = 1.5%	From Table C (see Appendix): Time-adjusted return$_{BT}$ = 20% Time-adjusted return$_{AT}$ = 8%

Table 14-3   Summary of Evaluation Data

Profitability measurement	Machine #1	Machine #2
Payback$_{BT}$	4.0 years	5.1 years
Av. annual rate of return$_{BT}$	10.0 percent	25.7 percent
Time-adjusted rate of return$_{BT}$	9.5 percent	20.0 percent
Payback$_{AT}$	4.8 years	8.8 years
Av. annual rate of return$_{AT}$	1.7 percent	9.3 percent
Time-adjusted rate of return$_{AT}$	1.5 percent	8.0 percent

purposes, it should be reduced by the amount of the forfeited tax liability. *Net, or incremental, costs and savings are those that are relevant in making equipment replacement decisions.* The accuracy with which such factors are analyzed determines in part the validity of the final computed data.

In summary, both payback and some type of rate of return calculation, preferably one recognizing the time value of money, have a place in the total analysis. The former is useful in evaluating a potential purchase in light of a firm's liquidity position. The latter is useful in giving a more complete picture of the total profitability of various alternatives. Several other good techniques have not been mentioned in this discussion. Notable among these are the net present value method, the net terminal value technique, and the MAPI approach (which is available from the Machinery and Allied Products Institute). The reader interested in a sophisticated treatment of the topic should review the source material cited.[10]

USED EQUIPMENT

A buyer is by no means restricted to the purchase of new capital equipment. Purchases of used machinery, in fact, constitute an important percentage of total machinery sales.

Reasons for Purchasing Used Equipment

A purchaser may contemplate buying used equipment for several reasons. First, the cost of used machinery is substantially less than that of new equipment. Analysis of payback or rate of return may well reveal that a piece of used equipment is a better buy than a new machine. Even if this is not the

---

[10]Robert N. Anthony, *Management Accounting*, Richard D. Irwin, Inc., Homewood, Ill., 1964, chap. 19; R. Lindsay and A. Sametz, *Financial Management*, Richard D. Irwin, Inc., Homewood, Ill., 1967, chaps. 10–15; George Terborgh, *Business Investment Management*, Machinery and Allied Products Institute, 1967; and J. T. S. Porterfield, *Investment Decisions and Capital Costs*, Prentice-Hall, Inc., Englewood Cliffs, N.J., 1965.

case, a firm's financial position may dictate the purchase of a lower-priced machine. Second, used equipment is frequently more quickly available than new equipment. In some situations, availability may override all other considerations.

A third and very common reason for the purchase of used equipment is that used equipment adequately satisfies the purchaser's need, in which case there is no point in buying new equipment. In cases where operating requirements are not severe, a used machine in sound operating condition frequently provides economical service for many years. In the event that equipment is needed for standby or peak-capacity operation, or for use on a short-lived project, more often than not used equipment satisfies the need adequately.

The Used Equipment Market

Used equipment becomes available for purchase for a number of legitimate reasons. When a firm buys a new machine, it frequently disposes of its old one. Although the old machine may be obsolete relative to the original owner's needs, it is often completely adequate for the needs of many potential buyers. If a firm extensively modifies its product design or its total production process, it may be advantageous to obtain more specialized production equipment. Finally, some used equipment becomes available because the owner lost a particular contract or has discontinued operation altogether.

Whatever the reason, a great deal of used equipment is available and is commonly purchased from one of four sources: (1) used equipment dealers, (2) directly from the owner, (3) brokers, and (4) auctions. The majority of purchases are made from used equipment dealers who specialize in buying, overhauling, and marketing certain types of equipment. Dealers are usually located in large industrial areas, and, as a rule, they periodically advertise the major equipment available.

Used equipment dealers sell two types of machines—"reconditioned" machines and "rebuilt" machines. Generally speaking, reconditioned machines carry a dealer guarantee and sell for approximately 40 to 50 percent of the price of a similar new machine. The machine has usually been cleaned and painted; broken and severely worn parts have been replaced; and the machine has been tested under power. A rebuilt machine typically carries a more inclusive dealer warranty and sells for perhaps 50 to 70 percent of a new machine's price. A rebuilt machine has usually been completely dismantled and built up from the base. All worn and broken parts have been replaced; wearing surfaces have been reground and realigned; the machine has been reassembled to hold original tolerances; and it has been tested under power.

Some owners prefer to sell their used equipment directly to the next user because they feel they can realize a higher price than they can by selling to a dealer. Some buyers also prefer this arrangement. It permits them to see the machine in operation and learn something about its usage history before making the purchasing decision.

Brokers sometimes liquidate large segments of the equipment of a complete plant. Occasionally, an industrial supply house or a manufacturer's agent will act as a broker for a good customer by helping him dispose of an odd piece of equipment which has a limited sales market.

Auctions represent still another source of used equipment. Generally speaking, buying at auction is somewhat more risky than the other supply sources because auctioned machines usually carry no warranty, and rarely is it possible to have the machine demonstrated. In some cases, however, machines can be purchased at auction via video tape, which permits the buyer to see the machine operating in a distant plant.

Cautions in Purchasing Used Equipment

It is difficult to determine the true condition of a used machine and to estimate the type and length of service it will provide. For this reason it is wise to have one buyer specialize in used equipment. Moreover, it is virtually essential to enlist the cooperation of an experienced production or maintenance specialist in appraising used equipment. It is always sound practice to check the reputation of a used equipment supplier and to "shop around," inspecting several machines before making a purchase. Whenever possible, a machine should be observed under power through a complete operating cycle. Finally, a prospective buyer should determine the age of a machine. If not available in the seller's records, the age of a machine can be traced through the manufacturer simply by serial number identification. The combined knowledge of age and usage history is a key guide in predicting the future performance of a used machine.

In preparing a purchase order for used capital equipment, care must be taken to include all essential data. In addition to an adequate description of the machine, an order should specify the accessories included, warranty provisions, services to be performed before shipment, and financing as well as shipping terms.

Generally speaking, sellers do not provide service for used equipment after the purchase. All transportation, handling, installation, and start-up costs, as well as risks, are usually borne by the purchaser.

LEASED EQUIPMENT

In addition to the possibilities of purchasing new or used capital equipment to fulfill his requirements, a buyer has a third alternative, that of *leasing* the equipment. In recent years leasing has become a popular method of acquiring the use of industrial equipment. Today, nearly half of our large corporations lease some of their equipment. Generally accepted reasons underlying this trend appear to be the heavy demand for capital, high corporate tax rates, and the fact that in an inflationary economy depreciation sometimes fails to produce sufficient funds to replace all the capital equipment that needs replacing.

Short-term leasing agreements are common for such equipment as automobiles, construction equipment, and small tools and mechanical devices. For many short-term projects, leasing is the most practical way to obtain the use of specialized tools for which a firm has no further need after completion of the project.

More important, however, is the consideration of major production equipment which can be leased for perhaps five to eight years. The most noteworthy advantages in leasing this type of equipment center on financial considerations.

Factors Favoring Leasing

The major advantage of leasing production equipment stems from the fact that leasing replaces a large capital outlay with much smaller, regularly spaced payments. This frees working capital for use in meeting expanded operating expenses or for additional investment.

A second and sometimes questionable benefit is the claim that leasing acts as a financial hedge against rising prices. Those who hold this view, however, fail to point out that fixed lease payments are an added burden during a deflationary period. Nevertheless, if the value of the dollar *does* shrink during the lease period, leasing (like debt financing) enables a firm to contract for the use of an asset with today's dollars and pay for it with cheaper dollars tomorrow. The important point to consider in assessing this situation, however, is the *total* "real" cost to the lessee. Any gain accruing to the lessee is at the same time a loss to the lessor. The lessor can protect himself against such a loss merely by setting the payments high enough to cover it. Thus, whether leasing really gives the buyer a hedge against inflation depends entirely on how the lease payments in each specific case are computed.

A third and certainly questionable reason for leasing centers on advantages in reporting company financial conditions to the firm's external publics. Leasing provides a popular, and *legally* acceptable, method of distorting a company's true debt condition in reports to stockholders and other external investors. Notations of many lease agreements are excluded from external financial statements or are reflected inconspicuously in footnotes to the statements. Consequently, the company's debt picture presented in this manner may appear considerably more favorable than it would under other alternative financing arrangements.

Finally, in some cases, leasing reduces the income tax burden. As long as lease payments exceed the value of allowable depreciation (were the asset owned), an additional "tax shield" is provided. The amount of taxable income is reduced by the difference between lease expense payments and allowable depreciation expenses. Some lease contracts, however, call for extremely low payments during the last few years. When this type of payment schedule prevails, the tax burden is simply deferred until the latter years. Further, the law views certain lease contracts as nothing more than disguised conditional sales contracts, in which case lease payments exceeding normal depreciation are not allowable as operating expense charges. In most cases, though, where the lease agreement is conventional in terms of the basis and timing of rental payments and where the conditions of any ultimate purchase are well established in advance, lease payments are generally approved as normal expense items. However, since the tax benefit is questionable in some cases, a buyer should obtain legal interpretation of a lease agreement before accepting it.

Two nonfinancial benefits frequently accrue from leasing capital equipment. The first is a substantially reduced risk of equipment obsolescence. In some industries, notably those using electronic devices, equipment is technologically obsoleted within a few years. When leasing such things as data processing equipment, for example, an arrangement can usually be made with the manufacturer to have leased equipment updated or replaced with a current model. In a competitive business this may well be an important reason for leasing equipment. The buyer must bear in mind, however, that lease payments for such equipment usually reflect the obsolescence risk. A second nonfinancial benefit stems from the fact that some lease contracts provide for maintenance of the equipment by the lessor. In the case of complex equipment requiring highly specialized maintenance skill, this can become a benefit of major importance. Even for such mundane things as automobiles and trucks, much managerial time can often be saved by passing related administrative burdens to a leasing company.

Factors Weighing against Leasing

As a general rule, the primary disadvantage of leasing is its cost. Interest rates are typically higher on leases than on direct loans. This is understandable, because in addition to covering financing charges, the lessor must also bear all the risks associated with ownership (including obsolescence and inflation risks). The typical lease runs for three-quarters of the equipment's estimated useful life, and monthly fees total approximately 120 to 135 percent of the purchase price.

A second disadvantage arises from the fact that the lessor retains control of the equipment. This loss of ownership usually places some restrictions on the manner in which the equipment is operated; it also requires that the lessee allow the lessor access to the equipment for inspection and maintenance. There are usually times when such control by the lessor creates inconveniences for the lessee. Closely related to this is the possibility that the lessee may have his purchasing prerogatives constrained in respect to the purchase of operating supplies for the leased equipment. A lessor normally desires to have the equipment operated with his own supplies. In the event that use of other manufacturers' supplies could conceivably impair the machine's performance, the lessor usually agress to such an arrangement.

In the final analysis, the decision to lease or buy should first be based on an evaluation of the relative costs and returns of alternative financing methods. Details involved in the computation vary from one situation to the next, depending upon numerous conditions within any particular firm. For this reason, each situation must be studied individually. The cost evaluation should then be considered in light of the existing qualitative factors before making the final decision.

FOR DISCUSSION

14-1   Explain how capital equipment purchases differ from purchases of production materials and supplies.

14-2   Discuss the role the purchasing department plays in capital equipment purchasing.

14-3   Discuss the major factors in selecting a source from which to purchase capital equipment.

14-4   What qualitative considerations relative to supplier capabilities are important in capital equipment purchasing? Compare these qualitative considerations with those important in production purchasing.

14-5   Explain the concepts underlying (1) payback analysis, (2) average annual rate of return analysis, and (3) time-adjusted rate of return analysis.

14-6   Why is a *total* economic analysis of alternative machines important in purchasing capital equipment?

14-7   What are the strengths and weaknesses of payback analysis? Of average annual rate of return analysis?

14-8   Define and show how to compute the following terms:
   a   Net investment required by a machine
   b   Annual operating savings produced by a machine
   c   Effective machine life
   d   Annual amortization for a machine
   What is the difference between the straight-line depreciation and annual amortization concepts?

14-9   Discuss the reasons why a company might want to purchase a used machine rather than a new machine.

14-10   What risks are involved in purchasing used equipment? Discuss.

14-11   Is economic analysis applicable in evaluating a used machine compared with a new machine? Discuss.

14-12   Discuss the advantages and disadvantages of leasing capital equipment.

CASES FOR CHAPTER 14

A Problem of Power, page 644
Winsmore Laboratory, page 669

Make or Buy

A purchasing department is responsible for investigating all potential suppliers and for placing the order with the supplier which will, in the long run, provide a satisfactory product at the lowest cost to the company. Among the potential suppliers that should be considered is the buyer's own firm. In some cases a company may be able to make a required component more economically than it can buy it. On the other hand, historical production-policy decisions may at times require a company to make certain parts that it could buy more effectively from outside suppliers. Deciding whether a part should be purchased or manufactured is known in industry as the *make-or-buy* problem.

A firm's objective is to arrive at make-or-buy decisions whose composite effect maximizes the utilization of its productive, managerial, and financial capabilities. Unfortunately, studies indicate that surprisingly few firms (large or small) give adequate objective study to their make-or-buy problems.

HOW MAKE-OR-BUY INVESTIGATIONS ORIGINATE

In a going concern, past managerial decisions establish the current operating pattern. This pattern dictates that some parts and components of the company's products will be made internally and that others will be purchased from outside suppliers. Within a particular operational pattern, make-or-buy investigations can originate in one of several ways.

The development of a new product and the substantial modification of an old one are typical situations requiring make-or-buy investigations. Every major part of the new product should be studied in advance of actual production. Careful analysis of a complete set of part requirements *prior* to pressing production demands is more effective than subsequent piecemeal analysis in obtaining optimum use of the firm's resources. For this reason, progressive firms include make-or-buy analysis as an integral part of their new product development procedures.

Unsatisfactory supplier performance for parts originally purchased is a second situation that gives rise to make-or-buy investigations. Less than desirable performance may occur for several reasons. It may stem from the supplier's inability to perform certain complex production operations satisfactorily, or from unstable quality performance. Often it results from poor service or from unreasonable price increases. Sometimes a firm's value analysis program uncovers a purchased part whose cost is disproportionate to its value. The possibility of making such parts should be investigated, as well as the possibilities of improving the present supplier's performance or finding a more efficient supplier.

Periods of significant sales growth or sales decline also generate situations that initiate make-or-buy analyses. Reduced sales result in reduced production activity, leaving plant facilities and workers idle. When this happens, management quite naturally attempts to bring into its own shops work previously performed by outside suppliers. During periods of rising sales, management seeks external assistance in satisfying the production demands made on its limited facilities. During such periods, make-or-buy analysis of individual parts discloses the parts which are most profitable to make within the company and those whose production should be left with outside suppliers.

TYPES OF MAKE-OR-BUY INVESTIGATIONS

Make-or-buy problems, when viewed in a broad sense, can be grouped in two general categories. The first category includes parts for which the using firm currently possesses the necessary major production potential. With only a *small* capital outlay for tooling and minor equipment, the firm can make each of these parts. The second category includes parts which the using firm cannot produce in its existing operations without making a sizable additional investment in tooling and facilities.

Investigation of problems in the second category extends far beyond the traditional make-or-buy analysis. Any "make" alternative requiring a significant capital investment becomes a matter of basic product determination, because it is directly related to long-range company objectives and financial plans. This second type of problem, therefore, calls for top management consideration, including extensive economic analysis of the type discussed in Chapter 14. Specifically, the investment required for production equipment to make the item and the savings produced by the decision must be expressed in the form of a net return to the business. This net return must be evaluated in terms of the risk involved and in the light of possible returns obtainable from alternative investments.

The make-or-buy problem requiring only a nominal expenditure of funds in the event of a "make" decision is the type most commonly encountered by materials and production managers. A decision of this type is important insofar as effective allocation of the firm's resources is concerned; however, its effect on the firm's future is less far-reaching than in the case of a decision requiring a major capital investment. Although the decision requiring a nominal expenditure of funds does not require *direct* top management participation, it does require coordinated study by several operating departments. Top management's responsibility is to develop an operating procedure which provides for the pooling of information from all departments affected by the decision. In other words, management should ensure that the decision is made after full consideration of all relevant facts.

FACTORS INFLUENCING MAKE-OR-BUY DECISIONS

Two factors stand out above all others when considering the make-or-buy question. These paramount considerations are *cost* and *availability of production capacity*. A good make-or-buy decision, nevertheless, requires the evaluation of many less tangible factors, in addition to the two basic factors. Several extensive surveys reveal that the following considerations influence firms to "make" or "buy" the parts used in assembling their finished products.

Considerations Which Favor Making the Part
1 Cost considerations (less expensive to make the part)
2 Desire to integrate plant operations
3 Productive use of excess plant capacity to help absorb fixed overhead
4 Need to exert direct control over production and/or quality
5 Design secrecy required
6 Unreliable suppliers
7 Desire to maintain a stable work force (in periods of declining sales)

Considerations Which Favor Buying the Part
1 Suppliers' research and specialized know-how
2 Cost considerations (less expensive to buy the part)
3 Small volume requirements
4 Limited production facilities

5   Desire to maintain a stable work force (in periods of rising sales)
6   Desire to maintain a multiple-source policy
7   Indirect managerial control considerations

Cost Considerations

In some cases cost considerations indicate that a part should be made in-house, and in others they reveal that it should be purchased externally. Cost is obviously important, yet no other factor is subject to more varied interpretation and to greater misunderstanding.

A make-or-buy cost analysis involves a determination of the cost to make an item and a comparison of this cost with the cost to buy it. The following checklist provides a summary of major elements which should be included in a make-or-buy cost estimate.

To Make
1   Delivered raw material costs
2   Direct labor costs[1]
3   Incremental factory overhead costs
4   Incremental managerial costs
5   Incremental purchasing costs
6   Incremental inventory carrying costs
7   Incremental costs of capital

To Buy
1   Purchase price of the part
2   Transportation costs
3   Receiving and inspection costs[1]

To see the comparative cost picture clearly, however, the analyst must carefully evaluate these costs, considering the effects of time and the ramifications of the production capacity situation existing in the user's plant.

The Time Factor   Costs can be computed on either a short-term or a long-term basis. Short-term calculations tend to focus on direct measurable costs. As such, they frequently understate tooling costs and overlook such indirect material costs as those incurred in storage, purchasing, inspection, and similar activities. Moreover, a short-term cost analysis fails to consider the probable future changes in the relative costs of labor, materials, transportation, and so on. It thus becomes clear that, in comparing the costs to make and to buy, the long-term view is the correct one. Cost figures must include all relevant costs, direct and indirect, and they must reflect the effect of anticipated cost changes.

---

[1]It is assumed that all inspection costs associated with the "make" operation are included in the direct labor costs.

Since it is difficult to predict future cost levels, *estimated average* cost figures for the total time period in question are generally used. Even though an estimate of future costs cannot be completely accurate, the following example illustrates its value.

Suppose the user of a particular stamped part develops permanent excess capacity in his general-purpose press department. He subsequently decides to make the stamped part which he had previously purchased from a specialized metalworking firm. Because this enables him to reactivate several otherwise useless presses, his additional cost to make the item is less than the cost to buy it. However, he finds that the labor segment of *his* total cost is much higher than the labor segment of his automated supplier's cost. Should labor costs continue to rise more rapidly than do the other costs of production, the user's cost advantage in making the part may soon disappear. Thus, an estimate of future cost behavior can prevent a "make" decision that might well prove unprofitable in the future.

The Capacity Factor   When the cost to make a part is computed, the determination of relevant overhead costs poses a difficult problem. The root of the problem lies in the user's *capacity utilization factor.* As is true in most managerial cost analyses, the costs relevant to a make-or-buy decision are the *incremental costs.* In this case, *incremental costs are those costs which would not be incurred if the part were purchased outside.* The overhead problem centers on the fact that the *incremental overhead* costs vary from time to time, depending upon the extent to which production facilities are utilized by existing products.

For example, assume that an automobile engine manufacturer currently buys his piston pins from a distant machine shop. For various reasons, the engine producer now decides that he wants to make the piston pins in his own shop. Investigation reveals that his machine shop is loaded to capacity with existing work and will remain in that condition throughout the foreseeable future. If the firm decides to make its own piston pins, it will have to either purchase additional machining equipment or free existing equipment by subcontracting to an outside supplier a part currently made in-house. In this situation, the incremental factory overhead cost figure should include the variable overhead caused by the production of piston pins, *plus* the full portion of fixed overhead allocable to the piston pin operation.[2]

Now assume that the same engine manufacturer wants to make his own piston pins and that he has enough excess capacity to make the pins in his machine shop with existing equipment. Investigation shows that the excess capacity will exist for at least the next two or three years. What are his

---

[2]In the event that piston pin production replaces production of another part, the piston pin operation should carry the same absolute amount of fixed overhead as was carried by the part replaced. In the case where new equipment is purchased to produce piston pins, the piston pin operation should be charged with the additional fixed overhead arising from acquisition of the new equipment.

incremental overhead costs to make the pins in this situation? *Only* the variable overhead caused by production of the piston pins! In this case fixed overhead represents sunk costs which continue to accumulate whether piston pins are produced in the shop or not. The total machine shop building continues to generate depreciation charges. Heat, light, and janitorial service are still furnished to the total machine shop area. Also, property taxes for the machine shop remain the same regardless of the number of machines productively employed. The firm incurs these same fixed costs regardless of the make-or-buy action it decides upon. Such costs, under conditions of idle capacity, are *not* incremental costs and, for purposes of the make-or-buy decision, must be omitted from computation of the cost to make a new part.

This concept can also be observed from a slightly different point of view in the graphic representation of Figure 15-1. Note that a 12$\frac{1}{2}$ percent increase in production volume (an increase from 80 to 90 percent of capacity) can be achieved by a total cost increase of only 10 percent. This favorable situation results simply because the 12$\frac{1}{2}$ percent increase in production is accomplished by activating unused capacity. Fixed overhead costs are incurred irrespective of the decision to make piston pins by utilizing unused capacity.

Finally, consider a third common situation in which the same engine manufacturer wants to make his own piston pins. Investigation in this case reveals that enough excess capacity currently exists in the machine shop to permit production of the piston pins. However, management expects a gradual increase in business during the next several years, which will eliminate all excess capacity by the end of the second year. How should the make-or-buy decision be approached in this particular case?

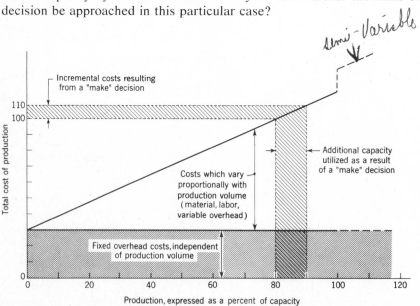

Figure 15-1 A representative case illustrating the incremental costs resulting from a "make" decision when operating at 80 percent of production capacity.

As always, the starting point of the analysis is an estimate of the costs to make versus the costs to buy. For the first $1^1/_2$ to 2 years, the cost to make piston pins will not include fixed overhead because excess capacity exists. Beyond two years, however, the cost to make must include fixed overhead; if piston pins are not made, increased production of some other part will, in the normal course of business, carry its full share of fixed overhead. One alternative is to consider the make-or-buy decision separately for each of the two time periods. While the analysis may indicate that it is profitable to make the pins in both cases, it will probably reveal that it is profitable to make the pins only for the first two years and to buy them beyond that date. In this case several qualitative factors must be investigated to determine the practical feasibility of a split course of action. If the split course of action does not prove practicable, a second alternative is to compute a weighted average cost to make the pins during both time periods. The cost data can then be used in considering the total make-or-buy question.

In practice, an infinite number of situations exist between the two extremes of excess capacity and full capacity. Any attempt to categorize these situations and apply rules of thumb in analyzing them is arbitrary (and sometimes dangerous). There is no simple, absolutely accurate solution to any of these problems. Each situation must be analyzed in its own dynamic context.

In summary, an analyst should be guided by several basic ideas. First, *incremental costs* are virtually always the costs germane to the managerial decision-making process. Second, the determination of a realistic cost to "make" an item requires a realistic estimate of the future conditions of capacity. When capacity can be utilized by existing business or by alternative new projects, incremental overhead costs to make a new item must reflect total overhead costs. During any period of time when this condition does not exist, the incremental overhead to "make" consists only of variable overhead. When conditions of capacity normally oscillate frequently between partial load and full load, it is likely that the make-or-buy decision for a new project of substantial duration will turn largely on considerations other than comparative cost.

Precautions in Developing Costs   In the event that a firm has in the past made a part but decides to purchase it in the future, it must exercise particular care in interpreting the quotations it receives from potential external suppliers. Some suppliers may prepare the quotation carelessly, with the mistaken idea that the user does not really intend to buy the part. Other suppliers may bid unrealistically low in an attempt to induce the user to discontinue making the part in favor of buying it. Once the user has discontinued his "make" operation, it can be costly to resume it. Thus, he may be at the mercy of the supplier in case the supplier later chooses to increase his price.[3] It is essential that the user

---

[3]A long-term requirements contract may be used as a device to help forestall such price increases.

carefully evaluate the reliability of all quotations in his attempt to determine a realistic estimate of the total cost to buy the part.

In estimating the cost to make a part, an analyst must ensure that the firm possesses adequate equipment and technical know-how to do the job. Moreover, in an industry where technological change occurs rapidly, a firm can find its equipment and know-how competitively outmoded in a few short years. Thus, the factor of obsolescence should also be given adequate consideration in determining the ultimate costs of equipment and personnel training.

The proper equipment to make any item may sometimes be easier to acquire than the properly skilled manpower. Large volume requirements, complex skill requirements, or unique geographic locations can precipitate shortages of adequately skilled manpower. In preparing "cost-to-make" estimates, the local manpower situation must be evaluated. Should it be necessary to import adequately skilled personnel, total labor costs can substantially exceed initial estimates.

In the case of a "make" decision, it is equally important to investigate the availability and price stability of required raw materials. Large users of particular materials generally find the availability and price structure of these materials much more favorable than do small unspecialized users. Wise analysts ensure that their estimates for raw material are realistic.

In estimating the cost to make a part for the first time, the analyst must also investigate several practical production matters. The first deals with the cost of unacceptable production work. What is the expected rate of rejected and spoiled parts? Equally important, what learning curve can the production department reasonably expect to apply? Answers to these questions may vary substantially, depending upon the complexity of the job and the type of workers and equipment available. The resultant influence on the make-buy cost comparison can be considerable, however, and realistic answers should be sought.

Finally, when a company decides to make a part, it assumes responsibility for all production problems stemming from the variability of the part's demand. Final cost estimates must therefore include any increased costs of production resulting from consequent production inefficiencies.

Control of Production or Quality

Consider now some of the factors other than direct costs which influence make-or-buy decisions. Two conditions, not uncommon in certain industries, weigh heavily in some firms' decisions to make a particular part.

Production Requirements The need for close control of production operations is particularly acute in some firms. A company whose sales demand is subject to extreme short-run fluctuations finds that its production department must operate on unusually tight time schedules. This kind of company typically produces for stock those parts used in several different products. However, it produces to individual customer order the parts unique to a particular product or customer specification. Sales fluctuations for products using unique parts therefore influence the planning and scheduling of numerous assembly and subassembly operations as well as single-part production operations. Efficient conduct of assembly operations thus depends upon the firm's ability to obtain the unique, unstocked parts on short notice.

Most suppliers serving a number of customers cannot normally tool up and fit an order for a unique part into existing schedules on a moment's notice. If the user cannot tolerate suppliers' lead time requirements, his only other major alternative is to control the part production operations himself. Thus, by making the item, the user acquires the needed control. He can quickly revise job priorities, reassign operators and machines to specific jobs, and require overtime work as conditions demand.

Some firms also choose to make certain critical parts to assure continuity of supply of these parts to succeeding production operations. This type of vertical integration guards against production shutdowns caused by supplier labor problems, local transportation strikes, and miscellaneous supplier service problems. These are particularly important considerations when dealing with parts that feed an automated production operation whose downtime is tremendously expensive. If such action reduces the risk of a production stoppage, it may well justify the incurrence of extra material costs.

Quality Requirements   A firm's unique quality requirements frequently represent a second condition requiring control of parts production operations. Certain parts in technical products are occasionally quite difficult to manufacture. Frequently, compounding this difficulty is an unusually exacting quality specification the part must meet. In certain technological fields or in particular geographical areas, a user may find that the uniqueness of the task results in unsatisfactory performance by an outside supplier. Some companies find that their own firm is in a better position to do an acceptable production job than are external suppliers.

A user normally understands more completely than an outside supplier the operational intricacies connected with usage of the part. Therefore, if he makes the part himself, there can be greater coordination between the assembly operation and the part production operation. Conducting both operations under one roof likewise eliminates many communications problems which can arise between a buyer and supplier whose operations are geographically separated. Finally, large users often possess technological resources superior to those of smaller vendors. Such resources may be needed in solving *new* technical problems in production.

For example, one producer of aircraft hydraulic systems makes a practice of subcontracting production of some of the valves used in its systems. The production of one particular subcontracted valve involved difficult interior machining operations as well as tight quality requirements. Of the supplier's first four shipments, the systems manufacturer rejected 80 percent of the valves for failure to meet quality specifications. During the ensuing months, the systems manufacturer worked closely with the subcontractor in an attempt to solve the quality problem. With the passage of time, however, it became clear that the systems manufacturer was contributing considerably more to solution of the problem than was the supplier. Eventually, the systems firm decided to make the valve. Although production of the valve still remained a difficult task, the systems manufacturer was able to develop the techniques necessary to produce a valve of acceptable quality, with a greatly reduced percentage of rejects.

Design Secrecy Required

Although their number is small, there are a few firms that make particular parts primarily because they want to keep secret certain aspects of the part's design or manufacture. The secrecy justification for making an item can be found in highly competitive industries where style and cost play unusually important roles. Also, a firm is more likely to "make" a key part for which patent protection does not provide effective protection against commercial emulation.

If design secrecy is really important, however, a firm may have nearly as much difficulty maintaining secrecy when it makes a part as it would when a supplier makes it. In either case, a large number of individuals must be taken into the firm's confidence, and once information leaks to a competitor, very little can be done about it. A firm can usually control security measures more easily and directly in its own plant, but it can never prevent an individual from becoming an informer if the person so chooses.

Unreliable Suppliers

A few firms decide to make specific parts because their experience has shown that the reliability record of available suppliers falls below the required level. The likelihood of encountering such a situation thirty years ago was infinitely greater than it is today. Competition in most industries today is so keen that grossly unreliable performers do not long survive the competitive struggle. With one major exception, unreliable delivery or unpredictable service is confined largely to isolated cases in new, highly specialized lines of business where competition has not yet become established. Such lines of business are usually characterized by low sales volumes, the requirement of highly specialized production equipment, or the unique possession of new technological capabilities.

The one major exception mentioned above is the case of the buyer who provides only an insignificant fraction of a specific supplier's total volume of business. Even the most reputable suppliers are forced at times to "short-change" very small accounts in order to give proper attention to their major accounts. Regardless of the reasonableness of the cause, however, consistently unreliable performance by a supplier is sufficient grounds for shifting vendors or possibly reconsidering the original make-buy decision.

Suppliers' Specialized Knowledge and Research

A primary reason underlying most decisions to buy a part rather than make it is the user's desire to take advantage of the specialized abilities and research efforts of various vendors.

Lest the preceding discussion of "make" decisions distort the total procurement picture, bear in mind that the typical American manufacturing firm spends more than 50 percent of its sales dollar for purchases from external suppliers. Modern industry is highly specialized. No ordinary firm, regardless of size, can hope to possess adequate facilities and technical know-how to make a majority of its production part requirements efficiently. Large corporations spend millions of dollars on product and process research each year. The fruits of this research and the ensuing technical know-how are available to customers in the form of highly developed and refined parts and component products. The firm that considers forgoing these benefits in favor of making an item should, before making its final decision, assess carefully the long-range values that accrue from industrial specialization.

Small-Volume Requirements

When a firm uses only a small quantity of a particular item, it usually decides to buy the item. The typical firm strives to concentrate its production efforts in areas where it is most efficient and in areas it finds most profitable. The work of designing, tooling, planning, and setting up for the production of a new part is time-consuming and costly. These fixed costs are recovered more easily from long production runs than from short ones. More often than not, the small-volume user consequently searches for a potential supplier who specializes in production of the given part and can economically produce it in large quantities. The specialty supplier can sell to a large number of users in almost any desired quantity.

Small-volume production of *unique, nonstandard* parts may likewise be unattractive to external suppliers. Every supplier is obligated to concentrate first on its high-volume, high-profit accounts. Thus, cases may develop in which a user is virtually *forced* to "make" a highly nonstandard part it uses in small quantities. Generally speaking, however, as the part tends toward a more common and finally a standard configuration, the tendency to "buy" increases proportionally.

Limited Facilities

Another reason for buying rather than making certain parts is the physical limitation imposed by the user's production facilities. A firm with limited facilities typically attempts to utilize them as fully as possible on its most profitable production work. It then depends upon external suppliers for the balance of its requirements. Thus, during peak periods a firm may purchase a substantial portion of its total requirements because of loaded production facilities, and during slack periods, as internal production capacity opens up, its purchases may decrease markedly.

Work Force Stability

Closely related to the matter of facilities is the factor of work force stability. A fluctuating production level compels a firm to face the continual problem of contracting and expanding its work force to keep in step with production demands. Significant continuing fluctuation, moreover, adversely affects the type of workers such a firm is able to employ. The less stable an operation, the more difficult it becomes to retain an efficient work force.

At the time when a firm "sizes" the various segments of its production operation, many make-buy decisions are made. One factor which often bears heavily on the decision is the firm's desire to develop an interested, responsible group of workers with a high degree of company loyalty. Awareness that stable employment facilitates the attainment of this objective frequently prompts a firm to undersize its production facility by a slight margin. Its plan is to maintain as stable an internal production operation as possible and to buy requirements in excess of its capacity from external suppliers. This policy is most effective in firms whose products require a considerable amount of general-purpose equipment in the manufacturing operation. Equipment, as well as personnel, that can perform a variety of different jobs provides the internal flexibility required to consolidate or split work among various production areas as business fluctuates. This capability is necessary for the successful implementation of such a policy, because it is not feasible to place small orders for a large number of different parts with outside suppliers as business increases. It is much more profitable to "farm out" large orders for a small number of parts.

Firms that successfully solve their work force problems in this way frequently create problems in the purchasing area. External suppliers are, in effect, used as "buffers" to absorb the shocks of production fluctuations. This action transfers many of the problems associated with production fluctuations from the user to the supplier. The supplier's ability to absorb these production shocks is therefore an important consideration. In some instances he may be able to absorb them reasonably well; in others, he may not.[4] In all cases, however, the supplier prefers, as does the user, to maintain a stable production operation. Consequently, many suppliers are not interested in the user who buys only his peak requirements. The question naturally arises: Will a supplier

---

[4]Two factors largely determine a supplier's ability to absorb fluctuating order requirements from a user. They are:

1   The similarity of the work involved in producing a particular user's requirement and in producing other customers' orders. The more similar the requirements are, the less is the expense of special planning and setup work for a particular user.
2   The extent to which other customers' orders offset the peaks and valleys in the supplier's production operation. The more stable his total production operation is, the less is the disturbing effect of an occasional fluctuating account.

ever be motivated to perform well for a buyer who uses him only for surplus work? This question should be considered carefully before a "buy" decision of this type is made.

Multiple-Source Policy

Some firms occasionally make *and* buy the same nonstandard part. This policy is followed for the explicit purpose of having available a reliable and experienced second source of supply. Firms adopting a make-and-buy policy recognize that they may not always be able to meet their internal production schedules for certain parts. In case of an emergency, an experienced outside source is usually willing to increase its delivery of the part in question on a temporary basis until the situation is under control.

Indirect Managerial Control Considerations

Companies occasionally buy and make the same part for the purpose of developing managerial control data. Some firms use outside suppliers' cost and quality performance as a check on their own internal production efficiency. If internal costs for a particular part rise above a supplier's cost, the user knows that somewhere in his own production system some element of cost is probably out of line. An investigation frequently uncovers one or more problems, some of which often extend to other production areas. Consequent improvements may therefore exhibit a compounding effect as they reach into other operations where inefficiencies might otherwise have gone undetected.

THE VOLATILE NATURE OF THE MAKE-OR-BUY SITUATION

Although make-or-buy investigations begin with a cost analysis, various qualitative factors frequently portend more far-reaching consequences than does the cost analysis. Therefore, a make-or-buy decision correctly approached considers the probable *composite effect* of all factors on the firm's total operation.

A thorough investigation is complicated considerably by the dynamics and uncertainties of business activity. Certain factors can hold quite different implications for a make-or-buy decision at different points in time and under different operating conditions. As pointed out, changing costs can turn a good decision into a bad one in a very short period of time. And future costs, complicated by numerous demand and capacity interrelationships, are influenced substantially by such variable factors as technological innovation and customer demand. The availability of expansion capital also influences make-or-buy decisions. An "easy money" policy, a liberal depreciation policy, or liberal government taxing policies tend to encourage "make" decisions. Contrary policies promote "buy" decisions. These federal policies fluctuate with economic conditions.

The tendency toward "make" decisions in order to stabilize production and work force fluctuation is usually greater in small firms than in large ones. In some small shops the loss of just a few orders results in the temporary layoff of a sizable percentage of the work force until additional orders can be obtained. Generally speaking, larger organizations do not have such severe labor force problems because their fluctuations in production volume relative to total capacity are smaller. As large firms adopt compensation plans such as the guaranteed annual wage, however, they too will feel a similar pressure to favor "make" decisions.

Finally, the labor-relations climate within a firm can influence its make-or-buy decisions. A hostile union may, on rational or other grounds, seize the opportunity to irritate management as a result of the decision to buy an item previously made in-house. An amicable labor-management climate may evoke a quite different union reaction.

To summarize, the point very briefly stated is this: Beware of rigid formulas and rules of thumb that claim to produce easy make-or-buy decisions. The make-or-buy question is influenced by a multitude of diverse factors that are in a constant state of change. Under such conditions, few easy decisions turn out well in both the short and the long run. Moreover, the relevant factors vary immensely from one firm to another. For these reasons, every company should periodically evaluate the effectiveness of its past decisions to generate information helpful in guiding future courses of make-buy action.

PROCEDURE AND PERSONNEL
INVOLVED IN MAKE-OR-BUY DECISIONS

It is not difficult to find otherwise well-managed firms in which most make-or-buy decisions are inadvertently delegated to a clerk in inventory control or production control. It should now be apparent that this is a poor practice. In the first place, such a person does not normally have adequate information with which to make an intelligent decision from a companywide point of view. Second, even if adequate information were available, a typical clerical employee lacks the breadth of experience to evaluate fully the significance of the information and the resultant decision.

In most cases, make-or-buy decisions should be made, or at least reviewed, at a managerial level. The decision maker must be able to view such problems with a broad companywide perspective. Many progressive firms use the committee approach to analyze make-or-buy alternatives. The committee is usually composed of department managers or high-level staff assistants. The important point to keep in mind is that all departments which can contribute to the decision or which are affected by it should have some voice in making it. The committee approach accomplishes this directly by committee activity. In other cases, a formal mechanism must be established which facilitates, and indeed requires, all interested departments to submit relevant data and suggestions to the decision maker. Moreover, to ensure thoroughness and consistency, the system must detail the cost computation procedures to be used and assign cost investigations to specific operating groups.

In addition to providing an operational framework within which make-or-buy alternatives are investigated, a complete review system is necessary. The system should provide definite procedures for three important additional activities: (1) the entry of projects into the investigatory system, (2) maintenance of essential records, and (3) a periodic audit of important decisions.

Procedures should be established as part of a firm's product development program, compelling high-value parts from new products to enter the make-or-buy investigation process. In some cases, this investigation can be effectively integrated with preproduction value analysis investigations. Similarly, existing production parts should be subjected to a systematic review which searches for borderline make-or-buy items warranting full investigation.

Regardless of the source of entry, all make-or-buy investigations should be classified as "major" or "minor," based upon the value of the part. In one firm all items involving expenditures under $25,000 are classed as "minor." Subsequent investigations of minor itemes involve personnel from production, purchasing, quality control, and occasionally design engineering. Major items entail expenditures over $25,000 and additionally involve personnel from finance, marketing, and other production areas.

Certain summary records are essential to full utilization of the data developed in make-or-buy investigations. The investigation record should be designed to serve as a useful future reference. A brief discussion of all factors pertinent to the decision that was made should be included, as well as the primary reasons for the decision. Assumptions about future conditions should be stated. And an accurate summary of cost data should always be included. Records of this type provide the information required when a firm is forced to make quick decisions about subcontracting work under peak operating conditions or about bringing work back into the shop when business slumps. Accurate records can mean the difference between a profitable decision based on *facts* or a hopeful decision based on intuition and hunches.

Finally, investigation records provide the basic data for postdecision audits. Because of the volatility of the make-buy situation, it behooves every firm to audit its major make-or-buy decisions from time to time. Only by conducting such audits can a firm detect significant changing influences, discover its errors, and benefit from such discoveries in improving future performance.

FOR DISCUSSION

15-1   Discuss briefly the basic objective of make-or-buy decisions.
15-2   Do all make-or-buy investigations require the same type of analysis? Explain.

15-3   Develop in detail a procedure to be followed in conducting a make-or-buy cost analysis. (Include explanations necessary for the reader's full understanding of the procedure.)

15-4   List and briefly discuss the major difficulties that may be encountered in making a valid make-or-buy cost analysis.

15-5   Why may fixed overhead expenses in a specific plant be an incremental cost in the case of one make-or-buy investigation and not in the case of a similar investigation made at a later date in the same plant? Explain.

15-6   Refer to Figure 15-1. How do you explain the fact that a 12½ percent increase in production produces only a 10 percent increase in production cost?

15-7   Are make-or-buy decisions influenced by the learning curve concept? Explain.

15-8   It has been said that make-or-buy decisions are much more critical in companies whose production operations are highly automated than in others. What is your reaction to this statement? Explain.

15-9   Some business executives strongly advocate vertical integration of production operations because they can eliminate payment of a profit to various middlemen. What is your reaction to this argument?

15-10   List and briefly discuss the major factors which tend to influence make-or-buy decisions in the direction of buying.

15-11   List and briefly discuss the major factors which tend to influence make-or-buy decisions in the direction of making.

15-12   Some companies claim that they can transfer much of the shock of sales fluctuations normally felt in the production operations to their suppliers. How can this be done? What problems frequently result when a firm attempts to do this?

15-13   The text states that most make-or-buy decisions are volatile in nature. What is meant by this statement? Explain.

15-14   To whom should a company assign the responsibility for make-or-buy decisions? Explain.

CASES FOR CHAPTER 15

Part Three

Related Materials Functions

Chapter 16

Traffic

KEY CONCEPTS

Carrier selection and routing
  Shipping terms
  Modes of transportation
  Types of carriers
  Class rates and commodity rates
Expediting and tracing shipments
Freight bill audits
Loss and damage of freight
Demurrage
Transportation cost reduction
Purchasing's role in traffic

The nature of the traffic function, particularly as related to inbound traffic, makes it an integral part of the larger materials management function. Its importance is magnified by the fact that transportation cost and service factors significantly affect a firm's total cost of materials, the efficiency of its production operation, and ultimately its ability to compete in the marketplace. Current estimates indicate that American industry spends approximately $100 billion per year for transportation services. By any criterion this is big business.

Business managers are concerned not only with the cost of transportation to their own firms, but also with the cost of transportation to their competitors. Assume, for example, that steel prices are approximately the same at two different mills. If the first mill can deliver steel more cheaply than the second because it has lower transportation costs, it has a distinct advantage over its competitor. If customers pay the freight charges, the first mill can expect to get proportionately more orders; if the mills pay the freight, the first mill will net a higher unit profit. For this reason, industrial traffic managers must be alert to actual changes in transportation regulations, and also to subtle changes in the general philosophy and views held by the various regulatory agencies.

The traffic function in an industrial firm includes responsibility for four areas of activity:

1   The transportation of incoming shipments
2   The transportation of outgoing shipments
3   Major internal transportation of materials and products on the firm's property
4   Participation in hearings before the Interstate Commerce Commission, congressional committees, and other governmental bodies on matters affecting transportation costs and the quality of transportation services

In his or her daily purchasing work, a buyer encounters traffic problems that focus primarily on incoming shipments of materials and equipment. This chapter consequently investigates the major traffic activities concerned with incoming shipments and views these activities in the light of their relationship to the purchasing function. It pinpoints the things a buyer should understand about traffic to do an effective purchasing job.

Transportation costs can be high; in some companies they may average as much as 20 to 40 percent of the product cost. This is often the case in firms producing heavy machinery or products requiring heavy or bulky production materials. In the steel, lumber, cement, and heavy chemical industries, for example, transportation frequently represents one of the largest elements of total cost. At the other end of the cost spectrum, in some light manufacturing firms transportation costs sometimes total substantially less than 1 percent of product cost. Electronics, pharmaceutical, and fur producers are good examples. Thus, transportation costs vary greatly, depending upon the nature of the materials a firm uses; the importance of the transportation function consequently varies from one industry to another.

Irrespective of direct transportation costs, transportation *service* is frequently a critical factor in the purchasing process. If shipments fail to arrive when scheduled, much of the preceding purchasing and production scheduling work can be nullified. Serious production delays may ensue because of transportation failures. Moreover, the general efficiency of any supply program can be significantly affected by the type of cooperation obtained from carriers. On matters of materials-handling methods, shipment tracing and expediting, and the allowance of various in-transit privileges, carrier cooperation is essential.

Transportation services should be purchased much as any material is purchased. After careful investigation of potential carriers, the selection decision should be based on proper evaluation of service, quality, and price.

CARRIER SELECTION

A purchaser frequently has the right to specify the carrier and the routing to be used in transporting the purchased material. When this prerogative exists, the buyer should view it as another purchase to be made. Too many buyers forfeit this responsibility and opportunity for savings by simply noting, "ship best way."

Shipping Terms

The shipping terms included in a sales contract determine who has the right to specify the carrier and routing. More precisely, shipping terms define three things:

1 The point at which the buyer takes legal title to the goods
2 Who is responsible for payment of freight charges
3 Who is responsible for prosecuting claims against carriers for loss or damage

Numerous terms of shipment can be used, but the most common are:

1 F.o.b. buyer's plant
2 F.o.b. seller's plant
3 F.o.b. seller's plant, freight allowed to buyer's plant
4 C.i.f. contracts

Under the first arrangement, legal title to the material passes from the seller to the buyer when the carrier delivers the material at the buyer's plant. Because the seller retains ownership of the material during transit, he has the right to select the carrier as well as the responsibility for paying the freight charges. Under the second arrangement, the buyer takes title when the carrier accepts the material for shipment at the seller's plant. In this case, the buyer assumes responsibility for carrier selection and payment of freight charges. The third arrangement is similar to the second, so far as legal liability is concerned; however, the shipper agrees to reimburse the buyer for the freight charges. The fourth type of contract is commonly used in international trade. The abbreviation c.i.f. stands for cost, insurance, and freight, which means that the contract price includes insurance and delivery charges, as well as the cost of the material.

Buying under the terms of f.o.b. seller's plant is common practice today among a large number of well-managed firms. These companies want control of an order during transit. Many purchasers feel that they can do a better job of carrier selection and routing, from either a cost or service standpoint, than their suppliers can. This is frequently true because many small shippers simply are not properly staffed to make such decisions for all of their geographically dispersed customers. Many purchasers also develop long-term relationships with carriers, just as they do with suppliers. Hence, the routing of each major production material, from various points across the country, is but one element of a total transportation purchasing program which is designed to serve the purchaser's long-range interests. Consequently, the purchaser frequently wants the prerogative of carrier selection because he plans to develop certain types of relationships with specific carriers.

There are situations, however, in which a supplier will be better informed than the buyer about traffic conditions and about the services offered by specific carriers in the supplier's area. In such cases, the intelligent buyer works with the supplier and utilizes the latter's capabilities to the fullest extent possible.

Occasionally, buyers are heard to say that they prefer to buy f.o.b. their plant. Their reasoning goes something like this. By so doing, they shift the burden of locating effective carriers to the supplier and do not have to concern themselves with the details of transportation investigations. Likewise, since the supplier has agreed to pay the freight charges, the buyer does not have to worry about costs of transportation. And finally, in the event that problems arise from shipping damage, etc., the buyer is not responsible for the time-consuming negotiation with the carrier which often ensues. This type of reasoning contains two fallacies. In the first place, there is no assurance that the supplier will accept the responsibility of finding an "effective" chain of carriers. The buyer, in effect, abdicates his responsibility for assuring his firm good transportation service. Second, even though the supplier pays the freight bill, in the long run freight charges are included and passed on to the buyer in the material selling price. Ultimately, the buyer pays the transportation bill, and he also bears any extra costs resulting from poor carrier selection.

Modes of Transportation

The bulk of United States intercity freight traffic is moved by rail, motor freight, oil pipeline, and water carriers. Although the railroads have continually lost ground to the motor freight industry since World War II, they still haul approximately 40 percent of the country's freight (nearly twice the amount moved by truck). Freight movement by air has increased at a fantastic rate during the same period, but it still amounts to slightly less than 1 percent of all freight moved.

A surprisingly large number of transportation methods are available. Most buyers, at one time or another, utilize a majority of the following specific methods:

1 Parcel post
2 Parcel delivery service
3 Bus service
4 Air cargo
5 Rail freight, carload (CL) and less than carload (LCL)
6 Motor freight, truckload (TL) and less than truckload (LTL)
7 Freight forwarder
8 Coastal, intercoastal, and inland water freight
9 Piggyback and fishyback
10 Pipeline

Generally speaking, a buyer of transportation finds that methods providing fast delivery cost more than slower methods. A West Coast firm, for example, buys heavy machine parts from a firm in Philadelphia. The parts can be shipped by water, by rail, by truck, or by some combination of these methods. If shipped by truck, delivery time is approximately eleven days. If shipped by intercoastal steamship, delivery takes roughly twice as long. Depending upon the specific part, however, the water freight rate ranges from 20 to 50 percent lower than the truck rate.

Exceptions to this rule, of course, do exist. A buyer may discover some isolated cases where a faster mode is also cheaper. For instance, for many years the air freight rate between San Diego and San Francisco was less than the Railway Express rate! Other similar exceptions undoubtedly exist.

When approaching a shipping problem for the first time, wise purchasers initially compare rates and delivery times of the feasible alternative shipping methods. Next they familiarize themselves with the applicable portion of the rate structure for each of the methods of shipment they use. In this way they can ensure that the item is in fact shipped under the most advantageous rate relative to their delivery requirements.

Buyers should bear in mind, however, that certain indirect cost factors may be just as important as the freight rate itself. Packaging and crating costs may vary from one mode to another. Also, the size and frequency of shipment is determined by the mode. Consequently, the necessity for warehousing and the cost of maintaining inventory may vary from one mode to another. Clearly, the buyer is concerned with *total costs* influenced by transportation, not direct transportation costs alone.

Parcel Post   Very little industrial freight travels by parcel post. However, this rather expensive service is a relatively fast and convenient method of shipping small packages. The United States postal service has placed the following size and weight limits on parcel post shipments:[1]

If mailed at a first-class post office for delivery at another first-class post office,

Weight limit = 40 pounds for all zone destinations

Size limit = 84-inch combined length and girth for all zone destinations

If mailed at or addressed for delivery to other than a first-class post office,

Weight limit = 70 pounds

Size limit = 100-inch combined length and girth

[1]These parcel post limitations were in effect Jan. 1, 1976. They may be changed from time to time by the Post Office Department.

Air parcel post service is also available at substantially higher rates. Shipping limits are 70 pounds and 100 inches.

Parcel Delivery Service   Privately operated parcel delivery services also provide important delivery services to major metropolitan and nearby areas. Some of these firms operate in interstate commerce. Others operate only intrastate or intracity. In recent years private parcel delivery services have grown rapidly in number and size, primarily because of their flexibility and strong service orientation. United Parcel Service is an outstanding example of this type of firm. Business customers have generally responded favorably to the wide range of specialized and custom-tailored services available.

Bus Service   Intercity bus transportation is another method used occasionally for shipping easily manageable packages over relatively short distances. Most bus lines accept packages larger than parcel post size, provided one person can handle them without difficulty. Although this too is an expensive service, delivery is usually fast for distances less than 200 miles because of the numerous scheduled runs between major cities. In an emergency situation the buyer sometimes finds this service to be extremely valuable. Some of its value, however, may be negated by the necessity for local delivery or pickup of the shipment at the bus terminal.

Air Cargo   Although air cargo movements have increased tremendously in recent years, high rates still prohibit regular use of air service for most industrial purchasers. As a general rule, freight rates are approximately twice as high for air cargo as for LCL and LTL movements. The continued development of high-capacity jet freighters, however, may permit further rate reductions in the future.

Because air travel produces a smooth ride compared with other methods of moving freight, it is an exceptionally good way to transport delicate equipment or perishable commodities. Because of this fact, if ground handling is not too rough, packaging and crating requirements for materials may be reduced substantially if they are shipped by air. This cost reduction partially offsets the higher freight rate in some cases.

One selling point emphasized by most air cargo carriers is the fact that the short delivery time afforded by air shipment permits a purchaser to carry smaller inventories. The rationale underlying this point is entirely valid. The final decision, however, still involves an analysis of *total* costs. Each purchaser must make his own analysis and determine in which cases a net saving in fact results.

Rail Freight   Rail carriers handle more freight than any other type of carrier. Generally speaking, rail rates *for full carload lots* are lower than those of any carrier discussed to this point in the chapter.

Rail shipments move as full carload (CL) shipments or as less than carload (LCL) shipments. For ordinary materials, a CL movement is considered to be approximately 30,000 pounds or more. When hauling a dense commodity such as grain, however, the figure might range from 60,000 to 100,000 pounds. The CL volume is usually sufficient to fill a car, so that it does not have to be opened until it reaches its destination. CL shipments move at a freight rate that is substantially below (in some cases approximately one-half) the LCL rate. As will become evident in the following paragraphs, LCL shipment frequently does not compete favorably with motor freight shipment. For this reason, the volume of LCL shipments is declining for most railroads.

To make effective use of CL movements, the shipper and purchaser should each have conveniently located spur tracks and loading facilities. If a purchaser has to unload a railcar at the freight yard and truck the material to his plant, the cost of double handling frequently makes it less costly to utilize a single truck haul all the way from the supplier's plant. On the other hand, for LCL shipments, the rate usually includes pickup and delivery service, provided the shipment moves more than 300 miles.

A railroad's major advantage over its trucking competitors is in the area of long intercity hauls. A railroad must make a huge investment in equipment, rolling stock, and trackage. While its fixed costs are high, its variable operating costs are relatively low. Once a train is loaded and rolling, it costs little more to move it 1,000 miles than to move it 100 miles. Hence, on long hauls, its total operating cost per ton-mile is typically lower than that of its motor freight competitors. For shipments moving less than 1,000 miles, the reverse situation occurs.

Railroads offer CL shippers two privileges that prove extremely valuable in some types of business: (1) in-transit privileges, and (2) diversion and reconsignment privileges.

Generally speaking, intransit privileges give a shippper the right to stop a shipment en route, unload it, perform certain processing operations on the material, reload the processed material, and continue the shipment at the original freight rate (subject to a small additional charge). The economics of the total operation become clear when one observes that freight rates on processed materials are usually higher than on corresponding raw materials. This means, for example, that a tank fabricator in Kansas City might purchase a car of steel in Chicago, ship it to Kansas City, fabricate tanks from the carload of steel, and then ship the tanks on to a customer in Denver. In doing this under a fabrication-in-transit agreement, the tank fabricator pays almost the same freight rate on tanks shipped from Kansas City to Denver as he paid on the steel shippped from Chicago to Kansas City.[2]

A similar type of agreement allows shippers to delay a shipment and use the railcar as a temporary storage facility until they wish to continue the movement.

Diversion privileges permit a shipper to divert a car in transit to a new

[2]An interesting application of the fabrication-in-transit privilege is discussed in an article by Peter Wulff, "There's More Than One Way to Cut a Freight Bill," *Purchasing Magazine,* June 27, 1968, pp. 54–56.

destination. This can be a very convenient prerogative when unexpected conditions in a multiplant company call for the shipment of an extra car of material to plant X, rather than to plant Y as scheduled. Reconsignment privileges allow the shipper to go a step further; he can also consign the car to a new customer, or consignee, at the same or at a different location. In certain types of businesses these privileges can be used to very definite advantage.[3]

Rail carriers also provide other privileges, for little or no additional cost. One of these services is pickup or loading at two separate points with a single delivery at destination. They also provide for a single pickup with delivery and unloading at two separate points. These privileges can be of particular value to multiplant companies.

Motor Freight   In this industry shipments move on either a truckload (TL) or less than truckload (LTL) basis. TL rates are substantially lower than LTL rates. In contrast with rail freight movement, approximately 20,000 pounds of ordinary material make up a full truckload. The definition of "a full truckload," however, varies somewhat among commodities and among carriers.

Comparison of truck rates with rail rates reveals that, in general, the difference between them depends on the length of the haul and the weight of the load. On movements of less than 1,000 miles, truck rates are occasionally somewhat lower than rail rates. On long hauls, however, the reverse is frequently true, notably for heavy, low-grade bulk materials.

A point of interest to purchasing personnel centers on the difference between weight requirements for TL and CL shipments. Suppose a buyer is considering shipping a 20,000-pound order by rail, LCL. If truck shipment is feasible, a TL rate will apply. In most cases, the TL rate will be considerably lower than the LCL rate. A similar situation may well exist when shipment weights are somewhat below 20,000 pounds. The freight bill for a 17,000-pound shipment which is moved and billed as a 20,000-pound truckload may well be lower in total than if it were actually billed as 17,000 pounds and moved at the higher LTL rate.

The most important advantage a truck line possesses over a rail line is its operating flexibility. For short hauls it has no peer. In contrast with a train, a truck is a small, flexible, self-contained unit. It can be loaded easily and less expensively (because less bracing is required) at a shipper's plant. Once on the road, a TL shipment can proceed directly to its destination. It does not have to wait in various classification yards across the country, as a railcar does, to be switched to a new train that moves it over the next leg of its journey. As a consequence, in almost all cases, motor freight delivery is faster than rail freight delivery.

For a short haul of 300 miles an LTL shipment should arrive in a day, while

---

[3]For an interesting discussion of some of the things which Sears, Roebuck and Company has done in this connection, see A. L. Russell, "Business Logistics in Action," in Karl Ruppenthal (ed.), *New Dimensions in Business Logistics*, Stanford Graduate School of Business, Stanford, Calif., 1963.

an LCL shipment typically requires three or four days. As the length of the haul increases, the truck advantage becomes less pronounced. Finally, on transcontinental CL hauls delivery performance tends to be about equal. Some of the aggressive railroads now offer improved service, on a limited basis, between selected metropolitan areas having high-density traffic movements. This service takes two forms: (1) fast "hi-ball" freight trains which bypass classification yards, and (2) scheduled "merchandise cars" which move immediately on through trains.

Freight Forwarder   The operations of rail freight forwarders are designed to provide a service to firms buying materials in less-than-carload lots. For distances over 300 miles, freight forwarding shipments should normally move much faster than ordinary LCL shipments, closely paralleling CL and LTL delivery service. Freight forwarders' rates, in virtually all cases, are at least as low as LCL and LTL rates, and on long hauls they are usually significantly lower.

A freight forwarder operates much like a broker. He accepts only less-than-carload shipments. He then combines such shipments into a full load and ships by rail at the CL rate. Thus, his operating margin is the difference between the rate he charges and the CL rate he pays for shipment. Long hauls are therefore most profitable for him. They frequently permit him to reduce his rate below the LCL level and still generate a reasonable profit.

Air freight forwarders operate in much the same way. Some air freight forwarders now offer a combination of air and surface movement for their shipments. These can be used to advantage when direct air shipments are not feasible, or when the combination provides advantageous movement at a lesser cost than direct air service.

Coastal, Intercoastal, and Inland Water Freight   Domestic ship lines, operating on inland as well as on coastal and intercoastal waterways, represent one of the earliest forms of American freight transportation. Because of infrequent sailing schedules and relatively slow speeds, water transportation is by far the slowest of all transportation methods. To compensate for slow deliveries, water carriers offer considerably lower rates than their rail and truck competitors.

The federal government considers domestic ship lines to be a vital part of the American Merchant Marine. It therefore protects their existence in various ways. The government, for example, legislates protection against competition from more cheaply operated foreign ships, it makes capital equipment available at reduced prices, and it partially subsidizes the harbors and docking facilities they use. Such actions permit domestic water carriers to remain financially sound and still quote freight rates substantially below competing rail and truck carriers.

Water transportation is frequently used by strategically located firms for moving raw materials, heavy items, and low-value materials, when shipments can be planned well in advance of operating requirements. In computing total shipping costs, the user should be aware that water freight rates do not include pickup and delivery service. The cost of transporting material to and from dockside must be added to the water carrier's quoted rates. Water carriers charge on the basis of weight or volume, depending on which yields the greater revenue. Consequently, shipping costs for bulky, low-density materials, relative to corresponding rail costs, are higher than for high-density materials.

Piggyback and Fishyback   These combination methods of freight transportation made their initial appearance on the commercial transportation scene during the mid-1950s. In both cases the cargo is loaded in truck trailers at the shipper's plant. In using piggyback, a truck tractor pulls the trailer from the plant to rail loading yards, where the trailer is placed on a flat car which holds several trailers. The long intercity haul is then made by rail. At the destination, truck tractors pick up the trailers and deliver them to the purchaser's plant.

This method of transportation actually combines the major advantages of both truck and rail movement. It utilizes the flexibility of trucks on pickup, delivery, and short off-line hauls, and it takes advantage of the railroads' favorable cost and speed performance on long hauls. This method of shipment usually cuts down loading and handling time, and it also frequently results in faster delivery for the purchaser. At times it results in a lower rate, particularly when shipment is made from or to plants without rail sidings.

Fishyback is similar to piggyback, except that it combines the use of truck and water carriers rather than truck and rail. While the main objective of piggyback is to utilize the strong features of both truck and rail movement, the major objective of fishyback is to reduce the extremely high costs of loading and unloading individually packaged items aboard ship. Fishyback replaces the handling of thousands of individual items with the handling of a relatively small number of previously loaded trailers or large standardized containers.

Pipeline   Pipelines are used primarily in transporting petroleum products, chemicals, and water. However, they are also being used increasingly for transporting cereal, coal, and certain ores. Movement of these materials is accomplished by pulverizing the solid material, mechanically suspending it in water, and pumping the resultant solution through a pipeline. Although pipelines of this kind are considered common carriers and are regulated by the Interstate Commerce Commission, they have very specialized uses when viewed as part of the total freight transportation picture.

Types of Carriers

The transportation buyer should be familiar with the basic legal status of the carriers being he deals with. The federal government recognizes three types of carriers: (1) common carriers, (2) contract carriers, and (3) private carriers.

A "common carrier" serves all customers but carries only that type of freight for which it is certified. Some truck certificates, for example, explicitly exclude specific types of freight, while others include only certain very limited types. The bulk of industrial freight moves by common carrier. The preceding discussion, with the exception of postal service, has dealt with freight movement by common carriers.

The Interstate Commerce Act of 1887 gives the federal government the right to regulate, in the "public interest," almost all common carriers engaging in *interstate* traffic. A host of subsequent legislation reinforces the basic intent and supplements the authority of the original act. All rail, motor, and intercoastal water common carriers are regulated by the Federal Interstate Commerce Commission. Ships in international commerce are regulated by the Federal Maritime Commission. Air common carriers are regulated by the Civil Aeronautics Board. Supplemental air carriers, popularly called the "non-scheds," are also regulated by the CAB.

The regulating agencies do two things. First, they prescribe a body of operating regulations constituting the legal framework within which carriers operate their businesses. The Interstate Commerce Commission, for example, issues all "certificates of convenience and necessity." The certificates give truck lines the authority to haul freight in a designated geographic area or over certain specific routes. No truck can operate as an interstate common carrier without a certificate. Second, they act as controllers of the freight rate structure to ensure that no carrier charges rates which discriminate against other carriers or against customers. All common carrier rates must be approved and published in "tariffs" legally filed with the Interstate Commerce Commission. Most states have state agencies which function in a similar manner for all carriers engaged in *intrastate* transportation.

A "contract carrier" does not provide service to the general public. Such carriers operate only under negotiated contractual agreements with specific customers. Although all contract carriers are regulated by the same agencies as common carriers, generally speaking, their regulation is less stringent. Each carrier must obtain an operating permit and also must file with the appropriate agency a schedule of minimum rates.

As a rule, contract carriers have no loading or terminal facilities. This usually lowers their operating costs. It also means that, by and large, contract carriers handle only truckload shipments. Unlike the liability of a common carrier, which is fixed by law, the liability of a contract carrier depends entirely upon the contractual arrangement made with the customer.

"Private carriers" are not subject to regulation by the Interstate Commerce Commission. A private carrier transports by motor vehicle property of which he is the owner, lessee, or bailee. Some industrial firms have thus become private carriers by operating their own fleets of trucks. A common problem such firms encounter in hauling their own production materials, though, is that of running the truck empty on one leg of the trip. Consequently, this type of private carrier generally tries to haul finished goods to customers traveling one way, and production materials to the plant going the other.

However, in such an operation scheduling becomes a major problem. Likewise, in the industrial relations area the company may find that it has an additional union—the Teamsters—to deal with. Thus, becoming a private carrier puts the firm in the trucking business as well as the manufacturing business, and it cannot escape certain problems unique to the transportation industry.

Purchasing people need not concern themselves with the plethora of legal details surrounding carrier operation, but they should be aware of the general framework within which carriers operate. Keeping out of legal difficulties in the transportation business is a complex problem in itself. Furthermore, the law holds a shipper equally liable with the carrier for violation of federal transportation regulations. Consequently, it behooves every buyer of transportation services to be generally familiar with the Interstate Commerce Act and the Motor Carrier Act of 1935. Against this background, then, buyers should investigate the carriers with whom they contemplate doing business.

Freight Rates

To the uninitiated, the structure of freight rates in the American transportation industry appears little short of chaotic. Unlike most business operations, the price charged for hauling freight does not and cannot bear a consistent relationship to the carrier's actual cost of providing the service. The difficulty of allocating operating costs to specific products carried, the debatable matter of "public interest," and rate cases of historic precedent all contribute to the inconsistent and confusing rate structure which now exists.

A brief review of the rough-and-tumble era during which railroads were laying the foundation for the nation's transportation system provides a clear explanation of how the complex rate system originated. The miscellany of rates developed during that period were, for the most part, created independently of each other as various needs arose. Little thought was given at that time to the rate structure for the total transportation system. Individual rates were based largely on "what the traffic would bear" and were conditioned by numerous economic and political pressures coming from different areas of the country.

Rates established today are based on cost to a greater extent than in past years. However, the following factors, some of them very subjective, are all considered in present-day rate making, which still appears to be much more an art than an exact science.

- Value of the service to the shipper
- Cost to the carrier of providing the service
- Special services involved, such as transit privileges
- Volume of traffic movement involved
- Rates on similar articles moving under similar conditions
- Rates of competing carriers
- Competitive conditons existing in the *shipper's* industry

Class Rates and Commodity Rates Generally speaking, freight moves under one of two types of rates: (1) class rates or (2) commodity rates. It was originally impossible to establish a rate for every individual commodity shipped. Consequently, similar commodities were grouped in classes, and rates were established for each *class* of commodity. These rates become known as "class rates."

If a commodity is shipped regularly in large volumes (even by only one producer) between the same origin and destination cities, it is possible to obtain a "commodity rate" for these shipments. Unique commodity rates are established to give special treatment to particular commodity movements which have economic or competitive importance in a certain market. Such rates apply only to carload, truckload, or planeload shipments. Approximately 90 percent of all rail freight and the majority of truck freight move under commodity rates. Commodity rates are important to the transportation buyer because they are usually lower than class rates.

A transportation buyer who wishes to obtain a rate adjustment or apply for a commodity rate generally proceeds in the following manner:

1 The buyer contacts the major carrier involved, explains the problem, and requests the carrier to initiate a proposal in his behalf.
2 If the carrier agrees, carrier representatives prepare a complete proposal for the requested rate change and submit it to the standing rate committee of the carrier's cooperative rate-making association.
3 This committee studies the proposal and accepts or rejects it. If accepted, the new rate is written and filed with the Interstate Commerce Commission.
4 If the proposal is rejected, the case can be appealed to an executive group of the rate-making association.
5 If the proposal is again rejected, final appeal can be made directly to the Interstate Commerce Commission for a hearing of the case.

One thing is clear. Rate making and commodity classification are extremely specialized activities. It is not uncommon for even a well-qualified general traffic manager to call upon a specialist for assistance.

Designating Carrier and Route

Not only do freight rates differ significantly between the modes of transportation which might be selected for a given shipment, but in some cases they also differ between the various routes over which the shipment might move. Hence, to minimize shipping costs, it is important that the right mode, carrier, and routing be designated.

To many transportation buyers the service factor is a more important consideration than cost in designating a specific carrier and routing. Service offered by different carriers can vary as much as that of different suppliers. In the case of shipment by motor freight, on long hauls a buyer may have the choice of using a dozen or more connecting carriers. Usually, he tries to involve as few separate carriers in the move as possible in order to reduce the number of transfers required. When a shipment passes from one carrier to another at the boundary of the first carrier's operating territory, the transfer can be made with varying degrees of efficiency. The time actually lost during the transfer depends upon running schedules and transfer facilities of the lines involved.[4]

A city in the Rocky Mountain area, for example, is served by three major motor carriers from Chicago. Because of differences in schedules and facilities at intermediate transfer points, normal delivery times for the alternative carriers range from three to six days. This difference can be quite significant if a firm operates with low inventories or needs an emergency shipment.

On many railroad runs between two points, the carrier can use several alternative routes. There is the fast, direct route, and usually there is a slower circuitous route designed to serve communities located off the direct route. So long as the carrier operates both routes, it can move unrouted shipments over either one. However, the railroad frequently sends unrouted shipments via the circuitous route to achieve a better load distribution among its trains. The informed buyer avoids this possibility by specifying the routing to be used.

A final reason for controlling carrier selection involves a principle well understood by purchasing people. If a company distributes its transportation business among a few selected carriers, in adequate volumes, it is possible to develop very favorable long-term relationships with the carriers. Relationships of this kind can be valuable to the buyer in many ways. When the buyer needs the best service possible for occasional urgent shipments, a favored and friendly carrier is much more inclined to provide the desired service willingly. Likewise, such a carrier is more prone to settle claims promptly and to provide assistance in obtaining justifiable rate adjustments.

EXPEDITING AND TRACING SHIPMENTS

When it is imperative that a purchaser receive a tightly scheduled shipment by a particular date, he or she may wish to "expedite" the shipment. In these cases, the purchaser advises the carrier of the situation *prior* to shipment and requests that arrangements be made for faster than normal movement. Most carriers are willing to expedite shipments if the purchaser requests the service *only* when really necessary. Like the proverbial boy who called "wolf" too often, the purchaser who makes frequent and unnecessary use of this service soon finds that the carrier pays little attention to repetitious demands.

[4]Between New York and Los Angeles there are over 300 possible rail carrier combinations. The number of possible truck combinations from New York to Los Angeles has never been calculated; there are thousands of possibilities.

"Tracing" is the process of following a shipment *after* its departure to obtain a record of the various steps of its movemnet. A purchaser finds that this activity is occasionally required to bring in an overdue shipment; it is inevitable that some shipments become misdirected or lost. In critical situations, tracing is necessary to ensure prompt delivery and continuity of manufacturing operations. Effective tracing work is contingent upon a rather detailed understanding of how various carriers handle their freight. In conducting expediting and tracing work, the purchaser may simply contact a carrier's general agent and ask him to handle the detailed investigation. If the matter is urgent, a purchaser's representative (usually a traffic specialist) may in fact participate in the detailed investigation with the carrier's personnel.

The ease with which a shipment can be traced depends largely upon two things: (1) the completeness and accuracy of the shipping information possessed by the tracer, and (2) the shipping records maintained by the carrier.

As an example, the following information is helpful in tracing a CL shipment:

- Description of material
- Date shipped
- Car number
- Train number
- Route
- Shipper
- Consignee
- Origin
- Destination

In tracing an LCL shipment, additional information typically required is the number of pieces, weight, waybill number, and the first transfer point for the shipment.

Rail CL shipments can be traced fairly easily because most railroads keep records of CL shipments by car initial and number. Passing reports are also maintained along the line, so that a particular car can usually be traced without difficulty from one classification yard to the next as it progresses across the country.

Rail LCL tracing is sometimes difficult. Some railroads keep records of the loading of LCL shipments, others do not. Where records are available, tracing can be accomplished. When no records are maintained, tracing is a nebulous task because of the guesswork involved, and frequently it is impossible.

Freight forwarders usually trace their own CL shipments. Forwarders maintain records which permit them to cross-check any individual shipment to the railcar in which it moved.

Express shipments, by rail and air, are very difficult to trace. Express companies usually maintain records by date and waybill number but frequently keep insufficient details about the movement of individual shipments to permit tracing. However, tracing service offered by these companies is improving.

Motor TL shipments can be traced quite easily because records are kept on every trailer. A trailer travels directly from origin to destination, with perhaps several tractor changes, and can be traced through its various checkpoints along the route.

Motor LTL shipments, as a rule, can be traced fairly easily. Most truck lines maintain a record of every LTL shipment handled.

Air cargo carriers, for the most part, keep records of individual shipments. When a plane takes off, most carriers teletype its entire manifest, giving individual shipment identification, to the destination stations. Consequently, tracing can usually be accomplished without difficulty.

Water carrier shipments can be located easily because, once loaded, they remain aboard the ship until it reaches its destination. The important point, however, is to ensure that the shipment is taken aboard in the first place! Occasionally, cargo is left behind because more material is delivered to the dock than the vessel can carry. In tracing, however, there should be no mystery as to whether cargo was in fact loaded, because the first mate (or a subordinate) is required to sign the waybill when the cargo is actually taken on board.

Parcel post shipments cannot be traced. The postal service keeps no records of individual shipments unless they are registered or insured.

FREIGHT BILL AUDITS

The purchaser of transportation services has the right to audit his freight bills and submit a claim for overcharge within a three-year period after payment of the bill. Most firms find it profitable to audit freight bills. Although such an audit is only prudent business practice, the complexities of freight rates provide a clue to a more compelling motive for scrutinizing freight bills.

The voluminous and complex commodity classification structure produces literally thousands of rates for the different materials moving between different geographical points. It is not uncommon, even for a skilled rate clerk, to make an error in commodity description or commodity classification. This results in an incorrect rate determination. For example, "asbestos blocks packed loosely in boxes" take one rate, while "asbestos shapes other than blocks packed loosely in boxes" take another rate. In thumbing through the Uniform Freight Classification, one finds a myriad of similar cases illustrating even finer distinctions between two classifications. It is, therefore, an understandably common occurrence for most firms to receive freight bills which are incorrect simply because the carrier's billing department applied the wrong rate.[5] If the item is purchased repetitively, errors of this kind may be repeated and a firm's loss compounded.

[5]Freight rate experts estimate that from 4 to 8 percent of all freight bills are rated in error. For more details see T. F. Dillon, "Today's Best Transportation Buy," *Purchasing,* July 23, 1974, pp. 59–62.

During the last several decades, numerous specialized audit bureaus and traffic consultants have developed profitable businesses by auditing their clients' freight bills on a 50 percent commission basis. Under this system the consultant audits all the firm's freight bills free of charge. If incorrect bills are detected, the firm pays the consultant 50 percent of all recoverable overcharges. The fact that more than two dozen independent rate consultants operate in the San Francisco area alone attests to the significance of this problem.

LOSS AND DAMAGE OF FREIGHT

Shipments sometimes get lost or arrive in damaged condition. Normally, the carrier is legally responsible for a shipment while it is in his possession. To obtain a satisfactory settlement for lost shipments, the purchaser should pursue the following procedures: If a shipment does not arrive within a few days of its expected delivery date, the purchaser should contact the supplier to determine definitely that the material was shipped—and if it was, also to obtain necessary tracing information. The purchaser should then contact the carrier and request that the shipment be traced. If the shipment cannot be located, a loss claim for a precise amount of money should be filed in writing with the carrier. It is mandatory that all claims be filed within nine months after the loss, or they may be outlawed. In the interest of prompt investigation and settlement, the sooner the claim is filed, the better.

A shipment can incur two types of damage in transit: (1) apparent damage and (2) concealed damage. If a shipment appears to be damaged or partly missing, these facts should be noted in writing before the shipment is accepted. This can be done on the delivery receipt or the freight bill. Generally, the carrier's driver signs the exception on the copy left with the cosignee, while the cosignee's receiving clerk signs the exception on the copy retained by the carrier. The purchaser should then contact the carrier's freight agent and request the latter to inspect the damage and prepare an inspection report.

Occasionally, damage is concealed and not discovered until a shipment is unpacked. When this happens, the unpacking operation should be discontinued immediately upon detection of damage. The purchaser should contact the carrier's freight agent when the damage is found, in no case more than fifteen days after delivery, and request an inspection of the shipment. The merchandise, as well as the packing material and container, should be left undisturbed for the agent's inspection. Claim settlement is dependent upon satisfactory determination of the party responsible for the damage. Consequently, it is to the purchaser's advantage to preserve all evidence for the carrier's inspection.

The following data are usually submitted in support of a damage claim filed with a carrier:

- The statement of claim, itemized and submitted on a standard claim form available from the carrier
- The carrier's inspection report
- A certified copy of the invoice indicating the value of the shipment
- The paid freight bill
- The original bill of lading

In the case of concealed damage, a statement from the supplier may also be required.

A claim should always be filed as quickly after the occurrence as is practical. The probability of obtaining a favorable settlement is usually greater while the facts of the case are still fresh and clear.

Responsibility for filing a claim rests *with the owner of the material at the time damage occurred.* Consequently, if the damaged material was shipped f.o.b. supplier's plant, the purchaser bears this responsibility. On the other hand, if the shipment was made f.o.b. purchaser's plant, the supplier is responsible for assembling supporting data and filing the claim. In either case, the purchaser must do most of the work preparatory to the actual filing of the claim because he discovered the damage and he has possession of the material.

It is very difficult for a claimant, even by resorting to legal action, to recover successfully from a carrier the cost of concealed damage to a shipment. A claimant must present evidence that the material was properly packed to withstand the normal rigors of shipment and that the merchandise was in undamaged condition at the time it was delivered to the carrier. A claimant must also show that loss or damage was not sustained after delivery while the shipment was in his custody. These are difficult matters to prove. The wise buyer therefore makes every effort to settle such claims out of court. The development of a good business relationship with carriers and a cooperative attitude in following carriers' regulations for reporting and inspecting damage can pay handsome dividends.

DEMURRAGE

When a purchaser receives a carload of material, the railroad allows him approximately two days to unload the car. If he retains the car beyond the allowable period, the carrier assesses a "demurrage" charge. The reason for such a penalty is clear. A freight car is a piece of productive equipment for the railroad; as long as it sits idle on a customer's siding it produces no revenue.

Straight demurrage charges are assessed in the following manner. After a car is received and properly placed for unloading, the purchaser is given forty-eight hours beyond the next 7:00 A.M. to unload the car. For instance, if the railroad delivers and positions a car at 1:00 P.M. Monday, the purchaser has until 7:00 A.M. Thursday to unload the car. For each day he keeps the car after

7:00 A.M. Thursday he must pay a demurrage charge. Although rates fluctuate with the supply and demand for cars, 1976 charges were as follows: first four days $10 per car per day; next two days $20 per car per day; $30 per car per day thereafter. Saturdays, Sundays, and holidays are considered free days and are excluded from demurrage computations.

If a company does much purchasing in carload lots, it may wish to enter into an "average demurrage agreement" with the carrier. Under such an agreement, one demurrage debit is assessed for each day one car is held beyond the allowable time period; one demurrage credit is allowed for each car released during the first twenty-four hours of the allowable forty-eight hour period. Each month the purchaser is billed for the debits in excess of his credits.

It becomes clear that a purchasing department should consult with the department responsible for car handling and unloading when it schedules carload shipments. Good coordination at this point can produce an orderly flow of cars which does not exceed the manpower and physical facilities available for unloading. Sound planning in this area minimizes congestion on the receiving docks, reduces demurrage charges, and reduces labor overtime costs.[6]

TRANSPORTATION COST REDUCTION

A skilled traffic specialist can contribute substantially to the reduction of ultimate material costs. The freight bill audit has already been discussed. In addition to this conventional cost reduction activity, other major approaches to the reduction of transportation costs are: (1) reclassification projects, (2) commodity rate investigations, (3) pool car arrangements, and (4) post performance audits.

Reclassification Projects

The numerous, closely related commodity classifications which have been devised for rate-making purposes present a fertile field for cost reduction investigation. Because many items do not fit neatly into a single classification, the elements of interpretation and judgment play a significant role in the final assignment of a classification number to a given item. Similarly, the method in which a material is packed influences the risk involved in transporting it and, consequently, the classification to which it is assigned.

An alert rate specialist frequently is able to negotiate the reclassification of certain materials into lower-rated classes. Ironically, this can often be accom-

---

[6]While most companies object to paying demurrage charges, at times a boxcar can serve effectively as a rolling warehouse. In certain planned situations it may be profitable to pay some demurrage charges and use a car for storage purposes.

plished merely by revising written descriptions of materials or by slightly modifying packing methods.

For example, one traffic manager in a small plant was successful in getting a regularly purchased casting reclassified as a lower-rated material. Upon investigation, he discovered that several different classifications were applicable to the casting; the classifications differed only with respect to the way in which the casting was crated. By eliminating only one board from the crate, the lower-rated classification was fully applicable. This was done, and the reclassification was approved by the carrier. The first year's savings on this simple project totaled over $10,000.

Commodity Rate Investigations

As stated previously, commodity rates exist as exceptions to class rates and are usually lower than class rates. Quite often, however, no commodity rate exists for the particular item a purchaser ships from a given city. If shipments are repetitive and the volume reasonably large, or if economic or competitive reasons justify it, the purchaser should negotiate with a carrier in an attempt to obtain a commodity rate. It is sometimes possible, too, for several small buyers to consolidate their regular shipments of like materials, and attain a volume sufficient to justify the establishment of a commodity rate.

The case of a large San Francisco firm illustrates the point. Although the firm purchased a large number of castings from a Chicago foundry, the volume was not sufficient to justify the establishment of a commodity rate. Consequently, the traffic manager studied the casting requirements of other manufacturers in the area. Fortunately, he found several who patronized Chicago foundries. By coordinating their plans, he and the traffic managers from the other firms worked out a shipping schedule which permitted them to combine shipments of similar castings to attain a large and consistent volume. A subsequent rate negotiation yielded a commodity rate for these shipments which was 40 percent below the previously paid class rate.

In a more widely publicized case, one large California winery, unable to negotiate what it considered to be a satisfactory commodity rate on East Coast shipments, designed and built a ship for the sole purpose of shipping its wine in bulk. This action gave the winery a significant shipping cost advantage over its competitors. However, as often happens with innovations, the loss of this large traffic movement prompted the railroad to establish a lower commodity rate for the remaining California wineries, to forestall further traffic losses.

Pool Car Arrangements

It is also possible for several buyers to consolidate their requirements for dissimilar items into one single shipment. The individual buyers' small shipments would each ordinarily move under LCL class rates. By combining the small shipments, however, it is often possible to move the *pooled* shipment under a lower CL class rate. Cost-conscious traffic personnel make it a point to know about other firms that patronize suppliers located in the same areas, and they are quick to take advantage of pool car opportunities. At the same time, alert suppliers should know about the availability of pool cars. This is one situation about which the seller may have better transportation information than the purchaser.

Postperformance Audits

Just as decisions concerning the repetitive purchase of materials are periodically reviewed, so should decisions for the purchase of transportation be studied from time to time to ensure that the best buy is in fact achieved. Material usage, delivery requirements, freight rates, carrier performance, service considerations, and various other relevant factors change with the passage of time. Such changes typically influence transportation purchasing decisions, and may necessitate the modification of previously determined shipping practices.

Generally speaking, each major transportation purchase should be reviewed in its entirety. The following checklist is suggested as a starting point for such an investigation:

- Is the most efficient and effective *method of transportation* being used, considering total annual cost of the material?
- Is the most advantageous *routing* specified on major recurring purchases?
- Is the material being purchased or released from suppliers in the *most economical quantities* from a total cost (including transportation) point of view?
- Are *suppliers utilized to best advantage* from a transportation point of view? Are nearest available supplierss used when it is most profitable to do so? Are distant suppliers required to equalize freight charges with the nearest competing source when possible?
- On major recurring purchases, are *shipping instructions followed consistently* by suppliers and carriers? Do carriers consistently strive to provide *good service*?

Critique

In summary, skilled traffic specialists use two techniques to reduce transportation costs. First, by operating within the present rate structure they utilize existing rates to best advantage for the firm. Second, they make full use of special rate services which carriers offer their customers.

PURCHASING'S ROLE

Two things should now be clear. First, the buyer in the purchasing department who has a basic understanding about the buying of transportation is in a position to do a more enlightened job. Second, the buying of transportation is, for the most part, a specialized task best handled by a trained specialist.

The purchasing department and the traffic department should jointly establish their firm's policy in regard to shipping terms and carrier development. Wise buyers consult frequently with traffic personnel on matters of carrier designation and routing; they also request estimates of realistic delivery times and costs via different methods when either is critical. Additionally, buyers must coordinate their efforts with those of traffic personnel in regard to expediting and tracing activities, the filing of loss and damage claims, and the scheduling of major incoming carload shipments. Finally, where appropriate, the buyer should participate with the traffic specialist in transportation-cost reduction projects.

CONCLUSION

Some people mistakenly believe that all carriers have one rigid rate structure for hauling material from one point to another. Although common carriers have fixed rates, there is considerable room for price variation in terms of which rates apply and in terms of what can be done to lower transportation costs by changing classifications, by shipping f.o.b. seller's plant rather than buyer's plant, and by shipping via different routes. Contract carriers have only a schedule of minimum rates. Hence, with these carriers, buyers can often save money by competitive bidding or negotiation.

Many people are not aware of the keen competition that exists in the transportation industry. Truck, rail, air, and water carriers all compete vigorously for tonnage. Progressive buyers understand the potential of this market and take full advantage of its competitive nature.

In the final analysis, purchasing and traffic have no logical alternative but to work together. Their interests are so interrelated that the performance of one department significantly influences the degree of success attained by the other. If purchasing ignores the principles of good traffic management in its daily work, it will in the long run inevitably pay an excessive price for the transportation segment of the materials it buys.

FOR DISCUSSION

16-1   What is the significance of the shipping terms (f.o.b. terms) which appear on a purchase order issued by the buyer?

16-2   Some firms prefer to buy f.o.b. supplier's plant. What do you see as the major arguments for and against this policy? Discuss.

16-3   When a buyer specifies the method of transportation to be used in shipping an order, he has at least a dozen different choices in some cases. What are the significant factors he considers when he views the possibility of shipping by each of the following methods? Discuss.

a Parcel post
b Intercity bus service
c Air cargo

16-4 Answer question 16-3 with respect to the following methods of transportation:
a Freight forwarder
b Intercoastal or inland water freight
c Piggyback and fishyback
d Pipeline

16-5 Recognizing that there may be many specific exceptions, if you were to state a general rule, under what conditions is it usually most advantageous to use rail freight, and under what conditions is it usually most advantageous to use truck freight?

16-6 List and discuss the major types of carriers as viewed by the federal government for regulatory purposes.

16-7 Which of the federal regulatory agencies has jurisdiction over the activities of each type of carrier listed in answer to question 16-6?

16-8 It has been said that in many cases there appears to be little logical relationship between the freight rates in effect for different commodities. What are some of the general reasons which might help to explain this situation?

16-9 What is the difference between a class rate and a commodity rate? Explain.

16-10 Is it very likely that a shipper will ever be billed incorrectly for the transportation service rendered by a carrier? Explain.

16-11 a Define the term "expedite."
b Define the term "trace."
c Under what conditions might a shipper or a purchaser engage in either of these activities?

16-12 In what way might a manufacturing firm employ the services of a traffic consultant or an audit bureau? Explain.

16-13 Outline in detail a receiving procedure which a firm might use to ensure proper handling of lost and damaged shipments.

16-14 a Define the term "demurrage."
b Explain the different types of demurrage agreements under which a firm may operate.

16-15 Discuss in detail the various things a firm might do to reduce its transportation costs.

16-16 "Generally speaking, transportation should be purchased much like any material, on the basis of service, quality, and price." Discuss this statement.

CASES FOR CHAPTER 16

Redi-Pore Filter Corporation, page 647
The Controversial Freight Bill Case, page 609

Receiving and Stores

Receiving and storage activities constitute the last link in the materials management chain. Regardless of the efficiency with which all preceding inventory management, procurement, and traffic activities have been conducted, the production department will be supplied satisfactorily only if the receiving and stores operations function effectively.

Because the purchasing department is normally responsible for materials up to the point where they are ready for production use, it is essential that purchasing managers understand the fundamentals of receiving and stores operations. Moreover, in nearly one-half of all industrial concerns in the United States, stores and receiving departments are either placed under the jurisdiction of the purchasing department or are grouped with purchasing and related materials activities in a materials management department.[1] Whether a firm adopts the materials management concept extensively or not, receiving and stores are a vital element in its total materials system. Effective coordination with the purchasing, inventory management, and traffic functions is imperative.

[1] Baer and Centamore, "Materials Management: Where It Stands and What It Needs," *Purchasing Magazine* (special report), 1970; Aljian, *Purchasing Handbook*, McGraw-Hill Book Company, New York, 1973, p. 14-3.

RESPONSIBILITIES OF RECEIVING AND STORES

Receiving and stores operations function is the capacity of service and control groups. From a managerial viewpoint, they exist for three reasons. First, they provide a service to the production operation. It is difficult for a production organization to operate efficiently unless someone is specifically designated to organize and control the physical flow of materials into production. Second, the stores organization acts as a custodial and controlling agency. It is responsible for the physical welfare and control of a substantial portion of a firm's current assets. Third, the existence of stores permits quantity buying and the attendant cost savings in price, paperwork, and handling.

Specific Responsibilities

The receiving department is responsible for the expeditious receipt, identification, and general inspection of all incoming materials. Receiving is also responsible for promptly notifying all interested parties of the receipt and condition of incoming material.

The stores department bears responsibility for safe and technically sound physical storage of all production materials, some in-process inventory, and most MRO items. In some companies, stores is also responsible for finished goods storage; in others, finished goods are handled by a different organizational group.

The stores department must protect materials in its custody against pilferage, unauthorized usage, and unnecessary damage or deterioration. It must also adequately classify, mark, and locate all materials in a manner which permits ready accessibility. Finally, the stores department must control the physical issuance of all items in a manner that provides effective service for the production operation and, at the same time, protects against unauthorized withdrawal of materials.

Cost Implications

Receiving and stores activities *indirectly* influence product costs in several ways. Inventory carrying costs stemming from deterioration and pilferage of materials, as well as indirect stores labor, are controllable to a great extent by these organizations. Moreover, an alert stores organization can help reduce the costs of obsolescence by developing check systems to detect inactive materials. Similarly, efficient use of scarce storage space can further reduce inventory carrying costs.

The stores operation also exerts a strong influence on *direct* labor costs. Strategically located storage facilities that provide prompt service for production personnel help reduce the unproductive time of production workers and equipment. Workers and machines waiting for the delivery of material add nothing to the productive effort of a firm.

RECEIVING OF MATERIALS

Receiving is essentially a clerical operation. Because many clerical functions are regarded as "routine," this fact often clouds the importance of receiving. It is at the receiving desk that papers directing the flow of purchased materials meet the physical materials themselves. Any problem or error in a specific purchase transaction should come to light during the receiving operation. If the problem (shortage in quantity, damaged material, wrong items shipped, etc.) is not detected and corrected during the receiving operation, the cost to correct the mistake later is much higher. If a shortage in quantity, for example, is not discovered at the time of receipt, any combination of departments can be drawn into the problem later. Many hours are frequently spent in determining what really happened and in rectifying the situation. Hours are required to correct an error that could have been corrected at the receiving station in minutes.

The receiving report which the clerk completes upon receipt of a shipment is the only document a firm possesses which details the material it has actually received. This document is used as the basis for invoice payment, for continued purchasing negotiation, and for closing the order. Accuracy is therefore essential. Clearly, poor receiving performance can produce costly consequences. For this reason, it should be supervised by a person who is reasonably familiar with the physical characteristics of the materials and who is capable of exercising sound judgment in situations where a choice of alternatives must be made.

Receiving is an important control point in a firm's materials system. The receiving clerk can detect those suppliers who meet only the minimum standards of quality and service. Receiving records show which suppliers are consistently late in their deliveries, which have the maximum number of rejects, and which deliver the greatest number of split shipments. Any of these supplier failures is costly to the buyer; hence, close coordination between purchasing and receiving usually pays dividends.

Receiving Procedure

A typical receiving procedure consists of four steps:

1   *Unloading and checking the shipment.* The number of containers unloaded from the carrier's vehicle should be checked against the carrier's manifest (freight bill) to make certain the full consignment has been delivered. All containers should also be inspected for external damage; any damage found should be inspected by the carrier's representative and noted on the receipt which the receiving clerk signs. Failure to follow this procedure before accepting a shipment can relieve the carrier of all liability, except liability for concealed damage not evident until the container is unpacked.

2 *Unpacking and inspecting the material.* A receiving clerk is held responsible for three verifications. He checks the material received against the seller's packing slip and against his copy of his firm's purchase order to verify that the correct items have been shipped. Second, he verifies the quantity of the shipment in the same manner. Finally, he inspects the general condition of the material to determine whether any damage was incurred during shipment.

3 *Completion of the receiving report.* In most companies, a document known as a "receiving report" is prepared as a by-product of the purchase order. Upon completion of his inspection, the receiving clerk completes this report, checking off what he has received and indicating which items, if any, on the order remain open. Four groups generally require notification that material has been received: the requisitioner (the inventory control section in the case of stock materials), the purchasing department, the accounting department, and the inspection department if technical inspection is required.

4 *Delivery of the material.* In the case of non-stock materials, the receiving department is usually responsible for delivering them to the requisitioner or for releasing them to an internal delivery service that transports them to the requisitioner. In the case of inventory materials, the practice varies. In some firms the receiving department is responsible for internal deliveries, while in others this function is performed by an internal transportation service; in still others, stores clerks are responsible for picking up their own materials. The delivery system depends somewhat upon the relative location of the receiving and the stores areas.

Upon delivery of the material, the recipient customarily signs the receiving report, relieving the receiving clerk of any further responsibility for the material.

Receiving Paperwork

The paperwork system used in the receiving operation varies substantially among different firms. In a majority of cases, the receiving department is notified of an impending shipment by a copy of the original purchase order. Some firms feel it is advantageous to omit purchase order quantities from receiving's copy of the order. The theory is that the receiving clerk is less likely to miscount the quantity of items received if he or she does not know how many there are supposed to be. Since most vendors provide an itemized packing list, however, this theory is open to question.

In some companies, the receiving clerk prepares a receiving report by manually writing the data on a multipart carboned form. An obvious disadvantage of this approach is the preparation time required and the increased opportunity for errors. To avoid this inefficiency, many firms type a multipart receiving form as part of the original purchase order. Using this form, the receiving clerk notes only quantities and occasional comments on the report form.

Firms controlling inventories with punched card equipment can use a punched card receiving report. When an order is placed, all records. including the receiving report, are prepared in punched card form. Upon receipt of the order, the receiving clerk simply notes any significant deviations on the punched receiving card and sends it to the data processing group for correction, reproduction, and distribution. With the increased use of electronic data processing equipment, application of this medium has become fairly common in large companies.

Many small firms with few incoming shipments simplify the receiving reporting procedure. Some firms use receiving's copy of the purchase order as the report, noting any deviations on the order form. This form is then routed sequentially to all interested parties to complete the communication procedure. Other firms simplify the procedure even further by similarly using the supplier's packing slip as a receiving report. Although these simplified systems do not provide each department with a complete set of records, many small firms have no need for more elaborate records.

IDENTIFICATION OF MATERIALS

Stores activities involve primarily the physical aspects of materials handling and storage. Management personnel are concerned not only with the physical operations, but more importantly with the design and control of the systems utilized in conducting these activities. Developing systems for effective identification of materials is the first responsibility confronting a stores manager.

A firm's stock catalog, prepared by the inventory management group, lists and describes every item normally carried in inventory. These descriptions, however, are somewhat lengthy and imprecise for use in identifying materials during daily operations. For this reason, most suppliers assign part numbers to their products. Because different suppliers use vastly different numbering systems, however, it is virtually impossible for a purchaser to develop a satisfactory material identification system based on suppliers' part numbers. Therefore a firm with a sizable production and MRO inventory is compelled to develop its own numerical identification system for its materials. The inventory catalog should be arranged and indexed by the purchaser's own part numbers. It should also include the supplier's part number along with a concise verbal description of each item. The catalog can be cross-indexed in alternative ways; certainly it should be cross-indexed by generic name of the items and perhaps also by suppliers and their part numbers.

The objective is to develop an unambiguous identification system that facilitates clear internal communication. Ideally, this system should be designed so that it can be used effectively by all departments in the firm. Clearly, the purchasing, inventory control, and stores departments are critical areas where the system must provide consistent and unambiguous identification of materials. If the system can also be integrated with the operations of design engineering, production, and cost accounting, improved communication and simplified clerical activities are almost certain to result.

System Design

Three basic approaches may be used in developing an identification system: (1) the arbitrary approach, (2) the symbolic approach, and (3) the use of engineering drawing numbers. Using the arbitrary approach, inventory items are simply assigned arbitrary numbers in sequence as they are added to a stores account. Each item thus has a discrete number, but it bears no systematic relationship to the numbers assigned to related items. For example, two similar pumps or two mating parts may have numbers several thousand digits apart. While this system is certainly better than none, if time is to be spent developing a system, a more useful one can be developed with a little extra effort.

The symbolic approach to system design is commonly used in American industry. Symbolic systems can be either *numerical* or *mnemonic*. A numerical system assigns a six- to ten-digit code number to each item. The first several numbers usually indicate the classification to which the item belongs, the next several numbers typically indicate the subclass, and the last three numbers are usually uncoded. The following example illustrates the concept:

2	137	019	508
General Class	Generic Class	Sub-Class	Specific Item number

This ten-digit code number is one firm's stock number for a ¹/₄- by ³/₄-inch stainless steel square-neck carriage bolt. The first digit indicates that the item is a purchased part, in accordance with the following general classification:

1 Raw materials
2 Purchased parts
3 Manufactured parts
4 Work in process
5 MRO supplies

The next three digits indicate the generic classification of the item. In this case it is a fastener, code number 137; it might have been a bearing, a pulley, a pump, an electric motor, etc. All items are generically classified by their nature and carry a number from 000 to 999.

The next three digits indicate the subclass to which the item belongs. In this case, number 019 is a carriage bolt with a square neck. It might have been a machine screw, a rivet, a nut, etc. All fasteners are subclassified into a class bearing a number from 000 to 999.

The last three digits indicate the specific part number of the item. In this case, all part numbers under 500 designate plain steel, and numbers over 500 represent various alloys; 508 is stainless steel, $1/4$ by $3/4$ inch. Other dimensional details can be determined only by referring to the inventory catalog.

This example and similar systems provide a complete and ordered framework within which all materials can be unambiguously identified and handled. As a rule, each company devises its own specific system to suit the needs of its own particular materials. A ten-digit number is long and cumbersome; a six-digit system is much easier to use if it provides adequate definition and contains enough unused numbers to accommodate future growth. A few companies structure their systems around finished products rather than generic classification. The subdivision distinctions can be made as fine or as broad as desired. A major criterion to guide these decisions should be the value of the utility the additional system refinement provides the user.

A mnemonic system functions much like a numerical system. However, it combines numeric and alphabetic notations in its symbols. For example, the preceding carriage bolt might be described this way in a mnemonic system:

P   Fa   BCS   508

P denotes a purchased part, Fa is a fastener, BCS stands for bolt, carriage, with a square neck, and 508 represents the specific number of the bolt.

Mnemonic systems, particularly where a small number of items are involved, frequently make visual identification easier because they are more descriptive and they are often shorter. As more and different types of items are added to the inventory, however, this advantage diminishes because the number of good symbols is limited. Telephone companies have encountered this coding problem. As a result, most have converted telephone dial codes from mnemonic to numeric.

Some firms identify the stock parts manufactured to their own engineering specifications by using the engineering drawing number as the part number. This system is effective because it is simple and it directly references the technical data source for the part. Moreover, it simplifies interdepartmental communications because all departments use the same system. On the other hand, the system has the nonsequencing disadvantages of the arbitrary system, and since it covers primarily manufactured parts, a separate system must be devised for many purchased parts.

Physical Identification

Even though a satisfactory identification system is developed, physical identification of materials in the storeroom may still be a problem. The first step in minimizing identification problems is to record the storage location of all items in an inventory catalog. When a storeroom is properly laid out, every storage location has a numerical designation. Each inventory item should be assigned a specific storage location. These locations can be noted in the catalog or in a separate storage locator index so that anyone should be able to locate any material with ease.

Each storage bin should be labeled with its part number. In some cases, an abbreviated description of the item may be helpful. All items which are not readily identifiable on sight should be tagged or marked with the part number by the storekeeper. On nonstandard items, suppliers can frequently mark an item during the manufacturing or shipping operation. Castings, stampings, and forgings are good examples of items which can be marked permanently for little or no extra cost. Some materials, such as steel plate, bars, special bolts, etc., are difficult to mark. Intercompany groups have done much to standardize identification markings for such material. One scheme involves the use of a standard color code; the ends or edges of the material are simply marked with the appropriate color to facilitate quick identification.

STORES SYSTEMS

Two basic systems can be used in physically controlling stores materials: (1) a closed stores system and (2) an open stores system. A single firm often employs both systems. The application of each system depends upon the nature of the production operation and the way in which materials are used in it.

Closed System

As its name indicates, a closed stores system is one in which all materials are physically stored in a closed or controlled area. Wherever possible, the general practice is to maintain physical control by locking the storage area. As a rule, no one other than stores personnel is permitted in the stores area. Material enters and leaves the area only with the accompaniment of an authorizing document. This system is designed to afford maximum physical security and to ensure tight accounting control of inventory material.

Records   In years past, each storekeeper was responsible for maintaining an inventory record for each of the items under his control. He posted all receipts and withdrawals on a "bin tag" which eventually became the firm's permanent record of activity for a given material.

Today, most firms maintain centralized perpetual inventory records independent of storeroom stock cards. Receipts are posted to the perpetual record from suppliers' invoices or from the firm's receiving reports. Withdrawals from stores are normally authorized and posted from one of two sources. The most common source is the stores requisition, which is made out by the user and signed by an authorized supervisor. This central record provides a running balance for each major inventory item.

Another commonly used source of withdrawal authorization is the engineering bill of materials. These lists of materials are developed along with the design drawings. After the design engineering work for a job has been completed, production control schedules the job and arranges for the release of the required materials to the shop. Instead of preparing a set of stores requisitions for these materials, production control may simply reproduce the engineering bill of materials and send a copy to stores as the document authorizing release of the materials. For effective use, this system requires clear and complete identification of all materials on the engineering bill of materials. For the materials involved, a single companywide inventory numbering system is a necessity when this system is used.

When the materials required for a job are to be withdrawn from stores over a period of time, using bills of material as withdrawal authorizations presents a problem. Unless a daily report of withdrawals for the job is prepared, it is difficult for the central inventory record section to keep its records current, because the stores department must retain its copy of the bill of materials until all withdrawals are made.

This problem can be circumvented, however, by using a material apportioning system. Under this system, the bill of materials goes first to the inventory record section, where the total requirement for each material needed on a job is deducted from the current inventory balance. The required amount is set aside, or apportioned (on the record card), so it will not be allocated for use on any other job before the current requirement materializes in the shop. When the apportioned material is actually used, the apportioned quantity on the inventory record is charged off to the job. The apportioning system, of course, can be used to assure material availability for specific jobs regardless of the method used to authorize stores withdrawals. The system is widely used among firms with job-shop-type operations.

Every firm uses many low-value inventory items. To maintain a perpetual inventory record for all low-value items may cost more than the control provided such a record is worth. To obtain a record of approximate usage, it is much cheaper to have the stores clerk record all receipts on a bin tag. To indicate when an item should be ordered, a bin level mark or some form of the two-bin control system can be used. Many firms simply place the reorder quantity of small items in a plastic bag; when the clerk has to use stock from the bag, he knows it is time to reorder. This method is frequently used for nuts, bolts, and other low-value hardware. If the accounting charge can be determined at the time an order is issued, the accounting department can pick up the proper distribution code from the purchase order. If not, the accounting department usually develops a method by which the expenditure can be allocated equitably among the users.

Physical Inventory   No matter how diligently a storekeeper performs the custodial job or how carefully an inventory control clerk maintains records (computerized or manual), some discrepancy between the actual and the book balances of inventories is bound to occur. The system is operated by people, and people occasionally make mistakes. For this reason, every inventory item should be physically counted and checked against its book balance at least once a year. The books are subsequently adjusted to match the actual count. Most companies create an "inventory short and over" account to absorb such

discrepancies; this account is eventually closed into the manufacturing overhead account.

The physical inventory can be conducted in one of three ways:

1 *Fixed annual inventory.* Many companies take physical inventory every
   year at the close of the fiscal period. This necessitates shutting down
   the production operation and organizing a special crew for the inventory job.
2 *Continuous inventory.* At the beginning of each year some firms divide
   their inventory into fifty-two equal groups and assign one of the
   fifty-two groups to be physically counted each week. Thus, the physical
   inventory operation goes on continuously without interrupting the
   production operation or upsetting storeroom activities.[2]
3 *Low-point inventory.* Some companies take physical inventory irregularly, i.e., whenever the stock level of an item reaches its lowest point.

All three methods are widely used; the selection of the most appropriate
one depends largely upon conditions in each individual business. The fixed
annual inventory can be troublesome because it is a major task which must be
accomplished in a short period of time. However, it is ideal for seasonal
businesses or for businesses that completely close down for an annual
vacation.

The continuous inventory approach possesses two important advantages.
It can be planned and worked into scheduled activities without a shutdown. It
can be conducted in an orderly and relaxed manner; these conditions are
always conducive to accurate work. This approach also facilitates efficient
utilization of stores personnel. In many storerooms, withdrawals are heavy
early in the day and are much lighter later on. Thus, when the stock clerks'
normal work slacks off, they always have a backlog of inventory work to do.

The low-point approach minimizes the time required for actual inventory
work because of the small quantities of materials involved. However, it has the
disadvantage of producing an irregular inventory schedule, which tends to peak
the work load for stores personnel.

Finally, before developing the details of any physical inventory method, a
company should consult the accounting firm that audits its books. A company
must be able to demonstrate to auditing firms, and to local and federal tax
officials, that the method finally selected is capable of producing accurate
inventory reports.

Storeroom Location   In laying out a manufacturing operation, a layout
engineer attempts to develop an efficient work flow that minimizes the
transportation and handling of materials. This means that materials should be

---

[2]This method is also called the "cycle-count" method. A major advantage it offers is the
possibility of detecting and eliminating basic causes of errors that might otherwise continue
throughout the year.

stored as close to their point of use as is feasible. Hence, the use of decentralized storage facilities frequently reduces manufacturing costs.

On the other hand, the centralization of storage facilities also yields significant benefits. From a managerial point of view, the major advantage of centralization is that it facilitates control of the total stores operation— manpower, materials, space utilization, and equipment. Whenever an activity is divided and conducted as a number of separate subactivities, supervision and coordination of the total operation become more difficult. Up to a point, the larger the storage area, the more efficiently space and equipment can be used. Similarly, a larger operation facilitates the balancing of individual work loads and permits more efficient utilization of personnel.

A company normally attempts to use both centralized and decentralized locations in its total stores operation. The objective is to secure the major advantages of both approaches to the extent possible in a particular situation. Most plants attempt to centralize as much material as is practical. The result, for example, may be two or three large storerooms strategically located near different manufacturing areas, the exact number depending upon the size and nature of the production operation. When possible, heavy or bulky materials that are costly to handle should be stored adjacent to the point of use. For example, in a processing plant it is quite common to find one or two large centralized storerooms handling small production items, packaging materials, tools, and MRO supplies. Scattered throughout the plant adjacent to the point at which they are put into the process are numerous stacks of large bags and drums containing such things as chemicals and additives.

Open System

The open system represents the second major type of stores system. It finds its widest use in highly repetitive, mass production types of operations exhibiting a continuous and predictable demand for the same materials.

In plants using the open stores system, no storeroom as such exists. Each material is stored as close to its point of use as is physically possible. Materials are stored in bins, on shelves, in racks, on pallets, in tote boxes, and so on, much as they would be stored in a storeroom. However, the storage configuration at each work station is arranged to fit the available space. Storage facilities are completely open, and any worker has access to any storage facility.

After material is received, stores personnel are usually responsible for its delivery to the production areas. They are further responsible for working out satisfactory physical storage arrangements with the production supervisors. After the material has been delivered, production supervisors assume responsibility for materials stored in their areas.

The open system is designed to expedite production activities. It places little emphasis on the physical security of materials. In ideal applications, there is considerable justification for this approach because the material is used relatively quickly, and it is not subject to a high rate of deterioration or obsolescence.

An automobile assembly plant offers the clearest example of an open stores system. Here daily production is high, and purchased parts and subassemblies flow into the plant in a steady stream. For higher-cost, bulky items, deliveries from vendors are scheduled at frequencies as high as several times per day. As a result, average inventory is extremely low relative to plant output. Such systems place unusually exacting demands for close cooperation on production control, purchasing, and suppliers' personnel.

The open system also places less emphasis on the accounting control of materials. Materials are usually put into production without the use of a requisition or a control document. No perpetual inventory records are kept in an open system. To determine the *actual* usage of a material during a given period, it is necessary to take a physical count of the material at the end of the period and to compare this figure with the similar beginning-period figure (which has been adjusted for material receipts during the period). Hence, accounting charges are determined indirectly rather than directly. As a result, the system provides control over material usage only if it is used in conjunction with an accounting system employing standard cost techniques.

To conclude, the open system is most applicable in situations where a repetitive production operation produces standardized products. Materials handled in an open system should not be subject to pilferage, nor should they be easily damaged. If production requires delicate or pilferable items, they should probably be controlled in a closed storeroom. Generally speaking, an open system is more likely to function successfully if it is not applied to a large number of items. Firms applying such a system to several hundred items typically experience better results than those applying it to several thousand items.

Random-Access Storage System

The random-access storage system is a unique type of closed stores system, employed by a relatively small number of large firms. In this system, no material has a fixed storage location. When an item enters the storeroom, it is stored in the first available bin or shelf suitable for its storage requirements. When the item is withdrawn from stores, the storage space is available for any other incoming item having similar physical storage requirements. All materials are thus stored at random locations throughout the storeroom. This means, for example, that a stock of nine 20-horsepower electric motors may be located at nine different places in the storeroom. However, *similar types and sizes of storage equipment* are grouped together. This has the effect of dividing the storeroom into areas of materials that are similar in size and storage requirements.

How does the storekeeper find an item once it has been stored? Items are located by means of a paper-work control system that utilizes punched card data processing equipment. When an item enters the storeroom, a punched record card is prepared. Included on the item's record card is its storage location address (each storage location is numbered). The record card is then filed. When a stores requisition (in punched card form) is received for an item, the requisition and the stored-material cards are run through an electronic matching device. The electronic unit locates a stored-material record that matches the requisition. When a corresponding record card is obtained, it contains the storage address where the item can be found.

The random-access storage system is clearly feasible only in large operations. It requires electronic data processing equipment, as well as an expensive control system. The system also has several significant disadvantages. For example, tight physical control of materials is more difficult to achieve. Clerks seldom become familiar with the total stock of any item. If a record card is lost, the item itself may literally be "lost" for an indefinite period of time. Additionally, when a physical inventory is taken, it clearly becomes a major and time-consuming project.

If properly designed and operated, a random-access storage system possesses two important advantages. First, it utilizes space much more efficiently than a fixed-location system. In arranging storage facilities, space for a fluctuating inventory level does not have to be left vacant for each individual material. Second, the system provides great flexibility. The same storage facilities can easily accommodate different materials, shifts in inventory mix, and unexpected increases in the stock level of an existing material.

STORING OF MATERIALS

Few things irritate a production supervisor more than an inefficient, poorly organized storeroom. A good storeroom layout and good storage methods yield the following benefits:

1. Ready accessibility of major materials, permitting efficient service to users
2. Efficient space utilization and flexibility of arrangement
3. A reduced need for materials handling equipment
4. Minimization of material deterioration and pilferage
5. Ease of physical counting

Methods and Equipment

Planning Planning is the key to consistent and efficient storeroom operation. What types and combinations of storage equipment should be used? How should the storeroom be laid out? These are key planning questions that must be answered.

The initial step in answering the first question is to compile a list of information about the materials to be stored. Using a current inventory catalog, the following data should be listed for each item carried:

1   How much space is required to store the item properly?
2   How many units are normally withdrawn at once? Should the item be stored singly, in pairs, in dozens?
3   What is the maximum number of units to be stored at one time?
4   What type of storage facility best suits the item (considering such things as weight, shape, and handling)?
5   What handling equipment is necessary to transport the item?
6   How often is the item withdrawn from stores?
7   Where is the item most frequently used in the production operation?

The numbers and types of storage facilities currently required can be determined fairly definitely if these seven questions are answered for all materials. At the same time, estimates of future needs should be made. By comparing future requirements with current requirements, a solution to the current problem can often be designed to include enough flexibility to permit relatively easy adaptation of the facilities to future needs when that time arrives.

Equipment   Eight general types of equipment are commonly used in storing materials:

1   Pallets and skids
2   Open and closed shelving
3   Cabinets (with or without counters)
4   Bins
5   Stacking boxes
6   Special storage racks
7   Gravity feed racks
8   Outdoor platforms and racks

Figures 17-1 and 17-2 illustrate several storage installations using some of the common types of storage and materials handling equipment.

Most industrial storerooms used to be equipped with wooden shelving and storage facilities. Wooden facilities still offer several advantages. Wood is softer than metal and provides safer storage for delicate items which might be dropped or scuffed in the bin. Wooden facilities can also be built to special configurations and can generally be installed quickly and inexpensively.

Wooden facilities are quite inflexible, however, and this causes problems as an a operation expands or as storage needs change. To overcome this disadvantage, most companies today use steel equipment of the "knock-down" variety. This equipment is designed so that it can be assembled and reassem-

Figure 17-1 A two-level storeroom using a combination of metal shelving, bins, and cabinets. Materials-handling equipment shown consists of roller conveyors joined by a belt conveyor. *(Courtesy of Lyon Metal Products Inc.).*

bled in shelf or bin form in numerous different standardized shapes and sizes. Although steel equipment is more expensive initially, its long-run advantages usually outweight the additional cost. Its configuration and location flexibility gives steel equipment a major advantage over wooden equipment. Steel equipment has the additional advantages of strength and fire resistance; it is also easy to keep clean.

Storage Methods An important objective of all stores operations is to minimize deterioration and spoilage. It is common practice, particularly when dealing with materials that tend to deteriorate or become obsolete, to issue old material ahead of new material. Numerous schemes can be devised for accomplishing this end. A very simple solution, however, is illustrated in Figure 17-3.

Figure 17-3 represents stacked boxes of material. As material is withdrawn, it is taken from the left end of the stack, moving progressively to the right. When new shipments arrive, they are stored on the right. Thus, by moving from left to right, older material is used first, leaving newer material for future use. This technique is commonly referred to as storage for "first-in, first-out" usage.

Special protection is occasionally required for some items. If metal parts are subject to rust or corrosion, they should be stored in dry areas. In some cases, they may have to be covered with suitable rust-inhibiting compounds.

Figure 17-2 Wooden pallets being used to provide efficient storage for heavy, unwieldy industrial valves. The materials-handling equipment is a gasoline-powered fork-lift type of stacking truck. *(Courtesy of the Clark Equipment Company).*

Likewise, dust may be harmful to certain items. Airtight containers or drawers are suitable for the storage of these items. In some cases, it is possible to purchase such items packaged in sealed plastic; this obviates the need for dust-free storage.

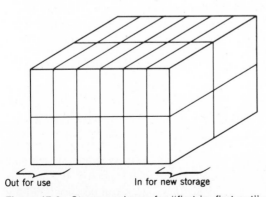

Out for use   In for new storage

Figure 17-3 Storage scheme for "first-in, first-out" usage.

Some liquids are sensitive to heat and cold; certain granulated materials are sensitive to moisture. Such items should be stored in suitable locations.

Obviously, items subject to pilferage should be stored in locked cabinets or other secure areas to reduce temptation and subsequent losses.

Units of Issue   A storeroom does not always issue a material in the same units in which it is purchased. Steel, for example, is usually purchased in tons or pounds and issued in sheets, bars, or feet. Some boxed materials are purchased by the gross and issued by the dozen. Record-keeping errors sometimes occur when specific units of issue are not clearly established for such materials.

To avoid possible communication difficulties, the standard unit of issue for a material is usually defined as the smallest quantity likely to be issued. The inventory record should be maintained in terms of the standard unit, and stores requisitions should state withdrawals in the same terms. Errors can be avoided by using the same unit of issue for similar materials. Likewise, units of issue involving calculations, such as square feet or board feet, should be avoided whenever possible. In cases where the unit of issue is not obvious to operating personnel, it should be clearly marked on the stock bin and on the inventory record.

Some items, such as powdered materials, nails, screws, and numerous small items, can be dispensed more efficiently by weight than by actual count. In such cases, weight-to-unit conversion tables should be developed so that records can be maintained in the same units as issues are made.

Layout

Good storeroom layout attempts to achieve five objectives:

1   A straight-line flow of activity through the storeroom with minimum backtracking
2   Minimum handling and transportation of materials
3   Minimum travel and waste motion for personnel
4   Efficient use of space
5   Provision for flexibility and expansion of layout

It is virtually impossible to attain all objectives completely. However, a carefully planned compromise solution can usually satisfy most layout objectives reasonably well.

The initial criteria used in laying out most storerooms are the size, shape, and type of material to be stored. Items are first analyzed to determine their storage facility requirements. Items with similar requirements are then grouped together. From this analysis, the total requirement *for each type of storage equipment* can be determined. Once this determination is made, it can be analyzed in conjunction with a floor plan of the available space. By making scaled templates of the equipment, various arrangements can be simulated on the floor plan until the one which most nearly satisfies the basic objectives is found.

Storage Location Address A well-worn but appropriate slogan seen in many storerooms is, "A place for everything and everything in its place." A "place for everything" can be planned. Keeping "everything in its place," though, is not always an easy job. The development of a good storage location address system provides assistance to those who try to keep everything in place.

There are numerous ways of addressing storage locations. One widely used system is illustrated in Figure 17-4. This system arranges the storeroom in "blocks" of storage units, much as a city is laid out in blocks of houses. Each

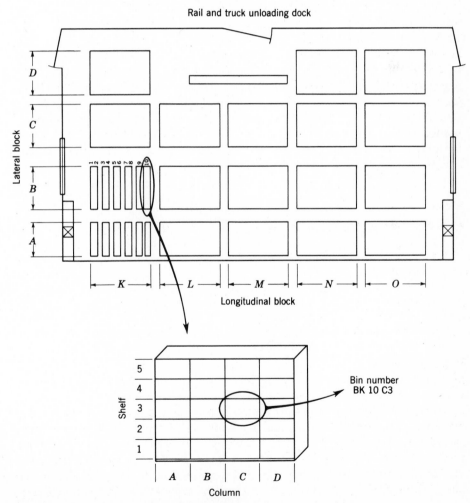

Figure 17-4 A common system used in addressing storage locations.

block is identified by a lateral block letter and a longitudinal block letter. Within each block, every row of shelves is given a number. Each row is divided vertically into columns and horizontally into shelves. A particular bin is identified by reading the letters and numbers in the following sequence: lateral block, longitudinal block, row, column, and shelf.

Blocks and rows should be clearly identified with painted signs. Columns and shelves are always read starting from the lower left corner. Frequently, the shelves are not labeled because shelves are added and taken away from time to time as storage requirements change.

Every item carried in stores thus has a specific storage location address. These location addresses should be listed in the inventory catalog if possible; if not, they should at least be listed in a stores location index.

ORGANIZATION

The stores and receiving jobs are closely related. Therefore, the receiving activity is often placed under jurisdiction of the storekeeper. As stated earlier, in nearly half of all United States industrial firms, stores either reports to the purchasing department or is grouped with purchasing in a materials management department. There are two strong arguments for such an organizational arrangement:

1   The stores activity is a materials-oriented activity; therefore, it should report to a department whose primary interest likewise lies in materials and supply operations. Supervisory personnel will thus recognize and be equipped to deal with the materials and supply problems encountered in receiving and stores.

2   Receiving is the last step in the material acquisition process, and stores is the last step in the material supply process. From the standpoint of the *total control of materials* these activities should be included with the rest of the materials activities. From an operating point of view, such a materials organization facilitates coordination among the related materials activities. Specifically, it ensures that the relationships between stores, inventory control, and purchasing will receive proper attention, as will the important factor of indirect material costs.

Other firms place the stores activity under the production department. In some cases, it is placed under a factory superintendent; in others, it reports to the production control manager; and in still others, it reports to the general production manager. Two common justifications for this form of organization are:

1   Production management is responsible for running the production operation smoothly and for meeting product delivery dates. Production should therefore have control of its immediate material supply group to ensure smooth delivery of material to the production work stations.

2 Receiving and stores should not be supervised by the department that buys and authorizes payment for the materials they receive and disburse. Collusion and embezzlement of materials are discouraged when stores and receiving personnel report to a manager outside the purchasing department.

Both preceding sets of arguments are valid, although in most firms the authors believe those supporting a materials management structure are more compelling. The final decision, however, will probably be heavily conditioned by other factors in a particular firm's organizational and operational pattern.

In making the organization decision, management's primary concern should be the fulfillment of three basic objectives. First, materials must be stored and managed so that they are immediately available and in good condition when the production organization needs them. Second, the order-filling and delivery system must efficiently supply the production organization in accordance with production schedules. Third, these and related activities must be accomplished at a minimum cost.

Under which manager (production or materials) will the three objectives in fact be realized to the fullest extent? The answer may vary with the basic orientation of a given firm. However, the responsible executive must be broad-gauged enough to see the importance of all three objectives clearly and fairly. Furthermore, consistent fulfillment of the second objective requires fulfillment of the first objective also. This means that the stores responsibility should rest with one individual who is qualified and primarily interested in doing a good stores job. Such a person must not be pressured unduly by short-term-oriented personnel who are interested primarily in "getting the finished product out the back door."

A final factor which conditions the decision is the location of the inventory control responsibility. While there is no requirement that stores and inventory control must report to the same department head, in practice the paperwork system of a closed stores operation demands close coordination between stores and inventory control. If the two groups do in fact report to the same department head, many mutual control problems can be solved quickly at a lower level before they become serious. Thus in a firm using a predominantly closed stores system, there is a legitimate tendency to place inventory control and stores under the same department head.

FOR DISCUSSION

17-1   "Receiving and stores activities indirectly influence product costs in several ways." Comment on this statement.

17-2   The receiving of material appears to be largely a routine clerical activity. Yet the statement is made that receiving should be conducted by a person who is capable of exercising sound judgment. Discuss.

17-3   Outline and discuss briefly a typical receiving procedure.

17-4   Prepare a complete flow chart for a receiving procedure to be used in a plant where inventory control is handled entirely on a computer. Supplement your flow chart with a brief description of the various documents you use and an explanation of their significance.

17-5   Discuss briefly the responsibilities of a typical stores department.

17-6   a What problems exist when a company attempts to use suppliers' part numbers in its material identification system?

   b What problems does a company encounter when it develops its own material identification system but develops the system only for its major production materials?

17-7   a Explain how a numerical material identification system works.

   b Explain how a mnemonic material identification system works.

   c Devise and explain an eight-digit numerical system which could be used for identifying production materials used in an automobile assembly plant.

17-8   a Explain how a closed stores system operates. How is accounting control maintained? Under what conditions should a closed stores system be used?

   b Explain how an open stores sytem operates. How is accounting control maintained? Under what conditions should an open stores system be used?

17-9   Discuss the use of a perpetual inventory record in both the closed and open stores systems.

17-10 Prepare a step-by-step procedure for use in conducting an annual physical inventory of materials. Make rough sketches of any forms required and include any instructions necessary for clerical personnel.

17-11 Describe and discuss the merits of the three methods which might be used in conducting a physical inventory of materials.

17-12 a Discuss the advantages and disadvantages of centralized storeroom facilities.

   b Discuss the advantages and disadvantages of decentralized storage facilities.

17-13 Assume that you have been given the responsibility of making a study of an existing storeroom and of taking charge of its reorganization. Outline and explain briefly the approach you would use in planning this undertaking.

17-14 What are the objectives of good storeroom layout? Explain.

17-15 Prepare for your boss a short report summarizing your analysis of the major factors involved in determining how stores and receiving should fit into the company organization.

CASE FOR CHAPTER 17

Monitor Manufacturing Company, page 631

Surplus Materials

Surplus is usually not an inspiring word. It frequently brings to mind thoughts of old pup tents, mess kits, and World War II gas masks. Even *industrial* surplus seems to imply mistakes in overprocurement, wasteful production processes, and inefficiencies in general. To make matters worse, surplus is often associated unglamorously with "junk" and scrap heaps. Consequently, surplus is seldom considered an enchanting business activity, and it rarely receives the management attention it deserves. This is regrettable because the total cost of production is the sum of the costs of labor, materials, and overhead *minus* any return from the successful sale of all kinds of surplus materials. Profits are maximized only when all elements affecting cost are fully controlled.

Regardless of the lack of glamor associated with surplus materials, effective disposal of surplus produces a very handsome payoff. For example, a large aircraft manufacturer recently increased its revenue from surplus sales by over $780,000 after instituting improved methods of surplus disposal. Similarly, a large chemical company increased its annual return on surplus at just one plant from $60,000 to $205,000. A large oil company recovered $286,000 the first year it reprocessed sludge and sediment that was formerly discarded as valueless.

With the explosion of concern for the environment in the 1970s came a change in the image and the scope of surplus operations and in the materials manager's responsibility for this activity. In signing the National Environmental Policy Act of 1970, former President Nixon said, "The 1970s absolutely must be the years when America pays its debt to the past by reclaiming the purity of its air, its water, and our living environment. It is literally now or never."

Because metals constitute such a significant part of the overall environmental and natural resources problem, they will be discussed as a representative example to illustrate the total problem with surpluses.

Ten metals are essential to a modern industrial society. The United States already has to import more than 75 percent of its requirements for five: aluminum, chromium, manganese, nickel, and tin. By 1985, over 50 percent of the nation's iron ore, zinc, lead, and tungsten will have to be imported, and by the year 2000 copper will join this list.[1] In the face of such circumstances, the necessity to conserve and reuse scrap metal is clear.

Consider the critical fact depicted in Table 18-1. Recycling steel, aluminum, and copper scrap compared with processing virgin ores results in energy savings of roughly 90 percent. In an era of energy shortages, this is not only a desirable but a mandatory saving.

In addition to energy savings, recycling yields many other desirable benefits. For example, when 1,000 tons of steel are produced from recycled scrap, rather than from virgin ore, the following benefits accrue: 6.7 million gallons of water are saved, because water usage is reduced from 16.6 million to 9.9 million gallons; 104 tons of air pollution effluents are avoided, because pollutant discharges are reduced from 121 tons to 17 tons; and 2,754 tons of mining wastes are avoided, because these wastes are reduced from 2,828 tons to 63 tons.[2]

In its totality, therefore, recycling reduces energy requirements, reduces gaseous and solid pollutants, and conserves raw materials.

The government wholeheartedly supports and encourages beneficial processes such as recycling. However, laws enacted before 1970 to achieve different objectives are temporarily thwarting the full implementation of environmental and conservation legislation. For example. trucks transport much freight that could more economically be transported by less polluting, less fuel-consuming railroads. Scrap iron is being exported, while at the same time less desirable virgin iron ore is being imported. Virgin iron ore moves at less than half the freight rate of scrap iron over the nation's rail system, which encourages use of the least desirable product, from an ecological point of view. Tax benefits are paid for depletion allowances of virgin ore to encourage

---

[1]*Phoenix Quarterly*, The Institute of Scrap Iron and Steel, Inc., Washington, D.C., Summer 1975, p. 5.

[2]Environmental Protection Agency, Report to Congress on Resource Recovery, April 1973, p. 12.

Table 18-1   Energy Requirements for Production of Metals

	Steel	Aluminum	Copper
Energy required in pounds of coal to produce one pound of material:			
From virgin ore	1.11	6.09	1.98
From recycled materials	0.22	0.17–0.26	0.11
Percent reduction in energy requirements with recycling	80	96–97	94

Source: Edmund Faltermayer, "Metals: The Warning Signals Are Up," *Fortune,* October 1972, p. 110.

discovery and production; no similar benefits are paid to encourage the increased use of environmentally and economically preferable scrap metals.

Congress is aware of these conflicting laws, and changes are in process. During the reconciliation period many opportunities will be created for the competent materials manager. He will have continuing opportunities to integrate more profitably a firm's goals of increased conservation, improved environment, and increased dollar return from recovery of surplus material.

PRIMARY SOURCES OF SURPLUSES

"Industrial surpluses" are defined as those materials which are in excess of a firm's operational requirements. Surpluses originate from three primary sources: (1) scrap and waste; (2) surplus, obsolete, or damaged stocks; and (3) surplus, obsolete, or damaged equipment. Each will be discussed in turn.

Surplus from Scrap and Waste

Surpluses from production processing are inevitable. Not all the materials a firm purchases are wholly consumed in production; a residue is left. For example, one company stamps disks from copper strip. From this operation, at least 15 percent of the copper left cannot be used elsewhere in the firm's production operations. This excess, which is called "scrap," must therefore be disposed of as surplus. It is impossible to eliminate this type of surplus; however, management attempts to minimize it by intelligent planning and effective production controls.

Surpluses also result from the inefficient use of production machinery, carelessness, and poor purchasing. This type of surplus is called "waste."

Effective management does everything possible to keep waste at a minimum.

The least costly method of controlling surplus is its elimination at the source. This is why effective value analysis programs which eliminate surpluses before they occur are so profitable. For example, the buyer of raw materials must be constantly alert to the need for buying the most efficient sizes and shapes of metals his firm uses. The authors recently observed a plant which was buying 1-foot-square metal sheets from which 6-inch disks were being stamped. This kind of waste is clearly avoidable.

The largest single category of salable surplus material is scrap metal.[3] This surplus exceeds 55 million tons annually, having an estimated value of well over $4 billion.[4] Because of its high dollar value, the disposal of this large quantity of scrap metal is an important part of the overall American economy. Scrap metal is also a necessary material in the operation of one of the nation's largest industries—the steel industry.

Precious metals are a growing source of profits from the proper recovery and disposal of scrap. These metals are especially important today because of their increasing rates of usage by many industries, including electronics, precision instruments, hospitals, photography, and industrial chemistry.

By comparing its results with those of other firms doing similar work, a firm can ascertain with reasonable accuracy the standard scrap rates for its production processes. When actual scrap rates vary from predetermined standards, or when learning experience does not reduce scrap losses, corrective action should be taken. Scrap losses should decrease with learning for the same reasons that production times decrease with learning. The learning curve concept, as discussed in Chapter 7, also applies to scrap rates. The curve which portrays the relationship between scrap rates and time is called the "efficiency curve." It is based on the theory that scrap losses will decline at a predictable percentage rate as the work force gains experience in manufacturing any specific product.

Surplus from Obsolete or Damaged Stocks

It is unreasonable to expect that sales forecasting and planning will always be 100 percent accurate. In cases of overanticipation, material excesses above actual requirements inevitably result. An automobile company, for example, may predict that consumers want seats of real leather, for which they will be willing to pay an extra charge. Time may well prove, however, that most consumers in fact prefer fabric or imitation leather, at no extra charge, thus

---

[3]Frequently, the word "scrap" is used to mean ferrous metals that are suitable for resmelting to produce iron and steel products. The word "metals" is used to identify surplus nonferrous materials.

[4]Ferrous metals represent roughly 92 percent, by weight, of the total scrap metal market; nonferrous metals represent the remaining 8 percent (Institute of Scrap Iron & Steel, Inc., Washington, D.C., 1969 Annual Report and 1974 Special Report on Reclamation, Conservation, and Beautification).

leaving the manufacturer with a surplus of real leather that must be disposed of.

Changes occur constantly in the designs and specifications of materials and components in a fast-moving technological society. As a consequence, obsolete products and their parts constitute a continuing source of surplus materials. Production planning normally takes place well in advance of the date when production actually begins. At any time prior to the commencement of the manufacturing operation, either technical or product changes can completely alter the schedule of materials required for any specific production run. Even after production begins, changes in highly technical items often make some inventory materials obsolete. The ease with which technological advancement can generate surpluses is highlighted by the single fact that in many firms today over 50 percent of the products they sell did not even exist ten years ago.

Excessive forward buying is another common source of surplus materials. Some firms forward-buy only under specific economic circumstances; others forward-buy as a matter of routine company policy. Regardless of the reason for using this type of buying, it entails the hazard of surpluses from obsolescence, deterioration, or excess carrying costs.

Planned overbuying represents still another source of surplus stocks. Some firms, such as automobile and aircraft manufacturers, produce more parts for specific models of automobiles and airplanes than they expect to sell because of what is called the "life of type" problem. It is more economical for an automobile manufacturer to produce an oversupply of certain replacement parts for new cars while the production line for those cars is in operation (and pay for their storage for as long as the manufacturer accepts the responsibility of furnishing parts for this model) than it is to pay the high start-up costs entailed with reestablishing production facilities for the same parts some years later.

Any warehousing inventory control operation, regardless of how efficiently it is controlled, will accumulate some surpluses from breakage, deterioration, and errors in record keeping.

Surplus from Obsolete or Damaged Equipment

All machine tools and equipment at some point in their life become surplus for one of two primary reasons: they wear out, or they become technologically obsolete. In today's rapidly advancing technological world, major machine tools seldom "wear out"; more frequently they are replaced because they have become technologically obsolete.

In addition to machine tools and plant equipment, most firms also have a large capital investment in many kinds of office equipment and furnishings, plus the physical plant itself. Competent management makes every practical effort to prolong the life of the firm's capital equipment as long as possible, but ultimately, because of obsolescence, breakdowns, the introduction of new products, or new methods of production, replacement of all capital assets—even buildings—becomes mandatory.

ORGANIZATION FOR SURPLUS DISPOSAL

Salvage and Reclamation Departments

Nearly all manufacturing firms (large and small) and many nonmanufacturing firms should have a salvage and reclamation (S&R) department. Depending on the quantity and value of the salvageable material involved, the department can operate full or part time from either a salvage yard or the department head's desk. Many small firms, unfortunately, fail to establish a salvage department, primarily because they believe their volume of surplus does not justify a full-time operation.

Industry loses millions of dollars annually by neglecting salvage and reclamation programs. For example, a large electrical company, by reorganizing its S&R department, recently increased its yearly savings by over 20 percent to roughly $700,000. A large university started a salvage program and had sales of over $150,000 and savings of over $90,000 in the program's first year. A bank created additional profits of over $60,000 per year by correctly salvaging its wastepaper. Many other firms could similarly benefit, but they forfeit such additional profits by inaction.

The basic charge management gives to its S&R department is to ensure that surpluses are disposed of with optimum profitability. To accomplish this, *all* of a firm's surplus materials should be handled by its S&R department.

Assume an obsolete motor-generator is to be disposed of. If there were no salvage yard, the S&R department head would dispose of the equipment "as is." If there were a salvage yard, the first determination to be made would be whether the machine could be sold as an operating machine, either in its present condition or after some repair work was done. If it could not be sold as an operating machine, the second determination would be to decide on the economic practicability of disassembling it and segregating it into its component parts and/or into its various kinds of metals, such as copper, steel, or aluminum. The component parts of some used machines can be quite valuable either for stock purposes or for sale. If the decision is against disassembly, the machine would be sold "as is" for its scrap metal value.

How best to salvage materials can sometimes be a challenging analytical exercise. A university had an old chapel organ to sell. The high bid was $6,000. The surplus and salvage manager thought the organ could be sold for more. Further analysis proved he was right. For a cost of $1,500, the organ was disassembled into its component parts. The tin from the pipes then sold for $16,000; the remainder of the material for $1,800.

Overall company salvage expense can frequently be reduced greatly by preplanning and instituting simple operating procedures. For example, sorting surplus metals by type can often be accomplished inexpensively simply by providing suitably marked containers at the point of accumulation. This simple procedure increases scrap value. For example, if high-carbon-steel cutting tools are mixed with less expensive grades of metal scrap, the money realized from selling the mixed scrap as a single lot will be considerably less than that which would result from selling the cutting tools as one lot and the remainder of the scrap as another. To simplify sorting of this type, barrels of different colors can be used for different kinds of scrap metals. Similarly, surplus paper, cardboard, and similar surplus materials should be segregated during accumulation by the method that will bring their highest selling price.

The salvage and reclamation department handles all three kinds of surplus: scrap, surplus stock, and surplus equipment.

Materials Management and Purchasing Departments

The materials cycle is not complete until all materials are disposed of in the most productive way. Consequently, surplus disposal is a basic function of the materials management department. In a large firm not having a materials manager, but having high dollar surpluses, the head of the S&R department traditionally reports to the plant manager. In the majority of firms not having either a materials manager or an *independent* S&R department, the responsibility for surplus disposal is assigned to the firm's purchasing department.[5]

There are many reasons for assigning this responsibility to purchasing. Usually, no other department in the firm is as well qualified as the purchasing department to perform this task. The professional and management skills required for a successful disposal operation are the very ones found in a competent purchasing department. No other department of a firm is as vitally concerned or as well informed as the purchasing department about materials, materials markets, and current economic market conditions. The firm's sales department focuses its energies on selling the firm's end products in the markets for these products. It is not normally familiar with or interested in surplus markets.

The purchasing department routinely buys a large variety of raw materials, component parts, and equipment. It has knowledge of who makes these materials, what other firms use them, how they are used in its own firm, and how much they cost. This is the precise knowledge needed to sell surpluses of these materials successfully. Also, a relatively large number of buyers in the metal industries regularly buy some form of scrap or other surplus material for their own manufacturing purposes. The vice-president for materials of one of the nation's largest steel companies reports that he considers the purchasing of scrap metal the key profit responsibility of his purchasing department. In this and similar situations, the purchasing department is particularly knowledgeable. Daily contact with many representatives from a large number of industries,

---

[5]National Association of Purchasing Management Survey of 1971 indicated 56 percent; Stanford University Survey of 1973 indicated 72 percent.

as well as the reading of purchasing and trade journals, keeps purchasing personnel informed of surplus price trends in many markets. Additionally, it is not at all unusual for a buyer to sell much of his firm's surplus materials back to the firm from which he originally bought the raw materials.

DISPOSING OF SURPLUS PROFITABLY

When material has been declared surplus, the materials management, purchasing, or salvage and reclamation departments, as appropriate, should be informed. From that point, disposal can take six routes:

1 Circulation within the company
2 Return to the supplier
3 Direct sale to another firm
4 Sale to a dealer or broker
5 Sale to employees
6 Donations to educational institutions

Circulation within the Company

At a well-known multiplant pump company, the usual method for circulation within the company is to prepare specifications on the surplus material or equipment for distribution to each division. If no request is forthcoming from United States divisions, the specifications are sent to the company's overseas subsidiaries.

At a large automobile manufacturing company, the disposal of fixed assets for all United States plants is the function of a three-man staff in the central office. When a surplus develops, it is the responsibility of the local plant manager to inform his division manager. The latter solicits all divisional facilities to determine whether the equipment can be used. If it cannot be used within the division, the matter is referred to the three-man disposal staff in the central office. This staff then initiates a companywide screening program that sometimes involves overseas divisions as well. If the screening steps fail to turn up a user, the local plant is given authority to sell the equipment as surplus.

Use within the firm is always the most profitable form of surplus disposal. This type of disposal utilizes 100 percent of the original cost, whereas returns to suppliers typically yield 80 to 90 percent of original cost, and sales to dealers and brokers only 10 to 40 percent.

Return to Suppliers

If the surplus material cannot be used within the firm, the return-to-supplier method of disposal is generally the next best method. Suppliers typically allow the return of both new and used surpluses as a courtesy to good accounts.

Salable materials returned from inventory are traditionally accepted at original cost, less a nominal restocking charge. Since all firms do not progress technically at the same rate, suppliers can frequently resell even obsolete inventory items at full price.

Scrap metals can sometimes be returned to suppliers, depending on the size of the buyer's account, the metal involved, its degree of contamination, and the current economics of the scrap market. When scrap is scarce, many suppliers routinely require the return of scrap as a precondition of further sales. Precious metals are traditionally returned to the supplier for reprocessing.

Supplier policies regarding return of used equipment vary widely with the economics of the used equipment market and the sales policies of manufacturers.

Selling to Other Firms

Some companies sell surplus materials and equipment directly to other firms. Sales of equipment to other firms depend primarily upon the condition of the equipment, the economics of price, and the availability of similar equipment from other sources.

Sales of production surpluses can be ideal when the surplus of one company is the raw material of another. For example, if a firm can sell its waste paper back to the paper mill, it will get the highest possible price and cause the least possible pollution.

Selling to Dealers and Brokers

Surplus dealers and brokers (hereinafter referred to as dealers) constitute an excellent outlet for surplus materials. When a firm advertises surplus materials for sale, dealers often respond. Transactions with dealers are usually "where is, as is," and most of the time they are for cash. Surplus machine tool dealers, for example, operate in two ways: by auction, which usually involves selling a plant's entire equipment inventory, or by purchase of small lots. For auctions the dealer receives a commission and seldom does more to the equipment than to show it to bidders. For small lot transactions, however, he pays the owners cash, and he often reconditions or rebuilds machine tools before he sells them. Normally, it is not profitable for the original owner himself to recondition equipment before selling it.

Although cooperative action among purchasing agents to sell surplus materials is rare, such a situation exists among members of the Cleveland Association of Purchasing Management. This group has a surplus commodity service available to its members. Purchasing agents send their lists of surplus commodities to the association office. The association approves the list, writes a covering letter, reproduces both, and distributes the information to all its members.

Interplay among dealers is more widespread than among purchasing associations. Through the Machinery Dealers' National Association, its members have what amounts to a single inventory pool. One dealer, for example, may have a customer for equipment not in his stock, but by knowing what other dealers have on hand, he can make a sale from another dealer's inventory. He learns what other dealers have on hand from an equipment listing that is published periodically by the association. Association members find such a reciprocal arrangement advantageous, because even the biggest dealer cannot carry everything in stock.

Selling to Employees

Many firms make it a practice to sell both the products they manufacture and their surpluses to their employees. If the surpluses are the result of overstocking or obsolescence and the materials are in new or good condition, or if they are odds and ends of scrap desired by do-it-yourself employees, this can be a satisfactory method of disposal. On the other hand, if the surpluses are not in fully satisfactory condition, such sales, regardless of their attractive prices, can be sources of resentment on the part of employees toward their employers. Used automobiles can be an especially dangerous item of equipment to sell to employees.

Because of the numerous potential disadvantages involved, many sophisticated firms will not sell *used* surpluses (especially equipment) to their employees. Besides possible dissatisfaction, selling to employees often entails a high cost of paperwork, and it always imposes an administrative burden on ensuring complete impartiality among employees. High administrative costs have caused some firms to set minimum dollar amounts for sales to employees. Other firms, to avoid administrative costs, give their employees surplus materials having only a nominal value.

Donations to Educational Institutions

Corporate income taxes create another basis for disposal of surplus materials—giving them away. At the present time, colleges and schools acutely need machine tools and other types of industrial materials for instructional use in laboratories. Although the 1969 Tax Reform Act reduced the tax benefits allowed for gifts to educational and other nonprofit institutions, desirable benefits still exist. Because the applicable tax laws and regulations are complicated, before making large gifts potential donors should consult their tax advisers to determine exactly what benefits are available.

Contractual Considerations

Generally speaking, the following contractual considerations apply to the three major categories of materials that are sold as surplus.

Scrap metals, depending on existing economic conditions, are best disposed of by either a short- or a long-term contract made with a local scrap dealer. The dealer getting the contract should be selected from an investigation of at least three dealers. Because of the breadth of scrap market activities, a purchasing department should generally experience little difficulty in interesting three or more capable dealers who will compete vigorously for the business. The highly competitive nature of the scrap business usually keeps the variation in bid prices within a narrow range. Local dealers have an operating and transportation advantage over more distant competitors; also, they can provide more frequent pickups and more personalized contract service. Published market prices are available for many varieties of scrap, and these prices are frequently used as the bases for long-term contract prices. Bid prices are normally used for short-term contract prices.

Surplus stock that cannot be returned to the supplier is best disposed of by sale to jobbers or second-hand dealers. Such sales are most frequently made on a competitive bid basis, and competition for these materials is usually keen.

Surplus equipment is usually best disposed of by competitive bids from dealers. However, on occasion negotiation is used. Intense competition is traditionally developed after a firm acquires a select group of dealers who are interested in bidding for its surplus equipment on a continuing basis. Fixed prices to dealers are satisfactory when a selling firm is sure of the equipment's fair selling price. Auction is frequently used as a quick and convenient method of disposing of large quantities of equipment. Occasionally, advertisements in trade journals or trade papers prove effective in selling this category of surplus.

BUYING SURPLUS MATERIAL

Purchasing departments not only *sell* surplus material; at times they also *buy* it. Purchasing executives can find many bargains by shopping among surplus dealers. These dealers can supply almost anything—from transistors to molding machines. The wide range of surplus goods now available to those looking for good buys is best illustrated by the yearly displays of the Institute of Surplus Dealers Trade Show. Exhibitors' booths are filled with an impressive variety of power tools, packaging materials, grinding wheels, pressure-sensitive tapes, electronic parts, and a multitude of other products.

The Advantages

Most dealers stress low price as their main selling point; however, a few extol the advantages of *immediate availability*, which is often an even more valuable advantage to a buyer. A company building a prototype product, for example, can often pick up suitable material immediately from a surplus dealer, whereas it might wait weeks or months to get the same material new. Amity Merchandise Products Corporation, for example, has on many occasions been able to supply such large and technically oriented companies as IBM with surplus parts they needed for immediate research work.

Specialized Dealers

The rapid increase in the variety of surplus products has led naturally to an increasing number of specialized dealers. Alben Packaging Corporation, for example, specializes in the sale of surplus paper and packaging materials. Specialists in hydraulic parts, nylon rope, bearings, marine supplies, machine tools, and many other fields are replacing those dealers who formerly sold everything.

Despite specialization, even those dealers who specialize still handle a wide range of material. Some dealers, such as The Tunnel Machinery Exchange, stand ready to equip an entire plant. "If you want to set up a factory to manufacture fluorescent light fixtures," an executive of Tunnel has said, "Tunnel Machinery Exchange can supply presses, molding machines, office equipment, typewriters—everything you need."

Where to Find Surplus Dealers

Buyers looking for a dealer—either for buying or selling—can contact the New York office of the Institute of Surplus Dealers. This office lists all members and their various specialties. Two regional associations can provide similar information: the Associated Surplus Dealers in Los Angeles and the National Surplus Dealers Association in Chicago. The Institute of Scrap Iron & Steel, Inc., in Washignton, D.C., can supply a list of dealers who buy and sell all types of ferrous metals. The National Association of Secondary Material Industries, Inc., in New York City, can furnish information regarding the disposal of nonferrous metals, paper, and many other surplus materials.

FOR DISCUSSION

18-1   Explain why surplus materials are important to the individual firms which create them, to the overall economy of the nation, and to the environment.

18-2   Why are metals so important to a modern industrial society? Explain.

18-3   If recycling scrap metal reduces energy requirements, reduces pollution, and conserves raw materials, why then in some cases is virgin ore smelted in place of available scrap?

18-4   What department in most companies do you feel is best qualified to handle surplus disposal? Why?

18-5   Why are a firm's buyers usually better informed about surplus than its sales personnel?

18-6   Discuss how surplus materials are created in the American economy. Can these surpluses be controlled?

18-7   The Soviet Union is at times held up as an example of what can result from poor economic planning. Is there faulty planning in the United States at times? Discuss. How does economic planning relate to surplus materials?

18-8   Explain why some companies engage in planned overbuying, thus possibly creating a disposal-of-surplus problem.

18-9   Why are there problems in attempting to use surplus material throughout a large multiplant company?

18-10   If you were the purchasing manager for the prime contractor for a Mach 3 commercial airliner, what thoughts would you have about the disposal of scrap metals that will need to be used in this 2,000-miles-an-hour plane?

18-11   Explain why purchasing executives follow scrap prices with such great interest.

18-12   Explain the traditional ways in which scrap is disposed of.

CASES FOR CHAPTER 18

Pacific Machine Shop, page 639
La Jolla Research Institute, page 627

Part Four

Management of Purchasing and Materials Activities

Chapter 19

Planning

> **KEY CONCEPTS**
>
> The management process
> Planning concepts
>   Decision-making process
> Planning techniques for materials management
>   Budgeting
>   Materials budget
>   Operating budget
>   Purchasing research
>   Purchasing library
>   Formalized program
>   Critical path scheduling
>   and analysis

The preceding chapters have dealt with the fundamentals of materials management—that is, the concepts involved in conducting the materials activities. Part Four is devoted to the management of these activities. Given a staff adequately skilled in the fundamentals, how do materials executives manage the departments for which they are responsible?

A materials executive's managerial responsibilities differ little from those of other functional executives. All executives function primarily as decision makers. Although the details involved in managing a purchasing department differ from those involved in managing an engineering or a production department, the basic managerial activities are the same. All executives develop the specific patterns of activity required in their own functional areas by applying the same general management concepts.

THE MANAGEMENT PROCESS

To ensure efficient performance of his staff, a manager plans the activities of his department, develops the required task relationships and communications links, hires and trains his employees, motivates and coordinates their efforts, and evaluates and controls their performance. The management process is thus made up of five interrelated, yet distinct, fundamental functions: planning, organizing, staffing, actuating and coordinating, and controlling. Figure 19-1 summarizes the management process and its associated activities in schematic form.

Different situations call for different "management mixes." In some cases planning demands primary attention; in others, coordinating or controlling may require major emphasis. The former is frequently the case at top management levels, while in first- and second-line supervisory situations the latter requirements may prevail.

In the course of their daily work, executives should concentrate on each of the five functions of management as distinctly separate phases of their managerial responsibility. Yet, in a going concern, the five functions cannot be handled sequentially or independently as though each operates in a vacuum. They are inextricably interrelated. A decision made in the planning phase affects future decisions in the other four phases. A decision to adopt a given form of organization can easily make it more difficult to staff the organization, to motivate particular workers, or to control the performance of a certain group. Similarly, decisions in the coordinating function may influence the effectiveness of a given control system or require a manager to reevaluate an existing plan or organizational structure. Finally, when corrective action is

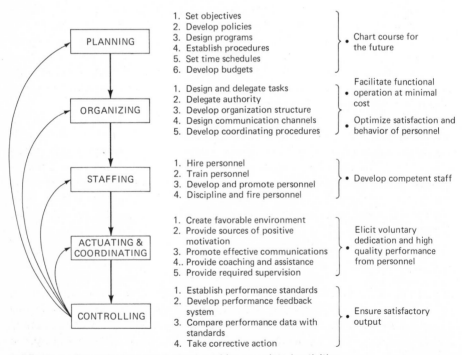

Figure 19-1   The management process and its associated activities.

required, it can frequently be effected by modifying prior decisions in any of the other four functions.

A manager's job is complicated by the fact that he or she must coordinate decisions with those made by other operating managers. The purchasing executive's plans and organization, for example, should be totally compatible with present and future plans of the executives in sales, engineering, and production. In a highly competitive business environment, the firms most likely to succeed are those that effectively integrate the efforts of their functional departments into a unified team effort.

PLANNING

The first function of management is the development of a series of plans that establish the framework within which future activities will be conducted. Initially, this process involves setting specific objectives and determining operating policies which guide all activities toward the attainment of these objectives. Subsequently, a group of detailed procedures must be developed to implement each policy. Finally, time schedules and financial budgets must be determined to ensure that each group of procedures can in fact be carried out. Every managerial job demands that planning be done before the other functions of management are executed.

A plan can be simple or complex. It can cover the short term or the long term. A first-line supervisor's plans, for example, usually cover short-range operating situations. As such, they tend to be fairly simple and concrete. A top-level executive, on the other hand, is charged primarily with the development of plans that reach farther into the future, and in this case the plans tend to be more complex and more abstract.

Regardless of its complexity, most planning can be done in a relatively simple series of steps. Like the other functions of management, planning is largely a decision-making process because it involves making choices among alternatives. The planning concept will therefore be discussed in the context of six basic steps which constitute the rational decision-making process: (1) define the problem; (2) gather data; (3) develop alternative solutions; (4) evaluate alternatives, test, and decide; (5) implement the solution; (6) follow up the results.

Define the Problem

Recognition of the need for a particular plan in a purchasing operation is not always as easy as it might at first appear. It is clear that a purchasing department must perform such functions as order processing, vendor selection, and order follow-up. And to accomplish these repetitive tasks smoothly, the purchasing executive must develop plans. However, all of purchasing's responsibilities are not this clearly delineated. Should a formal value analysis program be initiated? Should periodic vendor seminars be conducted? Should a purchasing research program be instituted? Should a program of vendor certification be established? Progressive executives in all functional areas continuously seek to discover hidden areas of need that their departments should fulfill. To answer the questions uncovered by such a search, the executive must first define in detail the specific problems which give rise to the questions.

Whether the problem is routine or unique, plans cannot be devised to solve it efficiently until its various elements have been separated and each carefully defined. *Specific plans* should be devised to cope with *specific segments* of a general problem. Only in this way, by concentrating on one specific problem at a time, can the planner establish the *specific objectives* he wants to achieve.

Gather Data

No problem can be defined until the facts which surround it are known. Similarly, no effective plan can be devised until certain relevant information is available. All plans are based on *premises*. Some planning premises stem from existing facts. Because plans deal with future events, however, other premises stem from forecasts and assumptions about the future. In both situations, relevant data from inside and outside the firm must be gathered and interpreted before a plan can be intelligently developed.

Develop Alternative Solutions

Rare, indeed, is the business problem that cannot be solved in a variety of ways. Before developing a detailed working plan, a wise manager attempts to develop several skeleton plans, each of which possesses reasonable potential for attaining satisfactory results. Different plans usually have associated with them different costs, time requirements, and resource requirements. From such alternative plans, a manager can then select (or synthesize) a plan whose requirements and expected effectiveness combine to yield the most advantageous course of action under current operating conditions.

Evaluate, Test, and Decide

The specific criteria used in evaluating alternative plans vary from one situation to another. The starting point, however, is normally an economic justification of the plan—a quantitative comparison of expected benefits with estimated costs. Following the quantitative investigation, analysis of qualitative features should be made. A good working plan represents a compromise between the planner's desire for precision and the need for flexibility. If certain premises prove to be invalid, the plan must be capable of adjustment to actual conditions. Even if all planning premises prove to be valid, the passage of time invariably produces some changes in operating conditions. A good plan must likewise adjust to these changes at minimum cost, without losing its effectiveness.

Testing Before placing a plan in operation, it is always desirable to pretest it so that any major difficulties can be detected and corrected. Although testing is difficult in a dynamic business situation, several approaches are feasible. In some cases, it is possible to test a plan's effectiveness by *simulating* operation of the plan. Consider, for example, a plan for a new inventory control system. The system might be given a "dry run" using historical data. Operation of the system could be studied for weaknesses under the simulated conditions, and the results could be compared with those of the existing system. If historical data were not available, the system might be operated simultaneously with the existing system on a selected group of materials. This would likewise permit comparison of the two systems and facilitate detection of weaknesses. Computer simulation is another feasible approach to the testing of many quantitatively oriented plans.

In cases where actual simulation is impossible, the planner must at least go through a general mental simulation process. He should mentally work through the complete plan, step by step, carefully checking the need for and the flow of all input and output data relative to the activities the plan involves. Additionally, the seasoned manager pays particular attention to the creation and modification of interpersonal relationships required by the plan. The types of action and interaction a plan imposes upon the personnel operating it vitally influence its effectiveness.

Implement and Follow Up

The best plan can fail if the planner overlooks the people who ultimately must operate it. Successful implementation is largely a matter of effective communication, education, and motivation. *During the developmental stages* plans should be discussed with the personnel they will affect. Such action promotes a *two-way* flow of information which is vital in developing and refining the details of a plan. If handled wisely, a discussion of the plan also gives those who will operate it an opportunity to contribute personally to its formulation. Such participation is desirable because it usually exerts a strong positive influence on an individual's ultimate acceptance of a plan.

To ensure clear communication, plans should always be stated in simple written form. Finally, when the new plan is implemented, it should be discussed fully with appropriate personnel. Necessary instruction should be given continuously during the break-in period.

Operating a plan is somewhat like navigating a sailboat. To reach the desired destination, the specific course must periodically be altered to compensate for gradually changing environmental conditions. The planner must regularly *follow up*, not only to see that the plan is functioning properly, but to detect the subtle changes in operating conditions which require a slight, temporary change of course.

PLANNING TECHNIQUES FOR MATERIALS MANAGEMENT

Materials executives apply the basic concepts of planning, formally and informally, in making a multitude of daily business decisions. They also use a number of specific planning techniques in considering longer-range activities. Three widely used techniques are *budgeting, purchasing research*, and *critical path scheduling and analysis*.

Budgeting

Budgeting has long been recognized as a basic tool in managerial planning and control. A company budget is a device which balances the planned allocation of expenses with forecasted income during a specified period of time (normally annually and monthly). As shown in Figure 19-2, a typical company budget is composed of numerous sub-budgets, each covering specific departmental operating activities.

   All department heads typically prepare a budget for their area of responsi-

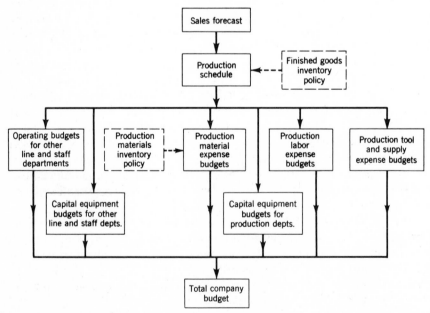

Figure 19-2   Major constituents of a total company budget.

bility and submit it to the controller. In most companies, the controller coordinates the sub-budgets and combines them into a total company budget. The total budget is usually submitted to a budget committee for study and final approval. Most budget committees are composed of a top management representative and the company's major department heads, including the purchasing executive or the materials manager.

The basic budget is developed from a sales forecast and a planned volume of production. Since sales forecasts can rarely be completely accurate, though, in practice production levels inevitably deviate from planned levels. When deviation occurs, the basic budget is in error for those items whose costs vary with the level of production (notably direct labor and material requirements). This unavoidable situation has led most companies to adopt some form of flexible budgeting practice. The flexible budget makes use of supplementary data which adjust variable costs in accordance with the production level actually experienced.

Materials executives are concerned primarily with two budgets—the *materials budget* and their respective *departmental operating budgets.*

The Materials Budget The materials budget is based entirely on the presumption that production will take place at a predetermined level. Preparation of a detailed annual materials budget is therefore practical only for those products whose sales can be forecast reasonably accurately, or for materials that are used in a variety of products whose aggregate demand can be forecast. This means that many companies find it impossible to develop a materials budget for the full year ahead, and that others may be able to budget only selected key materials (perhaps the class A inventory items). Nevertheless, whenever possible, most materials departments find it profitable to develop a materials budget expressed at least in terms of units, if not in terms of dollars.

Most materials executives have little control over the production schedule; it is normally prepared by the chief production executive. Once the production schedule is made available, however, it can be converted into a materials budget with the use of the various products' bills of material. Conversion simply entails an extension of material requirements for each product, followed by a consolidation of individual material requirements. At this point, the budget is expressed in units. Conversion of units into dollars is normally accomplished by applying either standard cost data or estimated actual cost figures.

When a materials budget is to be expressed in terms of dollars, the purchasing manager is normally called upon to supply the budget department with two types of information: (1) estimates of material *prices* during the coming year, and (2) plans for the specific *timing* of purchases. This information gives the finance department the necessary data to draw up a realistic schedule of cash requirements for each operating period.

Even when the materials budget is expressed only in terms of units, it still provides positive benefits in planning purchasing activities. Precise knowledge of material requirements over an extended period of time permits advantageous use of contract purchasing and blanket-order purchasing techniques. Quantity discounts can also be utilized more effectively. Inventory investment, and its associated risks, can likewise be reduced by advance planning of requirements. Material budgets provide maximum purchasing lead time. This benefit permits the careful selection of qualified suppliers, negotiation without the pressure of deadlines, and a better chance to obtain maximum value for each dollar spent. Additional lead time also produces savings by the use of routine rather than premium transportation, by a reduction in expediting costs, and by a smoothing of the purchasing work load. Vendor relationships are improved and costs can be reduced because time is available to optimally mesh purchasing requirements with the vendor's production schedule. Finally, in appropriate circumstances, the use of material budgets also facilitates intelligent forward buying.

Departmental Operating Budget   This budget is essential for the effective planning and control of departmental operations. It is normally constructed by adjusting historical operating costs for expected future changes in the scope and level of operations.

Among the multitude of items contained in the various materials departments' budgets, salaries and wages typically constitute approximately 80 percent of the operating expenses. A large portion of this outlay pays for the routine clerical work performed in the department. Consequently, a cost-conscious manager is compelled to appraise carefully the efficiency of such activities and to search constantly for ways of reducing clerical costs.

In a purchasing department, telephone and telegraph costs typically run from 3 to 6 percent of the operating budget, travel from 2 to 3.5 percent, printing and forms from 1.5 to 3 percent, and space rental from 1.5 to 5 percent. Expressed as a percent of the annual cost of materials, total costs of operating a purchasing department typically range from 0.3 to 4.3 percent. Clearly, costs vary widely among firms. However, small firms pay more per dollar purchased to operate their purchasing departments than do large firms, and operating costs tend to be higher among durable goods producers than among nondurable goods producers.

Conclusion   The major advantage of budgeting is that it forces a manager to plan ahead in precise terms. However, budgets must be developed and applied with care. Since a budget is based on quantitative estimates of the future, it can be no more accurate than the estimates on which it is based. The user must therefore be alert to detect inaccuracies resulting from forecasting errors and from changing conditions. Once established, a budget should *not* be allowed to exert inflexible control over an operation, particularly in the face of changing needs.

Finally, a budget is not a panacea for management ills. A budget helps a manager plan, and it reveals deficiencies as the plan materializes. But a budget cannot correct these deficiencies. This responsibility still rests with the manager.

Purchasing Research

In the planning stages, most purchasing actions require certain research investigations. Because he is confronted with numerous unknown facts, an industrial materials buyer cannot make an enlightened purchasing decision until these unknown areas are explored. The following questions should be answered when investigating a purchase request: What is the significance of the need relative to the company's long-range plans? Are standard materials available to do the job? Should the material be subjected to a formal value analysis study? What manufacturing processes are involved in the case of nonstandard items? How much should the item cost? Who are the suppliers best equipped to do the work? Are factors present that make one supplier more desirable than another in meeting the company's needs in the light of existing business conditions? What is the economic outlook for the industry involved? Answers to these types of questions require research effort by someone in the buyer's organization.

The Purchasing Library   A firm's purchasing library should contain a number of general sources of information that assist the buyer in answering many of the preceding questions. Required reference materials can be classified in four broad categories: technical, economic, commercial, and materials management. A complete and carefully indexed file of vendor catalogs and technical bulletins is essential. This file should be supplemented with various commodity, manufacturing, and engineering handbooks to provide basic, authoritative technical data relevant to the types of materials the firm purchases. Supporting these general references should be a current collection of selected trade magazines and technical journals that provide specialized information about relevant industries, processes, and materials. In addition to such technological information, the purchasing library should contain several good sources of current business and economic information. (A number of specific publications are listed in Chapter 12.) Subscription to a financial or investment service also often proves to be valuable in analyzing trends in commodity prices, production, and industry sales.

An essential inclusion in every purchasing library is a comprehensive purchasing directory and perhaps several specialized manufacturer's directories for the most heavily patronized industries. Such references are invaluable aids in locating potential suppliers for unique products. (Specific directories are discussed in Chapter 5.) Finally, no purchasing library should be without the services of a comprehensive collection of books and periodicals dealing with purchasing and materials management. It is particularly important that this collection include several good periodicals that report new concepts and techniques for conducting and managing purchasing and materials activities.

A Formal Purchasing Research Program   The current trend in industry is toward the production of highly specialized products. Compared with past practice, this means that most firms now produce fewer and buy more of the components used in the products they manufacture. This emerging pattern of operation broadens the scope of the purchasing department's buying activities. At the same time that individual buyers are purchasing a larger number of varied items, they are also buying more complex items produced by more complex manufacturing processes. Many companies have consequently discovered that the mounting pressure of daily buying activities tends to require an increasing amount of the individual buyer's time, leaving him without adequate time to conduct all the necessary prepurchase investigations. Instead of simply adding more buyers to the department, some companies have attacked the problem by creating a staff of purchasing research specialists to assist the buyers. This approach, it is claimed, solves the problem more efficiently. It ensures adequate time for thorough research, and it eliminates duplications of research effort. The approach effectively centralizes the required "in-depth" research activities within a small group of highly skilled specialists.

The concept of formalized purchasing research began to receive widespread attention by practitioners during the late 1950s and early 1960s. Since then, it has become widely accepted in American industry and is routinely practiced by most large firms. A formal purchasing research program serves as a procurement planning instrument. The general objective of such a program is to undertake in-depth investigations which improve total procurement performance and increase the function's contribution to company profits. Albert Kreig, manager of purchasing research for the American Cyanamid Company, developed the following classification of purchasing research staff functions, which has since been adopted by numerous firms.[1]

1   Procurement planning
2   Research on purchased materials
3   Research on the purchasing system
4   Special projects

Procurement planning involves a study of the firm's short- and long-range material requirements and a determination of acceptable cost objectives. Using these data as a base, further studies are undertaken by research specialists to

---

[1]Albert A. Kreig, "A Growing Concept: Purchasing Research," *Purchasing Research: Its Concept and Value*, American Management Association, 1962, pp. 1–2.

discover potential suppliers and to examine in depth the advantages and disadvantages of attempting to develop relationships with them. Procurement planning also includes the responsibility for developing cost estimates and other data required in planning for specific purchasing negotiations.

Since the early 1970s procurement planning has received increased emphasis in many American films. Extreme supply and price volatility, coupled with resulting sporadic shortages, in numerous basic materials markets has highlighted the necessity of thorough long-range procurement planning. Increased international business activity also has brought this need into sharper focus. The expansion of procurement responsibility and concomitant organizational changes at Du Pont, Champion International, Scott Paper, and other firms discussed in Chapter 2 are a direct result of industry's growing realization of the importance of this activity.

Research on purchased materials involves both economic and technical investigations. In the economic area, forecasts of general economic conditions are made, and studies of specific industries and commodity markets are undertaken. Price trends and technological developments in industries producing interchangeable materials are studied in an attempt to forecast future conditions in competitive industries. These forecasted conditions are then related to the firm's future needs. This type of analysis permits an assessment of current purchasing policy and points up the possible need for changes which may require careful advance planning. Technical investigations dovetail into two major programs which are frequently conducted on a companywide basis—*make-or-buy* and *value analysis.*

Research on the purchasing system involves studies of administrative problems. Specific activities include the analysis of such things as policies, procedures, reports, organization structures, job specifications, wage payment plans, and so on. Staff studies of this type materially assist the top purchasing executive in developing an effective operation.

Special projects is often a fourth area of formal purchasing research activity. Staff assistance is frequently needed to study a multitude of special problems that arise in areas such as inventory management, traffic management, quality control, and vendor relations, for example.

The specific investigations conducted by a formal purchasing research group naturally vary widely among companies, depending upon each firm's unique needs. The nature of the investigations may also vary due to the different ways in which various companies are organized to perform other related staff functions. The wide range of activities encompassed by the formal purchasing research concept may well overlap the activities of other existing staff groups in some companies. For example, some firms retain a staff of economists and statisticians at the corporate level to conduct economic analyses for top management. In such cases, the purchasing research group would normally work with this group in obtaining the data necessary for purchasing planning. A similar cooperating pattern of operation would be followed if the firm had a staff of systems analysts functioning at the corporate level. If a companywide value analysis program were centered in the engineering department, the purchasing research group would integrate its value analysis efforts with the existing program. If the value analysis program were centered in the purchasing department, purchasing research would normally assume responsibility for administration of the program.

The formal purchasing research concept recognizes the need for generating and analyzing a sizable amount of detailed data when planning procurement operations. If the required data are available or can be developed effectively in other existing departments, the job of the purchasing research group is to obtain such information and organize it for use in purchasing. If the information is nowhere available within the firm it is the purchasing research staff's job to generate it. In summary, the purchasing research staff is charged with the responsibility of obtaining, organizing, and interpreting data which facilitate procurement planning and hence improve the total materials management operation.

Critical Path Scheduling and Analysis

Critical path scheduling is a basic technique used for planning and controlling complex projects composed of a large number of interrelated and interdependent activities. A materials executive should understand the fundamentals of this technique for two reasons. First, his firm may at some time become a subcontractor on a job which requires the use of critical path scheduling. In this event, purchasing activities may be subjected to this type of scheduling and control procedure. Second, an increasing number of purchasing departments are finding the technique useful in scheduling and controlling the efforts of certain vendors. This technique is particularly applicable in subcontracting, project buying, construction contracts, and development work.

There are no fewer than fifteen specific techniques derived from the basic critical path scheduling concept.[2] The best known of these are CPM (critical path method) and PERT (program evaluation and review technique). CPM was originally developed in 1955 by the Du Pont and Remington Rand companies for use in coping with complex plant maintenance problems. PERT emerged in 1958 through the joint efforts of the United States Navy, the Booz, Allen & Hamilton consulting firm, and the Lockheed Missile and Space Division in connection with the Polaris weapons program. With the passage of time, PERT and CPM have become very similar in concept. Currently, they differ only with respect to various details of application.

The inclusion of critical path scheduling in this discussion serves only to introduce the *concept* to materials personnel—not to explore specific techniques in depth. The discussion therefore focuses on the basic concept, with but occasional reference to unique features of PERT and CPM.

[2]For a detailed comparison of these techniques see Thomas V. Sobczak, "Network Planning: The Continuing Revolution," presentation to the American Academy of Management, Boston, Dec. 28, 1963.

How Critical Path Scheduling Works Critical path scheduling begins with the identification and listing of all significant activities involved in the project to be planned and controlled. When the list of activities is complete, the sequential relationship between all activities is determined and shown graphically by constructing an activity network (see Figure 19-3a). The network shows the time required to complete each activity, and it explicitly indicates the relationship of each activity to all other activities. Finally, it establishes the sequence in which activities should be scheduled for efficient completion of the total project. Some activities can be paralleled, allowing many different jobs to be carried on simultaneously; other activities must be placed in series to allow step-by-step completion of interrelated tasks. The complete interrelationship of all project activities is the important feature that distinguishes critical path analysis from Gantt and other bar chart planning techniques.

Construction of the network permits determination of a project's "critical path"—the chain of activities requiring the most time for completion from start to finish of the project. Once the critical path is determined, the planner can identify precisely and completely the activities that require close control. He can also determine which activities permit the greatest latitude in scheduling and can, if necessary, most easily relinquish manpower to more urgent jobs. An activity network also highlights the activities that can be expedited most effectively in case a stepped-up pace becomes necessary.

Figure 19-3 illustrates the mechanics of network development. This simplified example shows a partial network of the major subcontracted activities involved in the construction of a new laboratory. Engineering and purchasing activities prior to site preparation have been omitted for reasons of simplification. The example shows only the major activities to be completed after the site has been excavated and prepared for the concrete subcontractor.

1 Column 1 (Figure 19-3b) lists the major activities to be completed.
2 Figure 19-3a shows the activities in network form. The required interdependencies and sequencing of operations have been determined and reviewed with the project engineer and the various subcontractors. Each arrow in the diagram represents an *activity* that will be conducted during a period of time. Each circle represents an *event* that will occur at a specific point in time (e.g., the start of an activity and the completion of an activity).
3 Careful estimates of the time required to complete each activity have been made by the respective contractors and are noted next to the appropriate arrows.[3]

[3]The PERT technique is often used for jobs whose time requirements cannot be accurately estimated. For this reason PERT requires three time estimates for each activity: (1) t_l = longest time required under the most difficult conditions (expect once in 100 times), (2) t_s = shortest time required under the best conditions (expect once in 100 times), (3) t_m = most likely time requirement. The expected time t_e, the figure actually used on the network, is a weighted average computed as:

$$t_e = \frac{t_l + t_s + 4t_m}{6}$$

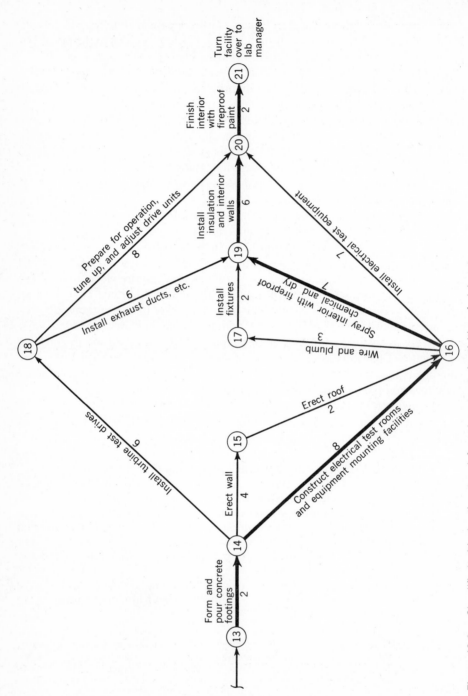

Figure 19-3a Simplified critical path network for subcontracted activities of a laboratory construction job.

Activity (1)	Earliest (2)		Latest (3)		Slack (4)
	Start	Complete	Start	Complete	
13–14 Form and pour concrete footings	0	2	0	2	0
14–16 Construct electrical test rooms and equipment mounting facilities	2	10	2	10	0
16–19 Spray interior with fireproof chemical and let dry	10	17	10	17	0
19–20 Install insulation and interior walls	17	23	17	23	0
20–21 Finish interior with fireproof paint	23	25	23	25	0
14–15 Erect walls	2	6	4	8	2
15–16 Erect roof	6	8	8	10	2
16–17 Install electrical wiring and plumbing	10	13	12	15	2
17–19 Install fixtures	13	15	15	17	2
14–18 Install turbine test drives	2	8	5	11	3
18–19 Install exhaust ducts, etc.	8	14	11	17	3
16–20 Install electrical test equipment	10	17	16	23	6
18–20 Prepare for operation, tune up, and adjust drive units	8	16	15	23	7

Figure 19-3b Data for Figures 19-3a and 19-3c.

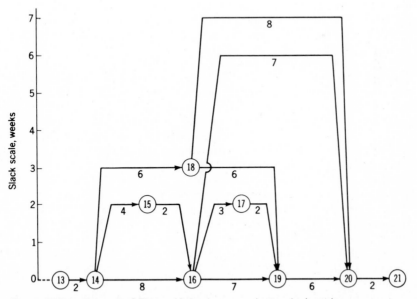

Figure 19-3c Network of Figure 19-3a drawn against a slack scale.

4 The critical path (longest chain of activities) consists of the activities 13-14-16-19-20-21; it will take 25 weeks to finish the project. The critical path is determined by totaling the time requirements for individual activities put together in every conceivable path from start to finish of the project. The critical path is the one requiring the longest time. Using the given time estimates, it is impossible to complete the project in less time.

5 At this point, the objective is to determine the amount of "slack time" (extra time, or leeway) existing in each of the noncritical paths. This is done by first developing the figures in column 2 (the earliest start and completion dates for each activity) and then those in column 3 (the latest possible start and completion dates for each activity) of Figure 19-3b.

The earliest start and completion date for each activity is determined by starting with the first activity and totaling the time requirements of the various paths through the network. If we say that the earliest start date for 13-14 (the concrete work) is today (the 0 point in time), the earliest completion date for 13-14 is the end of week 2 (0 + 2 = 2). Therefore, the earliest start date for both 14-15 and 14-16, which cannot begin before 13-14 is completed, is the end of week 2. The earliest completion date for 14-16 is the end of week 10 (2 + 8 = 10), and for 14-15 it is the end of week 6 (2 + 4 = 6). The earliest start date for 15-16 is the end of week 6, and the earliest completion date is the end of week 8 (6 + 2 = 8). What is the earliest start date for the electrical wiring and plumbing activity 16-17? Is it the end of week 8 or week 10? Clearly, it is the end of week 10, because the wiring cannot be started until the electrical test rooms and mounting facilities are completed. The analysis continues in this manner through the entire network until column 2 is complete.

The latest possible start and completion date for each activity (column 3) is determined in exactly the reverse manner. Begin with the completion date for the final activity and work backward through the network, determining the latest completion and start dates that can be used for each activity without delaying completion of the project. All activities on the critical path will have identical "earliest" and "latest" dates. This is not true, however, for the noncritical path activities.

The latest completion date for the final painting activity (20-21) is the end of week 25, and the latest start date is the end of week 23 (25 − 2 = 23). Therefore, the latest completion date for 18-20 is the end of week 23, and the latest start date is the end of week 15. Notice, however, that the latest completion date for 14-18 is not the end of week 15. Activity 14-18 must be completed by the latest start date for activity 18-19, which is the end of week 11 (23 − 6 − 6 = 11). This procedure, then, is followed back through the network to complete column 3.

6 The purpose in developing columns 2 and 3 is to determine the amount of "slack time" in each noncritical, or slack, path (column 4). The slack time existing for a particular activity is simply the difference between the earliest start date and the latest start date (or between the earliest completion date and the latest completion date). This important factor

represents leeway which can be used in scheduling the slack path activity most efficiently in light of other demands for facilities and manpower.[4]

7   Figure 19-3c represents the network in Figure 19-3a drawn against a vertical slack scale. Its purpose is merely to show, at a quick glance, how much slack is available in each slack-path activity. Such a chart frequently serves as a good visual planning aid.

Conclusion   The preceding discussion has dealt only with the rudiments of the critical path planning concept. In practice, performance is monitored, and progress data are periodically compared with the original plan. The technique is therefore an effective control device as well as an aid in making future planning decisions as changes in plans occur. The projects to which the technique is applied in practice are often made up of several thousand activities. After the initial network is constructed for such projects, a computer program is written, and the mechanics of preparing and monitoring progress reports are accomplished by computer.

The illustration depicted in Figure 19-3 considers the planning and controlling activities only with respect to the factor of time. Some techniques of critical path analysis add to this the factor of cost. These techniques integrate the two important variables in a single system, permitting virtually total managerial control.

A wise manager always raises two questions about the practicability of any planning or control concept. How accurate is it? How much does it cost? Like other planning techniques, critical path analysis is no more accurate than the data it manipulates. As for cost, some companies find it profitable; others do not. Generally speaking, the greatest profit potential for such a system lies in its application to projects too complex for adequate planning with bar charts. The basic question a firm must answer is: How important is the utlimate control the system affords? When management puts a price tag on this variable, it can then determine whether or not adoption of the system is likely to be profitable.

Its current popularity indicates that a large number of users find critical path analysis profitable primarily because it forces vendors to do more planning than they otherwise would do. Numerous governmental and industrial buyers require subcontractors to submit a critical path network (for major events, or "milestones") with their bids on subcontract and construction jobs. Some companies have found that the technique can pay off even without the use of computers. The Purchasing Department of the Ortho Pharmaceutical Corporation, for example, uses a manually operated PERT system to coordinate its buying activities with the activities of other departments when the firm introduces a new product.[5]

---

[4]Column 4 indicates that both activities 14-15 and 15-16 have two weeks' slack. Notice that this is an "either-or" situation. Two weeks' slack cannot be utilized in both activities; two weeks represents the total combined slack for both activities.

[5]"Purchasing Makes Time with PERT," *Purchasing*, vol. 54, no. 11, p. 85, June 3, 1964.

FOR DISCUSSION

19-1   Explain and discuss each of the managerial functions that make up the management process.

19-2   "In his daily work, an executive should concentrate on each of the five functions of management as distinctly separate phases of his managerial responsibility. Yet, in a going concern . . . they are inextricably interrelated." Comment.

19-3   Should a first-line foreman be able to use the management process as effectively in conducting his job as the plant manager uses it in conducting his? Explain.

19-4   What is planning? Discuss.

19-5   In the text, the planning function is discussed within the framework of the rational decision-making process. Define and discuss each step in the rational decision-making process.

19-6   List and discuss the minimum components a good working plan should include.

19-7   Discuss the "evaluation and testing" phase of the planning process.

19-8   What role does the purchasing department play in a company's budgeting procedures?

19-9   Discuss the benefits a purchasing department can derive from using a materials budget.

19-10 What are some of the potential problems associated with the use of budgets? Discuss.

19-11 "All good buyers engage in purchasing research." Explain.

19-12 Why do some companies find it desirable to institute a formal purchasing research program? Explain.

19-13 What problems might you expect to encounter in implementing a formal purchasing research program in a large, well-established company? Discuss.

19-14 Explain what critical path analysis is and what it is used for.

19-15 List and explain each step involved in making a critical path analysis.

19-16 In what ways might a purchasing department become involved in the use of critical path scheduling techniques?

19-17 What do you see as the primary advantages and problems associated with the use of critical path analysis in purchasing?

CASES FOR CHAPTER 19

Smithson Company, page 658
G. A. R. Manufacturing Company, page 616

Chapter 20

Basic Policies

KEY CONCEPTS

Centralization of purchasing
Policies affecting vendors
    Salesmen and orientation booklets
    Competitive bids
    Presale technical service
    Purchase of design work
    Samples
    Plant visits
The policy manual
Ethics in purchasing

Dozens of times each day, most managers utilize basic policies as guidelines in making operating decisions associated with their jobs. Precisely what is a policy? A policy is a statement which describes in very general terms an intended course of action. After the fundamental objectives of an activity are established during the planning process, policies are developed to serve as general guidelines in channeling future action toward the objectives. Policies, as distinguished from procedures, do not set down a series of explicit steps to be followed in performing a task. Rather, they state broadly the intended course of action. After a policy has been formulated, specific procedures are then developed for handling common recurring decisions.

From an operating manager's viewpoint, an established policy serves two functions. First, it serves as a base to be used in formulating operating procedures. Second, it serves as a general guide in making decisions about unusual problems which fall outside clear-cut procedural boundaries.

BASIC OPERATING POLICIES

To avoid misinterpretation of the title of this chapter, "Basic Policies," it should be emphasized that the entire book deals largely with matters of policy. Chapters 3, 4, and 9, for example, focus on numerous policies influencing the quality of materials. Chapters 6 and 7 investigate pricing policies, Chapters 10 and 11 consider policies of inventory management, and so on. Every chapter deals with various matters of policy which relate to a specific phase of materials management. This chapter is concerned with fundamental *operating* policies—broad policies of particular interest to top management. These policies deal with such things as purchasing authority, ethics, and vendor relations. All of these policies lie close to the heart of the purchasing operation, yet their influence permeates the entire company operation.

Policies Defining Purchasing Responsibility

Centralization of Purchasing To decentralize the purchasing function needlessly is to deny a firm some of its potential profits. Centralization of the purchasing function is essential for the attainment of both optimum operating efficiency and maximum profit.

Centralization of purchasing, as discussed in this book, is concerned solely with the placement of purchasing *authority.* It has nothing to do with the location of buying personnel. Centralization takes place when the entire purchasing function is made the responsibility of a single person. This person is held accountable by top management for proper performance of purchasing activities. Decentralization of purchasing occurs when personnel from other functional areas of a business—production, engineering, sales, finance, and personnel—decide on sources of supply, negotiate with vendors directly, or perform any of the other functions of purchasing.

Most companies today accept the centralization of purchasing as a logical extension of Frederick Taylor's basic concept of the specialization of labor. Whether the efficiencies of specialization that Taylor demonstrated nearly a century ago are realized when a firm creates a purchasing department, however, depends largely on the authority delegated to that department. When functioning properly, centralized purchasing produces the following benefits.

1 Duplication of effort and haphazard purchasing practices are minimized by the central coordination of all company purchases.
2 Quantity discounts are made possible by consolidating all company orders for the same and similar materials. In addition, a firm is able to develop and implement a unified procurement policy, enabling it to speak with a single voice to its vendors. In this way, the firm gains maximum competitive advantage from its total economic power.
3 Transportation savings are realized by the consolidation of orders and delivery schedules.
4 More effective inventory control is possible because of companywide knowledge of stock levels, material usage, lead times, and prices.
5 Centralization develops purchasing specialists whose primary concern is purchasing. Purchasing specialists inevitably buy more efficiently than less skilled persons who view purchasing as a secondary responsibility.

6 Line department managers do not have to spend their time purchasing. They can devote full time and effort to their basic responsibilities. (When given purchasing responsibility, too often the overriding concern of line managers is to get what they want when they want it, to the exclusion of all other purchasing considerations.)

7 Responsibility for the performance of the purchasing function is fixed with a single department head, thereby facilitating management control.

8 Suppliers are able to offer better prices and better service because their expenses are reduced. Their sales personnel have fewer persons to call on, fewer orders to prepare, fewer shipments to make, fewer invoices to prepare, and fewer financial records to keep. Under these conditions, supplier goodwill and responsiveness natually follow.

9 Record keeping is reduced and at the same time made significantly more effective.

10 Fewer orders are processed for the same quantity of goods purchased, thus reducing purchasing, receiving, inspection, and accounts payable expense, as well as prices.

Despite the general advantages of centralization, *complete* centralized purchasing is neither always possible nor always desirable. There are three major situations that justify some decentralization. The first of these is found in companies that process *single natural raw materials.* Many such firms separate the purchase of the key raw material from the purchase of other materials. Firms in the tobacco, textile, and leather industries are good examples.

In these industries, the raw materials are products of nature that are purchased in unstable markets whose prices fluctuate widely. Buying typically takes place at auctions conducted in small local warehouses. In such markets, a knowledge of grades is often as important as a knowledge of prices. Buyers of these commodities usually guard their knowledge with secrecy, frequently handing it down from one generation to the next.

The second situation justifying some decentralization of purchasing authority exists in *highly technically oriented firms that are heavily involved in research.* In these firms some exceptions to complete centralization are always desirable. Much buying in the research, design engineering, and quality control departments can be handled more effectively by professional personnel in these departments. Moreover, the dollar volume of such purchases is usually relatively small.

In the research situation, scientists often do not know exactly what they want. Consequently, they must frequently discuss concepts with a vendor before it is possible to select specific pieces of hardware. The design engineer concerned with developing a prototype must frequently talk with the vendor at the completion of each developmental step. These circumstances dictate giving engineers and scientists flexibility and a small portion of the firm's purchasing authority. *After specifications become firm,* however, the purchasing department should assume full responsibility for procurement.

The third situation justifying a different type of decentralization is found in the *operation of multiplant manufacturing firms.* This interesting topic is discussed fully in Chapter 22.

The purchase of nontechnical odds and ends also often calls for a partial decentralization of purchasing. Petty cash fund purchases of less than $25 are a good example. Decentralizing through the use of a petty cash fund can be a great money saver. It costs the average company from $7 to $12 to process a formal purchase order. For many small purchases, the cost of the paperwork exceeds the cost of the item purchased. Even though the user may pay more for the item if he buys it himself with funds from petty cash, the extra cost is more than offset by the saving in purchasing processing costs.

The danger of a firm's losing purchasing control (i.e., efficiency and profit) does not stem per se from a partial decentralization of the purchasing function. Some decentralization is necessary as a matter of common sense. The real danger of loss stems from *excessive* decentralization. What percentage of decentralization constitutes excess? Generally speaking, if 97 percent or more of the purchasing is performed by the purchasing department, decentralization should not be considered a problem. However, the correct extent of decentralization must be determined for each firm from an analysis of the individual factors involved in its operations. One fact is certain: operating departments seldom try to assume the functions of a purchasing department if the purchasing department is doing a good job for them.

Implementing and Maintaining Centralization   When a purchasing department is assigned responsibility for all or most of a firm's purchasing function, it is necessary to communicate this fact clearly internally and externally. Company personnel and vendors must know and accept this fact as a way of business life. Consequently, a firm's policy manual must contain a clear and cogent statement to the effect that the purchasing department holds full authority for negotiating, concluding, and following up purchases. This does not mean that the purchasing department should not call upon the operating departments for technical assistance. It does mean that normally purchasing should initiate, administer, and control all external inquiries and negotiations that ultimately lead to the purchase of a production material.

Stemming from this basic policy, most companies issue a series of additional policy statements which give more precise guidance in specific situations. For example, when an operating department head wishes to talk with a vendor's salesman or technical representative, the request should normally be made to the purchasing department. The appropriate buyer then makes the initial contact, arranges the appointment, and keeps informed of significant aspects of the discussion that might influence future purchasing activity. Channeling such external contacts through the purchasing department serves several useful functions. It permits buyers to maintain reasonable control of vendor relations—one of their major responsibilities. The operating department head, for example, may not know about other commitments the buyer has made on related matters with other suppliers. The buyer thus acts as a company coordinator. Moreover, the procedure keeps buyers aware of pending discussions and enables them to plan for and integrate these activities into related purchasing activities already under way. The same logic applies to correspondence between operating departments and vendors.

Clearly, except in predetermined situations, no one outside the purchasing department should be given the authority to commit the firm to a purchase. Various unique or emergency conditions, however, may produce a situation where it is in the firm's best interest to delegate specific purchasing authority. In such cases, delegation of the authority should be accompanied with adequate plans and constraints to ensure that the purchasing department does not lose control of its purchasing responsibilities. A firm must also make certain that its purchasing department is placed in the best possible bargaining position. Toward this end, it should be clearly understood that no one outside of purchasing is to give vendors any indication of product preference, current sources of supply, price or performance data for competing products, or any other information which would weaken the firm's purchasing position.

The purchasing department's authority to *challenge* material specifications and purchase requests is a policy of paramount importance that must be included in the policy manual. One company phrases its policy this way:

> The purchasing department and . . . subsidiary purchasing agents have the *duty* and *authority* to ask reconsideration of specifications or quantity of material requisitioned if, in the opinion of the buyer, the interest of the company or its subsidiaries may be better served. Any change in the requisition is prohibited unless it is approved by the person or department initiating the requisition.

Without the establishment of this basic policy, the profit-making potential of centralized purchasing is severly curtailed. Its importance cannot be overemphasized. In some companies the purchasing department is required to review and approve all material specifications before a new product leaves the drawing boards.

In the interest of controlling expenditures, a firm should delegate the authority to approve purchase requisitions only to specified individuals in each department. This practice establishes the groundwork for a policy requiring that all requests for purchase be submitted in writing, usually on a printed purchase requisition form. Except in an emergency, oral requisitions should not be accepted. This policy obviously eliminates numerous costly communication errors. More important, however, is the fact that it requires operating departments to plan their material requirements more carefully. This in turn results in less ill-advised impulse buying, and it also reduces costly "rush buying" activities in the purchasing department.

Policies Affecting Vendors

Most companies spend a great deal of money to develop a favorable public image. Madison Avenue derives its livelihood from the efforts of American business executives to convince the public that their companies are "good citizens" producing good products. Irrespective of public relations and advertising expenditures, however, a firm's purchasing and sales departments contribute heavily to the shaping of its public image. Most of a firm's contacts with the business community are managed by these two departments.

The development of sound vendor relations is a major responsibility of the purchasing department, for two reasons. First, good vendor relations contribute to the formation of a good public image. Second, the treatment and service that a supplier gives a customer depends to a great extent on the way the supplier feels about the customer. However the matter is viewed, it is in purchasing's best interest to establish policies that promote favorable vendor relations.

Salespeople   Perhaps the simplest thing a purchasing department can do to promote favorable vendor relations is to treat all salespeople fairly and courteously. Most companies make it a policy to see all salespeople who call, as long as their products are remotely relevant to the firm's needs. To permit more efficient planning and utilization of a buyer's time, many companies establish regular calling hours for salesmen (perhaps four hours a day, four or five days a week). As a rule, this conserves time for buyers and salesmen alike.

Orientation and Policy Booklets   Careful and complete communication with vendors greatly facilitates the development of good relations. Toward this end, many companies prepare an orientation booklet which is given to all vendors calling on the purchasing department. Such booklets typically contain a brief description of the company's products and manufacturing operations, a directory of buyers and the types of materials they buy, and a statement of major purchasing policies and practices that vendors should know about.

The Kaiser Corporation distributes a small booklet which, in addition to explaining the purchasing department's calling hours, sets forth a number of "Ground Rules" which affect the company's relationships with vendors. Several key policies are as follows:[1]

> Our purchasing departments are the sole agents at the plant who have authority to commit the company to purchases, large or small.
> We prefer to limit the number of our suppliers to an extent that those suppliers will value our business and will endeavor to meet legitimate competition.
> We secure competitive prices whenever possible, giving due consideration to assurance of supply and prompt delivery.
> We buy from vendors nearest the point of use, other considerations being equal.
> Suppliers' representatives can deal with our plant Purchasing Agents secure in the knowledge that they are protected from any unfair advantage of competing suppliers through "second looks" or personal relationships.

[1]*Welcome to Kaiser Aluminum & Chemical Corporation Purchasing Department*, Kaiser Aluminum & Chemical Corporation.

To the extent that orientation booklets apprise a firm's vendors of the basic policies and procedures under which it operates, they can be of great assistance to vendors and can prevent exasperating misunderstandings. A buyer must always bear in mind that statements which are *not* made in oral discussions with a vendor's representatives may tell the vendor more than statements that are made. Incomplete communication can give rise to incorrect rumors and speculations highly detrimental to the relationship. For these reasons, many firms follow the policy of communicating relevant purchasing policies to their vendors by means of the written word stated in a precise yet congenial manner.

Competitive Bids   Nothing offers more potential danger to a firm's reputation for fair dealing than a poorly handled competitive-bidding situation. Consequently, most firms establish definite policies to guide all buying personnel in handling bidding activities, both *before* and *after* the issuance of requests for bid.

Despite the fact that no legal requirements compel a private firm to award a contract to the low bidder, the competitive-bidding process itself implies that the lowest qualified bidder will get the contract. It is this expectation that motivates a supplier to compute his costs and assess his competitive position carefully before submitting his bid. To consistently obtain vendors' best prices on the first bid, a buyer should therefore, in most cases, award the contract to the low bidder. This situation gives rise to two important policies:

1   Sound competitive-bidding practice demands that a buyer be willing to do business with every vendor from whom he solicits a bid (or with every vendor from whom he accepts a bid). The resulting policy states that all vendors requested to bid must be determined *in advance* to be *qualified* suppliers for the job in question.
2   Whenever the lowest bidder does not receive the contract, the buyer is required to explain his decision. A short memorandum to this effect should be filed with the order or with the quotation analysis.

As simple as they sound, the preceding two policies can be quite difficult to follow in practice. The fact that very few vendors are *equally* qualified or motivated to handle a specific purchase makes it virtually impossible to evaluate bidders on the basis of price alone (except for highly standardized, off-the-shelf products). This situation, at times, justifies the selection of someone other than the low bidder. Even though justified, such a decision is often difficult to explain satisfactorily to the unsuccessful bidders who quoted lower prices than the successful bidder. And try as he may, a buyer is usually unable to prevent unsuccessful bidders from learning the successful bid price. In a competitive industry, "grapevines" are too numerous and too effective to permit the keeping of many price secrets. Thus, even when the decision to award the contract to a high bidder is fully justified by a combined evaluation of quality, service, and price, it can still produce unfavorable vendor relations. Hence, the need for the policies and their enlightened observance is clear.

Chapter 6 stresses the importance of allowing each vendor only one bid on a competitively bid contract. In the interest of fairness, all vendors must be accorded the same treatment. The buyer should treat all bid data confidentially and should not divulge one bidder's data to another bidder, either before or after the contract has been awarded. All bidders should be advised of the bid closing date, and no bids should be accepted after this date. If, for extraordinary reasons, the bid date is extended to give an interested vendor more time, it is the buyer's responsibility to notify *all* bidders of the new bid closing date.

The rules of common courtesy require the buyer to notify all unsuccessful bidders that the contract has been awarded. This allows those vendors to release production capacity that may have been reserved for this potential contract. It is most important that bidders be told of their failure to get the contract in a courteous and objective manner. Although a vendor realizes that he cannot get every order, he is likely to be more competitive on future jobs if he is not dissatisfied with his treatment on the current job.

Presale Technical Service   The purchase of certain technical materials and components requires the vendor to conduct a presale study of the buyer's specific application of the items to be purchased. Vendors in some industries customarily make such studies as part of their regular sales efforts. Selling prices in these industries are set so that the revenue from successful efforts covers the cost of unsuccessful presale studies.

In other industries, however, vendors' prices provide for very little presale engineering work. Purchasing policy must therefore establish distinct limits with respect to the acceptance of presale technical services. While the buyer wants all the assistance he can get, he cannot afford to place his company under obligation to a vendor by accepting an unreasonable amount of presale service.[2]

The incurrence of such an obligation usually leads to one of two undesirable results. First, the buyer can place the order with the vendor to whom he is obligated; however, he may suffer some disadvantage if another vendor proves to be more desirable. Second, he can place the order with the most favorable supplier, regardless of his obligation to the vendor providing the unusual service. Even though the latter may have no legal claim to the order or to compensation for his services, he may frequently feel or say that the buyer has taken unfair advantage of him. Whether or not this is true, of course, depends upon the explicit agreement reached in prior negotiations. In reality, however, at this point the truth of the matter is of little significance to the buyer. What is important is the fact that, as a result of the ensuing rumor, the buyer's firm may be viewed with suspicion by some members of the business community.

---

[2]Unfortunately, some salesmen deliberately employ this technique to gain a psychological advantage. If, for any reason, a buyer is under obligation to a seller, the buyer's conscience may well compel him to evaluate the relative positions of various vendors differently than he would were he under obligation to none of the vendors.

Purchasing policy must guard against such problems, however innocently they may arise. Before accepting a seller's offer to make a presale study, the buyer must ascertain the amount of money involved and determine whether the offer is consistent with standard practice in the industry. Any service exceeding normal industry practice should be *purchased* completely apart from the basic purchase of material or equipment.

Purchase of Design Work   When a buyer contracts for the *design* as well as the manufacturer of a special component, he must be careful not to create a future supplier relations problem. One facet of the potential problem centers about the matter of ownership of the special design. Another phase of the problem concerns the supplier's recovery of sunk costs in design work and tooling.

When a supplier agrees to design and manufacture a special component, who owns the resulting design—the supplier or the buyer? Who has the right to apply for a patent on the item? Further, who owns the special tooling the supplier must obtain to produce the item? The answers to these basic questions should be specified unequivocally in the purchase contract. By taking this precaution, the buyer can avoid the uncertainties and distasteful misunderstandings which at times accompany such purchases.

The purchase price stated in the contract should reflect the decision regarding ownership of the design and tooling. From a buyer's standpoint, the most desirable method of pricing is one which separates the supplier's charges into three categories: (1) price for design and development work, (2) price for special tooling and equipment, and (3) price for manufacturing. Under these circumstances, both parties know precisely what the buyer is paying for and what he should get in return.

If a buyer can purchase design work and tooling completely apart from the manufactured components, the contract is usually clear-cut and no problems ensue. The buyer can do whatever he wishes with the design or the tooling without infringing upon the prerogatives of the supplier. Other things being equal, this is by far the most desirable type of contract. It makes the buyer less dependent on a single supplier; it gives him more leverage, which can be used in stimulating competition among additional potential suppliers.

As anyone with good business sense would suspect, many vendors are unwilling to accept contracts for continuing business on the basis just described. A shrewd vendor may well prefer to develop a proprietary product, and, for a limited period of time, establish himself in a monopolistic position. It is this type of contract that generates supplier relations problems. Clearly, the buyer does not want to remain a captive customer of one supplier indefinitely. On the other hand, in the interest of fairness, he is obligated to see that the supplier is adequately compensated for his original design and development work. Therefore, if the supplier will not divulge his design and tooling costs, the buyer should write the purchase contract in a manner which compels the supplier to price the job so as to recover these costs within a reasonable period of time (usually within a year). For example, the contract might guarantee the purchase of a specified number of units, or it might state that the job will be opened for bid on an annual basis.

Although the original supplier has an inherent advantage over future bidders, it is nevertheless essential that the buyer state at the outset his intention to open the job to competition as soon as the original contractor has recovered his sunk costs and earned a reasonable profit. This approach is in keeping with the buyer's responsibility to treat all vendors fairly and at the same time to seek out the efficient, low-cost producer.

Samples   One way to assess the quality of a product is to actually use or test a sample before ordering a significant quantity. In an effort to "get a foot in the door," many sales people request a buyer to accept a free sample of a product and "try it out."

The buyer may find it advantageous to accept such an invitation. It is an inexpensive and effortless way of learning about new, potentially useful products. If the cost of the sample is more than a dollar or two, the buyer should elect to pay for the sample. Such prudence removes any possible obligation that could accrue from accepting free material.

On the other hand, if the buyer sees no possible value in investigating a salesman's product, he should explain the reason to the salesman and refuse to accept the sample. Once a buyer does accept a sample, he is obligated to see that it gets a prompt and fair test. He is further obligated to give the salesman a complete report of the test as well as an evaluation of his potential use for the product. This procedure requires time and administrative effort. Under the constant pressures of daily business, buyers occasionally tend to handle samples in a haphazard and inconsistent fashion. Yet nothing irritates a supplier more than to learn two months later that his sample has not even been tested. Such irritation inevitably influences his attitude toward the buyer's firm. In the interest of good vendor relations, therefore, a definite policy (and related procedures) should be established to ensure fair and uniform treatment of all samples by all buyers.

Plant Visits   Every company should require its buyers to visit periodically the plants of major suppliers. Plant visits yield three distinct benefits. First, they provide an opportunity for a buyer to learn more about the current technical and manufacturing aspects of the materials he buys. Second, such visits enable a buyer to discover a great deal of "inside" information about specific suppliers. In no other way can a buyer become intimately acquainted with his suppliers' strengths and weaknesses, or with the unique conditions under which each supplier operates. Third, plant visits permit a buyer to develop valuable personal acquaintances and friendships among suppliers' personnel.

Despite the impersonal nature of most major business decisions, daily business activities and negotiations are conducted by people who prefer to deal with someone they know and like. A buyer who is known personally in a supplier's plant sheds his inconspicuous role as a name on the customer mailing list and becomes a living personality. When a buyer has to expedite an order, ask a special favor, or ask a delicate question to which he wants a frank answer, there is no substitute for honest and friendly communication on a first-name basis with someone in the supplier's organization. Any purchasing department that fails to recognize this basic truth deprives itself of some of the "fun" of business, as well as some very tangible benefits.

Policies on Supply Sources

Source-of-supply decisions frequently produce substantial impact both inside and outside the buyer's firm. For this reason, it is essential that carefully conceived policies be included in the policy manual to facilitate sound and consistent decisions in this important area. Specific topics which should be covered include the number of sources, the size of sources, the matter of reciprocity, local sources, foreign sources, and the development of new sources. These topics are discussed in depth in Chapter 5.

THE POLICY MANUAL

It is appropriate at this point to state explicitly an underlying concept which has only been implied in the preceding discussions of policies. If policies are to function effectively, it is imperative that they be placed in written form. A policy is a communication—an important one. It is important that the message reach those who are to receive it as clearly and accurately as possible. The complexity of a modern firm necessitates the establishment of many diverse policies, all of which cannot possibly be remembered with accuracy. The normal turnover of employees and managers compounds the difficulty. More-over, because policies are general statements, minor differences in interpretation are inevitable. It is essential, therefore, that care be taken to ensure the accuracy of policy communications.

Consequently, most firms disseminate policy statements to their employees via some type of written policy manual. A policy manual typically has at least two distinct sections, one containing company policies and one containing department policies. The section on company policies spells out in unmistakable terms the responsibility and authority of all other departments. It is essential that these policies carry top management approval and that they be communicated to every department head.

The second section of the manual contains departmental policies that are directed to the personnel of each respective operating department. In the case of purchasing, departmental policies inform personnel of the expected patterns of conduct for major buying activities and for relations with vendors and external personnel. The use of a policy manual clearly facilitates consistent basic conduct among all departmental personnel. It is particularly important to foster consistent performance among buyers because their dealings with vendors can significantly influence the firm's public image. A policy manual also facilitates the training of personnel.

The specific style, format, and contents of purchasing manuals vary widely. Some firms include only policies, while others include policies and procedures. Still others add organization charts, job descriptions, sample departmental forms, and other detailed data which, in total, completely describe the purchasing department's operation. The particular format used is of little importance. One style may fit one company's need better than another. What is important is that all major policies and operating procedures be committed to writing. They must be stated simply and unambiguously in a manual that is easy to use and that is kept current.

ETHICS IN PURCHASING

The following statements appear among the guidelines for purchasing personnel stated in the *National Association of Purchasing Management Standards of Conduct:*[3]

1 To provide justice to those with whom he deals
2 To buy without prejudice, seeking to obtain the maximum ultimate value for each dollar of expenditure
3 To subscribe to and work for honesty and truth in buying and selling, and to denounce all forms and manifestations of commercial bribery
4 To respect his obligation and to require that obligations to himself and to his concern be respected, consistent with good business practice
5 To avoid sharp (questionable or unethical) practice

It is not surprising that these specific references to ethics appear in the official *NAPM Standards of Conduct.* Purchasing executives and their buyers must be above suspicion in matters of ethics. Even though a buyer's actions are in fact ethical, if a vendor *believes* a buyer has not been entirely ethical, the buyer and his firm both suffer as a result of the vendor's false impression. Whenever honesty or ethics are involved, purchasing personnel cannot afford to give anyone the slightest reason to question their actions.

How do purchasing executives ensure that their department's performance will be above suspicion? This is no easy task because of the difficulty in classifying some activities as being distinctly ethical or unethical. Two approaches, however, can be used as "starters" in seeking to achieve this objective. First, *definite policies on all matters involving ethics should be*

---

[3]H. W. Christensen, Chairman, N. J. Gibbons, and H. F. Jones, NAPM Special Committee, *NAPM Standards of Conduct,* adopted by the NAPM Executive Committee, June 11, 1959, p. 1.

formulated and clearly communicated to all personnel. Second, an attempt should be made to *create a working atmosphere where unethical temptations seldom become realities.*

Departmental policy should make it clear that buying personnel engage in any unethical activity at the risk of losing their jobs. These activities should then be defined as completely as possible. Commercial bribery (accepting "kickbacks" from suppliers) obviously falls in this category. Although many firms fail to recognize it, the acceptance of gifts and entertainment simply constitutes a subtle, though lesser, form of bribery. Any action which places a buyer under obligation to a vendor can influence buying decisions. Even though the obligation is not explicit, it has the same effect as a minor form of bribery. For this reason, progressive company policy prohibits the acceptance of all gifts other than advertising novelties. The acceptance of any entertainment other than a simple meal should also be prohibited.

It is a generally accepted premise that a relatively small percentage of American citizens are basically dishonest, that an equally small percentage are completely honest, and that the great bulk of people are honest or dishonest, depending upon the circumstances. Consequently, after the basic policy framework has been established, it appears that the surest way to encourage ethical conduct is to develop a working environment conducive to such conduct.

The foundation for such an environment consists of the personnel themselves. Purchasing management will be repaid many times for the effort put into thorough, careful investigation and selection of buying personnel. Habits and attitudes are "catching" in the close working environment of a purchasing department. If the bulk of the personnel are basically honest, the purchasing executive has the major portion of the ethics battle won.

One businessman has said that "the way to keep employees honest is to pay them enough to live a decent life." There is obviously room for debate about the exact definition of a "decent life," but the idea is basically sound. It makes little sense to place someone who has significant unfilled material needs in a position where he or she is deliberately confronted with the temptations inherent in an industrial purchasing job. The implication for purchasing salaries is clear. Furthermore, many companies now provide buyers with modest expense accounts so they can reciprocate with salespersons in paying luncheon checks.

The age-old adage "monkey see, monkey do" has great relevance in the matter of ethical conduct. The purchasing executive and his supervisors must *live*, to the letter, the department's policies and ideals. Numerous studies have confirmed beyond doubt that the actions and attitudes of supervisors are the most influential single factor in determining the attitudes of a work group.

No discussion of ethics is complete without at least a brief review of situations that can create a "conflict of interest" for purchasing personnel. Such a situation occurs when a buyer's loyalty is divided between his firm and an external organization with which he has an opportunity to do business.

Perhaps the most common example is the case in which a buyer is a substantial stockholder in a supplier's firm. By placing a large volume of business with that supplier, the buyer could possibly benefit personally. Consequently, to prevent the possibility of personal gain from influencing buying decisions, most companies do not permit purchasing personnel to hold significant investments in potential suppliers' firms. The critical factors are (1) the relative size of the buyer's investment, and (2) the buyer's ability (through his purchases) to influence the supplier's profit position. Clearly, a buyer who purchases 25 automobiles per year, and also owns 50 shares of General Motors stock, does not have to worry about a conflict of interest.

Buying from friends or relatives may also create potential conflicts of interest. If the supplying firm is owned by a friend or relative, a variation of the situation just duscussed exists. If the friend or relative serves in a sales or high-level managerial capacity, a less obvious but equally dangerous potential conflict is present. A wise purchasing person clearly should make every effort to avoid buying situations that have even the slightest possibility for producing a conflict of interest.

Whenever purchasing executives must take action in a "gray area" not clearly covered by policy, they may find guidance by considering whether the action is completely compatible with the firm's overall responsibilities to its customers, employees, suppliers, and stockholders. In making the final decision, a few moments' thought may well be devoted to the following lines, entitled "What Makes a Profession."[4]

If there is such a thing as a profession as a concept distinct from a vocation, it must consist in the ideals which its members maintain, the dignity of character they bring to the performance of their duties, and the austerity of the self-imposed ethical standards. To constitute a true profession, there must be ethical tradition so potent as to bring into conformity members whose personal standards of conduct are at a lower level, and to have an elevating and ennobling effect on those members. A profession cannot be created by resolution, or become such overnight. It requires many years for its development, and they must be years of self-denial, years when success by base means is scorned, years when no results bring honor except those free from the taint of unworthy methods.

FOR DISCUSSION

20-1   Define a policy. Define a procedure.
20-2   Some business executives believe that a company should operate with as few policies and procedures as possible, because they think policies and procedures inhibit the creative thinking of managers and employees. Comment on this idea in general. Comment on the idea as it relates specifically to purchasing policies.

[4]Author unknown, quoted in NAPM Standards of Conduct, 1959.

20-3   Assume that you have just become the purchasing manager for an electric appliance manufacturer employing 4,000 people. You have been asked to rewrite the section of the company's policy manual that includes policies defining the purchasing department's responsibilities. Write these policies as you think they should appear in the company manual.

20-4   Assuming the same conditions as in question 20-3, write a policy for the complete handling of competitive bids in your firm.

20-5   What problems can arise in the handling of presale technical services? Discuss.

20-6   What problems can arise in the purchasing of design services? Discuss.

20-7   Prepare for your boss (the vice-president for purchasing in a medium-size machinery manufacturing firm) a detailed report discussing the concept of centralized purchasing including its strengths and weaknesses.

20-8   Assume you are the purchasing manager for a machinery manufacturing firm of 700 employees. Every year you use approximately $300,000 worth of lubricants, which you purchase from one supplier who is selected on the basis of competitive bids every January.

   The salesman for your current supplier makes his usual monthly call to your office on the first day of October. After discussing the normal business problems, he extends an invitation (through your office) to a group of your company executives and supervisors to attend a party.

   Those invited are:

1   The purchasing manager, his assistant, and his three buyers
2   The plant manager and his assistant
3   The chief design engineer and his four section heads
4   The maintenance superintendent and his three foremen
5   The production manager and his staff assistant
6   The controller and his assistant
7   The sales manager
8   The industrial relations manager

   Vendor's personnel attending are:

1   Two corporate sales managers and the district manager
2   Several salesmen
3   A representative from the corporate research department
4   Two representatives from the corporate technical applications department

   The party is planned for Friday evening in the private dining room of a local hotel and includes the following program:

6:30– 7:30   Cocktail hour
7:30– 8:30   Dinner

8:30– 9:00	Informal discussion and slides of the supplier's technical research activities and achievements
9:00– 9:30	Film of the Olympic Games
9:30–10:00	Film—"New Dimensions in Musical Entertainment"
10:00–	Adjourn for continuation of the cocktail hour

Discuss in detail how (and why) you would handle this situation.

CASES FOR CHAPTER 20

Basic Procedures

After a policy has been formulated to guide departmental action toward a basic company objective, detailed operating procedures must be developed to implement the policy. A procedure outlines in detail the specific action to be taken. In short, it establishes the way of doing things.

Procurement executives should develop their departments' procedures in accordance with four fundamental concepts. First, procedures are not ends unto themselves. They are means to an end. The objective is to develop a series of procedures that facilitate accomplishment of a task with minimum effort and "red tape." This means that procedures should be as simply defined as possible and should be placed in writing to ensure accurate communication.

Second, procedures must be designed to facilitate communication and coordination of the efforts of one work group with another. Figure 21-1 identifies the numerous departments that are affected by procurement procudures. In developing a procedure, it is essential that an executive look beyond the procedure itself. He must consider its relationship to existing procedures, particularly with respect to the matter of timing, and then design the new procedure to ensure efficient integration with the other parts of the total system. The development of a flow chart, such as the one shown in Figure 21-1, is extremely helpful in making such an analysis.

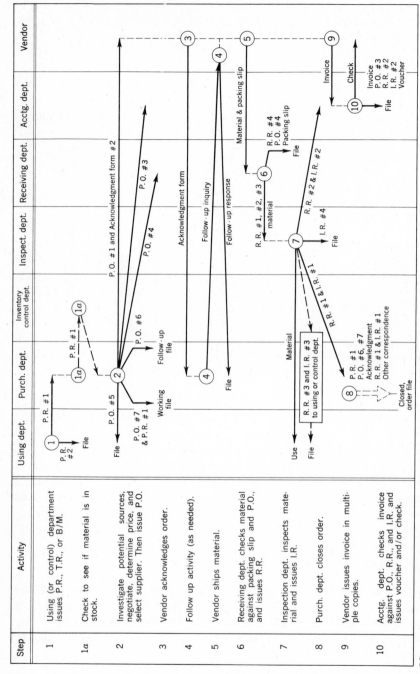

Step	Activity	Using dept.	Purch. dept.	Inventory control dept.	Inspect. dept.	Receiving dept.	Acctg. dept.	Vendor

Figure with document flow chart (see image).

Figure 21-1 General procedure and document flow chart for a typical purchasing cycle.

Step 1 — Using (or control) department issues P.R., T.R., or B/M.

1a — Check to see if material is in stock.

2 — Investigate potential sources, negotiate, determine price, and select supplier. Then issue P.O.

3 — Vendor acknowledges order.

4 — Follow up activity (as needed).

5 — Vendor ships material.

6 — Receiving dept. checks material against packing slip and P.O., and issues R.R.

7 — Inspection dept. inspects material and issues I.R.

8 — Purch. dept. closes order.

9 — Vendor issues invoice in multiple copies.

10 — Acctg. dept. checks invoice against P.O., R.R., and I.R. and issues voucher and/or check.

P.R. = purchase requisition; T.R. = traveling requisition; B.M. = bill of materials; P.O. = purchase order; R.R. = receiving report; I.R. = inspection report.

414

Third, effective operation requires that responsibility be clearly designated for the accomplishment of each step of each procedure. Failure to do so results in the overlapping of effort and in troublesome conflicts between operating personnel.[1]

Finally, procedures permit "management by exception." A procedure should establish at the lowest possible organizational level the best method for conducting a routine activity. A procedure thus enables an employee to handle the activity with a minimum of direct supervision. Consultation with a manager is required only when conditions arise that are not covered by the procedure.

GENERAL PROCUREMENT PROCEDURES

A purchasing department buys many different types of materials and services, and the procedures used in completing a total transaction normally vary among the different types of purchases. However, the general cycle of activities in purchasing most production materials is fairly standardized. The following steps constitute the typical purchasing cycle: (1) recognize, define, and describe the need; (2) transmit the need; (3) investigate and select the supplier; (4) prepare and issue the purchase order; (5) follow up the order; (6) receive and inspect the material; (7) audit the invoice; and (8) close the order. Figure 21-1 outlines these steps in operational form. More important, it details the *minimum* flow of communication documents required for a system to function smoothly and efficiently. The precise form the documents take varies widely from one company to another. The important point to note, however, is that a properly controlled purchase requires extensive communication with numerous work groups. Procurement procedures constitute the framework within which this task is accomplished.

Chapters 3 to 18 suggest policies and procedures for the specific materials activities covered by those chapters. The purpose of this chapter is to investigate the *operating* procedures, documents, and records that integrate the specialized activities of those chapters into a complete operational purchasing cycle.

Recognition, Definition, Description, and Transmission of the Need

The need for a purchase typically originates in one of a firm's operating departments or in its inventory control section. Transmission of the need to the purchasing department is usually accomplished by one of three forms: (1) a standard purchase requisition, (2) a traveling purchase requisition, or (3) a bill of materials.

---

[1]The problems resulting from procedures that cut across departmental lines have led many firms to create a small corporate staff of systems analysts. This approach ensures that procedures and systems are developed in the best interests of the *total* operation.

Standard Purchase Requisition   The purchase requisition is an "internal" document, in contrast with the purchase order, which is basically an external document. Most companies use a standard, serially numbered purchase requisition form for requests originating in the operating departments. The user generally makes a minimum of two copies. One copy is sent to purchasing; the other is retained in the using department's file. Some companies use as many as nine copies of the requisition for communication with other interested departments. Purchase requisition formats vary widely because each company designs its format to simplify its own particular communication problems. The essential information which every requisition should contain, however, includes a description of the material, quantity and date required, estimated unit cost, operating account to be charged, the date, and an authorized signature.

Traveling Purchase Requisition   Many companies use a "traveling requisition" to communicate to purchasing the material needs that originate in the inventory control section. In a manually operated system, a traveling requisition is a simple printed card that is usually filed with the inventory control record for each item carried in inventory. The following data typically appear on a traveling requisition: (1) a complete description of the item, including reference to applicable specifications; (2) a numbered list of potential suppliers and their addresses; (3) last prices paid to various suppliers; (4) reorder point and order quantity values; and (5) a record of usage. If desired, the card can also include vendor performance information and other historical data.

When the stock level drops to the reorder point, an inventory clerk takes the traveling requisition from the file, notes the current stock level and the desired delivery date on the card, and sends it to the purchasing department. To indicate that the requisition has been sent to purchasing, a colored signal clip is usually attached to the inventory record card. This procedure eliminates the typing of a purchase requisition. Since the traveling requisition contains information the buyer would otherwise have to locate in his own files, it also conserves his time. After reviewing the requisition, the buyer pencils the small quantity of required order data in the provided columns. The purchase order is then typed directly from the traveling requisition. After the buyer signs the purchase order, the traveling requisition is returned to the inventory control section and refiled with its respective inventory record card.

In companies using computerized inventory control systems, the work of the inventory control clerk is done automatically by a computer. In such cases, the computer typically produces a purchase requisition (in printed or punched card form) that replaces and contains essentially the same information as the traveling requisition.

Bill of Materials   When a design engineer completes the design of a part or an assembly, he makes a list of all the materials (and the quantity of each) required to manufacture the item. This list is called a "bill of materials." (In some cases it is possible to include the bill of materials directly on the engineering drawing.) The bill of materials, along with a production schedule, can be sent directly to purchasing as notification of the production department's need for materials. Total requirements are obtained by simply extending the bill of materials for the production quantity scheduled. In many companies using computerized production and inventory control systems, this entire procedure is accomplished by the computer. It produces a single print-out containing the information required by the buyer.

This procedure eliminates the necessity of typing numerous purchase requisitions and is an efficient method of transmitting the need for standard or easily described materials. It is used most effectively in situations involving special one-time projects or in firms operating on a job-shop basis.

Definition and Description of the Need   Chapter 4 discusses in depth the formulation and utilization of material specifications and standards; Chapter 3 deals extensively with the various methods of describing quality. Regardless of the form of transmission used, material requirements must be defined effectively, and the most appropriate methods of description should be selected for the situation at hand. The point to be made here is that *clear, complete, appropriate* definition and description is a joint responsibility of the user and the buyer. One of the reasons why every purchase requisition should be approved by designated departmental supervisors is to ensure that requisitions are initially reviewed by qualified individuals and subsequently come to purchasing in correct form. The buyer's responsibility is then twofold. First, he must check the requisition for accuracy and completeness, including internal data such as the account to which the purchase will be charged. Second, he must ascertain that the need has been adequately defined and that the appropriate method of description has been used to guarantee a satisfactory purchase for the user and, at the same time, provide all possible latitude in the selection of vendors.

The Stock Check   With the exception of traveling requisitions that originate in the inventory control section, when purchase requests arrive in the purchasing department, they are checked to see if the requested item is carried in stock. In many cases, a buyer can tell simply by looking at the requisition whether it involves a stock material. If adequate stock is on hand, no purchase is necessary.

Some companies route all requisitions for tools, supplies, and production-type materials to inventory control before they are sent to purchasing. If a sizable percentage of a firm's requisitions involve stores-type items, this procedure expedites the supply process and reduces clerical work in the purchasing department. It also apprises inventory control of the non-stock items that are being ordered repetitively and therefore might advantageously be carried in stock.

Supplier Selection and Preparation of the Purchase Order

As soon as a need has been established and precisely described, the buyer begins the investigation of vendors to select a source of supply. In the case of routine items for which supplier relationships have already been developed, little additional investigation may be required to select a good source. The purchase of a new or a high-value item, on the other hand, may require a lengthy investigation of potential suppliers. After selecting a preliminary group of potential sources, the buyer may employ the techniques of competitive bidding or negotiation, or both. When competitive bidding is used, the buyer initiates the procedure by requesting quotations from a selected group of vendors with whom he is willing to do business. Although "request for quotation" forms vary widely among firms, typically they contain the same basic information that will subsequently be included on the purchase order.

Once a supplier has been selected, the purchasing department prepares and issues a serially numbered purchase order. It should be emphasized that in most cases the purchase order becomes a legal contract document. For this reason, the buyer should take great care in preparing and wording the order. Quantity requirements, price, and delivery requirements must be specified accurately. Quality specifications must be precisely described. If blueprints and other specification documents are to be considered an integral part of the order, they should be clearly incorporated by reference. In the event sampling inspection is to be used, sampling plans and conditions of acceptance should be stated or referenced on the order. Similarly, any other important factor affecting the acceptability of the product should be precisely stated. In short, the order should include all data required to ensure a satisfactory contract, and it should be worded in a manner which leaves little room for misinterpretation by either party.

In addition to those provisions which are unique to each contract, most firms also include as a part of every contract a series of terms and conditions that are standard for all orders. These terms and conditions are designed to give legal protection to the buyer regarding such matters as contract acceptance, delivery performance and contract termination, shipment rejections, assignment and subcontracting of the order, patent rights and infringements, warranties, compliance with legal regulations, and invoicing and payment procedures. Each company develops its terms and conditions of purchase in accordance with its own unique needs. Consequently, much variation exists among firms. The terms and conditions which are printed on the back of one firm's purchase order form are reproduced in Figure 21-2.

Most companies prepare their purchase orders on multipart "snap-out" forms that provide enough copies of the order to satisfy both internal and external communication needs. Although one preparation completes all copies, the various copies of the form may be printed with slightly different formats as the use of each demands. Seven is the *minimum* number of copies most commonly required. The typical distribution procedure is as follows:

- Copy 1 and copy 2 (the acknowledgment copy) are sent to the supplier.
- Copy 3 informs the accounting department of the purchase. It is used by accounting in checking and issuing payment for the seller's invoice.
- Copy 4 advises the receiving department that it can expect to receive shipment of the order on a particular date. Receiving uses its copy to identify and check the incoming shipment.
- Copy 5 informs the user of the details of the order so he can plan his work and budget accordingly.
- Copy 6 remains in the purchasing department open-order file and is often used for purposes of order follow-up and expediting. (See p. 420.)

Figure 21-2   Terms and Conditions of Purchase Appearing on the Back of a Typical Purchase Order

Terms and conditions

The following terms and conditions and any specifications, drawings, and additional terms and conditions which may be incorporated by reference or appended hereto are part of this purchase order. By accepting the order or any part thereof, the Seller agrees to and accepts all terms and conditions.

1   The cash discount period available to Buyer shall commence on the date of the receipt of the merchandise or on the date of receipt of the invoice, whichever may be the later.

2   In the event of Seller's failure to deliver as and when specified, Buyer reserves the right to cancel this order or any part thereof without prejudice to its other rights, and Seller agrees that Buyer may return part or all of any shipment so made and may charge Seller with any loss or expense sustained as a result of such failure to deliver.

3   In the event any article sold and delivered hereunder shall be covered by any patent, copyright, or application therefore, Seller will indemnify and save harmless Buyer from any and all loss, cost, or expense on account of any and all claims, suits, or judgments on account of the use or sale of such article in violation of rights under such patent, copyright, or application.

4   Seller guarantees that the design of all equipment being purchased conforms with all regulations of the Federal Occupational Safety and Health Act of time of delivery.

5   Seller agrees not to use the name of Buyer or to quote the opinion of any of Buyer's employees in any advertising without obtaining the prior written consent of Buyer.

6   Buyer may at any time insist upon strict compliance with these terms and conditions notwithstanding any previous custom, practice, or course of dealing to the contrary.

7   Seller agrees to indemnify, defend, and hold harmless Buyer, its trustees, officers, agents, and employees, of, from, and against any and all claims and demands which may arise in any way out of the furnishing of goods or services hereunder, including, without limitation, claims and demands arising from injury to or death of personnel of Buyer or for damage to the property of Buyer, except those arising by reason of the negligent or willful act of Buyer, its officers, agents, or employees.

8   It is the policy of the Buyer to give favorable consideration to those suppliers who do not discriminate against any employee or applicant for employment because of race, creed, color, or national origin.

- Copy 7 becomes the buyer's working document and is filed in purchasing's open-order file.

Some companies organize their personnel into a larger number of specialized work groups and therefore require more copies of the order to complete the communication system. In any event, all parties involved in the transaction should receive a copy of the order. This communication has two objectives: (1) to permit planning and efficient conduct of the individual activities, and (2) to integrate the efforts of the individual groups into a smoothly functioning supply operation.

After an order has been issued, changes in company requirements frequently require a change in the contract. In such cases, the buyer issues a "change order," following the same procedures as were followed for the original order. When accepted by the supplier, the change order either supplements or replaces the original order.

Acknowledgment and Follow-up of the Order

In most cases, the original copy of the purchase order which is sent to the supplier constitutes a legal "offer" to buy. No purchase "contract" exists, however, until the seller "accepts" the buyer's offer. The seller's acceptance can take one of two forms: (1) performance of the contract, or (2) formal notification that he accepts the offer.

The purpose of sending the supplier an acknowledgment form along with the purchase order is twofold. First, it is a form he can conveniently complete and return to the buyer, acknowledging acceptance of the order. At the same time, he can indicate whether or not he is able to meet the desired delivery date. If a supplier ships the ordered item immediately from stock, he frequently disregards the acknowledgment form.

If shipment is *not* made immediately, an acceptance should be sent to the buyer. Although the acknowledgment form usually serves this purpose, some sellers prefer to use their own forms, which state their terms and conditions of sale. In either event, the buyer should check the acceptance closely to see that the supplier has not taken exception to any provisions of the order. If the seller's terms are different from those on the buyer's order, the law holds that they will automatically be incorporated in the contract unless they materially alter the intent of the offer or unless the buyer files a written objection to their inclusion. In cases where the seller's and the buyer's terms are in direct conflict, the law omits such terms from the contract, leaving settlement of the differences to private negotiation or legal adjudication.[2] In view of the posture adopted by the courts on this matter, it is amply clear that a buyer must review suppliers' order acceptances with great care.

The purchasing department's responsibility for an order does not termi-

---

[2]This subject is discussed in greater depth in Chapter 25.

nate with the making of a satisfactory contract. Purchasing bears full responsibility for an order until the material is received, inspected, and accepted.

Even though a supplier intends to meet a required delivery date, many problems can arise to prevent him from doing so. When there is a reasonable probability that such conditions may develop, important orders with critical delivery dates should receive active follow-up attention. When such orders are placed, the buyer should determine specific dates on which checks are to be made.

Numerous specific follow-up systems can be used. In one system, the follow-up copy of the order is simply filed in a calendar file under the date the order is to be checked. Each day a clerk withdraws the orders to be checked that day. In a second system, the orders are filed alphabetically by vendor. The upper edge of each order has numbers from one to thirty-one printed on it; a colored flag is subsequently attached to each order at the number corresponding with the next follow-up date. A clerk reviews these files daily or semiweekly to withdraw the orders requiring follow-up. In an automated purchasing system, the computer checks the programmed follow-up dates and notifies the buyer when follow-up is required.

In all systems, follow-up communication with the supplier usually takes two forms. A letter, a wire, or a telephone call is typically used for most critical orders. Routine follow-up for the less critical orders is usually accomplished by mailing a preprinted inquiry or postal card to the supplier.

In some companies, follow-up procedures are conducted by the buyer handling the order. In other companies, follow-up activities are conducted by a separate expediting group. This subject is discussed in the following chapter.

Although relatively few in number, some companies maintain a force of field expediters (follow-up personnel). Such companies are typically in various kinds of contracting businesses and purchase a great deal of major equipment on very tight delivery schedules. To ensure that all equipment is available when needed, these firms follow up critical purchases by having traveling expediters personally visit suppliers' plants.

Receipt and Inspection

The next step in the purchasing cycle is receipt and inspection of the order. When a supplier ships material, he includes in the shipping container a packing slip which itemizes and describes the contents of the shipment. The receiving clerk uses this packing slip in conjunction with his copy of the purchase order to verify that the correct material has been received. (For a complete discussion of the receiving procedure, the reader may wish to review Chapter 17. Chapter 16 outlines in detail the procedures to be followed when short or damaged shipments are received.)

After a shipment has been inspected for quantity and for general condition of the material, the receiving clerk prepares a receiving report. In some cases, the report is prepared on separate receiving department forms. However, the trend in most companies today is to reduce the clerical work by preparing the receiving report forms during the same typing or printing operation that prepares the purchase order. In these situations, the receiving report forms are included in the purchase order snap-out form. To complete the report, the receiving clerk merely writes the identification and receiving figures in the appropriate spaces included on the form.

Copies of the receiving report are typically distributed as follows:

- Copy 1 is used by the purchasing department in closing out its working file of the order.
- Copy 2 is used by the accounting department in reviewing the order for payment.
- Copy 3 is sent to the user as notification that the material has arrived, or as a delivery copy if immediate delivery is made. (If another notification system is used, this copy can be omitted.)
- Copy 4 is retained in the receiving department's operating record file.

Before some shipments can be accepted, technical inspection is necessary. (A discussion of these procedures is found in Chapter 9.) In some companies, distribution of the receiving report is withheld until the technical inspection report has been prepared. In other companies, distribution of the receiving report precedes distribution of the inspection report. Some firms send an inspection report to every department that gets a receiving report, so their records of *actual* receipts will be complete. Other companies provide copies only to purchasing, accounting, and inspection.

The Invoice Audit and Completion of the Order

Occasionally, a supplier's billing department makes an error in preparing an invoice, or its shipping department makes an incorrect or incomplete shipment. To ensure that the purchaser makes proper payment for the materials actually received, sound accounting practice dictates that some type of review procedure precede payment to the supplier.

A typical procedure involves a simultaneous review of the purchase order, the receiving report, and the invoice. By checking the receiving report against the purchase order, the purchaser determines whether the quantity and type of material ordered was in fact received. Then by comparing the invoice with the purchase order and receiving report, he verifies that the supplier's bill is priced correctly and that it covers the proper quantity of acceptable material. Finally, by verifying the arithmetic accuracy of the invoice, he determines the correctness of the total invoice figure. Auditing invoices is a repetitive, time-consuming task that should be handled as efficiently as possible. It should also be conducted soon after receipt of the invoice to permit the accounting department to make prompt payment and obtain any applicable cash discounts. Because of the high cost of auditing invoices, many companies do not verify the accuracy of low-dollar-value invoices.

Invoice auditing is technically an accounting function. Theoretically, the purchasing department's job is completed when an order has been received in the plant and is ready for use. In practice, however, some firms assign the invoice auditing responsibility to accounting, while others assign it to purchasing. A difference of opinion centers about questions concerning the efficiency and accuracy with which invoices can be checked when the task is assigned to the accounting department.

In the purchase of complex or technical materials, a strong case can be made for assigning the auditing task to the buyer who handled the order. This individual is familiar with the materials and their technical nomenclature, with prices and contract provisions, and with all ensuing negotiations. Invoices for such orders are usually difficult to interpret and evaluate without a detailed knowledge of these things. Hence, an audit done by an accounting clerk is frequently open to question. Auditing invoices for the purchase of most standard materials, on the other hand, is a routine clerical task. Moreover, a high percentage of most firms' orders are of this latter type. There is no reason to burden a buyer with this job, which can be done satisfactorily by clerical personnel.

Figure 21-1 indicates that the purchasing department closes its order before the invoice is audited. This is usually the case if accounting audits the invoice. When purchasing audits the invoice, its records are closed after the audit. Closing the order simply entails a consolidation of all documents and correspondence relevant to the order; the completed order is then filed in the closed-order file. In most firms, a completed order consists of the purchase requisition, the open-order file copy of the purchase order, the acknowledgment, the receiving report, the inspection report, and any notes or correspondence pertaining to the order. The completed order thus constitutes a historical record of activities encompassing the total purchasing cycle.

PURCHASING DEPARTMENT RECORDS

The files of a purchasing department contain an endless flow of operating data. Despite its huge volume, much of this information can be useless in daily operations unless it is organized in a manner which makes it readily accessible. Although the unique needs of each purchasing department dictate the specific structure of its records system, the following basic records are essential for the effective operation of most purchasing departments:

- File of open orders
- File of closed orders
- Purchase log
- Commodity record
- Supplier record
- Contract record
- Special tool record

File of Open Orders

All buyers must have immediate access to all information concerning the status of their outstanding orders. Because reference to these orders most frequently requires identification by the supplier's name, the filing system is customarily indexed alphabetically by suppliers' names. Within each supplier's subfile, orders are arranged in ascending numerical sequence.

Although practice varies widely, each order folder commonly contains the purchase requisition, the working copy of the order, the returned acknowledgment form, follow-up data, and all notes and correspondence that pertain to the order. Some companies also file competitive bids with the order. Others prefer to file bids in a separate price file or with the commodity record. When the bid is not filed with the order, the order folder must contain a cross-indexing reference.

Some firms also maintain a separate numerical file of purchase requisitions. This file makes it easy to locate a purchase order needed to answer questions from a requisitioner who can identify the order only by requisition number. In such situations, it is essential to note the purchase order number on the requisition. When follow-up activities are conducted by a separate expediter, all information pertaining to the purchase is contained in his working file. To reduce paperwork, duplicate information is frequently omitted from the open-order file.

File of Closed Orders

The closed-order file provides a historical record of all completed purchases. It frequently serves as a useful reference when questions arise concerning past orders and when certain historical data are needed to guide future decisions. Specific inclusions of the file were discussed on page 423.

It is difficult to generalize about the length of time such records should be kept. Nearly all companies retain their closed orders at least three years. Normally, any order files kept beyond three years should be retained only on a highly selective basis. In a large firm, records retention is costly. Therefore, if commodity and vendor records are properly maintained, only unique and high-value orders are generally worth keeping longer than three years.

Purchase Log

Every purchasing department should maintain a numerical record of all purchase orders issued. The record need not be elaborate, but it should contain the purchase order number, the vendor's name, a brief description of the material purchased, and the total value of the order. Such a record summarizes the commitments for which the purchasing executive is responsible. In the event that the working copy of an order is misplaced, basic data concerning the purchase can be found in the log. The log further serves as a convenient record from which summary administrative data can be extracted concerning such matters as the number of small orders, rush orders, and total orders issued; the volume of purchases from various suppliers; the value of outstanding commitments; and so forth.

Some companies' purchase logs consist of a sequential list of purchase orders recorded in a journal, with one line devoted to each order. Other firms accomplish the same objective simply by filing, in numerical sequence, the follow-up copy or an additional copy of the order.

Commodity Record

The file of commodity records constitutes the vast reservoir of materials data that makes possible efficient mass production purchasing. A commodity record card should be maintained for each major material and service that is purchased repetitively. Typically included on the card is a complete description of the material or service, with full reference to necessary engineering drawings and specifications which might be filed elsewhere. Also included should be a list of approved suppliers and their price schedules. Competitive quotations may be included in the file, although it is more common to summarize bid data on the card, note a cross reference to the original quotation, and place all quotations in a separate file.

The preceding data provide a buyer with the basic information initially required in a repetitive purchase investigation. In making the purchase decision, he supplements this information with numerous qualitative considerations concerning individual suppliers, such as their current work loads, internal problems, quality performance, and so on. Some companies, however, also include on the card a complete purchase history for the item. For every purchase, the purchase order number, purchase quantity, price, delivery performance, and quality performance are recorded. In deciding how much detailed information to record on its commodity cards, each firm must weigh the value of the information against the cost of transcribing it.

When a firm uses a traveling requisition system for repetitively purchased inventory items, the traveling requisition and inventory record cards duplicate the commodity record. In such cases, there is no need to maintain a separate commodity record card.

Supplier Record

To provide quick access to information about suppliers, most companies centralize such information in a single supplier record file. A separate card is maintained for each major supplier. On this card is recorded his address, telephone number, and the names of personnel to contact on specific matters of inquiry. Selling terms and routing instructions for shipping purposes are also usually included. Although the practice varies, many companies additionally summarize on this record the supplier's delivery and quality performance, as well as the annual volume of materials purchased from him.

In a matter of seconds, these records enable a buyer to obtain a wealth of summary information about any important supplier.

Contract Record

Most firms purchase some items on a long-term contractual basis. In such cases, it is usually convenient to consolidate all contracts in a separate file. In addition to providing immediate access to all contract documents, this file also apprises all buying personnel of the materials that are purchased in this manner. If the number of contracts is large, it is desirable to list them on summary sheets to provide a bird's-eye view of all contract purchases and their expiration dates.

Special Tool Record

Many companies have no need for this record. However, such a record is essential to those firms that purchase many items requiring special tooling for their manufacture. On some orders the purchaser buys the required dies, jigs, fixtures, and patterns; on others he does not. By maintaining a record of special tools, he can summarize for quick reference the special tools owned, the age and location of each, and the essential mounting and operating characteristics of each.

"RUSH" ORDERS

Every departmental executive seeks to develop an orderly and systematic pattern of operation that efficiently utilizes the resources of that department. In a well-run purchasing department, systematic analysis and processing of most orders is completed in two to four days after the requisition is received.

How should purchasing handle the emergency needs that inevitably arise in any business operation? Clearly, a special procedure for processing "rush" requisitions is needed. Key elements of such a procedure are discussed in the following paragraphs.

Even in the case of emergencies, it is unwise to accept verbal requisitions over the telephone. Too much chance for erroneous interpretation of the requirement exists. The requisitioner should state the need in writing and have a messenger deliver it to the buyer. For purposes of identification, emergency requisitions can be printed on paper of a different color, or they can be identified with a colored emergency sticker. Typically, the buyer should process these requisitions immediately and telephone emergency orders to the supplier. In no case, however, should an order be placed without assigning it a purchase order number. Subsequently, for most purchases, a confirming purchase order should be mailed to the supplier. In cases where the emergency is less urgent, the buyer may process such requisitions at appointed times twice daily (say at 10:30 A.M. and 2:30 P.M.).

Purchasing's basic responsibility is to the departments it serves. Yet purchasing should not permit users to take unfair advantage of its emergency service. Only justifiable requests should receive this service. Rush orders almost always cost more than if they were handled through the normal purchasing system. Higher prices are frequently paid because rush purchases are not investigated as thoroughly as routine purchases, and premium-cost transportation is frequently used. Furthermore, the interruption of a buyer's scheduled work by the emergency request invariably produces inefficiency in normal purchasing department activity.

Steps should therefore be taken to discourage all rush orders that arise because of poor planning in the using departments. In practice, three approaches have proved successful. The first involves a concerted effort to coordinate the activities of production control and purchasing. Some companies require that realistic order points for inventory materials be established jointly by production control and purchasing. In other firms operating on a job-order basis, purchasing is required to issue periodic lead time reports to production control for all major classes of materials. A second approach, designed to reduce unjustifiable requests, requires the requisitioner to obtain approval from a general management executive for all emergency requisitions. Still another approach assesses the requisitioning department a predetermined service charge for each emergency requisition processed.

THE SMALL-ORDER PROBLEM

Small orders are a perennial problem in every business. Examination of a typical company's purchase order file reveals that a sizable percentage of its purchases involve an expenditure of less than $100; in total, however, these purchases constitute a small percentage of the firm's annual dollar expenditures. Clearly, no manager wants to devote as much buying and clerical effort to the expenditure of 10 percent of his funds as he does to expenditure of the other 90 percent. Yet this is frequently what happens. The very nature of business requires the purchase of many low-value items. Nevertheless, small orders are costly to buyer and seller alike. It costs a seller only a few cents more to process a $1,000 order than it does to process a $5 order. The following sections discuss various methods that a purchasing executive can use to minimize the small-order problem.

Centralized Stores System

A stores system represents the first approach typically used to reduce the volume of a firm's small-order purchasing activity. When experience shows that the same supply items are ordered in small quantities time after time, the logical solution is to order such items in larger quantities and place them in a centralized inventory for withdrawal as needed. An ABC analysis of repetitively used production materials leads to the same action for the multitude of low-value C items. If usage of the item is reasonably stable, an optimum order quantity can be computed using the EOQ approach.

"Blanket," or "Open-End," Order System

A stores system solves the small-order problem only for items that are used repetitively. Every company buys thousands of items it cannot carry in inventory. The most common method of purchasing these items is by means of a "blanket order" (also called an "open-end order").

Briefly, the general procedure used for this type of purchase is as follows. Based on an analysis of past purchases, the buyer determines which materials should be handled in this manner. After selecting a supplier for each item, he issues a blanket order to each supplier (this may involve price negotiation when it is possible to group a number of similar items on the same order). The order includes a description of each item, a unit price for each item when possible, and the other customary contract provisions. However, no specific order quantities are noted. The order typically indicates only an estimated usage during the period of coverage. It also states that all requirements are to be delivered upon receipt of an authorized release from the buyer. On receiving a requisition for one of these materials, the buyer merely sends a brief release form to the supplier. On the release form are noted the purchase order number, the item number, and the quantity to be delivered. Receiving reports are filed with the original order, and at the end of the month are checked against the supplier's monthly invoice. At the end of the period, the order may be renewed or placed with another vendor, depending upon the supplier's performance record.

Most companies develop their own unique modifications of the basic procedure. For example, instead of advising suppliers of order releases by means of a written form, some companies simply issue releases to local suppliers by telephone. By noting such releases on the order, the buyer still retains adequate control.

In the event that material is needed immediately (and the supplier is nearby), some firms allow the using department to pick up the material without notifying the purchasing department. The employee getting the material simply endorses and enters the proper accounting charge on the sales receipt, a copy of which is sent to the buyer. This document then serves as the receiving report. This procedure is particularly applicable to the frequent purchase of various repair parts, when specific needs are not known until the equipment is dismantled. It also works well for purchasing special processing services, such as heat-treating and plating, when the service is required quickly but cannot be planned in advance. This variation of the basic blanket order procedure can easily be abused and can possibly lead to petty fraud. It is therfore important to

entrust its use only to responsible operating personnel and to review periodically the endorsed sales receipts.

The blanket order system offers six important benefits:

1   It requires fewer purchase orders and reduces clerical work in purchas-
    ing, accounting, and receiving.
2   It releases buyers from routine work, giving them more time to
    concentrate on major problems.
3   It permits volume pricing by consolidating and grouping requireents.
4   It sometimes ensures protection against price rises during the period of
    coverage.
5   It centralizes purchasing control of similar commodities.
6   It can improve the flow of feedback information, because of the
    grouping of materials and suppliers.

To function effectively in the long run, however, any blanket order system
must provide adequate internal control. Absence of the control element
encourages petty fraud and poor supplier performance. The elements essential
to effective control are (1) a numbered purchase order including proper internal
accounting charge notations, (2) a record of authorized delivery releases, and
(3) bona fide evidence of receipt of the material.

Telephone Order System

An increasing number of companies now use a telephone ordering system to
reduce the paperwork associated with small-order purchasing. Under this
system, when the purchasing department receives a requisition, it does not
prepare a formal purchase order. Instead, the order is placed by telephone, and
the requisition is used in the receiving procedure.

Although many variations of this system are in use, it is important that the
requisition form be designed to provide all data necessary for internal control.
One company uses a six-part form which includes all data normally included on
a conventional purchase order. When the order is placed, one copy of the
requisition is sent to the requisitioner, one goes to accounting, one remains in
purchasing, and three copies are sent to receiving. When the material arrives,
all receiving data are noted on the latter copies. One of these copies is sent to
accounting, one is sent to purchasing, and the final copy either goes to the
requisitioner or remains in a permanent receiving file.

The Atomic Power Equipment Department of the General Electric Company purchases approximately 60 percent of its requirements by telephone.[3] Its
system goes one step further in the elimination of paperwork; its suppliers send
no invoices for telephone purchases. A firm price is determined during the
initial telephone conversation and is recorded on the requisition. When the

[3]Harold Stephens, "Purchasing by Telephone without Confirmation or Invoice," *NAA
Bulletin*, June 1963, p. 55.

material is received as ordered, the accounting department issues payment on
the basis of the purchase requisition.

Electronic Ordering System

A number of electronic communication systems are currently available to
transmit material purchase requests without writing orders or talking on the
telephone. The best known of these systems, perhaps, is the Data-Phone
"Ten-O-One." This equipment is the product of a joint venture of IBM and the
Bell Telephone System. The hardware consists of (1) an IBM punched card
reader connected to a telephone in the purchaser's office, and (2) an interpreting
unit connected to a telephone in the supplier's office. With this system, the
buyer simply places a purchase requisition (in punched card form) in his card
reader and dials the supplier's telephone number. The requisition data are then
transmitted over telephone lines to the supplier's interpreting unit.

Such electronic systems are relatively new, and they have limited use for
general purchasing activity until most of a buyer's major suppliers acquire the
necessary equipment. Rapid growth in usage, however, *is* occurring among
industrial supply firms. In situations where buyers find their use feasible, such
systems can expedite the purchasing process, reduce paperwork, and simplify
internal accounting and control. They are particularly applicable to the
purchase of repetitively used items whose recurring orders can be placed using
the same punched card. Clearly, the use of an electronic ordering system
requires a blanket order, or similar contractual agreement, with the supplier.

Petty Cash System

Many firms use a petty cash fund for making small one-time purchases. It is
often less expensive for an individual user (or a purchasing delivery employee)
to buy minor items personally and pay for them from a petty cash fund, than it
is to buy them through the conventional purchasing system. Any inefficiencies
that may arise because of a lack of buying skill are more than compensated for
by saving the costs of placing a purchase order.

C.O.D. System

Some firms find it economical to make small one-time purchases on a C.O.D.
basis. Material can be ordered by telephone and paid for on arrival. Payment
can be made with petty cash or with a departmental check written on an
account set up for such use.

Purchase Order Draft System

Some years ago the Kaiser Aluminum and Chemical Corporation instituted a
blank check type of ordering system to reduce the paperwork required by its

numerous small purchases.[4] The system has since been adopted by a number of companies. Unlike the preceding systems, the draft system requires preparation of a formal purchase order for every purchase. However, the bottom quarter of the purchase order is a bank draft—a blank check to be filled in by the supplier. When he receives the order, the supplier detaches the draft and fills it in for the exact amount of the invoice, less the cash discount. The draft is actually constructed in the form of an envelope. The supplier then places one copy of his invoice in the envelope and deposits it in his bank as an immediate cash payment. The draft can only be deposited, not cashed. The purchaser's bank pays the draft when received and bills the purchaser daily for the total number of drafts paid.

Each draft is usually limited to a sum of $1,000 (or some other predetermined figure printed on the face of the draft). To provide adequate control, the amount of each returned draft can be checked against its accompanying invoice or receiving report. Kaiser performs this audit by computer. Like the telephone system, the draft system does not permit back ordering. Each order is considered complete as it is shipped. This system does not significantly reduce the purchasing work associated with small orders, but it virtually eliminates the work of the accounts payable section.

Supplier Stores System

If a purchaser buys miscellaneous supplies from a single supplier, the supplier can sometimes afford to staff a small "store" at the purchaser's plant. Some suppliers find that $100,000 of business annually justifies such a branch operation. Users then simply go to the store and "sign" for their purchases. At the end of the month the company is billed for its purchases just as if the user had "gone down town" to buy the material.

This system is clearly not a short-term arrangement. The purchaser, therefore, must take great care in selecting the supplier and in negotiating the terms of the agreement.

Supplier Delivery System

The supplier delivery system is somewhat similar to a supplier stores system, but it is more feasible for firms with a smaller volume of purchases. Many suppliers who are not willing to set up a store at the plant are willing to stock numerous miscellaneous materials and make daily or semiweekly deliveries. The buyer typically reviews and accumulates purchase requisitions for such materials. The supplier's delivery person then picks them up on the specified day, and at the same time delivers the material ordered on the preceding batch of requisitions. This automatic shuttle service provides reasonably fast deliv-

---

[4]For a complete discussion of this system see "Blank Check Solves Small Order Problem," *Purchasing,* vol. 53, no. 10, pp. 78–82, Nov. 5, 1962.

ery and also reduces the purchaser's paperwork and inventory problems. Properly designed, the system can provide for adequate accounting control.

FOR DISCUSSION

21-1   One executive has said that the development of many of his company's procedures was a waste of time. Could there be any merit to this statement? Why do executives develop procedures and record them in procedure manuals? Explain.

21-2   What basic objectives should a good procedure fulfill?

21-3   List and discuss the steps in the purchasing cycle.

21-4   What improvements can you make to the procedures illustrated in Figure 21-1? Explain.

21-5   Write a series of procedures for the tasks constituting the complete purchasing cycle when a bill of materials is used to transmit the need to the purchasing department.

21-6   How does a traveling purchase requisition differ from a standard purchase requisition?

21-7   Write a procedure for auditing invoices.

21-8   Design a commodity record card (include related requirements). Design a contract record summary sheet.

21-9   Design a supplier record card (include related requirements). Design a special tool record.

21-10   Assume that you are a maintenance supplies buyer. A maintenance foreman calls you to inquire about a purchase order you placed two weeks ago. The foreman has lost his copy of the order, but he does have his copy of the requisition. How would you locate your copy of the purchase order to get the information he requests? Explain.

21-11   What is the value of maintaining a purchase log?

21-12   Write a procedure to be used in handling rush orders.

21-13   What does a purchasing executive mean when he refers to the "small-order problem"? Explain.

21-14   Explain briefly the various techniques that might be used to help solve the small-order problem.

21-15   How does a blanket purchase order system work? What are its advantages? What are its disadvantages?

CASES FOR CHAPTER 21

Blozis Company, page 588
Relbod Company, page 648
Seyah Electro-Devices Company, page 656
Monitor Manufacturing Company, page 631

Organization

Assume for a moment that you and nine business associates have in your possession the engineering design for a new consumer product which you believe to be a "sure-fire" success. You have decided to form a company to manufacture and market the product. You are so sure the venture will succeed that you and each of your associates are willing to contribute $10,000 and full-time effort to the formation and operation of the company. Once you and your colleagues have conceived a general plan for your undertaking, what do you do next? Two questions logically arise at this point: What specific work has to be done to make the company go? And what job does each partner do? Thus, the matter of organization becomes a key concern.

An organization structure should be devised to define clearly the operating tasks and to delineate the responsibilities associated with each task. How important is the organization structure? Much greater than many managers historically have realized.

Three principal factors largely determine the level of performance attained by a group of people: (1) capabilities of the personnel, (2) motivation of the personnel, and (3) the organizational structure within which the personnel function. Dr. Harry Hopf stated the idea concisely some twenty-five years ago:[1]

[1]Harry A. Hopf, as quoted by Ernest Dale, *Planning and Developing the Company Organization Structure*, American Management Association Research Report 20, New York, 1952, p. 17.

That a business cannot permanently occupy levels of effectiveness higher than those clearly determined by the capacity of its executives is self-evident, but it is not generally understood that the influence of a superior organization upon the accomplishments of mediocre executives can raise the enterprise to heights not otherwise attainable.

Peter Drucker, a widely recognized authority on management, states the case even more forcefully:[2]

Good organization structure does not by itself produce good performance—just as a good constitution does not guarantee great presidents, or good laws, or a moral society. But a poor organization structure makes good performance impossible, no matter how good the individual managers may be. To improve organization structure . . . will therefore always improve performance.

CONCEPTS FOR ORGANIZATION

The structure of a firm's organization establishes the authority and responsibility relationships among its personnel. It constitutes a framework that determines to a great extent the manner in which various groups of people work together. The underlying purpose of organization is, logically, to facilitate cooperation among the firm's variously skilled personnel and to channel their efforts toward a common goal.

In fitting the operating tasks into an effective organizational framework, a manager should consider the implications of three basic concepts: (1) functionalization and human needs, (2) control, and (3) coordination.

Functionalization and Human Needs

The concept of functionalization has evolved from Frederick Taylor's experiments with the specialization of factory work. The essence of the concept is this: The overall objectives of an organization tend to be achieved most efficiently when the organization is structured by grouping similar activities together. The process begins by dividing the total operation into its basic functional components. Each component, in turn, is divided into a number of subfunctions. This process is continued until each individual job encompasses a reasonable number of related tasks.

The efficiency of the functional approach to organization stems from two factors. First, it limits the scope of activities performed by each person and by each operating group. Personnel therefore become specialists and usually perform their jobs with greater skill and efficiency. Second, because of the narrower scope of each job, functionalization tends to gear each job more closely to the level of the job holder's ability. This means that for each

[2]Peter F. Drucker, *The Practice of Management,* Harper & Row, New York, 1954, p. 225.

individual job, a company can pay a wage commensurate with the value of the job and, in total, receive more productive work for its labor dollar.

Every company utilizes the concept of functionalization to a certain extent. However, the basic question each firm must answer is this: To what extent is job functionalization actually profitable as it interacts with the desires and expectations of the people doing each of the jobs? When departments and operating groups are functionalized too narrowly, they tend to lose sight of the overall objectives of the firm. As C. Northcote Parkinson wittily points out, such groups may focus on their own narrow activities to the extent that they see their activities as ends in themselves, rather than as means to greater ends. Thus, some department managers devote more effort to building their own "empires" than to coordinating their work with that of other departments.[3]

Individual jobs that are too highly specialized become monotonous and boring to some people. A clerical filing job, for example, may call upon a very small segment of an individual's total abilities. Although some people enjoy such limited activity, many others prefer more varied work. The individual who feels like a very small cog in a huge, impersonal organizational wheel may have very little desire to accept and work toward the objectives of the organization. Extreme functionalization can therefore be counterproductive in terms of the lack of motivation provided for individuals doing the jobs.

Application of the functional concept can produce significant advantages at the group level and at the individual level. As functionalization increases, however, its advantages tend increasingly to be offset by its disadvantages. The seriousness of the disadvantages varies from one department to another, depending on the nature of the work and the expectations of personnel involved.

Control

The way in which a manager organizes his department greatly influences his ability to control departmental operations. Foremost among his organizational considerations is the question of how many employees a manager should supervise (the span of managerial control). If he employs a large number of subordinate managers, each supervising a relatively small number of personnel, activities can be closely supervised and controlled. Under such an arrangement, supervisory costs are higher and the number of levels in the organizational structure is greater than if fewer managers were employed. Additionally, a deep organization with many levels of managers poses numerous communication problems.

On the other hand, if a small number of managers is used, each manager supervises more employees. A manager in this situation tends to focus on a broader range of activities and becomes more of a generalist. Because his

[3]For a humorous and revealing insight into the general topic of administration, see C. Northcote Parkinson, *Parkinson's Law and Other Studies in Administration*, Houghton Mifflin Company, Boston, 1957.

employees are closer to top management, they tend to view their jobs in the broader context of the total company operation. Although this type of organization clearly permits less direct supervision and control, the resulting situation provides good experience for employees with managerial potential. However, it also requires that operating personnel be *capable* of making a broader range of decisions. This type of operating situation consequently forces management to rely more heavily on a system of operating reports as a basis for control.

Because of the complexity of the tasks involved and the complexity of the supervision required, the span of control should be narrower at the top of an organization than at the lower echelons. However, only experience can tell an executive exactly how many people a manager should supervise at various levels in a specific organization. The final decision is influenced by the nature of the work, the personnel involved, and the specific needs of management. Moreover, the decision is conditioned heavily by the chief executive's philosophical views concerning the use and development of the firm's human resources.

Another factor which influences operational control is the clarity with which an organization structure specifies authority and responsibility for each operating activity. Ideally, an organization structure should clearly specify that each operating task is the responsibility of one individual who reports to only one supervisor. In practice, however, this ideal is seldom attainable. Consider, for example, a purchasing department that places responsibility for all expediting activities with a group of expediters who report to an expediting supervisor. The purchasing executive also properly holds each buyer responsible for his orders until they are correctly received. Suppose a critical order does not arrive as scheduled. How does the purchasing manager determine who is at fault? Is it the buyer who failed to negotiate the lead time properly in the first place? Or is it the expediting supervisor who failed to see that the order was expedited properly? Problems arising from a dual assignment of responsibility can be resolved, but whenever possible the organization should be structured so as to avoid the creation of such problems. When an operating situation makes such assignments unavoidable, specific procedures should be established beforehand to govern the resolution of anticipated conflicts.

The preceding example illustrates the desirability of grouping assigned *operating tasks* in a manner that facilitates managerial control. The same idea can be expanded and applied to the grouping of *work groups into larger sections or departments.* In some companies, for example, inventory levels can be controlled most easily if the inventory control section reports to purchasing. In other companies, they can be controlled most easily if inventory control reports to production control.

A firm's organization structure is designed to fulfill a number of different needs. It must facilitate efficient operation of each work group. It should satisfy to a resonable extent the human needs of each group's operating personnel. At the same time, a good structure must satisfy management's need for control.

Coordination

Some authorities hold that coordination is the keystone of good organization. Indeed, the fundamental purpose of organization is to provide a stucture that facilitates coordination and channels the efforts of all individuals toward the common goals of the firm.

Consider again the functions of purchasing, inventory control, and production control. The efficiency with which purchasing utilizes its personnel and procures production materials depends upon the quantities in which materials are ordered, the frequency with which orders are placed, and the lead time allowed to make each purchase. In most companies, many of these decisions are made by the inventory control and production control departments. Hence, the actions of these departments can determine the efficiency with which the purchasing department operates. Production control, on the other hand, can plan production to utilize shop facilities and personnel efficiently only if materials are available when needed. Hence, to perform its function efficiently, it is dependent upon effective performance by the inventory control and purchasing departments.

The need for coordination between the three departments is obvious. Can the organization structure facilitate coordination? It can—by optimal grouping of units and placement of operating authority. After determining which department's needs are most critical and most difficult to fulfill (this varies from firm to firm), one solution might place inventory control under the jurisdiction of that department. Another solution might merge all three departments into a single operating unit. It is clear that various organizational arrangements are possible and that each possesses a different potential for effective coordination.

It is equally clear that optimum coordination also requires the establishment of certain operating procedures to compensate for the inevitable shortcomings of the organization structure. Hence, for operating purposes, the structure is complete only when supplemented with the necessary coordinating procedures.

**LOCATION OF THE PURCHASING FUNCTION
IN AN INDUSTRIAL ORGANIZATION**

A firm's organizational structure reflects management's basic attitudes toward the major activities involved in its operation. Where should the purchasing function fit in a firm's organizational structure? To answer this question a choice must be made between two basic alternatives illustrated in simplified form in Figures 22-1 and 22-2. Is purchasing a top-level function that should report to a general management executive, as do sales and production? Or is it a subfunction that should report to one of the top functional executives (generally, though not always, the manufacturing executive)? Answers to these questions can be determined only by finding the answers to more basic

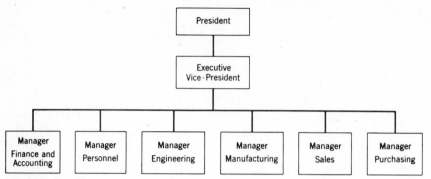

Figure 22-1 Skeleton organization for a medium-sized firm, with purchasing as a top-level function.

questions. How important is the purchasing activity to the total company operation? Will the company suffer significantly if purchasing does not perform as effectively as it might? How important is it that purchasing activities be closely coordinated with engineering and finance activities? Is it essential that material costs be tightly controlled?

Due to the nature of a company's products and its operations, answers to the preceding questions differ among companies. The importance of purchasing in any specific company is determined largely by three factors.

1 *Absolute dollar volume of purchases.* If a company spends a large amount of money for materials, the sheer magnitude of the expenditure means that top-flight purchasing can usually produce significant profit. Small unit savings add up quickly when thousands of units are purchased.

2 *Percent of product cost represented by materials.* When a firm's material costs are approximately 40 percent or more of its product cost, small reductions in material costs increase profit significantly. Top-level purchasing usually pays off in such companies.

3 *Types of material purchased.* Perhaps even more important than the preceding considerations is the amount of control purchasing personnel actually have over material costs. Most large companies use a wide range of materials, many of whose prices can definitely be influenced by creative purchasing performance. Some companies, on the other hand, use primarily a small number of standard production and supply materials, from which even a top-flight purchasing department can produce little profit as a result of its vendor selection and negotiation activities.

Value analysis and purchasing-engineering coordination activities produce handsome profits for a company like General Electric. On the other hand, the types of materials required by some companies leave little room for savings to

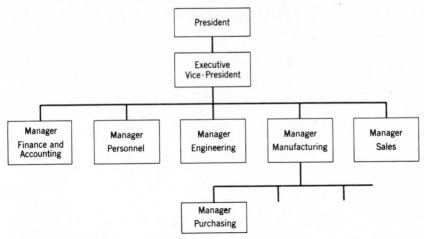

Figure 22-2 Skeleton organization for a medium-sized firm, with purchasing as a second-level function.

be produced by such creative effort. A manufacturer of storage batteries, for example, would appear to have little need for sophisticated value analysis work after product designs have been refined several times.

Economic analysis and other profit-oriented activities conducted by purchasing research groups are likewise much more lucrative when dealing with some materials and markets than with others. Purchasing for a technical research and development organization, for example, is often primarily a service activity. In such a firm, material costs and market trends are not the important concerns they are in a production-oriented firm.

When business operations are viewed in the light of the preceding criteria, it is evident that many companies can benefit from a high-caliber, creative purchasing department. In such companies purchasing should be a top-level, profit-making function that receives close attention from general management. In other firms, purchasing performs primarily a service activity for a major operating function. In such cases, purchasing should properly report to that functional executive. Similar types of considerations dictate the location of all departments in an organization. In most companies, for example, engineering and sales are top-level functions; in some companies, however, they perform a secondary function and are organized accordingly.

Recent surveys[4] indicate that in well over half the nation's manufacturing firms, the purchasing function reports directly to a general management executive. This is a growing trend which is accentuated by sporadic shortage conditions in major materials markets.

[4]The results of two surveys are reported in George W. Aljian (ed.), *Purchasing Handbook*, McGraw-Hill Book Company, New York, 1973, pp. 2–6; and J. H. Westing, I. V. Fine, and G. J. Zenz, *Purchasing Management*, John Wiley & Sons, Inc., New York, 1969, p. 27.

ORGANIZATION FOR PURCHASING IN A SINGLE-PLANT COMPANY

A Basic Approach to Organization

The nature of purchasing activity permits effective use of the functionalization concept. Purchasing work divides naturally into five distinct classifications, each of which encompasses a fairly wide range of activities. In most cases the classifications can be further divided into more specialized tasks, each of which still involves working with different problems, different products, and different vendors. This happy circumstance permits the attainment of a high degree of specialization, without creating serious personnel motivation problems. Moreover, as will be seen later, this type of functionalization permits reasonable flexibility in expanding the work force to meet operational demands.

The five classifications of work found in a purchasing operation are:

1 *Administrative.* Purchasing administration involves all the tasks associated with the management process, with emphasis on the development of policies, procedures, controls, and mechanics for coordinating purchasing operations with those of other departments.
2 *Buying.* This includes a wide variety of activities such as reviewing requisitions, analyzing specifications, doing informal value analysis, investigating vendors, interviewing salespeople, studying costs and prices, and negotiating.
3 *Expediting.* This order follow-up activity involves various types of vendor liaison work, such as reviewing the status of orders, writing letters, telephoning and telegraphing vendors, and occasionally visiting vendors' plants.
4 *Special staff work.* Any well-developed purchasing operation has an unending number of special projects or studies requiring specialized knowledge and uninterrupted effort. Such projects are commonly found in the areas of formal value analysis, economic and market studies, special cost studies, special vendor investigations, and systems studies.
5 *Clerical.* Every department must write orders, maintain working files, maintain catalog and library materials, and maintain records for commodities, vendors, prices, and so on.

The precise manner in which purchasing work is subdivided and grouped depends on the size of the department, which in turn depends on the size of the company. The size of the purchasing department typically runs from 1 to 1.5 percent of the company work force in small companies to substantially less than 1 percent of the work force in large companies. Considering just the professional buying staff, a recent survey by George Aljian reports that most companies with annual sales of less than $5 million employ one to three buyers, while over one-third of the companies with sales from $5 to $50 million employ from four to ten buyers. Virtually all companies with sales exceeding $50 million employ more than ten buyers.[5]

In a small company, say 150 employees, purchasing is frequently a two-person department. The purchasing manager handles all work in the first four classifications, and a secretary performs the clerical work. As the size of the department increases, additional personnel are usually assigned joint buying and expediting duties. At this point, buyers begin to specialize on the basis of broad classifications of the commodities which they buy, and each buyer typically does his or her own expediting work. As the department grows, buyers continue to specialize in increasingly narrower commodity classifications. Eventually, the expediting work may be withdrawn from the buyers and assigned to expediters, who may specialize in somewhat the same manner as buyers. Continued growth finally results in the addition of one or more staff personnel who tend to specialize in various kinds of special projects.

The Typical Organization Structure

Figure 22-3 illustrates a typical structure for the internal organization of a medium-sized purchasing department.[6]

Manager of Purchasing The chief purchasing executive assumes various titles in different companies, such as manager of purchasing, purchasing agent, or director of purchases. In a small department, he usually performs major buying activities as well as the required administrative duties. As the department grows, he devotes more of his time to administration. Finally, in a large department his work is nearly all administrative, except for the negotiation of a few major contracts.

Buyers Buyers and their assistants perform the actual buying activity. Each buyer, and his assistant if the job requires one, handles a specific group of materials.

For buying purposes, materials can be grouped in two ways: (1) materials whose purchase requires similar buying skills and technical knowledge can be grouped together, or (2) materials that are used in the same finished product (or by the same operating department) can be grouped together. The former practice is the more common. Grouping materials that have similar buying and technical characteristics permits a buyer to become a technical specialist. For

---

[5]Aljian, *op. cit.*, pp. 2–12.

[6]A common modification of this basic pattern entails the assignment of expediting personnel and clerical personnel to each buying group. This kind of structure is sometimes called the commodity-type organization. It reduces the possibility of divided responsibility among buyers and expediters, and some firms feel that it tends to increase employee job satisfaction. On the other hand, the commodity-type organization can be more costly and less flexible, especially in small companies.

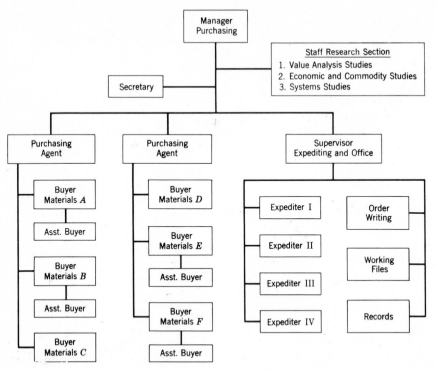

Figure 22-3 A typical basic structure for the internal organization of a medium-sized single-plant purchasing department.

example, he may specialize in buying electronic parts, metal castings, or abrasive materials. In most companies today this is highly desirable. As materials continue to become more complex, specialized knowledge of their characteristics, manufacturing processes, and markets is indeed required to purchase them intelligently. Table 22-1 illustrates a classification of materials used in a typical production operation. For assignment to buyers, these classifications are organized into larger groups on the basis of required buying skills. Exact groupings depend upon the size of the department and the volume of material usage.

If a buyer's materials are grouped by similarity of end use, one buyer may buy some or all of the parts for finished product A and another buyer may buy the parts for finished product B. Or one buyer may handle the materials used by the fabrication department and another may handle the components for the assembly department. Generally speaking, when materials are grouped by end use, the buyer buys a wider range of items and becomes less of a specialist than he would under the preceding method. This arrangement also produces some duplication of effort because several different buyers invariably buy some of the same types of materials.

A major advantage of grouping materials by end use, however, is the fact that buyers do not become immersed in their own technical specialities. They have a tendency to identify to a greater extent with the product or the department for which they are buying. In these circumstances, the buyer frequently feels that he is an integral part of a *specific* production effort. Companies favoring this form of organization believe that the loss of technical buying specialization is more than compensated for by the added effectiveness of the purchasing-production team effort that results. The extent to which this is actually true in a specific situation depends upon the range and complexity of materials purchased by each buyer and upon the effectiveness achieved by the team effort.

Buying Supervisors   The size of the buying staff and the complexity of the purchases handled determine the need for buying supervision. In some departments eight or ten buyers can report directly to the purchasing manager or to a line assistant. In other cases, each commodity buying group is headed by a senior buyer who reports to the chief purchasing executive. Possibly the most common arrangement is depicted in Figure 22-3. In this case, buyers are organized into larger groups on the basis of similar commodity characteristics. An intermediate manager, who reports to the chief executive, is assigned to each group (sometimes called a buying department). These managers are variously titled assistant purchasing agents, purchasing agents, or buying department managers, consistent with the title of the top purchasing executive. The duties of these managers typically encompass both administrative and actual buying activities.

Table 22-1   A Classification of Materials Used in a Typical Manufacturing Operation.

1	Abrasives	17	Machined parts
2	Adhesives	18	Machine tools
3	Bearings	19	Office furniture and equipment
4	Castings	20	Office supplies
5	Chemicals	21	Packaging material
6	Coal	22	Paint
7	Containers	23	Plastic parts
8	Electrical and electronic components	24	Powdered metal parts
9	Electrical and electronic assemblies	25	Printed materials
		26	Power sources
10	Electrical cable and wire	27	Pumps
11	Fasteners	28	Rubber parts
12	Forgings	29	Safety clothing
13	Fuel oil	30	Sheet metal parts
14	Hardware	31	Shop supplies
15	Laboratory supplies	32	Stampings
16	Lubricants	33	Tooling

Expediters The most common form of organization for the expediting activity is shown in Figure 22-3. Formation of a separate expediting department permits a high degree of specialization; additionally, it facilitates an even distribution of the work load and efficient utilization of expediting personnel. However, a great difference of opinion exists concerning the most effective arrangement for handling the expediting activity. Some firms require each buyer to do his own expediting. Because of his status and his intimate knowledge of the order, they believe that a buyer can obtain more effective results from suppliers than can a person of lesser status in the organization. More important, companies using this approach want the buyer to assume *total* responsibility for each of his orders. They feel he can do this best by personally participating in all phases of the purchase. Additionally, if a buyer is responsible for all phases of his orders and for all vendor contacts, it is easier to measure and control his performance.

Since much expediting is routine work, however, it often represents an inefficient use of a buyer's time. Some companies therefore adopt a compromise form of organization. To achieve the benefits of specialization, they assign expediting work to a separate expediter. So the buyer can retain full control of his orders, though, each expediter is assigned directly to one buyer (or a buying group). Thus, the expediter does his work as directed by the buyer, and the buyer is held fully accountable for his orders. In practice, the expediter usually handles all routine follow-up inquiries and calls upon the buyer for assistance with the difficult or delicate expediting problems. This form of organization, when fully developed, produces a commodity-type organization structure that minimizes the division of responsibility between buyers and expediters and tends to produce a beneficial esprit de corps among buyers, exediters, and clerical personnel assigned to a particular commodity group. This form of organization clearly may also be less flexible and more costly, especially in small companies.

Staff Research Personnel The number of staff specialists employed depends on the size of the department, the complexity of its operation, and the types of material it purchases. Theoretically, in making prepurchase investigations good buyers should perform nearly all the activities such staff specialists are hired to do. However, most companies now realize that under the pressure of daily operations, most buyers simply do not have time to conduct all desired investigations in adequate depth. This is particularly true for complicated purchases that influence future procurement efficiency. This fact, coupled with an awareness of the great benefits specialization can produce in the areas of planning and research, has led many firms to organize such activities functionally within a special staff group. The specific activities of this group are discussed in the chapters dealing with value analysis and purchasing research. For these activities to yield optimum benefits, it is essential that their organization and implementation be carefully planned from a *companywide* point of view.

Organization by Product or Project

Few single-plant companies are large enough to organize the total purchasing activity profitably on the basis of product. A few large firms making only several major products, however, do utilize a separate purchasing department for each product they manufacture. In such companies, each product division is largely autonomous and to a great extent operates its own manufacturing facility, complete with all supporting functions. The basic objective of this type of organization is to develop a group of employees whose interests and identification with a specific *production effort* transcend their identification with a department. This attempt to motivate individuals and to develop a smoothly coordinated team effort is based on the same reasoning as that involved in grouping buyers' materials by end use. Viewing the total operation from the standpoint of each product manager, this form of organization permits more effective coordination and control of all operating functions contributing to his production responsibility.

As top management views the purchasing activity, however, this decentralized form of organization can possess two disadvantages. First, when the autonomous divisions use many of the same materials, savings can be lost through the failure to consolidate requirements and exploit the company's full buying potential. Second, some duplication of buying effort always exists. Given a fixed number of buying personnel, this means that the firm is not taking full advantage of the potential benefits afforded by increased buyer specialization that would be possible under a consolidated purchasing effort. The seriousness of these two disadvantages depends largely on the size of the individual product divisions.

ORGANIZATION FOR PURCHASING IN A MULTIPLANT COMPANY

A multiplant company faces one additional organizational problem that does not concern most single-plant companies: To what extent should purchasing activity be centralized at the corporate level? In practice, virtually every company answers this question differently. Some firms centralize the activity completely, doing the buying for all plants at a central headquarters office. Others decentralize the function entirely, giving each plant full authority to conduct all its purchasing activities. Still other firms—the majority of them—develop an organization somewhere between these two extremes. Each extreme approach offers significant benefits that are discussed in the following sections.

Advantages of Multiplant Centralization

Greater Specialization Perhaps the greatest benefit of centralization stems from the fact that it permits greater technical specialization among buyers. This leads to the development of more knowledgeable and more highly skilled buying personnel.

Assume that a firm has three plants, each employing a decentralized purchasing department of six buyers. Assume further that each plant uses eighteen different classes of materials and that each buyer is responsible for materials in three classes. It is not unusual to find that half of the material classes used by each plant are also used by the other plants. If the eighteen buyers were combined in a central department, they would have only thirty-six classes of material to purchase [9 common + (3 × 9) unique]. Thus, each buyer would have only two material classes to handle (36/18); each buyer's degree of specialization would be increased by one-third. Because materials purchased in the different classes normally vary in complexity and volume, the transformation does not occur this simply in practice. However, the example illustrates an important point. Centralization enables a firm to do a better technical job of buying, or it permits a job of buying comparable with that under decentralization to be accomplished with fewer buyers. It also provides for the capable buying of major capital equipment and construction services which are required only intermittently by any single plant, but which on a companywide basis represent a continuing purchasing activity.

In most companies, the importance of buying specialization cannot be overvalued. The complexity of industrial materials increases constantly. A buyer who does not fully comprehend the significance of a material's major technical and manufacturing characteristics cannot perform effectively. If buyers fail to perform with technical competence, the important buying decisions will ultimately be made in the using departments, and buyers will be relegated to a glorified clerical status.

Consolidation of Requirements   Just as single-plant centralization facilitates the consolidation of plant requirements, multiplant centralization facilitates the consolidation of material requirements at the corporate level. In most situations, such consolidation results in larger purchases from a smaller number of suppliers, yielding more favorable prices and increased supplier service. Increased purchase volumes also permit the negotiation of highly profitable *long-term* contracts for many production materials.

Easier Purchasing Coordination and Control   When all company purchasing activities are consolidated in one office, procedures for coordinating and controlling individual segments of activity can be effected more quickly and with less paperwork. Consolidation permits more direct administration and control of such important policies as those affecting supplier selection procedures, supplier relations, reciprocity, purchasing ethics, budget compliance, and the consistency of general purchasing practices among the various buying groups. In general, under this type of organization, the chief purchasing executive finds it easier to control the total efficiency of the corporate purchasing activity.

Advantages of Multiplant Decentralization

Easier Coordination with Operating Departments From an operating standpoint, the greatest advantage of decentralization is that it facilitates the coordination of purchasing activities with the activities of using departments within each plant. When a complete purchasing unit is located at each plant site, purchasing personnel are close to the users' operating problems and develop a much better "feel" for unique plant needs and their implications in the purchasing area. Buyers can personally discuss purchasing matters with using supervisors any time they wish. Value analysts and technical coordinators can work daily with engineering personnel whenever necessary. Also, a plant purchasing department can develop a much closer working relationship among suppliers' technical representatives, buyers, and plant engineers than is possible under a centralized organization.

In brief, under a decentralized arrangement, purchasing personnel can participate more fully as members of a specific purchasing-production team.[7]

Speed of Operation A purchasing department located at the plant clearly can respond more quickly to users' needs. The transmittal of information from plant to headquarters by means of a conventional paperwork system typically lengthens the purchasing procedure by one or two days. Of course, telephone and teletype services can be used in many cases, but often these are not practical as a regular method of communication. If most operating needs could be adequately planned, and plans always functioned according to schedule, the time delay factor would be a minor problem. In a dynamic business situation, however, unforeseen events cause enough deviations from schedule so that this is rarely the case.

Effective Use of Local Sources If a firm's plants are geographically dispersed, it can be difficult for a centralized purchasing department to locate and develop potentially good suppliers in the locale of each plant. At times this difficulty deprives a plant of various technical and purchasing benefits resulting from close working relationships between plant personnel and suppliers. If plants are separated by great distances, decentralized purchasing departments in many cases may also be able to reduce material transportation costs by the wise use of local suppliers.

Plant Autonomy A fundamental principle of management states that the delegation of responsibility must be accompanied by the delegation of adequate authority to carry out that responsibility. If a plant manager is given full

---

[7]To prevent each plant from losing its identification in a *centralized* purchasing office, some companies using centralization locate a "plant coordinator" for each plant in the purchasing office. The coordinator's job is to act as a liaison between plant users and centralized purchasing; he looks after the procurement interests of his plant.

responsibility for the operation and profit performance of a plant, he can properly contend that he should have full authority over the expenditures for materials. Decentralization of purchasing gives a plant manager this authority.

Although entirely valid, the preceding idea implies that a plant manager has no control over material expenditures if purchasing is centralized. This need not be true. While a plant manager has no line control over a centralized purchasing department, many companies develop coordinating committees to correct purchasing situations that are unsatisfactory to plant management. If these are established within the proper framework, a plant manager, through such a mechanism, can exercise satisfactory indirect control over the performance of a centralized purchasing department.

Factors Affecting Feasibility and Desirability of Centralization

Three factors determine how feasible or desirable centralization of the purchasing function may be in a given situation: (1) similarity of the *classes* of materials used in each of the plants, (2) size of each individual plant purchasing department, and (3) distance separating the individual plants.

Similarity of Material Usage   If a firm's plants use entirely different materials, centralization of purchasing offers only minimal benefits; the major benefits of increased specialization and requirement consolidation cannot be achieved. In such cases, potential disadvantages of centralization usually outweigh the advantages gained from better coordination and control.

Most firms, however, generally have a greater similarity of material usage among plants than is at first apparent. To make specialization profitable, various plants do not have to use exactly the same *items*. The important thing is the similarity of *types* of materials (or markets). Specialization of buyers is accomplished on the basis of material (or market) *classifications*. Most firms find that their plants do use a number of the same classifications of material. The J. I. Case Company, for example, found that only about 5 percent of the 16,000 items it purchases were used by more than one of its five plants (each plant makes a different line of products—agricultural machinery, industrial tractors, materials-handling equipment, and construction equipment). However, analysis of these items by material classification revealed that of the total 191 classifications of material, over 75 percent were used by at least several plants. Further study of the situation led the Case Company to centralize its purchasing operation, whereas the initial decision had been to decentralize because of the dissimilarity of the items purchased.[8]

Plant Department Size   As a general rule, centralization is more advantageous when a firm's individual plant purchasing departments are not large. If

---

[8]For a complete account of the Case Company's reorganization see "J. I. Case Switches to Centralized Purchasing," *Purchasing Week,* May 6, 1963, pp. 18–19.

plant purchasing operations are large, a high degree of buyer specialization may already have been achieved. Similarly, the benefits to be gained from consolidating requirements of large departments are less significant than those gained from consolidating the requirements of small plants. This is not to say that consolidation of large departments does not yield benefits. It usually does. The benefits, however, are not as significant as in the case of small departments, and they are frequently outweighed by the concomitant disadvantages.

Geographic Dispersion of Plants   The closer a firm's plants are situated geographically, the more feasible centralization becomes. Conversely, the wider the plants are dispersed, the more serious the disadvantages of centralization become. Even if a centralized purchasing office has direct telephone service to the production control offices at each plant, when a plant is 1,000 miles distant, the problems of communication and coordination with that plant are difficult indeed.

The Trend in Industry

While the purchasing organizations of some multiplant firms are found at both ends of the centralization continuum, most are located somewhere between these two extremes. The trend appears to be toward the general type of organization shown in Figure 22-4. This organization includes elements of both centralization and decentralization. Its objective is to reap the major benefits offered by both approaches.

A centralized purchasing office is established at the corporate level, with the chief purchasing executive usually reporting to the president or executive vice-president. Duties of the centralized office include planning, research, and specialized buying. Economic and industry analyses, technical commodity research, systems planning, and government contract regulation work are the most common types of planning and research activities. Buying activities conducted centrally vary widely from firm to firm, but they focus on the material classifications for which highly specialized buying and requirements consolidation produce the greatest profit. In addition, most long-term contracts are negotiated centrally on a companywide basis. Plant purchasing departments then issue orders against these contracts in accordance with their needs.

In most cases, the relationship between the central purchasing office and the plant purchasing departments is a "functional" relationship. This means that each plant has its own purchasing department, whose manager usually reports directly to the plant manager. By explicit agreement, however, the plant purchasing department relinquishes to the central purchasing department certain planning and buying responsibilities. The central department generally has no line authority over the plant manager of purchasing, but typically, it does have the authority to determine specifically which materials will be purchased locally and which centrally. The central department also serves in a coordinating capacity by formulating and enforcing basic purchasing policy and by designing purchasing systems and procedures for all plants.

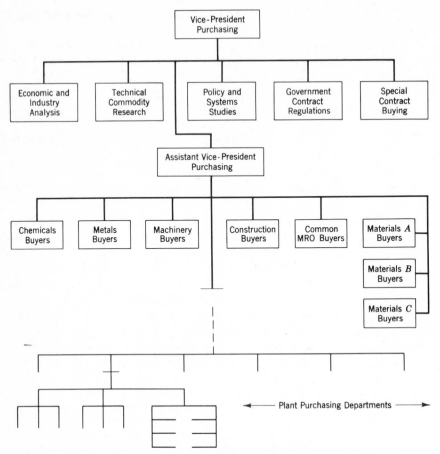

Figure 22-4 A multiplant purchasing organization with some activities centralized and some decentralized.

THE MATERIALS MANAGEMENT CONCEPT

To this point, we have discussed only the organization of the purchasing function. In designing an organization structure for the total plant, management must decide how to group and coordinate the other activities whose primary interest also focuses on the company's materials problems. In addition to purchasing, the departments that are primarily concerned with materials are inventory control, stores, receiving, production control, and traffic. To which functional executives should these departments report?

Chapter 2 discussed the materials management concept and its growing application in American industry. Historically, firms have divided responsibility for the various materials activities among two or three functional departments (i.e., purchasing, production, and sales). This division of responsibility makes it difficult to coordinate the interrelated activities of the materials-oriented departments. More important, it makes effective identification and control of *total* materials costs extremely difficult, if not impossible. The materials management concept, and subsequent form of organization, has evolved in response to these needs. Materials management provides an *integrated, systems approach* to the coordination of materials activities and the control of total materials costs. It advocates assigning to a single operating department all major activities which contribute to materials cost. The objective is to optimize performance of the materials *system*, as opposed to suboptimization of the performance of individual operating units that are major parts of the materials system (but are also minor parts of other subsystems). The resulting organization of the materials activities takes the general form shown in Figure 22-5.

Among top executives and management consultants, however, there is not complete agreement concerning the operational details of the materials management form of organization. In many cases, these differences in application of the concept are quite legitimate simply because each firm is somewhat unique in terms of its specific orientation, its operating environment, and its specific problems. Consequently, some companies do not include all of the materials activities in the materials management department. In fact, the title of the department responsible for most materials activities may vary considerably among firms. Some firms adopt the *philosophy* underlying the concept, but for various internal reasons assign the materials activities to a strong existing department (often the purchasing department), without creating a department bearing the materials management name.

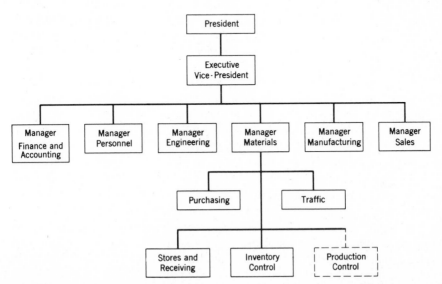

Figure 22-5 The general structure of an organization using the materials management concept.

Strengths and Weaknesses

Abundant evidence supports the claim that a materials management type of organization improves coordination and control of the activities that contribute to total material costs. The need for such coordination and control has been emphasized repeatedly in preceding chapters; the operating effectiveness of each materials activity depends heavily upon the policies and performance of the other materials activities. Under a materials management organization, these matters become the responsibility of one top-level executive. If inventory levels or material costs are out of line, top management can immediately pinpoint the weak link in the materials chain. This type of organization eliminates the "buck passing" possibilities prevalent in an organization that divides the responsibility for total material costs.

What must management give up to obtain the benefits of a materials management organization? In most firms little or no sacrifice is required. If anything must be given up, it is only a small amount of coordination between the materials activities and the departments in which they might otherwise be located. As for stores, there is no difficulty under materials management in providing adequate service to the production department. In fact, most companies find that materials management improves stores' service to production, because internal stores operations tend to improve when they are under the control of a person whose primatry interest is materials. In the case of traffic, the significance of the coordination problem depends on the quantity of outbound shipments the traffic department handles. In most companies, traffic's work is approximately equally divided between incoming and outgoing activities. If this typical situation prevails, a strong case can be made for locating traffic in the materials management group. On the other hand, if traffic deals largely with outbound shipments, the purchase of transportation services constitutes its major tie to the materials management group. In such cases, traffic bears a greater functional responsibility to sales than to materials, and it might well be part of the sales organization.

From the standpoint of materials control, production control should definitely be located in the materials department, because it *controls the scheduling* of manufacturing's material requirements. In Figure 22-5, however, the status of production control is shown as indefinite (indicated by dashed lines). The reason for this is that in many companies production control *must* be located in the production department, since the major portion of its work relates to production activieies. In such cases, if production control were located in the materials department, coordination with production would be a monumental task. As a general rule, production control can function effectively as a member of the materials department when its major responsibility is scheduling production and assuring the availability of materials. When its major responsibility focuses on controlling and expediting production orders through the shop, production control is usually more effectively located in the production organization.

When production control is part of the materials department, the location of inventory control presents no problem. Even when production control reports to production, the stronger case can usually be made for locating inventory control in the materials department rather than in the production department. In most companies, effective coordination is easier to achieve with this arrangement. The materials manager and the production manager are equally concerned about coordinating lead time and material availability requirements with inventory control operations. The materials manager, however, must also coordinate with inventory control activities his requirements for economic order quantities and for ordering patterns that facilitate efficient procurement and efficient use of materials department personnel. In total, material requirements are generally more difficult to coordinate with inventory control than are production control requirements.

A strong, integrated materials department, whose manager has equal status with the engineering and production managers, offers one intangible yet important benefit which is not apparent on an organization chart. Such a department possesses the potential to exert a strong influence on such indirect materials activities as the standards program, the material specifications program, and the value analysis program. An organization structure containing a top executive whose primary responsibility is the *total* cost of materials without doubt establishes the foundation for developing profitable interdepartmental participation in these activities.

Effect on Purchasing Organization

What effect does the adoption of a materials management organization have on purchasing? It has no effect on the purchasing function per se. Internal organization of the purchasing department, in most cases, should change very little.[9] With respect to the purchasing function's status in the organization, if any change occurs, its status should be enhanced because of the greater attention management gives to material costs.

The position of the chief purchasing exucutive does change, however, if he previously reported to a general management executive. He automatically moves down the executive hierarchy one level. Under the new organization, the purchasing manager reports to a materials manager, who now occupies his previous location on the organization chart. Although the materials manager has responsibilities that are considerably broader than purchasing, purchasing is the focal point of activity in the new department. For this reason, the competent purchasing executive may well be a logical candidate to fill the materials manager's position when the transition is made.

In a multiplant company, the central purchasing office experiences approximately the same type of transition as the plant purchasing departments.

[9]To facilitate coordination of buyers and production control analysts, material groupings may be modified so that buyers and analysts tend to handle the same groups of materials.

However, the additional centralized activities for inventory control, production control, and stores tend to focus on the development of policies and systems; most operating activities usually remain decentralized.

The Future

As detailed in Chapter 2, the number of companies employing the materials management concept has literally skyrocketed during the past decade. Current estimates indicate that approximately 70 percent of America's industrial firms, large and small, utilize the organizational concept in either complete or modified form. Although the growth rate will be less spectacular, it appears that this general trend will continue in the future.

In addition to the benefits inherent in the materials management concept itself, four emerging forces will make this form of organization even more attractive in the future. The first of these forces is the trend in industry toward the production of an increasing number of highly specialized, complex materials and components. As a result of this development, most firms in the future will make fewer and buy more of their material requirements. Consequently, materials will continue to represent an increasing percentage of total product cost. Hence, the control of materials activities and materials costs will be even more important than it is today.

The second force is generated by the recurring shortages of basic materials evident in today's economy. Such volatile supply situations are bound to continue and become more complex in the future. This phenomenon demands increasingly sophisticated planning for long-range material sources and acquisition, within increasingly severe cost constraints. Efficient organization and operation of all materials activities will be a requirement for business survival.

The third force is the increasing use in business of computers and related electronic data processing equipment. Effective use of this equipment requires the integration of interrelated operating systems within the firm. This means that, in the materials area of a business, the operating records of purchasing, inventory control, production control, and stores will in most cases be integrated to a significant extent. The most feasible organization for efficient daily operation under this arrangement is a structure based on the materials management concept.

The fourth force stems from the current trend toward factory automation. As a buyer's own production departments automate their manufacturing processes, material specification requirements become more stringent and the range of acceptable quality usually becomes narrower. An automated production operation also demands an uninterrupted flow of production materials. Failure of a single production material of the proper quality to arrive on time in the right quantity can shut down an entire segment of the production operation. Both of these factors magnify considerably the importance of total integrated planning and control of material requirements and acquisition, as well as effective purchasing performance.

FOR DISCUSSION

22-1   How do you distinguish between a good organization and a poor organization?

22-2   Some business executives say that overorganization is just as bad as underorganization. What is your reaction to this idea? Explain.

22-3   What factors determine how wide a manager's span of control should be? Explain.

22-4   Where in a single-plant manufacturing company's organizational structure should the purchasing department be located? Explain.

22-5   Assume that you have been asked to study a plant's purchasing department and recommend an ideal organization to the manager. Describe exactly what you would do and how you would conduct the study.

22-6   On what bases are materials grouped for buying purposes? Explain the strengths and weaknesses of each approach.

22-7   How and by whom should the expediting function be conducted in a purchasing department? Explain.

22-8   Discuss the advantages and disadvantages of centralized purchasing in a multiplant company.

22-9   When is it neither feasible nor desirable to centralize the purchasing activity in a multiplant company? Explain.

22-10   Discuss the major weaknesses you see in the organization structure shown in Figure 22-5.

22-11   How does the materials management concept affect a firm's organization structure?

22-12   From an operating point of view, discuss the pros and cons of the materials management concept.

22-13   What factors tend to favor increased future use of the materials management type of organization? What factors tend to impede its future use? Explain.

CASES FOR CHAPTER 22

Northeastern Equipment Company, page 634
G.A.R. Manufacturing Company, page 616
Smithson Company, page 658
Blozis Company, page 588
State Research Laboratories, page 660

Managing Personnel

A sound organization, refined policies and procedures, and knowledge of sophisticated procurement practices cannot alone make a successful purchasing and materials operation. Competent and willing personnel serve as the catalyst that provides the lifeblood for these important elements. The effectiveness of any business enterprise is limited invariably by the abilities and motivation of the people operating it.

The management of personnel enters the total management process at three important points—organization, staffing, and coordination. In the organization phase of the management activity, specific materials job requirements and consequent manpower needs should be determined in detail. This is the starting point for the development of sound personnel management. After satisfactory personnel have been obtained through effective staffing, their ultimate performance is influenced substantially by the way management performs the "coordinating" function of its responsibility.

Personnel management is an extremely broad field of study; nevertheless, it is one with which every materials executive should be familiar. The purpose of this chapter is to review briefly those key personnel concepts which are of paramount importance to purchasing and materials managers.

PURCHASING JOB REQUIREMENTS

Planning and Job Design

Purchasing executives cannot optimally staff their departments simply by hiring intelligent, responsible individuals. The wise manager knows that successful long-run performance depends heavily on the job satisfaction of the employees. Consequently, the first step is to determine precisely what the department's work requirements are. Next, a good manager attempts to package these requirements into specific jobs that provide reasonable levels of interest, diversity, and challenge for the individuals performing them. Over the long run, most people perform better when they enjoy their work. And people tend to enjoy a job more when their abilities and interests are fully utilized and challenged by the requirements of the job. This is not to say that all jobs should be designed to be highly creative and individualistic. This is neither practical nor desirable. Different individuals have differing levels of abilities and aspirations. The combined objective in job design and staffing, considering individual differences, is to match the total qualifications of an employee to the requirements of the job. In most cases, an optimal fit ultimately requires some modification of both elements—job structure and employee capability.

A departmental organization plan should serve as the blueprint from which all employee selection activities are developed. The generalized purchasing jobs appearing on the plan were discussed in the preceding chapter. To determine the most effective organizational and authority relationships within the department, each individual job must be carefully analyzed and described. This type of job analysis pinpoints the specific duties and responsibilities the job entails, any unusual working conditions involved, and any special qualifications and characteristics required of the person holding the job. The latter determination focuses on abilities, knowledge, training, experience, and personal qualities necessary to do the job satisfactorily. While actual practice differs from firm to firm, most companies condense all these findings and include them, for each job, in a written "job description."

General Qualifications for Buying

In addition to the specific qualifications indicated on job descriptions, two important general qualifications for buyers and purchasing managers deserve special consideration. These focus on the personal characteristics and background experience which a purchasing person must develop to achieve stature in the profession.

Personal Characteristics   Many of the characteristics required for success in purchasing are the same as those required for success in most professional areas: for example, integrity, dependability, initiative, human relations skills, analytical ability, and an inquiring mind. Several types of characteristics, however, receive greater emphasis in purchasing and therefore warrant further comment. Most purchasing authorities agree that top-flight buying requires an unusually high degree of *initiative*. The total framework within which a buyer operates is largly unstructured. He must depend upon his own initiative and imagination in developing sources of supply, good vendor relations, alternative materials, value analysis projects, and cooperative investigations with other operating departments. The extent to which a buyer is a "self-starter" greatly influences his success in these areas. A good buyer must also be especially *tactful* and must display genuine *cooperative ability*. A buyer's success depends ultimately upon the effectiveness of the relationships he develops with suppliers and with technical personnel in his own organization. Such relationships can be achieved only through the use of tact and cooperative abilities of a high order.

Although a buyer spends considerable time dealing with people, much of his work also involves detailed analyses. Without *patience* and an *aptitude for detailed investigation*, a buyer would find it difficult indeed to arrive consistently at sound decisions. Finally, a *mechanical aptitude* usually proves to be a definite asset in most industrial buying jobs. Many items purchased are themselves mechanical or semitechnical in nature, and they are frequently produced by technical manufacturing processes which the buyer should understand. Quite apart from the characteristics of the material purchased, a buyer should also understand how the material is handled and processed in his own manufacturing operation.

Background Experience   A successful buyer or purchasing manager must develop two types of "know-how"—business and technical. Business know-how is composed of a thorough understanding of purchasing principles and their applications, as well as a general understanding of the business functions involved in and related to purchasing. Technical know-how involves an understanding of materials and manufacturing processes.

The proportions in which a buyer combines the two types of experience vary from one company to another, depending upon the nature of the firm's products. The need for technical know-how increases proportionately as a firm's products and materials exhibit greater technical complexity. Moreover, the specific technical know-how required in each different industry is usually highly specialized (e.g., electronic, chemical).

How is this broad and rather formidable aggregation of experience acquired? Usually, it is obtained by a combination of academic training and practical expereince. A college degree is helpful and usually desirable, but it is not always essential. Selected college courses, however, are by far the fastest method of acquiring a fairly *complete* exposure to the *principles* of purchasing, general business functions, and general manufacturing processes. Subsequent to this type of formal schooling, practical experience and selected reading in specialized areas then combine to provide the detailed knowledge required for effective buying performance.

If a purchasing department establishes educational requirements for new employees, what should they be? Most purchasing authorities now believe that an academic major in business administration, with elective courses in selected technical and mathematics areas, is very helpful. This means that the student will have to acquire most of his technical know-how on the job. A second approach, with growing support in some industries, favors an academic major in general engineering. This approach forces the student to acquire most of his business know-how on the job. Joint business-engineering training (such as a B.S. in engineering and an M.B.A. in business) is, of course, an ideal educational combination.[1]

In some technically oriented companies a buyer is required to have an engineering background. In most companies, however, this requirement is not necessary. Engineering training very rarely provides the *specialized* technical know-how required for a buyer of any specific material. The real value of engineering training to a buyer is twofold. It provides him with a technical orientation, and through its rigorous curriculum it develops his analytical abilities for dealing with quantitative problems.

To conclude, it appears that it is generally easier for a young buyer to obtain the required technical know-how on the job than it is to obtain the required business know-how on the job. The business requirement consists of a broad understanding of a myriad of general, interrelated principles of business. On the other hand, the technical requirements consist largely of knowledge of a body of highly specialized, detailed, factual information about a specific group of materials. The latter, because of its limited scope for a given group of materials, can usually be acquired more easily than the former from selected evening courses, directed reading, and practical experience.

SELECTION OF PERSONNEL

Basic Policy

In terms of personnel, most purchasing/materials departments are relatively small, usually employing from 0.5 to 1.5 percent of the total number of employees in the firm. In addition, purchasing employee turnover typically is low. Hence, advancement of personnel through the procurement ranks, although steady, does not occur rapidly in most established companies.

Every purchasing department strives to hire and develop a number of ambitious, promotable personnel to build a creative, management-oriented organization. However, *not all* expediters', assistant buyers', and buyers' jobs should be filled with individuals who will become readily promotable. Usually, there are not enough vacancies into which all can be promoted. And when a person's job no longer offers him a challenge, he soon becomes discontented and either leaves the company or performs in only a mediocre fashion. For

---

[1]Lamar Lee, Jr., "Purchasing Education," unpublished research study conducted at Stanford University, Stanford, Calif., 1968.

these reasons it is essential that personnel be selected with care. During the selection process, most executives attempt to match an individual's qualifications *both* to current and to anticipated future job requirements of the department. It is much easier and less costly to weed out marginal performers *before* rather than after selection. A good purchasing person properly trained is invaluable to the firm; a poor one is a major liability.

Sources of Personnel

Purchasing/materials personnel at all levels can be acquired either from within the firm or from external sources. When vacancies occur above the expediter's level, the common practice in most companies is to promote personnel from within the department when it is feasible to do so. Promotion from within produces several distinct benefits. First, the practice tends to keep morale high because employees know they are not "trapped" in dead-end jobs. It stimulates individual performance by offering an avenue of advancement for the better career employees. Second, promotion from within reduces total training costs. It entails a minimum of training for the person in the new position because his past experience in the organization is generally useful in his new job. If a person is hired from the outside to replace the promoted individual, he can thus be brought in at a lower level. This, too, requires less training.

Promotion from within can also produce problems. The first promotion may result in a chain of lower-level promotions, simultaneously moving several people one step up the organizational ladder. If chain promotions occur frequently, the organization tends to lose its stability because a large number of individuals are continuously learning new jobs. When a company is growing rapidly, this policy sometimes results in the promotion of people who are not ready to be promoted. The mediocre performance resulting from such action simply compounds the problem of instability. Finally, promotion from within produces "inbreeding," and if carried to extremes it may jeopardize the flow of new ideas into the organization.

A wise manager promotes from within when it is practicable. When such action tends to generate problems, however, he draws personnel from external sources to fill his needs. To fill lower-level jobs, young people are frequently hired directly upon graduation from college. At higher levels, persons with purchasing/materials experience are sometimes hired from other firms when no one in the department is qualified to fill the position. This practice has considerable merit in the case of special staff and managerial jobs, because it brings new blood and new ideas into the organization, and it prevents the substituting of seniority for management ability.

When a procurement executive must go outside his department to find personnel, he may acquire them from other departments in his own firm. Transfers of this type usually occur at the lower levels. Such action is usually viewed with favor by management. It tends to stabilize the firm's total employment pattern, and it offers career opportunities to deserving employees who may be blocked from promotion in their present positions. In addition to these considerations, interdepartmental transfers may also be advantageous to the purchasing/materials department. In the first place, the person transferred is familiar with company operations and can usually assume full job responsibility sooner than a new employee. Second, and more important, it is the fact that such a transfer brings to the purchasing/materials department experience in a related functional area. Coming from important related areas in the plant, this experience may be useful in buying activities, and it may also provide stronger liaison with a cooperating department.

ORIENTATION OF PERSONNEL

New employees become oriented, one way or another, whether or not the supervisor makes any attempt to orient them. The important question is: *How* are they oriented and what are their resulting *attitudes* toward the organization and toward the job?

Experience indicates that first impressions are important to a new employee. They create an initial working atmosphere which lays a foundation for the satisfaction and security that will be derived from the job. It consequently behooves every materials supervisor to give more than casual thought to orientation activities; careful planning pays future dividends. Thorough orientation facilitates psychological adjustment, which, in turn, enables a person to approach his or her job confidently and to become fully productive at an early date.

Generally speaking, purchasing orientation consists of two distinct phases of activity: (1) general orientation and (2) functional orientation.

General Orientation

General orientation consists largely of "get acquainted" activities conducted during the first several days a new person is on the job. As a rule, the personnel department initiates this activity with a formal orientation interview. In larger companies, during the interview the following written information is typically given to new employees and discussed with them.

- A brief write-up of the company's history, its progress, and its products
- A pamphlet discussing insurance programs and employee fringe benefits
- A booklet discussing general company policies and work regulations as they affect the employee
- A booklet discussing safety regulations as they affect the employee
- Wage scale information
- A map of the plant and an abbreviated company organization chart

The purpose of this interview is to acquaint the individual with the general aspects of his new working environment and to facilitate his adjustment to it. After the new employee has studied the written material, an alert supervisor should volunteer further assistance in explaining and interpreting any items still not clear. If this initial orientation is not conducted by the personnel department, the immediate supervisor should see that it is done by a capable person, preferably himself.

When the new employee reports to the purchasing/materials department, his supervisor should continue the orientation process, focusing on more specific factors and activities that relate to departmental operations and the individual's job. The purpose of the procurement supervisor's orientation activities is threefold. First, it enables the new employee to "get his feet on the ground" and learn his way around the total company operation. Second, it provides an abbreviated view of the intricacies of the purchasing/materials organization and its operation. Finally, it reveals the interrelationships of these departments with other departments, showing the materials function in context as an integral part of the total company operation. The new person should see a detailed picture of his job, and he should also see his job as a part of "the big picture."

Functional Orientation

Functional orientation, focusing primarily on initial job training, constitutes the second phase of a new employee's total orientation program. Three basic approaches can be used: (1) learning by doing, (2) the sponsor system, (3) functional rotation.

Learning by Doing   One school of thought holds that a person can learn best by actually doing the work himself. This approach employs almost no training at all; a new employee is immediately assigned to a job and is expected to perform it with a minimum of guidance from his supervisor. He either "sinks or swims," depending upon his own ingenuity and ability to handle the job.

There is little doubt than an individual can learn a job well by doing it. Likewise, practice in figuring things out for himself undoubtedly develops his ingenuity and analytical ability. However, most authorities believe that this approach should be employed *after* a person is well grounded in the basics of the job, not before. Most procurement jobs are too complex to be learned thoroughly by the sink-or-swim approach. After mastering the fundamentals of his job, a procurement employee has an infinite number of opportunities to handle problems "on his own" without detailed guidance by his supervisor.

Some small companies justify the use of the sink-or-swim approach by saying they cannot afford the luxury of a training program or the loss of a person's productivity while he is in training. In most cases, however, a good training program more than pays for itself by teaching an employee to do the job *right,* thus nurturing him to full productive capacity sooner and reducing the number of costly errors committed in the process. Most companies manage to get along without a new person for some time before he is hired; in most cases, they can also get along without a portion of his productive services for another month or so while he is being properly trained.

The Sponsor System   A second commonly used orientation practice involves the assignment of a sponsor (or a "buddy") to the newly hired person. After initial orientation, the new employee is assigned to a specific job where he frequently receives basic job instruction from this supervisor. The bulk of the training load, however, rests with the individual's sponsor, who is an employee doing similar work. His sponsor acts as an informal trainer during the entire period the new person is learning the job. A sponsor should be chosen for his experience and, more important, his teaching ability.

This approach can be quite effective *if* the sponsor is a good teacher. It has the probable disadvantage, however, of restricting the new person's orientation training to a single job. Some time may elapse before he realizes fully the implications of his activities for related departments outside the procurement area. Also, the time devoted to such training activities may significantly reduce the sponsor's productive output.

Functional Rotation   Before a new employee is assigned to a specific job. many companies consider him as a trainee for a period varying from several weeks to several months. Much of this initial training period is frequently spent in departments other than purchasing/materials. The basic idea is to expose the individual to a number of functional activities to facilitate his understanding of the various procurement functions and their relationships to other operating functions. A typical program includes assignments in such areas as:

- Receiving and stores departments
- Purchasing records section
- Expediting section
- Assistant buying activities
- Buying activities (perhaps one assignment with an MRO buyer and one assignment with a production parts buyer)
- Inventory control department
- Production control department
- Quality control department
- Line production department
- Traffic department

Specific assignments vary, depending upon the person's background and upon his first permanent job assignment. The program objective, however, is to develop a general understanding of the complete materials cycle in the firm. Upon completion of rotational orientation, the new employee is assigned to a specific job where he may receive further job training from a sponsor or from his supervisor.

Classroom Training Some large companies either precede or follow orientation training with approximately a month of theoretical training. This activity may be viewed as a training or as an orientation activity. It is discussed at this point, however, because in a broad sense it simply represents further orientation for procurement work.

This type of training consists of a series of brief classroom courses dealing with the theoretical principles underlying purchasing and related activities. It is given to new employees who show promise of advancing to responsible materials jobs in the near future. Typical subjects studied include inventory control, production control, quality control, traffic, manufacturing processes, value analysis, purchasing principles, human relations, public speaking, and salesmanship. The objective of this type of training closely parallels the objective of functional rotation, except that it focuses on theory rather than practice. Companies using such a program feel that it prepares the new purchasing/materials employee to do a better job, and that it also aids him in establishing rapport with personnel in related departments.

Conclusion

The concept of orientation is based on two major premises: (1) that experience during the first several weeks on a job strongly influences a new person's attitude toward permanency and career ambitions with the firm, and (2) that it costs most companies a substantial sum of money to acquire a new professional employee and a substantial sum to lose him, and at times it costs even more to retain a disgruntled employee. If these premises are valid—and experience indicates they are—a prudent manager can justify a reasonable expenditure of time to ensure that new employees are properly oriented.

CONTINUOUS PROFESSIONAL TRAINING

The need for continuous training in materials management, as in most professions, never ceases. The National Association of Purchasing Management has long been noted for its active interest in and promotion of professional development activities among its members. Although content details of the training programs differ among the various materials functions, the basic methods and approaches to training are essentially the same. Discussion throughout the next several pages focuses on training in the purchasing function, and also serves as a general guide for training in the other materials functions.

After an employee has completed the initial academic and orientation training, four methods are commonly used to further his professional development: (1) job rotation training, (2) on-the-job training, (3) self-training, and (4) management development training.

Job Rotation Training

Job rotation training can take several forms. Young purchasing employees often begin their careers in the expediting section of the purchasing department. After a year or so in this work, the able individual progresses to an assistant buyer's job. Following several years of assistant buying experience, the competent person moves on to assume a buyer's responsibilities. A logical starting point at the buyer's level is the MRO section or the general-purpose materials section. These buying jobs typically involve less complex materials than specialized production buying jobs, yet they provide good initial buying experience. From this poisition the individual may elect to specialize in buying a particular type of raw material or production part. Such job progression training thus provides the maturing purchasing person with experience in various types of departmental activity, each with increasing complexity.

Job rotation training finds its second major application at the buyer's level. Although each production buyer is a skilled specialist, his capabilities can be expanded by providing experience in several specialized buying jobs. This type of rotation naturally occurs slowly because of the extensive background and knowledge required in each buying area. Conducted wisely, the technique not only fosters professional development of personnel but also provides buying flexibility within the department. However, one danger must be avoided. Care must be taken not to dilute technical buying competence by rotating buyers too frequently.

On-the-Job Training

Most on-the-job training is conducted informally. It can be initiated by various members of purchasing management in response to observed needs among departmental personnel. Such training may simply consist of supervisory coaching for selected individuals. In some companies, it takes the form of periodic discussion sessions among management and selected groups of personnel. Each session is conducted in seminar fashion and focuses on the exchange of ideas about relevant purchasing topics.

On-the-job training in many progressive companies also includes periodic lectures and demonstrations. Such firms frequently engage consultants to conduct refresher sessions on such topics as value analysis, cost estimating, negotiations, human relations, and similar practical purchasing skills and techniques.

Self-Training

Professional competence is a matter of unique concern to each individual. Responsibility for the recognition of specific needs lies with individuals and their supervisors. Much of a mature buyer's professional development, for this reason, is acquired through self-training. Self-training takes many forms, but commonly involves the following approaches:

- Studying purchasing periodicals, books, and research reports
- Studying selected business publications
- Studying trade magazines and special resource books on materials
- Attending purchasing association meetings and special commodity group meetings
- Enrolling in selected university evening courses and correspondence courses
- Attending special seminars and workshops sponsored by universities and professional societies

During the course of his self-training endeavors, a professional purchasing person must strive to attain a balance between the development of his business skills and his technical knowledge of materials.

Management Development Training

In addition to the acquisition of professional procurement competence, individuals aspiring to managerial positions must also develop general administrative and managerial skills. Development of these skills comes largely through self-training activities and through practice.

Procurement management programs now sponsored jointly by the NAPM and several leading universities represent a significant innovation in the management training area. These programs are designed for practicing materials executives and involve from one to two weeks of intensive study on a university campus. Program content typically focuses on management and decision-making concepts outside of, but related to, the materials functions.

More broadly based management development seminars offered by the American Management Association, as well as by numerous professional societies and universities, provide many opportunities for materials executives to continue their professional education.

APPRAISING PERSONNEL PERFORMANCE

Need for Appraisal

It is essential that every materials manager develop a carefully structured and continuing program for appraising the performance of personnel. Nothing is more disastrous to the morale of a department than haphazard and inconsistent evaluation of individual employee performance. A well-designed appraisal program systematically reviews each individual's performance at least once each year. Such a program provides information which can be used for four important managerial purposes: (1) to evaluate selection and training programs,

(2) to determine which employees are promotable, (3) to develop a fair salary structure, and (4) to help in the personal development of all employees.

How do managers measure the effectiveness of their employee selection and training programs? How do they determine where improvement is needed? Their most important feedback comes from an appraisal of employee performance. A systematic study of employee performance data and trends provides a method by which strengths and weaknesses in selection and training activities can be pinpointed. Such information can be used to strengthen these programs and ultimately to improve the total performance level within the department.

How do managers know which people in their departments are likely to become candidates for the top jobs? They determine this by analyzing each aspect of an individual's performance record. It is clearly imperative that such analyses be made using detailed and accurate written data which have been collected over a period of years. A well-designed appraisal program provides the required data.

No department operates at its full potential for long if its salary structure fails to reward individuals in relationship to their respective performance levels. A good performance appraisal program does not guarantee an equitable salary structure. It does, however, provide data which can be used in developing a sound compensation plan or in correcting an inadequate one.

The most important benefit that can come from a good employee evaluation program is the information needed to stimulate and direct individual employee development. A supervisor's prime responsibility is to develop capable and effective personnel. The data provided by appraisals can be analyzed to determine each employee's strengths and weaknesses. This determination facilitates the development of a realistic professional improvement program for each individual.

Appraisal Concepts

Factors Appraised   When developing a personnel appraisal program, questions invariably arise concerning the precise factors on which employees should be evaluated. The National Industrial Conference Board sought answers to these questions by analyzing the appraisal forms used in fifty leading companies. The most commonly used factors are noted below.

- Quality of work
- Quantity of work
- Knowledge of specific job activities
- Cooperativeness
- Dependability
- Initiative
- Accuracy
- Adaptability
- Attitude

Each materials department must choose the factors that are related to its specific job responsibilities. The foregoing factors constitute a good general list from which a core group of factors can be developed.

Who Evaluates Currently, the most common practice in industry is to assign the evaluation responsibility to the employee's supervisor. A second, less widely used approach is that of committee evaluation. Even though the committee approach is the more time-consuming of the two methods, it possesses several distinct advantages in evaluating materials personnel. The committee typically includes the employee's supervisor and two other supervisors with whom the employee has frequent contact outside of his specific work area. As a rule, the general observations of members outside of the employee's own department are quite helpful in developing a complete appraisal. Equally important is the fact that an employee frequently accepts an evaluation with greater objectivity when it represents the consensus of a group rather than the opinion of just one individual.

Regardless of the appraisal method used, it is essential that those doing the evaluating be fully qualified. First, they must be familiar enough with the employee's performance to make a valid evaluation of it. Second, they must be adequately trained in appraisal work. The personnel department of most companies assumes responsibility for this kind of training.

Discussion with the Employee Some companies discuss an employee's performance appraisal with him; others do not. The former practice appears to be the more advantageous one. Most employees want to know "where they stand." Such knowledge is essential to the development of an individual's feeling of security and confidence in his work.

A primary benefit accruing from an employee appraisal program is the development of a professional improvement plan for each employee. This benefit can hardly be realized if an employee does not clearly see and understand his or her weaknesses. A good supervisor constantly helps those under him achieve this understanding and whenever possible suggests courses of action for improvement.

THE MANPOWER PLAN

The forward-looking executive prepares a long-range manpower plan for his total operation. After developing a current organization chart, complete with job descriptions for each position, a wise manager looks to the future. Based on future company plans, he anticipates possible expansion and organizational changes within the materials activity during the next five years. He defines these changes, to the extent possible, in terms of specific jobs and personnel requirements. For planning purposes, these changes can then be superimposed upon the existing organization chart.

Next, the status and career potential of all individuals currently in the organization must be determined. Which are promotable and which are not?

Which position might each individual occupy in the future? In each case, what type of training will be required prior to promotion? Answers to these questions constitute the basis for development of a long-range timetable for training, promotion, and hiring.

Plans for meeting future manpower needs, however, should not be allowed to remain static. They are based on predictions of the future, which can never be made with precision. Therefore, as the future unfolds, the materials executive should review his plans and modify them in the light of new conditions and changing expectations.

FOR DISCUSSION

23-1   Discuss the relationship between the total management process and the function of personnel management.

23-2   How important is the management of personnel in a purchasing/materials operation? Explain.

23-3   How does job analysis fit into the overall manpower management plan?

23-4   What type of background should a buyer possess? Discuss.

23-5   What does engineering training contribute to a buyer's competence? What does training in business administration contribute to a buyer's competence?

23-6   Develop a basic policy for the selection of purchasing personnel.

23-7   From what sources can purchasing personnel be acquired? Discuss pros and cons of each.

23-8   Why is orientation important?

23-9   What role should the immediate supervisor play in orientation?

23-10   Discuss the pros and cons of the various methods of orientation training.

23-11   Discuss the various methods of continuing professional training. What are the strengths and weaknesses of job rotation training? Explain.

23-12   Assume that your ultimate career goal is to become a senior buyer of castings and machined parts. Outline a five-year self-training program which will help you attain your goal.

23-13   Why is employee performance appraisal important? For what purposes can it be used? What possible problems do you see in discussing the results of an employee's appraisal with him?

23-14   What does an overall manpower plan include? How is it used by the manager of a purchasing department?

CASES FOR CHAPTER 23

Allied Industries, page 584
Career Crossroads, page 593
The Case of Mr. Adams, page 595
Picking a Buyer—What Really Counts? page 642

Control

How do managers know when their departments are performing satisfactorily? What do they do when performance is not satisfactory? Appraisal and control is the final essential step in the management process.

CONCEPTS FOR CONTROL

Why Control?

When a manager delegates to a subordinate the responsibility and authority for performing a particular job, the manager is still responsible for seeing that the job is done properly. It is therefore essential that he develop some system of control. The system should enable him to appraise the subordinate's perform-ance and control it to the extent that unsatisfactory performance can be detected and rectified before it causes serious damage.

A good control system achieves another highly desirable goal—self-control. Whenever possible, the control system for a job should utilize objective standards of performance. When a delegate knows the specific level of performance expected and also knows that his performance is being evaluated, he normally exercises more self-control than he otherwise would.

Stimulating employees to exercise a high degree of self-control should be every manager's ultimate goal. As discussed in several preceding chapters, a primary managerial responsibility is the creation of a work environment and a reward system that produces strong positive motivation for employees. This situation can contribute significantly to effective development of self-control. When each individual willingly and continuously exercises adequate control over his or her own performance, controlling the total operation becomes a relatively easy job.

There are basically two types of formal control a manager can employ: (1) preaction control, and (2) postaction control.

Preaction Control

Preaction control is accomplished in two ways. The most common method is by means of personal supervision (which is always most effective in a work climate characterized by openness, honesty, and mutual respect among supervisors and employees). A second approach utilizes control checks built into the operating procedures for a given task.

Aircraft operating procedures provide an illustration of the second method. Before a plane leaves the ground, for example, preflight procedure requires that engines, alternators, pumps, and other vital pieces of equipment be tested to ensure that they function properly. In a purchasing operation, the commitment of large sums can be controlled by requiring that, as a matter of procedure, all purchase orders exceeding a stipulated figure be approved by the director of purchasing. Control of competitive-bid awards can be strengthened by requiring buyers to prepare a written justification, based on predetermined control criteria, for any contract awarded to a vendor other than the low bidder. This type of control measure is preventive in nature and, whenever practical, is preferable to postaction control. Numerous specific preaction control techniques are discussed in the preceding chapters dealing with purchasing fundamentals and procedures.

Postaction Control

Preaction control techniques seldom provide *completely* satisfactory control, and they are always subject to human error. Therefore, they should be supplemented with a postaction control system. This chapter deals primarily with postaction control.

The post action control process consists of four activities:

1   Establishing a workable standard of performance
2   Developing procedures for "feeding back" actual performance data to the administrator
3   Comparing actual performance with the standard and appraising the results
4   Taking corrective action when necessary

Establishing Performance Standards It is imperative that performance standards be determined as objectively as possible and that they be fair; otherwise, individuals will refuse to have their performance evaluated against the standards. Establishing a realistic standard which is accurate and readily accepted by operating personnel is usually the most difficult part of the control process. The degree of difficulty depends upon the nature of the job. Acceptable standards can be set with little difficulty for repetitive manual or machine-paced jobs (e.g., the production of a stamped part on a punch press or the filing of purchasing documents). As job duties become more varied and require more individual creativity, however, determination of a workable control standard becomes increasingly difficult.

The effectiveness with which standards can be determined also depends on the extent to which prior plans and procedures have been developed. It is extremely difficult to develop a meaningful standard for a job whose content and scope have not been clearly defined. If a job has not been precisely defined, each person performing the job will define its responsibilities slightly differently. Under these conditions, no single performance standard can be determined for the job because, in practice, the job itself undergoes constant change. Similarly, it is difficult to establish a workable standard for a job whose operating procedure has not been standardized. If different employees use significantly different procedures in performing the same job, their performances will usually differ because of this fact. Hence, if there is significant variation among the procedures used, no single performance standard is appropriate or valid.

Whenever possible, performance standards should be expressed in quantitative terms; such measurements are exact, and they facilitate comparison. The performance of individuals or groups can thus be expressed precisely as a percentage of the standard. This, in turn, facilitates a comparison of performance among different operating groups or among individuals in the same group. Such comparisons can be used as a powerful motivating stimulus for most individuals and groups.

In practice, performance comparisons cannot always be made so simply. It is frequently difficult to establish for different groups *absolute standards that are in fact comparable.* For example, in establishing a performance standard for negotiation cost savings, an equipment-buying group clearly has more opportunity to generate such savings than does an MRO-buying group. To be truly comparable, therefore, the equipment group's standard must bear the same relationship to its opportunity to generate savings as the MRO group's standard bears to its opportunity. Only under these conditions can each group's performance (expressed as a percentage of its standard) be validly compared with the other. Thus, while performance standards constitute a convenient basis on which to compare the performances of different operating groups, a manager must interpret such comparisons cautiously when there is any question about the basic comparability of the standards themselves.

Priorities for Control In embarking upon a control program for his department, how does a manager determine which activities to control? Typically, he begins by listing the potentially controllable activities in the order of their importance relative to departmental objectives. Since the development of standards and the accumulation of feedback data entail both clerical and managerial costs, standards should first be developed for the most important activities. As he works down the list, the manager ultimately reaches a point where the cost of control exceeds the benefits of control. This, then, should be the cutoff point for the development of control standards until changing conditions dictate otherwise.

In subsequently designing the individual control system for each activity to be controlled, the manager must also answer this question: *At which point in the activity's action sequence does a dollar buy the most effective control?* The activity's performance relative to a given objective can be controlled at various points in the sequence of actions that comprise the complete activity. However, both the cost and the effectiveness of control differ at the various points. It is essential, in the design of each individual system, that a manager select those points of control which provide, at the least expense, the control he considers adequate.

Developing Performance Feedback Most of the raw data required for the appraisal of performance are scattered throughout a department's various operating records. The information frequently requires tabulation and/or arithmetic manipulation before it can be used effectively in a control system. Since feedback must be timely if control is to be effective (i.e., result in corrective action before a situation becomes serious), data accumulation and preparation can become excessively expensive if not properly planned. A department should therefore coordinate the development of its operating procedures and departmental records with development of the control system and its required performance feedback reports. The objective of such coordination is to provide the feedback data for control as inexpensively as possible, as by byproduct of normal operations. The increasing use of computerized systems in industry today facilitates attainment of this objective, provided coordination occurs at an early stage in the systems design process.

Evaluating and Taking Corrective Action An effective control system permits a manager to manage by exception, concentrating primarily on those situations requiring corrective or commendatory action. The data-producing elements of a control system alone, however, do not provide control. These elements, performance standards and the flow of feedback data, merely provide a manager with the information required for control. To control, the manager must first compare performance data with the established standard. Then he must determine the significance of the comparison. This requires thorough consideration of any unusual circumstances which might have caused current performance to vary from the standard. The most demanding phase of managerial control is the diagnosis of the cause of the deviation from desired performance. After carefully interpreting the meaning of nonstandard performance, *the manager* must *decide* upon and *initiate* the most appropriate course of action.

The ease with which corrective action can be effected depends in part upon how precisely responsibility for the problem can be traced to a specific work group or a specific individual. The precision with which the problem can be pinpointed is, in turn, dependent upon the way in which the organization structure and the operating procedures were developed. Clearly, the ideal situation is to have established in the organization a unity of command that permits each responsibility to be traced directly to a specific individual. Such a situation avoids, for example, the difficulties encountered in attempting to pinpoint responsibility for an excessive inventory level, when inventory determination is the *joint* responsibility of a buyer and a production control analyst.

To summarize, an effective control system must provide realistic performance standards, it must feed back timely operating data, and it must ensure reasonably clear-cut responsibility for operating activities. A system without these characteristics retards the timely detection and correction of operating problems.

APPRAISING AND CONTROLLING PROCUREMENT PERFORMANCE

In developing a system to appraise and control the performance of a department, the logical starting point is an analysis of the objectives of the department. Once this has been done, the organization structure and the responsibilities assigned to each work group should be examined to determine the impact each operating activity has on the attainment of each departmental objective. This procedure discloses the critical points (or activities) in the operation where control is most important and can be most effective.

Problems in Controlling Purchasing Performance

When an analysis of objectives is made in a purchasing department, it reveals one unfortunate fact. Most of the critical control points lie in a single activity—the buying activity. A wide range of extremely variable activities are placed under the jurisdiction of each commodity buyer. Moreover, examination of the basic responsibilities of each buyer reveals that performance in most areas is quite difficult to express in quantitative terms. Thus, the very nature of the purchasing function makes it unusually difficult to establish workable performance standards. Consequently, development of an effective control system is a difficult task.

Several examples illustrate the problems involved. Suppose a manager attempts to control the quality of a cast-steel valve purchased repetitively by a particular buyer. What performance standard can be used? Probably the most feasible quantitative standard is the percentage (or number) of valves rejected per month by the inspection department. Thus, if the vendor's rejection rate remains at or below the standard, this fact indicates that the buyer has selected a valve and a vendor that satisfy the using department's requirements. So far, so good. However, is this accomplishment the extent of the buyer's responsibility? Who knows whether it is possible for the buyer to locate a more satisfactory valve (considering the quality of the valve related to the function for which it is used)? If he studied the user's need more carefully, and if he investigated the valves of additional suppliers, it is possible that a more suitable valve would be found. By far the most important part of the buyer's performance results from his ability to go beyond the simple purchase of a valve whose quality is "satisfactory."

In the preceding example, the factor of price is clearly interrelated with the factor of quality. Suppose the manager also wants to control the price paid for the valve. By studying the market he can probably establish a target (or standard) price for the type of valve selected by the buyer. However, how meaningful will this standard be? Does it reflect the fact that a valve of lower quality and lower price might be acceptable? Does it reflect the potential price reduction the buyer might obtain by using a detailed cost analysis in negotiating with the vendor? Does it reflect the pricing improvement that might be gained from more skillful grouping of commodities or timing of purchases? A perceptive observer can ask many such questions which tend to place the validity of the standard in doubt.

Assume, further, that the manager wants to control his departmental operating costs. As part of this objective, he wants to set a standard time (or cost) that a buyer should expend, on the average, in processing a purchase request. Again, the important question is: How can a standard that will be useful for control purposes be determined? At what level should the standard be set so that it does not deter a buyer from making a thorough prepurchase investigation of specifications and vendors? To compound the problem, time requirements vary widely for making different types of purchases. This situation makes it even more difficult to establish a meaningful average time standard.

The preceding examples illustrate one cardinal point. Although it is usually difficult to establish absolute quantitative standards of performance for purchasing responsibilities, in many cases it can be done. *However, control systems based on such standards are much less precise and meaningful than their quantitative character might indicate.* In the first place, the *accuracy* of the standards is in many cases open to question. More significant than this fact is the question of the *validity of* many standards themselves. The intangible nature of purchasing's primary responsibilities prohibits the *direct measurement* of purchasing accomplishment. Most standards and measurements therefore focus on secondary factors that are only *indirect indicators* of true accomplishment. The secondary factors that can be measured (e.g., quality rejection rate and price paid) are useful in determing *trends* of performance. In appraising the absolute level of accomplishment, however, secondary factors may or may not be useful. The validity of each factor must be assessed in each specific case; it varies with materials, markets, and vendors.

A Basic Approach to Purchasing Control

Because of the difficulties encountered in developing precise purchasing control systems, many companies have adopted a fairly broad approach to the control of their purchasing activities. Such an approach possesses three distinctive features. First, it includes *a qualitative assessment of a number of broad managerial responsibilities,* such as the capabilities of personnel, the soundness of the organization structure, purchasing plans, policies, procedures, and so on. The theory underlying the use of such an evaluation is this: These factors control the *potential* level of a department's performance; as such they are useful indirect indicators of performance.

The second feature of the broad approach focuses on *buying proficiency.* Attempts are made to establish performance targets (standards) for the measurable secondary factors that relate to primary buying objectives. Recognizing that a single factor may not provide an accurate indication of creative buying performance, most companies develop a cross check by measuring several factors that relate to the same primary objective. For example, buying performance relative to the price objective can be checked from two standpoints: (1) actual prices paid can be compared with target prices, and (2) targets for cost savings resulting from negotiation and from value analysis can be established and actual savings compared with these targets. Thus, two measurements provide a cross check on the same primary objective—price. A similar approach can be used in evaluating buying performance relative to each of its other basic objectives.

The third feature of the broad approach deals separately with *purchasing efficiency.* Proficiency in buying and efficiency in buying are two distinctly different elements. Control of efficiency involves evaluation of work loads, personnel utilization, operating costs, and processing times as related to specific volumes of purchasing operations. Clearly, a purchasing executive wants to achieve a high degree of operating efficiency—*but not at the expense of buying proficiency.* The latter element offers far more opportunity for cost savings than the former.

Appraising Managerial Effort

The broad appraisal of managerial effort is, in essence, a management audit of the purchasing operation. Because of the subjectivity involved in this kind of evaluation, it can usually be conducted most effectively by someone outside the purchasing department. Persons normally called upon to make such audits are private consultants, staff systems specialists, staff management engineers, and internal staff auditors. This does not mean that purchasing management should not make such evaluations. On the contrary, to improve the operation, purchasing management should continuously ask itself the same types of questions that management consultants ask.

The areas investigated and the types of questions raised during the evaluation are similar to those discussed in the preceding five chapters. Without repeating the details, the list that follows outlines the general areas of inquiry.

1 *Scope of the purchasing function.* How important does management consider the purchasing activity in the total operation? Is purchasing properly located in the organizational hierarchy? Does purchasing participate in the formulation of policies on forward buying, reciprocity, and inventory levels? To what extent does purchasing participate in make-or-buy decisions, in the material standards program, in the value analysis program?

2 *Evaluation of purchasing managerial personnel.* Are purchasing managers adequately qualified? Do they fully understand the economic and business intricacies of their company and industry? Are they qualified administrators? Do they have adequate knowledge of relevant materials and manufacturing processes? Do they have adequate knowledge of the suppliers and markets with which they deal?

3 *Organization.* Does purchasing have a complete and current organization chart? Is all purchasing activity centralized in the purchasing department? Have clear lines of responsibility and authority been established? Is sufficient authority delegated along with responsibility? Are the operating activities logically grouped for purposes of functional operation, coordination, and control? Has the department developed adequate job descriptions and employee qualifications for its jobs? Is adequate organization planning being done to meet future needs?

4 *Personnel.* Do employees' qualifications match job requirements? Are adequate selection criteria used in hiring personnel? What job training is given personnel? What professional development training is afforded and required of personnel? What planning and preparation is done for the advancement and replacement of personnel? Are compensation levels adequate to retain good personnel? Is the employee turnover rate reasonable?

5 *Policies.* Is a well-defined basic purchasing policy, outlining purchasing responsibility and authority, well known and accepted throughout the company? Is a well-developed policy manual in use? What policy has been adopted regarding purchasing research activities (economic research, commodity research, systems research)? Do buyers concentrate time and effort on materials proportionate to their respective dollar-volume values? Is adequate advance material planning done to permit effective purchasing? Do satisfactory policies exist concerning forward buying and speculative purchasing? Do satisfactory policies exist for the following activities: new vendor identification, vendor

evaluation and selection, use of competitive bids, use of negotiation (cost analysis and price analysis), and vendor relations? Have satisfactory policies been developed concerning terms of purchase, routing of shipments, types of inspection (and coordination with vendors), personal purchases, local purchases, and the use of multiple sources?

6 *Procedures.* Have all procedures been mechanized and automated to the extent reasonably possible? Is a well-developed procedure manual in use (simple, clear, complete)? Have procedure flow charts been developed? Are all forms well designed, simple, and effective? Are procedures in operation that effectively coordinate purchasing with using departments, the data processing division, inventory control, receiving and stores, traffic, engineering (as regards value analysis work), and inspection? Are adequate procedures used to handle rush orders and small orders? Are sound procedures in existence for such activities as negotiation, competitive bidding, vendor selection, and order follow-up? Are complete procedures available for controlling the receiving activity and for handling loss and damage claims? Do adequate stores procedures exist for receiving, storing, and disbursing materials? Have procedures been developed for evaluating capital equipment purchase alternatives? Have procedures been developed for evaluating capital equipment purchase alternatives? Are sound procedures used in managing inventory, in determining ordering quantities (EOQ used?), and in determing safety stock levels (probability concept used?)?

7 *Records and reports.* Are adequate records maintained to facilitate effective purchasing (emphasis on commodity records and vendor records)? Do operating records contain necessary data for control purposes? What reports are submitted to purchasing management to facilitate managerial control by exception? How frequently are such reports submitted? What reports are submitted to top management?

Controlling Buying Proficiency

A number of different performance factors can be measured to provide a basis for appraising and controlling buying proficiency. The factors differ in importance among different companies, depending upon the nature of the business and the materials purchased. Most firms, therefore, do not use *all* the measures discussed in this section. Similarly, to pinpoint certain problems more precisely, some firms find it desirable to divide certain individual measurements into several more detailed measurements.

In the following discussion, measurement factors are classified according to the primary purchasing objectives whose attainment they help achieve.

Control of the Time Factor   A purchasing department's first responsibility is to support the production operation. The following measurements indicate how effectively this responsibility is fulfilled:

1 Percentage of overdue orders. To provide more direct control, a weekly list of overdue orders can be reported.
2 Percentage of stock-outs caused by late deliveries.
3 Number of production stoppages caused by late deliveries.

An initial categorization of these data by material classification usually provides an adequate basis from which subsequent control action can be taken.

Control of Quantity and Inventory Investment Closely related to the preceding measures of production support effectiveness are the following two measures:

1 Percentage of stock-outs caused by underbuying
2 Number of production stoppages caused by underbuying

Other measurements useful in controlling the quantity factor are:

3 A chart showing target and actual inventory levels in the aggregate and by major material classification. This chart is most useful when supplemented with a chart showing inventory turnover rates (annual material usage divided by average inventory) for the same material classifications. When analyzed together, these charts point up imbalances between inventory carrying costs and material acquisition costs.
4 A report of "dead stock" materials in stores, resulting from overbuying. The report should be classified by major material classes, listing the items in each class and their respective dollar values.
5 A list of vendor stocking arrangements which have been negotiated and an estimate of resulting inventory savings.

Control of Prices Paid for Materials The following techniques provide a cross check on the reasonableness of prices paid for materials:

1 Standard or target prices can be established for major materials. Prices actually paid can then be charted against the target figures to display any significant differences.
2 A materials budget, utilizing standard price data, can be used to achieve the same result. However, the preceding technique provides a more direct measurement which can be more easily and quickly interpreted.
3 A firm can develop its own average "price paid" indexes for major classes of materials. The trends of such price indexes are valuable guides to control. If developed on a comparable basis, these indexes can also be charted against various national commodity price indexes published by the Bureau of Labor Statistics and the Department of Commerce. This comparison reveals cases in which a firm's material costs are rising or declining more than market prices during an inflationary or deflationary period.

4　Periodic cost savings figures can be individually charted for savings arising from such activities as negotiation, value analysis design changes, value analysis material changes, vendor suggestions, change of vendors, packaging improvements, and transportation cost-reduction projects.

　　The development of accurate figures for such projects frequently poses a problem because of the variables involved. Numerous individuals and departments sometimes contribute to the solution of a single problem, making it difficult to allocate fairly credit for the savings. Also, questions often arise concerning the magnitude of savings figures and the validity of the time period used in computing repetitive savings. For these reasons, it is wise to have a separate auditing group coordinate the development of the actual figures.

5　Gains and losses from forward-buying activities should periodically be reported to determine forecasting effectiveness. Again, a major problem is the determination of a standard figure to use as a basis for comparison. Typically, prices paid during a period are compared with the average market price during the period. While this is a feasible approach, in reality it produces only approximate savings figures. A more precise approach compares prices paid with prices that would have been paid had the conventional buying schedule been followed. However, this approach requires more clerical effort than can typically be justified.

6　A report of the percentage of purchase orders that are issued without firm prices provides another basis for controlling material cost.

All the preceding measurements can be classified and subclassified in various ways to pinpoint responsibility for the problems they reveal. The most useful initial classification, however, is by major material groupings.

Control of Material Quality　Once material specifications have been established, the most direct measure of quality performance is the percentage or number of delivered materials that are rejected by the inspection and production departments. To check on the improvement of quality specifications, the purchasing executive can also review the value analysis reports dealing with component design changes and material substitutions.

Control of Source Reliability　The following measurements can be used to indicate the reliability of major suppliers:

1　Reports dealing with percentage of late deliveries and percentage of rejected items can be further analyzed and classified by supplier.
2　Percentage of orders on which incorrect materials were shipped.
3　Percentage of orders on which incorrect quantities of materials were shipped.
4　Percentage of orders on which split shipments were made.
5　Some firms combine these and other measurements, by means of a

formula, into a single vendor rating which is published and used for control purposes. This approach is discussed in detail in Chapter 5.

6 To provide close control of sole-source suppliers of nonstandard materials, a periodic report should be made summarizing for each supplier the percentage of rejected materials, the percentage of late deliveries, and the dollar volume of business handled.

7 The quality of transportation service offered by various carriers can be partially appraised by maintaining a record of transit times and of damaged shipments.

Control of Vendor Relations   This intangible factor is extremely difficult to control because of the numerous nebulous activities that combine to shape vendors' opinions. A periodic vendor survey is the most common method used to measure performance in this area. The survey is typically conducted by means of a mail questionnaire. Although responding vendors normally remain anonymous, various techniques can be used to relate responses to material classifications or to buyers for control purposes. The following questions appear on one firm's questionnaire:

1 Are your salesmen always received in a friendly, courteous, business-like manner by our purchasing personnel?

2 Are your personnel kept waiting in our reception room longer than is necessary?

3 Do our buyers devote full attention to the interview, with only a reasonable number of distractions?

4 Are you allowed a sufficient amount of time in each interview?

5 Are our buyers eager to hear your suggestions and ideas?

6 Are you continually urged by our buyers to develop new ideas and methods that will help us cut costs?

7 Do buyers with whom you do business have a satisfactory knowledge of the items they purchase?

8 Do you believe that our buyers are concerned only with price considerations?

9 Do you consider our buyers' negotiation techniques to be satisfactory?

10 Are our buyers overly critical of your products and services?

11 Do you believe that our buyers all have high ethical standards?

12 How could we make better use of your firm's know-how and experience?

13 Do you always receive fair treatment in your dealings with our purchasing personnel?

14 Do we place too many rush orders with you?

15 Do we expect only services that are reasonably justified?

16 How would you rate our purchasing department as compared with other departments with which you are familiar?

17 With which buyers do you normally come in contact?

18 We would appreciate any additional comments or suggestions.

Control of Coordination A purchasing department can partially determine how successfully it coordinates its efforts with those of other departments by evaluating the effectiveness of certain joint activities (e.g., the joint development of material standards with users, joint value analysis investigations with engineering, joint establishment of order quantities with production control). Unfortunately, these assessments tend to be somewhat haphazard and difficult to make. Moreover, they cover only a few isolated cases out of the many potential possibilities for coordination.

Consequently, some purchasing departments have turned to the use of periodic surveys of other departments to supplement their own subjective assessments of performance in this area. By means of a biennial questionnaire, one firm asks its using departments the following questions:

1 Has the purchasing department provided you with a list of estimated lead times for the items you use?

2 Do you believe that the buyers who handle your requirements know enough about the items to make intelligent purchasing decisions?

3 Is the quality of material the purchasing department obtains for you always suitable for your needs?

4 Does the buyer who handles your requirements occasionally visit your department?

5 Is he familiar with the operation of your department?

6 Does he assist you in planning your material requirements?

7 Does he keep you informed regarding delays, estimated delivery dates, etc., for materials that you have requisitioned?

8 Does he occasionally bring a supplier's representative to your department to discuss cost-saving proposals?

9 Are you always treated in a friendly, courteous, businesslike manner by purchasing personnel?

10 Do you believe that purchasing personnel are taking advantage of cost-saving ideas and recommendations of suppliers?

11 Do you feel that purchasing personnel continually urge suppliers to develop new methods and ideas that will help you cut your costs and improve your operations?

12 Do the materials you requisition usually arrive on time?

13 How often do the buyers arbitrarily change the quality specifications on your purchases without consulting you?

14 How long does it take, on the average, for the stores department to fill your requisition for items that are carried in inventory?

15 Additional comments and suggestions.

The success of interdepartmental coordination is evidenced by the extent to which using departments follow published purchasing policies and procedures. To check on this phase of coordination, some firms periodically have buyers formally evaluate using departments' performance on such matters as unauthorized negotiations with vendors, cooperativeness in reducing material costs by changing specifications and vendors, allowance for sufficient purchasing lead time in planning requirements, correctness and completeness of requisitions, and so on.

When used together, the preceding three techniques provide a reasonably good measurement of purchasing's performance in the area of coordination.

Composite Audit of Buying Performance To supplement the use of selected techniques from the preceding lists, some firms continually audit a small random sample of completed orders in each major material classification. Such an audit is typically conducted on a weekly basis and entails a careful evaluation of total buying performance. Each order reviewed is scrutinized closely to determine if the buyer used the correct method of purchase, consolidated order requirements advantageously, handled bids properly, selected the vendor wisely, devoted sufficient value analysis effort to the order, and obtained the appropriate quality of material at the right price.

When conducted on a continuing basis, such an audit frequently detects newly developing problems more quickly than do the other techniques using aggregate measurements. Moreover, the psychological effect of the audit usually stimulates buyers to higher and more consistent levels of performance.

Conclusion Valid and accurate *absolute* standards are difficult to determine for many of the preceding measurements. Even so, most firms find it helpful to compare present performance with past performance. Although a firm has no assurance that past performance occurred at an optimum level, such a comparison does indicate the *trend* of performance and serves as a basis for effecting improvement. In addition, graphing each measurement over a period of time is an excellent method of portraying performance to facilitate quick visualization and comprehension of progress.

The need for careful interpretation of the preceding statistical measurements cannot be overemphasized. Many of the performance measures are interrelated in such a manner that improvement of one factor may contribute to poorer performance of another factor (e.g., the relationship of material quality measurements and delivery time measurements in the case of certain materials or vendors). Further, the behavior of numerous operating variables (production demands, departmental work loads, suppliers' problems, etc.) significantly influences short-run performance. The administrator must look behind the statistics carefully if their true meanings are to be assessed.

Controlling Procurement Efficiency

Every purchasing executive wants to achieve a high degree of buying proficiency and, at the same time, utilize the department's resources as efficiently as possible. A number of measurements can be used as guides in controlling departmental efficiency, but they must be used in a very general way. Too much much emphasis on efficiency can easily decrease buying proficiency. The problem is that of finding the optimum level of operating efficiency that still permits personnel to do a thorough, proficient job of buying. Because this problem can never be completely solved, few *absolute* standards of efficiency are used in practice. The executive customarily compares *trends* of his efficiency measurements with *trends* of proficiency measurements, in an attempt to determine the optimum combination which yields a maximum net purchasing profit.

Buying Efficiency   Although a variety of statistics is used to reflect buying efficiency, some combination of the following measurements is most common:

1   Number of purchase orders issued per period and per working day (frequently broken down by buying group).
2   Total dollars committed per period (frequently broken down by by buying group).
3   Average number of dollars expended per purchase order per buying group. Changes in this value provide an indication of buyers' ability to control low-value purchases. More important, when used in conjunction with the average number of purchase orders issued per day, this statistic helps a manager plan work loards and staffing requirements as operating conditions change.
4   Incidence of purchase order value. Every month (or quarter) some firms sample the orders issued to determine the percentage of orders for purchases under $50, the percentage of orders for purchases between $50 and $100, $100 and $500, and so on, for the various value classifications they find useful. When possible, it is usually useful to categorize the data also by material classification and by vendor.[1]
     These data are extremely useful to purchasing management. They provide specific information required for controlling the allocation of buying time, for initiating standardization projects, for initiating stock level changes, for developing more effective consolidation of requirements, and for making more effective use of blanket orders.
5   Number of blanket order releases issued during the period (usually categorized by order).
6   Number of orders placed against long-term contracts during the period (usually categorized by contract). This and the preceding statistic indicate the extent to which such negotiated arrangements are used to reduce buying time.
7   Number of rush orders issued during the period. Although this statistic cannot be completely controlled by buyers, it indicates to some extent how effectively rush order control procedures preserve buying efficiency. The number of rush orders also indicates how satisfactorily the routine system is working.
8   Number of change orders issued during the period. This statistic partially measures the thoroughness with which original buying activities are conducted.

---

[1] In automated records systems, a complete tabulation of summary data can be inexpensively obtained as a byproduct of normal operation.

9   Purchasing processing time report (frequently categorized by buying group). Many firms periodically sample the orders issued to determine the percentage of purchase requests processed in one day, two days, three days, and so on. This report provides data useful in detecting imbalanced work loads and purchasing bottlenecks. Moreover, it provides another indication of purchasing service to the using departments.

10 Department operating cost report. A majority of firms use a departmental operating budget categorized by nature of expenditure (salaries, travel, telephone, etc.) and by work group. Actual expenditures can thus be charted against planned expenditures for control purposes.

Using these cost data, the *operating cost per purchase order* and the *operating cost per dollar expended* can be computed. Alone, these statistics have little meaning.[2] When their trends are carefully analyzed in conjunction with the trends of other efficiency and proficiency statistics, however, they provide a good indication of the control of costs in relation to business volume.

Efficiency of Personnel   The following techniques and records are helpful in controlling performance in this area:

1   Performance standards for clerical jobs. It is entirely feasible to develop performance standards that are acceptable to employees for the repetitive jobs in purchasing, receiving, stores, and inventory control.[3] Although most standards for such work are not as precise as factory standards, they can nevertheless be used very effectively in controlling the volume of clerical performance over the period of a week or longer.[4]

2   Study of time utilization for nonrepetitive jobs. Although satisfactory performance standards (for the volume of work done) can rarely be developed for jobs requiring creative intellectual activity, an executive can take a step in this direction which definitely facilitates control. The work habits of buyers and managers (including the chief purchasing executive) should be studied periodically to detect inefficiencies in their patterns of activity.

A work sampling study, for example, can accurately reveal to a buyer the proportion of his time he devotes to the various activities of

---

[2]Good buying efficiency in terms of cost per purchase order may in reality represent only a decrease in the dollar amount of each purchase order and an accompanying increase in the number of purchase orders issued. Similarly, a reduction in the cost of committing each purchase dollar may merely be the result of spending more than necessary for some of the items purchased.

[3]Of the numerous available techniques, work sampling, predetermined standard data, and time study are the most commonly used for determining clerical performance standards.

[4]During the past few years, a large insurance firm (with an increasing work load) has reduced the number of clerical jobs in its 3,500 district offices by approximately 35 percent. It has achieved this $5 million annual saving solely by refining procedures and systems and by establishing standards for repetitive clerical jobs.

his job. He may well find that he is spending too much time on relatively inconsequential matters. Such knowledge would call for a reallocation of his time. This knowledge might also lead to a study and modification of various office and paperwork systems which compel the buyer to perform as he does. Inefficiency in a purchasing office is frequently due more to the use of inefficiently designed systems (management's responsibility) than to ineffective or lackadaisical performance by employees.

3   A record of the number of employees in each work group.
4   A daily record of absences and tardy arrivals for each employee.
5   Monthly computation of employee turnover rate, using the formula:

$$\frac{\text{Monthly number of terminations}}{\text{Average total number of employees}} \times 100$$

This and the preceding statistic provide an indirect measure of the departmental morale and the adequacy of compensation.

Receiving and stores   The key measurements used in planning work loads and controlling efficiency in receiving and stores are as follows:

1   Average number of incoming shipments received daily.
2   Average time required to receive and process incoming shipmants.
3   Average number of stores requisitions processed daily.
4   Stores loss, obsolescence, and damage report. A periodic report listing damaged, obsolete, and lost items (traced to stores activities) is helpful in appraising the efficiency of storage methods and handling procedures.
5   Periodic personal inspection of stores. The stores operation should be inspected periodically to ensure that materials are properly marked, easily located, and adequately protected. Such an inspection also permits an appraisal of safety procedures and general housekeeping practices.

Reports to Management

The measurements discussed to this point provide purchasing management with the detailed data required to appraise and control purchasing activities. The purchasing executive, in turn, should summarize the most significant features of this information in periodic reports to top management. Reports for top management should serve two purposes. First, they should provide *new* information that management can use in controlling company operations and in planning future company activities. Second, such reports should apprise management of purchasing's contribution to the entire company operation.

Purchasing reports to management can take two forms. The first is a monthly (or biweekly) report containing the following types of information:

1 A summary of general business conditions in the major markets the company patronizes
2 A list of specific price increases or decreases for the major materials purchased
3 A summary of trends in lead time requirements for major materials
4 A list of materials that are in short supply and a statement of purchasing's strategy for coping with each individual problem

This report is designed to inform management of conditions in the materials area that potentially could affect seriously the company's total operation.

The second report, usually issued quarterly (or monthly), apprises management of matters dealing primarily with purchasing performance and administrative programs. Typically, it contains the following kinds of information:

1 A summary of how well purchasing has performed during the period. This summary should include indications of both purchasing proficiency and purchasing efficiency. In the section on proficiency, it is usually desirable to summarize savings resulting from negotiation, value analysis, and so forth. The summary figure for savings may be reported as a percentage of total annual purchasing expenditures.
2 Selected but *very brief* physical statistics that are useful to management. Typically, the following items are included: number of purchasing department employees, number of purchase orders issued during the period, and total dollars committed during the period (usually broken down by major material classifications).
3 A brief discussion of department status and problems. This section should summarize progress made on projects and undertakings previously reported. It should also point up existing problems in the materials function and indicate what action is being taken to alleviate them.
4 Future plans. Plans for significant procurement projects and administrative activities should be summarized to provide clear communication with management on matters which management may want to coordinate with other plans.

Reports to top management should contain only timely information that is of definite value to the recipient. Functional managers at times seem to have difficulty in discriminating between the data they need to appraise and control performance of their departments and the data the president needs to appraise and control the operations of the total firm. Whenever possible, data should be presented graphically to facilitate interpretation. The objective of management reports is to present key departmental facts in concise form so that they can be quickly and clearly understood.

FOR DISCUSSION

24-1   Define and discuss the use of "preaction control."

24-2   Define and discuss the use of a "postaction control" system. What are the objectives of postaction control?

24-3   What general criteria should a manager use in determining the points at which to control the performance of his organization? Explain.

24-4   "Establishing a realistic performance standard against which to compare actual performance is usually the most difficult part of the control process." Explain this statement.

24-5   List and discuss the major problems involved in controlling purchasing performance.

24-6   Explain the difference between purchasing efficiency and purchasing proficiency. Which is more important? Explain.

24-7   Is a management audit of the purchasing department useful in controlling purchasing performance? Explain.

24-8   Assume that as a purchasing manager you have just received a production report which indicates that your department has caused an excessive number of material stock-outs and an excessive number of production stoppages due to material shortages. Outline in step-by-step fashion exactly how you would proceed to correct the situation. What additional facts must you know? Discuss.

24-9   Develop three additional questions that could be used advantageously on the vendor relations survey questionnaire shown in the text.

24-10   Develop three additional questions that could be used advantageously on the departmental coordination survey questionnaire shown in the text.

24-11   Why is it difficult to appraise purchasing efficiency?

24-12   What problems arise in establishing value analysis cost-savings targets (or standards) for buyers? What problems arise in administering such a control program? Discuss.

24-13   Assume you are a purchasing manager. Outline how you would proceed to establish and place in operation performance standards for the clerical personnel in the purchasing office. Discuss not only what you would do but also the problems you anticipate and how you would overcome them.

24-14   Develop a reporting system for the materials manager of a steel-fabricating firm (employing 110 people) to use in reporting to the company president. Design the system completely, including forms and any explanations required.

CASES FOR CHAPTER 24

Chapter 25

Legal Considerations

KEY CONCEPTS

The Uniform Sales Act
The Uniform Commercial Code
Status of an agent
The purchase contract
Inspection and rejection rights
Warranties
Order cancelation and breach of contract
Honest mistakes
Patent infringement
Restraint of trade laws
The buyer's responsibility

In professional life most purchasing executives seldom, if ever, become involved in legal actions. Yet their daily activities are subject to two major areas of the law—the law of agency and the law of contracts. A purchasing officer acts as an agent for his firm. Legally, this relationship is defined and governed by the law of agency. When a purchasing officer buys materials and services from other firms, each purchase involves the formation of a purchase contract. Should a serious disagreement arise between the purchaser and supplier, the dispute would normally be settled by a court of law or, if the purchase contract provides for arbitration, by an arbiter. In either case, the dispute would be resolved in accordance with the law of contracts.

A purchasing officer's basic responsibility is to conduct the firm's procurement business as efficiently and expeditiously as possible. Buying policies and practices are therefore predicated primarily on business requirements and business judgment, rather than on legal considerations. As Professor Dean Ammer has aptly stated, "A highly legalistic approach is both unnecessary and unprofitable." From a business standpoint, contractual disputes can normally be resolved much more effectively and with less cost by friendly negotiation than by litigation. A lawsuit almost always alienates a good supplier. Additionally, the outcome of any court case is usually uncertain; otherwise there would be little need for court action. Litigation is also costly, even in the event of a favorable decision. The total cost of legal fees, executive time diverted to the dispute, and disrupted business operations is seldom recovered from damage awards. For these reasons, in settling disputes, most business firms utilize litigation only as a last resort.

The fact that a purchasing executive tries to avoid litigation, however, does not mean that he can be oblivious to the law. On the contrary, a basic knowledge of relevant legal principles is essential to his success. Unless a purchasing executive understands the legal implications of his job and his actions, he is indeed likely to stumble into legal entanglements.

The purpose of this chapter is to review briefly some of the principal legal concepts as they relate to an industrial purchasing executive's responsibilities. The chapter does not attempt to provide a complete discussion of these concepts. All buying personnel should seek such knowledge through a thorough study of commercial law.

DEVELOPMENT OF COMMERCIAL LAW

Historically, each state developed its own bodies of statutes and common law to deal with the problems prevalent in its particular spheres of activity. This ultimately led to the creation of a series of commercial laws that varied widely from state to state—a situation that obviously produced difficulties for businesses involved in interstate commerce.

In an attempt to promote uniformity among the laws applicable to business transactions, the American Bar Association created a committee known as the National Conference of Commissioners on Uniform State Laws (NCCUSL). The assignment of this group was to codify (i.e., set forth in writing) the laws applying to various business transactions. Its first product was the Uniform Negotiable Instruments Law, followed by the Uniform Stock Transfer Act, the Uniform Conditional Sales Act, the Uniform Bills of Lading Act, the Uniform Warehouse Receipts Act, and the Uniform Sales Act.

The work of purchasing executives has been most heavily influenced by the Uniform Sales Act, which contributed substantially to the uniformity of laws affecting sales and contracts. Unfortunately, however, in practice, the act still left much to be desired. It permitted each state considerable latitude in applying its own laws of contract, and decisions on legal interpretations still varied widely among state courts. Moreover, only approximately three-quarters of the states adopted the Uniform Sales Act.

Recognizing the need for modernization and noting the sporadic adoption of the act in the face of increasing interstate trade, the NCCUSL joined with the American Law Institute in the early 1940s to formulate a new uniform code. The resulting code, entitled the Uniform Commercial Code, was published in 1952; refined versions of the code followed in 1958 and 1962. Although the Uniform Commercial Code deals with a wide range of commercial problems, Article 2 deals specifically with sales.

A fundamental difference between the Uniform Commercial Code and the

Uniform Sales Act lies in the basic underpinnings of the acts themselves. The Uniform Sales Act determined many rights and obligations of contract parties on the basis of title; that is, such decisions depended heavily upon which party possessed title to the material. The Uniform Commercial Code, on the other hand, determines rights and obligations on the basis of fairness and reasonableness in the light of accepted business practice. Thus, the code is geared more closely to the needs and circumstances found in daily business operations.

Today, the Uniform Commercial Code has been adopted by all the states except Louisiana. It has effectively eliminated a majority of the important differences that existed among the commercial laws of the various states, and has also provided new statutory provisions to fill many of the gaps in the prior laws. It should be noted, however, that the new code is silent on some matters covered by earlier laws. Consequently, unless superseded by provisions of the new code, earlier laws dealing with matters such as principal and agent, fraud, mistakes, coercion, and misrepresentation continue in effect and supplement the provisions of the code.

Topics treated throughout the rest of the chapter therefore reflect the provisions of the Uniform Commercial Code where applicable, as well as the provisions of earlier laws not displaced by the code.

BASIC LEGAL CONSIDERATIONS

Status of an Agent

In the legal sense, an agent is a person who, by express or implied agreement, is authorized to *act for* someone else in business dealings with a third party. Regardless of the job title, this is precisely what a purchasing executive does. A purchasing agent is not a *legal party* to his business transactions, but rather serves as an intermediary. In this capacity, the *law requires him* to be loyal to his employer (the principal) and to perform his duties with diligence to the best of his ability. Because his employer has contracted for his services, the law further permits the employer to hold its purchasing agent personally liable for any secret advantages gained for himself, or for any aid given to competitors.

The authority under which a purchasing agent functions is delegated by his employer. Since the law requires him to operate within the bounds of this authority, it behooves every purchasing agent to know as precisely as possible the types of transactions in which he can and cannot legally represent his firm. In practice, the amount of authority delegated to purchasing agents varies among companies. Hence, it is difficult for sellers to know the exact limits of a particular purchasing agent's authority. Consequently, under the law, a purchasing agent operates under two types of authority—*actual* authority and *apparent* authority. Although the agent's actual authority may be unknown, a seller acting in good faith can reasonably assume that he has apparent authority comparable with that of similar agents in similar companies.

The significance of "apparent authority" becomes evident upon examination of a purchasing agent's legal liability. For example, if an agent acts outside his actual authority but within what can reasonably be inferred as his apparent authority, the seller can generally hold the agent's firm liable for his action. However, the firm, in turn, can legally bring suit against the agent for acting beyond the limit of his actual authority. On the other hand, if an agent exceeds the limits of both his actual and his apparent authority, a seller usually cannot hold the firm liable, but he may be able to hold the agent personally liable for his action. In both of the above situations, however, if the seller knows at the time of the act that the agent is exceeding his authority, the seller generally has no legal recourse against either the agent or his firm.

Just as purchasing officers occupy the legal status of buying agents for their firms, sales personnel similarly hold the status of selling agents for their firms. In most cases, however, a salesman or saleswoman does not have the authority to bind a company to a sales contract or to a warranty. The courts usually hold that, unless otherwise stated, sales personnel have authority only to solicit orders. It is important that buyers recognize this fact. To ensure that a satisfactory contract does in fact exist, a buyer should insist upon acceptance of an order by an authorized company official or by the vendor's sales office. (The sales manager customarily serves as his company's agent for this purpose.)

The Purchase Contract

Although a legalistic approach to purchasing is in most cases unnecessary, every purchasing agent must nevertheless protect his company against potential legal problems. His major responsibility in this regard is to ensure that each purchase contract is satisfactorily drawn and that it is legally binding on the supplier. To be valid and enforceable, a contract must contain four basic elements: (1) agreement ("meeting of the minds") resulting from an offer and an acceptance; (2) consideration, or obligation; (3) competent parties; and (4) a lawful purpose.

Offer and Acceptance   When a buyer sends a purchase order to a vendor, this act usually constitutes a legal offer to buy materials in accordance with the terms stated on the order. Agreement does not exist, however, until the vendor accepts the offer; when this occurs, the law deems that a "meeting of the minds" exists regarding the proposed contract. In the event that a buyer requests a quotation from a vendor, the vendor's quotation usually constitutes an offer. Agreement then exists when the buyer accepts the quotation.

Under the Uniform Sales Act, the law required acceptance of an offer in terms that were identical and the terms of the offer. The Uniform Commercial Code, however, eliminates this stringent requirement. The code states that "conduct by both parties which recognizes the existence of a contract is sufficient to establish a contract or sale although the writings of the parties do not otherwise establish a contract." The code also recognizes vendors' standard confirmation forms and acknowledgment forms as a valid acceptance, *even if the terms stated thereon are different from the terms of the offer.*

When the terms of an acceptance differ from the terms of the offer, they will automatically be incorporated in the contract unless one of three conditions exists: (1) unless they materially alter the intent of the offer, (2) unless the offeror objects in writing, or (3) unless the offer explicitly states that no different terms will be accepted. What happens when an offer and an acceptance contain *conflicting terms*, and yet none of the preceding conditions exist? All terms except the conflicting terms become part of the contract, and the conflicting terms are simply omitted from the contract. This provision of the code substantially clarifies the legal position of many such purchase orders. Moreover, the provision indicates clearly the action a buyer should take to protect himself in such matters.

The code contains another important provision relating to the acceptance of an offer to buy. It recognizes as valid the communication of an acceptance in "any manner and by any medium reasonable to the circumstances." Consequently, when a supplier receives an order for the purchase of material for immediate delivery, he can accept the offer either by prompt acknowledgment of the order or by prompt shipment of the material. The code thus permits prompt supplier performance of such proposed contracts to constitute acceptance of the offer. The contract becomes effective when the supplier ships the material.

A hitherto long-standing principle of commercial law stated that an offer could be revoked by the offeror at any time before it had been accepted, regardless of the time period stipulated in the offer. The Uniform Commercial Code has changed this principle with respect to the commercial purchase or sale of goods. The code states that a *written* offer to buy or sell material must give the offeree assurance that the offer will be held open as long as it is stipulated in the offer. If no time period is stipulated, the offer can be assumed firm for a reasonable period of time, not to exceed three months.

This provision of the code has significant implications for industrial purchasers and their potential suppliers. Purchasers can use vendors' quotations in making precise manufacturing cost calculations and *rely on the fact* that the quotations cannot be revoked before a certain date. Without the code, no such assurance existed. On the other hand, this provision prevents a buyer from canceling an order, without legal obligation, prior to vendor acceptance. An offer to buy, like an offer to sell, must also remain firm for a stated or a reasonable period of time. To maintain firm control, it is now doubly important that the buyer state on the order the length of time for which the offer is valid (or the date by which acceptance of the order is required).

Consideration   In addition to a meeting of minds, a valid contract must also contain the element of obligation. Most purchase contracts are bilateral; that is, *both parties* agree to do something they would not otherwise be required to do. The buyer promises to buy from the vendor certain material at a stated price; the vendor promises to deliver the material in accordance with stated contract conditions. The important point is the *mutuality of obligation.* The contract must be drawn so that each party (or promissor) is bound. If both are not bound, in the eyes of the law neither is bound. Hence, no contract exists.

A buyer is confronted with the practical significance of the "mutual obligation" concept when he formulates his terms of purchase. His statements regarding material quantity, price, delivery, and so on, must be specific enough to bind both his firm and the supplier to definable levels of performance. In writing a blanket purchase order for pipe fittings, for example, it is not sufficient to state the quantity as "all company X desires." Such a statement is too indefinite to bind company X to any specific purchase. However, if the requirement were stated as "the quantity company X uses during the month of March," most courts would consider this sufficient to define X's purchase obligation. It is also prudent to qualify such a statement by indicating approximate minimum and maximum levels of consumption.

Similar situations arise in specifying prices and delivery dates. Some companies, for example, occasionally issue unpriced purchase orders. Aside from the questionable wisdom of such a business practice, a legal question concerning the definiteness of the offer also exists. From a legal standpoint, the question which must be answered is: Under existing conditions, can the price be determined precisely enough to define the obligations of both parties? The Uniform Commercial Code provides more latitude in answering this question than did the Uniform Sales Act. The code specifically says that a buyer and a vendor can make a binding contract without agreeing on an exact price until a later date. If at the time of shipment a price cannot be agreed upon, the code includes provisions by which a fair price shall be determined. On such orders, however, a buyer should protect himself by noting a precise price range or by stating how the price is to be determined.

Competent Parties   A valid contract must be made by persons having full contractual capacity. If a purchasing agent exceeds his actual and his apparent authority in making a contract, under most circumstances his company is not bound by the contract, even though the purchasing agent may be held personally liable for his actions. A contract made by a minor or by an insane or intoxicated person is usually entirely void or voidable at the option of the incompetent party.

Legality of Purpose   A contract whose purpose is illegal is automatically illegal and void. A contract whose primary purpose is legal, but one of whose ancillary terms is illegal, may be either void or valid, depending upon the seriousness of the illegality and the extent to which the illegal part can be separated from the legal part of the contract. The latter situation may occasionally have relevance for purchasing agents. Such would be the case, for example, if a material were purchased at a price which violated restraint of trade or price discrimination laws.

The Written and the Spoken Word   Purchasing agents should be aware of several basic concepts concerning the construction of a contract. Contrary to common belief, a contract is not a physical thing. It is actually a relationship which exists between the parties making the contract. When a contract is reduced to writing, the written document is not in fact the contract; it is simply evidence of the contract. Hence, a contract may be supported by either written or oral evidence. In most cases, courts hold an oral contract to be just as binding as a written one, although it may be substantially more difficult to prove the facts upon which an oral contract is based. However, the law requires some types of agreements to be in writing. In the case of sales transactions between qualified "merchants,"[1] for example, the Uniform Commercial Code specifically states that when a selling price of $500 or more is involved, the contract must be reduced to writing to be enforceable.[2] In the event an oral contract between a supplier and a buyer is later confirmed in writing, the *written confirmation* is binding on both parties if no objection is raised within ten days.

Hence, it is important to note that when a contract is reduced to writing, the written evidence supersedes all prior oral evidence. The courts generally hold that a contract expressed in writing embodies all preceding oral discussion pertinent to the agreement. This means that a buyer cannot legally rely upon a vendor's oral statements concerning a material's performance or warranty unless the statements have been included in the written agreement. Consequently, from a legal standpoint, a buyer should consider carefully the content of his oral negotiations with a vendor and ensure that he has reduced to writing the relevant data which he wants to include as part of the contract. The buyer should also be aware of the fact that courts have ruled that written or typed statements take precedence over printed statements on the contract form, should conflicting statements appear in the document.

Finally, in signing a written contract, a purchasing agent should specifically indicate on the document that he is acting in the capacity of an agent for his firm. This avoids any possible misinterpretation as to the identity of the parties making the contract. Moreover, all data to be included as part of the contract should appear above the agent's signature. Courts have ruled that data

---

[1]Section 2-104 of the code defines a "merchant" as one who deals in goods; one who holds himself out as having particular skill in the subject matter; or one who uses a person who holds himself out as having such knowledge or skill. Hence, it is generally held under this broad definition that almost every person in business, including a purchasing officer, is a "merchant." Even a person not in business may be classified as a "merchant" if he employes a purchasing officer or broker.

[2]Prior to enactment of the Uniform Commercial Code, the Statute of Frauds required contracts relating to personal property, for which neither delivery nor payment had been made, to be in writing if the value of the sale exceeded a specified amount; this specified amount varied widely among states.

appearing below the signature is informational only and not part of the contract.

SPECIAL LEGAL CONSIDERATIONS

Inspection Rights

If a purchaser has not previously inspected the material purchased to ensure that it conforms with the terms of the contract, the law gives him a reasonable period of time to inspect the material after it is received. If the purchaser raises no objection to the material within a reasonable period of time, he is deemed to have accepted it. In court decisions on this matter, it has been largely industry practice which sets the standard for "reasonable" time.

Rights of Rejection

A purchaser has the right to reject material if it does not conform with the terms of the contract. If an overshipment is received, the purchaser can either reject the complete shipment or reject the quantity in excess of the contract. When a purchaser does not wish to accept wrongly delivered material, he is required only to notify the supplier; he is not legally bound to return the rejected material. If he neither returns the material or notifies the supplier of his rejection within a reasonable period of time, however, he is then obligated to pay for the material.

Title

As discussed previously, the question of which party has title to purchased materials is normally answered by defining the f.o.b. point of purchase. A complete discussion of this matter is presented in Chapter 16, "Traffic."

Warranties

The sale of a material may involve two types of warranties—*implied* and *express.* When a vendor agrees to sell a particular item, he implies that he (or his principal) has title to the item and that he has legal authority to sell it. In cases where material is sold by catalog or by oral description, the vendor implies that the material is of "merchantable quality."[3] In cases where, by discussion or observation, the buyer apprises a vendor of his functional needs and subsequently relies on the vendor's skill or judgment in selecting a specific material, the material usually carries an implied warranty of fitness for the stated need. For this reason, in buying expensive or complicated machinery, a

[3] Under the Uniform Sales Act, courts held that "merchantable quality" meant "fair, average quality." The Uniform Commercial Code gives much more precise definition to the term.

wise buyer specifies in writing the performance required from the machine. Finally, in cases where a sale is made on the basis of a sample, the vendor implies that the sample is representative of the total quantity to be sold.

Numerous variable factors influence the extent to which a buyer can rely on an implied warranty in a specific situation. The knowledge and conduct of both buyer and seller, as well as the specific conditions surrounding a transaction, are taken into consideration by the court in resolving a dispute over warranty. Generally speaking, if a buyer acts in good faith and has no knowledge of conditions contrary to an implied warranty, the law holds a vendor liable for such implied warranties, unless otherwise stated in the contract.

Vendors frequently make express warranties for their products in sales and technical literature. Such warranties typically refer to the product's capacity, performance characteristics, and so on. If a buyer has no way of determining the facts of the matter and consequently relies on such warranties, the vendor is usually held liable for them. The buyer should also realize that an express warranty nullifies an implied warranty to the extent that it conflicts with the implied warranty.

Recent legislation[4] has tended to increase warranty protection for buyers by strengthening and expanding the liability of manufacturers and sellers with respect to warranty performance. A buyer should recognize, however, that the Uniform Commercial Code permits a seller to exclude or modify the implied warranty for a product. A vendor can do this by including a conspicuous written statement in the sales contract. Statements commonly used to accomplish warranty exclusion are: "this item is offered for sale 'as is,' " or "there are no warranties which extend beyond the description on the face here of." In several states, however, such warranty disclaimers have been declared invalid, as being contrary to public policy.

Order Cancelation and Breach of Contract

If a supplier fails to deliver an order by the delivery date agreed upon in the contract, or if he fails to perform in accordance with contract conditions, legally he has breached the contract. The breach usually gives the purchaser the right to cancel the order. In addition, the purchaser can sue for damages if he wishes. In practice the latter right is infrequently exercised because a more effective settlement can usually be negotiated directly with the supplier. Nevertheless, under the law, a buyer may be able to recover damages if he actually suffers injury as a result of a breach of contract. In the case of delivery failure, if the buyer subsequently purchases the material elsewhere, damages are generally limited to the difference between the contract price and the price paid the new vendor. If the material is not available elsewhere, actual damages

[4]The Consumer Product Safety Act and the Federal Warranties Act, as well as the Uniform Commercial Code.

may be difficult to determine. In any case, the courts usually follow the general rule of attempting to place the injured party in the same financial position he would have been in had the contract not been breached.

When no specific delivery date is stated in a contract, the law requires the supplier to deliver within a reasonable period of time. What the buyer thinks is a reasonable period of time may or may not coincide with what the supplier or the court deems to be a reasonable period of time. Hence, in such a situation, a buyer may be on uncertain ground if he decides to cancel an order because of nondelivery and subsequently places the order with another vendor. He may or may not have the legal right to do so. The desirability of including a specific delivery date in the contract thus becomes amply clear.

Situations sometimes arise that compel a buyer to cancel an order before the supplier is obligated to supply the material. In making such a cancellation, the *buyer* breaches the purchase contract. This act legally is termed anticipatory breach, and it makes the purchaser liable for any resulting injury to the supplier. If the cancellation results in no real injury to the supplier (as is often the case with orders for standard materials), he can collect no damages. On the other hand, if the cancellation leaves the supplier with semifinished goods in his shop, he frequently does suffer injury. In such cases, if the in-process material is salable, the purchaser is usually held liable for the difference between the prorated contract value and the market value of the in-process material. If the material is not salable, the purchaser's liability usually covers the supplier's costs prior to termination plus a reasonable profit on the contract.

If it is evident at the time a major contract is drawn that breach of the contract would severely injure one or both parties and that damages would be difficult to determine, it is wise to include in the contract itself a termination or liquidated damages provision. Such provisions stipulate *in advance* the procedures to be used in determining costs and damages. In some cases, specific damage payments are stated. For example, if the contract is for the purchase of power-generating equipment to be used on a large construction project, the date of delivery may be critical for the purchaser. Perhaps installation of the equipment must precede other important phases of the construction work. If the project is delayed by late delivery of the generating equipment, the purchaser might well incur heavy financial losses. It is therefore normally sound practice on such a contract to include a liquidated damages clause that requires the supplier to pay the purchaser damages of x dollars per day for late delivery. It is essential, however, that the damage figure specified be a reasonable estimate of the probable loss to the buyer, and not be calculated simply to impose a penalty on the supplier. Courts generally refuse to enforce a penalty provision.

A termination or liquidated damages provision represents prior agreement by both parties on the ground rules to be followed in case of a breach of contract. If such a breach subsequently occurs, the provision minimizes the possibility of misunderstandings and the generation of ill will between the two firms.

Honest Mistakes

When an honest mistake is made in drawing up a purchase contract, the conditions surrounding each specific case weigh heavily in determining whether the contract is valid or void. As a general rule, a mistake made by only one party does not render a contract void, unless the other party is aware or should be aware of the mistake. To affect a contract, the mistake usually must be made by both parties. Even then, not every mutual mistake invalidates the contract.

Assume, for example, that in submitting a quotation a vendor intends to quote a price of $260. Through an error, the price is typed on the quotation as $250 and is so transmitted to the buyer. In such cases, courts have held that if the buyer accepts the offer, without knowledge of the error, a valid contract exists. The magnitude of the error is deemed insufficient to affect agreement materially. On the other hand, if the $260 price were incorrectly typed as $26, the court would probably hold that a competent buyer should recognize the error, and if one party knows or should know of the other's error, the contract is void.

Mutual mistakes concerning matters of opinion usually do not affect a contract. Neither is a contract affected by immaterial mutual mistakes about matters of fact. However, a mutual mistake concerning *matters of fact that materially affect agreement* usually renders a contract void. Assume, for example, that a buyer and a vendor agree on the sale of specific machinery. If, unknown to either, the machinery has been destroyed or for some other reason is not available for sale, the contract is void.

Generally speaking, a buyer should not assume that a mistake, however innocent, will release him from a contractual obligation. In the majority of cases, it will not do so. A prudent buyer employs all reasonable means to minimize the possibility of committing contractual mistakes.

Patent Infringement

The law gives a patent holder the exclusive right to manufacture, sell, and use the patented device for a specified number of years. A purchaser who engages in any of these activities during the period of patent protection without permission from the patent holder is guilty of patent infringement and can be sued for damages by the patent holder.

Buyers frequently have no way of knowing whether their suppliers are selling patented materials with or without authorization from the patent holder. If a purchaser unknowingly buys an item from a vendor who has infringed the patent holder's rights, the purchaser is also guilty of infringement if he uses the item. To protect against such unintentional violations, most companies include a protective clause in their purchase orders which states that the seller will indemnify the purchaser for all expenses and damages resulting from patent infringement. Clauses of this type do not prevent the patent holder from suing the user. If properly stated, however, they can require the seller to defend the user in such legal proceedings and can give the user legal recourse to recover any resulting losses from the seller.

Infringement suits are rare in the normal course of business activities. However, one area where most manufacturing firms frequently encounter potential infringement problems is in the maintenance of productive equipment. In some cases, a complete machine is patented, but its individual parts are not. In other cases, individual parts are patented. In cases where the individual part is not patented, the owner of the machine usually has the right to make a replacement part or to have it made by a vendor. When the individual part is patented, however, this cannot be done legally without permission from the patent holder.

On the other hand, if the owner of a patented machine wishes to rebuild the machine substantially, such activity is not considered within the range of normal maintenance and repair activity. To accomplish a rebuilding job, the owner must either have it done by the patent holder or obtain the patent holder's permission to do the job himself.

Restraint of Trade Laws

The Robinson-Patman Act is a federal statute designed to prevent price discrimination that reduces competition in interstate commerce. Generally speaking, the act prevents a vendor from offering the same quantity of a specific materail to competing buyers at different prices, unless: (1) one buyer is offered a lower price because his purchases entail lower manufacturing or distribution costs for the vendor, or (2) one buyer is offered a lower price in order to meet the legitimate bid of a competing vendor.

It is important that all buyers be familiar with the detailed provisions of the act, because it also makes it *unlawful for any buyer knowingly to induce or receive a discriminatory price.* Thus, if a buyer accepts a price that he knows is in fact discriminatory, he violates the law to the same extent as the vendor.

To date, no industrial purchasing agent has been prosecuted under the Robinson-Patman Act. The act does not prevent a buyer from seeking legitimate price concessions. It is imperative, however, for a buyer to ensure that any price concessions gained are in fact justifiable under the act.

Nearly every state also has its own price discrimination legislation applicable to intrastate transactions. Since these laws vary widely from state to state, each buyer should likewise be familiar with the regulations in his state.

CONCLUSION

The purpose of this chapter has been simply to alert buyers and potential purchasing professionals to the most basic legal considerations that relate to the purchasing function. Yet there is danger in doing this. No author can briefly accomplish this objective without simplifying the issues. And such simplification may at times leave the reader with an incomplete understanding which lulls him into a false feeling of security.

Even though adoption of the Uniform Commercial Code by all but one of the states creates greater uniformity among state commercial laws than ever before, it is unreasonable to assume that interpretations of the laws by the various states will not exhibit some variation. Only time can reveal how significant such variations will be. Moreover, the interpretation of circumstances surrounding each specific case weighs heavily in the analysis of that particular case. These factors virtually defy a definite and unqualified analysis of a legal controversy by anyone who is not a highly skilled professional in the legal field. Stuart Heinritz states the matter cogently in saying that "the layman who tries to be his own lawyer has a fool for a client." Perhaps the most important function of this chapter is to underscore the fact that purchasing executives should seek sound legal counsel whenever potential legal problems arise.

Just as a lawyer is expected to exhibit skill in extricating his client from legal entanglements, so a purchasing executive is expected to exhibit skill in avoiding legal controversies. A purchasing executive must understand basic legal concepts well enough to detect potential problems before they become realities. At the same time, the most powerful tool he can utilize to avoid legal problems is skill in selecting sound, cooperative, and reliable suppliers. Vigilance in this area of responsibility minimizes the need for legal assistance.

FOR DISCUSSION

25-1   "A highly legalistic approach to purchasing is both unnecessary and unprofitable." Comment on this statement.

25-2   It has been said that the purchasing agent who tries to be his own lawyer has a fool for a client. If this is true, why do purchasing people study commercial law? Discuss.

25-3   Discuss the legal responsibilities of a purchasing agent to his or her firm. To what extent are purchasing agents liable for their actions?

25-4   Purchasing executives and sales personnel are both "agents" for their respective firms. Is there usually any significant difference in the authority they possess as agents? Explain.

25-5   List and discuss the four essential elements of a contract.

25-6   When a purchase (or sales) contract is created, what specific actions constitute the "offer" and the "acceptance"? Explain.

25-7   What is the Uniform Sales Act?

25-8   What is the Uniform Commercial Code?

25-9   What is the legal status of a purchase order which has been accepted by a vendor who used an acceptance form containing terms that conflict with the terms that are stated on the purchase order? Explain.

25-10 Would the answer to question 25-9 be different if the Uniform Sales Act were still in effect? Explain.

25-11   What is meant by the term "mutuality of obligation"? What is its significance for normal purchasing transactions?

25-12   What inspection rights does a purchaser have? Explain.

25-13   Under what conditions can purchasers reject materials they have purchased?

25-14   Discuss the warranty protection purchasers have when they make a purchase.

25-15   What are a buyer's legal rights and obligations when canceling an order if:

a. The vendor has failed to make delivery by the agreed delivery date?

b. The delivery date is three weeks in the future?

c. No delivery date has been specified on the order?

25-16   Discuss "liquidated damages" in relation to purchase contracts.

25-17   How do "honest mistakes" affect purchase contracts? Discuss.

25-18   How can a purchaser infringe the rights of a patent holder?

25-19   Discuss the significance of the Robinson-Patman Act for the industrial buyer.

CASES FOR CHAPTER 25

The Pricing Sandtrap, page 643
Congressman Tardy, page 608
Too Much, Too Soon, page 663
Redi-Pore Filter Corporation, page 647

Automation and Computer-based Systems

WHAT IS AUTOMATION?

What is automation? A tour of the engine-block line in a Ford Motor Company plant illustrates one striking form of automation. An operator pushes a button and a series of machine tools, with connecting transfer machines, begin their day's work. Each machine performs several operations on an engine block. An automatic transfer machine then conveys the block to the next machine, where several more operations are performed, and so the process continues until a finished block leaves the last machine on the line. Not only are machining operations done automatically, but in many cases gauges automatically check the work. If an out-of-tolerance operation is found, the gauge may stop the line and signal trouble. In other cases it may activate a device that automatically removes the part from the line, or it may automatically reset the cutting tool which produced the defective work. Thus, engine blocks are produced by the push of a button, never having been touched by human hands in the process.

A traveler approaches an American Airlines reservation counter located in a metropolitan hotel and asks for a ticket on a particular flight the following week. The agent presses several keys on the keyboard of an interactive computer terminal at the desk, and within a matter of seconds knows whether a seat is available on the requested flight. If all seats are sold, the information source responds instantly, informing the agent of alternative flights that are open. Thus, the traveler can obtain, at any of more than 3,000 reservation offices across the country, a seat on any of American's different flights (over 1,000 daily) several weeks in advance. All this can be performed in less than a minute! How is this possible? American Airlines, like many major carriers, uses a computer-automated reservations system. American's is one of the largest commercial real-time data processing systems ever built. The central computer contains a file of passenger lists on every flight for approximately the next two weeks. When operating the terminal keyboard, the agent simply asks the computer if there is a vacant seat on a specific flight for a particular day. The computer checks its perpetual inventory of available seats, determines whether any vacant seats are left, and communicates this information to the agent via an electronic signal.

Still another use of automation can be seen in the computer-automated inventory control system of a western military depot. This particular depot controls the disbursement of supplies and equipment used at all military bases in the Pacific area. Complicating its operation is the fact that it has numerous warehousing operations located throughout the geographical area it serves. Using a computerized inventory control system, however, the depot is able to process within a matter of minutes a supply order from a base in the Orient. A random-access memory system instantly locates warehouses which have the required material on hand. It also determines from which warehouse the material should be shipped to minimize costs; and to complete the job, it produces the necessary paperwork to conclude the transaction! Once it has been properly instructed by means of a "program," the system accomplishes this feat with virtually no human intervention.

As the invention of machines freed people from laborious, back-breaking work during the past century, so various forms of automation are now freeing people, in factory and office alike, from many dull, repetitive manufacturing and clerical tasks. In its broadest sense, automation involves the use of machines to run and control other machines doing the work. This is true whether the production machine is a machine tool or office calculating equipment. These feats are accomplished in part by an extension of the mechanization process. Predominantly, however, they are accomplished by employing control devices (electronic, pneumatic, and mechanical) that utilize the "feedback" concept. This means that the automated process does a job, measures the critical feature of the work performed, compares the measurement with a predetermined standard, and feeds this information back to the process or to the manager in charge of the process.[1] It thus permits operation and management of the operation by the "exception principle." (That is, positive action is taken only when operations are no longer being performed within predetermined limits.)

IMPLICATIONS FOR MATERIALS MANAGEMENT

What does all this mean to an industrial materials manager? Automation has a two-dimensional implication of the utmost significance for the materials

---

[1]If the process is self-correcting, it is considered to be a "closed-loop" system. If a person intervenes to handle the exception, it said to be an "open-loop" system.

executive. First, it means that there is a good probability that some of the materials activities themselves can be automated. While automation does not change the various materials *functions,* it does involve substantial modification of the procedures used in performing the routine, repetitive tasks of the functions. The application of automation concepts to such tasks can produce two significant results: (1) a possible reduction in departmental operating costs, and (2) the generation of more complete and more timely data with which to make materials decisions.

Second, even if a materials department is unable to apply automated techniques in its own operations, it cannot escape certain effects of factory automation. As its own production department automates its manufacturing processes, for example, purchasing finds that material specification requirements become more stringent. The range of acceptable quality usually becomes narrower. Automated production processes, as a rule, cannot accept nonuniform materials to the degree a manually controlled process can. An operator of a machine can compensate for variability in work materials to a significant extent; it is often impracticable to build such capability into an automated process. In some cases automation may require an upgrading of the quality level itself. The final effect of these requirements is felt sharply in the areas of value analysis and supplier selection. Purchasing's flexibility is reduced. At the same time, more precise and rigorous performance is required.

An automated production operation also demands an uninterrupted flow of production materials. While this requirement is not new to most purchasing and production control departments, automation makes it much more critical. A stock-out of a single production material shuts down an entire segment of the production operation. Shutdowns of automated production lines are tremendously expensive. While no firm can afford to have high-priced equipment idle, the operational inflexibility and the high setup costs associated with automated equipment usually make it impractical to use the equipment for other jobs while waiting for materials to arrive. Supplier reliability, delivery scheduling, and traffic considerations therefore demand increased attention in a firm using automated production facilities.

THE COMPUTER

Automation of the materials activities[2] centers about the use of high-speed data processing equipment. When extended to completion, it requires access to an electronic digital computer. To the uninitiated, a computer in operation can be an awesome sight. Its futuristic physical appearance and its numerous blinking lights can conjure up disquieting and apprehensive reactions. A person can watch in near disbelief as it digests punched cards or magnetic tape at a fantastic speed and simultaneously produces reams of printed sheets. Although its achievements are indeed astounding, the computer is really not as mysteri-

[2]With the exception of physical materials-handling activities.

ous or overwhelming as it might appear at first glance. Those contemplating the use of a computer in a materials management system can quickly dispel its aura of mystery by reviewing the fundamental ideas which underlie its operation.

The *digital* computer is an electronic data processing machine which receives, stores, and performs arithmetic operations on discrete numerical data at extremely high speeds. It manipulates the data and produces results with precise digital accuracy. Digital computers are designed for both scientific and business applications. Business machines are equipped to receive huge volumes of input data, to manipulate the data using a relatively small number of simple arithemtic operations, and to turn out results in the form of reports, account records, purchase orders, etc., in mass volume. Such a machine is particularly adaptable to business activities of a periodic recurring nature. This is the type of computer used in automating the various materials activities.

Communicating with a Computer

Edison's original "talking machines" talked *at* their audiences, and so do their descendants, today's hi-fi and stereo sets. In a very broad sense, the computer is also a special type of "talking machine." It is unique as a communication device, however, because it will respond to instructions, and will in fact talk *with* its user—if the user knows how to talk its language.

If a company has access to a computer, then, and the materials executive wants to utilize it in his departmental operating activities, how does he go about it? How does he ultimatly communicate with the computer? To begin with, he should have a thorough study made of the complete operating system being considered for computerization. The complex system should first be broken down into individual activities, each of which must be carefully studied to determine and chart how the functions within the department relate to each other, and in what specific ways the department relates to other departments in the organization. Each activity must then be analyzed, and input and output data necessary for effective operation must be determined with respect to quality, quantity, and timing.

At this point, the materials manager will review his system with a systems analyst who is familiar with computer requirements and capabilities. The system must be studied again in detail to determine the problems and possible changes involved in adapting it to computer operation. During this study, the systems analyst prepares the final flow chart (or model) of the system. He then takes the information in this form to a computer programmer, who translates the general operation of the system into a precise "program" the computer understands. The program is actually a lengthy series of instructions that tell the machine in minute detail exactly what operations it is to perform, the sequence in which they are to be performed, and where in its memory it will find the data required to perform each operation.

As noted previously, the first step in developing a computer program, which will in effect "run" a department's computerized operating system, is the preparation of an operational flow chart of the entire system. Figure 26-1 illustrates the flow-charting concept and applies it to one segment of the system, a simplified inventory posting and ordering operation. After this general procedure has been applied to all segments of the system whose operations are to be computerized, a complete program can be developed that will in fact permit operating personnel and the computer to talk to each other.

For those readers who are interested, a detailed explanation of the flow-charting activity shown in Figure 26-1 is provided in the footnote below.[3]

Advantages for Materials Management

Materials executives who wish to utilize a computer in the operation of their departments do not have to understand its electronic intricacies any more than they have to understand the mechanical intricacies of their automobiles. They should, however, understand the fundamentals of computer operation; they should know generally what a computer can do, what it cannot do, and how their departmental procedures must be designed so as to be compatible with computer operation.

Effective use of a computer offers a manager several significant advantages. Because of its ability to process huge volumes of data rapidly, the computer can do much routine clerical work, thus freeing departmental personnel from many dull, repetitive tasks. This means, for example, that a purchaisng department can operate with fewer clerical personnel or that the personnel can spend their time on more creative purchasing work. This does not mean, however, that departmental operating costs will necessarily fall. They may or they may not decline, depending on how effectively the total system is designed and on the volume and frequency of output data (reports, etc.) purchasing managers desire. The costs of computer time, programming work, and transferring operating data to punched cards, etc., at least partially offset the gains.

Perhaps the primary advantage a computer offers a materials manager is the immediate availability of much more complete data for use in making purchasing and related materials decisions. Because of its fantastic speed, the computer can supply management with virtually instantaneous reports which might otherwise take an army of clerks weeks or months to prepare and update. The timeliness of such reports enables a materials executive to manage by exception and to do a more effective and economical job of purchasing and managing the flow of materials throughout the operation.

AUTOMATING THE MATERIALS OPERATIONS

The Approach to System Design

Historically, the system of materials activities in many companies has, like Topsy, "just growed." Various elements of the system have progressed from

---

[3]Figure 26-1 assumes that the inventory records are available in the machine's memory. It also assumes that each inventory withdrawal requisition has been punched into a separate card and that all cards are ready for processing. (Continued on page 509.)

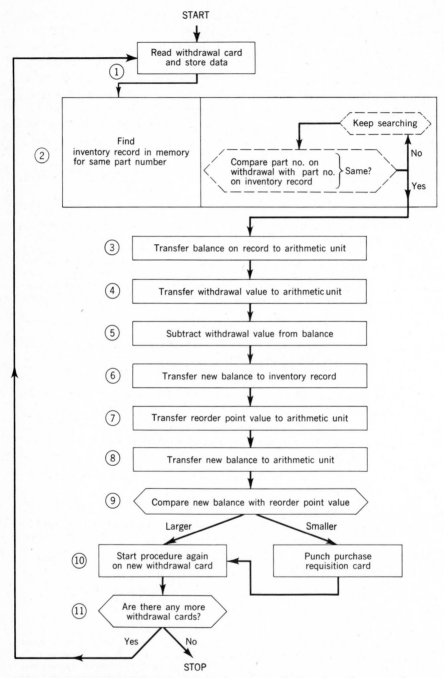

Figure 26-1 Operational flow chart for an inventory withdrawal posting operation.

manual to automated operation by means of a relatively unplanned, evolutionary process. For most pioneers, the first step was the development of various types of unit-record subsystems (such as inventory posting, vendor performance posting, etc.) which could be processed on sorting, collating, accounting, and related punched-card data processing machines. As the computer became a fixture of business life, these systems were modified for individual processing on a computer. Until then, little thought was given to the interrelationships existing among these operating subsystems; each was viewed primarily as an independent operating unit. In reality, however, all of the materials subsystems

---

1   The programmer must first instruct the machine to read a withdrawal card and store the data for immediate use.
2   The programmer then tells the machine to find in memory the inventory record for the same part number as the requisition being processed. If the programmer does not know in advance which part numbers will be processed, he will not know in which memory location to tell the machine to find the corresponding inventory record. In this case, however, since the machine utilizes a random-access memory system, it can find the correct record simply by searching its memory. It can do this by subtracting the requisitioned part number from the part number for the inventory record stored in each of its memory locations (remember, the machine can do this with lightening speed). It keeps searching until the result of its subtraction is zero, thus indicating that the requisitioned part number and the part number of the inventory record found in memory are the same.
3   When the machine has found the correct inventory record, the programmer tells it to transfer the balance-on-hand figure to the arithmetic unit for processing.
4   The programmer also tells the machine to transfer to the arithmetic unit the number of units withdrawn, as noted on the withdrawal requisition.
5   When both values have been transferred to the arithmetic unit, the unit is instructed to subtract the withdrawal value from the balance value.
6   After the subtraction has been completed, the programmer instructs the machine to store the result (the new balance) in place of the old balance on the inventory record.
7   Updating the inventory record is now complete. However, before processing the next withdrawal card, the present part should be checked to see if it is time to reorder. The programmer therefore tells the machine to transfer the part's reorder point value to the arithmetic unit.
8   The machine is instructed to transfer the new balance to the arithmetic unit.
9   The programmer then tells the arithmetic unit to subtract the new balance value from the reorder point value.
10 Instructions tell the machine to do one of two things at this point. If the new balance is larger than the reorder point value, the machine is to accept the next withdrawal card and start the posting process all over again. If the new balance is smaller than the reorder point value, the machine is to punch out a purchase requisition card for the part and then go on to the next withdrawal card.
11 Finally, the programmer must tell the machine to see if there are any more withdrawal cards to be processed. One way of doing this is to punch a predetermined signal number in the last card to indicate that it is the last card. If the machine does not find this signal in the card just processed, it reads the next card. If it does find the signal, it knows that this particular posting job is completed and stops the processing routine.

The amount of detail the programmer must actually include in the instructions depends upon the specific computer being used and the programming language it is designed to accept. Early computers required virtually every machine operation to be actuated by a numerical code contained in the program. In such cases, programming was an extremely time-consuming and tedious chore. In recent years computer operating systems and compilers have been developed that will, in effect, do some of the detailed programming for the programmer. As a result, the programmer can communicate with the machine by using more sophisticated mnemonic languages which involve the writing of fewer detailed instructions.

are interrelated in terms of the sources and uses of data required in their operation. Consequently, the next step in the development process—one involving a great deal of redesign effort—was the *integration* of existing unit subsystems into a single operating system.

Today, the advantage of hindsight reveals clearly the value of planning for the total operating system at the outset. A sensible *total system* approach should attempt to interrelate the activities and needs of *all* possible subsystems in the design of an efficient overall system which tends to optimize the results for the *total* materials operation. No wise manager would deliberately choose to experience at some future date the problems of integrating independently designed unit-systems when these problems can be avoided by adequate planning for a total system in the beginning.

The nature of many companies' operations will never permit them to develop a completely automated materials operation. Nevertheless, as computer technology and availability progress, and as their own businesses develop, most companies will advance beyond the initial design of their first automated system. For this reason, the system should be conceived to *include all* possible purchasing and related materials activities and to *integrate* them properly at the outset. It should further provide for easy integration of other possible additions at future dates.

An Automated Materials Management System

Every company that automates its materials activities utilizes the computer in a slightly different manner. The data inputs vary from company to company, as do the desired data outputs. The form and timing of various reports depend to a great extent upon the operating needs of each particular company. Generally speaking, however, the *basic* materials activities which can be performed well by an automated system are the same in all cases. They are:

1 Posting of inventory records
2 Computation of order quantities
3 Preparation of purchase requisitions
4 Preparation of purchase orders
5 Distribution of accounting charges
6 Automatic preparation of follow-up memos
7 Posting of delivery and quality records, by part and by supplier
8 Preparation of numerous operating reports for management
9 Auditing of invoices and preparation of the check for payment of invoice

Figure 26-2 shows in schematic form the general operation of a computerized integrated materials management system.

Inventory Control and Purchase Requisitions   In an automated system, all inventory and part records are filed in the computer's memory. For each part,

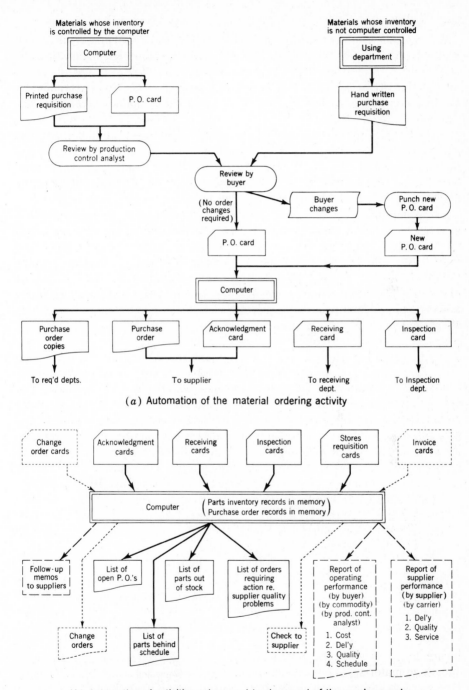

(a) Automation of the material ordering activity

(b) Automation of activities subsequent to placement of the purchase order

Figure 26-2 Schematic diagram of the general operation of a computerized materials management system.

either one record or several different records can be maintained. In either case, certain standard information is included, such as the part number, its name, required descriptive data, historical usage data, and the current balance. Additionally, price data from recent purchases as well as price quotation information are also on file. Just as in a manual system, the computer memory likewise contains such information as a vendor file of names and addresses, shipping terms, and open orders.

Each time the machine posts a stores withdrawal requisition for a particular part, it updates the balance on hand and compares this figure with a predetermined reorder point figure. When the balance falls below the order point, the computer prints out a purchase requisition. The quantity that the machine orders may be a predetermined order quantity. If desired, however, it can be programmed to compute and order the most economical quantity, just as a buyer might do manually, based on predetermined figures for inventory carrying costs and acquisition costs and current figures for part usage and price.[4] Thus, the computer automatically produces printed purchase requisitions which contain most of the information (including the appropriate accounting charge) that would normally appear on a manually prepared requisition. For the buyer's use, the requisition can also contain monthly usage data for the past year, a listing of past purchase orders and prices, and a summary of the most recent price quotations from different vendors.

The computer, however, cannot determine the urgency of the firm's need for a part. Consequently, for other than normal delivery requirements, exact shipping dates and order follow-up dates must be specified by the buyer. For this reason and for purposes of control, an automated system usually provides for a review of all purchase requisitions by the production control analyst and by the buyer. In the event that production needs (quantity and time requirements) fluctuate, the production control analyst changes the requisition accordingly before sending it to the buyer. The buyer analyzes the requisition in terms of potential suppliers' performances under current conditions. He also considers future quantity and quality requirements, as well as other intangible factors, and makes any changes he deems appropriate. The buyer likewise specifies unique delivery dates, shipping routings, the dates on which follow-up inquiries should be made, and a purchase order number.

Once an automated system is installed, the peculiarities of human nature occasionally pose a problem for the administrator. In most cases requisitions are reviewed by the same individuals who used to make the computations now performed by the computer. Some buyers inevitably resent the new system and cannot resist the temptation to change "machine-made decisions," whether

---

[4]This discussion assumes the use of a fixed order quantity inventory control system. The operation can be automated just as easily for items that are controlled under a cyclical review or MRP system of inventory control. The cyclical review system is frequently used extensively in companies that cannot accurately forecast production demands more than a month or two in advance. In fact, computerization of inventory control in such cases reduces clerical costs of operating the inventory control system immensely.

such changes are justified or not. A wise manager guards against the possibility of generating feelings of dissatisfaction and insecurity among his employees, by providing a thorough program of education and orientation prior to and during the transition period.

Note that all purchase requisitions for parts whose inventory is not controlled by the computer must be completed manually by the buyer. From this point on, however, a purchase order (PO) card can be made for the order, and it can be handled in the automated system without difficulty.

Purchase Orders At the time the computer prints the purchase requisition, it can also punch a corresponding purchase order card containing the data to be printed on the purchase order. If the buyer does not change the original requisition, the purchase order can be prepared simply by adding the PO number and feeding this purchase order card back into the computer. Additional data the buyer adds to the requisition, such as follow-up dates, must likewise be added to the PO card for the computer's use in producing future follow-up memos. Of course, if the requisition is altered by the buyer, a new PO card must be punched to reflect the changes.

At the same time that the computer prepares the purchase order to be mailed to the supplier, it can produce an acknowledgment card for the supplier, copies of the purchase order for internal distribution, a punched card to be used as the receiving report, and a punched card to be used as the inspection report. While producing purchase orders, the machine also produces and files in its memory unit a cumulative list of all outstanding purchase orders. This becomes the major "working" order file.

Change Orders In the event that an order is changed after it has been issued, a change order card (punched card) is prepared by the buyer and processed by the computer. The change order card is processed by the machine in the same way as the original purchase order. With accompanying documents, it simply replaces the original order.

Follow-up and Expediting The file of open purchase orders can be processed as frequently as is desirable (or possible, considering the computer work load) to produce current information for purchasing personnel. Most firms update open orders once a day to provide purchasing with "up-to-the-minute" status reports.

One of the most important outputs of the open-order processing operation is the follow-up memorandum. At the time a purchase requisition is converted into an order, the buyer instructs the computer to print out a follow-up memo at certain specified dates prior to scheduled delivery. Such a system assures periodic review of every purchase order, regardless of departmental work load or absenteeism. The computer, as instructed, faithfully produces follow-up memos, according to a predetermined format; hence, mailing the memos is the only clerical effort required of purchasing personnel. Upon receipt of the supplier's response, the buyer or expediter gives attention only to those orders requiring expediting.

Orders whose delivery is behind schedule are brought to the attention of the buyer by a "behind schedule" report.

Receiving, Inspection, and Stores Requisitions   When an order is received, the receiving clerk can report conventional receiving information in several ways. In one system, he uses the receiving card (punched card) for the order as the receiving report. His handwritten data are then punched into the card by a keypunch operator. In another system, he transmits the receiving information for an order by means of a teleprocessing unit which is connected to several machines that automatically punch and print the receiving card for the order. In still another newly introduced system, the receiving clerk utilizes a remote computer terminal and a cathode ray tube display unit to enter the information directly in the computer's order record, while simultaneously producing the punched and printed reports required for the use of other company personnel. In any case, receiving cards can thus be generated in multiple copies for the buyer, the production control analyst, and the computer. Inspection reports for those orders requiring technical inspection cards are processed daily by the computer to update the open-order file and the inventory record file.

As previously indicated, stores requisitions are also prepared in punched card form and processed daily to update inventory records.

Daily updating of the open-order records and the parts inventory records, coupled with the computer's fantastic speed, permits the preparation of numerous daily operating reports to facilitate the buyer's job. Four commonly used reports are:

1   List of open purchase orders
2   List of orders or parts that are behind schedule
3   List of parts that are out of stock
4   List of orders or parts that require action because of supplier quality problems

Such reports are of tremendous value to individual buyers. They provide the buyer with a summary of critical, up-to-the-minute information about his orders that is virtually impossible to obtain manually. Such summary reports also permit the buyer to manage by exception, that is, to concentrate his efforts on those orders requiring attention in time to prevent the development of serious purchasing problems.

Invoices and Payment   When an invoice for an order is received, typically it is reproduced in punched card form. The computer then audits the invoice by comparing the item, the quantity, and the price with corresponding information recorded on the purchase order and the receiving card. It likewise verifies the price extension. Any discrepancies are noted on an output error card or list. If no discrepancies are found, the unit signals a printer to write a check to the supplier for the amount of the invoice less the discount.

Accounting charges for the order can be distributed in the conventional manner from a printed copy of the purchase order, or they may be distributed by the computer. If the accounting system is computerized, distributions can be made by the machine during processing of the accounting records.

Management Reports   In its initial design an automated materials management system can be developed to accumulate various data useful to managerial personnel for control purposes. The computer's speed permits monthly or semimonthly analysis and summary of much information that is outside the realm of feasibility in a manually operated system. While managers in different firms may desire different types of reports, most materials executives want to evaluate the performance of suppliers, carriers, and commodities, as well as their own individual personnel and departments.

It is entirely possible to program the computer to provide periodic reports of each supplier's and carrier's performance with respect to such things a volume of business, late deliveries, rejected shipments (because of poor quality), transit damage, or price trends. Such reports can even be broken down by product lines, in the case of multiproduct suppliers. Likewise, the computer can prepare reports on the performance of individual buyers, production control analysts, and departments. Such reports can include figures on number of orders and materials handled, dollar volume of orders by commodity, percentage of open orders, prices paid versus target prices, percentage of late deliveries, percentage of rejected shipments, percentage of schedules missed, etc. Some companies even develop formulas for determining performance indexes for suppliers and buyers and have the computer automatically compute the indexes every month. The computer offers materials executives many other possibilities for developing data to improve management decisions and control.

THE EFFECT OF AUTOMATION ON DAILY OPERATIONS

An automated materials management system is most beneficial to the company that carries a large number of diversified materials in inventory, that processes a large number of purchase orders, that buys a large number of different items, or that deals with a large number of different suppliers. Nevertheless, automation can be profitable in small companies too. It can pay off in companies with a small dollar volume of purchases just as handsomely as in a corporate giant.

Reports from companies using automated systems indicate that approximately half of their purchase requisitions are prepared by the computer. This means that the computer performs the routine inventory control activities for at least 50 percent, and probably much more (up to 90 percent in some cases), of the production and nonproduction materials carried in inventory. Items whose inventory cannot be controlled effectively by a computer on a continuing basis are primarily those whose usage fluctuates rapidly and extensively. Requisitions for these items as well as for new items and normal "one-time" purchases are usually generated manually.

Regardless of how the purchase requisition is generated, however, after leaving the buyer's desk, *all* orders can enter the system and be controlled automatically until the order is closed (refer to Figure 26-2). There are occasions, of course, when it may be desirable to handle certain "rush" or critical orders manually. In such cases, the buyer can handle them in the conventional manner.

The volume of activity of even the largest purchasing and related materials departments is not adequate to utilize a computer on a full-time basis. The materials functions, therefore, typically share the use of a computer with accounting and finance, production, and engineering. Since computers are expensive to buy or to lease, joint use of the machine usually reduces each department's operating cost to a reasonable level. One large automated purchasing department has reported computer operating costs of several thousand dollars a month. On the other hand, a two-man purchasing department processing fifty orders a day reported some years ago that it automated its operation at a computer cost of $425 per month.[5]

Perhaps system conversion and start-up problems pose the most formidable obstacle to a management considering the automation of its materials activities for the first time. A large aircraft manufacturer invested approximately 5,000 man-hours in converting materials records into satisfactory form for an automated system. Considering the time required for systems analysis and programming, one authority estimates the total time requirement to be in excess of 25,000 man-hours. Further, since no system operates perfectly at first, management can anticipate numerous problems during the initial period of operation. Most of these problems can usually be overcome as a system is "debugged" and "refined." Nevertheless, they are time-consuming and troublesome.

Compensation for these initial costs and problems takes three forms. First, as discussed, the system regularly provides management with a large quantity of new and valuable detailed control data. One aircraft manufacturer found that such report data enabled it to reduce delays in manufacturing because of fewer late shipments, reduce its inventory investment, reduce average material costs, do a better job of planning cash flow, improve its cost accounting control, and increase the speed and effectiveness of the total procurement operation.[6]

Second, the system *may* permit a significant saving in the clerical costs of operating the materials departments. Reports from some companies with automated systems, for example, indicate that the clerical work force require-

[5]Somerby Dowst, "What the Computer Can Do for the Small Company," *Purchasing*, vol 55, no. 5, p. 74, Sept. 9, 1963.
[6]For a detailed discussion of this case see D. S. Ammer, *Materials Management*, rev. ed., Richard D. Irwin, Inc., Homewood, Ill., 1968, pp. 524–529.

ment drops from 20 to 50 percent. Whether or not such a saving materializes, however, depends upon the unique characteristics of a given operation and a given system. Such savings may or may not actually be generated by an automated system.

Third, and more important, is the fact that an automated system frees buyers and other professional personnel from a vast amount of routine work associated with the initiating and processing of requisitions. One company found that prior to the installation of an automated system, the average buyer spent nearly 50 percent of his time processing purchase requisitions. After installation of the system, requisition processing required only a fraction of this time. Automation thus permitted the buyer to devote the majority of his time to creative buying activities such as vendor investigation, negotiation, value analysis, and various types of purchasing research.

Finally, the relationship between purchasing and other materials activities, particularly production control, is somewhat closer under an automated system. The computer is the common bond which draws all materials activities into an integrated system. The resultant tendency is toward the development of a materials management type of organization. Even where the traditional forms of organization persist, buyers find themselves working more closely with their counterparts in the production control department. The design of the system and the speed with which it functions minimize "buck passing" between the two and tend to make specific materials problems mutual purchasing–production control problems.

Compared with a conventional purchasing operation, the general tenor of activities in an automated department is upgraded and focuses more sharply on the managerial and creative responsibilities of the purchasing function. Fewer clerks and expediters are required. The buyer's role, if developed as a logical extension of the old one, involves more analytical work and more purchasing research. Looking at the total picture, however, automation does not come as an unmixed blessing. Personnel problems arise that are similar to those encountered in automating production operations. What happens to displaced clerical personnel? What is the fate of buyers who do not have the ability to meet the stepped-up demands of the newly expanded jobs? The growing firm that engages in forward planning can anticipate such personnel problems and eliminate most of them by normal attrition, planned transfers, and careful personnel selection and promotion. The company that fails to do adequate planning for either personnel requirements or system requirements, however, is unlikely to develop a highly effective automated operation.

AUTOMATION AND INVENTORY MANAGEMENT

Automation may, in the future, have far-reaching effects on the management of production and finished-goods inventories alike. The computer's ability to handle mathematical computations with lightning speed facilitates an entirely new approach to the solution of inventory problems. It permits the repetitive daily use of sophisticated mathematical models in making inventory decisions at a practical, operating level.

This approach to inventory management can result first in a reduction of inventory levels through the more frequent use of more precise (and complicated) economic lot size formulas. Secondly, the approach *may* permit the reduction of inventory levels by facilitating a reduction in safety stock. The use of probability theory in safety stock determination (as discussed in Chapter 11) is possible with a computer *if* realistic stock-out costs can be determined. Likewise, computer simulation techniques can be employed to determine near-optimum safety stock levels in complex situations. In both of the above cases, the difficulty and time involved in manually making the calculations on a repetitive basis renders the techniques impractical as management decision-making tools. The computer eliminates this impracticality, and it will doubtless alter the course of inventory management practice in many companies.

FOR DISCUSSION

26-1   Define automation. What feature distinguishes a highly automated production process from a highly mechanized production process? Explain.

26-2   Discuss the general effects of automation on an industrial purchasing department.

26-3   Assume that the inventory posting routine in a company is handled on a "batch" basis by a computer. Explain the procedure and the specific input data required in making an inventory posting "run."

26-4   How does a computer determine when the order point has been reached in an automated inventory control operation? Explain how this computer capability is used in developing other operating elements of an automated purchasing system.

26-5   Explain how an automated purchasing system such as that shown in Figure 26-2 works in practice.

26-6   The uninformed person sometimes envisions an automated purchasing system as one in which most purchasing personnel are simply replaced by a huge computer. Comment. Discuss the jobs people do in operating an automated purchasing system.

26-7   In what ways does a buyer's job change when his or her company automates the purchasing operation?

26-8   Explain how a computer can calculate the economic order quantity for a particular material. From a buyer's point of view, what problems might you anticipate regarding the computer's ability to calculate accurate and valid EOQ values? Explain.

26-9   Discuss in detail the benefits a purchasing department might expect to obtain from automating its operation. What problems or disadvantages might be expected?

26-10   It is frequently said that managers and buyers can truly "manage by exception" in a purchasing department that is automated. What is your reaction to this statement?

26-11 "The design of an integrated, automated purchasing operation, and the speed with which it functions, minimize 'buck passing' between purchasing and production control personnel." Comment.

CASE FOR CHAPTER 26

A Computer for Purchasing, page 606

Part Five

Institutional and Government Purchasing

Chapter 27

Purchasing for Institutions

KEY CONCEPTS

Differences in institutional and industrial purchasing
    Control of budgets
    Challenging specifications
    Conflict of interest; reciprocity
    Organization; centralization
    Back-door selling
    Inspection
    Teachers and scientists
    Government research contracts
    Cooperative purchasing
    Insurance
    Remodeling and construction
    Auxiliary functions

One of the most noteworthy developments in the United States economy in recent years has been its transtition from a production economy to a service economy. By spending more for *services* than for *goods*, the United States has become the world's first nation having a service economy. Because the national demand for services continues to rise faster than the demand for goods, the economy is becoming increasingly service-oriented with the passage of time. This phenomenon places new emphasis on purchasing and what it can contribute to the nation's prosperity.

This chapter focuses on purchasing for education and health care institutions—two of the fast-growing service industries. Most of what is said here, however, applies to all other types of institutions as well, for example, penal institutions, art galleries, and libraries. When discussing educational institutions, colleges and universities will be stressed. Because the purchasing operations of these institutions cover the entire spectrum of educational buying, a discussion of purchasing at this level also includes the purchasing considerations of elementary and secondary school levels as well. Purchasing differences which exist among educational institutions at various academic levels are generally ones of degree, rather than substance.

Buying for institutions is big business! Schools and hospitals[1] are a rapidly growing segment of the American economy. Their economic size alone makes them important. In 1973–1974, the cost of United States education at all levels exceeded $96 billion.[2] This was 7.9 percent of the 1973 gross national product (GNP). Medical services are growing at an even faster rate than education. In fact, medical services now represent the nation's fastest growing industry. In 1973, the cost of health care was just over $94 billion, or 7.7 percent of the GNP.[3] The magnitude of these sums is seen clearly when they are compared with the combined 1974 income of the nation's fifteen most profitable corporations. This total was only $18.3 billion.[4]

Every principle of good purchasing discussed in the preceding chapters applies to purchases made for institutions. All buying activities—whether industrial, governmental, or institutional—have one cardinal objective: to obtain the maximum value for each dollar spent. There is no separate group of principles for institutional buying. When compared with industrial purchasing, however, institutional purchasing places different emphasis on some of the considerations of good purchasing. This chapter critically examines these differences.

DIFFERENCES IN INSTITUTIONAL AND INDUSTRIAL PURCHASING EMPHASES

Control of Budgets

Parkinson's Law on Budgets states that "expenditures will always rise to exceed income." This "law" could apply to all business operations; however, it seems especially applicable to institutions. In most institutions, the determination to control expenditures is not as strong as it is in industry. Thus far it has proved easier for schools to raise tuition rates and for hospitals to raise room and service rates than it has for industrial companies to raise the selling prices of their products. Consequently, institutions in many cases have not been motivated to control purchasing costs in the same way that competitive industry has. However, it appears that this situation may be changing. The federal government and individual tax payers alike are becoming increasingly concerned about the high cost of education and medical care. This concern is being forcefully communicated to hospital and school administrators. As costs for these services continue to rise, Congress can be expected to direct a larger part of its investigatory time to these areas of expenditure. Congressional investigations, in turn, invariably result in closer control over the expenditures

---

[1]The term "hospital(s)" in this discussion is used generically to include many types of medical institutions, such as clinics, convalescent homes, nursing homes, and similar health care facilities.

[2]"Education," U.S. Bureau of the Census, *Statistical Abstract of the United States*, 1974, p. 109.

[3]"Health," U.S. Bureau of the Census, *Statistical Abstract of the United States, 1974, p. 69.*

[4]*Forbes*, May 15, 1975, p. 186.

of government funds—which represent a significant portion of total educational and medical expense.

Savings

Purchasing savings are as valuable to institutions as they are to industry. In industry these savings increase profits and, therefore, increase a firm's capability to survive in a competitive society. In education and health care, purchasing savings permit the college or hospital to further accomplish its goals of better education, better patient care, better physical facilities, better salaries, etc. Because most purchasing savings recur year after year, such savings work like a gift to an institution's endowment fund. For example, a leading university recently achieved purchasing savings of approximately $640,000. With its endowment income generated at roughly a 5 percent earning rate, the $640,000 recurring savings is equivalent to an endowment gift of $12,800,000 ($640,000/0.05 = $12,800,000). Stated differently, each $1 saved by wise purchasing has the same budgetary effect as a $20 gift to the institution's endowment fund.

Challenging Specifications

The benefits from the purchasing department's responsibility to challenge specifications are especially important to colleges and hospitals. These institutions purchase a much broader spectrum of materials and services than does the average industrial company. Further, teachers and medical personnel tend to become even more specialized than their industrial counterparts. Most researchers are exceedingly knowledgeable concerning their professional activities. Unfortunately, they are not always equally knowledgeable concerning the economics and market availability of research equipment and supplies needed to help achieve their goals. For example, assume that a chemistry teacher or a medical biologist wishes to acquire a new, complex microscope. The purchasing department can help this individual by arranging for demonstrations of competing microscopes from several major manufacturers. This is something that teachers or researchers usually cannot accomplish by themselves simply because they do not have enough economic leverage.

Because of this economic capability, the purchasing department is in a logical position to challenge restrictive specifications for microscopes. Stated a little differently, the microscope buyer in the purchasing department learns much about many types of microscopes because he continually deals in them. He knows what models are available, who sells them, and which distributor has the best facilities for servicing and pricing them most economically. Also, he discusses technical and marketing changes and improvements with all manufacturers' sales representatives on a continual basis. On the other hand, even constant users of microscopes make only infrequent purchases; therefore, they cannot possibly keep up with the many advancements and changes of all major manufacturers. Because the purchasing department buys many things in addition to microscopes from the distributor of scientific equipment, it can obtain from the distributor a superior response in terms of sales effort, timing, and price.

When it comes to the purchase of unique or seldom-purchased capital equipment, the situation is usually different. In these cases, the technical competence of the academician must be relied upon heavily. The purchasing staff can help, however, by working with the academician well "upstream" in planning the procurement. Purchasing can help with the economic problems of capacity, prices, and obtaining favorable terms and conditions in general. For example, in the purchase of high-speed computer memory units, a competent university purchasing specialist was able to combine his skills effectively with the technical know-how of an EDP systems engineer and with the professional needs of a professor. The professor wanted to purchase memory units that would increase the capability of his computer-assisted instruction project. Among the problems included in this procurement were: funding of the purchase, possible contract cancellation at no cost, deferred delivery of some units, and an option to increase the number of units at the original price one or two years later. The purchasing specialist was invited to enter the procurement picture as soon as the requirement was known. He prepared the request for proposals to be sent to six major manufacturing firms, participated in the evaluation of the proposals, negotiated at length with the two firms whose proposals were most favorable, and suggested in detail a possible basis for the manufacturers' financing of the sale. The contract award ultimately was made on the basis of the quality of one manufacturer's product, together with the consideration of his responsiveness to the nontechnical aspects of funding, and to other desired contractual provisions. The final unit price, a six-digit figure, was approximately 15 percent below the best quotation among the other five initial competitive proposals.

Conflicts of Interest

Conflicts of interest in educational and medical purchasing are probably even more critical than in industry. Medical scientists and college professors control millions of research dollars, often flowing from the federal government and philanthropic foundations. The individuals receiving these grants, in addition to doing teaching and research, also frequently serve as consultants to industrial companies. Such companies in turn, are often working on projects similar, if not identical, to those the scientists are working on in connection with their research grants. Additionally, some of these same people serve on boards of directors of still other companies that are also searching for answers to comparable questions because they have similar types of research projects. These relationships can raise many delicate questions of propriety. Consider, for example, patents and royalties. Who owns the patents to and who gets the royalties from a product developed by a consulting professor or researcher while working under a government research contract or grant? Is it the professor, the government agency, or the firm for which he is consulting? To compound a situation which at best is already vague, various agencies of the federal government answer these questions differently! The Atomic Energy Commission, the Department of Defense, and the Department of Health, Education and Welfare all view patent rights differently.

In his book, *The Closed Corporation—American University in Crisis,* James Ridgeway discusses many questions of this type. Rigeway points out such interesting facts as the following: the number of professors involved in industry as consultants and directors is growing; an increasing number of dealings between business institutions and university officials has caused an increasing number of conflicts of interest; professors and scientists are increasingly using their prestige as scholars to advance the interests of specific business firms, industries, and governmental organizations. This situation tends to make the persons involved biased rather than objective in their views. In such circumstances, conflicts of interest can easily follow.

Few institutions have developed clearly defined and effective policies concerning conflicts of interest. They are, however, now being forced from several fronts to do so. The federal government especially desires such policies, and it will press harder in the future to get them. Congress has historically demanded tight controls in areas where public expenditures are high, and private foundations are now starting to examine very closely the ethical implications of their grants.

Inspection of Materials and Services

Schools and hospitals often have a more difficult problem in inspecting purchased items than do industrial organizations. A large university, for example, deals in nearly every field of human knowledge. This requires the purchase of practically the entire range of materials, services, and products developed by man. The very range of incoming materials, therefore, makes centralized inspection practically impossible. Too many different kinds of inspectors and too much expensive inspection equipment would be required to perform the function at reasonable cost.

In most universities and medical centers, therefore, receiving departments inspect only for bulk quantity and outward evidences of physical damage. The inspection for unit quantity, quality, and compliance with specifications is made by the scientist or professor who originated the request for the material. When desired, the receiving department can, of course, inspect for general stores-type or common-use items. It should be remembered, however, that these types of items now represent only a small dollar percentage of a research-oriented institution's total purchases and receipts.

Back-Door Selling

Controlling the visits of sales personnel is considerably more difficult in schools and medical centers than it is in industry. Most scientists and professors are extremely individualistic and tend not to be organization-oriented. This fact at times creates vexing problems in establishing and enforcing effective business procedures. Coupled with this, the physical layout of most institutional facilities compounds the problem. For example, most industrial concerns have a reception room, and visitors cannot get past this room without clearance. Such is not the case in most colleges and hospitals; here visitors are "free to roam." Consequently, and because controls can seldom be accomplished by fiat in an academic-scientific environment, the purchasing department must use the techniques of persuasion to convince researchers and faculty members that using proper purchasing procedures is to their advantage.

Naturally, there are many situations in which academic people and researchers have a genuine and sometimes urgent need to talk with sales representatives. Indeed, as noted previously, institutions must rely upon the technical competence of their academicians and scientists to develop specifications and to recommend suppliers in those instances where the subject matter is highly unique or complex. In such situations, the purchasing staff should do everything possible to bring competent sales personnel (generally sales engineers) and the academicians and scientists together.

Controlling salesmen properly involves scheduling them in accordance with two common-sense alternatives: (1) salesmen who, from an institutional point of view, can be utilized most effectively in the purchasing department should be handled there; and (2) salesmen who can be utilized most effectively by appropriate technical personnel should be assisted in establishing such relationships.

Reciprocity

In theory, reciprocity should be easier to control in schools and hospitals than it is in industry; in practice, this is often not the case. Trustees, donors, and alumni on occasion bring great pressure on institutions for the purchase of a particular company's products. Normally, such pressures should be resisted. By its very nature, a school or a hospital has nothing to sell back to its potential suppliers. Therefore, when a vendor says, "Give me your business because I gave you a donation of $10,000," he could in effect be saying, "I really did not want to give you $10,000, but some unstated lesser amount." If the business the donor demands for his firm yields a profit in excess of $10,000, then he is actually asking the institution to give him a gift. Institutional buyers should always be alert to this questionable practice, because potential opportunities of this type abound. This obviously is quite a different situation from that which exists in industrial reciprocity. There the objective of reciprocity is, in theory at least, for the buyer and seller to reach an agreement on an exchange of business that is mutually beneficial. The preceding discussion of reciprocity is not meant to imply that donors cannot be good suppliers. They certainly can be. In fact, where they are willing to compete on quality, service, and price, they can be the very best suppliers. It is only when they are not willing to compete freely that their motives become suspicious.

What then is the answer to proposals of reciprocity in institutions? The answer to the vendor's statement in the preceding paragraph could be something like this: "Yes, you did give the college $10,000, and your generosity is appreciated. However, the school has many benefactors, and it must give impartial treatment to all of its supporters if it is to maintain a reputation for integrity, fair dealing, and progressiveness. Consequently, it really has no practical alternative to selecting its suppliers on any basis other than the best combination of quality, service, and price."

Personnel

Despite their rapid growth thus far, many schools and hospitals have lagged behind industry and government in recruiting the most competent purchasing personnel. Institutional salary levels historically have been lower than industry's. As they "grew up," hospitals and schools were considered places of service that primarily attracted employees who were not materially oriented. For example, until very recently, nurses were paid less than clerk-typists, and college professors' salaries were lower than some of their graduate students' immediately after graduation.

Fortunately institutional salaries are now becoming more competitive with industrial salaries. With competitive salaries, plus the additional satisfaction that comes from public service, institutions in the future should be able to attract personnel with top-flight qualifications.

There is no need for institutions to deceive themselves about purchasing salaries. Good purchasing results primarily from professional competence. Determining the best combination of quality, service, and price is the result of actions such as effective negotiation, value analysis, vendor analysis, cost analysis, and price analysis—all actions requiring a high level of competence. Purchasing personnel who lack such competence serve as order placers, not as creative buyers.

Organization

Where a purchasing department is located within the organizational structure greatly influences the department's ability to function optimally and influence its firm's decision-making process. As discussed in Chapter 20, a large percentage of industrial purchasing managers report directly to the chief executive of their companies or to a senior vice president. In government, purchasing invariably reports to the chief executive officer of the unit to which the purchasing department is attached. Institutions have routinely placed their purchasing departments too low in the management structure. Hospitals particularly have been guilty of this error. Undoubtedly, this is a primary reason why some hospitals have experienced difficulty in attracting top purchasing talent.

The pursuit of and the administration of government research contracts frequently entail organizational problems that also lead to ineffective procurement performance. Traditionally, one organizational unit of the university (often called research administration) is charged with the responsibility of negotiating the university's research contracts with the government. Another organizational unit (the purchasing department) is responsible for negotiating the subcontracts for all goods and services purchased from outside suppliers with funds from the above prime contracts. Close coordination between these two university offices—research administration and purchasing—is essential to ensure that the funds allocated under various government research contracts are: (1) handled properly within the constraints of government procurement regulations; (2) expended properly in accordance with the terms of the contract; and (3) processed expeditiously to accomplish the institution's goals. In practice, such coordination frequently does not exist. Too often the two organizational units even report to different functional heads. Consequently, many universities fail to gain the benefits which can result from an effective organization of their total government research procurement effort.

Teachers and Scientists

Teachers and scientists are the paramount resource of teaching and research institutions. They have no exact counterparts in industry. It is true that scholars do work in industry, as well as in the academic world, but when they do, they usually change their orientation. Holders of a Ph.D. or M.D. who are working at their profession at an institution of learning are basically more concerned with their professional accomplishments than with the institution's for which they are working. If they are offered a better laboratory, better teaching conditions, or better assistants at another institution, more often than not they will accept the offer. This is not to imply that such individuals are not loyal to their institutions. They are. Typically, however, their loyalties are first to their professions, and second to their schools. This is the reverse of business loyalty priorities. This reversal of priorities is an important reason why business people sometimes find it difficult to understand institutions.

A business executive's loyalty must be first to his or her firm and then to his or her profession; otherwise, neither the executive nor the firm can be *fully* successful. If any single, basic business function in a firm (finance, purchasing, personnel, production, engineering, and sales) fails or weakens, the firm as a whole suffers similar consequences. This is why business managers cannot achieve optimum individual success unless they cooperate and become team players.

The basic functions of business are similar to the basic organs of the human body in that both are integral parts of a unified whole. Unless all applicable parts function properly, all inevitably die or function at reduced efficiency. Scientists and teachers are different; they can be entities unto themselves. They can succeed or fail individually, without regard to the success or failure of the institutions that employ them.

The business people working in schools and hospitals, consequently, deal with unique people—people who frequently are in great demand and short supply. As a rule, these people are motivated less by material rewards than are their colleagues in industry. Rather, it is typically intellectual recognition that inspires them most to pursue their research and teaching activities.

Working successfully with this kind of person requires different appeals and techniques from those used successfully in industry. These professionals, however, *are* concerned with getting the greatest possible mileage from their research and teaching dollars. The purchasing department that proves its ability to help them achieve *this* goal will be welcome as a member of their team. Most scientific and educational people publish books, papers, and journal articles. It is often possible for purchasing managers and buyers to gain rapport with them by the simple technique of reading some of their publications, becoming familiar with their work, and then discussing these things with them. It is amazing how often this simple technique is overlooked by the personnel of institutional purchasing departments. Yet this kind of interest from purchasing people not only assures them of doing better purchasing, but it also permits them to share in the exhilaration that comes from intellectual achievement. This is but one of many possible get-acquainted techniques, and it is only a first step. In the end, the only thing that will keep academic people returning to the purchasing department, or any business department, is professional business competence.

Differences between Public and Private Institutions

There can be notable differences between the purchasing responsibilities of public and private institutions. Some public schools and hospitals are completely free from political purchasing constraints. Such freedom, however, is not typical; rather, most public institutions are tightly constrained in their operations by governmental regulations. Private institutions, on the other hand, are usually free to use their economic power in the way they deem most desirable.

To the extent possible, the procedures selected to operate either a public or private institution should be directed toward creating goodwill for the institution. Goodwill is achieved when the public feels assured that an institution treats all interested parties impartially. To satisfy such diverse institutional groups as alumni, trustees, donors, business firms, and governmental agencies, a private institution has no rational alternative but to buy without favoritism—just as public institutions are required to do by law. The difference between purchasing for public and private institutions is not a matter of concept; rather, it is a matter of how to implement the concept of buying without favoritism. Political pressures frequently cause public institutions to carry otherwise sound concepts to ridiculous extremes. For example, public institutions are often forced to use competitive bidding in situations where negotiation would produce both better prices and better service.

Centralization of Purchasing

In a large, research-oriented institution, the broad scope of its technical effort and the complete lack of departmental routine in many situations make it difficult to centralize purchasing. To complicate matters further, universities tend to spread themselves over large physical areas. (A wit once defined a university as a "collection of colleges and schools connected more or less by inadequate plumbing.")

It is difficult to coordinate widely separated organizational units under any circumstances; in an atmosphere of academic freedom, it is especially difficult. In an academic environment, very few things can be accomplished by edict. Consequently, it is extremely difficult and generally unwise to attempt a *total* centralization of the institution's purchasing activities. Nevertheless, the centralization benefits described in Chapters 1, 20, and 22 are as valid in an institutional setting as in a business setting. Competent institutional management, therefore, should strive to achieve purchasing centralization to the greatest degree that is *practical*.

It has been conservatively estimated that a centralized purchasing operation yields savings of at least 10 to 15 percent over a decentralized operation.[5] Centralized purchasing additionally allows suppliers to give institutions better service as well as better prices because their expenses are reduced. Specifically, their sales people have fewer persons to call on, fewer orders have to be serviced, fewer invoices have to be prepared, fewer shipments have to be made, fewer financial records have to be kept, and so on.

Cooperative Purchasing

When properly guided, cooperative institutional purchasing can be most beneficial. Many colleges and universities have affiliated with the Educational and Institutional Purchasing Cooperative (E&I), an activity of the National Association of Educational Buyers of Garden City, New York. This national organization provides many useful services to its members. Because of the nominal cost of affiliation, a college or university cannot prudently take the financial risk of not joining E&I. Even one small purchase against any E&I contract will result in savings well in excess of the small affiliation fee.

Hospital Bureau, Pleasantville, New York, is an outstanding national cooperative serving hospitals. A number of hospitals have also formed regional purchasing cooperatives which also sometimes engage in regional service ventures such as laundries. Successes of regional ventures have been proportional to the skill with which the cooperatives have been conceived and managed. There is no doubt that savings can result from the proper cooperative grouping of economic power and professional talent. However, many coopera-

[5]George W. Aljian, Ed., *Purchasing Handbook*, 2d ed., McGraw-Hill Book Company, New York, 1966, pp. 18–19.

tives fail because they are ill conceived, poorly managed, and too small to reap the rewards resulting from large dollar volume contracts.

Price

Until rather recently, many suppliers granted special prices to institutions, especially to schools and hospitals. Suppliers used to feel it was their philanthropic and patriotic duty to help these institutions financially. However, that was when the institutional market was small and financially unimportant. The present market has changed. Today, most suppliers view the institutional market as large, choice, highly profitable, and one worthy of their best sales effort. To obtain fair prices in such a market, institutions must have buyers and materials managers who have the knowledge and intellectual capacity to negotiate effectively with their highly competent sales counterparts.

Institutions, as a group, continue to violate one of the basic principles of good purchasing—that of not disclosing prices. Many small institutions (especially hospitals) waste their time and money trying to improve their prices by making price comparisons with other institutions. Additionally, the practice frequently penalizes the efficient institution while seldom helping the inefficient one. No rational sales representative will offer a price concession to a buyer whom he or she suspects will advertise this fact to other buyers, who in turn would soon pressure the sales representative for the same low price. Institutions should follow the pricing practices set forth in Chapters 6 and 7. These are the only effective practices for achieving good pricing.

Government Research Contracts

Universities and medical centers are becoming increasingly dependent on government sponsored research contracts. Such contracts generally entail a highly sophisticated procurement activity. Any research effort can require complex negotiation, plus the preparation and management of complex cost-type and other involved types of contracts. Government research can be even more complex because it involves increasingly severe government constraints. As a contractor with the United States, an institution must comply with government regulations and undergo a periodic government review of its purchasing system. Usually, this review is made under the auspices of the Department of Defense, as set forth in Section XXIII of the Armed Services Procurement Regulations (ASPR). These regulations require a review of an institution's purchasing techniques when "the procurement work being done is complex and the dollar value is substantial."

It is highly desirable for an institution to get its purchasing techniques approved by the government because without such approval, the government will examine each subcontract involving government funds. ASPR states: "Reliance upon a contractor's approved procurement system will usually obviate the need for reviewing and consenting to individual subcontracts."

An institution can best satisfy the government's requirements for good purchasing by hiring personnel who have recognized competence in the field of government procurement. Also, as discussed earlier in this chapter (under the subheading Organization), institutions can optimize their benefits from government contracts if all institutional operations regarding government contracts are coordinated and controlled by a single organizational unit.

Insurance

Institutions are concerned with a large variety of activities, ranging from the operation of small electrical shops to the operation of huge linear accelerators. Also, colleges and hospitals are concerned with the physical presence of large and diverse groups of people, including faculty, staff, students, patients, and a continuous stream of visitors. For these reasons, the insurance requirements for institutions are normally more complex than those of industry.

Purchasing insurance involves the application of the same principles used to purchase other services and commodities. The first procedural step—and the critical one—is to prepare a list of exactly what categories of insurance are needed. A competent broker or agent (the supplier) can assist in this step. Specifically, he can caution institutions not to overlook their unusual and unique risks. For example, a college should insure against the risk of a chartered airplane crashing with its football team aboard. In the event of such a tragedy, claims far in excess of the insurance carried by the airline would result.

After an institution's insurance needs have been determined and listed, an effective broker or general agent can assist the institution in developing competition among appropriate underwriters. Competition for insurance coverage is not confined to price alone; traditionally reliability and service are more important than price. Hence, in evaluating insurance agents and brokers, an institution must consider not only their ability to assist in selecting the correct coverage, but also their capability to help in settling claims quickly and inexpensively.

Remodeling and New Construction

New construction and remodeling programs at medical and educational institutions constitute a significant part of their total expenses. Furthermore, because construction costs are rising at a rate considerably above the average of other operational costs, in the future these costs are destined to become even more significant. Despite the economic importance of construction buying, space limitations dictate that only an overview of the subject be presented in this chapter.

Purchasing's Interest in Construction   In most institutions, the purchasing department does not contract for new buildings. However, in some—particularly in large government institutions—they do. Most purchasing departments do routinely contract for: (1) the interior furnishings of new buildings, (furniture, equipment of all types, carpets, desks, library shelving, etc.); (2) routine construction repairs; and (3) minor construction alterations. The following remodeling and new construction discussion, therefore, focuses primarily on these areas of purchasing and materials management interest.

Purchase of Interior Furnishings Is Profitable   It is often profitable for an institution itself to buy such interior furnishings of a new building as chalkboards, classroom and office furniture, carpets, drapes, laboratory equipment, and scientific instruments. If such interior furnishings are purchased by an architect, a general contractor, or a contract furnisher, the institution invariably pays marked-up prices. Such prices could be 40 percent above those at which the institution itself could purchase such materials. Typically, the mark-up would be less than 40 percent, but not less than 10 percent.

Naturally, when an institution's purchasing department contracts for the interior furnishings of a building, additional work results. However, as previously discussed, this additional work can be financially rewarding. Purchasing departments do not always confine their new building purchases to interior furnishings. One college purchasing department recently ordered more than two million bricks to be used in the construction of several new campus buildings. The savings from this purchase was $20 per thousand bricks, a total of $40,000.

One category of interior furnishings deserves special mention because typically as much as 90 percent of the total demand for educational office, classroom, and library furniture occurs in the summer and early fall months. Consequently, significant savings can result when orders for such furnishings are placed as far as possible in advance of desired delivery dates. With long leadtime orders, furniture manufacturers can schedule the production of such orders at times when factory workloads are light. This, in turn, makes it possible for manufacturers to price on a marginal cost basis (as discussed in Chapter 6) and for institutions to receive the ultimate in good pricing. One college saved over 30 percent ($165,000) on the cost of its new married-student housing furniture by placing its order eight months in advance of the date the furniture was actually needed. This saving was made after the payment of five months commercial storage charges.

Construction Purchasing Entails Unique Problems   Construction purchasing is a highly specialized field of buying entailing unique problems. For example it is not unusual for an institution to discover that after completion of a new building or a major alteration it has a mechanic's lien filed against it. In such cases, the institution has typically paid the general contractor, but the general has not paid his subcontractors. Under the law of mechanics' liens, if a general does not pay his subs, the institution is financially responsible. Proper financial and legal steps, therefore, must be taken in advance to prevent this kind of loss. What constitutes "proper steps" differs among various states and municipalities; hence, the precise steps must be determined by each purchasing department for itself. In general, an institution achieves financial protection by carefully analyzing the financial status of all prospective contractors before making any contract award. Legal protection is achieved by the institution's properly filing all required completion and other reports, at the appropriate times, at the appropriate courthouse.

Construction Insurance   Because construction is often a high-risk business, insurance is sometimes an especially important consideration. Contractors should be required to furnish the institution with copies of all required insurance policies and certificates. The coverage should include such things as workmen's compensation, and general and public liability insurance. Most importantly, each policy should contain a provision that the policy cannot be canceled by the insurance company before giving ten days written notice of such action to the *institution.* Failure to have this provision can be very costly. Without it, a thinly financed contractor developing a need for cash can cancel a policy without the institution's knowing it.

Selection of the Right Architect Is Important   Selecting an architect is a very important construction buying decision because a mistake here is certain to result in increased construction costs and increased operational difficulties. It is especially important for institutions to select architects that have a paramount interest in the interior design of buildings. It is the correct design of its buildings' interior spaces that assures an institution the proper use of its equipment and space, the regulated flow of its traffic, and the timely execution of its educational and medical functions. Attractive exteriors are desirable; functional interiors are essential.

Cost Controls Are Profitable   Establishing cost control policies for purchases of interior furnishings, routine repairs, and minor alterations is most advisable. Consider the benefits of one such policy—a competitive bidding policy. Such a policy would, among other things, require that the architect and interior decorator specify only products for interior furnishings that can be purchased competitively from at least three sources of supply. With such a policy, who does the actual buying (the architect, the decorator, or the institution's purchasing department) becomes much less important. Competitive prices are assured in any case. In addition to improved pricing, an effective competitive bidding policy concurrently produces other desirable objectives: conflicts of interest are reduced, unreasonable personal bias is eliminated, and the frequent practice of some architects and decorators specifying low volume, high dollar value proprietary items is precluded.

Stores

Institutions have the same reasons as industry for carrying items in stores: economy and service. Economy results from savings made through quantity buying with its resultant savings in paperwork, handling, and prices. Service results from having items immediately available. Stores items provide a buffer between fluctuations in demand and changes in lead time; thus they protect an institution's using department against uncertainty and delay.

In addition to economy and service, the modern college campus has engendered another very practical reason for having a stores system, i.e., campus congestion. If materials were to be delivered by suppliers as needed to each using department, most schools would substantially increase their traffic congestion.

Hospitals must have access to immediate emergency reserves of patient-care materials. Loss of life cannot be risked because of such inevitable business failures as strikes, transportation breakdowns, and fires. However, this does not mean that the required emergency supplies must all be stocked by the hospital itself in its own storerooms. Quite the contrary: suppliers can stock many medical supplies for the hospital in the supplier's storeroom. The specific items the hospital needs to have stocked, together with their exact quantities, must, of course, be determined in advance. The material so determined can be included as a legal requirement in the procurement contract. The supplier, therefore, becomes legally bound not only to have this material on hand, but also to earmark it for the hospital making the purchase.

Under this concept of supply, the supplier's stores system literally becomes an extension of the hospital's stores system. In many situations, application of this concept permits the hospital to achieve its needed reserve supply protection at much lower warehousing costs than it could by stocking the same supplies in its own storerooms. The economic advantages of the concept can be illustrated by one fact. Storage space in most medical centers located in metropolitan areas costs more than $45 per square foot to build.[6] The usual commercial warehousing on the periphery of similar areas costs less than $15 per square foot to build.[7]

This concept of the supplier's stores system serving as an extension of the institution's stores system is not limited to medical supplies. It is equally applicable to supplies for biology, chemistry, engineering, maintenance, etc.

Auxiliary Functions

Many institutions have found it organizationally desirable to group their auxiliary purchasing functions—traffic, receiving, delivery, and surplus—together in what can appropriately be called the "Purchasing Services Division."

Traffic Many institutions, as contrasted with industry and government, do not have a traffic specialist. Outgoing shipments in many institutions are small in number, and incoming shipments are usually consigned f.o.b. the

---

[6] *Dodge Digest of Building Costs and Specifications*, "Section G, Office and Manufacturing," *Warehouse Construction* (Medical Centers), McGraw-Hill, New York, 1974.

[7] *Ibid.* (Warehouses).

institution. Nonetheless, at the appropriate stage of their development, all institutions should consider seriously the advantages of having a traffic specialist.

An institution cannot avoid paying a reasonable salary to an intelligent clerk for processing its freight bills for payment (which by law must be paid within five days) and for initiating settlement of its freight claims. For not many additional dollars in salary, a skilled traffic specialist can be hired. In all likelihood, this individual will generate cash savings that will recover his salary several times over. In addition, improved traffic and damage claims service will be gained for the institution. For example, one college's traffic manager, after checking the classification guide for a shipment, challenged the carrier on the classification of a $5,400 shipment. As a result of this challenge, the classification was changed from "electronics" to "radio repair parts mounted on a truck or trailer." The bill was lowered from $5,400 to $2,230, a saving of $3,170.

Receiving   Because institutions do not have production schedules to meet, they sometimes underestimate the importance of the receiving function. Poor receiving can produce costly consequences for institutions, just as it can for industry. Receiving is a critical control point in an institution's materials system. It is at the receiving dock that the papers directing the flow of purchased materials and the physical materials themselves meet for the first time. At this meeting, if the receiving function is performed correctly, any existing discrepancies will be uncovered. Errors are easily corrected at this time. If they are not corrected then, however, the cost to correct them later is certain to be higher. Because of this fact, the importance of the receiving function should not be underestimated by management.

Delivery   Many of the materials received by purchases from outside suppliers and all materials requisitioned from stores must be delivered to using departments. To the extent possible, the delivery of these two categories of materials should be combined into a single, integrated delivery system. Mail and other items to be delivered to using departments should also be included in the above delivery system if such action prevents duplication of effort.

Failing to plan ahead for their material requirements is a common shortcoming of many institutional departments. To compensate for this shortcoming, frequently they want immediate delivery of all materials they requisition, especially stores items. Putting all other aspects of the problem aside, institutions simply cannot afford the cost of making continuous deliveries. Schools especially can support only a "reasonable" delivery system, not an "express" delivery system. Each school must determine for itself what is reasonable. This is not always easy to do. Sears, Penney's, and other similarly successful retailers have found a weekly delivery schedule to be satisfactory to their customers. Some successfully managed industrial firms now operate on a weekly delivery system from stores to various shops in their plants. At one time, all of these companies thought that daily deliveries were essential for customer and production scheduling satisfaction. There appears to be no reason why institutions should not pattern their delivery systems along industrial lines.

Surplus and Salvage In institutions, surplus and salvage sales are not usually handled with the dispatch industry directs to these activities. Institutions, however, are generating larger and larger surpluses of increasing value. Last year, for example, one university's surplus and salvage section returned over $140,000 in cash to the university. Nearly all of this money came from sales that formerly were not made or from sales of surplus material and equipment that formerly were made to employees for a token payment. Without a formalized surplus and salvage program, institutions tend to sell surplus materials to employees and friends on a subjective rather than a business basis.

CONCLUSION

Educational and medical costs already represent a significant portion of the nation's gross national product (GNP). Because their joint costs are growing faster than the GNP, they will in the future represent an even larger portion.[8] The United States Office of Education estimates that in 1980 national education costs will exceed $107 billion.[9] The United States Social Security Administration estimates that in 1980 health care costs will exceed $155 billion.[10] Together these two costs will total more than 18.7 percent of the 1980 estimated GNP of $1,400 billion.[11] This is in contrast to 1973–1974 education and 1974 health care expenditures which totaled only 15.1 percent of the GNP. (See footnotes 3 and 4.) Typically, between 20 and 25 percent of an institution's total expenditures are for the purchase of materials and services. Hence, 1980 purchases made by schools and hospitals will range between $52.4 and $65.5 billion. To help insure against needless rising hospital and tuition bills, and to assist in assuring the optimum results from teaching, medical, and research expenditures, it is desirable, if not imperative, that this large sum of money be spent competently.

All purchasing savings available to industry are also available to schools and hospitals. To attain these benefits, a school or hospital must take three actions:

1 Hire *enough* people to perform the purchasing job well.
2 Compete with industry for *competent* purchasing personnel.
3 Provide a *stimulating environment* in which the people hired will be motivated to do excellent work.

[8]There is already much evidence to indicate that as the nation approaches zero population growth, schools will come under more personal and government pressure to reduce expenditures than will medical facilities. As indicated by footnotes 3 and 10 of this report, the federal government expects only an 11.4 percent growth in education from 1974 to 1980.

[9]U.S. Office of Education, *Projection of Educational Statistics to 1982–83*, 1974, p. 90.

[10]U.S. Social Security Administration, *Office of Research and Statistics, Medical Care Costs and Prices: Background Look*, 1972, p. 90.

[11]U.S. Bureau of Labor Statistics, *The Economy in 1980: A Summary of BLS Projections*, 1970, p. 6.

The American Management Association's "Management Bulletin 33" states that every dollar invested wisely in purchasing should return $3 to $5. Schools and hospitals must understand what industry has understood for a number of years—money spent intelligently for good purchasing is not an *expense*, it is an *investment!*

FOR DISCUSSION

27-1   Explain what a service economy is, and discuss the two fastest-growing service industries in the United States economy.

27-2   Explain why challenging specifications is as important for colleges and hospitals as it is for industrial firms.

27-3   Discuss why conflicts of interest can be more critical in educational and medical purchasing than in industrial purchasing.

27-4   Why is inspection of materials and services sometimes so difficult in universities and hospitals? Explain.

27-5   Explain why reciprocity can take a different form in institutions than in industry.

27-6   What is the most common organizational problem in institutional purchasing? Explain.

27-7   Discuss how the orientation of teachers and scientists who serve in an academic environment differs from that of those who serve in industry. What unique problems does an academic orientation create for purchasing? Discuss.

27-8   Discuss the difficulties of centralizing purchasing in large, research-oriented institutions.

27-9   Explain why pricing for institutions has changed greatly in recent years.

27-10 Explain why materials management progress in institutions usually appears much more advanced than it really is.

27-11 Insurance for institutions can be very important for many reasons. Discuss briefly as many of these reasons as you can.

27-12 Discuss the major problems of institutional purchasing in the areas of remodeling, repair, and new construction.

27-13 Why do institutions operate storerooms? Do required stores stocks have to be physically located at the institution? Explain.

27-14 Discuss the primary auxiliary functions normally associated with institutional purchasing. Why are they important?

27-15 All purchasing savings available to industrial firms are also available to institutions; to attain these benefits, an institution usually must take three actions. Name and discuss these three actions.

CASES FOR CHAPTER 27

Government Purchasing

There is a widespread impression that government purchasing is totally different from industrial purchasing. This impression is not altogether valid. Both government and industrial purchasing are concerned with buying the right quality, in the right quantity, at the right price and time, and from the right source. Government purchasing, however, frequently involves special considerations which are not usually applicable to the purchaser in private industry. It is the purpose of this chapter to examine these considerations and to discuss the major differences and similarities of government and industrial purchasing.

One major government consideration stems from the nature of the items purchased. Federal government purchases include items ranging from the mundane to the exotic—from pencils and paper to supersonic aircraft, sophisticated missiles, and space vehicles. The major portion of military and space purchasing is for technical items involving extensive research and development. Roughly 75 percent of federal government purchasing by dollar value is for *sophisticated and complicated major weapons and space systems* and 25 percent is for *civilian-type commodities.* In state and local governments, purchases are almost exclusively limited to civilian-type commodities. Interestingly, the largest single expenditure of local governments is for construction contracts.

The technical nature of the products purchased is a primary factor which characterizes the federal government purchasing market. The importance of technology in this market can be pinpointed by two facts. First, the money in the federal budget for research and development (R&D) exceeds that spent for R&D by all private industry in the United States. In 1975, R&D expenditures for the Department of Defense (DOD) alone were roughly $17.1 billion; in this same year they were $15.9 billion for all private industry.[1] Second, defense-related industries spend substantially more for R&D than do non-defense industries. Federal government purchasing is greatly influenced by these two facts. For example, in purchasing weapons and space systems, there is almost always a product in view, but the specific nature of the product, for R&D reasons, is generally not known when contractual negotiations take place. When the need for a space vehicle capable of going to the moon first originated, no one knew its final form, what metals would be used in its construction, what instruments would be required for its operation, and so forth.

Another critical difference between industrial and government purchasing is the source of the funds used for the purchases. At all levels of government, taxes paid by citizens and businesses are used to purchase the required materials and services. Usually, government procedures allow the government purchasing manager considerably less freedom of action and discretion than business allows his industrial counterpart. Government procedures stem from specific laws and regulations which require competitive bidding, fixed budgetary limitations, rigid auditing of accounts, and the use of prescribed standard specifications. While these procedures are designed to protect the interests of the taxpayers, they generally result in less flexibility and, in many cases, purchases whose total cost (considering purchase price, inspection costs, installation costs, maintenance costs, and service life) is greater than it would have been had the government used profit-oriented business buying techniques.

For example, over ten years ago, DOD introduced the Life Cycle Costing (LCC) concept of procurement. LCC takes into consideration the total cost of a product over its useful life, not just its purchase price. Under this concept at the time of purchase, DOD considers reliability and maintainability of a product. It also considers the costs of training personnel to operate and maintain differently designed equipments. Additionally, the cost of buying new spare and repair parts for inventory and managing inventories are also considered. The logic of LCC is compelling. It is simply basic, effective purchasing, the kind which industry uses routinely.

DOD's attempt to buy "value" has met with difficulty since its inception. A 1972 GAO report to Congress (B-179214), submitted to encourage the increased use of LCC, reported that during the prior four years only the Air Force could document any savings from LCC, and these savings totaled only $25 million.

DOD is making a concerted effort toward broadening its use of LCC. Success has been achieved for simple procurements such as tires, batteries,

---

[1]U.S. Bureau of the Census, *Statistical Abstract of the United States: 1975.*

filters, and similar items. Success has been more elusive for procurements of complex systems and subsystems. DOD's ability to model and project total ownership costs needs further development. Failure of DOD to more fully utilize LCC constitutes a fundamental difference between government and industrial purchasing.

BACKGROUND

History

The first law dealing with government procurement in the United States was a federal law passed by Congress in 1792. Under this law, the Departments of War and Treasury were given responsibility to make purchases and contracts in the name of the United States. In 1795, a Purveyor of Public Supplies was established in the Treasury Department to act as the government's purchasing agent. In 1798 a separate Department of the Navy was established, and Congress declared "that all purchases and contracts for supplies or services for the military and naval services of the United States should be made by or under the direction of the chief officers of the Departments of War and Navy respectively."

Considering the historic interest of Congress in the profits of contractors, it is interesting to note that the first procurement problems and abuses in government arose out of the activities of congressmen. They used their influence and offices to secure government contracts for their friends and for the firms with which they were associated. This situation resulted in an 1808 law which required the inclusion of a clause in every government contract to stipulate that no member of Congress might benefit therefrom. This clause is still required; it is now known as the "Officials Not to Benefit" clause.

In the early days of the republic, the conduct of both public officials and private business managers left much to be desired. Graft and favoritism in the award of government contracts were commonplace. Incoming administrations investigated the activities of the former administration. The political party out of power kept a watchful eye on the activities of the "ins." Congress soon concluded that the most effective way to prevent procurement abuses was to require that government purchases be made by competitive bids. To implement this conclusion, Congress passed the Procurement Act of March 3, 1809.

The Procurement Act of 1809 established a general requirement that formal advertising be used in the procurement of supplies and services for the government of the United States. Over the next fifty years, a series of additional acts extended and sharpened the requirements for formal advertising to include such techniques as the use of sealed proposals, public bid openings, and financial security from bidders for ensuring contract performance. Most state, county, and city governments have adopted the same principles that have been incorporated into the federal government procurement legislation.

Competitive bidding,[2] with relatively few exceptions, served the federal government effectively and adequately for well over 100 years. The increasing complexities of a rapidly growing technology, however, combined with a dollar volume of purchases undreamed of in the past, caused the competitive bidding system of purchasing to break down (almost to the point of collapse) at the beginning of World War II. As a result of this breakdown, negotiated purchasing, as will be discussed later in the chapter, was in many instances substituted for competitive bidding. Local government procurement was not affected by this circumstance because states and cities do not have the technical problems inherent in federal government procurement.

Public Funds

All buyers are constrained by budgets. Government buyers, however, are constrained to a much greater degree than industrial buyers. For example, industrial buyers typically do not encounter difficulty in obtaining funds to purchase larger quantities of materials unexpectedly offered at greatly reduced prices. Corporate funds can usually be released readily for such advantageous purposes. This is not always the case with government funds. Government buyers operate under a budget which is fixed by a legislative body. To make major changes in government budgets requires additional legislative action, and getting such action is often impossible. The introduction of new legislation can be blocked by established priority procedures, or in some cases the legislature may already have recessed.

Because of a strong desire to control public funds, in approving budgets legislatures often prescribe the precise kinds of materials that can be purchased and the precise ranges of inventories that can be carried. A similar type of restrictive budgetary control is often extended to the internal operations of government purchasing offices. As a result of such controls, one government purchasing office observed by the authors wasted thousands of dollars making automobile trips to convey messages that could have been conveyed at a fraction of the cost by telephone. In this case, the telephone budget was exhausted, but the automobile operating budget was not. Strict audits of government budgets force departmental budgetary compliance, regardless of any innate inefficiencies which exist in the budgets.

The distinction between governmental borrowing power and governmental taxing power also serves as a funding constraint that sometimes results in inefficient purchasing. Traditionally, the borrowing power of governments (particularly local governments) is more tightly restricted than their more flexible taxing power. This distinction in methods of acquiring funds forces many local governments to purchase low-quality, low-priced capital items which have high

---

[2]Formal advertising and competitive bidding over the years grew to be synonymous terms. Actually, competitive bidding can be used in either the formal advertising or the negotiation method of purchasing. The primary difference is that in formal advertising the competitive bids are the last step in price determination, whereas in negotiation they are only the first step.

operating costs and high total costs. In most of these governmental units, the difference between price and value is clearly understood. However, the realities of the political situation sometimes dictate that purchases be made on the basis of price rather than on the basis of value. Voters just naturally resist bond issues.

Personnel

The recruitment, training, and retention of competent personnel, especially at *local* levels of government, often pose a major obstacle to increased efficiency in government purchasing. A personnel system which allows political appointees to fill positions such as "Director of Procurement" or "Director of Supply Management," or even as a purchasing agent, certainly does not enhance the professionalism of the purchasing and materials management function. Even if competent business managers are appointed to these purchasing positions, a person whose tenure is at the sufferance of a political official may have neither the time nor the incentive to do his best. Some steps have been taken to take the politics out of local government purchasing and to improve this problem, but much still remains to be accomplished. Federal government civilian buyers and top supervisors, including even the Deputy Assistant Secretary of Defense for Procurement, are civil service employees, not political appointees. A personnel weakness in the DOD involves the assignment of *unqualified* military officers to key purchasing positions. This practice, however, has been greatly alleviated in recent years. Many military officers currently are eminently qualified by education, training, and experience for procurement assignments.

Standardization

Standardization programs are generally more effective in government than in industry. Centralized public purchasing necessitates standardization. The purchasing requirements of government departments can be effectively consolidated only after it is agreed that all departments will use equipment and supplies having the same specifications. Also, standard specifications are an essential for the widespread use of the competitive bid method of purchasing. Without standardization, the various units of government would inevitably be purchasing myriad different types of equipment and supplies with a resultant high cost of purchasing, inspection, warehousing, and inventory control.

Both the federal government and local governments have standing committees on standards and specifications. On the whole, these committees are extremely effective. The General Services Administration (GSA) of the federal government issues federal specifications for a wide range of common, commercial-type items which are used regularly by all or a large number of federal agencies. To date, GSA has issued roughly 13,260 specifications to cover about 19,340 items. The quality of these specifications is attested by the fact that many have been adopted as industry standards. An index of federal specifications may be obtained from the Government Printing Office, Washington, D.C. Individual specifications may be inspected at the Regional Offices of the GSA and purchased from the General Services Administration Regional Business Service Center, Washington, D.C.

The military departments, under the coordination of the Department of Defense, have also developed large numbers of standardized specifications for technical military supplies and equipments. These specifications (called MIL specs) describe the essential and technical requirements for numerous military items, materials, and services. MIL specs also include inspection procedures, and they may contain preservation, packaging, packing, and marking instructions. In total, there are approximately 17,000 military specifications covering materials in more than 600 federal supply classes. These specifications may be obtained from the Naval Publications and Forms Center, 5801 Tabor Avenue, Philadelphia, Pennsylvania (no charge for individual copies), and from the Global Engineering Documents Services, Inc., 3950 Campus Drive, Newport Beach, California (approximately 10 cents per page).

STATE AND LOCAL GOVERNMENT PURCHASING

General Problems

According to the latest issue of the *Statistical Abstract of the United States*, there are approximately 80,000 governmental bodies in the United States which possess the power to spend. In many states, the chief purchasing officer reports to the Governor. In most of the remainder, he reports to an administrative officer who in turn reports to the Governor. In most county and city governments, the chief purchasing officer reports to the chief administrative officer of those units of government. Hence, the level of reporting in government purchasing is not one of its areas of weakness.

The dollar volume of local government expenditures is considerably higher than is generally believed. Its growing importance is verified by two facts. First, in 1970 for the first time in history, the total dollar value of state and local purchasing exceeded the federal government total. Second, in 1974 it exceeded the federal government total by 35 percent.[3]

The quality of state and local purchasing varies widely, as does the quality of industrial purchasing. There is, however, one significant fact that affects the long-range outcome of these quality differences. If purchasing is not handled with competence in a private business, that particular business generally cannot survive indefinitely. Unfortunately, this is not true in the case of governmental units, since the power to collect taxes is not dependent on the ability to spend tax monies either wisely or efficiently!

There are two continuing factors which especially detract from efficient

---

[3]U.S. Department of Commerce, Bureau of the Census, *Statistical Abstract of the United States*, 1971 and 1974.

and economical purchasing at the state and local level: (1) decentralization, and (2) overly inclusive requirements for competitive bidding. The advantages of centralization are discussed in Chapter 20; therefore, they will not be repeated here. The governmental practice of decentralizing the purchase of major items of equipment, mostly by small political units, is extremely costly. When items such as school buses, bulldozers, and fire engines are authorized for purchase, local government agencies frequently organize "selection committees." These committees are usually composed of the mayor and other town officials. The committees often visit a number of potential suppliers to investigate their plants and products. These visits are supposedly at no expense to the political agency or the committee since the prospective suppliers "pay" all the bills. But the question must be asked: "Who really pays for such trips?" Would their elimination save the taxpayers money? One medium-sized city made known its intention not to accept such "free" trips and saved roughly $5,000 on the purchase price of a new fire engine.

Competitive bidding can and frequently does lengthen the time required to obtain supplies; also, it usually necessitates a need for larger stocks of supplies. Additionally, this method of purchase increases administrative costs because of the need for detailed specifications and increased administrative work. Detailed specifications are designed to protect the purchaser's interest without being overly restrictive, but their preparation presents local engineering staffs with a most difficult challenge. To preclude such difficulties, the Department of Defense raised its limit on the amount of supplies and services which may be purchased through informal competition from $2,500 to $10,000.[4] The National Institute of Municipal Law Officers now recommends that the use of formal bid practices be restricted for most local government requirements to those in excess of $5,000. Nonetheless, some local governments have limits as low as $100.

One of the most widespread and least justifiable practices commonly found in government purchasing is that of protectionism. Examples of this practice include the Buy American Act at the federal level, and the granting of price advantages (averaging roughly 5 percent) to companies within the political jurisdiction of a number of state and city governments. The basic argument for free trade, both domestic and international, was made by Adam Smith in his *Wealth of Nations* in 1776. Smith concluded that specialization and the division of labor with the free exchange of the resulting products makes possible a higher standard of living for everyone. A provision favoring local manufacturers or suppliers over "outside" suppliers is, in effect, a subsidy to the local firms financed directly by the taxpayers. The State of Pennsylvania dramatized its protest of protectionism most effectively by refusing to do business with firms located in states having protectionistic laws favoring

---

[4]A GAO study participated in by one of the authors estimated $270 million could be saved annually in processing costs alone if informal competition limits were raised from $2,500 to $10,000. On July 25, 1974, the President signed into law the bill raising the $2,500 figure to $10,000.

in-state bidders. Protectionism, of course, is sometimes justified for national defense reasons.

Many encouraging trends are taking place in the field of state and local government purchasing. Cities are revising their charters to provide for centralization of the purchasing function. The dollar limit at which formal competitive bidding procedures are required is being raised. Recognition of the importance of purchasing is being reflected in the establishment of important new purchasing positions with top-level salaries and civil service status.

Cooperative Purchasing

Local governments are overcoming some of their purchasing problems through cooperative purchasing. Such purchasing takes one of three forms: (1) full purchasing service, (2) cooperative open-end contracts, and (3) consolidation of requirements under joint bid procedures.

Under *full purchasing service,* local governments purchase from a common warehouse which is operated by another government agency. For example, cities purchase from county warehouses. The prices charged the cities are the same as those charged the county agencies that use the warehouse. Because prices are lower and deliveries often quicker, local governments have a strong incentive to use such warehouses.

Under *cooperative open-end contracts,* the central agency (i.e., city, county, or state) awards contracts which permit other local governments to order directly from the contractor at the same prices quoted to the central agency. Under contracts of this type, local governments gain the advantages of price and service which are the natural result of large-volume contracts. Also, local governments gain the convenience and economies of placing their orders as the items needed are required, rather than having to accumulate their requirements in order to get quantity price breaks.

Under the *joint bid procedure,* a number of government units consolidate their requirements for large joint bids. This procedure necessitates an agreement on the standardization of items and their descriptions, a collection and collation of each individual government's requirements, and a joint call for competitive bids. Thus, an extra administrative workload is imposed on the central activity coordinating the joint bid procedure, but the resultant reductions in prices more than compensate for the added expense. Joint bidding is most effective in the procurement of large items of equipment, such as buses or fire engines, but it is also advantageous for many consumable supplies.

FEDERAL GOVERNMENT PURCHASING

The technical nature of the products purchased and the unique nature of the federal government as a customer combine to distinguish the federal government purchasing market from all other purchasing markets. Much of the distinction between industrial and federal government purchasing stems from the fact that the federal government plays a dual role in contracting. In one role, the government is a sovereign, and as such can determine the *conditions* for doing business in the government market. The government, for example, regulates the actions of its prime contractors, even to the point of determining the manner in which they do business with their subcontractors. As a buyer, the government is unique in its ability to pass laws that influence purchasing transactions. For instance, the government has passed a law that gives its buyers the right to examine its suppliers' records, operating costs, and even their techniques for making management decisions.

In addition to the constraints on the market imposed by the government as a sovereign, there is still another controlling fact that influences government purchasing—the environment of the *technical defense industry* is a "non-market" environment.[5] Many products the government buys are characterized by a marketplace where there are few sellers. "Technological monopoly," therefore, in some sectors of the government market is commonplace. In these sectors, the classical economic guarantee provided by the price mechanism of a free, competitive market structure is often totally lacking. Despite these imperfections of the market, it is a basic objective of the federal government to rely on private industry for government requirements. To achieve this objective, the government has established policies and procedures designed to assure that "the initiative and interest of the individual corporation can be more effectively harnessed to serve the interests of national security."[6]

Procurement Agencies

The four primary agencies of the federal government responsible for procurement are: the General Services Administration (GSA), the Department of Defense (DOD), the National Aeronautics and Space Administration (NASA), and the Energy Research and Development Agency (ERDA).

The General Services Administration is basically responsible for the purchasing of all government departments and agencies except that of the other three primary procurement agencies. Even these three agencies get many of their common supply items from orders placed against numerous GSA open-end contracts. Assume that the NASA facility in Houston, Texas wants to buy a new truck tire. The tire could be obtained by placing an order with a local dealer of one of the national tire companies having a GSA contract. A naval station in California can buy tires under the same type of contract from a local dealer in its area. GSA has many similar open-end contracts for thousands of other common items which are available to all government agencies

---

[5]J. Ronald Fox, *Arming America: How the U.S. Buys Weapons*, Harvard University Press, Cambridge, Mass., 1974. Merton J. Peck and Frederic Scherer, *The Weapons Acquisition Process: An Economic Analysis*, Division of Research, Graduate School of Business Administration, Harvard University, Boston, Mass., 1962.

[6]Ibid., especially chap. 3.

throughout the United States. These contracts are generally made as a result of nationwide, advertised, competitive bidding.

The Department of Defense is the major government procurement agency. Its economic importance is attested by the fact that its annual budget for 1976–1977 exceeds $100 billion, approximately one-third of the total federal budget. Approximately $46 billion of the DOD budget will be used for purchasing materials and services.[7] This is equivalent to approximately 55 percent of total personal consumption expenditures for durable goods in the United States. Despite the size of these figures, the DOD budget as a percentage of the GNP has decreased markedly in recent years. For example, for the past ten years, the DOD budget has averaged roughly 8 percent of the GNP. For the 1976–1977 fiscal year, it will be only 5.9 percent of the GNP—the lowest since 1950. In terms of percentage of the labor force, it will be 4.8 percent for fiscal 1976–1977, the lowest since 1940.[8] Regardless of its significant percentage reduction, DOD remains the largest single purchaser in the United States, and its purchases because of their size are certain to have a significant impact on the nation's business.

Because of its magnitude, the focus of this part of the chapter will be primarily on DOD purchasing. The major problems and principles influencing sophisticated, complicated, major weapons purchasing will be emphasized. However, the problems of commodity-type purchasing will also be explored. This dual treatment of the subject permits a discussion of the many purchasing problems faced by the nontechnical departments of the federal government as well as the technical DOD problems.

Major Defense Contractors

History is replete with society's condemnations of the "munitions makers" of old. Today's munitions maker plays a more acceptable role in society. Regardless of the community in which he is located, he is apt to be that community's major employer. His ability to stay in business no longer depends on a state of war. Rather, he is kept in business by an armed peace. His success in business depends on his ability to hire a diverse but complementary group of highly creative personnel which he can coordinate to produce marketable defense products. Major defense programs such as Minuteman III, Polaris, Poseidon, and Air Combat Fighter (F-16) are typical products of such achievement. These are the kinds of products for which the most successful companies get contracts in the intense, nonprice competition of today's technical defense environment.

Only a very small, select group—the nation's major defense contractors—

---

[7]Another way of highlighting how DOD dominates federal contracting is to realize that in fiscal year 1975 it represented approximately 70 percent of the federal total. The second largest federal contractor, NASA, was only roughly 20 percent as large as any one of the three military departments.

[8]DOD appropriations, Senate Hearings, Part I, 94th Cong., 1st Sess. p. 250.

perceived and acted on the formula for successful government technical contracting in the new era of missiles and satellites. This group, largely the airframe producers of World War II, realized that the contracts of the future would flow to those companies capable of offering an imposing array of top scientific talent, combined with a demonstrated ability to manage complex endeavors. As part of their strategy, these major contractors also developed a strong group of small subcontractors. The perceptiveness of these defense contractors has been rewarded. Since World War II, the bulk of military expenditures has gone to them. During the past five years, the top five defense contractors received an average of 20 percent of all military prime contracts; the top twenty-five contractors received an average of roughly 50 percent; the top 100 received an average of 70 percent (see Table 28-1).

None of the top five companies for defense sales in 1975 can be categorized as nondefense business firms. The companies making up the top five are Lockheed, Boeing, United Technologies, McDonnell-Douglas, and Grumman. Exxon and General Motors, which ranked first and second among United States firms in sales in 1974, ranked nineteenth and twentieth in the list of top defense contractors.[9]

The inherent nature of the goods purchased by DOD assures a skewed distribution of contract dollars. Major weapon and space systems account for many millions of dollars each. Few firms have the manpower, physical capacity, and technological virtuosity required to participate in the research,

Table 28-1   Percentage of DOD Procurement Dollars
Awarded to Contractors Ranked by Dollar Share (FY 1965–1975)*

Rank of company	Fiscal year					
	1965	1971	1972	1973	1974	1975
1st	5.5	5.1	5.1	5.3	5.4	5.3
2nd	4.2	5.0	5.1	4.5	4.3	4.0
3rd	3.4	4.0	3.9	3.9	3.8	3.5
4th	3.5	3.7	3.7	3.6	3.5	3.5
5th	3.2	3.5	3.5	2.8	3.5	3.4
1–5	19.8	21.3	21.3	20.1	20.5	19.7
6–10	11.2	13.5	13.9	11.7	12.8	13.6
11–25	—	17.3	16.0	17.0	17.1	15.3
1–25	48.2	52.1	51.2	48.8	50.4	48.6
26–50	13.0	11.0	11.5	10.4	10.7	11.2
51–75	5.2	5.8	6.0	5.9	5.6	5.6
76–100	2.5	3.2	3.4	3.5	3.2	3.3
1–100	68.9	72.1	72.1	68.6	69.9	68.7

*All procurement actions $10,000 or more.
Source: 100 Companies Receiving the Largest Dollar Volume of Prime Contract Awards, Directorate of Statistical Services, Office of the Secretary of Defense, 1975, p. 1.

[9]"The Forbes Sales 500," *Forbes,* May 15, 1975, p. 159. See Table 28-1.

definition, and production cycle of major weapon and space systems. As a result, there are substantial barriers to both entry into and exit from the markets for major weapon and space systems. Therefore, it should not be surprising that names such as General Dynamics, Lockheed, United Technologies, McDonnell-Douglas, Boeing, and Rockwell International appear year after year in the roster of firms obtaining the largest portion of DOD dollars.

While concentration of economic power is a fact of current American industrial life, there is no other economic concentration as great as that represented by the top defense contractors. Also, no other economic block of comparable size sells to only one customer. The economic and political power potential of this group of concentrated sellers and a single buyer is one which requires constant vigilance. Former President Eisenhower highlighted the importance of this unique situation as follows in his now-famous Farewell Speech as president:[10]

> Now this conjunction of an immense military establishment and a large arms industry is new in the American experience. The total influence—economic, political, and spiritual—is felt in every city, every state, every house, every office of the Federal Government. We recognize the imperative need for this development. Yet we must not fail to comprehend its grave implications. Our toil, resources, and livelihood are all involved; so is the very structure of our society.

The Role of Congress

From the founding of the United States to the beginning of World War II, congressional legislation authorizing and controlling federal procurement was a mass of uncoordinated laws. Each commodity tended to have its own individual set of guidelines. However, there was policy consistency in one respect— advertised bidding was the generally approved method of purchasing. In 1941, immediately following the outbreak of World War II, the First War Powers Act (which authorized negotiation) was hurriedly passed by Congress. Rapidly changing technology made advertised purchasing an unacceptable technique in modern warfare; negotiation had to be authorized.

The General Accounting Office

The General Accounting Office (GAO), an agency of Congress, is headed by the Comptroller General of the United States. The GAO is responsible for auditing the expenditures of the government's executive departments and for ensuring that they have been made in accordance with applicable statutes and appropria-

---

[10]President Dwight D. Eisenhower, Farewell Address, 1961.

tion acts. After examining payments made under government contracts, the Comptroller General may disallow any payment he deems improper. In conducting the examination, he has the authority to audit the books of contractors for some fixed-price and all cost-type contracts. If he finds that a contract is in any way contrary to federal statutes, he has the authority to void the contract. The GAO is commonly called the "watchdog" of the Treasury. GAO auditing methods are strongly disapproved by some members of the business world. They contend that the GAO, under the pretext of validating costs, often in reality is second-guessing past management decisions and attempting to influence future management decisions. The GAO strongly denies this allegation.

In recent years, the character of the GAO has undergone a perceptible change. The GAO is now as concerned with improving the practices under which funds are expended as it is in determining that funds are spent properly. In executing this new, progressive responsibility, the GAO makes in-depth research studies in basic areas of purchasing and materials management. These GAO research studies seek answers to fundamental questions such as, "What dollar limit for purchases made in a manner common in the business world would most ideally balance administrative, control, and pricing costs?" "What effect are budgetary restraints having on proper control of inventories?" "Can effective purchasing be accomplished with lower administrative costs?" As a result of such studies, recommendations for improvement are submitted to the government department(s) concerned, to Congress, or to both—depending on whether administrative or legislative action, or both, are required to effect the recommended improvements. One of the authors participated in several of these studies. From this participation, he can attest to both their high quality and the fact that they have resulted in savings to the government of tens of millions of dollars.

Armed Services Procurement Act of 1947

After World War II, the government faced the problem of returning to peacetime operations and peacetime procurement. To prosecute the war effectively, the rules for government purchasing had been temporarily liberalized. The question raised in 1946 was what rules should apply now that peace had been restored. The war and its realignment of world power produced permanent changes in the mission and responsibilities of the United States government. The nation's armed forces were destined to remain at roughly ten times their prewar size. These forces, spread throughout the entire world, would need vast quantities of supplies and equipment to support them. In addition to changes in size and responsibilities, constantly changing technology also complicated and enlarged the scope of postwar government purchasing. Return to the limited provisions of prewar purchasing legislation was simply out of the question. But what should the new procurement policy be?

After protracted study to determine the best course of action, Congress in 1947 passed the Armed Services Procurement Act.[11] Later in the same year, it passed Public Law 152, which granted the General Services Administration and other federal purchasing agencies permission to negotiate contracts under specific circumstances.

The Armed Services Procurement Act accomplished two major objectives. First, it established workable procurement policies for periods of national emergencies. Either the President or the Congress can put these policies into immediate effect when either thinks the nation is threatened. Second, the law recognized that *negotiated procurement* is a required method of purchase in peacetime as well as in wartime.

The Armed Services Procurement Act of 1947 is part of a new era—an era characterized by unbelievable changes in technology. The act is a compromise, but it is a good, progressive compromise. The act establishes negotiation as a permanent technique, but it retains the advertising procedures as the preferred method of purchasing.

METHODS OF PURCHASING

In recent years, roughly between 12 and 16 percent of the total dollar value of government procurement has been spent by formal advertising; military procurement has averaged roughly 10 percent. The remaining 84 to 88 percent has been spent by negotiation.

Formal Advertising

"Advertised bidding" and "negotiation" have specialized meanings in government purchasing. A knowledge of these meanings is essential to understanding government purchasing. Advertised bidding requires five steps. First, preparation of an invitation for bids (IFB). (The IFB is a complete purchasing package, including all contractual requirements and terms.) Second, distribution of the IFBs to a wide number of bidders. Third, a public opening, reading, and recording of the bids at the place and time set forth in the IFB. Fourth, evaluation of the bids. (Bidders not conforming precisely to the IFB are eliminated. No bidder can change his bid or withdraw from competition once the bids are opened.) Fifth, award of the contract to that responsible bidder whose price is lowest, provided it is deemed reasonable and most advantageous to the government, all factors considered.

In government purchasing there are four widely recognized criteria for

---

[11]This act, now codified as Chapter 137, title 10 of the United States Code, is quite short. It is implemented within the Department of Defense by the Armed Services Procurement Regulations, a ponderous volume of over 3,000 pages, including appendices. In addition, the Army, Navy, and the Air Force each have their own procurement regulations which, in turn, implement the DOD regulations.

using formal advertising. Interestingly, these criteria are not a part of any law or regulation.

1 *Bidder interest.* Two or more suppliers must be capable of supplying the wanted item and be interested in doing so.
2 *Adequate time.* There must be time for formal solicitation and for the delays that frequently develop when procurements are advertised.
3 *Definitive specifications.* The items to be purchased must be so accurately described that all bidders understand precisely what the government wants.
4 *Terms and conditions.* The provision of the purchase must be such that award can normally be made on the basis of the lowest price.

Federal law requires that under formal advertising "award be made to that *responsible* bidder whose bid, *conforming* to the invitation for bids, is most advantageous to the government, *Price and other factors considered."* Despite the broad interpretation which could reasonably be deduced from the language of the law, the common interpretation is that the lowest bidder gets the contract.

The key words in the law are "conforming" and "responsible"; they require amplification. The word conforming means that the bid must be identical or responsive in all major aspects to the invitation for bids. Any major exception makes the bid nonconforming, in which case it must be rejected.[12] The word responsible has been given a similar, rather rigid interpretation. As a result, the natural human response has been a tendency on the part of most contracting officers to follow the line of least resistance. Consequently, most exceptions are treated as disqualifying.

In borderline cases, when marginal suppliers are low bidders, they are often given the contract because of the difficulty of proving "nonresponsibility." The Department of Defense is aware of this problem. To effect progress, major efforts have been made to improve the policy for screening and selecting contractors to ensure that the government deals only with responsible contractors. While these efforts constitute an admission of past difficulties in this important area, it is hoped that they will result in continuing progress.

The key prerequisite to formal advertising is that usually the successful bidder is determined on the basis of price alone. A major shortcoming of this concept can be illustrated by a recent government purchase. The government formally advertised a procurement for steel-tipped cutting tools using a federal specification. The award was made to the low bidder. Industry had lately changed to carbide-tipped tools. The carbide-tipped tools were priced higher than the steel-tipped tools, but their total cost was considerably less. They returned their extra cost by longer life and reduced downtime for setup.

---

[12]It is true that certain minor exceptions can be waived by the government; however, this is a complicated subject, which is greatly influenced by past decisions of the Comptroller General of the United States.

Competitive negotiation would have developed these facts and resulted in the purchase of a higher-priced but a lower-cost item for the government.

There are many cases in which giving a vendor latitude in bidding can save the buyer money. Most purchasing problems have alternative solutions. One university in California, for example, in purchasing its fleet of automobiles, does not restrict the bidding to any specific model or type of car. Dealers and distributors of many cars are requested to bid. The university in evaluating the bids determines the operating cost per mile for each car offered. The determination includes a consideration of initial price, operating cost, depreciation, repair, and trade-in price. Often brands other than the "low-priced three" and models other than the cheapest turn out to be the most economical for the university. Restricting bidding to any group, type, or model of cars would preclude considering such alternatives. In this example of a more flexible type of competitive purchasing, price competition is still important, but other value factors in addition to price are also considered in determining total value and the successful supplier.

The preceding two examples are not intended to imply that there are not many instances in which price can be the controlling factor of a purchase. Rather the examples are cited to point out that governments at all levels frequently and unnecessarily restrict their procedures for competitive bidding. Such restrictions do permit simpler procedures, which in turn can be implemented by buyers with less training and experience. The restrictions in some cases, however, also entail a higher overall cost for materials.

Two-step formal advertising is a relatively new procedure designed to obtain competition under a sealed bid procedure when available specifications are not adequate for conventional formal advertising. In the first step of two-step formal advertising, unpriced technical proposals are solicited and then evaluated to screen out unresponsive proposals and technically nonqualified suppliers. The second step is a competitive sealed bid procedure similar to regular formal advertising, but participation in the second step is limited to those firms that submitted acceptable technical proposals in the first step.

Procurement by Negotiation

In government purchasing by formal bidding, all actions are taken publicly, many suppliers participate, and the contract is awarded to the lowest responsive and responsible bidder. Government purchasing by negotiation is much more flexible. The contracting officer has more freedom in selecting the suppliers to whom he will send invitations. He can negotiate with any offeror submitting a fair offer. Neither the identity nor the number of offerors participating in a purchase must be made public. Offerors can submit revised pricing and technical information as a result of negotiations, as initial bids are not final bids. In short, under negotiated purchasing, the government buyer is less restricted by formal rules and regulations than under formal advertised purchasing. In most negotiated purchases, he is free to act much like an industrial buyer.

The Armed Services Procurement Act permits purchases to be negotiated when certain conditions, or "exceptions," exist. The act states that all procurement will be made by formal advertising unless one of the following seventeen "exceptions" permits negotiation:

Exception 1: a national emergency declared by either Congress or the President. This exception primarily permits the government to act immediately in emergencies without special congressional legislation.

Exception 2: a public exigency. This exception is designed to cover unusual urgencies which, if unsatisfied, will result in the government's being injured, financially or otherwise. This exception typically accounts for less than 5 percent of negotiated expenditures.

Exception 3: purchases of not more than $10,000. This exception reflects congressional recognition that in purchases of relatively small dollar value, the costly and time-consuming requirements of formal advertising should be waived. In a typical procurement year, over 85 percent of all military purchase orders fall within this exception. The total dollars represented by this large percentage of orders, however, is usually only 4 to 5 percent of the total negotiated dollars.

Exception 4: Personal or professional services. This is an insignificant exception from the standpoint of use. It typically accounts for much less than 1 percent of total negotiations.

Exception 5: services of educational institutions. This exception is used to pay tuition fees and to place research contracts with colleges and universities. Typically, around $0.5 billion per year is spent under this exception. This amount is just under 2 percent of the total dollars expended by negotiation.

Exception 6: purchases made outside the United States. This exception covers supplies delivered and used outside the United States, regardless of where the procurement is actually negotiated or executed. Petroleum products account for the largest dollar volume under this exception. In recent years, this exception has accounted for between 3 and 5 percent of total negotiated dollars.

Exception 7: medicines or medical supplies. This exception in total usage accounts for only a small fraction of 1 percent of total negotiations.

Exception 8: supplies purchased for authorized resale. These supplies include brand-name articles demanded by patrons of ships' stores and post exchanges outside the United States. This exception accounts for roughly 1 percent of all negotiated purchases.

Exception 9: perishable or nonperishable subsistence supplies. In a typical year, approximately 4 percent of total negotiations involve such expenditures.

Exception 10: supplies or services impracticable to secure by formal advertising. In a typical year, approximately 150,000 contracts totaling between $8 and $5 billion (30 percent of total negotiations) are placed under this exception. This is the most important exception which can be exercised by a military contracting officer without approval of his service secretary (Secretary of Navy, etc.). As a consequence, this exception is policed stringently by the Department of Defense and by the General Accounting Office.

Exceptions 11 to 15 account for approximately 40 percent of a typical year's negotiated dollar expenditures. Anticipating the importance of these five exceptions, Congress requires all purchases made thereunder to be authorized by Departmental Secretaries. In actual practice, the Assistant Secretary for Installations and Logistics (commonly referred to as the Procurement Secretary) signs the authorizing documents.

Exception 11: experimental, developmental, or research work. This exception is not used for quantity production. However, a research and development contract for a reasonable number of prototypes is not regarded as a production contract. Approximately 15 percent of negotiated dollars are spent under this exception.

Exception 12: classified purchases, or purchases the service secretary determines should not be disclosed for security reasons. This exception is not used when the use of any other exception is possible; consequently, contracts for classified material are usually made under one of the other exceptions. This exception typically accounts for between 1 and 2 percent of the total negotiated dollars.

Exception 13: technical equipment requiring standardization and interchangeability of parts. The purpose of this exception is to permit the armed services to standardize on certain types of equipment to achieve savings in maintenance, inventory, and repair part costs. Since standardization for some types of major equipment restricts competition, this exception has been administered rigidly, with the result that its use has been negligible (less than 1 percent).

Exception 14: technical or specialized supplies whose production requires a substantial initial investment or an extended period of preparation. This exception is used when competitive bidding might require duplication of investment, or preparation already made, or might unduly delay procurement. This important exception typically accounts for 15 to 20 percent of the total negotiated dollars. It is frequently used as an extension of Exception 11. For example, a major weapon system program is usually initiated by using the research and development exception (Exception 11). As the program passes from the test and evaluation stage into production, the negotiation authority would change to Exception 14.

Exception 15: negotiation after advertising. This little-used exception is a safety valve against unreasonable prices and collusion. If a service secretary after formal advertising determines that bid prices are not reasonable, or that they were not arrived at in open competition, he may authorize rejection of all bids, and direct completion of the purchase by negotiation. Use of this exception is limited to a very few cases per year.

Exception 16: purchases in the interest of national defense or industrial mobilization. The intent of this exception is to permit contracts that keep vital production lines in partial or standby operation or that keep a trained nucleus of vital skills available as a basis for industrial mobilization. The exception accounts for 3 to 5 percent of all total negotiated dollars.

Exception 17: as otherwise authorized by law. This exception preserves the statutory authority to negotiate contracts under laws not repealed by the Armed Services Procurement Act. One to two percent of the negotiated dollars are normally expended under this exception.

In summary, the exceptions to formal advertising granted by the Armed Services Procurement Act of 1947 are a recognition that, under some circumstances, competitive bidding is an inefficient way of purchasing. More importantly, the act recognizes the technological realities of the twentieth century. Complex items such as weapon systems whose ultimate designs cannot be known in advance simply cannot be purchased intelligently or economically under advertised procurement. Also, the legislation recognizes negotiation as being economical in the purchase of some commercial-type items.

Despite its legal acceptance, negotiation remains an ugly and misunderstood word in some government and publishing circles, where the term is treated as a synonym for secrecy. The impression is fancifully created that the government contracting officer, using negotiation as a guise, furtively meets with a favored contractor and offers him a contract, in preference to more worthy competitors who would surely "win" the contract under formal bidding. When reviewed objectively, this implication is found to have no basis in fact, as the discussion to follow will clearly show.

Sole-Source Negotiation

Negotiation takes two basic forms: *sole-source* and *competitive.* Sole-source negotiation is negotiation with a single supplier. The high dollar contracts for major weapon systems fall into this category. Such negotiations, however, do not start as sole-source negotiations. Rather, they start as intensely competitive negotiations. All potential suppliers considered capable of designing and manufacturing a desired weapon system compete. Competition is primarily in the design and management areas. Only after the overall most competent supplier is selected from among all competitors do sole-source negotiations commence. It is important for the reader to understand that in large weapon systems contracts many business review boards, many technical review boards, and finally the service secretaries themselves participate in contractor selection. In extremely important cases, the selection is made by the Secretary of Defense or by the President.[13] The contracting officer does not by himself make major decisions concerning large or important sole-source–negotiated weapon systems contracts.

It is also important for the reader to understand that weapon systems

---

[13]For an interesting account of this process, the reader is referred to "The $7-Billion Contract That Changed the Rules," *Fortune*, April 1963, p. 110.

purchases are all made at the highest levels of the Military Services. Also, at these levels, the Services' top managerial, technical, purchasing, financial, and production talent are all available, and all are heavily involved with these purchases. Weapon systems purchases consist of a small number of contracts, which average tens of millions of dollars, and which collectively total billions of dollars. These purchases are at one extreme of a range of DOD purchases, with the minor purchases made for ship and base operations being at the other extreme.

Detailed procedures for conducting actual negotiations vary slightly among the three military departments, but all use the "team approach." The negotiating team consists of a combination of engineers, technicians, lawyers, and accountants, with the contracting officer serving as team captain. The captain's primary responsibility is to weld this group of highly individualistic professional people into an effective negotiating unit for the government. The contractor has a team, similarly staffed, to conduct his end of the negotiations.

Chapter 6 explored in depth the superiority of effective competition as the most practical single means of establishing a reasonable price. Despite competition's superiority in this regard, approximately 40 percent of all defense contract dollars are placed by using sole-source negotiation—theoretically the least desirable method of DOD purchasing. Two compelling and overriding facts dictate this situation:

1 Price competition is impossible when the ultimate design of the product being purchased is not known. Weapon systems purchases are further complicated because traditionally these purchases take four to ten years to complete, and technical advances continually evolve all during this period.
2 Because of the complexity and cost of the special equipment required to manufacture most weapon systems, not to mention set-up and personnel training costs, duplication of this costly equipment to obtain two suppliers can seldom be economically justified.

Sole-source negotiation, however, does not mean that the government does not buy at reasonable prices. Instead, it means that prices must be negotiated, rather than determined by competition and the free market. Generally speaking, for sole-source negotiations, the government relies on price analysis for pricing purchases of under $100,000 and cost analysis for pricing purchases exceeding $100,000.

Estimating the cost of a weapon system is obviously very different from estimating the cost of a product whose design has been firmly established. A good cost estimator can reliably price most industrial items having firm designs within an error range ± 10 percent. However, errors in estimating the cost of a new weapon system on occasion have run to 10 times (1,000 percent of) the original estimate.[14] Although errors of 300 percent have not been uncommon, most errors are well below 100 percent. With errors of this magnitude possible, however, placing contracts for such materials on a basis of competitive bidding would be foolhardy. The primary reason errors of such magnitudes are possible is that weapon systems contractors do not usually have a firm statement of the work involved. Nor can they have such a statement in most cases; hence, they cannot estimate costs accurately. Military urgency frequently does not permit waiting for a firm "definition of requirements." The DOD is acutely aware of this situation, and weapon systems plans, whenever possible, are being made further in advance. As a result, cost estimating is becoming increasingly more accurate.[15]

A weapon system supplier for the most part is evaluated according to its ability to perform within each of three parameters: time, quality, and cost. The government assigns different weights to each of these parameters, but in total they determine the satisfactory fulfillment of a contract. For one contract, ability to produce at a low cost may be more important than ability to meet a rigorous delivery schedule. For another contract, the major factor may be the ability of the contractor to produce a desired technological advance. The relative importance of time, cost, and quality depends upon each specific procurement situation, as does the amount of uncertainty associated with anticipated R&D results.

Despite its shortcomings, the best minds of government and industry have not been able to develop a better purchasing method than sole-source negotiation for purchasing weapon systems and similar industrial items involving design and production unknowns.

Competitive Negotiation

Government sole-source negotiated procurement, as previously indicated, is unique. Government competitive negotiated procurement, on the other hand, is quite similar to industrial procurement. The major difference between industrial and government competitive negotiation lies in the extent rather than in the form of its use. Industry uses competitive negotiation much more extensively than does government. For large purchases, government is forced to use advertised procurement in some situations where negotiation is obviously

[14]Charles H. Hitch and Roland N. McKean, *The Economics of Defense in the Nuclear Age,* Harvard University Press, Cambridge, Mass., 1960, p. 189.

[15]These large errors are factual; however, it is important to note that they are principally program and budget estimating errors. They are not contract pricing errors. Also, it is interesting to note that large cost errors for systems contracts are not limited to government contracts. Industry makes many similar errors. For example, the percentage cost error of building the San Francisco Bay Area Rapid Transit System far exceeded most comparable DOD errors. Many new atomic generating plants are missing their estimated costs by several hundred percent. The simple fact is that estimating costs for complex, technical systems of any kind for which no previous production experience exists entails an error risk of considerable magnitude.

preferable from a professional purchasing viewpoint. For negotiations under $10,000, government procedures are very similar to industry's. Competitive negotiations are used principally for purchasing commercial-type items; however, they are also used for purchasing some military items.

Publicity is a problem in some government competitive negotiations. All unclassified negotiated awards of more than $25,000 are publicized in the Department of Commerce's *Commerce Business Daily.* This means that competitors know the prices at which awards for these contracts are made. The prices of all offerors are not publicized (as in the case of advertised bidding), only the price of the successful firm. Revealing prices is a practice that seldom helps a buyer; however, in some situations it can hurt him badly. For many reasons, a vendor may be willing temporarily to price specific materials substantially "below the market." However, the vendor does not want either his other customers (who might demand similar prices) or his competitors (who might take economic advantage of him) to know this fact. Knowing that the government reveals prices, a vendor when having a choice would normally prefer to do business with an industrial buyer. If he does bid on a government competitive negotiated procurement, it will possibly be at prices higher than would be the case were there no fear of price disclosure.

Preaward Approval

A government contract bears but a single signature for the government, the signature of the contracting officer. Before signing negotiated contracts over a certain dollar value, however, the contracting officer must get approval from higher management levels. Requests for approval take the form of lengthy justifications, including all pertinent background information on the price and other important considerations of the negotiations. The approval itself is called preaward approval or clearance. The contracting officer, therefore, must not only reach agreement with the contractor, he must also obtain approval for the agreement he has negotiated from professional reviewers in his own department.

It should now be evident that there can be nothing secret or preferential in a procurement system that involves so many individuals and groups of individuals from source selection, through negotiation, through chains of review, to final approval. The question is really not one of secrecy, but rather how does anything ever get accomplished with so many people in the act! *A letter contract* (though generally disliked by the government) is one key. This instrument is a practical device for getting things started, while still preserving time for negotiation of price and other contractual terms later. Letter contracts authorize contractors to proceed with development and production preliminaries while the actual details of a final contract are being worked out. Although many major military contracts begin with letter contracts, and their extensive use in wartime is inevitable, greater use of advanced planning has meaningfully reduced their numbers in peacetime.

Purchasing Safeguards

Members of Congress and the nation's press have made repeated charges concerning excessive profits from government *negotiated* contracts. These charges have led to congressional investigations and corrective legislation. The fact per se that the dollar value of purchases by the federal government is so large—over $60 billion in 1975—makes potential profiteering by government contractors a problem of enormous dimensions. Because defense purchases represent the largest single part of federal government expenditures for materials and services, congressional attention directly and through its audit agency, the GAO, has logically focused on DOD procurement activities.

The DOD purchases a large number of unique or semiunique products or weapon systems. These items frequently are being manufactured for the first time; therefore, the normal economic factors of supply and demand seldom create a competitive price environment for such purchases. Because of the unique technical skills required to manufacture these items, or because of a particular kind of product, there is frequently only one acceptable supplier. As a result of a lack of market competition, prices have to be determined from extensive negotiations—negotiations which are based on analyzing previous costs of similar items or projections of future costs extrapolated from known costs. The critical cost data controlling these negotiations are invaribly provided by the contractors. These firms are naturally much better informed than the government concerning the specific cost patterns of the products they manufacture. Purchases of these unique-type items represent many billions of dollars (roughly one-third of the DOD total). Consequently, these purchases provide dishonest, misinformed, or inefficient contractors an opportunity for making excessive profits by simply overstating their cost and pricing data.

To help overcome this undesirable situation, Congress, in 1962, passed Public Law 87–653, better known as the Truth in Negotiations Act. This act was designed to place the government buyer in a more equal bargaining position with the contractor (who in the past held all the trump cards of cost). The act established the requirement that for *noncompetitive* negotiated contracts of over $100,000, contractors must furnish the government buyer complete, accurate, and current data on appropriate costs. Additionally, the act requires contractors to certify that, to the best of their knowledge and belief, all data furnished is current, accurate, and complete. Lastly, the act provides that all applicable contracts must contain a clause requiring readjustment of the contract price whenever it can be shown that the contracting data were noncurrent, inaccurate, or incomplete.

The DOD is intensely interested in the capabilities of the purchasing departments of its contractors. This is as it should be, for these departments actually spend about one-half of the total DOD contract dollars. To ensure contractor efficiency, DOD makes regular reviews of the purchasing departments of all its suppliers with contracts totaling $5 million or more per year. Also, DOD reviews all their proposed subcontracts when the dollar value is substantial, or when there is inadequate price competition. Among the key elements reviewed by DOD when evaluating its contractors' purchasing departments are the degree of price competition obtained, the educational and experiential level of the purchasing department's top managers, where the departments report in the organizational structure of the firm (if it's too low, the contractor's top management is urged to raise it); the adequacy of the department's policies and procedures, top management's attitude toward its firm's purchasing operations, the extent to which purchasing participates in make-or-buy decisions, the extent to which purchasing controls the administration of subcontracts, and the effectiveness of the contractor's value analysis program and the extent of his suppliers' participation in it. In this excellent practice of evaluating thoroughly the purchasing departments of its largest suppliers, government leads industry.

Negotiation Not Favored

Regardless of the financial and business advantages that negotiation frequently offers the government, Congress simply does not seem to favor negotiated procurement. In the light of this fact, most government contracting officers, to escape criticism, lean over backward to use formal advertised procurement whenever possible. *This approach to selecting purchasing methods is in marked contrast to industrial purchasing practice and sound purchasing theory. The practice constitutes a major difference between industrial and government purchasing.*

SOURCES OF SUPPLY

Source Selection

The degree of freedom that exists in selecting sources of supply offers another excellent example in contrast between industrial and government buying. The industrial buyer is free to choose suppliers on the basis of total value. In addition to price, total value includes factors such as quality, responsiveness, capability, dependability, service, maintenance costs, attitude toward customers, competitive prices, and reciprocity.

Under formal advertising, source selection by a government buyer is largely an automatic process, quite independent of his decision-making authority, except in nonresponsive and nonresponsible situations. Under negotiated procurement, the contracting officer in theory has authority to select the suppliers with whom he feels it is best for the government to do business. In actual practice, the freedom afforded in negotiation is directly restricted by legislation and indirectly restricted by various procedural requirements.

For example, most purchases exceeding $10,000 must be given advance publicity in the *Commerce Business Daily.* Advance publicity on purchases of lesser amounts, although not required, is strongly encouraged. In addition, Small

Business Seminars are continually held to encourage small suppliers to join the ranks of government contractors. The inevitable effect of this open—door policy of bidder recruitment is to load bidders' lists with suppliers of marginal and submarginal ability. This is not to imply that awards must be made to marginal suppliers, or that they are routinely low bidders, or that the seminars attract only inept suppliers. Fortunately, none of these situations is factual. Nevertheless, a policy of constantly increasing the bidders' lists adds to the cost of government overhead and tends to create an "unreliable bidders" problem.

Much emphasis is given to the *rights* of a citizen to share in the government's procurement dollar. Unfortunately, very little emphasis is given to his *responsibilities*. When government contracts are given to inefficient or high-cost producers, the excess costs of such actions are paid with taxes from the pockets of all citizens.

Laws Affecting Sources

Many laws and executive orders influence government purchasing. A large number of these laws and orders are designed to achieve socioeconomic goals. Examples of laws and executive orders with such goals are the Walsh-Healey Act, Davis-Bacon Act, Fair Employment Practices Act, Buy American Act, and Equal Employment Opportunity Executive Order.

There are, however, two laws in addition to the Armed Services Procurement Act that have special impact on government purchasing operations. These laws are the Small Business Act and the Labor Surplus Area Section of the Defense Production Act.

Small Business Act: Set Aside and Non-Set Aside Procurement   The desire of Congress that small business should receive a fair share of the government's procurement dollar is expressed in the Armed Services Procurement Regulations and the Small Business Act.[16] Procurement requirements selected as having small-business application are of two types: those assigned solely to small-business competition and those divided between big and small business.

If previous experience indicates that there are enough small firms interested in and capable of performing any given procurement, that procurement can be assigned to small business only. Theoretically, the government might pay premium prices for materials purchased in this manner since big business could conceivably supply such materials at lower prices. Although sufficient evidence is not available to support a definite conclusion that higher prices are paid, enough real and circumstantial evidence does exist to support a logical

---

[16]A small business is defined in general terms as a firm independently owned and operated, not dominant in the field in which it is bidding, and having total dollar receipts, depending on the industry, below an amount specified by the Small Business Administration. There are special definitions tailored to the peculiarities of specific industries, e.g., construction, dredging, petroleum, and small arms.

suspicion that higher prices probably are paid. Consider the following example of existing evidence: contrary to instructions, big business firms on occasion unwittingly bid on purchases restricted solely to small business firms. In these cases, the prices bid by the larger firms invariably are lower then those bid by competing small firms. Consider an example of existing circumstantial evidence, which stems from a research study (of numerous small-business contracts for repairs to major weapon systems) in which one of the authors participated. The prices paid under many of these contracts were compared with the prices paid to big business for similar contracts. In many instances, the prices paid to the small business firms appeared to be substantially higher than those paid to big business firms for similar purchases. Conclusive research studies, based on incontrovertible evidence, seem highly desirable in this important area of government purchasing.

If the total quantity to be purchased is too large for small business alone, but small business can handle part of it, the procurement is divided. Divided requirements are portioned on a *set aside* and *non-set aside basis.* The non-set aside portion is solicited by free, competitive advertised procurement. All small business firms wishing to be considered for the set aside portion must bid with big business on the non-set aside portion. When award prices for the non-set aside portion are known, the small business concerns whose bids are not more than 30 percent above these prices are given the opportunity of matching them, i.e., small business can have the set aside portion of the contract at the same price paid for the non-set aside portion. As awards to small and big business are made at identical prices, the government does not pay a premium price for materials purchased in this manner.

The Labor Surplus Program　This program provides special consideration to firms in areas designated as labor surplus areas by the Labor Department. Essentially, all purchases exceeding $10,000 are screened to ensure that portions of these purchases are set aside for suppliers in labor surplus areas. A firm that is a small business and is also located in a surplus area gets top priority in a set-aside purchase.

In recent years, the DOD has become active in the government's efforts to create employment in areas of concentrated unemployment or underemployment where the problem is particularly acute with respect to the hard-core disadvantaged. Such areas, when so designated by the Secretary of Labor, "take priority over the present types of persistent and substantial labor surplus area concerns in partial set-aside sections.[17]

Perspective　To keep this part of the discussion in perspective, the reader should understand that socioeconomic programs are important, but not vital in their effect on government purchasing. This is because these programs affect only a very small portion of total government procurement dollars. The

---

[17]*Armed Services Procurement Regulations,* 1975.

programs do increase administrative expense, and in some cases they increase prices, but their greatest impact is to frustrate government buyers. Any restriction that limits a buyer's use of judgment in selecting suppliers (a basic purchasing responsibility) tends to make the buyer an automaton, rather than an intelligent, imaginative contracting officer. Unfortunately, this damaging side effect to government purchasing is not always considered or understood by legislators and administrators when they dictate additional buyer constraints.

Small-business and labor surplus area programs are typical of the programs that have been superimposed upon the government's purchasing effort. Whether these programs produce sufficient national political and social advantages to offset their additional costs to procurement is unknown. However, the basic questions are, "Should the government deliberately use its business functions inefficiently to accomplish political and social goals? Or, would it really be more economical to accomplish these same goals by other methods?" Unfortunately, those who attempt to answer these questions speak usually more from intuition and emotion than from an exhaustive body of evidence. It is unfortunate, indeed, that comprehensive research studies have not been made to assist in directing national policy in this important and potentially costly area of government responsibility.

Summary of Source Selection

It is clear that under advertised procurement government buyers do not have the same freedom as industrial buyers to choose sources of supply. In some cases under negotiated procurement, government buyers have complete freedom of choice; in others they do not. Therefore, in the aggregate, *the industrial buyer enjoys a far greater degree of freedom in choosing his suppliers than does his government counterpart.* This freedom to select suppliers, which in industry is considered a basic purchasing prerogative, is another major difference between government and industrial purchasing.

GOVERNMENT CONTRACTS

Types of Contracts

During the past ten years, the government in some degree has used the entire range of contract types discussed in Chapter 7. Fixed-price-type contracts were used for roughly 75 percent of the total dollar value of all purchases. Cost reimbursement contracts were used for roughly 24 percent, and the time and materials and labor hour contracts were used for the remaining 1 percent.[18] During these ten years, government procurement officials strived diligently to maintain the above percentage distribution and to minimize the use of cost-type

[18]*Military Prime Contract Awards*, DOD, Office of The Secretary of Defense, pp. 60–62, 1974.

contracts (it was only a short time ago that cost-type contracts equaled 50 percent of total dollar purchases). Also, during the past ten years, top DOD procurement officials introduced many policy changes to assist in minimizing the use of cost-type contracts. These procurement officials also successfully implemented a new dimension in DOD purchasing—the use of advanced business management techniques (i.e., a rigorous, tough-minded, quantitative approach to decision making). These techniques provide, first, for unprecedented *preplanning* in weapons development and, second, for close observance of each stage of a major contract's progress, from design through production. By requiring contractor's cost and schedule control systems to meet specified criteria, DOD is increasingly able to monitor a supplier's production efficiency and production costs. As a result of this DOD capability, suppliers are forced to analyze, to innovate, and thus to become capable of producing an increasing number of high-quality products at firm prices.

For example, in purchasing the nuclear-power aircraft carrier *Enterprise,* it took the Navy's Ship Systems Command and the Newport News Shipbuilding Company nine months of preplanning to formalize a contract. To permit the cost calculations required to use a fixed-price incentive contract, 4,500 individual cost centers were isolated. Preplanning in this purchase rewarded both the government and the supplier. The cost of the *Enterprise* to the government was well below the target price of $209 million. The profit to the supplier, as a result of his efficiencies, was well above that originally estimated.

On its effort to shift from cost to fixed-price contracts whenever possible, DOD achieved a reduction of "sole sources" for many repair parts. Repair parts were separated from their sole-source equipments and identified either by design specifications or by their original manufacturer's description. The separation of parts from equipment and the use of commercial identification permitted competition. This in turn produced price reductions that average 25 to 50 percent.

Because the majority of defense dollars are spent through negotiated contracts, great emphasis is rightly placed on a careful selection of the best type of contract to use. The cost-plus-fixed-fee (CPFF) contract offers the contractor little incentive to reduce the costs incurred in the performance of a contract. In fact, negative incentives may develop which lead to increased costs. Nonetheless, when proper controls and surveillance are established, this method of contracting is effective.

The paramount advantage of all fixed-price contracts (and cost incentive contracts to a degree) is that a contractor's profit is not a predetermined amount which remains unchanged regardless of how well or how poorly he performs his contractual obligations. Rather, under these contracts profit is an amount which varies proportionally to the contractor's efficiency or ineffiency. This method of determining profit is in consonance with capitalism's basic premise that the reward of profit and the fear of loss are the best possible motivators for stimulating production efficiency.

DOD has not solved the basic problem of the correct contract types to use in purchasing major weapons. In fact, this is a problem which can never be fully solved. Solution of the problem is impossible because the basic responsibility of the nation's largest buyer is to *defend* well—to buy well must come second.

Renegotiation

The Renegotiation Act gives the government the authority to examine the costs of sales to the government in those companies whose aggregate government business exceeds $1 million a year. The act also allows the government to renegotiate any "excess" profits resulting from such sales. Any profit considered to be in excess of a "fair profit" is recaptured by this process and deposited in the public treasury. The primary purposes of the Renegotiation Act are to provide a substitute for competitive pressures on prices and costs and to prevent profiteering. Renegotiation is not performed on a contract by contract basis. Rather, all of a firm's business subject to renegotiation is examined as a whole. Excessive profits on one contract can be balanced by losses on other contracts.

In contrast to the Renegotiation Board's authority to view contracts as a whole, the military services are compelled to view each contract individually. The money recovered from renegotiation is deposited in the United States Treasury; it is not returned to the appropriate service. Hence, renegotiation does not provide a basis for the services to neglect close pricing on the premise that "we will recover our mistakes later." There is no "later" for the individual services.

GOVERNMENT SPECIFICATIONS AND QUALITY

Design Specifications

A design specification provides a complete description of the item wanted. It also lists the composition of the materials to be used, their size, shape, and method of fabrication. Any competent manufacturer having the specifications and the required equipment can make the item. When a purchaser develops his own design specifications, he avoids the duplication of development work by the bidders. Additionally, the use of such specifications permits wide competition among firms not having the scientific or engineering staffs to do their own product development work. Further, design specifications permit formal advertising as an appropriate method of purchase because bidders can quote on exactly the same item.

During a *seller's market*, buyers usually, but not always, get reasonable prices on materials purchased by design specifications. Profits are generally fair, and both efficient and inefficient producers get orders.

During a *buyer's market*, the situation usually changes. Bidding on design specifications normally becomes extremely keen. To be low bidder in such a market, few firms are able to quote prices which permit the recovery of all costs, much less include a profit. Competition sometimes forces suppliers to quote prices that cover all out-of-pocket costs, but only as much overhead cost as they think necessary to get the contracts. Economic survival forces normally disinterested firms to seek government business. Although this system of purchasing does assure the lowest possible prices to the government, it also creates problems. When faced with tight contract prices, suppliers natually take every possible measure to minimize costs (and sometimes losses).[19] Ethical manufacturers are stimulated to operate as efficiently as possible. Less scrupulous suppliers have an incentive to cut every possible corner on quality. Industrial purchasers can avoid this latter problem of less desirable suppliers by a careful preselection of prospective suppliers, but the government cannot.

The government is frequently criticized for its elaborate and lengthy specifications. Such specifications are a normal outgrowth of the advertising method of purchase and its overemphasis on the lowest price. To be the low bidder, advertised purchasing practically challenges marginal manufacturers to find and exploit loopholes in government specifications. As these manufacturers are successful in their search, the practice is detected, and the loophole is closed. This process breeds a sequential cycle of evasion and detection which generates increasingly detailed specifications.

Performance Specifications

A performance specification expresses the government's requirement in terms such as capacity, function, or operation. Under this type of specification, the details of design, fabrication, and internal structure are left primarily to the option of the contractor. For common equipment such as automobiles, tractors, and trailers, performance specifications permit competition among manufacturers already having products available in the commercial market. Each manufacturer's equipment can differ in design specifications, yet still compete under the government's performance specifications. For most standard commercial products, each manufacturer is tooled up to make equipment to his own design. The cost of changing this tooling to permit equipment to be manufactured to government design specifications would be a needless waste. It is more logical for Caterpillar, International Harvester, and John Deere to compete on performance specifications than it is for the government to design a tractor and then pay the higher prices that would attend nonstandard production.[20]

---

[19]One of the authors is familiar with an example that illustrates this point. The Navy gradually converted almost all of its shipboard lighting from incandescent to fluorescent. A series of lighting fixtures were developed, tested, and completely described by drawings and specifications. The initial purchase price for a 4-foot fixture was $40 per unit. Unit costs were successively reduced over a six-year period (during which time raw material prices were gradually increasing) to $36, $32, $28, $24, and finally to a price of $16.75 for a quantity of 20,000. A audit of production costs on this last contract showed that tooling, direct labor, and material costs alone amounted to $17.12 per unit.

[20]A typical exception to this general rule is the purchase of certain military trucks. These trucks purchased to detailed military specifications can be purchased at low prices because of their great volume.

Performance specifications are used almost exclusively in the procurement of major weapon systems, as no commercial designs are available for these products. In using performance specifications for weapon systems, the principal problem is to select a supplier who is technically, managerially, and financially qualified to design and manufacture the product wanted.

Quality of Government-purchased Items

To obtain materials of the desired quality, it is essential in government purchasing that specifications be developed with great care and completeness. However, some quality characteristics are extremely difficult to define precisely. For example, how sharp is "sharp"? How free of defects is "reasonably free of defects"? Or where does a "minor defect" end and a "major defect" begin? How can such qualities be measured? These questions illustrate why writing specifications is so difficult.

In industry, suppliers have a strong incentive to interpret specifications in a way that is fully satisfactory to the buyers. If a supplier's product turns out to be unsuitable for the purpose intended, the supplier knows the buyer is free to take his future business elsewhere. This ability motivates a rational supplier to take the initiative in clarifying questionable specifications or to make adjustments when failures do occur. For example, a household furnishings contractor recently supplied the draperies for a plush new apartment house in San Francisco. A few weeks after installation, the draperies shrank 9 inches. The apartment-house owner asked the contractor for a replacement. The contractor made the same request to the textile mill that manufactured the cloth. The mill initially refused, explaining that the cloth was not preshrunk because the specifications did not call for preshrinking. The contractor admitted the mill was technically right, but implied that if the mill stood on this "technically right" position, future business relationships could be affected. The contractor contended that the mill, as a capable supplier, should have known that preshrunk cloth is a necessity for foggy areas such as San Francisco, regardless of any omission in the specifications. The mill subsequently replaced the drapery material.

The government, on the other hand, is normally not free to take its business elsewhere as a result of such experiences. In similar situations involving the government, a contractor can, and often does, contend that his product meets the specifications and that he is a fully reliable supplier. He disclaims any responsibility for his product not being serviceable, maintaining that his responsibility does not extend beyond meeting the specifications. He challenges the government to prove otherwise. The government's usual recourse to such experiences is to redraft the specifications in the hope that next time there will be no loopholes. In the absence of being able to prove clearly that the contractor has not met the specifications, the government must accept delivery of the product, and keep the supplier on the bidders' list as a qualified vendor in good standing.

Despite the government's difficulties in preparing foolproof design specifications, the conclusion should not be drawn that the government routinely gets cheated on quality. That government specifications are not perfect is undeniable. The government's cost of inspection to enforce compliance of quality, under a system that lets sellers choose the buyer rather than vice versa, is obviously high. On the other hand, the quality of many government specifications is attested by the fact that private industry accepts many of these specifications as its own standard of quality. On a product-by-product basis, the prices the government pays and the quality it receives are generally satisfactory—in most cases, both compare favorably with those of private industry. In some cases, however, government prices are higher than industry's; in others, they are lower. Generally speaking, most industrial purchasing managers can learn much about the difficult art of specifications writing from their government counterparts, who perforce must truly be experts in this field.

VOLUME OF PAPERWORK

Critics frequently suggest that the government reduce the size of its paper volume (red tape). It is true that for large purchases the government frequently uses 12,000 sheets of paper in situations where industry would use less than 100 sheets of paper. It must be remembered, however, that in a typical year roughly 90 percent of all government purchases (by numbers) are under $10,000, and these purchases are made in essentially the same manner as industry would make them.

A common item such as paint can be used to illustrate the paperwork involved in a typical commodity-type purchase of large dollar value. For such a purchase, the government would use advertised purchasing. The invitation for bids would consist of at least three parts: cover sheet, mandatory clauses, and a schedule. On the average, these three parts would require 10 to 12 pages. If special instructions were necessary, the number of parts and pages would increase.

Part I, the cover sheet, gives the vendors broad general information such as the name of the buying agency, where to send the bids, and the time of bid openings. Part II includes the mandatory clauses commonly called "boiler plate." These clauses are those required either by statute or by executive order (the examination of records clause, Buy American Act, the Eight-Hour Law, etc.). Part III, the schedule, sets forth the most important port of the invitation. It includes specifications, quantities, delivery dates, delivery locations, marking and shipping instructions, inspection instructions, and so forth. Invitations for bids (remember each set has roughly 10 to 12 pages) are normally prepared in sets of three or four (30 to 48 pages) per bidder.

For large procurements, bids are usually sent to all firms on the bidders' list. The bidder gets one to three sets, depending on the issuing agency or department. Customarily, for supply-type items, only 15 to 20 percent of the bidders respond. This means that 80 to 85 percent of those on the bidders' list do not choose to participate in any specific procurement. The question natually arises, "Why then send bids to the entire list?" The answer: For large purchases, it is cheaper and more efficient to do this than to attempt selectivity.

For small purchases, government buyers can send bids to a selective group of bidders—provided the list is rotated in such a manner as to assure equal opportunity eventually to all bidders. For common items with many manufacturers, such as paint, the bidders' list frequently consists of 500 or more firms. To attempt to use a selected group from such a list for a large purchase would be unsuccessful, harrowing, and costly. The national publicity given to procurements over $10,000 would quickly inform the omitted vendors that they did not receive an invitation to bid. Almost in unison, with self-righteous indignation, they would, via telegram, letter, or their congressmen, demand an opportuntity to participate. The purchasing officer would have no alternative but to grant their requests, and most likely he would have to postpone the bid opening to do so. In many cases, he would also have to write letters explaining why the suppliers did not get a bid form in the first place. Most government buyers have only to suffer such an experience once to learn the wisdom of overusing rather than underusing the bid list.

After the awards are made, the paper mill again starts grinding. Multiple awards are commonplace, and each award produces a need for at least fifty copies of each contract. Inspectors, receiving personnel, inventory managers, supply managers, and finance officers must all be provided with copies.

On occasion, short cuts to paper usage are achieved. Nonetheless, when it comes to paper consumption, the government procurement system stands guilty as charged. It does use considerably more paper than industry uses to process similar purchases. Nonetheless, in recent years the government has made noteworthy progress in reducing its annual purchasing administrative costs by many millions of dollars. These savings have resulted from actions such as reducing the size of solicitation packages, reducing the number of solicitation packages sent to vendors, referencing required clauses rather than detailing them in their entirety, not furnishing solicitation packages to requesting firms that obviously do not have a technical capability to perform the contract, and by using the master solicitation technique (distributing to firms on a one-time basis any clauses, certifications, representations, and requirements that are repeated in solicitation after solicitation).

What about pricing for purchases involving high paper usage? The government generally gets excellent pricing for its large purchases. As a matter of policy, some companies (particularly the industrial giants) offer their lowest prices to the government. It is a statistical truth that the larger the number of bidders solicited the greater is the probability of obtaining a lower price. For this reason, an industrial buyer increases his number of bidders for large purchases, but he seldom uses more than six to eight bidders. The increased cost of dealing with a much larger number of bidders would ordinarily offset the advantage of a slightly lower price.

AWARD LEAD TIME

Total procurement lead time includes administrative lead time. Therefore, total lead time for requisitioners can be reduced by either improved administrative scheduling or by carrying larger inventories of materials in stock.

As insurance against national emergencies, the military services must carry large inventories of many strategic items. No one questions the necessity for these inventories. However, perceptive government critics do question whether the government always differentiates wisely between "strategic military items" and "common items." The strategic items must be carried in inventory. The common items do not have to be so carried; they are kept in inventory out of choice, not necessity. The critical question is, "Cannot the needed reserves of common items be carried more economically in the nation's regular distribution channels than in government warehouses?" The DOD recognizes this problem, and its recent policy guidelines favor a greater use of commercial facilities. However, this is another significant government materials management area where sufficient evidence is lacking to answer realistically this critical question. Additional research studies in this important area could be helpful in directing national policy.

A representative example can illustrate the lead time problem. Suppose a government purchasing agency receives a requisition for a large quantity of hand tools for delivery at twenty-five different locations. The specifications are clear, and bidder interest is keen. Advertised purchasing is therefore mandatory. The total quantity, however, cannot be solicited by the invitation for bids (IFB). A portion of the total must be set aside for later negotiation with labor surplus areas or small business. Two weeks are needed to develop the IFB and determine the percentage of set-asides. The bids are in the hands of all the suppliers for four and a half weeks. One week is needed to abstract the bids and select the tentative low bidders (multiple awards would be almost a certainty). One to two weeks are needed to check the competency of those bidders who were successful, but who had not had a previous contract with the buying agency. Another week is required to prepare the contracts.

A military contracting officer would be fortunate indeed if he could process a large advertised procurement for hand tools in less than sixty days; 90 days would not be uncommon. For cost and competitive reasons, private enterprise could not tolerate such a long lead time for the routine purchases of hand tools, or anything else. It is conservatively estimated that industry would process this purchase in less than 14 days, using fewer than 75 sheets of paper. The government used over 12,000 sheets.

Lead time is another phase of purchasing in which government and industry differ. Here again, the government, for other than business reasons, has added additional costs to its purchasing operation. It should be understood clearly that without restraints government buyers could purchase hand tools just as quickly as industrial buyers, and with just as few pieces of paper. Government buyers are fully knowledgeable concerning the hand tools industry and the low-cost producers in the industry. In *emergencies* and by using *negotiation*, government buyers do purchase supplies with the same speed as industry.

DIFFERENCES BETWEEN GOVERNMENT AND INDUSTRIAL PURCHASING SUMMARIZED

To this point, the discussion has briefly covered the history of government purchasing, its scope, its conflicts, its "body of law," and the major areas of difference between government and industrial purchasing. Before discussing government and industrial purchasing similarities, it seems appropriate to summarize their differences. Remember, these differences are normally matters of degree, not direct opposites (e.g., both government and industry use negotiation and competitive bidding, but industry tends to use negotiation more freely than government). The principal differences between government and industrial purchasing center on the following facts:

1 Inflexible budgets sometimes preclude large governmental purchasing offices from taking advantage of exceptionally valued, one-shot buying opportunities.

2 In borderline situations, the government is frequently forced to use marginal suppliers.

3 Because of unknowns in design, there are inherent difficulties of costing government purchases of major weapon systems. Competition for such purchases focuses on technical and managerial competence, rather than price.

4 Government loses some pricing effectiveness because, in accordance with law, it reveals pricing information.

5 Buyer frustration, increased administrative expense, and possible price premiums result from the government's using some of its purchasing dollars to assist in implementing its social and economic policies, e.g., small business and distressed labor areas.

6 The government can recover "excessive profits" from those purchases covered by the Renegotiation Act.

7 Suppliers are generally motivated to interpret an industrial buyer's design specifications favorably because of this buyer's capability of withholding future business. These same suppliers are not equally motivated to do the same for government buyers who in most cases do not have a similar withholding capability.

8 The government uses considerably more paper than industry in effecting all large and some small purchases.

9 For high dollar purchases, the government uses considerably more lead time than industry. As a consequence, the government is forced to carry higher safety stocks than industry for many items.

10 Some observers contend that the government carries needlessly high inventories of common items that are readily available in commercial channels.

11 Because of the size of the federal government, and because a specific buying agency may not be a part of the requisitioning agency, its buyers do not always participate in the key decisions which influence good purchasing. For this reason, industry and smaller government buyers who participate in the development of specifications, quantity determinations, schedules, etc. often influence the underlying factors which cause good or bad purchasing to a greater extent than their federal government counterparts.

12 Federal government buyers, because of the complexity of the items they buy, frequently become more skilled in areas such as cost and price analysis than their industrial and small government counterparts.

SIMILARITIES BETWEEN GOVERNMENT AND INDUSTRIAL PURCHASING

The basic objectives of government and industrial purchasing are the same. Both seek to support operations, buy competitively and wisely, keep minimum inventories, develop reliable sources of supply, and hire and train competent personnel.

There is much evidence to indicate that government and industrial purchasing officers are equally competent and equally motivated. Each can help the other by a sharing of different viewpoints. Some of purchasing's most advanced techniques and concepts, such as the learning curve, cost analysis, statistical quality control, advanced inventory control, PERT, integrated use of electronic data processing, materials management, and team negotiation were first used by military buyers.[21] Industrial buyers introduced such advances as value analysis; standardization; centralization of purchasing; coordination among departments; and a professional association to permit the accumulation and sharing of purchasing knowledge, to publish a professional journal and a professional trade bulletin, and to increase the overall professional competence of purchasing personnel. Despite its constraints, government purchasing offers an intellectual challenge essentially equal to that of industrial purchasing. The obstacles imposed by government constraints serve as a challenge for competent purchasing personnel to overcome.

In addition to having common major objectives, and a common need for highly capable personnel, successful government and industrial purchasing both need buyers who understand thoroughly and employ profitably the fundamental concepts of purchasing discussed in Part Two of this book. The Armed Services Procurement Regulation and corporate purchasing policy manuals alike contain ample flexibility for the intelligent application of

---

[21]This is not to imply that all these techniques were conceived and developed by government buyers, however; some were. All were initially applied to purchasing problems by government buyers.

purchasing theory. To attain optimum administrative capability, both governmental and industrial purchasing executives must understand and be able to skillfully employ the basic concepts of management discussed in Part Four of this book.

FOR DISCUSSION

28-1   What are the two types of products the government purchases? Discuss the primary factors distinguishing the products that are unique to government purchasing.

28-2   Briefly relate the history of government purchasing.

28-3   Discuss the major personnel problems in both federal and local government purchasing.

28-4   Discuss the factors which tend to make local government purchasing inefficient. What changes would you recommend?

28-5   Discuss the market environment in which federal purchases for weapon and space systems are made.

28-6   Discuss briefly the four primary purchasing agencies of the federal government, giving emphasis to the DOD.

28-7   Why do the major defense contractors have such a concentration of economic power? What could this mean to the nation? Do you see any alternative to this situation?

28-8   Evaluate the Armed Services Procurement Act of 1947 in terms of what it accomplishes.

28-9   Discuss the differences between sole-source negotiation and competitive negotiation.

28-10   Discuss the purposes of the Truth in Negotiations Act. Do you believe the purposes are accomplished?

28-11   Discuss the differences between government and industrial purchasing with respect to the freedom of buyers to select sources of supply and choose contract types.

28-12   Do you believe the government's decision to use its purchasing dollars to aid its social and economic policies is an overall wise decision? Explain your position.

28-13   What do you think about the government's right to recover "excessive profits" through renegotiation and the General Accounting Office's right to audit all cost-type contracts?

28-14   What price and quality problems does the government experience with design specifications? Discuss.

28-15   Do you think the government uses excessive paper work in its purchasing operations? Explain.

28-16   Some observers believe that the government unnecessarily warehouses items immediately available in normal industrial channels of trade. Others go further and contend that for commercial items there is no necessity for large military depots, such as the Naval Supply Centers in Norfolk, San Diego, and Oakland. These observers believe the local distributors of commercial items can supply these items on a round-the-clock basis to the ships and shore stations in the area just as reliably as the government depots, and at a lower price. What is your reaction to this problem?

28-17   Considering the extensive degree of documentation and the numerous review board approvals (both business and technical) required for high-dollar-value government negotiated purchases, why do you think some reporters and politicians continue to pronounce negotiated purchases as undesirable and furtive?

28-18   Why are government award lead times of 90 days not uncommon for purchases that are made in 10 days in industry? Discuss. What price do you estimate the government pays for this practice?

28-19   Discuss the major areas of similarity and difference between government and industrial purchasing. Which do you feel are overriding—the similarities or the differences? Why?

28-20   Discuss the contributions industrial purchasing makes to the proficiency of government purchasing and vice versa.

CASES FOR CHAPTER 28

Part Six

Cases for Study
and Analysis

ACME WIRE PRODUCTS COMPANY

The jet airplane created new and varied material problems for the aircraft industry. Many of the new problems were associated with the high temperatures generated by jet engines. Materials that had performed satisfactorily in piston-powered aircraft were in many instances no longer useful.

Among the conventional materials no longer useful were many of the types of wire used in the electrical systems of aircraft. Fortunately, however, the electrical wire manufacturers had been brought in on the problem at an early date so that before long many of them could offer for sale a standard stock electrical wire capable of withstanding unusually high temperatures.

One leading electrical wire firm, the Acme Wire Products Company of Chicago, Illinois, had developed a ceramic-coated wire. Other wire sources had tackled the problem in different ways. The representatives of all these companies were anxious to demonstrate their products to the engineering departments of the aircraft companies.

The engineers at the Universal Aircraft Company, a large airframe manufacturer, were quite favorably impressed with Acme's ceramic-coated wire. They knew from previous experience that Acme had a reputation as a quality supplier of electrical wiring for Universal Aircraft and the aircraft industry as a whole. Believing that Acme's wire was the highest quality obtainable, the engineers specified it on the bill of materials.

Mr. Stan Geralds bought wire and related items for the Universal Aircraft Company. An experienced buyer, Mr. Geralds had a reputation for conscientiousness and knowledge of the commodities that he purchased. When the requisition came to him to buy Acme's ceramic-coated wire, he immediately wondered why Acme had been designated as a sole source. From his experience in buying wire, he knew Acme on occasion to be a high-cost producer. Moreover, he always attempted to follow the Universal Aircraft Company policy of dealing with more than one source whenever possible.

Believing that engineering may have been "sold a bill of goods" by the Acme salesman, Mr. Geralds decided to telephone the engineering department to learn what specifications governed the wire in question. Mr. Geralds did not want the engineer he was telephoning to think that despite the fact that the current instance was typical of a number of similar instances, he was in any way censuring him for specifying Acme as a sole source. The engineer explained that the wire was of a special nature, designed to withstand extremely high temperatures. He also said that Acme's wire was the highest quality obtainable and that in his judgment, it should be purchased to fill the current need.

Mr. Geralds pointed out to the engineer that there were many thousands of types of electrical wiring. He said that all of these types were made according to some sort of specification, either military, wire industry specifications, or specifications established by the purchaser. Mr. Geralds also said that a rule of the Universal Aircraft purchasing department required a buyer to know about any governing specifications before issuing a purchaser order. After a few minutes more of conversation, the engineer said that he would attempt to locate the governing specifications and send them over to Mr. Geralds.

In the meantime, Mr. Geralds got in touch with the local representative of Acme Wire to request samples of its ceramic-coated wire and price quotations. When the quotations were submitted, Mr. Geralds felt that once again Acme's prices were higher than those of the industry in general. Yet, he realized that this particular wire might well be a more expensive item to manufacture as a result of its ceramic-coating feature.

Several days later, Mr. Geralds received the specifications for the wire. The specifications were of the Army-Navy joint type and listed the performance requirements that the wire was to meet. They said nothing about whether the wire was to have a ceramic coating. Accordingly, Mr. Geralds solicited quotations from the other qualified vendors and asked that samples be submitted to him that would meet the performance requirements of the specifications.

Five other vendors submitted samples and price quotations. Upon receipt of the samples, Mr. Geralds forwarded them, along with Acme's sample, to the production development laboratory of Universal Aircraft for analysis and evaluation. The production development laboratory was under the direction of Universal Aircraft's inspection department and was separated both physically and organizationally from the engineering department.

A week later the report of the production development laboratory was in Mr. Geralds' hands. The samples submitted by the six vendors had undergone exhaustive tests, particularly with regard to their ability to withstand high temperatures for prolonged periods of time. One of the vendors was eliminated from consideration when his product failed to meet performance specifications. The other five samples, including Acme's, were found to exceed minimum performance requirements, and at extremely high temperatures ranges the ceramic coating of Acme's sample made it superior to the others.

With regard to the weight of the samples (another important consideration) Acme's wire was found to be heavier than the others. Furthermore, the conductivity characteristics of Acme's wire were rated as inferior to the other samples, although all of the samples exceeded the minimum performance requirements and were rated as acceptable. On the abrasiveness test, Acme's wire was found to be slightly less durable than the other vendors' samples but, nevertheless, acceptable.

These laboratory findings tended to confirm Mr. Geralds' belief that the engineering department had been "sold a bill of goods" in specifying Acme as the sole supplier. The samples submitted by four of the other suppliers had met the governing Army-Navy specifications and in some ways were superior to Acme's. While Acme's wire withstood higher temperatures, Mr. Geralds saw no need to pay a premium price for it since the wire supplied by the other vendors met the specifications which engineering had submitted to him.

With regard to price, the Excello Wire & Tubing Company was the lowest bidder and Acme was the highest. The high and low bidders compared dollarwise as follows on the quantities to be purchased:

Size	Acme	Excello	Quantity to be purchased	Difference in price
20-gauge	$27.60*	$10.50*	100,000 ft	$1,710.00
12-gauge	51.00	25.20	70,000 ft	1,806.00
10-gauge	62.30	38.45	120,000 ft	2,982.00
8-gauge	121.80	64.80	40,000 ft	2,280.00
4-gauge	199.95	124.20	20,000 ft	1,515.00
				$10,293.00

*Prices quoted are for 1,000 ft.

The delivery schedules required by Universal Aircraft posed no particular problem since all five of the qualified vendors seemed capable of meeting required delivery dates.

The laboratory report and the price quotations were then sent by Mr. Geralds to the engineering department, along with a request that the purchasing department be authorized to place the order with any company that could meet the Army-Navy joint specifications.

The engineering department refused Mr. Geralds' request, maintaining that Acme was the only company which could manufacture wiring that would meet the requirements of Universal's engineering department. The engineers stated further that since Acme had been the first company to develop this particular wiring, the purchase order should be placed with Acme. In conclusion, they reiterated their claim that Acme had a superior product that would justify any price differential.

1 If you were Mr. Geralds, what action would you take now?
2 Should Mr. Geralds have challenged the engineering department's specification of Acme's wire?

ALLIED INDUSTRIES

Following the regular Friday meeting of Allied Industries' Plans Committee, the company president took his vice president for purchasing to one side. "Harry," he said, "we're happy to have you back and well. I'm sorry the lad you had pinch hit for you while you were away didn't make the impression in our meetings that I know you wanted and expected. He's good in many ways, but he has a pretty narrow viewpoint technically and doesn't see the over-all company picture. I wonder if he can make the grade to follow you when you retire in two years? Sometime ago I asked you to select and train a successor, and I think you should take another look at the situation."

Harry was disappointed. He had high hopes for Gene Wilson, director of purchasing of Allied's Chicago Division, which makes bulk chemicals for industry.

There were three other divisions in the decentralized company—the Pharmaceutical Division, a Forest Products Division (pulp, paper, chip board and fiber containers), and a small but fast-growing Aerospace Materials Division. Each was headed by a vice president, but purchasing reported to the division manufacturing manager. The divisions, while largely autonomous, were expected to follow the broad policy and procedure outlines set forth by the corporate staff. The vice president of purchasing's principal job was policy coordination and staff advice to the president. Harry had only a junior assistant and a clerk for his staff.

Harry had been purchasing director at the Chicago Division and had been promoted to vice president in the course of the mergers that had built the company to $220 million in sales. He had the Chicago purchasing director sit in during his illness for convenience and because he had confidence in Wilson's ability. The 42-year-old Wilson, a chemical engineer, had been the Chicago Division purchasing director for four years. Before that he had been a buyer for eight years.

The Forest Products Division man, nearly 60, was considered an "old timer." The purchasing director for the Pharmaceutical Division was 35, a chemist with a graduate degree in business, plus experience in sales and finance. The Aerospace Materials Division purchasing manager was 32, an engineer, with production experience in new metals and materials. Also, he had been a government procurement officer on missile programs, and this background fitted into the company's plans to expand its space business.

Harry thought it might be possible to broaden Wilson's experience in the remaining two years by quick rotation through the other divisions and management courses at a business school. Harry might be able to give Wilson some special assignments which would show the president that Wilson could measure up to broad vice presidential responsibilities.

Or perhaps Harry should groom one of the younger men, with the Forest Products man as a stop-gap figurehead in the purchasing vice president slot. Harry could recommend bringing in someone from the outside via direct recruitment advertising or through Allied's management consultant. Or he could approach some of his friends in the local purchasing association who could handle a top-level job. There might be other alternatives, too.

The president would make the final decision, but Harry felt that his own recommendation would be a big factor. He knew that the company was growing fast and that his successor would have to demonstrate successful managerial ability. There might be a need for a whole new purchasing organization, for example, to meet greater demands for managerial expertise than required in Harry's time.

1   What overall considerations should Harry review in picking a successor?
2   What should he recommend?

BALDWIN COMPUTER CORPORATION

The Baldwin Computer Corporation produced a wide line of data processing equipment. A new addition to the product line was the Baldwin model 99, a high-speed card-sorting unit. Production of the entire model 99 was scheduled to be done at Baldwin's East Coast facility. The assembly unit was completely Baldwin-designed, and the company tooled up for frames, plates, cam shafts, vertical and horizontal spacers. All other components were purchased from outside vendors.

Machine sales increased, and requirements for these assemblies grew beyond the capacity of the plant to produce them. Accordingly, the decision was made to subcontract the overall assembly to an assembly supplier. Baldwin would select and qualify all components going into the assemblies. On the basis of competitive bidding, Murray Manufacturing Company was selected to produce the item. It agreed to buy directly all components from sources shown on the Baldwin print.

One of the components in the assembly was a phenolic plastic base, molded to Baldwin design, and produced on Baldwin-owned tooling. Three vendors had been invited by Baldwin to quote against the moldprint in lots of 5,000 to 100,000, at a rate of 5,000 units per month. Tooling was to be quoted separately. The low bidder was Peerless Plastics, a leader in the field of precision molding, and a long-time supplier to Baldwin on plastic parts. Its bid was $1.85 a unit for the quantities quoted, and a tooling charge of $23,750.

A purchase order was issued by Baldwin to Peerless for two sample pieces, each sample consisting of 5 four-cavity molds. The samples were submitted and approved. Peerless was qualified as a source for the base and its name inserted on the assembly drawing. Following approval by Baldwin,

Murray placed production orders directly with Peerless for 15,000 units, or a three-month supply.

Within thirty days, plastic parts were received, and within sixty days completed assemblies were shipped by Murray to Baldwin. Upon inspection, however, the assemblies were rejected. The cause of rejection was a dimensional error in the plastic base, and this was determined only after detailed inspection of the base. Baldwin had set up an inspection procedure whereby duplicate gauges and fixtures were provided to both Murray and Peerless, and these were patterned to master gauges and fixtures at Baldwin.

The value of the completed assembly was $72.75; the value of the base, as quoted by Peerless, was $1.85.

1   What was the extent of Murray's liability? of Peerless' liability?
2   Comment on the manner in which the purchase was made. Could the problems have been minimized—or eliminated—by some different approach?

THE BAYFLEET MACHINING COMPANY

Mr. Fingold, a buying supervisor at the Frick Turbo Engine Company, was responsible for the purchase of valves and other items for low-pressure assemblies in the company's engines. He had handled numerous valve procurements and had found that the designs were subject to considerable variation. He had found it useful, therefore, whenever he was required to initiate procurement of a new design, to make an estimate of the probable cost of the item from historical costs of similar equipment and from his own wide experience with machine shop practice and with conditions in the industry. He found that this method enabled him to question vendors' cost estimates effectively and to negotiate good prices even on initial procurements, with a corresponding saving in subsequent purchases of the same item.

In February, Mr. Fingold received a purchase request for 10,000 low-pressure valves of a new design. The engineering department was proud of the new design, which called for a valve made largely of stamped parts to replace an older type of valve which had involved a number of casting and machining processes. The last procurement of the old valve in November had been at a unit price of $1.32, and it was anticipated that substitution of the new process would result in a considerably lower unit price.

Mr. Fingold realized that prospective suppliers for the procurement would include a group different from his usual suppliers and decided for that reason to make an extremely careful estimate of the probable cost. After performing research and analyzing the processes and materials to be used, he arrived at a figure of approximately $0.87 per unit as a reasonable price for the item, made up as follows:

Material	$0.224
Direct Labor	0.172
Mfg. overhead	0.258 (assumed to be 150% of D.L.)
Tooling	0.096
G&A	0.0376 (assumed to be 5% of total cost)
Profit	0.0788 (assumed to be 10% of total cost)
Selling Price	$0.8664

Meanwhile, requests for proposals were sent out to eighteen companies. The closing date for submission of proposals was set at May 1. By the middle of April, Mr. Fingold had received thirteen proposals, of which nine were in the range from $0.92 to $1.04 per unit, while the other four ranged from $1.16 to $1.52. Mr. Fingold was pleased with the indication that his estimate had "pegged" the low range of quotations, and as each of the quotations came in, he examined each vendor's cost breakdown with a view to points for questioning and negotiation. Between April 20 and 23, however, two more companies submitted proposals. One of these, the Bayfleet Machining Company, quoted a unit price of $0.616, and the other, the Union Stamping Company, $0.752. Mr. Fingold was surprised, to say the least, at these low figures, and was inclined to think that they represented unrealistic estimates. Upon investigation, however, he found that both vendors were large, well-established metal forming companies with good reputations for satisfactory performance on previous contracts. The cost breakdowns for the two low proposals are reproduced below.

	Bayfleet Machining	Union Stamping	Mr. Fingold's estimate
Direct material	$0.172	$0.204	$0.224
Subcontracted parts	0.040	—	—
Direct labor	0.144	0.200	0.172
Manufacturing overhead	0.148 (103%)	0.152 (76%)	0.258 (150%)
Tooling	0.052	0.116	0.096
G&A	0.032 (6%)	0.012 (2%)	0.0376 (5%)
Profit	0.028 (5%)	0.060 (9%)	0.0788 (10%)
Selling price	0.616	0.744	0.8664

1 What factors might have caused the variance between Bayfleet's quotation and Mr. Fingold's estimate? Between Bayfleet's quotation and Union's quotation?
2 In light of your answer to the above question, what conclusions can you draw concerning (a) the reliability and usefulness of cost estimates made by the buyer, and (b) the value to be gained from the comparison of one vendor's quotation with that of another?

BLOZIS COMPANY

The Blozis Company was a small manufacturer of highly technical equipment. The $8,000,000 gross sales of the company consisted primarily of units designed to customer specifications by the engineering department and produced on a job-shop basis by the production department. The engineering department also designed highly complex control equipment of general industrial application to be sold by the Blozis Company on an off-the-shelf basis.

The purchasing department was comprised of the purchasing agent, a buyer, and two women who handled typing and filing. Although many of the items purchased were of a highly technical nature, the purchasing agent had no technical training. He had picked up through the years a fair grasp of the engineering terminology used in the field, but had made no attempt to keep up with the specialized design problems of the company. The buyer was a woman who was known in the trade as "hard-boiled but big-hearted," and was generally considered a competent general supplies buyer. Without great ingenuity, the buyer also handled technical items if detailed specifications were supplied by engineering or production.

An expediter was attached to production. He had formerly been one of the technicians in the production shop and had picked up some technical training in the Army. Because he could understand verbal descriptions of items needed by engineering and production, these groups often contacted him on ordering problems before submitting a requisition to purchasing. He would frequently suggest substitute components which could be drawn immediately from the stock room; or he would convert the oral description into a commercial specification, type a requisition, and submit it to purchasing. The expediter had two primary responsibilities: to pick up rush orders and to supervise the stock room. He spent about 50 percent of each day picking up items at nearby suppliers, at railroad terminals, or airports, or carrying materials to subcontractors, to platers, or to various carriers for shipment. In the stock room, a clerk kept up the facilities, issued supplies to engineering and production personnel, and kept stock records. The clerk reported to the expediter, who reviewed the stock records, prepared requisitions for items at their reorder points, and disposed of items which were turning too slowly or had deteriorated.

Frequent problems had arisen when suppliers claimed long overdue payments on materials which had been received by the Blozis Company. In these cases it always developed that someone had forgotten to make up a receiving report. Since purchasing only passed bills for payment after receipt of the receiving report, several sizable discounts had been missed and the company had been substantially tardy in meeting the net date on several bills. In these cases, the expediter was always sure that the item had come over the receiving dock, and the receiving clerk was just as sure that the expediter had brought it into the plant in the back of his station wagon.

A particularly unfortunate incident had occurred when two special micrometers disappeared within the plant after the Blozis Company had waited six months to receive them. The supplier could prove receipt by the bill of lading signed by the receiving clerk. The receiving clerk claimed the expediter had picked up the micrometers on the receiving dock to carry them to the engineers as quickly as possible. The expediter claimed he had never seen the micrometers. Both the production and plant maintenance managers had backed their respective men to the fullest. No disciplinary action had been taken since there were no signatures on the receiving reports to prove either case.

The expediter periodically typed up purchase orders for rush items. In other cases he picked up the desired items and informed the suppliers that they would receive "confirming orders" from the Blozis Company purchasing department. When the expediter forgot to ask purchasing for a confirming order, the purchasing department was occasionally distressed to be processing invoices for which it had no corresponding orders. Some suppliers were also mildly petulant when a promised purchase order was not forthcoming. Although suppliers had been warned not to honor an order from the Blozis Company unless it bore the purchasing agent's signature, it was considered poor business to penalize the suppliers who had honored the expediter's request in good faith. Consequently, purchase orders were often made up to match invoices if the material had obviously been received from the supplier.

The president liked to operate "informally" and allowed anyone in the company to initiate requisitions. The only approval signature required on orders up to $5,000 was the purchasing agent's. Orders over $5,000 required the president's approval on requisitions, but, in practice, all orders for more than $5,000 were approved by the president either in the materials budget or the capital budget long before requisitions were made out.

The president had heard something of the micrometer incident from his brother, but had dismissed the whole matter as "one of those unfortunate interdepartmental squabbles." However, when his engineering manager and his production manager began to complain of the difficulties of staying within the materials budget, he looked further into the matter. In subsequent talks with both men he drew up the following summary list of complaints:

1 The managers did not know what materials were being charged to their departments until the monthly accounting statement came out.
2 The engineering and operating personnel were not notified when materials came in unless the expediter dropped the material on the desk of the requisitioner.
3 The purchasing department was entirely too slow in processing orders. It took almost a full day just to get the order to the telephone.
4 The purchasing department did not understand technical specifica-

tions, and the expediter was being overworked by handling all technical orders.

The president presented these complaints to the purchasing agent and asked him for a solution.

1   If you were the purchasing agent, what recommendations would you have made?
2   At what points does this purchasing department exhibit weak control over (a) materials, (b) overall purchasing performance?
3   How could these weaknesses be corrected?
4   What activities should the expediter be responsible for in this organization?
5   What is the purchasing department's responsibility in establishing and interpreting technical specifications?

THE BUY-AT-HOME UPROAR

Elmville is getting to be as big and sturdy as the tree after which it is named. Recently it needed three mobile air compressors for its Street Department. A battle for the business loomed between a local manufacturer and out-of-town competitors.

Under the touchy circumstances, Harry O'Donnell, Elmville's municipal Purchasing Manager, did the best he could: he issued specifications and told bidders they could submit two sets of figures—a single price for a single unit, and a bulk price for the three compressors.

Groundhog Machinery, the local firm, bid $22,000 per single machine and $66,000 for the lot. Supra Equipment—a rival in Gotham City 200 miles away—also bid $22,000 per machine, but submitted a package price of only $60,000.

Harry checked the Street Department and found that the Superintendent thought Supra and Groundhog compressors to be about equal in quality, performance, and maintenance costs. Other bidders did not meet specifications or were much higher in price.

Years of precedent, plus the City Administrative Code, gave Harry clear authority to award the contract to Supra—the lowest bulk bidder. Yet, the haunting buy-at-home issue could not be quelled.

When the contents of the bids were made public, Groundhog's sales manager threatened, "Sure, our blanket price is higher than Supra's. But remember, we've had to lay off workers because of slack orders. How do you expect us, or anybody else, to say in Elmville when you act so hostilely?

Anyhow, our unit bid of $22,000 was the same as Supra's, so we ought to get at least part of the order. Let's keep as many tax dollars at home as we can!"

The Supra representative was just as emphatic. "Forget about Groundhog's dirty remarks. Do you realize how many components Supra buys in Elmville? We make just as many jobs here as Groundhog. We put in the low bid fair and square. Your reputation with every vendor will be shot if you throw our bid out!"

That evening Harry went to a meeting of the Elmville Purchasing Managers Association. He asked his fellow purchasing managers what they would do if they were in his shoes.

Sam Wilson, Purchasing Director of XYZ Company, had this opinion. "Sure, I'd give the order to Groundhog! You've got to do business with your friends here in Elmville and keep dollars circulating at home. It's the same as reciprocity. Our company has operated this way for years."

On the other hand, Chuck Connors of ABC, Inc., insisted "Harry, if you compromise now, you'll start something you can't stop. Every fly-by-night outfit in town will hound you for a piece of city business. I'd keep Elmville's good name in mind. Vendors tell me they think we're an honest bunch. That's why they always give us such good service and help so much on the standardization and value analysis committees."

Roscoe Stevens of NPQ Corporation added this diplomatic note. "You can't throw the bids out, Harry, but you've got to watch your step. The Taxpayers' League and the papers will scream if you give the whole order to Groundhog, because Groundhog really wasn't low bidder. On the other hand, you can't be unpatriotic, either. I'd split the business. After all, both bidders had a $22,000 unit figure."

1   What factors should Harry consider in making a decision?
2   What should that decision be?

CAMPBELL TYPEWRITER CORPORATION

The Campbell Typewriter Corporation was enjoying the biggest year in its history. High production made its unit costs low. It was the successful bidder for the National Mail Order Corporation's annual typewriter contract—the largest single typewriter sale in the world each year.

Campbell Typewriter Corporation, in order not to interfere with the sales of typewriters under the "Campbell" brand name, modified the appearance of the "National" model from the appearance of the Campbell regular line of typewriters. Part of the appearance change was in the color and shape of the keyboard key tops.

Typewriter key tops are usually double-injection-molded. This means that first, the individual letters themselves are injection-molded, for instance, in a light color such as white. Then, the white letters are used as inserts around which the body of the key is molded, for instance, in a dark color such as green. It is a patented art in which there are a small number of skilled suppliers. Campbell Typewriter molded its own key tops, except under overload conditions.

In order to meet the initial delivery deadline to National Mail Order Corporation, the Campbell Typewriter Corporation had to "put a new dress on the old lady" in a hurry—by changing the housing, the key tops, and the carrying case. The shape of the carrying case was a rather simple matter to change, since it was fabricated by hand on a bent plywood frame. It was decided to change the appearance of the housing by using the lower portion of the housing from the preceding model, and just building one new tool for the "mask"—the top part of the housing that covers the type basket and the ribbon spools. This meant that the time squeeze would be concentrated on the double-injection-molded key tops. Campbell Typewriter's own key top molding department could not handle the National order. It would have to be placed outside.

Because of the tight schedule, it was essential that purchasing delay as little as possible in selecting a source for the key tops and placing the purchase order. Of the double-injection-molding plants available, only four were large enough to handle the key tops in the necessary quantities. Three of the four sources contacted either refused to quote on so short a schedule, or else were fully loaded and unable to consider the order. The only exception was the Ingborg Key Top Company, a highly reputable concern with a wide reputation for reliable work and strict adherence to promised delivery dates.

The Ingborg Key Top Company was run by Niels Ingborg, a Swede by birth, who was indeed a master craftsman and a man of personal integrity and honesty. However, Ingborg was a businessman of the old school, and ran his operation on a tight-fisted, closed-mouth basis. He knew his business, and insisted upon running his business as he saw fit. He sought advice from no one, and recently, when he was told by one of his customers that his prices were too high, he was heard to have said, "I produce a quality product, and I meet my delivery dates. I know my business, and I know what I should charge as a price. You get what you pay for, and if you're looking for bargains or cut-rate prices, I would rather not have your business."

This, then, was the only supplier willing and able to consider the key-top procurement. Jim Smith, the Campbell Typewriter purchasing manager, opened discussions with Ingborg expecting at best a difficult time. At the outset, the meeting was noticeably strained. Several months previously, Campbell Typewriter canceled a sizable order with Niels Ingborg and returned the work to its own shops to relieve what was then an underload condition. As could be expected, Ingborg was most unhappy on that occasion, and Smith was aware that now the shoe was on the other foot.

It was with a sense of uneasiness, therefore, that Smith asked Ingborg to submit a quotation on the mold-making and molding of the key tops. However, Ingborg was the epitome of politeness and seemed anxious and sincere to be helpful and cooperative. The key top letters were a fancy style—created by Campbell's industrial designer and approved by National Mail Order. Ingborg cited the fact that the Campbell letters were difficult to make, and that more time was needed than Smith was prepared to allow in order to develop a realistic quotation. As a consequence, he proposed that Smith tell him what the job was worth, and that would be the price he would quote. This approach on the part of Ingborg caught Smith completely off balance. It was the last thing he expected to hear, and although he liked to believe that the "old man had mellowed," his intuition told him to be more wary.

Smith knew that manufacturing engineering had estimated the molds at 2,600 man-hours, but this style of letter had never been produced before. Further, it was estimated on internal facilities, and could be either much above or much below what actually might be experienced. It was, at best, a "guesstimate," and Smith knew from experience how unrealistic such "guesstimates" could be. If he accepted the 2,600-man-hour figure, he could be paying more than what might be reasonable, or again on the other hand, he might be causing Ingborg a loss to pull Campbell Typewriter out of a hole. To aggravate Smith's dilemma futher, Ingborg then proposed an alternative—$13 per hour straight time and $20 for overtime, based on the actual hours spent on the job.

1 What is your opinion of Ingborg's two proposals? Which, if either, would you accept, and why?
2 Are there any other choices open to Smith for arriving at an equitable agreement?
3 How would you have handled the procurement if you were Smith?

CAREER CROSSROADS

Bill Winters, a bright young purchasing manager, stood at a big turning point in his professional purchasing career. Over a long lunch at a plush club, George Snell of Management Research Associates, an executive recruiting service, had painted for Bill a space-age rainbow complete with pot of gold. . . . "Bill, we want you for the top purchasing job at Electro Products, a new company that will sweep the market. You'll be in on the ground floor from the beginning and build your own department. Materials are 65 percent of the Flanistor cost, and we need your practical buying know-how to make the thing profitable!

"It's a great team we're building. The scientists who invented the Flanistor will be president and secretary-treasurer, and we have top men picked for the sales and manufacturing manager slots. Your title will be Director of Purchases, and you'll report to the President. The sky's the limit on opportunity here!"

The Flanistor had been incubating in a local university laboratory for four years with backing by a wealthy investor. Now Snell reported a major scientific breakthrough and said studies indicated a large sales potential. The backers had decided to go into production as soon as possible and hired Management Research Associates to assemble top candidates for the management. An extensive survey spotlighted Winters as the best purchasing choice. Snell continued . . . "We picked you because you have a smart reputation in buying Gladstone, a major component in the Flanistor. Also, your cost reduction record and the way you set up Marshall's branch purchasing operations have convinced us that you can handle a brand-new operation from the word go."

Bill had been sitting pretty at Marshall Manufacturing Company, a firm with $60 million sales in tools and general products. Marshall's sales were steady, and its conservatively made products enjoyed a reputation for quality and service. But it was not a growth company by any means, although the future did seem to hold continued profitable operations.

Six years of experience in engineering and five years' experience in purchasing had put him in the No. 2 spot as the assistant director under a director of purchases who would retire in two years. Marshall had a promotion-from-within policy, and Bill clearly was being groomed for the top job. His salary was low, but a promotion might increase it by $8,000 a year.

Snell said . . . "We are convinced you can do the job at Electro, but to get the company on its feet, we'll have to conserve cash. So starting salaries will be low. We will pay you what you are getting now at Marshall but your salary should increase fast as the company grows. Think the deal over a few days and give me a call."

Bill wondered out loud what he should do. . . . "Marshall is a solid firm, and my course upward looks clear. I've got security, status, and recognition from top management. Purchasing is running well, but I'm sure I can still score some big dollar savings.

"But the Electro job might be a once-in-a-lifetime chance, even though it is a risky new situation. The salary is the same, but there's promise of a lot more, plus an inside spot in top management."

1   What actions should Bill take to properly weigh the pros and cons of the offer?
2   How should he go about making up his mind? (Note: Consider the case only from the professional career side; don't bring in family or personal factors.)

THE CASE OF MR. ADAMS

Mr. Adams was the supervisory buyer for all the final assembly material required to build television sets in the television division of the American Manufacturing Company. A sudden increase in activity required that he hire an assistant. He found the man that he wanted in one of the other divisions of his company—an experienced buyer who had been purchasing metal stampings, die castings, and all of the finished metal parts of industrial control apparatus.

Mr. Smith, the new buyer, received as his first major buying assignment the purchase of a metal cabinet for a 14-inch portable television set. His previous experience had given him a familiarity with drawings and specifications, particularly as they were related to sheet metal work. He was not disturbed at all by the magnitude of the assignment. It involved not only a high-priced assembly, but a major investment in tools. The type of finishing operation, however, which was applied to the cabinet removed most of his old sources from the picture, and he requested advice from Mr. Adams as to those sources who could not only fabricate a box at low cost but could finish it in a variety of ways. Mr. Adams gave him the names, addresses and contacts for four companies currently in the business of manufacturing this type of product, and recommended that they be sent drawings and specifications.

Upon receipt of the drawings, all the suppliers visited Mr. Smith to make sure that all details were understood and to offer helpful suggestions as to ways in which the cabinet could be made at lower cost. In the meetings which ensued, both Mr. Smith and Mr. Adams discussed the details with the suppliers and the cabinet engineer. At that time it was pointed out very clearly by Mr. Adams that this cabinet purchase was highly competitive, that other sources were also quoting on the same drawings and specifications, and that the set was a low-profit-margin item. Accordingly, the company was forced to make every conceivable effort by negotiation of design and price to purchase the cabinet at the rock-bottom price. He also pointed out that there would be substantial volume over a period of twelve to eighteen months, which should make the business very attractive. In a few days following these separate meetings, quotations were received from the suppliers. They were carefully reviewed by Mr. Smith, with a resultant determination on his part to place the business with the lowest bidder who apparently would meet all the drawing and specification requirements. The low bidder, the Pennsylvania Cabinet Company, quoted $19.56. The next lowest bidder, the Ohio Cabinet Company, quoted $19.80. The other two companies were over $21.00 and were not given any consideration whatsoever by Mr. Smith.

In the course of a discussion of the placement of this business, Mr. Smith was quite surprised to find that Mr. Adams did not consider that the business was ready for placement, that the price of $19.56 was too high, and that the business should really be placed with the Ohio Cabinet Company. Mr. Smith argued with Mr. Adams that, inasmuch as the suppliers had been told that they must bid at the lowest possible price, they had negotiated out all of the design features possible. The price must be right. He saw no reason for procrastination or further discussion. Mr. Adams, on the other hand, calmly stated that they were now in a position for the first time really to negotiate the purchase and that Mr. Smith should go back to both the Pennsylvania and the Ohio Cabinet Companies, and tell them that their prices were too high and that they should submit new quotations. Mr. Smith stated that he was of the opinion that this was unfair to the Pennsylvania Cabinet Company. He felt the quotations were already based upon the suppliers' making a fair profit, and that such a quotation might injure their opportunity to negotiate satisfactorily further business with these suppliers. Mr. Adams agreed that any company who does not receive the business is apt to be unhappy regardless of the circumstances, but he would not agree that the question of profit should concern the buyer as there was no consideration being given to the profitability of the end product which had already been clearly defined as marginal.

Mr. Adams further explained to Mr. Smith that it was highly desirable for the business to be placed with the Ohio Cabinet Company as the Pennsylvania Company was already making all the other metal cabinets. Unless the company provided some split of the business, they would lose their negotiating effectiveness for future business (it being accepted by the suppliers that no one but the Pennsylvania Company could get business from the American Manufacturing Company). Mr. Adams further explained that the company was not in a position to pay Ohio more than Pennsylvania and that the negotiation should be so conducted as to be sure that Ohio not only received the business but that they were the low bidders. The degree of determination on the part of Mr. Adams that this must be true, and the lack of acceptance by Mr. Smith of the fact that it either could or should be done resulted in Mr. Adams taking over the completion of the negotiation with both the Pennsylvania and Ohio Cabinet Companies.

The net result of this second-look negotiation was that the business was placed with the Ohio Cabinet Company at a price of $18.60 as compared with the Pennsylvania Cabinet Company's second quotation of $18.75. Mr. Smith was disturbed by this not only because his supervisor had proved that additional cost could be taken out of the part, but also because supplier relations had in no way been disturbed.

1   Why was Mr. Adams able to reduce the price of the metal cabinet purchase, and how did he know that a reduction was possible?
2   Did Adams treat Smith fairly?
3   Can this type of buying approach be broadly applied to all commodities and industries?
4   Do you believe that either Mr. Adams or Mr. Smith was right in disregarding the high initial bids submitted by the third and fourth companies?

THE CASE OF THE UNRULY SPIDER

Allen Jones, the buyer of tooling and subcontract material for Alex Precision Manufacturing Company, received a routine rejection notice from the Inspection Department. This notified him that thirty-two spider gears, which had recently been received from the Speedy Tool Company, had been rejected. There were two reasons for the rejection. First, the 1¹/₈-inch diameter holes had a rough finish on the bore. Second, the magnaflux mark was not clearly legible on all of the pieces. Before Jones had a chance to go to the receiving department to examine the pieces, he received a telephone call from the production superintendent demanding immediate replacement of the parts because they were holding up the shipment of a substantial spare parts order. The parts were needed for a foreign shipment.

As soon as he got a chance, Jones went to the receiving department and examined the spider gears. He called to the attention of the chief inspector the fact that there was no notation on the drawing calling for any finish on the bore of the three holes. This dimension called for a 0.0004-inch tolerance, and all the parts met this requirement when measured with an inside micrometer. However, he could see that the inside surface of these holes was slightly rough from the boring operation. Jones did not feel that this roughness was adequate grounds for rejection; however, he suggested that the inspector call the engineer responsible for the part to see if it would be possible to use the part.

A meeting was quickly arranged with the engineer. He took one look at the spiders and said that they were absolutely unsuitable for use because the dimension he objected to was a bearing seat. The engineer said that he could not afford to take a chance on a fit which could become loose in service. He felt that any respectable supplier would produce a smooth surface on this type of hole without any notification on the drawing. He felt that the rough surface showed inferior workmanship. The engineer refused to accept the parts as they were, and suggested that the supplier prepare new ones with a ground finish on the bores. Jones asked the engineer to add a suitable finish indication on the drawing, so the supplier would know exactly what finish was required. This indication would give the inspection department a definite standard for inspection. The request was refused because the engineer felt that any good subcontractor would immediately identify the holes as bearing seats and would produce a 64-micro-inch finish without any special note. Moreover, these parts had been in production for several years and he had never experienced this trouble before; the engineer felt that it must be the fact that there was a new supplier who was causing the trouble.

Allen Jones put a telephone call to Mr. Speed of the Speedy Tool Company and described the situation to him. Mr. Speed objected strenuously to the rejection on the basis of the rough finish. He said that he had been furnished a plug gauge to check this dimension and that the parts had all been checked satisfactorily with this gauge before they had been shipped. Nothing had ever been said to Mr. Speed about the necessity for a ground finish on the bores.

Since the holes were already at the proper dimension, it would be impossible to grind them further to salvage the 32 units without an expensive chromeplating operation. Mr. Speed agreed to change his procedure in the future, so that these holes would have a ground finish. The fixture for this operation would cost at least $1,050, and Speed felt that he would probably have to spend about $12 a unit for additional labor in the grinding operation.

In regard to the magnaflux marking, Mr. Speed pointed out that the marking stamp had been furnished by the Alex Company and that the drawing called for it to be applied to a curved surface. Mr. Speed agreed that it was not very legible, but said that it was the best they could do under the circumstances without damaging the stamp.

Mr. Speed said that he was able to make the new grinding operation effective on 100 pieces that were in process, and thought that he could deliver these within a week.

The Speedy Tool Company was a major supplier of production tooling, particularly dies, jigs, and fixtures. The two companies had had a very favorable relationship for ten or twelve years. Mr. Speed called on Mr. Jones about once a week in regard to the many items of tooling which were on order, and the two men had come to know each other very well. Speedy Tool had done very little production work for Jones, but their precision work on tooling had always been well done and they had a very good delivery and quality record.

The spider had become active at the time of the introduction of the Alex offset press. It had been necessary to subcontract this item because no facilities were available internally. At that time, the drawings, specifications, and gauges were furnished to the original subcontractor, the Wilson Automatic Machine Company. Wilson had built the original tooling. When Alex had dropped this press from the product line, the part had become inactive, and a demand had only recently occurred for spare parts. Jones had found that Wilson had virtually gone out of business on subcontract precision work. In fact, he had had considerable difficulty in getting the original gauges and tooling back from the Wilson Company. Speedy had quoted on the basis of tooling to be furnished, but when the tools had been received from Wilson, they were found to be in very poor condition. In fact, some of the tooling had not been modified to bring it up to the marked revision of the drawing. It had been necessary for Mr. Speed to spend over $12,000 in repairing the tooling before he could use it.

Allen Jones was puzzled as to the action he should take. He did not think it would be completely fair to reject the thirty-two units to Speedy, because he felt that Alex Precision Manufacturing Company had some responsibility for the loss. He also knew that Mr. Speed had spent considerably more than he had anticipated on getting adequately tooled for the job. He was debating in his own mind the advisability of permitting Mr. Speed to raise his price to compensate him for this change in circumstances.

1 What do you think would be an equitable solution to this problem?

CLIFTON MACHINERY COMPANY

What is a fair profit for a manufacturer? Is it a fixed amount? Should it vary with total sales or total capital invested? Is a percentage of cost an adequate way of computing profit when one manufacturer may spend $100 to produce an item and a competitor may be able to produce the same item for, perhaps, $80? If a profit of 10 percent of cost is allowed, should the high cost producer receive $10 for his inefficient work and the low cost producer only $8 for his efforts? Is a percentage of profit based upon selling price a more satisfactory method of determining a fair profit than one based on cost? Or as Joe Johnston, one of the equipment buyers at the Sirius Aircraft Company, put it, "What is a fair profit anyway?"

Mr. Johnston, along with a number of his fellow buyers, had always considered that a fixed price contract under competitive bidding conditions was the best possible method of arriving at a price which would be fair to both the seller and the buyer. It was Mr. Johnston's contention that under these conditions a bidder would receive a fair profit on his work, since he would not reduce his bid below a point which enabled him to make a fair return. A bidder might make more than a "fair" profit, Mr. Johnston realized, when an industry as a whole fixed prices. Conditions of this sort were rare, however, Mr. Johnston believed. A bidder might make less than a fair profit, or no profit at all, under conditions of fixed price and competitive bidding when he needed work to keep his plant operating and bid abnormally low. Yet, in most cases, Mr. Johnston believed that the lowest bidder was the most efficient bidder and as a result was able to make a satisfactory dollar profit. This profit, by the very nature of a competition, was also fair to the buyer, since he was still obtaining the item at a lower price than competing firms could offer.

Such were Joe Johnston's beliefs on profit until he was rudely exposed to another theory on a fine spring morning.

For several years, Mr. Johnston had been purchasing a number of different items from the Clifton Machinery Company. Clifton was a leader in the field of automatic controls, although it manufactured a wide and diversified line of other products including such items as machine tools, hand tools, motors, and special machinery. It sold these items on a nationwide basis to almost every industry in the country. Most of the articles which Sirius Aircraft purchased from the Clifton Machinery Company were specially designed aircraft items, but a few were standard items that Clifton sold to the general commercial market.

Mr. Johnston had always purchased from Clifton Machinery Company on a fixed price basis. As might be imagined, Clifton's competition consisted of some of the largest and most successful corporations in the United States. Thus, it was with some surprise that the management of the Sirius Aircraft Company in general and Mr. Johnston in particular received a sharply worded letter from the Air Force. The letter pointed out that a team of Air Force auditors had just completed an audit of all Air Force work in the Clifton plant. The Air Force was extremely perturbed to discover from its audit that the Clifton Machinery Company was making on the average, a profit of about 45 percent on its sales to the Sirius Aircraft Company.

Enclosed with the letter was a complete list of all the purchase orders issued to Clifton by Sirius Aircraft, and the amount of profit that had been made on each one. For example, the following figures were submitted on one item, a switch block:

Amount	Manufacturing cost	General expense	Development expense	Total	Price to Sirius
50 blocks	$22.02	$4.18	$1.44	$27.64	$102

On another item, the profit was a percent of sales was 60.8 percent, and on still another, 73.7 percent. The Air Force intimated that the high profit figures were the result of poor buying on the part of Sirius Aircraft, and requested that the Sirius Aircraft Company take immediate steps to improve the situation on future orders.

Mr. Johnston and the Sirius Aircraft management had no way of knowing why the Air Force audit had been held in the first place. They were inclined to feel that, if Clifton was so efficient that it could consistently bid low against difficult competition and still make a 45 percent profit on sales, more power to the company. On the other hand, the Air Force was still the Sirius Aircraft Company's best customer and it was thought wise to call a conference with the management of Clifton Machinery Company to discuss the problem posed by the Air Force auditors.

At the conference purchasing personnel of Sirius were puzzled as to just what approach to take to the problem. As Joe Johnston put it, "How the devil are we going to tell another private corporation that it isn't enough just to be the low bidder. Now we've got to tell them that they can't get our business unless they're at least 20 percent to 30 percent lower than everyone else."

As might be expected, the Clifton management objected to the findings of the Air Force audit. They pointed out that the Air Force had disallowed a whole series of costs which Clifton's public accountants had accepted as being fully justified. In particular, the Air Force auditors had disallowed large sums for development of new items.

The Air Force administrative contracting officer at the Sirius Aircraft Company was satisfied with the explanation made by the Clifton management. Basically, he agreed with the general feeling of the Sirius purchasing department that Sirius was in no position to dictate to another company what it could charge for an item after a fixed price bid had been accepted. It was pointed out to the Clifton people, however, that their contracts with Sirius were subject to renegotiation by the government (under the authority of the Renegotiation Act because their total yearly government business exceeded $1 million) and, if they were making a profit that was in excess of what the government auditors considered fair, it would probably be recaptured. The meeting ended on a friendly note, with the Clifton Machinery Company representatives promising to review their whole cost structure in the near future.

A few weeks later, Mr. Johnston received the following letter from the Clifton Company.

Gentlemen:
We are about to announce a price reduction on some of our basic control units, retroactive to the first of this year. A voluntary price reduction following on the heels of a long period of rising costs, and a cost future which is still anything but clear, calls for some explanation.

Our policy over the years has been a conservative one with respect to the risk factors involved in the aircraft business. We speak of risk in the sense that it is not uncommon for vendors to be called upon to establish prices on the basis of specifications which do not lend themselves to accurate cost analysis. Design costs, not to mention the expenses connected with correcting difficulties which appear only after the equipment is in service, result in a quoted price based on considerable guess work.

The situation is further aggravated by the fact that the rapidly changing character of the aircraft business has created entirely new problems for which there is no experience to draw from. Nevertheless, the last few years in particular have better prepared us to appraise the risk aspects involved, and we have a better understanding of what aircraft manufacturers must require of their vendors. Moreover, we have had the benefit of the costly education entailed in becoming familiar with inspection, performance, and qualification test procedures, necessary to satisfy the government authorities as well as our customers.

In addition to improving our position with respect to the factors which affect costs, we have been urged to rebate to our prime contractors any cost savings we were able to effect, so as to assure the Air Force the use of funds appropriated to it, as opposed to allowing part of the profit to be recaptured by renegotiation. Henceforth, it will be our policy to review all government contracts as production progresses and our actual costs become known. Whenever possible, price adjustments will be volunteered for the benefit of the Air Force, or whichever branch of the service is affected.

Price reductions we are about to make now, retroactive to January 1, will result in a saving to the Air Force of about $79,000. The rebate to Sirius Aircraft Company will amount to approximately $16,000 and affects quite a number of different contracts.

Very truly yours,
Clifton Machinery Company

In line with the policy expressed in the above-quoted letter, reductions were continued throughout the year and amounted, on the average, to about 10 percent of the original selling price. For example, one unit had been priced at $164 at the beginning of the year. Later in the year, Sirius bought 600 of these same items at a price of $144. During the period that the order was being produced, the Clifton Machinery Company made a voluntary reduction in the price of this item, reducing it to $130.

In February of the following year, Mr. Johnston requested bids for 100 units of the item mentioned above which had finally been priced at $130. As usual, the Clifton Machinery Company was low bidder, at a fixed price of $138.70. While this price was lower than the $144 price quoted seven months earlier, it was higher than the last quotation of $130.

Mr. Johnston placed the order at the $138.70 price and scheduled deliveries at the rate of 50 units in April, and the remaining 50 in December. He expected the Clifton Machinery Company to offer a voluntary price reduction on the new order, but some months went by with no word from Clifton regarding a price cut. In the early fall, Mr. Johnston met with the Clifton sales manager to discuss the matter. The sales manager pointed out that the present order was only a sixth as large as the one on which the last price reduction had been granted. Costs had risen since then, the sales manager pointed out, and some consideration had to be given to possibly higher costs later in the year, when the remainder of the order was scheduled to be delivered. Furthermore, the policy expressed in Clifton's letter, quoted above, specifically stated that reduction would be given when the actual costs were known. These actual costs would not be known for some time, on the order in question. As the meeting with the sales manager drew to a close, Mr. Johnston suggested that he be supplied with a cost breakdown to support the $138.70 price.

The answer to Mr. Johnston's request for a cost breakdown was formally presented in a letter Mr. Johnston received a few days after his meeting with the Clifton sales manager. The letter said:

> *Gentlemen:*
> If for no other reason, we should like to comply with your request in the interest of maintaining the pleasant relations that have existed between us over a period of years. Needless to say, we are greatly concerned about any situation which tends to jeopardize our standing with a desirable customer. Nevertheless, we feel called upon to stand by our opinion that cost breakdowns in conjunction with fixed price contracts are inconsistent with the risks that competitive bidding entails.
>
> Since our discussion of last year, we have made voluntary rebates and price reductions to prime contractors and to the Air Force, amounting to more than $670,000 and we shall continue to lower prices as costs permit.
>
> *Very truly yours,*
> *Clifton Machinery Company.*

1 What is the purpose of a "profit"?
2 When a buyer is deciding upon an adequate profit to promote his own interests, what points should be kept in mind?
3 In this case, should a cost breakdown have been considered?
4 Discuss ways of obtaining fair and reasonable prices as applied to this case.
5 What method of pricing do you believe should have been used?

COLLIER COMPANY I

The Collier Company is a large electrical manufacturer. Recently, a new division of the company was started, and entirely new facilities were required. In equipping the new plant, it was decided that for certain subassembly operations it would be desirable to have production employees seated at high stools instead of standing at their work benches. Eight hundred and fifty employees were to be so seated in the new plant.

After investigating many possible stool designs, the plant engineering department and the personnel department agreed on a certain style of stool which was easily described to the trade as "Carter's 816 or equal." Bids were requested by purchasing from most major fabricators of this type of item, and bids from nine suppliers were received more than ten days before the announced closing date.

Several days before the final bid date these suppliers started to call the purchasing manager to see how they ranked. The purchasing manager answered their questions honestly with phrases like:

"You are not low bidder, but you are fairly competitive."

"You are not low bidder. You are way out of line."

"You are presently low bidder, but others seem to be revising their bids."

By April 23, the day originally chosen to close bidding, every supplier except vendor C had submitted at least one revised quotation. (See Exhibit I.) In most cases, the prices quoted were substantially below the initial bids.

Late in the afternoon on April 23, two suppliers asked for special permission to make a final bid on April 24. Since these two firms had been favorable suppliers of the Collier Company for years, the purchasing manager was anxious to give them any opportunity to keep their facilities operating in the depressed conditions which then characterized their industry. He gave them a special extension of one day. By the next afternoon, the purchasing

Exhibit I   Unit Prices Quoted by Vendors

	Original bid	April 23 bid	May 7 bid
Vendor A	$27.96	$20.55	$17.04
Vendor B	22.35	18.75	15.81
Vendor C	19.74	19.74	19.74
Vendor D	22.68	17.94	15.03
Vendor E	21.93	19.29	15.99
Vendor F	19.35	18.96	14.94
Vendor G	19.50	17.70	15.30
Vendor H	21.39	19.80	15.75
Vendor I	24.30	20.67	16.59

manager had heard from three more firms who wanted the same privileges as the two concerns who had rebid. Firms kept asking for special extensions or equal bid privileges until the purchasing manager finally said to all who called that May 7 was the last day he would entertain bids. On May 7 several suppliers asked for special permission to bid late and were refused. Vendor C still had not called in to change its original bid.

By May 7, the purchasing manager felt that all of the firms were bidding at less than their total costs in order to keep their facilities operating at the highest possible volume in this slack period. He also felt that further price adjustments would be negligible. However, not wanting any vendor to go out of pocket on the order, the purchasing manager asked the plant engineers to make a cost estimate on the chairs. The engineers estimated costs as follows:

Labor	$ 6.00
Materials	6.81
Overhead : 150% of direct labor	9.00
Total cost (excluding profit)	$21.81

Having satisfied himself that all vendors were making some contribution to overhead at the quoted prices, the purchasing manager awarded the order to vendor D, who had done business with the Collier Company in the past and was considered as one of the best fabricators in its field.

On May 9, two days after making the award, the purchasing manager heard from both vendor C and vendor F.

Vendor C was extremely angry that he had not been told of the acceptance of new bids. He said that he would write a letter to the vice president of purchasing requesting a review of this "entire deplorable situation." The purchasing manager informed vendor C that reasonable follow-up on the latter's part would have given him any information available to other vendors. Vendor C was not at all satisfied with this answer and again expressed his intention to contact the vice president of purchasing.

Vendor F asked why the purchasing manager had requested bids at all if his "mind had been made up all along." Vendor F said that the order should have gone to the lowest bidder who could provide the object desired. He said he could meet the specifications and could deliver to any schedule vendor D could meet. He demanded the order, and, when the purchasing manager informed vendor F that "final selection of the vendor is entirely my province," the vendor raged that he would "spread the word to the trade" and would write the Collier Company president, who "should know of such favoritism and incompetence." The vendor even suspected strongly that money had passed hands for this order.

The purchasing manager was upset by these calls and did not at all enjoy his supper on May 9.

1   What suggestions might you have made in the purchasing manager's handling of this matter?

2   What would you recommend that he do now?

3 To what extent would you concur in the purchasing manager's belief that vendors should at least be allowed to recover direct costs?
4 Who do you feel should have received the order?

COLLIER COMPANY II

Assume that instead of pricing the purchase for stools by competitive bidding, as was done in Collier Company I, the purchasing manager (PM) decided to negotiate this purchase. All of the facts that applied to Collier Company I (see page 603) also apply to this case with one exception. Instead of requesting bids, the PM requested quotations, and all vendors were advised that the purchase would be negotiated.

After receiving the quotations from the competing vendors, the PM made the following listing to help him start his analysis:

Vendor A's price of $27.96 is 140% of G's price of $19.50.
Vendor B's price of $22.35 is 115% of G's price.
Vendor C's price of $19.74 is 100.13% of G's price.
Vendor D's price of $22.68 is 116% of G's price.
Vendor E's price of $21.93 is 112% of G's price.
Vendor F's price of $19.35 is 99% of G's price.
Vendor H's price of $21.35 is 110% of G's price.
Vendor I's price of $24.30 is 124% of G's price.

From the above listing, it was clear to the PM that vendors C and G were the vendors with whom he should negotiate. Other vendors were asking from 10 to 40 percent more money than these vendors. Although vendor F submitted the low bid, this vendor was considered to be unsatisfactory because of labor troubles; therefore, his bid was rejected.

After carefully considering his initial analysis, the PM decided that his first negotiation step would be to request a cost breakdown from vendors C and G. At this point, the PM did not know how much lower he could get these companies to go. However, he did know the pricing theory involved, and he did know that he must apply this theory to the practical situation at hand. For good negotiation, he also knew that a knowledge of variable and fixed costs was essential.

In response to the PM's request for cost breakdowns, he received the following information:

	Company C cost	Company G cost
Labor	$ 6.60	$ 4.50
Material	6.54	6.00
Overhead	6.60	9.00
	$19.74	$19.50

1   What are some of the most important factors that will influence the cost of both C and G of the stools that are being purchased?
2   How can the PM use the cost breakdown information that he has available to help him negotiate the price he wants?
3   What principal negotiation arguments should the PM present to the two low bidders before requesting their final quotations?
4   Approximately what dollar profit do you believe the successful supplier will most likely receive from this order?

A COMPUTER FOR PURCHASING?

A New England manufacturer of hardware and small tools has decided to install a computer. The firm has sales of about $100,000,000 a year, and employs about 2,500 people, including blue-collar workers and office and executive personnel. The firm's one plant is devoted to general metalworking, finishing, assembly, and packaging operations. It has its own brass and bronze foundry, stamping, screw machine, and machine tool shops, but all ferrous castings, forgings, sheets, rods or rolls are purchased, as are packaging supplies.

The purchasing department consists of ten people, including clerical personnel. It buys, in varying quantities and at varying times, about 30,000 items. However, production control handles raw material inventory records, and the warehouse and stores department does the receiving and storage job. Traffic also is a separate department. When material is needed, production control sends a requisition to purchasing.

One day the president of the company approached the purchasing manager and said, "You know we have just contracted for an electronic computer. We think it will be great for payroll and accounting and other uses, but that won't take up all the computer's time. So your purchasing department can have a hour a week on the computer beginning about a year from now when the machine is fully installed. Let me know in two months if you want the hour each week and what you want it for."

1   If you were the purchasing manager of the company, how would you go about analyzing your situation?
2   What would you tell the president at the end of your two-month grace period?

CONFLICT OF INTEREST

Charlie Winslow, Purchasing Director for Monitor Manufacturing Company, had to make a decision which would tax the judgment of a Solomon. Charlie had found that Harry Starr, Monitor's top buyer, was purchasing components from Electro Products, Inc., a firm in which his brother was vice president and chief research wizard.

Monitor had never had a conflict of interest problem before, since the company bought most of its metals, plastics, and chemicals from giants of the industry or other widely held companies. Winslow was surprised that there was any family connection between one of his buyers and a supplier, but then he had not figured that such a relationship could enter the picture on Monitor contracts. At a recent, monthly dinner for purchasing and sales managers, Starr had introduced Winslow to his brother, Elwood. "Charlie, this is my brother Elwood, the gee-whiz type of the family. He's the brains behind the control switch we're putting in the new 'Monitron' line. Elwood developed it for us right on our kitchen table over coffee after I told him what our problems were. It's great being able to tap a local outfit for research and development help. This development has saved us a good *35 percent a year* on that product and given us a real jump on the competition!"

The product Harry Starr had brought in had really met a definite need and added another cost-cutting laurel to Starr's already impressive record in value analysis and all-around good purchasing know-how. But Winslow began to have qualms about the situation, even though Starr's performance on the contract—and all others—was above reproach.

He discussed the problem in conference with several company executives.

Kingsby Blackstone, Company attorney—"This is a serious case, Charlie. That buyer has entered a conspiracy to defraud this company by routing orders to his brother's outfit. He probably owns a good chunk of Electro stock besides. We should fire him and take quick action to recover damages. You have to prohibit buyers from having any interest in supplier firms."

Roger Goodbody, Manufacturing Manager—"You're making a mountain out of a molehill! I grew up with the Starr brothers and they are solid citizens. We're darn lucky to have one of them working for this firm. Besides, only Harry Starr could have gotten that genius interested in our problem. It's a darn good thing when our buyers can get that close to a supplier."

Charlie Winslow—"If it were anybody else but Harry, I'd be suspicious of his intentions. But I am sure he has acted in the best interest of the company, even though the situation does look a bit fishy. If we unfairly crack down on him, it will look as if we are punishing initiative. Also, if we kick up a fuss over the situation, aren't we trying to close the barn door after the horse has been stolen? I'll check into the situation a bit further and talk it over with you next week."

1 What should Charlie do about Harry now?
2 What should Charlie do about this problem in the future?

CONGRESSMAN TARDY

Congressman Tardy was a powerful political figure from the South who secretly enjoyed Yankee land far more than he could ever let anybody know. During his stay in Washington, he made some important business and political connections. As a result, when the year came in which he was not reelected, he was able to secure several positions as a director for large companies and banks. This served as a sufficient excuse to keep him from going back to the South.

It was not too long a time until he was able to acquire the complete stock of a plating plant in New Jersey. The plant had good facilities and some excellent customers. The congressman naturally wished to expand its operation and started to use some of his political influence in business contacts to that end.

The congressman was also able to get himself enmeshed in a very large housing project in Washington. Through his business affiliations and political contacts, at local, county, state and national levels, Congressman Tardy maintained that he could exert powerful pressures on the architect and contractors for the housing project to buy from manufacturers of his selection. He said they were very receptive to pressure of this type. His recommendations carried much weight, said Congressman Tardy, and would be the deciding factor in the selection of suppliers on the housing project. With this in mind he approached selected manufacturers to obtain business for his plating plant and offered them in return his help in obtaining orders for the housing project.

One of the companies he approached was Keystone Electric. They were in a position to supply all the electrical equipment and all the electrical appliances that would be required for the housing project. The congressman went to see several vice presidents of Keystone, as well as Mr. Selby (in charge of trade relations), and explained that he was in a position to influence greatly the placement of the electrical work. While he did not say so, he intimated that he could almost guarantee it. Knowing that such influence did not come gratuitously, Mr. Selby tried to probe the congressman for the amount and the form of the return favor. His answer was a detailed explanation of the fine plating plant the congressman had and the excellent quality of the plating it produced.

Mr. Selby knew that the amount of business that Keystone would have to place with the plating plant would be considerable in view of the fact that the order for the electrical equipment and appliances would run into several million dollars. The completely decentralized operation of Keystone posed a problem in such cases, because, to act on it, many division managers and purchasing managers would have to be sold on the advantages of such a move.

In addition, Keystone owned its own plating facility, which was currently producing more than 75 percent of the company's requirements. The plating facility was operating at 60 percent of capacity at best, and it was trying to secure more work. In spite of these problems, Mr. Selby decided to investigate the possibilities of using the congressman's plant. This investigation showed that the 25 percent of the company plating requirements that were bought "outside" were purchased from basic raw material producers or from highly specialized platers who did nothing but intricate work, all of whom were good Keystone customers.

Several months passed and Mr. Selby was still unable to resolve the problem. Naturally, he wanted to participate in the housing development, but there was no easy way of giving Tardy's plating plant any of Keystone's business. During this period Congressman Tardy had produced a very good contract for Keystone in molded plastic parts. He had done this, he said, to prove his value and show his good intentions toward Keystone. In addition, he spoke of other contracts, including one for an extremely large hydroelectric project in Asia. Mr. Selby about this time learned that Mr. Johnson, a recently retired president of one of the largest mail-order companies in the world, had joined forces with Congressman Tardy. The mail-order company handled Keystone equipment exclusively, and the retired president had been singly responsible for this purchasing agreement. Mr. Johnson visited Mr. Selby and reiterated the great influence that Congressman Tardy had with the housing project contracts, as well as his many other areas of influence.

1   Should Keystone become involved with Congressman Tardy? If so, to what degree?
2   Should business be taken from Keystone's own plating plant or regularly good sources of supply to satisfy Congressman Tardy?

THE CONTROVERSIAL FREIGHT BILL CASE

THE CAST

PRESIDENT, Creston Phillip—old-line type. Extremely successful. Has just attended an American Management Association seminar and is throwing a lot of new words around. From his subordinates' point of view, he is dangerous.
TRAFFIC MANAGER, Harold Britton—another old-liner. Is not good at

verbalizing, except to quote percentage increases. His freight bills are going up and he is being made to look bad by comparison.

PRODUCTION MANAGER, Joseph Scherf—blue-collar. Loves his machines and hates to see them idle. But beneath this exterior lies the soul of a power maniac, seeking control over traffic and purchasing.

SALES MANAGER, Samuel Foss—a stereotype. Is afraid of losing sales because of late deliveries. Echoes presidential statements. Appears ready to support Joe Scherf's plan for a power play.

PURCHASING MANAGER, Parker Young—much younger than his associates. Does his best. Understands President Phillip's words and tries to put some of them into action. Extremely inventory-conscious.

THE SITUATION

In this $75 million company, up to now things appear to have been going smoothly. Production does an efficient job and inventories have been reduced. But danger signs have just cropped up: though salesman Sam Foss has not lost any orders yet, he has missed quite a few deadlines; customers are starting to put the pressure on; a startling increase in transportation costs is discovered by President Phillip. He summons the group to his office.

President Phillip says, "Look at these air freight bills! There's one for $567—more than the part is worth. I know, I checked. These things are murdering us. You must realize that in our business today, transportation is a spot with great cost-cutting potential!"

Traffic Manager Britton replies, "I know our freight bills have risen 30 percent in the last six months, but what can I do? Young here is cutting inventories so hard he never has anything in stock. His short lead times force me to use air freight. And the way he spreads small orders, I almost never find a way to consolidate them to get volume rates."

Purchasing Manager Parker Young interrupts to say, "Harold, we're operating on low inventories because we save money doing it. Many times air freight is the only way I can be sure of getting what I need on time."

At this point Production Manager Scherf comments, "And when I need something, I need it. Take spares. This downtime is an awfully expensive proposition, and you both know it."

Sales Manager Foss joins in, "Whatever the trouble, it seems there must be a way to get an efficient pipeline. If Joe's late, then I'm late. Then we lose our image as a reliable supplier."

Traffic Manager Britton defends himself by saying "I don't want to seem bitter, but it looks like I'm getting the short end of the stick."

President Phillip then says that costs must come down. He asks for *action*!

Purchasing Manager Young defends himself by saying that the lead time problem goes right back through production, and eventually to Sam's sales. Young says that he needs earlier information.

Sales Manager Foss says that he has to promise prompt delivery. He thinks the problem is on the other end.

Production Manager Scherf suggests that the company combine Purchasing and Traffic and then find a way to get them closer to production.

At this point Purchasing Manager Young sounds frustrated when he says, "Joe, we're right back where we started. We need lower freight costs, but at the same time we must keep inventory down."

President Phillip concludes the meeting by saying "Joe's idea is a possibility. We could create a Materials Manager. I'll give you one week to put all your ideas on paper. Deliver your report at our next meeting. I want us out of this fix!"

1 What should Parker Young do?
2 Should Young suggest a Materials Manager?
3 Should Young build up his inventories?

DELTA STEEL COMPANY

The Delta Steel Company produces a large annual tonnage of sheet steel, tin plate, galvanized sheets, black plate, merchant bar, and other products. Company operations are on a substantial scale, as indicated by the fact that annual purchases, exclusive of capital equipment, average $100 million.

Purchasing is centralized in a department headed by the director of purchasing, who reports directly to the president of the company. The director of purchasing, is therefore, on a coordinate organizational level with the executives in charge, respectively, of operations, engineering, sales, and finance. The purchasing department personnel consists of the director, the assistant director, buyers, clerks, and typists. The director, in addition to his responsibility for general administration of the purchasing function, formulates purchasing policies, handles the major problems of coordination with various departments of the company, and represents his company in those industrial governmental, and other external activities involving important procurement matters. Although thousands of different items are bought during the course of a year, the director concerns himself with the purchase of such principal items as major capital equipment, construction, and raw materials, including those requiring contract negotiation, such as steel scrap and sulphuric acid.

It was the purchasing department's normal practice to have several sources of supply for all important materials and continuously to seek new and better sources. For the past fourteen years, however, the Delta Steel Company had contracted for its entire requirements of sulphuric acid from the Eureka

Reprinted by permission of Prentice-Hall, Inc., from *Selected Case Problems in Industrial Management*, (2d ed.), by Holden, Shallenberger, and Diehm.

Chemical Corporation, a subsidiary of a large metal mining and smelting company. Because of the fact that the Eureka Chemical Corporation produced sulphuric acid as a by-product from smelter stack fumes, its costs were appreciably less than those of several local chemical companies which manufactured the acid from natural sulphur. In fact, the price of locally produced sulphuric acid was from 15 to 20 percent higher than the delivered price of the Eureka Chemical Corporation, although its plant was several hundred miles distant.

Despite the price disadvantage which they faced, the local chemical companies had regularly and aggressively solicited the sulphuric acid business of the Delta Steel Company. They pointed out the hazards of a single source of supply and the propriety of patronizing local industry. Sulphuric acid is not only a critical item in the manufacture of certain steel products, but one involving considerable annual expenditure. In the case of the Delta Steel Company, purchases of this acid amounted to $825,000 or more in a year of capacity operation.

Sulphuric acid is used for the pickling of strip steel after the steel has been hot rolled. The long strips of steel are passed through a 25 percent solution of acid which removes scale, oil, grease, and dirt. This surface cleansing is essential before tin plate or galvanized sheets can be made, since otherwise tin or zinc would not adhere properly to the steel. Even for steel sold in the form of black or uncoated sheets, the surface must be similarly pickled before the subsequent operation of cold rolling. For pickling purposes, only the highest grade of sulphuric acid is usable. In trade terms this grade is specified as pure virgin acid or 100 percent H_2SO_4.

Sulphuric acid is essential to the manufacture of a wide variety of products other than steel. Among them are gasoline, paper, fertilizer, and chemical products ranging from rayon to explosives, dyes, rubber, and paint.

During a current period of scarcity of sulphuric acid, the plant of the Eureka Chemical Corporation was closed down by a strike. The Delta Steel Company had experienced no shortage, however, as the Eureka Chemical Company, in order to fulfill its contract obligations, had purchased sulphuric acid from the local manufacturers and absorbed the difference in price.

As the strike extended well into the second month, the vice president of operations of the Delta Steel Company became increasingly concerned over the situation. He voiced anxiety as to whether there would be an interruption in the shipments of acid. Steel companies do not store large quantities of sulphuric acid, depending instead upon scheduled daily receipts.

The director of purchases stated that he had implicit confidence in the Eureka Chemical Corporation's management and that, in accordance with the terms of the contract, three tank cars of acid had been received at the steel mill daily. Moreover, he said that the contract contained a cancellation clause which permitted either party to withdraw from the agreement upon ninety days' notice and, as yet, the supplier had not availed itself of this privilege. The vice president of operations still had some misgivings. He argued that the strike could well be a protracted one, and the Eureka Chemical Corporation could properly exercise the ninety-day cancellation provision. At the end of that period, the Delta Steel Company would have to rely upon local suppliers. The present scarcity of acid, together with the vulnerable position of the company, might well mean a substantial increase in the price of acid, with a resultant increase in steel production costs.

The director of purchases took the position that his company had benefited financially and in other ways from its long and satisfactory relationship with the Eureka Chemical Corporation. He did not feel, after fourteen years, that such a relationship should be abandoned when that particular supplier had the misfortune to be shut down by a strike which might be settled at any time. He also pointed out that any purchasing transaction is a two-way proposition, and should be mutually advantageous to buyer and seller. He stated that trade relationships developed on this basis are invaluable, and related the instance in which he had voluntarily testified in a freight-rate case on behalf of the Eureka Chemical Corporation a year or so ago. The local manufacturers of sulphuric acid had petitioned the Interstate Commerce Commission for an increase in freight rates on acid into the local territory. If the increase had been granted, the delivered price of sulphuric acid for the Eureka Chemical Corporation to the plant of the Delta Steel Company would have been 10 percent more than that of the local manufacturers. This would undoubtedly have precluded the Eureka Chemical Corporation from participation in the local business. Finally, the director of purchases expressed confidence in being able to negotiate a contract with either or both of the local suppliers in the event that the Eureka Chemical Corporation terminated its contract.

The vice president of operations remained unconvinced and continued to question the practice of concentrating the purchases of a vital commodity with a single supplier—a commodity, furthermore, for which there was no substitute. In his judgment there was a long but indefinite period of capacity operations ahead, and every means practicable should be taken to prevent any interruption to production. He suggested that, in view of their opposed opinions, he and the director of purchasing take the matter before the president of the company.

1 If you were the president of the Delta Steel Company, what decision would you make regarding this controversy? Explain why.
2 With respect to sulphuric acid or any other item of major importance, what are the advantages and the disadvantages of concentrating purchases with a single supplier?
3 What are your reactions to the proposition of patronizing home industries as advanced by the salesmen of the local acid manufacturers?
4 The director of purchasing in the Delta Steel Company reported to the president. Under what circumstances do you think the purchasing function should enjoy equal organizational status with such other functions as engineering, production, sales, and finance?

THE EEL CASE

Jack Smith is the purchasing director of the Eel Company, which manufactures heavy machinery and equipment. His department consists of 20 employees, which is just a little less than 2 percent of the company's 1,100 employees. The total annual costs of operating Smith's department are $450,000. The department annually buys about $45 million worth of materials for the enterprise, whose gross income is somewhat over $150 million a year. Jack Smith feels that this is a very satisfactory performance.

The company's one plant has a central warehouse and receiving department which reports to Smith. He is responsible for inventory control of raw material, subcomponent, and MRO inventories of $15 million. However, Smith is not in charge of materials handling, production scheduling, or incoming traffic, since these functions report to the manufacturing manager.

One day an alert young man presented himself to Smith and said, "I'm a member of the XYZ firm of management consultants. Your company has just retained us to check over its operations—including the purchasing department. My job is to discuss and analyze with you the importance and general performance of your department.

"Frankly, I come to you with a completely open mind. I don't know, for example, whether your department has enough authority or too little. I don't know whether its record is good or bad—or how your internal costs compare with your competitors'.

"My task is to find out from you how you appraise—and justify—what you are doing. I'm sure you'll welcome this chance to go into self-analysis. Would you be good enough to give me a brief report in about a week which capsules your operation and makes any recommendations for changes you think are necessary."

1   If you were Jack Smith, what would you include in this report?

THE FLANISTOR PROBLEM

Harper W. Beardsley, executive vice president of the Killington Company, a medium-sized maker of industrial products, studied a report from Chuck Martin, sales manager of the flanistor, the company's major product. It stated that a flood of recent customer complaints about flanistor breakdowns could be traced to several subassemblies, purchased from outside suppliers, which had been subsequently machined in Killington's plant. Martin's caustic note blamed both "sloppy manufacturing and poor-quality materials" for the failures, and stated that the product's success was built on "a reputation for quality, precision, and trouble-free operation."

Another memorandum was clipped to a monthly manufacturing cost report that detailed expenses for quality control and inspection, rework on rejected assemblies, and overtime chargeable to production shutdown from poor materials. Harry O'Brien, the manufacturing manager, had circled several items in red, and scribbled, "Quality control and inspection costs have soared since I have had to put three extra girls on inspection, as subassembly and material quality has deteriorated. There is $2,827 in rework and overtime here that has ruined my budget."

Then Bob Johnson, purchasing manager, called Beardsley. He said, "Several of our suppliers have told me that they have had bitter complaints on the quality of their products from the crowd in the quality control and inspection and receiving departments in manufacturing. According to them, the material was all right as shipped. It's not my job to receive and inspect materials—that's up to manufacturing. But if suppliers are not living up to the specifications on the purchasing order, I want to know about it. Manufacturing should not go behind my back to bawl out suppliers. This has got to stop, or I'll never be able to get consistent quality from suppliers with everybody calling them."

Beardsley recognized that he had not yet resolved these interdepartmental conflicts. Sales would try to set specifications as high as possible to ensure 100 percent customer satisfaction; manufacturing would try to pass rework costs and responsibility for any materials troubles onto purchasing as poor supplier quality, or to the sales department as setting unattainable standards; and purchasing would complain that sloppy machining and assembly or careless inspection caused the trouble.

Another approach was necessary, Beardsley decided, but he felt that the department managers would have to devise it themselves. He dictated this note:

To Messrs. Martin, O'Brien, and Johnson: The flanistor quality problem has apparently gotten out of hand all along the line from materials to product installation. Please meet with me in my office at 9:00 Monday, prepared to recommend and discuss means of correcting the present situation.

1 How should Bob Johnson, purchasing manager, prepare for this meeting?
2 What recommendations should he bring up at the meeting?

G.A.R. MANUFACTURING COMPANY

The G.A.R. Manufacturing Company is a producer of toys and small appliances with a seasonal sales pattern. Its sales are about $60 million a year. Recently the board of directors decided that G.A.R. should diversify, so it acquired the Wonder Chemical Company, a firm with $20 million sales of resins and chemicals. Wonder's market is mainly industrial, with an even year-round sales pattern, and the company has the reputation of being a fast-growing outfit in the field. Its one plant is located about 100 miles from G.A.R.'s factory and in the same state.

When the acquisition was completed, the president of G.A.R. said to Ralph Foster, his purchasing director, "I wonder if we should combine the purchasing departments of the two companies. I know both companies make widely different product lines, but there ought to be some economies, maybe in personnel and paperwork. Perhaps we could work out some transportation deals. For that matter, there may be some overlap in buying of maintenance supplies.

"I understand that Wonder's purchasing manager is a very good man, and of course, you know that we've promised to retain all their executives. But I would like you to look into the situation and let us know what you recommend. I've told them you'll be coming over."

Ralph's department consists of himself, four buyers, and five clerks and secretaries. It is responsible for buying all materials, components, and operating supplies, as well as inbound traffic. However, Ralph knows that his department has no experience in purchasing chemical industry raw materials, equipment, or supplies. Wonder's purchasing department includes five people, and is responsible only for buying.

1 If you were Ralph Foster, what facets of the situation would you explore in order to make an intelligent report?
2 What recommendations would you put into a formal report to your president?

GREAT WESTERN UNIVERSITY

Dan Summerfield just recently took over as director of purchasing for Great Western University. Great Western spent roughly $200,000 a year for the purchase of various kinds of plumbing supplies. These supplies included such items as pipe, tees, elbows, and many small plumbing repair parts. However, they also include some expensive items such as large valves and water heaters.

Because its plumbers were poor planners, Great Western maintained approximately a $120,000 inventory of plumbing supplies in its stores system. The university purchased its plumbing requirements from four plumbing supply houses.

Mr. Summerfield believed that if the university could consolidate its plumbing purchases with a single supplier who could supply all of its needs, Great Western could save money two ways: first, by getting lower prices, and second, by reducing inventories. Within the geographical area where Great Western is located, there were two very large plumbing suppliers and six small plumbing suppliers. Mr. Summerfield visited each supplier and carefully reviewed its managerial, technical, and financial capabilities.

The closest plumbing supplier to Great Western University was Bumble Bee Plumbing Supplies. This company was owned by the Bee family, and last year sales were roughly $32 million. Although Bumble Bee had many warehouses and offices throughout the state, one of its largest outlets was in Red City, just a few miles from Great Western. In fact, it was so close to the University that the plumbers regularly went there to pick up plumbing parts and participate in the free coffee and Cokes Bumble Bee made available for its pick-up customers.

Bumble Bee was managed by Mr. John Bee, age 74, and senior member of the Bee family. John Bee had worked in the family business since he was fifteen years old. His desk was located just inside the front door of the company's largest branch, where he was readily available to all who wanted to see him. Also, as he stated, "From here I can keep an eye on everything going on in the business." When questioned about the size of Bumble Bee's inventory by Dan Summerfield, Mr. Bee stated that he didn't know the exact size because he used no formal inventory control system, but he figured the inventory to be about $40 million, or a little over a year's supply of *everything.* Bumble Bee had excellent young managers, but for the most part Mr. Bee would not let them manage. For example, the purchasing manager told Dan Summerfield that only a few months ago he showed Mr. Bee a plan for reducing inventory by $10 million with little or no loss in customer effectiveness or product cost. Mr. Bee would have none of the plan. The company's controller told Summerfield that Bumble Bee's financial position was unbelievable. The "Old Man" had no interest in financial ventures outside the company, and for years he had just let its cash position grow until it now exceeded $15 million in cash assets. Total liabilities were less than $2 million.

After proposing an annual contract with Bumble Bee, Mr. Summerfield was told by Mr. Bee that his firm *never* sold for less than wholesale list price, and it would not sell to Great Western for anything less than that. With great pride Mr. Bee stated that Great Western might pay a little more for material from Bumble Bee, but his company *never* would be out of anything Great Western might need. Although Mr. Bee would not reduce prices to get an annual contract, he would give daily delivery service to Great Western in consideration for such a contract. Mr. Summerfield estimated that daily delivery from Bumble Bee's huge back-up inventory would permit him to reduce his own inventory from the present $120,000 to $40,000.

The largest plumbing supplier in Great Western's area was Automated Plumbing Supply. This was a widely held corporation with a staff of professional managers, and the majority having been trained in well-known graduate schools of business. Automated's sales throughout the state last year totaled $50 million. Automated's closest outlet to Great Western was 12 miles away in the city of Dumbarton. That branch was not large; however, it could be resupplied daily from Automated's large central warehouse in the city of Field. Field is a large industrial center about 30 miles from Great Western.

Automated had experienced rapid growth during the past ten years, its compounded growth rate being approximately 20 percent per year. Members of the management team at Automated pointed with pride to their new IBM computer, which was located at their headquarters in Field. The computer, in addition to providing reports to guide the company's overall operations, controlled the inventory in all twelve Automated branch warehouses. By use of the computer, Automated was able to turn its inventory roughly five times per year, which meant it had on hand about $10 of inventory at all times. Mr. Summerfield was told that stockouts averaged about 5 percent. However, use of the computer might lower the percentage of stockouts for the specific items Great Western buys. Automated's management was superb. Their capability and drive really impressed Summerfield. The management was young, aggressive, and very knowledgeable concerning the company's problems, how they could be solved, and where they were trying to take the company. Because of the company's rapid growth, finances in terms of accounting ratios appeared weak. Summerfield commented on this fact to the financial vice president. The latter readily admitted the weakness, explaining how the company planned to handle its finances to assure continued rapid growth. So sure of ultimate success were the managers that all had agreed to relatively low salaries with high stock options. This faith removed Summerfield's doubts.

Because of Automated's efficient operations, the company felt able to offer Mr. Summerfield a very attractive discount schedule, averaging 15 percent below wholesale list price, if he would sign a year's contract to purchase all of his plumbing supplies from Automated. Under the contract, Automated would deliver twice a week. Mr. Summerfield believed that semiweekly deliveries and a 5 percent stockout level at Automated would enable him to reduce his inventory from $120,000 to $80,000.

The other plumbing supply firms in the area typically had sales of less than $2 million. Some of these firms had only one office, but others had several branches. All of them were owner-managed and prided themselves on their "personalized" service. Several of these firms offer Mr. Summerfield a flat 25 percent discount if he would sign up with them. Typically, these firms had average stockout levels exceeding 10 percent. Each of these firms could deliver only once weekly to Great Western. Therefore, Summerfield could not reduce his inventory meaningfully, if at all, were he to contract with one of the smaller firms. However, the substantial 25 percent discount was attractive and interesting to Summerfield.

1   What should Dan Summerfield do? Should he contract with Bumble Bee? Automated? A small supplier?

GOTHAM CITY BUYS FIRE ENGINES

Mayor Harold Goodfellow of Gotham City is faced with a touchy situation involving a City Hall dispute between his newly appointed city purchasing manager, Ed Frisby, and Gotham's venerable fire chief, Willard Clark.

It all started soon after Mayer Goodfellow hired Frisby following a favoritism scandal linked to the purchases of the previous city purchasing manager. To prevent a recurrence of the problem, the Mayer gave Frisby instructions to set up a standards committee and gave the new city purchasing manager full backing in enlisting assistance from other city employees.

In accordance with the Mayor's instructions, Frisby formed a committee consisting of a Fire Department representative selected by Chief Clark, an engineer from the Public Works Department, a man from the Finance Department, and himself. The group began working on the high value purchases, and the first on the agenda was the purchase of ten new fire pumping engines and five extension ladder trucks, involving an estimated expenditure of approximately $300,000 for the pumpers and another $500,000 for the ladder trucks.

Frisby got together with the standards committee and representatives of fire-fighting equipment suppliers. Through these meetings the committee prepared open specifications, to which all agreed.

Bids were received, opened publicly, and then analyzed. The purchasing manager, in accordance with the unanimous findings of the committee, recommended that the city accept the lowest bid which met the minimum specifications in all respects. There was considerable spread between the lowest and the next lowest bids.

Then the trouble began. Shortly after making this recommendation, purchasing manager Frisby learned that Chief Clark had sent a resolution to the City Council recommending rejection of all the bids and award of the contract to another higher-priced supplier. Clark told the City Council that he would not be responsible for fighting fires unless his selection of equipment was approved by the Council.

The Mayor called Frisby. "Look, Ed," he said, "I'm in the middle of this fire equipment dispute. I think you're right in this hassle, and I want to support your work on the standards committee. But Chief Clark is a respected old-timer around here, and I think he's got some of the City Council on his side. Do you have any ideas on how to settle this difficulty and keep the Chief happy too?"

1   What should Frisby tell the mayor?
2   How should the city purchasing manager help solve the fire equipment dispute to the satisfaction of the fire chief and the city council?

HARDY COMPANY

The Hardy Company manufactures small electrical appliances, including electric shavers, electric mixers for the home, blenders, and irons. The company had recently introduced a new line of electric shavers for women. In the product design stage of the new product, the sales department had conducted an extensive marketing research survey to determine exactly what style-color combinations best suited the market for this new product. The style finally selected was an extremely modish plastic case with an entirely new shape of cutting head.

Unfortunately, no commercially available fractional horsepower motor could be fitted into the desired style of case. It was, therefore, necessary to have one of the Hardy Company's suppliers develop the required motor.

The vice president of purchasing of the Hardy Company, Mr. Monaghan, discussed the problem with the sales representatives of several of Hardy's best motor suppliers. One of the persons contacted was the sales vice president of the Centennial Electric Company, which had been one of Hardy's suppliers for years and which was known to have one of the best developmental groups in the small motor field. In his conversation with Mr. Monaghan, the Centennial Electric vice president expressed confidence that his firm could do the job, and he even roughed out a proposed method of attacking the problem.

Mr. Monaghan and the engineering manager were so impressed by the approach of the Centennial Company, as compared to presentations of the other companies contacted, that it was decided to award the development work to Centennial. In setting up the contract for this development work, it was discovered that the Centennial Electric Company had a rigid policy of billing separately for developmental services only on government contracts. For all other work, the Company recovered development costs through sale of the motors developed. Consequently, the shaver motor was developed by Centennial on a "no charge" basis simultaneously with the product design work at Hardy. Centennial was very cooperative and made several modifications to the original design specifications. Finally, ten handmade motors of the final design passed rigorous quality control checks by Hardy engineers. These motors were also provided on a "no charge" basis.

A purchase contract was then placed with Centennial Electric for the first production run of 100,000 units. The price of the motors was slightly above the price of a standard motor of equivalent horsepower ratings, but Mr. Monaghan felt that the differential was certainly not enough for Centennial to recover the entire development cost over the run of 100,000. He knew that Centennial had also made a sizable additional investment in special tools, dies, and fixtures for this motor.

The shaver was a great success and another 100,000 units were produced in the first year. Centennial had been given the order for these motors on a proprietary basis when it quoted a price equal to the price of standard motors of the same horsepower rating. A blanket order of 150,000 units for the second year's production was also awarded to Centennial without competitive bids.

When the contract for the third year's production was being considered, sales representatives of four different companies requested the right to bid on motors for the shaver. One salesman was very indignant and said that his company had been discriminated against all along and that he knew that his company could make a better motor for the job and sell it for less than Centennial's price. Although Mr. Monaghan felt that Centennial had done an excellent development job and was providing good service on the contract, he wondered how long he should allow Centennial to have this business on a proprietary basis. He was certain Centennial's price was not substantially out of line, but he was not at all certain that Centennial had recovered all of its investment in development, tools, dies, and fixtures.

1 Do you feel that the purchasing of this motor was properly handled? How would you have handled it?
2 Should the Hardy Company have solicited competitive bids on this item?
3 What would you do if you were in Mr. Monaghan's position now?

HARVEY COMPANY

Joe was foreman of the Harvey Company's small machine shop. When a small Excelsior bed lathe started to lose tolerances, he ordered a Benson 506 chuck (net price $89.52) to replace the Excelsior chuck on the lathe. Joe had used Benson chucks for years. They were a little more expensive than most competing lines, but the Benson chucks had stood up well, and the Benson Company had been a very helpful and cooperative supplier.

A new buyer, Eddie Atkins, had interviewed a chuck salesman from Jackson Company the day before he received Joe's requisition. Eddie reviewed the requisition and found that the Jackson 460 chuck had exactly the same specifications as the Benson 506. Upon checking with the sales office of Jackson Company, he was told that the Benson 506 and the Jackson 460 were completely interchangeable. The Jackson salesman thought the 460 held tolerances longer than the Benson 506 and was easier to adjust for all work. The Jackson chuck was quoted at $67.71 net.

Eddie called Joe into his office and pointed out the savings that could be made with the Jackson chuck. He showed Joe the two sets of specifications and asked Joe what he thought about the Jackson chuck. Joe was sure it wouldn't work. After fifteen minutes of unsuccessfully trying to convince Joe of the merits of the Jackson chuck, Eddie finally said that he thought the machine shop "ought to give it a try." The company normally bought 60 to 90 replacement chucks a year and Eddie thought a reasonable saving could be made if the Jackson line worked well. Joe left his office in a good humor saying, "Okay, but I know it won't work."

The Jackson 460 chuck was ordered and operated for almost three weeks before a requisition was received for a Benson 506. Upon checking, Eddie found that the Jackson chuck looked battered and would hold ±.01″ only if great care were taken. The Benson 506 was being requisitioned as a replacement for the Jackson 460. Eddie was convinced that the boys in the shop had "seen to it" that the Jackson chuck had not operated satisfactorily.

1 What should Eddie have done?
2 What should he do now?

HEATHE COMPANY

The Heathe Company is a highly successful manufacturer of smokestacks and unit heating devices. The smokestacks are made to customer specifications on a job shop basis for direct shipment to the customer. The unit heating devices are produced for inventory and are sold through wholesalers to industrial accounts and retailers. Most of the operations on both lines consist of cutting, shaping, and joining sheet metal and metal tubing.

About $30 million of the company's annual gross sales of $50 million is paid out to suppliers. Purchasing is centralized and the purchasing department handles all materials, supplies, and service orders placed with outside concerns. The purchasing manager is a member of the top management team consisting of himself, the engineering manager, the sales manager, the production manager, and the executive vice president.

Six months ago a new sales manager, Charles Johnson, was hired. He had a very successful sales background in major industrial equipment. After ten years as "star salesman" of the Smithson Company, a large manufacturer of stoves and heaters, he became sales vice president of that concern. In his five years as sales vice president, Johnson's primary responsibility had been the solicitation and negotiation of large government prime contracts. Since he had been personally involved in most of the contacts and discussions relative to these contracts, Johnson had had relatively few executive responsibilities even in his position as sales vice president. On the other hand, his talent for meeting people and putting across his product had enabled him to triple government sales for the Smithson Company in his five years as sales vice president.

Last year, the Heathe Company had begun an expansion which was intended to double sales in five years. Poor health had forced the former sales manager of the Heathe Company to retire near the end of the year. In recognition of the need for an aggressive sales program to accomplish the objectives of the proposed expansion, Mr. Johnson was hired to fill the vacancy left by the retirement of the former sales manager.

After one of the first executive meetings, Johnson had expressed his feeling that the purchasing manager "had no place in top management meetings." He felt that the purchasing manager could only inject a conservative vote in a situation which required "dynamism." Shortly thereafter, Mr. Johnson had become openly antagonistic to the purchasing manager. He had railed violently in an executive meeting once when the purchasing manager had made cost-saving suggestions on a new line and again when the purchasing manager had recommended holding up the introduction of new heater models by two weeks in order to ensure that adequate production inventories of steel and copper, which were then in short supply, could be accumulated. Mr. Johnson had said that specifications were up to him and engineering, that the line had to be introduced on schedule, and that purchasing should get the materials when they were needed rather than meddle in sales planning.

After this outburst Johnson had coldly refused to discuss sales matters with the purchasing manager present. He submitted requisitions for clerical and operating supplies to purchasing in a civilized manner, but took every possible occasion to criticize purchasing to the top management team. At all executive committee meetings Johnson announced "stock-outs," production delays, orders lost by lead time delays in ordering materials, and any other purchasing problem he had heard about. Any suggested change in a specification by purchasing was open to the heaviest barrage.

The purchasing manager did not become upset by these attacks because he was willing to take responsibility for any errors his group made. Despite the personal embarrassment these scenes caused, the purchasing manager felt that Johnson was not attacking him personally, but was attacking his position in the organization. The purchasing manager even felt that Johnson liked him personally, but was of "the old school" and thought of purchasing as a clerical operation.

On the other hand, the purchasing manager felt that his effectiveness was being impaired by Johnson's attitude. Several of the problems Johnson had announced had come about because of the lack of communication between sales and purchasing. Sufficient lead time for ordering materials had not been allowed in quoting delivery schedules. Specification changes were made on in-process items without considering materials availability, lead time, or costs. Purchasing was never apprised of quotations-in-process or of projected sales plans. In essence, the purchasing manager felt he was operating with no assistance or cooperation from sales.

Despite these difficulties sales were expanding and profits were increasing. The purchasing manager felt that considerably higher profits could be made if he could obtain full cooperation from sales.

1   In this kind of company what information and assistance does the purchasing manager need from sales?
2   How can he obtain this cooperation in the present situation?

THE INVENTORY OCTOPUS

Tom Johnson, newly hired purchasing director at Smithers Industries, Inc., was about to tackle an inventory octopus. Word had just come from the board room that the directors had decreed a $700,000 raw materials and supplies inventory reduction to conserve the company's working capital.

Smithers' president, Brashly Wintersee, had told him during the hiring interview that inventory was one of their biggest problems, and that's why they were looking for a purchasing and inventory control man who could show them how to work some of the fat off the company's inventories. Johnson's background and experience were expected to turn the trick.

Johnson started to dig into the problem via a visit to each of Smithers' divisions: Mill Machinery Division, Whizzo Tool Division, and Aerlectro Division.

At the Mill Machinery Division, he heard from Elihu Adams, purchasing superintendent, "Don't know as how the home office can give us much help on inventory, Johnson. We've been making machinery here since 1887, and every customer knows he can get a replacement part from us for almost every machine we've ever made. That's the real service that sells our machines. See that pile of raw castings and plates out there? Don't imagine there's another company in the country that has such a complete stock of material all ready to be made up to customer orders. It's taken years to build this up, and it's worth millions! We figure it's all gravy after depreciation, too."

George Rogers, the purchasing manager at Whizzo Tool Division, told him,

"Sure, I'm trying to get our inventory-sales in line with what the top brass at headquarters want. It's not purchased materials that's out of the line now on Whizzo home hobby shop tools. Our big materials stock last quarter is now in production or in finished tools. Look at them in the warehouse, all backed up for the Christmas selling rush. We've been building up finished stock for a big season all summer. I sure hope our sales forecast is right."

Their Aerlectro purchasing manager, Nelson Briteway, told Johnson, "We don't have any inventory problem here in purchasing. All our money is out there on the shop floor in custom-built components. All gear we buy goes directly into a government space black box. Since our customer is Uncle Sam, we don't have any finished goods inventory and darn little in the stockroom."

Smithers' divisions ran under separate division vice presidents, so Tom couldn't tackle the inventory problem himself at each plant. Because he was close to the top brass as a brand-new, high-powered expert, he was expected to help the purchasing managers come up with some results—and fast.

1   What are the company's inventory troubles?
2   How can Tom cure them?

THE IRATE VENDOR

Tom Jones, recently hired purchasing director at a medium-sized food products firm, received a memorandum from the company president, with a letter from an old supplier attached. The supplier's letter read: "I have just lost a $30,000 order from your company because my bid was $90 over the lowest quotation. I have been supplying your firm for over 30 years and I don't understand why I've been cut off without even the chance of discussing my bid. Most of the people I used to do business with in the purchasing department are dead or retired. We used to talk over your company's needs and I often advised them on how much to buy and at what price.

"Now I am asked only to bid on a set amount by a set date, and any remarks by me as to quantity greater or less than the set amount apparently are not wanted. I have tried to talk with these young and vigorous squirts now on the job as I used to with the old timers, but they want none of it. They tell me the policy of the company is to keep a minimum inventory and buy on bids, and the lowest bidder gets the business.

"In time they will find that buying on price alone will be an expensive business. It may fit some things, but it will not work for the kind of stuff I furnish. And, the outfit that undercut my bid shows a loss for last year and so far this year. How can you depend on a firm like that? I'm not going to do business unless there is a reasonable profit over a period. Certainly, I have got to be competitive, but I think my whole performance and capability should be considered. I have saved you thousands of dollars, and it's unfair to cut me out for only $90."

The president's memorandum said, "We may have treated this supplier unfairly, and I would like to see if this complaint is justified. His letter suggests that we do not yet have a policy on evaluating our vendors, particularly where intangibles like service, technical information, and advice are important. Just how should we weigh these points along with financial stability, delivery performance, price and quality? I know you are planning some changes in purchasing policy, and I would like to be brought up to date on what you have in mind.

"We buy about $150,000 a year of this supplier's product and we could give him an order for next month's requirements if he has been hurt. Send me a memorandum on what you think we should do."

Jones had been brought in by a management consultant to centralize the department's buying activities and improve purchasing efficiency. He had added a number of younger, technically trained men to the department and instituted competitive bidding on many items. Jones was convinced that his reorganization and new purchasing procedures were sound.

1 What should Jones's memorandum to the president contain?
2 Who should answer the supplier's letter, and what should the answer say?

JUSTIFYING POLICIES TO TOP MANAGEMENT

Tom Nelson, purchasing director of a medium-sized company making industrial machinery and processing equipment, was called into the president's office on Friday following the annual stockholders' meeting.

The president said, "You've probably heard about the ruckus we had at the meeting yesterday. One of the stockholders was disturbed over all this talk about price fixing, collusion, payola, extravagant business gifts, and conflicts of interest. He raised the question, 'How do we know that we aren't being taken for a ride on any of our big money purchases? How do we know that we are getting the right price for the right supplies on an ethical basis?'

"Now, Tom, you have my confidence, or you wouldn't have the top purchasing job. But the stockholders—all of them—deserve an answer to these questions, and I wasn't able to come up with an adequate one at the meeting.

"I am going to pass the ball to you. Please prepare a short report to present to the board of directors next week on your policies. There are a lot of things on the agenda so you'll have to be concise and to the point. I'll see you at 10:00 A.M. in the board room next Thursday."

Nelson's department spent about $132 million worth a year for a wide range of both standard and special-order items from motors and electronic subassemblies to sheet steel and pipe. Total purchases comprised 55 percent of sales. Nelson's buyers used bids and negotiation on both individual contracts and blanket orders. The firm's 1,800 suppliers were of all sizes and scattered across the country. The purchasing department had twelve buyers in the main office and eight others at the three branch plants.

1 What information and evidence would you, as Tom Nelson, gather to present to the board of directors?

LA JOLLA RESEARCH INSTITUTE

The La Jolla Research Institute (LJRI) is a large, independent research and development company. The company contracts to solve the scientific and economic problems of many clients. Among the company's satisfied customers are some of the largest industrial, transportation, and utility companies in the country. Now LJRI is faced with an interesting internal problem.

Mr. Irwin, the vice president for business at LJRI, said to Bill Wells, his purchasing director, "Bill, we have a problem to solve. Last year our gross purchases exceed $18 million, and they are still going up. I see many trucks delivering material to our receiving dock every day, but I have yet to see an entry in our financial statements showing any funds received from the sale of obsolete, salvage, or scrap material. What happens to the material for which we no longer have a use? Should someone in your department coordinate the disposal of material in a way more beneficial to LJRI? Give this problem your attention and let's see if we can add a new black figure to our financial statements."

Wells immediately started to investigate the disposition of LJRI surplus material. He found that most of the small material for which there was no further use was placed in trash containers located throughout the institute. These containers were hauled away several times a week. Wells noted that one-gallon cans, one-gallon jugs, used X-ray film, and all paper cartons were included in the material that went into the trash containers. These items had a potential value.

One of the buildings at LJRI was being remodeled, and it was found that employees were taking the used lumber, old lighting fixtures, used wiring, and other items home at night in their cars. This had been standard practice at LJRI.

In one research shop, the supervisor was selling the shop's scrap metal to a salvage man. The money received from these sales was going into a shop party fund.

Used equipment being replaced was often purchased by a shop machinist who would usually offer his supervisor $25 for an old lathe, drill press, and so forth. The proceeds of these sales also went into a party fund.

Wells observed that in all these cases the sales were made for cash, no attempt was made to appraise the value of items sold, no records were kept, and no money was being funded to the general account of LJRI. Wells also noted that department heads would give old items no longer in service to employees. This practice had come to be considered a fringe benefit.

As Mr. Wells turned the information he had gathered over in his mind, he was very conscious of the individuals concerned. He realized that the old-timers with twenty or more years' service were set in their ways and would resent the loss of income to their party funds. The employees who had been buying used equipment at reduced prices would not want to lose this fringe benefit. Also, the scientists in charge of research units typically resisted organizational discipline. They would undoubtedly oppose any encroachment on what they considered their own independent domain. In spite of these problems and sensitivities, Mr. Wells knew that he must make a complete report to Mr. Irwin, including a detailed recommendation for establishing control over disposal functions.

1   As Mr. Wells, what would you report?

LASTING LEVER COMPANY

For some time the Lasting Lever Company has been faced with the problem of defective castings. The manager of manufacturing claims that "these casting defects are costing us too much money to repair, they're chewing up all our profits." The problem is that most of the defects are hidden and are not discovered until machining has already taken place. When defects are discovered, the piece has to be taken off the machine, the defect chipped out, repair welded, and the piece remachined when possible. Even with this process approximately 12 percent of the incoming castings end up as scrap. Raw castings, when purchased in lots of 20, cost $4,000 each from any one of two or three suppliers.

Jack Hill, the purchasing manager, feels that Lasting should purchase machined castings, thus putting the responsibility of finding hidden defects on the supplier. Lasting would only receive and pay for finished, acceptable castings. This would reduce to a minimum the disruption of final maching and assembly operations scheduling, encourage the supplier to improve the casting quality, and increase the capacity of the Lasting shop, since both machines used for rough maching and welders used on repair work could be released for more productive work. It is obvious to Hill that such an arrangement would solve the most disrupting feature of all—the continual changes necessary in production scheduling now necessary to allow for repair and rework time.

The internal cost of maching each incoming rough casting had been figured at approximately $1,560 per casting. Machining consumed one man-month per casting, overhead was currently running at 100 percent of direct labor, and the total fixed overhead at 100 percent capacity was projected as $400,000. No estimate was available on the cost of disrupted production schedules because much of the impact of this, such as changing customer attitudes due to delays, could not be measured in dollars and cents alone.

Hill approached all his major suppliers for castings in an attempt to generate interest in his plan. Only one supplier, Hardness Foundry, showed interest. Of major concern to all of the foundries was the $60,000 to $80,000 investment necessary to set themselves up to machine the raw castings. Hardness was willing both to invest in the necessary machines and to guarantee immediate delivery of finished castings up to 15 units per month if Lasting would contract with them as a sole source for castings for the next three years. The price per casting would be $5,540 the first year, with an annual increase or decrease in price tied to one of the popular economic indexes.

Hill was faced with the problem of deciding whether to contract with Hardness for his castings, continue as in the past buying raw castings, or develop an alternative, more attractive solution. The Lasting machine shop was currently operating at 90 percent of capacity, but no one could give him any good estimation of what would be happening in the next few months, let alone the next three years. The decision was of major dollar importance in that Lasting used at least 100 finished castings per year and would continue using this many for at least five more years.

1 Should Hill contract with Hardness Foundry for finished castings?
2 Would there be any dollar savings by contracting with Hardness if the Lasting machine shop was operating at full capacity? At 50 percent capacity? At what point does it become "economical" for Lasting to contract for finished castings?
3 What are the dangers involved if Hardness becomes the sole source for Lasting's castings?

MANSFIELD WASHING MACHINE COMPANY

Part C-316 is a plastic faceplate for the control panel used on the low-priced "Challenger" washer of the Mansfield Company line. The Challenger has been popular over the years and recently won *Consumer Research's* highest rating for washers in its price class. This year's production schedule of the Challenger appears in Exhibit I. The production cycle for washers starts in August and continues to June, when the Mansfield Company shuts down for retooling and maintenance. The faceplates are used equally in each week of a given production month. One C-316 is used on each washer.

Part C-316 is one of the major style characteristics of the washer. It has, therefore, been modified several times in recent years and was radically changed only last year from the old C-315. Frequently production scheduling for the Challenger is not completely accurate. Schedules often vary ±50 percent from original estimates. Last year, the production schedule had to be doubled after the washer received the *Consumer Research* commendation. On the other hand, being a consumer capital item the Challenger has seen dramatic sales declines during periods of general economic recession. One such period saw a pile-up of finished washer inventory even after production was cut by two-thirds.

Because of space and funds limitations, management has set a maximum stock level for this kind of production part. The maximum level is 2,000 units or one month's supply, whichever is smaller.

The quantity discount schedule for C-316s is (including transportation):

Less than 1,000: 90¢ each
1,000–25,000: 75¢ each
25,000–75,000: 66¢ each
75,000–125,000: 60¢ each
125,000 or over: 54¢ each

The Supplier Record reveals frequency of deliveries between date of order placement and date of receipt of C-316s to have been:

	Supplier A	Supplier B	Supplier C
1–10 days	0	2	1
11–15 days	3	4	7
16–20 days	25	10	38
21–25 days	22	13	2
26–30 days	6	0	0
31–40 days	2	0	1

In each case delays of over 30 days had been caused by strikes.

Exhibit I   Production Schedule for Challenger Washers

August	5,000	February	5,000
September	10,000	March	4,000
October	15,000	April	3,000
November	20,000	May	3,000
December	15,000	June	
January	5,000	July	

1 Assume that you are considering purchase of C-316s in the June before the above production schedule is to go into effect. How should you schedule deliveries for C-316s? Describe the inventory control system you would use for this part.

MONITOR MANUFACTURING COMPANY

The Monitor Manufacturing Company was located in the Middle West. It developed, manufactured, and sold metering and flow-control devices used in chemical industries. Founded thirty years ago, the company was conservatively managed and had grown slowly to its current employment of about 100. The company was family-owned, and expansion had been financed entirely out of earnings. As it grew, the company found that its operating practices, developed in the company's early years, frequently had to be reexamined and modified to fit the more complex problems arising out of the company's growth. Recently, the management considered whether it might be advisable to install a more formal system of inventory control.

The company's product line contained about forty items, ranging in size from gauges and simple fittings to large flow meters weighing up to 150 pounds. Most of these were made in a number of different models and sizes, so that the total number of separate products was about 300. About half were standard models whose design had not changed greatly in the last ten years; others were subject to considerable technological change; a few involved special features for different customers, sometimes being made of special alloys to resist corrosive action of certain chemicals. Some of the more complex items were supplied with or without certain fittings and refinements. The company's position in the industry depended upon its ability to keep ahead of its competitors in design, quality of product, customer service, and price—roughly in that order.

The company had no formal inventory control system. No record was kept of raw materials, purchased parts, or manufactured parts on hand. An informal tabulation of finished goods, the Sales and Production Record, was maintained for each item. This showed the balance on hand, the amount currently being manufactured, orders received, customers' names, and dates of shipments made. It also showed the minimum stock balance and the standard manufacturing quantity. These had been determined at a top management level, taking into consideration past sales of the item, the time required for a production run, manufacturing economies, potential obsolescence, storage space available, and the financial resources of the company. In the last year, the minimum stock balance and the manufacturing quantity on most items had been revised

Reprinted by permission of Prentice-Hall, Inc., from *Selected Case Problems in Industrial Management* (2d ed.,), by Holden, Shallenberger and Diehm.

upward because of a substantial increase in volume, delivery delays, and more frequent manufacturing runs. The company felt that about three to four runs per year was about right for each item. A typical manufacturing run required about 9 to 12 weeks, most of which was consumed in obtaining castings. Actual processing in the plant required 2 to 4 weeks. Recently, it was found that jobs were frequently sold before completion and a second lot started before the first lot was finished. Currently, about 50 to 60 shop orders were initiated each month.

As customer orders were received, they were posted to the Sales and Production Record. When such orders reduced the balance on hand and in process to the predetermined minimum, a notice of depletions was prepared, showing the balance on hand and the standard manufacturing quantity. This notice was sent to the plant superintendent.

The plant superintendent, in determining the exact quantity to manufacture, was guided by the previously set quantities but consulted informally with the engineer, development, sales, and finance departments before each run. He then made out a make and buy sheet showing for the item in question the various parts required, the shop print numbers, the materials from which the parts were made, the quantity of each part required per completed unit, and the estimated completion date.

The make and buy sheet was forwarded to the assembly foreman, who checked off for each part the quantity of that part which had been accumulated from overruns on previous orders. There were no records kept on such accumulated parts. The parts were stored in bins in the assembly department, and those counted out against the make and buy sheet were separated in a tote box against the time when that order would be assembled.

The make and buy sheet was returned to the plant superintendent, who edited it to determine whether certain parts should be made or ordered in larger quantity than required for that particular order. Where parts were interchangeable, he might also consolidate them with other orders. The plant superintendent was familiar with the manufacturing process and set-ups involved, knew the price breaks on materials, and had a general knowledge of probable future demand. Before forwarding the make and buy sheet to the purchasing manager, the superintendent entered an estimated completion date, which in turn was posted to the sales and production record.

It was the responsibility of the purchasing manager to obtain the castings, materials, and parts indicated. Castings were purchased in the exact quantity required for the manufacturing order. For the most part, the same was true as to bar stock, plate, and similar materials. On the highly standard material sizes, more than enough for one order might be purchased, and in most cases full lengths would be ordered, rather than the exact fraction required. On odd sizes of expensive alloys, the exact amount would be purchased even down to the inch. Standard nuts, bolts, studs, pipefittings, and similar items were usually bought in standard commercial lot quantities, but even here the quantities did not greatly exceed immediate requirements, and frequently even these items were bought by the piece. Molded plastics and special fittings or stampings were sometimes bought in excess of immediate needs, especially when costs of small lot procurement were prohibitive. The purchasing manager did not alter the quantities shown on the make and buy sheet without discussion with the superintendent.

When materials began to come in, they were checked off the make and buy sheet and taken to the storeroom, to the production floor, or, if they were finished parts, to assembly.

Little attempt was made to schedule work to the shop, and the machine shop foreman was free to work on any manufacturing orders on which materials had been received. It was up to him to keep his men and machines busy and to meeting the estimated completion dates. As parts were completed, they moved on to assembly, where they were placed in the tote box with other parts accumulated against that order. When all parts were completed, assembly could take place. Finished units were placed in stock in the shipping room or were shipped out immediately against orders.

Completion of the lot was not posted to the sales and production record until the entire lot was finished. Inasmuch as some units were often assembled well in advance of the completion of the entire lot, the sales and production record frequently indicated earliest delivery as some time in the future when in fact completed units were in storage on the shipping room shelves. In this way sales had been lost to competitors who quoted earlier deliveries. Other sales had been lost because in setting estimated completion dates the superintendent usually allowed himself more time than was necessary for ordering, machining, and assembly.

Certain executives felt that the company should establish a more systematic control over raw material, manufactured and finished parts, and finished goods inventory. They pointed to the orders lost, the wastes of purchasing and producing in small quantities, delays in production and assembly occasioned by absence of materials and parts, and losses by misplacement, breakage, and pilferage. No survey had been made to evaluate potential savings in purchasing and manufacturing, and, since no records were kept, the inventory losses could not be measured. Pilferage was probably negligible, because the only items having real intrinsic value (thermometers and similar components) were kept in a locked cabinet by the assembly foreman.

Those who opposed changing the inventory control procedure pointed out the risks of obsolescence in any inventory accumulation, and, more importantly, the amount of funds which might be tied up in inventory and the space which would be necessary if substantial stocks of materials, parts, or finished assemblies were to be built up. They also pointed out that other uses of company funds—buildings, equipment, research and development—would yield greater returns.

1   What specific action should the company take? Support your proposal with an analysis of its strengths and weaknesses.

2   What is your reaction to the argument of those who oppose tighter controls?
3   How would your recommendation in answering question 1 differ if this
    company were making a single product?
4   How does the inventory control problem change as the company's overall
    volume of business increases?

NORTHEASTERN EQUIPMENT COMPANY

The Northeastern Equipment Company manufactured goods for the consumer,
government, and industrial markets. The company was organized on a divisional basis according to product lines. Each of the four division managers reported
to the executive vice president, as did the personnel director and controller.
Each division manager was expected to operate his division as a separate
business on a profitable basis. (See Exhibit I.) Each division occupied a
separate building containing its entire production facility, home sales office,
etc. The divisional plants were all within a 15-mile radius of the executive
offices where the president, vice president, personnel department, and accounting department were housed.

THE TEST EQUIPMENT DIVISION

The Test Equipment Division manufactured electrical and mechanical test
equipment for industrial, government, and laboratory use. The products of the

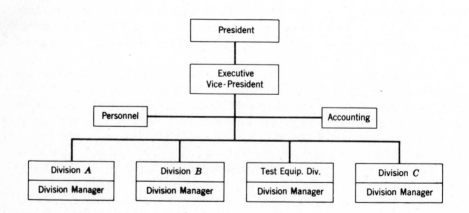

Exhibit I   Northeastern Equipment Company Organization Chart

division fell into two broad classes, relatively inexpensive mass-produced units and expensive highly engineering units which were manufactured on a low-volume or single-unit basis. Manufacturing, therefore, was placed under two foremen: one who was responsible for low-volume or "specialty products" and another who was responsible for the high-volume or "mass production" items. These two groups were supported by a metal shop and a machine shop, each of which was responsible for fabrication of subassemblies for both the specialty products group and the mass production group. (See Exhibit II.)

PURCHASING—TEST EQUIPMENT DIVISION

The purchasing manager, who was very competent and had twenty years' experience in production, engineering and purchasing, reported to the production manager because the division manager felt that the purchasing manager's primary function was to "see that production had what it needed when it needed it." The production manager was held responsible by the division manager for keeping all production costs in line.

On the other hand the sales manager exercised functional authority over the purchasing manager on all specialty products. These products, which were frequently large equipment installations such as automation devices and communication systems, were normally made on a job shop basis to customer specifications. Success in the sale of these products depended upon the ability of the division to produce efficiently to tight customer specifications and to deliver more quickly than competitors. The sales manager, therefore, could specify brands and suppliers for component parts, and he frequently negotiated directly with suppliers and supplier salesmen prior to placing an order through purchasing. The purchasing manager had repeatedly tried to eliminate these direct contacts between the sales manager and the suppliers since several expensive duplicate orders and contract complications had arisen as a result of purchasing's not being properly consulted or informed.

As a result of his resistance to the sales manager's activities, the purchasing manager and the sales manager were hardly on speaking terms. Whenever the sales manager did want purchasing assistance, he always went to the assistant to the purchasing manager, who was a very competent engineer and former lawyer and was known to be able to obtain excellent cooperation from all suppliers. Because of frequent favors asked by the sales manager in expediting and straightening out orders, the assistant to the purchasing manager had only one other set of assigned activities. These duties were the keeping up with special features of government contracts in process or negotiation, government regulations concerning procurement, and government liaison.

The internal organization of purchasing is shown in Exhibit II. The metal buyer bought castings, bar, plate, and extruded stock for the four production groups. His responsibilities included all basic metals and alloys which were to

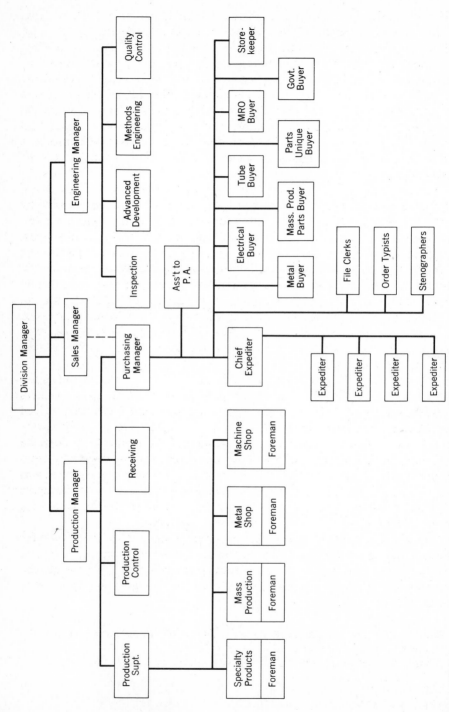

Exhibit II Northeastern Equipment Company Organization Chart, Test Equipment Division

be further fabricated in the division. The electrical buyer bought meters, wire, resistors, capacitors, and all similar fabricated electrical parts, except tubes, for both the speciality products and mass production sections. The mass production parts buyer bought all fabricated parts for the mass production section, other than electrical parts including tubes. The tube buyer bought cathode ray and miscellaneous tubes for both production sections. These tubes ranged in unit price from a few cents to $4,000, some tubes being off-the-shelf items and others being special development jobs. The parts unique buyer bought all fabricated parts other than electrical parts and tubes for the speciality products section. The MRO buyer handled all operating and clerical supplies for the entire division.

The government buyer handled subcontracts and purchase orders placed under government prime or subcontracts. Government work was handled by both production sections and accounted for 40 percent of the division's sales. Since government work was carried on in the production section simultaneously with civilian orders and since many parts were interchangeable, the government buyer only placed orders for parts unique to government orders. For standard items which would be included in government orders, he merely insured that the other buyers included proper clauses in the orders they placed. The government buyer worked closely with the assistant to the purchasing manager, with the sales department, and will all other buyers. He was well thought of by the entire division and handled government contract materials with a minimum of friction.

The storekeeper kept all records on preproduction inventories and supervised the stock clerks in the various storerooms of the plant. The expediters helped the buyers by following up on material orders until they were received in the plant and by picking up rush orders, etc., on request. Once materials were drawn from stores they became the responsibility of the production foreman who had drawn them from stock. Since some materials went directly from boxcars into product, rather than through stores, the receiving department was placed under the production manager. Inspection was performed by engineers assigned to the job by the engineering manager upon request by the purchasing manager. There was no full-time inspection department.

The Test Equipment Division had been operating at a low profit ratio for several years. Inventories of raw materials, goods in process, and final inventories were turning slowly, and orders were being lost because of high quoted prices and slow deliveries. A new division manager was appointed to clear up the situation.

1 What would you recommend the new division manager do to make the materials management operation more efficient?
2 What could be done to make purchasing operations more efficient?

OVERLAND EQUIPMENT COMPANY

Lieutenant James Essick, a contracting officer at a Navy Purchasing Office, was considering what action, if any, he could take in negotiating a contract with the Overland Equipment Company.

The Overland Equipment Company was the only supplier of a special machine costing several thousand dollars. This machine was useful in the maintenance and repair of naval aircraft. Using the machine, it was possible for three or four mechanics to complete in an afternoon a job that would otherwise require a week or more. Thus, the purchase of Overland machines would not only save the Navy money, but would also reduce substantially the "down-time" on aircraft. The Navy Purchasing Office had been requested to obtain 150 Overland machines.

In conducting the negotiations, Lt. Essick encountered the following overhead rates which the company willingly provided as part of a cost breakdown to explain its fixed price quotation, which the Navy considered too high.

> Manufacturing overhead—170 percent of direct labor
> Engineering overhead—93 percent of direct engineering labor
> General and administrative expenses—25 percent of operating cost (i.e., materials, direct labor, and manufacturing overhead)

Additionally the company had included a contingency allowance of approximately 3.3 percent of all other costs.

Compared with other firms in the same general line of business, the overhead rates seemed unusually high. Therefore, Lt. Essick requested detailed statements of the cost included in each of these overhead pools. After receipt and review of this information, Lt. Essick concluded that many of the costs were highly questionable. An inspection of the company's facilities further confirmed this conclusion. It was the inspector's impression that inattention to duties, loafing around the soft drink machines, and similar practices were standard operating procedures. For these reasons, Lt. Essick asked a representative of the Overland Company to come to Washington to discuss the breakdown of costs with him.

When the representative arrived, Lt. Essick pointed out to him the items which he regarded as questionable. He questioned the necessity for the company to employ one stenographer for every five production workers. He questioned the need in a small company for Overland's elaborate management structure with its three separate echelons of management. Moreover, Lt. Essick pointed out that members of the Cawthon family, who owned the enterprise, seemed to occupy positions in management which duplicated those of other people in the management hierarchy. Lieutenant Essick was particularly interested in one item of salary which he learned was being paid to the estate of an individual who had died over two years ago. When Lt. Essick suggested that the Overland Company must be a most pleasant place to work, the representative smiled and agreed with him. "People have a good time at the company," he said, "and there are lots of opportunities for relaxation and sociability."

Throughout the negotiation, the Overland representative was pleasant and amiable, but he insisted that the costs the company had submitted were necessary and justified. Although Lt. Essick succeeded in eliminating a few dollars in the cost of producing the item, he was unable to achieve any substantial reduction. He realized that the Navy needed the equipment and that use of the machines would save the Navy many times their cost. Yet, he also recognized that the Navy's purchasing policy was based on the assumption that prices should reflect reasonable costs. With these factors in mind. Lt. Essick, as the negotiator, wondered what his next step should be.

1 Should Lt. Essick question costs that appear to be caused by "inefficient management"?
2 What action should Lt. Essick take with respect to the contingency allowance of 3.3 percent?
3 What can Lt. Essick do if the Overland representative is unwilling to eliminate some of the unusual cost items?

PACIFIC MACHINE SHOP

Pacific Machine Shop is a small machine shop that derives the bulk of its business from large- and medium-size electronic companies. The major part of Pacific's work is building prototypes from rough blueprints. From time to time, production runs have been undertaken; however, Pacific's machines, layout, and space do not lend themselves to line production.

In the twenty-five years of its life, the Pacific Machine Shop has grown slowly, but continuously. Employment has increased from 20 to 150 employees, and the company is very successful financially. A new treasurer, Don Nix, has just been hired. Don, a young man, five years out of college, is full of new ideas and questions. One of the questions bothering him is the company's method of disposing of its scrap metal.

Because of its type of specialized manufacturing, Pacific Machine did not use a large quantity of metal. However, it did use several types, including iron, steel, monel, lead, copper, and brass. The total usage of all types would amount to about $3\frac{1}{2}$ tons of scrap per quarter. Roughly 10 percent of this total was brass and copper.

The shop foreman set aside two 55-gallon metal drums in which his men were to place their scrap brass and copper. Scrap lead was kept in a box so the scrap could be melted and used again. All other metal scrap was put into a general trash container. Around the first of every month, the foreman had the brass and copper drums loaded in the company pick-up. After the truck was loaded, the foreman drove to the plant of the metal supplier from whom Pacific purchased its new metal stock. The supplier would allow credit equal to the market price for the scrap. To offset the credit, the shop foreman would usually shop around to find items he wanted to take back to the shop.

Don was curious about this procedure. Could the company realize some value by saving its ferrous metal? Should the foreman, the highest-paid man in the shop, spend his time this way and also tie up a company truck for two or three hours while handling scrap metal?

Don was also curious about the method being used to liquidate the credit allowed for scrap. He did not like the idea of any representative of the company buying items without a purchase order. He also realized there was no way of verifying that the foreman returned to the shop with all the items he had purchased. It seemed to Don that more control should be exercised to eliminate the possibility of the foreman's being accused of wrongdoing.

Don placed all his thoughts on paper with his recommendations. He then went to see Mr. Sell, the owner-manager of Pacific Machine Shop.

1 Would a small quantity of metal be worth the trouble of setting up a good procedure to handle it?
2 Should the foreman handle surplus disposal?
3 What should Don recommend to Mr. Sell?

THE PERILS OF PRESUMPTION

This is the sad story of Tom Rogers, purchasing manager of the Buzzy Tool Company, who found out that a little knowledge is a dangerous thing. His company makes do-it-yourself power tools. After its president went on a cost-cutting rampage, Tom desperately embraced value analysis.

Tom set up a lobby exhibit which showed the most important components and subassemblies that Buzzy Tool bought. Salesmen were invited to come up with better ways of making these repetitive items. Whenever visiting suppliers showed interest in this new potential market, Tom gave them the following clues, "Fellows, we used to make a lot of these items ourselves. But our business grew so fast that we eventually had to farm them out. We're satisfied with present designs and quality, but our potential is such that we now are shopping around in all directions for new suppliers, designs, prices—everything."

The fancy Drill-A-Thon drew most attention. Made of castings, stampings, and turnings, it had been designed and turned over to a supplier before purchasing became a separate profit center under the president.

Three firms promptly came up with proposals. The first company said, "Tom, the ABC Company can give you a really swell price if you accept plastics instead of metal. Quality will be tops."

The second company said, "Our engineers at XYZ Company have figured out a way to use fewer parts. You know what a cost saving that will be!"

The third company said, "Tom, we at PDQ Company feel your best bet is to do your own assembling again. We'll supply the parts and give you a rock-bottom price because, as you know, we can make all kinds of economies on a big, continuing order."

Tom then got a hot telephone call from the sales vice president of his present supplier, Dandy Products, Inc.: "Tom, I think Dandy Products has a right to get upset when you put an assembly we've been making a long time up for grabs—without even giving us a chance to discuss the situation with you. What do you think a newcomer could possibly offer you? You know we've tried to get your people to talk value analysis time and again. No soap. Now all of a sudden everybody is invited to the party. We understand your product better than anybody else. How about giving us a chance to put our know-how together with any ideas you have floating around and come up with a price—and a job—that you can depend on?"

Then the chief design engineer came in. "Say, Tom what's all that stuff you have rigged up out there in the lobby? Is it true that you have a bunch of unknowns fooling with the Drill-A-Thon design? Don't tell me you've got some of those plastic peddlers trying to cheapen our merchandise! Over my dead body!"

Tom saw that he was in the middle of a four-way crossfire from his president who wanted a 5 percent cost reduction, his company's design experts who were uneasy about outside interference, would-be suppliers who were anxious to re-engineer Drill-A-Thon to fit their own shops, and his current supplier who could count on considerable loyalty throughout Buzzy Tool.

1   How can Tom start a sound value analysis program?
2   How should he inform the suppliers who can be genuinely helpful in this program?
3   What should Tom tell Dandy Products?

PICKING A BUYER—WHAT REALLY COUNTS

Alex Morrison, purchasing manager at the Flaxton Company, was trying to choose between two well-qualified candidates for a new buying job on his purchasing staff. Both were new college graduates; one was an engineering major, and the other a business major. Morrison recently had received a budget increase to add another buyer to his purchasing staff of five.

Morrison had organized his department on a specialty basis, with each man responsible for purchases in one of five groups: (1) special custom-built projects, (2) machine tools and capital equipment, (3) raw materials and commodities, including fuel, (4) pre-processed materials and components, and (5) MRO (maintenance, repair and operating) supplies, service materials, office equipment, and stationery. The new buyer would fill a slot formed by splitting groups 4 and 5 into three groups, with his first assignment being MRO supplies and service materials.

Morrison envisioned the new buyer as a future backstop for all buyers in value analysis, cost analysis, and negotiations. The new buyer would serve as an information center for new products, market development, commercial intelligence, and routing appropriate news to other buyers. In short, a new person was wanted who would develop into a broad-gauge purchasing executive, but assume specific buying jobs now. Morrison, as the department supervisor, would make the final choice among the candidates recruited by the personnel department. Morrison told personnel: "Sorry I can't give you people a better idea of the person I'm looking for. The job description will change with training and experience; no purpose would be served, therefore, in drawing up a long series of requirements. What I want is a good person who is interested in a career in purchasing at Flaxton."

Flaxton was a leader in its field of light machinery, and though still a medium-size company with $60 million in sales, it was growing nicely. Flaxton made several models of off-the-shelf tools and also designed and built special equipment layouts on contract, servicing them with parts and operating supplies. The company both made parts and components from a variety of metals and plastics, and bought parts and components from suppliers. Morrison reported to the president and played a key role in buying and planning decisions.

Although Flaxton was basically a small centralized organization with management and manufacturing under one roof at the home plant, it had eight sales and service centers located throughout the country. Management under President Harrison MacKlingle was excellent. It was strong on team decisions to produce quality at a profit. As Mr. MacKlingle advised Morrison, "You've got the green light for your department expansion, Alex, but remember a blue-chip company must have blue-chip people in blue-chip positions. You don't get something for nothing in any purchase of quality, dependability, and reliability. Sure, go ahead and tap this year's crop of college grads for your candidates, but a buyer who doesn't have what it takes to go higher is a poor investment."

Personnel did a fine screening job, and after several conferences and interviews, Alex had two choice candidates as nearly alike as peas in a pod, with good personality, education, background, age, health and character:

1 JONES
  Class of '75, State Poly Tech
  Major: Mechanical Engineering, with rank in top third of class
  Work Experience: Summer jobs in machine design, engineering drafting, and on a manufacturing production line as a drill press operator
2 SMITH
  Class of '75, University Business School
  Major: Business Administration, with rank in top third of class
  Work Experience: Summer jobs in an accounting office, retail sales in a hardware store, and statistical clerking in data processing

Both were willing to work for Flaxton at the starting salary offered, and both saw a career potential in purchasing.

1 What factors should Alex consider in making his choice?
2 Which person should he choose and why?

THE PRICING SANDTRAP

Leonard King, wide-awake chief of the ABC Chemical Company, which grosses around $100 million a year, and Dan Marshall, president of General Manufacturing Products, Inc., are long-time golf companions—and shop talkers. One day while playing golf, Leonard brought up the subject of price discrimination. "Say, Dan did you hear that Supra Equipment got tagged for price discrimination? The Justice Department claims they were giving some customers a special break on standard components. I've got a hunch Washington is going to get pretty rough in this whole area of prices and discounts."

Dan replied, "Yeah, I know. A fellow is a sucker these days if he starts doing favors to hold his customers. We're pretty careful to keep our hands clean. I've told our sales manager over and over: 'Your job isn't worth a dime if you start any funny price stuff—you can't play golf in jail, you know.'"

Leonard: "Sure, but that's only half the story. Do you know that your purchasing department can get you into the jug as fast if it puts the screws on vendors too tightly? My lawyers tell me that beating down prices too far can be construed as demanding an unfair advantage over competitors. Had you thought of that?"

Dan: "No, I hadn't. I know our purchasing boys are paid to get the best buys they can, and I know they've been crowing about how much they contribute to profits. But I suppose if they get too rough—especially if one of our competitors starts screaming about 'chiseling'—we may have some fast explaining to do. I think I'll look into this tomorrow."

General Manufacturing Products, Inc., is a diversified metalworking firm with annual sales of around $115 million. Each of its three plants has its own purchasing setup, staffed by 30 buyers in all. They do business with 2,000 vendors, contracting for $55-million worth of bearings, motors, electrical equipment, and supplies per year. The plant purchasing agents report to the local plant manager and are responsible to him for cost and size of purchase.

Jim Downes is the director of purchases at headquarters. He has two assistants to help on policy and research. He reports to President Marshall. After the golf match, Marshall called in Downes. "Jim, all the talk you hear these days about selling—and buying—at unfair prices has me on edge. Take our case. We're buying for three locations, and I know every one of our purchasing men is under the gun from the plant manager to reduce material costs and inventories. As a matter of fact, I know our boys saved $270,000 for us last year alone. That's great, but do our buyers really have any clear idea of the law? Do you have any general policies on proper prices? What I'm really driving at is this: If a fellow from the Justice Department walked in here tomorrow morning and said 'You're violating this or that law,' could we defend ourselves? I want to be absolutely sure we know what we're doing."

1   What should Jim Downes tell his president?

A PROBLEM OF POWER

George Bronson, director of purchases for a medium-sized manufacturing firm, received an urgent phone call from Jim Smith, purchasing manager at one of his company's five plants. "George," said Smith, "I'm up a tree and I need your help. Our company's chief facilities engineer and a salesman from the Supra Electric Company have just come to me with a sales contract for the big turbo-generator that's been authorized for the power house. They want me to sign it to 'firm up' the verbal commitment that the engineer has already made to Supra for the equipment. Supra says it has already begun work on the generator, and it looks as if the job is well on the way, although this is the first I've heard of it.

"I know the project is a rush job, and the appropriation has already been cleared with top management, but we haven't even had the specifications to get bids, much less write a purchase contract.

"The engineer says there wasn't time or need to get bids. He says we have to go along with Supra if the job is to be completed on time and that every day we hold back costs us money. Anyway, he insists we would end up buying the Supra equipment, as he thinks it's the best available.

"They're down the hall in the conference room, and want an answer right away. They're really putting the heat on me to sign. What should I tell them?"

Under their centralized system, purchasing managers in the plants reported to Bronson, and plant managers were under a corporation manufacturing manager. The facilities engineer was on the staff of the manufacturing manager. Bronson and the manufacturing manager both reported to the company president.

Bronson thought he had made it quite clear through information meetings, that, in accordance with company policy, negotiations leading to the purchase of any capital equipment were not to be initiated outside the purchasing department, or that any employee outside purchasing should not express preference for a particular supplier or commit the company in any way. He had no doubt that Supra was capable of doing the job, but it was company policy for the purchasing department to secure competitive bids from all suitable suppliers.

This was not the first instance of trouble with the chief engineer or others in manufacturing. It had happened before over capital equipment items, and other materials and supplies. However, Bronson thought his policy manual had settled the procedure with both his own management and with suppliers. He wanted to maintain good relations with the engineer and suppliers, but he wondered what to say.

1   What should Bronson tell Smith?
2   What steps should Bronson take to handle the immediate requirements for a generator?
3   How can Bronson prevent a recurrence of this type of situation?

THE R&D HASSLE

In September of last year, the Towne Equipment Company was faced with the urgent necessity of developing a prototype hydraulic mechanism. This mechanism was required for a special type of materials-handling equipment. Towne was producing for the Navy. Only one model hydraulic mechanism was to be produced. Only one company, the Fortech Corporation, was considered to have the engineering skill and experience necessary to develop the prototype model. The Fortech Corporation was a large manufacturing concern specializing in hydraulic equipment. Although the major portion of its business was the manufacture and sale of equipment listed in the company's catalog, Fortech also developed special machinery to solve unusual engineering problems. Because of the urgency of the work, the Towne purchasing manager sent a letter contract to the Fortech Corporation. This authorized starting design and development work, at the same time permitting the complete details of the formal contract to be worked out by negotiation while the work progressed.

In early December, the negotiation of the contract terms began. Fortech was asked to supply a cost breakdown for the firm's estimate of prototype cost. From their analysis of the breakdown, Towne believed the overhead charges excessively high, with general and administrative expenses accounting for 28 percent of direct costs plus manufacturing overhead. While discussing the most suitable type of contract, Towne was able to scale the G&A cost down to 22 percent. Although this was still thought to be excessive by Towne, the Fortech Company refused to accept any further reduction at this time. Both parties agreed that Towne would have to know more about Fortech's costs before a fair overhead rate could be ultimately negotiated. In view of the cost experience acquired during the two months the company had been at work on the project, Towne suggested the letter contract be converted into a fixed price contract with a redetermination downward-only clause. Fortech agreed. Both parties further agreed that an audit of the company's records would be necessary to obtain the needed costing information after completion of the contract.

Fortech did successfully develop a completely acceptable prototype model of the hydraulic mechanism in the time allotted. The audit was made shortly thereafter. The audit report focused especially on the G&A overhead expenses. Among these, one item of $14,000 was listed for "general research and development." Towne wanted to disallow this item entirely, saying that this research was in no way connected with the contract work done for Towne, and ultimately the Navy. Towne said that the charge for engineering overhead, already included in the company's estimates, was adequate to cover the costs of engineering talent applied to this project.

Towne also questioned an $8,000 charge for pro rata expenses for maintaining the company's sales engineering branches in twelve cities throughout the country. Since Towne had not used the sales services of the company, Towne asked that this charge be disallowed. The total reduction in G&A costs requested amounted to $22,000, or, in percentage terms, a reduction from 22 percent to 13 percent.

Fortech was adamant in insisting that both the research and development and the sales engineers' expenses were not only allowable but that they were fully justified. Fortech pointed out that its corporation had reached a very high level of proficiency in its work under the contract. The pure research workers, though they were not tied down to specific product development, were the backbone of the company's preeminence in hydraulic engineering. The pure research workers were constantly developing new materials, processes, and ideas which turned out to have valuable practical application. The prototype hydraulic mechanism could not have been made, by this or any other company, without such an accumulated body of theory and experience. Exactly the same relationship between general research and specific production problems was encountered in commercial development work, Fortech stated. In all the company's commercial contracts, the general research item was included as part of the cost. Fortech saw no reason for making an exception in this case. The Fortech staff claimed further that they had been able to avoid several unfruitful approaches to the Navy's problem, and had been able to finish work more efficiently and at less cost to the government than if they had not had the advantage of the company's accumulated research skill and experience.

In the matter of branch sales offices, the company representatives stated that these offices were not maintained merely as selling outlets. Rather, all their sales personnel were engineers who were prepared to examine the customer's plants, assess his needs and capabilities, and contribute to his product development and production techniques. In this way, the sales group formed an essential part of the company's development team. Its activities, therefore, like those of the general research men, should be legitimately included in the contract costs. Fortech further pointed out that engineers from both the main sales office and from the sales office in Washington, D.C., had been constantly in touch with technical personnel of Towne during work on the contract. These contacts had ironed out many difficulties through an exchange of ideas. Thus, in Fortech's view, Towne was receiving the sales engineering services as much as any other customer and should pay for them on the same basis.

1   As the purchasing manager for Towne, what factors would you consider in evaluating the position taken by Fortech?
2   What are the advantages and dangers of letter contracts in general and as related to this case specifically?

REDI-PORE FILTER CORPORATION

The Redi-Pore Filter Corporation of San Francisco, California, placed an order for seven filter-packing machines with the Sunland Manufacturing Company. The order was on a fixed price basis of $10,000 per unit, f.o.b. Los Angeles (shipping point). The Redi-Pore traffic manager designated a carrier and routes, and Sunland acknowledged the order without change.

Within six months the filter-packing machines were completed and shipped by Sunland to San Francisco. However, instead of shipping via the Southern Pacific R.R., Redi-Pore's designated carrier, Sunland shipped by truck. As was customary, it invoiced Redi-Pore immediately and, to take advantage of the cash discount, Redi-Pore paid immediately.

En route to San Francisco, the truck, a common carrier, collided with a tractor-trailer. The truck rolled over an embankment causing total loss of the seven filter-packing machines.

When the buyer contacted Sunland concerning the loss-in-transit, he was told that Sunland disclaimed all responsibility. "The units were sold f.o.b., Los Angeles, and title passed to Redi-Pore at that time." When the buyer pointed out that Sunland did not ship via Redi-Pore routes or carrier, he was told, "We saved Redi-Pore transportation costs by shipping via a less expensive carrier. You acknowledged that fact by paying our invoice. The responsibility of filing a claim with the trucker clearly must be yours."

1 What is the significance of f.o.b. point? What are the advantages and disadvantages of f.o.b. delivery; f.o.b. shipping point?
2 Whose responsibility is it to file claim with the carrier?

RELBOD COMPANY

The Relbod Company is trapped. This maker of small appliances and electrical equipment is taking in about $36 million, but the sales pattern has flattened while costs continue to go up. A consultant is called in to hunt for a remedy. . . .

Consultant—"Mr. President, here's your trouble: Your department heads don't have any profit-improvement program. They're just drifting. As your consultant, I say, 'Give 'em definite goals.' "

The president laid it on the line at a special management meeting. He demanded a 5 percent increase in profits for the remaining quarter of the year. For next year, he called for a 10 percent increase in profits, a 20 percent increase in sales, and deeper cuts in labor, material and overhead. The president then went to Larry Peters, director of purchasing.

President—"Larry, I want you purchasing fellows to carry the ball at the start of this game. We can't get sales moving for six months. *But you can improve your housekeeping—and Relbod's profits—right away.* Remember— out of every dollar we take in, 60¢ goes for purchases. Just think what you can do to that chart! *Every penny you save is profit!* So take a close look at what you buy. I don't care how you make your savings—by negotiations, imports, anything. But put the screws on tight—right away!

"Start with inventories. Our consultant says they're sky-high. So get together with the manufacturing boys on a 10 percent cut! We've got $6 million worth of stuff stashed away around here, and a 10 percent cut would save at least $150,000 a year in carrying charges. At the same time, *get your payroll and operating expenses down 10 percent.* That's in line with our companywide cutback. I know this hurts, Larry, because you've got some mighty fine men here in purchasing, but we can't be sentimental these days. Our overhead has got to come down—or we're dead!

"I'm having an executive committee meeting in two weeks. Have your plans ready by that time! We're betting on you, Larry. You've got to get us out of the hole. I know you can do it."

Larry Peters started a review of his purchases, which totaled $21,600,000 per year. Relbod bought a wide variety of materials ranging from a few pounds of rare earths to sizable quantities of sheet metal. A big part of the dollar volume was in nonferrous castings, forgings and stampings, fasteners, and subassemblies.

His department consisted of three buyers and four clerks. Salaries, fringes, and expenses came to $185,000 a year. The purchasing department was responsible only for buying; the manufacturing manager handled production and inventory control, receiving and traffic. Larry reported to the president, as did other department heads.

Larry learned from inventory control that raw stock inventory was $3,600,000. The sales manager controlled finished goods stocks. The company did not have a computer, but Larry thought he could work up the figures he needed by some hand computations.

Larry wondered how he could deliver the cost reduction and still keep his department and supplier relations in shape for the long pull.

1   What should Larry Peters do?

REPORTING PURCHASING PERFORMANCE

Marshall Fadler, the company president, handed a folder of purchasing department reports to purchasing manager George Harrison. In his usual cordial tone, Fadler said, "Where did you get the idea that I want to read these reams of reports about our purchasing activities, George? You are paid to run that department, and, when I think you are falling down on the job, you can expect me to be down there raising a storm. I would need a 48-hour day to read everything that everybody else thinks the president must have.

"You can save the time and effort that go into this one. I am interested in performance that shows up on the profit and loss statement, but I can't be bothered with a raft of figures cooked up by every Tom, Dick and Harry to help him run his job."

Harrison was bruised by the brush-off. Since his promotion to purchasing manager last year after two years in purchasing and three years in engineering, he believed the department was operating in an efficient, professional manner. To get his story over to management, he had been sending Fadler monthly reports on the dollar volume of purchases, with breakdowns by suppliers, and classified into raw materials, components, and supplies, the number of requisitions and purchase orders handled, and the departmental operating expense with a comparison to previous periods.

Harrison spent about $22.8 million a year for the company, which manufactured parts for a variety of industries, including the appliance, auto, and metal products fields. His buying list included aluminum and steel sheets, die-casting metals, forgings, turnings, copper, tin and zinc, and a wide range of maintenance items, as well as an occasional new machine tool. His buying staff included three buyers, an assistant buyer, and three clerks. Departmental salaries and operating expenses ran about $280,000 per year. He had some responsibility for inventory and receiving, and had taken on the traffic job more or less by default. An informal program of value analysis had been started in purchasing. Buyers interviewed 75 or more salesmen a week, and the most appropriate publications in their field were read and discussed.

The management group consisted of a vice president for sales and a vice president for manufacturing, with several department heads such as engineering, accounting, and purchasing being part of the management group. There were no formal line-staff relationships, although George more or less reported to the president. The weekly management meetings ran more to bull sessions than formal affairs with an agenda. Apparently, the president was satisfied with the operating results and the information picked up in the meetings. The firm was growing rapidly, and there had been talk of installing an electronic data processing system, though this was several years away. George wondered what he could report to the president that would be interesting and meaningful to him.

1 What information would you, as George Harrison, gather, and how would you report it?

SELECTION OF A PRESSURE VESSEL MANUFACTURER

Mid-Term
Case problem

On August 1, the engineering department hand-carried a purchase requisition to Jack Toole, buyer, purchasing department, Oceanics, Inc. The requisition covered the purchase of one pressure vessel to Oceanics' specifications as outlined in the requisition. Immediately, Jack went to work. He prepared a request for quotations asking 20 major pressure vessel manufacturers to have their proposals in his hands no later than Wednesday, August 31st. The response to Jack's request for quotations was amazing.

During the month of August, 18 of the 20 companies hurriedly prepared their proposals and submitted them to Jack within the allotted bidding time. As each proposal was received on Jack's desk, copies were forwarded to the engineer and manufacturing engineer for preliminary evaluation. By September 5, Jack called a meeting in his office with the engineer, Mr. Holpine, and the manufacturing engineer, Mr. Grinn.

During the course of this meeting, proposals were carefully screened and bidders were eliminated one by one until only two companies remained. It was a difficult decision for the group to decide which of the two companies submitted the best proposal. The advantages and disadvantages were about equal. Jack pointed out that Atomic Products Company submitted a lower estimated price, guaranteed the equipment, was more suitably located, and would meet the required delivery date. Jack also pointed out to Grinn and Holpine that Nuclear Vessels, Inc. offered Oceanics lower hourly and overhead rates, a minimum amount of subcontracting, and excellent past experience in making similar vessels. Jack stated that a field trip would be necessary to talk with both suppliers to determine which one was best qualified. At this point the meeting was adjourned and plans were made to visit both companies the following week. (See Exhibits I and II.)

In following through with purchasing policy, Jack called the vice president of Oceanics' New York sales office and advised him of the potential trip. Jack learned that Atomic Products was a potential customer for Oceanics' products, but Oceanics' salesmen were unable to get into the plant to meet key people responsible for procurement of major equipment. The vice president of sales stated that a salesman would be at the airport to meet Oceanics' representatives and take them to the Atomic Products Company first thing Monday morning. Jack phoned the President, Mr. Wilcox, and advised him that representatives from Oceanics would like to be at his plant Monday morning to review his plant facilities and meet the responsible people. The president did not appear to be enthusiastic, but said that he would be pleased to see them when they arrived.

Another call was also made to Nuclear Vessels' president, Mr. Winninghoff, who was quite enthusiastic about the potential visit and asked if he could meet the group at the airport, make hotel reservations, or perform other courtesies. Jack advised Mr. Winninghoff that these matters were taken care of and that an Oceanics' sales representative for the Houston, Texas area would accompany the group during the visit.

Monday morning, Messrs. Toole, Grinn, and Holpine took off from Pittsburgh and arrived at Kennedy Airport in New York. Mr. Morgan, the sales manager of Oceanics' New York office, met the group and drove them to the main office of the Atomic Products Company. The group registered, obtained passes, and went to the conference room. Shortly thereafter, the manager of production, Mr. Strickland, entered, introduced himself, and stated that the president was tied up but would see them later in the day. Jack Toole opened the meeting by stating that Atomic Products' proposal was among the top contenders for purchase of a pressure vessel and it was Oceanics' decision to take a field trip to look over the facilities and meet the people responsible for the job. Jack Toole asked Holpine to explain in greater detail the use of the vessel in the reactor system, and to give Mr. Strickland some background on the engineering work relating to the vessel. Mr. Grinn reviewed the manufacturing aspects of the vessel as required by the basic specifications. Near the end of this discussion, Jack Toole asked Mr. Strickland if Holpine's and Grinn's comments had the same meaning as Atomic Products' interpretation of the specifications. Mr. Strickland agreed, but was somewhat concerned over the rigid cleaning specification. As he told the group, "It is difficult for a shop our size to construct a temporary building around the pressure vessel, make such a building airtight, and compel our workmen to wear white coveralls, gloves, and to adhere to surgical cleanliness requirements. I doubt if we can erect such a building in our present shop area. Instead, we may add a lean-to to the outside of our existing buildings."

The meeting with the production manager lasted one hour; then the group commenced to tour the shop. Grinn noted that most of the machines, such as the vertical boring mill, horizontal mill planer, radial drills, and beam press, were comparatively new and well maintained.

Jack Toole wondered why Atomic Products' estimated cost was lower than Nuclear Vessels', yet Atomic Products' costing rates were somewhat higher. With this thought in mind, he asked Mr. Strickland, "Do you consider your shop to be better equipped than your competitors'?" Mr. Strickland replied that it was their management's feeling that this shop was the best equipped in the United States to handle such vessels, and that even though their shop rates were higher than other shops, they would turn out more work in less time than any competitor. Holpine asked Mr. Strickland why their past experience was limited to smaller-sized vessels, to which Mr. Strickland replied that they could handle any size vessel up to and beyond the one required by Oceanics, but had never received a contract for such vessels.

Atomic Products Company was a union shop which had had several major strikes occurring during the past few years. There were a total of 2,000 people employed, and the plant covered approximately 470,000 square feet of floor area.

The general appearance of the shop was excellent. The group noticed that the aisles were clean, there was ample lighting, adequate ventilation, up-to-date laboratories, good inspection facilities, and that the overall appearance of the building was extremely neat and well ordered.

The group pointed out several items in production and asked Mr. Strickland the ultimate use of these products. The group received a vague reply, such as, "These are a number of special jobs we have in the shop which we can handle without any trouble."

Mr. Strickland interrupted a group of employees standing in a corner and asked one of them to show the group the inspection and quality control departments. Both departments were well staffed and had up-to-date equipment.

The group asked Mr. Strickland to show them control of incoming materials vital to potential Oceanics' work. Wrong material which might possibly get into such a pressure vessel would contaminate the entire nuclear system. Mr. Strickland did not offer the group any evidence of material control, but stated that they had produced hundreds of smaller vessels and had no trouble in the segregation of material.

The metallurgical and chemical laboratories were well staffed and could provide Oceanics with adequate test specimens required by the specifications.

At the end of the tour, the group met with the president, who asked, "Do you think that our facilities are adequate to do the job?" Jack Toole replied that the facilities were impressive, but that the final selection of the supplier would be determined by many factors and that facilities were only part of the total evaluation. The president then replied, "If you want us to do the work, let us know and we will commence contract negotiations."

Several days later, Messrs. Toole, Grinn, and Holpine left New York and flew to Houston, Texas, for a visit to Nuclear Vessels, Inc. When the group registered in the hotel at 5 P.M., they found a call waiting for them from Mr. Winninghoff, president of Nuclear Vessels. Mr. Winninghoff asked the group to meet that evening at the Houston Country Club for business discussions. At 1:30 A.M., the group returned to the hotel.

The following morning, the Nuclear Vessels' chauffeur met Oceanics' team and the representative from Oceanics' sales office at the hotel and took them to Mr. Winninghoff's office. In the office, Mr. Winninghoff was waiting with the vice president of engineering, vice president of sales, vice president of manufacturing, and other key men in the organization. Mr. Toole opened the meeting in much the same manner as was done at the Atomic Products Company. After the Oceanics' people had gone into detail on the vessel, Jack Toole asked Mr. Winninghoff if they had any questions concerning the specifications. There were no comments, so the entire group commenced to tour the shop.

Mr. Grinn immediately noticed that the company's machines were of considerable age and not of large capacity, but adequate for the job. Some outside subcontracting work for the close machining tolerances would be required. Mr. Winninghoff stated: "True, we may not have all the necessary machines here, but there are ample machines available at other divisions, such as the large vertical boring mill at our El Paso, Texas, subsidiary plant. The schedule is such that we can move work into other divisions without delay." It was noted that general working conditions such as heating, lighting, ventilation, and cleanliness, were not as adequate as Atomic Products'. Jack Toole noted that the higher estimated cost resulted from more man-hours required to make the vessel because of less adequate machines.

Mr. Winninghoff stopped by one of the shop foremen and asked, "Say, Sam, how about giving these gentlemen from Oceanics an idea of what your group will be doing in the forming and rolling of the pressure vessel?" Sam had several of his men stop work to show the equipment available and its intended use. Mr. Winninghoff mentioned to the group that their plant had been on a profit-sharing plan since it was organized. The employees never organized a union.

There appeared to be effective control between management and the shop. For instance, to carry out the work fully, one member each from purchasing, expediting, quality control, and scheduling was assigned to a task force headed by a project engineer. It was the responsibility of this task force to follow the entire project through the shop and keep the project engineer informed on a day-to-day basis.

Nuclear Vessels had constructed one vessel considerably larger than the vessel required by Oceanics. Mr. Winnighoff claimed that they ran into numerous problems at the beginning of manufacturing and that the experience gained in the production of such a large vessel made them change their organization for closer follow-up. They also changed the type of paperwork and records for better control of material. The group noticed that each piece of material in the shop was marked for the project of its intended use. The metallurgical and chemical laboratories were very large, but much of their equipment was old. They appeared to have adequate room for the location of a cleaning room.

On Friday of the same week, Mr. Toole called a meeting of Holpine and Grinn to evaluate the two companies being considered. Holpine argued strongly that Nuclear Vessels should be given a contract because of their extreme enthusiasm to carry out the job, their past experience in manufacturing pressure vessels of equal size, and their previous Oceanics experience. Said Holpine, "Atomic Products has not had experience with our rigid specifications and the price and delivery will probably slip." Grinn argued that Atomic Products should be the company selected because of their adequate shop and laboratory facilities, location, ability to meet delivery date, and ability to guarantee the vessel.

Neither Holpine nor Grinn took into consideration the cost, the company's organization, guarantees, and other business considerations. It was Jack Toole's responsibility to evaluate both of these companies and show which company should be given the contract.

1   Let's assume as Jack did that both written proposals were equally acceptable, and that a visit to the plants would determine the successful supplier.
Prepare a list of points which the Oceanics' group observed in the suppliers'
plants to be used to evaluate each supplier.

2   Were there other facilities or information which the Oceanics' group failed
to secure which would help in evaluating each supplier's plant?

3   Based on the face value of the written proposals, which company appeared
to submit the best offer? Do not include information learned from the case
history.

4   Based on the proposal plus information obtained from the case history,
which company is likely to be the best supplier?

Exhibit I   Atomic Products Company, New York, N.Y.

We are pleased to submit a proposal in accordance with your request for the manufacture
of one pressure vessel in accordance with your sketch # 835 and all referenced specifications
pointed out in your letter of August 2.

PRICE

Because of the potential changes pointed out in your invitation to bid, and in line with
your request, the work will be performed on a cost-plus-a-fixed-fee contract detailed as
follows:

a. Total price:	Estimated cost	$560,000
	Fixed Fee	56,000
	Total	$616,000
b. Costing rate:	Estimated shop rate	$12/hour
	Shop overhead	180%
	Material	Cost + 10% handling charge

SHOP FACILITIES

There are adequate facilities at our New York Plant to manufacture the vessel and meet the
specifications to the fullest extent possible. We invite you and your associates to visit our
facilities.

PAST EXPERIENCE

Our company has not made vessels of this size but does have the equipment and know-how
necessary to perform the work. Our experience has been in working with vessels up to 60" in
length, I.D. 30" and 3" wall.

SUBCONTRACTING

We will be able to fabricate the entire vessel without exception in our shop.

ORGANIZATION

A total of 2000 employees is directly associated with our division.

DELIVERY

The pressure vessel will be shipped f.o.b. shipping point via rail in 6 months providing there
are no engineering changes.

GUARANTEE

We will guarantee workmanship and materials to be in accordance with the specifications
which were supplied to us at the time of this proposal.

Exhibit II Nuclear Vessels, Inc., Houston, Texas

Reference is made to your invitation to bid dated August 2 to manufacture the pressure vessel in accordance with your negative #835, and referenced specifications and any future changes necessary.

PRICE

The work will be performed on a cost-plus-a-fixed-fee basis, broken down as follows:

a. Total price: Estimated cost $780,000
                    Fixed fee   1

                    Total $780,001
b. Costing rates: Estimated shop rate $8/hour
                    Shop overhead   160%
                    Material   At cost

SHOP FACILITIES

We have adequate shop facilities to manufacture and deliver the vessel and would be pleased to have representatives from your company visit our facilities at any time.

PAST EXPERIENCE

The company has had extensive experience in manufacturing pressure vessels of heavy plate. Vessels 80" I.D., 49' long, 5" thick and many others have been handled by this company.

SUBCONTRACTING

It will not be necessary for the company to subcontract any of the forming, welding, machining, or testing for this work. However, forgings will be purchased from a competent vendor after he has satisfied the company's metallurgist that his forgings will meet the specifications.

ORGANIZATION

The Purchasing, Expediting, Quality Control, Production and other departments will each have one man assigned to follow this project from start to finish. Forms and records are available for your review. Our organization is familiar with Oceanics' requirements from knowledge gained as a result of previous work accomplished for your division.

DELIVERY

The pressure vessel will be shipped f.o.b. shipping point, Houston, Texas, to your Pittsburgh location within your required delivery time of six months or shortly thereafter.

GUARANTEE

This company will guarantee only workmanship. The rigid material specifications make it difficult for our supplier to furnish plate without any inclusion of slag deposits. Oceanics will have to stand the costs of any plate rejected or repaired after being tested by ultrasonic methods. Such costs can be negotiated after such defects are found.

SEYAH ELECTRO-DEVICES COMPANY

Gene Smith, purchasing agent at Seyah Electro-Devices Company, has just completed an analysis of his purchasing paperwork load. His staff, consisting of a buyer, an assistant, a clerk, and a stenographer, had complained of the steadily growing number of orders that the department had to process. The company, a maker of relays, subcomponents, and small control devices, had mushroomed in recent years to the point where 11,164 purchase orders (exclusive of changes and adjustments) were placed, spending $5,405,678 with 796 suppliers. Another breakdown by Gene showed that 15.2 percent of the suppliers received 82.5 percent of the dollar volume purchased.

A further analysis found the average value of all orders placed was $484.21, but 35 percent of them ranged between $30 and $100 and totaled 2.8 percent of the dollars spent. In fact, 23 percent of the purchases were for less than $30 and added only 0.35 percent to the dollar volume. Purchase orders were evenly spread throughout the year, running about 930 per month.

One cause for the numerous orders, he told the manufacturing manager, was the "daily need for rubber stamps, small parts, special screws, electronic tubes, MRO supplies, and other miscellaneous items" in his customer job shop operation. "The various departments write requisitions for purchasing because they want records for their files, and this conforms with accounting procedure."

Gene had asked Harry Flint, the accountant, to reduce some of the documentation required. He was told that "it's necessary to have proper records to control expenses, and the extra orders are not extra expenses because you would be on the payroll anyway."

The accountant also pointed out that the storekeeper, who initiated many of the orders, was following present company policy to keep only very active inventory items in stock and to make direct purchases of all others. Both the accountant and storekeeper were under the treasurer's office, which in turn reported to the president.

Another problem was the unpredictable number of change orders resulting from engineering modifications of original requisitions, and changes in quality, specifications, actual amount delivered, and date of delivery as specified by stores or production control. Accounting insisted that it would not pay invoices which did not completely match a confirmed purchase order or supporting changes. During the past year, 2,678 change orders had been issued, of which 1,946 had been due to relatively minor variations.

Smith knew that local suppliers and distributors had complained of the burden of small orders and that some were considering a minimum charge of $20 per order. Smith thought that small orders were not economical for the buyer or the seller, and he had asked the accountant and storekeeper to aid him, but neither would suggest to his superior, the treasurer, any change in policy or procedure. Smith's boss, the manufacturing manager, also reported to the president, and had expressed interest in trying to update the growing firm's management methods.

1   What other information should Smith muster to solve this problem?
2   How should he go about bringing the matter to a conclusion?

SMITHSON COMPANY

Smithson is a growth company. Last year it sold $40 million in electromechanical components. Smithson knows that continued success hinges on its ability to turn out "sophisticated" products made from sophisticated parts. Thus new ideas—and particularly new products—are a big factor in Smithson's well-being.

Because of Smithson's open-minded attitude toward suppliers, purchasing director Bob Finlay was swamped by a growing flood of ideas and items. Merely keeping track of them was a chore. Evaluating them was next to impossible.

But Bob was conscientious. He knew his company depended on fresh material. So he waded through the printed matter as best he could, attended several trade shows a year, and—with the help of his six buyers—saw 30 salesmen a day. In fact, Bob made it a policy that every supplier—known or unknown—would receive a courteous hearing. He reasoned that this would guarantee Smithson first crack at any new item as soon as it came on the market.

One day a salesman from Techno-Electronics, a small supplier, turned up. . . ."Bob, this is the performance graph on our new Bi-Polar Thermotron. It's just what Smithson has been looking for. Of course, it's terribly complicated, so I think you can save yourself some time if you let me talk directly to your Dr. Jones in research and development."

Bob debated with himself. . . ."Should I call Dr. Jones? He's always so busy. I'll make a fool of myself if this thing is a dud. But what if it's just what we need? It's way over my head. I'd better not take a chance. I'll call the old boy and ask him to look at it."

A few minutes later Dr. Jones called back. "Bob, please keep these peddlers out of my lab! That fellow you just sent down is a nut, and so is his company. Why do I have to waste my high-priced time talking to crackpots? Anyhow, I don't want salesmen poking around in the confidential information I keep down here. You can't trust 'em an inch and I don't want to see any more of them!"

Dr. Jones's remarks hurt. Bob and his buyers knew their engineering training was skimpy, but all had plant production experience, and they felt they had been doing a good job of scouting and screening.

Bob reflected, "That old Doc Jones burns me up! I can't figure him out. He's sure forgotten in a hurry the time purchasing discovered the key sub-component that put our control devices on the map. I practically had to ram that gadget down his throat. He kept grumbling that he hadn't heard of the supplier. So what happens? The discovery is worth a couple of million dollars!"

Another recollection rankled Bob. At a staff meeting a few days ago, Smithson's president had complained, "How come purchasing and research and development slipped up on that new aglutinizor? Our competitors got hold of it and are building their entire line around it. If we catch up in two years, we're lucky! What's happened to our policy of getting new products first?"

1 How can Bob devise an effective new-product screening system?

SPRINGER MANUFACTURING COMPANY

The Springer Manufacturing Company, a producer of computer components, has a requirement for 1,200 different types of plug-in control units, each having a different part number, and each with its own quantity and delivery schedule. Although these units entail the same cam shafts, bases, and frames, their wiring and components differ, so that each item would have its own requisition and purchase order number. Initial deliveries would be at the rate of 5,000 per month, total for all types, with quantities going eventually to 8,000 or 9,000 per month. A schedule would be established for a six-month period, but revisions would be frequent within any one-month period. On the basis of internal estimates, costs should average out to $60/unit with labor accounting for 70 percent and materials 30 percent of manufacturing costs. Tolerances are critical, and delivery to schedule is of the essence. To ensure against unforeseen contingencies, a small percentage of units of each type will be produced in the Springer Company's own facilities.

On the basis of engineering approval, five suppliers were asked to bid on all 1,200 different units at the rate of 2,500 total units per month, for a total annual requirement of 30,000 units. It was intended by Springer to establish dual sources, and as quantities increased, consider the advantages of a third source.

The bids received were as follows:

Popular Machine: $60.00/unit
Sterling Products: $57.00/unit
Taylor Manufacturing: $64.00/unit
Wright Manufacturing: $58.50/unit
Melville Products: $60.00/unit

Two days after the bids had been submitted—but before an award was made—Melville contacted the buyer and submitted an alternate proposal. If Springer would estimate its annual requirements of pluggable units and agree to purchase them all from Melville, the unit price would be reduced to $47.50. Springer would be free to release delivery quantities at its own convenience, and Melville would guarantee to meet them immediately. To assure this,

Melville would carry three months' inventory of each unit and increase its capacity, if quantities warranted.

1 What consideration, if any, would you give to Melville's alternate proposal?

2 Comment on the practice of dual sourcing, when part of the requirement is produced internally. Relate this practice to the advantages and disadvantages of a 100 percent requirements contract.

STATE RESEARCH LABORATORIES

The State Motor Company has annual sales of roughly $200 million. It expends approximately $10 million annually on basic research and advanced development projects. Most of these activities are centralized in a single research division, which employs approximately 70 people, including 22 engineers, 38 technicians, 5 stenos and clerks, and 5 administrative people.

The engineers and administrative staff of the research division, who were formerly engineers also, tend to look down upon nontechnical personnel and have a distinct bias toward high-quality developmental models and an extremely flexible operating technique. The 38 technical personnel are primarily high school or specialty-trained technicians, whose function is to construct prototypes of the designs created in the engineering department.

The purchasing department serving the research division reports to a central vice president of purchasing. The employees of the purchasing department are not employees of the research division, but of the purchasing department. The department consists of six people: a purchasing manager, a buyer, an assistant buyer, and three file girls and typists.

The purchasing department processes annually orders totaling about $3 million. The majority of these purchases consist of unit or small lots of unique and highly technical electrical and mechanical components and pieces of test equipment. On the other hand, about $600,000 per year is spent on more common parts and operating supplies, such as nuts, bolts, screws, switches, relays, and clerical supplies.

The primary difficulty faced by the purchasing department is the solicitation of bids on the complex technical materials required by the engineering staff. In most cases the purchasing manager and buyers, who are not technically trained, must rely upon the specifications and statements of the engineering staff of the research division. The research division staff feels that the purchasing department should not have any prerogatives regarding source, specifications, quantity ordered, or even price on the special materials required by the division.

On the other hand, the engineers and technicians raise no questions about the stock room items unless there is a "stock out" situation, in which case the engineer or technician informs the director of research that his activities have been interrupted by the stock shortage. The director of research has frequently stormed into the purchasing manager's office to inform the latter that "valuable engineers should not be left idle because some 2¢ part is not available in stock." The engineers have consistently refused to make any forecasts on use of stock room items. The purchasing manager is forced by company policy to control these items on a max-min basis, with a six-month average use as maximum. In items with low average use, an entire six-month supply may be withdrawn on a single requisition without further use of the item for another two years.

To complicate matters further, the engineers abhor "paperwork." They frequently go out and buy materials from petty cash or bring materials into the plant after promising an order to a supplier. In many cases, the purchasing manager does not know of the supplier contact or the receipt of materials until he receives an invoice. By the time the purchasing manager receives a purchase requisition, the engineer has frequently contacted several suppliers and promised the order to one. A further problem arises in the case of materials on supplier premises. At one time the engineers and technical personnel had over $550,000 worth of materials being assembled on supplier premises with no covering paperwork. Materials, including items "borrowed" from suppliers are brought in and out of the plant in briefcases and in the division's field truck with no approvals or paperwork required by any of the executives. The technical staff takes pride in this "freedom from detail" and "flexibility." The department heads and the director of research share their feelings on this matter and participate in the activities.

1   If you were the purchasing manager in this situation, what would you do?

2   What do you feel ought to be the functions and purposes of the purchasing department in such a division?

3   What prerogatives do you feel must be left to purchasing?

THREE VENDORS AND A TUB

Charlie Harris, tub buyer at Rub-A-Dub Washing Machine Company, faced a tough negotiation problem. Rub-A-Dub needed major tub assemblies for a new, low-priced model designed to improve Rub-A-Dub's share of the market. Quality and reliability were musts. But so were rock-bottom costs. Not a penny could be wasted.

In fact, purchasing and engineering had developed a cost program for vendors which they felt was tight, but fair. Harris emphatically was told to stay within the maximum that they had worked out.

The figure was $80 per unit, broken down thus:

Estimated vendor costs	
Material	$20
Labor	30
Overhead and profit	30
	$80

Harris first asked himself, "What if we make our own assemblies?" But he discarded this idea when he found out that Rub-A-Dub's tooling costs would be twice those of outside suppliers.

Meantime the sales department was flowing with enthusiasm, hoping Harris would come through.

Sales target	
1st year	50,000
2nd year	150,000
3rd year	300,000
4th and 5th years	200,000

Harris figured the sales projections were impressive enough to make the tub contract very attractive. So he invited three old-time suppliers to review the specifications and submit informal proposals for 50,000 units.

Joe Wilson of BMT Company presented setback No. 1. He said that his company could not go lower than $90. He stated that packaging costs were higher than Harris figured. If a three-year contract for 500,000 units was given, Wilson thought he could spread tooling costs and get the price down to $84.

Sam Newson of IND Company was disappointment No. 2. Newson offered a 100 percent return policy on rejects and quoted $88. Newson said that anything cheaper would just be junk, and that Harris wouldn't dare put it on the market.

George Withers of IRT Company would not quote at all. Withers told Harris that he thought the engineering department was pulling his leg. Withers suggested that Harris and Slim Boggs, IRT sales manager, get together to review the prints and the figures.

Harris told the three salesmen he would think over their proposals and get in touch with them soon. Then he wrote a digest of the situation and showed it to Donald Kingman, purchasing director. Kingman reiterated the fact that if they could not get $80 tubs, the new machine would be dead (and so would Purchasing!). Kingman felt that the suppliers were a pretty short-sighted crowd, and maybe purchasing should teach them a lesson. In any event, Rub-A-Dub needed good $80 tubs—and fast!

1   What factor must Charlie consider now?
2   How should Charlie prepare for and conduct new negotiations?

TOO MUCH, TOO SOON

The Space View Missile Company manufactures much of the ground control equipment used to launch and guide intercontinental ballistic missiles. One of the most difficult items to manufacture for all systems was the comb-bar in an input-control panel. The comb-bar was fabricated from a malleable iron casting, and comprised hundreds of finely cut slots. These were machined to extremely close tolerances, and the slightest discrepancy in either material or machining meant a total loss. Machine cycle time on the comb-bar was approximately sixteen weeks.

For nearly two years, castings had been purchased from the Richardson Foundries in Utah. Richardson had been a Space View source for many years and since that time had produced thousands of castings at suitable quality levels. Eight months ago, however, Richardson went out of business when its founder and president, Charles Richardson, died.

At the time of Richardson's death, two other foundries were also supplying castings for the comb-bar. Although they were capable suppliers, they could not assume the additional load created by Richardson's withdrawal from the business. Accordingly, a search for new sources was made. At first, few suppliers could be found who were either capable or willing to meet the exacting specifications and tolerances required. Ultimately, however, three foundries were selected, and invited to submit bids on 8,500 castings.

The low bidder, at $21.85 a unit, was Lawrence Foundry of Boise, Idaho. Lawrence was a medium-size concern with a good reputation for doing quality work and never failing to meet a delivery promise. Lawrence was given a purchase order for the full 8,500 units, with the stipulation that Space View approve the first 100 units produced.

Within two weeks the first 100 castings were received. They were subjected to initial inspection, and then dispatched to the floor for machining. In the words of the shop foreman, "They machined like butter," so that Lawrence was told to proceed with the entire order and a four-month delivery schedule.

It was about this time that problems began to develop in the shop. Some hard castings had damaged both grinding wheels and cutting tools. Also, cracks from casting porosity appeared on newly machined surfaces and slots. Although these conditions were not present in all castings, they occurred in a sufficient number to warrant action. It was determined that quality standards tighter than those of the existing Procurement Standard would be required. All suppliers were to be notified immediately.

Accordingly, the buyer contacted Lawrence, and told him to stop production of castings to the old standard, advising that new specifications were now being completed and would be issued within the next two days. To the buyer's shock, he learned that Lawrence had completed all 8,500 castings. Having had approval on the first 100 units, Lawrence established production on a continuous-line basis, and turned out castings at a fast, steady rate. Although the order called for deliveries to extend over the next four months, Lawrence was holding the castings and shipping them in accordance with the schedule. To meet the new Procurement Standard, it was obvious that Lawrence would either have to scrap all old castings and produce new ones, or undergo an expensive process of reannealing.

1 What are Lawrence's legal obligations in this matter?
2 Comment on the fact that Lawrence had already produced the full order quantity of 8,500 well in advance of actual delivery requirements.
3 What does the buyer do now?

VIGARD MANUFACTURING COMPANY

Mr. Jesse Krause, purchasing manager of the Vigard Manufacturing Company, was faced with the problem of selecting a source to prepare a technical manual for a winder that the company was planning to sell nationally.

The Vigard Manufacturing Company was formed four years ago by Edward Vigard, an engineer who had previously been employed by a large electronics manufacturer in the New Jersey area. Mr. Vigard's company concentrated on the production of a special type of wound magnet that had wide application in military and commercial electronics equipment. The company had grown from two employees to a present work force of seventy-five. In addition to Mr. Vigard and Mr. Krause, the management of the company included a sales manager and a production manager. The president, Mr. Vigard, handled design and engineering matters.

The magnets which the company produced were wound on a machine which Mr. Vigard had designed. The machine consisted of a specially designed casting, a high-speed motor, and a small core around which the finely spun copper wire was wound in order to produce the magnet. Mr. Vigard had fabricated a number of these winders for use by his company. Successful production of the magnets required proper operation of the winders and this, in turn, depended upon continual servicing to maintain required speeds and accuracy.

Last year Mr. Vigard and his management group decided to manufacture the winders for sale to electronics, aircraft, missile, and instrumentation firms, many of which produced their own magnets on equipment that Mr. Vigard believed was inferior to his own winder. Cost analyses and projections indicated to Mr. Vigard that sales of the winders might constitute a substantial new source of volume and profit. When a decision to produce the winder had been reached, Mr. Vigard invested a substantial portion of the company's funds in the castings and other components needed to manufacture the winders. As production proceeded, the sales manager made preparations for marketing the new product. First, he undertook exploratory discussions with potential customers in the immediate area of the Vigard plant. Secondly, he negotiated an agreement with a sales representative to handle sales in the western part of the United States. Thirdly, he initiated an advertising campaign, by means of direct mail and announcements in trade papers, stating that the winders would be ready for delivery on June 1st of that year.

The Vigard Manufacturing Company proceeded satisfactorily with the manufacture of the winders. Although the sales manager found that there was a substantial amount of interest in the new product, he learned that the winders could not be sold unless they were accompanied by an illustrated operation and maintenance manual. For example, the western sales representative informed him that the manual was not only essential to the user but also needed for demonstrating the winder. Moreover, an eastern customer, had placed an order for several of the winders contingent upon their being delivered with a suitable manual. These contingent orders were of great importance to the Vigard Company because the cost of the manufacturing program had required an additional bank loan and had seriously depleted the company's working capital.

Accordingly, Mr. Vigard and his associates prepared the technical descriptions that the manual would contain. Mr. Krause, the purchasing manager, was directed to locate a source that could prepare approximately 180 illustrations and technical drawings and have the manual ready for the printer on the first of May, in order that it would be available for the June 1 deadline.

Although he had never before had occasion to place art work contracts, Mr. Krause found that he was able to locate a number of potential sources through the use of the "yellow pages" and the telephone. The companies that he located were of two general types: (1) commercial art companies that prepared mail order catalogs; and (2) art companies that specialized in the preparation of technical manuals. He found that most of the commercial art companies showed little interest in the work because they were busy preparing catalogs and promotional pamphlets for their regular clients. Two large concerns which specialized in the preparation of technical manuals seemed anxious to obtain the work.

In addition to these two broad classes of companies, Bullock Art, a small organization that was attempting to expand, gave promise of being able to handle the work. This company consisted of Mr. Bullock and a group of free-lance artists whom he employed whenever he obtained a contract requiring their help. Mr. Bullock had been employed as a free-lance artist by several companies, which, upon telephone inquiries by Mr. Krause, reported favorably on the quality of Mr. Bullock's work. In addition, he taught commercial art at a well known trade school and had developed his own production methods, which appeared to be superior to those used by most other art concerns.

Mr. Krause's preliminary survey indicated that four companies were interested in undertaking the work: Bullock Art, Webster, Inc., and Hershey Associates (the two concerns specializing in the production of technical manuals) and The Catalogue Corporation, a large commercial art concern. Mr. Krause decided to visit each of these companies.

Webster, Inc., the first company visited, was the largest art concern in the city, employing approximately 150 artists and book designers. The company had excellent facilities, including the latest art and layout equipment and its own photographic laboratories. The operations of the company appeared to be efficiently organized and well managed. Although the company was then operating at capacity. Mr. Krause learned that approximately 80 percent of its business had been with one large manufacturer which had recently informed the Webster management that it was shifting its technical manual and work to another firm. The general manager of the company estimated that he could complete Mr. Krause's work on schedule. He stated further that the company would undertake the work on an hourly basis with a guarantee that the total time would not exceed a specified number of hours. He informed Mr. Krause that he could submit a definite quotation within forty-eight hours.

Hershey Associates was visited next. Although considerably smaller than Webster, Inc., the company had been doing the same general type of work. After examining samples of the company's previous work, Mr. Krause concluded that Hershey Associates was qualified to prepare the art work for the manual, and invited the company to submit a quotation.

Mr. Krause then called upon The Catalogue Corporation. Although this company was well-known as a publisher of mail order catalogs, it had never produced a technical manual. The company representative saw no problem in meeting Mr. Krause's requirements, however. He said that if any specialized talent was required, he would have no difficulty in obtaining needed personnel inasmuch as several qualified people had called upon him that week in search of employment. In view of these assertions and the general reputation of the company, Mr. Krause asked The Catalogue Corporation to submit a quotation.

The pressure of other work prevented Mr. Krause from visiting Bullock Art. However, Mr. Bullock telephoned to ask if he might visit the Vigard Manufacturing Company to analyze the job and submit a quotation. He stated that if he were given an opportunity to study the work, he was confident he could demonstrate his ability to handle the contract within the time limit and at a lower cost than his competitors. Although Mr. Krause did not believe that an additional quotation was necessary, he agreed to let Mr. Bullock analyze the work and submit a quotation.

The following day the general manager of Webster, Inc., called upon Mr. Krause to present his quotation. The quotation stipulated a rate of $8.70 per man-hour with a maximum guarantee of $36,000. The quotation was contingent, however, upon weekly progress payments based upon the number of hours spent on the contract. In submitting the quotation, the general manager stated that the hourly rate should be considered as the significant figure, since the maximum guarantee provided a margin of safety for contingencies. Mr. Krause took exception to this statement, pointing out that a company employing more highly skilled personnel might complete the job in fewer hours and at a lower total cost, even though it had a higher hourly rate. He concluded, therefore, that the maximum guarantee was the more important figure. In addition, Mr. Krause stated that although the art work would not necessarily be awarded to the lowest bidder, it was going to be placed on a competitive basis, and he advised the Webster general manager to eliminate any "water" that might be in his bid. After making a few computations on a scratch pad, the general manager stated that he could reduce the maximum guarantee to $24,000. Thereupon Mr. Krause told him to prepare a new quotation and to submit it as soon as possible. The following morning, the general manager returned with a new quotation containing the same hourly rate but with a new maximum guarantee of only $11,250. When Mr. Krause remarked, "There must have been enough 'water' in the previous quotation to float the manual," the general manager replied that he expected to lose money if he received the contract. He said that in view of this, he was unwilling to assume the burden of financing the work. Mr. Krause explained that this was an important issue to him and that his award of the contract might well hinge on this provision. The general manager pointed out that his company typically received weekly progress payments and that without them, he was not willing to accept the contract. Mr. Krause then stated that he would make his decision and place the contract within forty-eight hours.

In the meantime, Mr. Bullock had visited the Vigard Company and had spent several hours analyzing the work and preparing his quotation. In the course of his analysis, Mr. Bullock made a number of suggestions which not only improved the style of the manual but simplified the production of the art work. For example, Mr. Bullock suggested that certain expensive airbrush operations could be replaced by relatively inexpensive screening techniques. He also demonstrated that through more careful "eye control" many of the sketches could be improved; this would result from a rearrangement of details so that they were placed at a point in the illustration where the eye naturally fell first. He stated that if he were given the contract, he would improve the layout and general appearance of the manual and eliminate difficult production problems. Mr. Bullock examined the rough sketches for the manual and discussed them briefly with Mr. Vigard and the sales manager. When Mr. Krause discussed Mr. Bullock's qualifications with these two officers of the company, they both expressed the opinion that he possessed an unusual ability and seemed to be well qualified to undertake the work.

Bullock Art's quotation specified an hourly rate of $9 and a maximum guarantee of $10,530. Mr. Bullock explained in detail how he had prepared the quotation and how the production shortcuts he had developed would enable him to make a fair profit on the contract. Although Mr. Krause was convinced that Mr. Bullock had a better understanding of the job to be done than any other bidder, he questioned his ability to acquire an organization and get it in operation in time to meet the required production schedule. Mr. Bullock countered by saying that this was the normal manner in which he worked and that he was confident that he could get the personnel and equipment needed on a moment's notice. He stated further that if he needed additional funds to finance the work, he could borrow the money from his brother-in-law. In the event that he fell behind schedule, he could work nights and weekends.

During the day, the quotations of the the other two companies were received. The Catalogue Corporation offered to take the contract at an hourly rate of $10.50 and a maximum guarantee of $16,065. The quotation of Hershey Associates stipulated an hourly rate of $9.45 and a maximum guarantee of $16,875.

Although Bullock Art submitted the low quotation, Mr. Krause was somewhat reluctant to place the contract with the company. He did not question Mr. Bullock's personal ability, but doubted that he could expand his organization fast enough to meet the desired production schedule. On March 22, because of this doubt, Mr. Krause decided to visit Bullock Art. His visit disclosed that Bullock Art did not possess adequate space in which to do the work. However, Mr. Bullock showed him an unoccupied basement in a building down the street that could be rented, cleaned up, and put to use if needed.

After his visit to Bullock Art, Mr. Krause wondered if the potential savings of an award to Bullock justified the risks that were involved. He needed to place the contract immediately in order to allow sufficient time for the completion of the art work and delivery of the manual to the printer by May 1. Unless the manual reached the printer by this date, it would not be available on the first of June, the day on which the winders had been promised for delivery.

1   If you were Mr. Krause, what action would you take and why?

THE WIDE, WIDE WORLD OF PURCHASING

Charley Ruggles, purchasing manager at the Newton Manufacturing Company, was wondering whether to take the plunge into worldwide purchasing. A salesman from Eurofabrik, Ltd., a foreign producer of small assemblies and stamps, had just left a proposal on his desk for one of Newton's major purchases, the transklutch. Eurofabrik's price was 35 percent below what Charley was paying to a local supplier—even figuring in the extra cost of duty, ocean freight, and overland transportation to the Newton plant.

Newton used this assembly, a combination of stampings and turnings, in all of its "Powermaster" assemblies sold both for use in consumer and industrial end-products. The transklutch was half of the unit cost of a Powermaster final assembly. Charley had instructions from Slaterer P. Colby, Newton's president, to cut costs. "Charley, the cost-price squeeze on the Powermaster really hurts. Purchasing is responsible for half the cost of this product, and you have got to get your material cost down. *But don't cut corners on quality!* We can't afford to lose our reputation for a quality Powermaster! Give me a report at our meeting in two weeks!"

Ruggles had just started to work on the problem when the Eurofabrik salesman called. "Our plant is one of the most modern in the Common Market, and that's why we can give you such a low price. We have all the latest equipment, and our quality reputation is well-known. In three months you will have the first shipment made exactly to your specifications."

Charley talked it over with several of his closest purchasing management friends at lunch: Ralph Wilson, purchasing director of ABC; Gene Nelson, purchasing manager for Universal Manufacturing; and Larry Smith, purchasing manager for the local electric utility.

RALPH—"I'd rather look into it, Charley. You know we have been buying foreign on some of our raw materials and metals for years. You have to get used to some of the delays and red tape, *but it's sure worth it!* I got a promotion out of my foreign buying record."

GENE—"Whoa! That's just on commodities, Ralph, not components! We got stung when we couldn't get foreign suppliers to stick to our specifications on components. The late deliveries and headaches aren't worth it. We had to go back to our U.S. suppliers after that adventure!"

LARRY—"There's another side, too, Charley. We believe in 'buying American' and supporting local industry. Say, don't you purchase trans-klutches from Merit Machine here in town? That makes it a pretty touchy political issue then, I'd say."

Transklutch quality was important. If a Powermaster failed in service, the final customer usually complained to Newton. Deliveries had to be on schedule to prevent assembly line downtime and minimize expensive safety stock inventory. Technical service had never been a problem, as their supplier, Merit, was just down the street.

Ruggles knew he had to have an answer for the president in ten days, and the Eurofabrik proposal might be it. He could not go in half-cocked, but neither could he look into all aspects of the problem in this short a time.

1   What key issues and figures and information should Charley pull together?
2   What sources should Charley use for his information?
3   What should Charley recommend?

WINSMORE LABORATORY

Last spring the Winsmore Laboratory purchased the vessel *Joie,* a World War II freighter which had been in the "moth-ball" fleet for over twenty years. *Joie* was purchased for use as an off-shore exploration station. Winsmore budgeted $1,500,000 to convert *Joie* for this research work.

One major expense item of the conversion was the purchase of a complete range of electronic navigation, detection, and analysis devices. These devices included radars, sonars, precision depth recorders, gyroscopes, loran, and radio transmitting and receiving equipment. Outfitted with them, *Joie* would be one of the best-equipped floating laboratories in the world.

Six prominent scientists from the Winsmore staff were charged with selecting, by brand name, those electronic equipments best suited to accomplish the research projects planned for *Joie*. After three months of much disagreement among the scientists, a listing of the items needed was completed and forwarded to David Rice, director of purchasing for the Winsmore Laboratory. The listing consisted of seven items, each manufactured by a different company. Two manufacturers were in foreign countries. The catalog price for the equipment totaled $159,314. Installation and necessary spare parts would be additional.

After receiving the listing, Mr. Rice immediately contacted the sales representative handling each piece of equipment to determine delivery availability for each item. The shipyard converting the vessel needed this information to complete a critical path analysis of the conversion. Mr. Rice had included this provision in the conversion contract to expedite and smooth the ship's conversion schedule.

Because of the nature of the marine electronics industry, no discounting of list prices was available to Mr. Rice, other than the normal 2 percent, 10-day discount for prompt payment. Each manufacturer was willing to sell and install its own equipment for the price outlined in Schedule A. The shipyard conversion contract was written to allow Winsmore the option of buying and installing the electronic gear on an "owner-supplied" basis, if Winsmore so wished.

The sonar and depth recorder required hull fittings and retractable transducers. Therefore, it was necessary to install these units during the initial phase of the six-month overhaul period. During this period the vessel would be in dry dock. Any delay in mounting these units as scheduled would prove costly. If nonreceipt of the units did take place, work would either have to be suspended until the units arrived, or the vessel would have to be placed in dry dock a second time.

Another problem facing Mr. Rice was the need for a precise, high-quality installation. The performance and radiation characteristics of each unit were such that electronic interference problems would ensue if the units were not properly fitted and shielded.

The nature of the research work to be performed by *Joie* entailed long cruises of a year or more in waters far from the United States. With highly sophisticated electronic gear, failures are inevitable. Therefore, having the capability to effectuate timely repairs was a must. Winsmore's cost in operating expenses alone to keep *Joie* "on station" was estimated to be $3,000 per day.

While Dave Rice was considering possible solutions to these problems, he received a telephone call from the superintendent of the shipyard where *Joie* was to be converted. The superintendent offered to provide, install, and

Schedule A

Item	Unit price	Installation cost
Radar	$ 51,374	$14,400
Sonar	43,126	12,238
Gyroscope	19,756	6,444
Radio gear	18,012	3,536
Loran	10,800	1,978
Depth recorder	11,390	4,952
Portable recorder	4,856	—
Subtotal	$159,314	$43,548
Spares 10%	15,930	—
Total	$175,244	$43,548

Factory warranties	
Radar	6 months parts only
Sonar	3 months parts and labor
Gyroscope	9 months parts
Radio gear	9 months parts
Loran	2 months parts
Depth recorder	3 months parts
Portable recorder	3 months replacement of unit

warrant for six months all of the units listed in Schedule A, including $15,930 of spare parts, for a package price of $290,000.

1 What action should Dave Rice take?
2 How can the value of service be evaluated?
3 In situations such as this, who should select the equipment, the scientists or purchasing?

175.248
43.548
15.930
234.726
,80 - 000
4,4,726

Selected Bibliography

GENERAL PURCHASING AND MATERIALS REFERENCES

Aljian, George W. (ed.): *Purchasing Handbook,* 3d ed., McGraw-Hill Book Company, New York, 1973.

Ammer, Dean S.: *Materials Management,* 3d ed., Richard D. Irwin, Inc., Homewood, Ill., 1974.

Bailey, Peter, and David Farmer: *Managing Materials in Industry,* Gower Press Ltd., London, England, 1972.

———: *Purchasing Principles and Techniques,* Sir Isaac Pitman and Sons Ltd. (for the British Institute of Purchasing and Supply), London, England, 1968.

England, Wilbur. B., and Michiel R. Leenders: *Purchasing and Materials Management,* 6th ed., Richard D. Irwin, Inc., Homewood, Ill., 1975.

Ericsson, Dag: *Materials Administration,* McGraw-Hill Book Company, London, England. English trans. 1974, Swedish ed. 1971.

Heinritz, Stuart F., and P. V. Farrell: *Purchasing Principles and Applications,* 5th ed., Prentice-Hall, Inc., Englewood Cliffs, N.J., 1971.

McElhinney, Paul T., and R. I. Cook: *The Logistics of Materials Management: Readings in Modern Purchasing,* Houghton Mifflin Company, Boston, 1969.

Murray, John E., Jr.: *Purchasing and the Law,* Purchasing Management Association, Pittsburgh, Pa., 1973.

National Association of Purchasing Management: *Guide to Purchasing,* NAPM, New York, 1965, plus quarterly loose-leaf supplements.

Pingeot, Michel: *Purchase Negotiation,* IFE, Paris, France, 1972.

Pooler, Victor H., Jr.: *The Purchasing Man and His Job,* American Management Association, New York, 1964.

Westing, J. H., I. V. Fine, and G. J. Zenz: *Purchasing Management: Materials in Motion,* 3rd ed., John Wiley & Sons, Inc., New York, 1969.

SELECTED TOPICAL REFERENCES

Ammer, Dean S.: *Purchasing and Materials Management for Health Care Institutions,* D. C. Heath and Company, Lexington, Mass., 1975.

Anthony, Robert N.: *Management Accounting,* Richard D. Irwin, Inc., Homewood, Ill., 1969.

Bach, George Leland: *Economics—An Introduction to Analysis and Policy,* 7th ed., Prentice-Hall, Inc., Englewood Cliffs, N.J., 1971.

Baer, S. B., and O. G. Saxon: *Commodity Exchanges and Futures Trading,* Harper and Brothers, New York, 1949.

Silk, Leonard S., and M. Louise Curley: *A Primer on Business Forecasting,* Random House, Inc., New York, 1970.

Spurr, W. A., and C. P. Bonini: *Statistical Analysis for Business Decisions,* Richard D. Irwin, Inc., Homewood, Ill., 1967, chaps. 18–24.

Armed Services Procurement Regulations (ASPR): U.S. Superintendent of Documents, Washington, D.C., published annually.

McDonald, Paul R.: *Government Prime Contracts and Subcontracts,* Procurement Associates, Glendora, Calif., revised annually.

Buffa, E. S., and W. H. Taubert: *Production—Inventory Systems; Planning and Control,* Richard D. Irwin, Inc., Homewood, Ill., 1972.

Orlicky, Joseph: *Material Requirements Planning,* McGraw-Hill Book Company, New York, 1975.

Drucker, Peter F.: *Managing for Results,* Harper & Row, Publishers, Inc., New York, 1964.

McGregor, D.: *The Human Side of Enterprise,* McGraw-Hill Book Company, New York, 1960.

Newman, W. H., C. E. Summer, and W. E. Kirby: *The Process of Management: Concepts, Behavior and Practice,* 3d ed., Prentice-Hall, Inc., Englewood Cliffs, N.J., 1971.

Grant, Eugene L., and R. S. Leavenworth: *Statistical Quality Control,* 4th ed., McGraw-Hill Book Company, New York, 1971.

Lochlin, D. P.: *Economics of Transportation,* 7th ed., Richard D. Irwin, Inc., Homewood, Ill., 1971.

National Motor Freight Classification, American Trucking Association, Washington, D.C., published annually.
Uniform Freight Classification, Tariff Publishing Office, Chicago, published periodically.

Miles, Lawrence D.: *Techniques of Value Analysis and Engineering,* McGraw-Hill Book Company, New York, 1961.
Purchasing, annual Value Analysis Issue, published each May.

Appendix

678

TABLE A   Present Value of $1

Years hence	1%	2%	4%	6%	8%	10%	12%	14%	15%	16%	18%	20%	22%	24%	25%	26%	28%	30%	35%	40%	45%	50%
1	0.990	0.980	0.962	0.943	0.926	0.909	0.893	0.877	0.870	0.862	0.847	0.833	0.820	0.806	0.800	0.794	0.781	0.769	0.741	0.714	0.690	0.667
2	0.980	0.961	0.925	0.890	0.857	0.826	0.797	0.769	0.756	0.743	0.718	0.694	0.672	0.650	0.640	0.630	0.610	0.592	0.549	0.510	0.476	0.444
3	0.971	0.942	0.889	0.840	0.794	0.751	0.712	0.675	0.658	0.641	0.609	0.579	0.551	0.524	0.512	0.500	0.477	0.455	0.406	0.364	0.328	0.296
4	0.961	0.924	0.855	0.792	0.735	0.683	0.636	0.592	0.572	0.552	0.516	0.482	0.451	0.423	0.410	0.397	0.373	0.350	0.301	0.260	0.226	0.198
5	0.951	0.906	0.822	0.747	0.681	0.621	0.567	0.519	0.497	0.476	0.437	0.402	0.370	0.341	0.328	0.315	0.291	0.269	0.223	0.186	0.156	0.132
6	0.942	0.888	0.790	0.705	0.630	0.564	0.507	0.456	0.432	0.410	0.370	0.335	0.303	0.275	0.262	0.250	0.227	0.207	0.165	0.133	0.108	0.088
7	0.933	0.871	0.760	0.665	0.583	0.513	0.452	0.400	0.376	0.354	0.314	0.279	0.249	0.222	0.210	0.198	0.178	0.159	0.122	0.095	0.074	0.059
8	0.923	0.853	0.731	0.627	0.540	0.467	0.404	0.351	0.327	0.305	0.266	0.233	0.204	0.179	0.168	0.157	0.139	0.123	0.091	0.068	0.051	0.039
9	0.914	0.837	0.703	0.592	0.500	0.424	0.361	0.308	0.284	0.263	0.225	0.194	0.167	0.144	0.134	0.125	0.108	0.094	0.067	0.048	0.035	0.026
10	0.905	0.820	0.676	0.558	0.463	0.386	0.322	0.270	0.247	0.227	0.191	0.162	0.137	0.116	0.107	0.099	0.085	0.073	0.050	0.035	0.024	0.017
11	0.896	0.804	0.650	0.527	0.429	0.350	0.287	0.237	0.215	0.195	0.162	0.135	0.112	0.094	0.086	0.079	0.066	0.056	0.037	0.025	0.017	0.012
12	0.887	0.788	0.625	0.497	0.397	0.319	0.257	0.208	0.187	0.168	0.137	0.112	0.092	0.076	0.069	0.062	0.052	0.043	0.027	0.018	0.012	0.008
13	0.879	0.773	0.601	0.469	0.368	0.290	0.229	0.182	0.163	0.145	0.116	0.093	0.075	0.061	0.055	0.050	0.040	0.033	0.020	0.013	0.008	0.005
14	0.870	0.758	0.577	0.442	0.340	0.263	0.205	0.160	0.141	0.125	0.099	0.078	0.062	0.049	0.044	0.039	0.032	0.025	0.015	0.009	0.006	0.003
15	0.861	0.743	0.555	0.417	0.315	0.239	0.183	0.140	0.123	0.108	0.084	0.065	0.051	0.040	0.035	0.031	0.025	0.020	0.011	0.006	0.004	0.002
16	0.853	0.728	0.534	0.394	0.292	0.218	0.163	0.123	0.107	0.093	0.071	0.054	0.042	0.032	0.028	0.025	0.019	0.015	0.008	0.005	0.003	0.002
17	0.844	0.714	0.513	0.371	0.270	0.198	0.146	0.108	0.093	0.080	0.060	0.045	0.034	0.026	0.023	0.020	0.015	0.012	0.006	0.003	0.002	0.001
18	0.836	0.700	0.494	0.350	0.250	0.180	0.130	0.095	0.081	0.069	0.051	0.038	0.028	0.021	0.018	0.016	0.012	0.009	0.005	0.002	0.001	0.001
19	0.828	0.686	0.475	0.331	0.232	0.164	0.116	0.083	0.070	0.060	0.043	0.031	0.023	0.017	0.014	0.012	0.009	0.007	0.003	0.002	0.001	0.001
20	0.820	0.673	0.456	0.312	0.215	0.149	0.104	0.073	0.061	0.051	0.037	0.026	0.019	0.014	0.012	0.010	0.007	0.005	0.002	0.001	0.001	
21	0.811	0.660	0.439	0.294	0.199	0.135	0.093	0.064	0.053	0.044	0.031	0.022	0.015	0.011	0.009	0.008	0.006	0.004	0.002	0.001		
22	0.803	0.647	0.422	0.278	0.184	0.123	0.083	0.056	0.046	0.038	0.026	0.018	0.013	0.009	0.007	0.006	0.004	0.003	0.001	0.001		
23	0.795	0.634	0.406	0.262	0.170	0.112	0.074	0.049	0.040	0.033	0.022	0.015	0.010	0.007	0.006	0.005	0.003	0.002	0.001			
24	0.788	0.622	0.390	0.247	0.158	0.102	0.066	0.043	0.035	0.028	0.019	0.013	0.008	0.006	0.005	0.004	0.003	0.002	0.001			
25	0.780	0.610	0.375	0.233	0.146	0.092	0.059	0.038	0.030	0.024	0.016	0.010	0.007	0.005	0.004	0.003	0.002	0.001	0.001			
26	0.772	0.598	0.361	0.220	0.135	0.084	0.053	0.033	0.026	0.021	0.014	0.009	0.006	0.004	0.003	0.002	0.002	0.001				
27	0.764	0.586	0.347	0.207	0.125	0.076	0.047	0.029	0.023	0.018	0.011	0.007	0.005	0.003	0.002	0.002	0.001	0.001				
28	0.757	0.574	0.333	0.196	0.116	0.069	0.042	0.026	0.020	0.016	0.010	0.006	0.004	0.002	0.002	0.002	0.001	0.001				
29	0.749	0.563	0.321	0.185	0.107	0.063	0.037	0.022	0.017	0.014	0.008	0.005	0.003	0.002	0.002	0.001	0.001					
30	0.742	0.552	0.308	0.174	0.099	0.057	0.033	0.020	0.015	0.012	0.007	0.004	0.003	0.002	0.001	0.001	0.001					
40	0.672	0.453	0.208	0.097	0.046	0.022	0.011	0.005	0.004	0.003	0.001	0.001										
50	0.608	0.372	0.141	0.054	0.021	0.009	0.003	0.001	0.001	0.001												

Source: *Management Accounting,* Richard D. Irwin, Inc., Homewood, Ill., 1960.   Reproduced by Permission from Robert N. Anthony.

TABLE B   Present Value of $1 Received Annually for N Years

Years (N)	1%	2%	4%	6%	8%	10%	12%	14%	15%	16%	18%	20%	22%	24%	25%	26%	28%	30%	35%	40%	45%	50%
1	0.990	0.980	0.962	0.943	0.926	0.909	0.893	0.877	0.870	0.862	0.847	0.833	0.820	0.806	0.800	0.794	0.781	0.769	0.741	0.714	0.690	0.667
2	1.970	1.942	1.886	1.833	1.783	1.736	1.690	1.647	1.626	1.605	1.566	1.528	1.492	1.457	1.440	1.424	1.392	1.361	1.289	1.224	1.165	1.111
3	2.941	2.884	2.775	2.673	2.577	2.487	2.402	2.322	2.283	2.246	2.174	2.106	2.042	1.981	1.952	1.923	1.868	1.816	1.696	1.589	1.493	1.407
4	3.902	3.808	3.630	3.465	3.312	3.170	3.037	2.914	2.855	2.798	2.690	2.589	2.494	2.404	2.362	2.320	2.241	2.166	1.997	1.849	1.720	1.605
5	4.853	4.713	4.452	4.212	3.993	3.791	3.605	3.433	3.352	3.274	3.127	2.991	2.864	2.745	2.689	2.635	2.532	2.436	2.220	2.035	1.876	1.737
6	5.795	5.601	5.242	4.917	4.623	4.355	4.111	3.889	3.784	3.685	3.498	3.326	3.167	3.020	2.951	2.885	2.759	2.643	2.385	2.168	1.983	1.824
7	6.728	6.472	6.002	5.582	5.206	4.868	4.564	4.288	4.160	4.039	3.812	3.605	3.416	3.242	3.161	3.083	2.937	2.802	2.508	2.263	2.057	1.883
8	7.652	7.325	6.733	6.210	5.747	5.335	4.968	4.639	4.487	4.344	4.078	3.837	3.619	3.421	3.329	3.241	3.076	2.925	2.598	2.331	2.108	1.922
9	8.566	8.162	7.435	6.802	6.247	5.759	5.328	4.946	4.772	4.607	4.303	4.031	3.786	3.566	3.463	3.366	3.184	3.019	2.665	2.379	2.144	1.948
10	9.471	8.983	8.111	7.360	6.710	6.145	5.650	5.216	5.019	4.833	4.494	4.192	3.923	3.682	3.571	3.465	3.269	3.092	2.715	2.414	2.168	1.965
11	10.368	9.787	8.760	7.887	7.139	6.495	5.988	5.453	5.234	5.029	4.656	4.327	4.035	3.776	3.656	3.544	3.335	3.147	2.752	2.438	2.185	1.977
12	11.255	10.575	9.385	8.384	7.536	6.814	6.194	5.660	5.421	5.197	4.793	4.439	4.127	3.851	3.725	3.606	3.387	3.190	2.779	2.456	2.196	1.985
13	12.134	11.343	9.986	8.853	7.904	7.103	6.424	5.842	5.583	5.342	4.910	4.533	4.203	3.912	3.780	3.656	3.427	3.223	2.799	2.468	2.204	1.990
14	13.004	12.106	10.563	9.295	8.244	7.367	6.628	6.002	5.724	5.468	5.008	4.611	4.265	3.962	3.824	3.695	3.459	3.249	2.814	2.477	2.210	1.993
15	13.865	12.849	11.118	9.712	8.559	7.606	6.811	6.142	5.847	5.575	5.092	4.675	4.315	4.001	3.859	3.726	3.483	3.268	2.825	2.484	2.214	1.995
16	14.718	13.578	11.652	10.106	8.851	7.824	6.974	6.265	5.954	5.669	5.162	4.730	4.357	4.033	3.887	3.751	3.503	3.283	2.834	2.489	2.216	1.997
17	15.562	14.292	12.166	10.477	9.122	8.022	7.120	6.373	6.047	5.749	5.222	4.775	4.391	4.059	3.910	3.771	3.518	3.295	2.840	2.492	2.218	1.998
18	16.398	14.992	12.659	10.828	9.372	8.201	7.250	6.467	6.128	5.818	5.273	4.812	4.419	4.080	3.928	3.786	3.529	3.304	2.844	2.494	2.219	1.999
19	17.226	15.678	13.134	11.158	9.604	8.365	7.366	6.550	6.198	5.877	5.316	4.844	4.442	4.097	3.942	3.799	3.539	3.311	2.848	2.496	2.220	1.999
20	18.046	16.351	13.590	11.470	9.818	8.514	7.469	6.623	6.259	5.929	5.353	4.870	4.460	4.110	3.954	3.808	3.546	3.316	2.850	2.497	2.221	1.999
21	18.857	17.011	14.029	11.764	10.017	8.649	7.562	6.687	6.312	5.973	5.384	4.891	4.476	4.121	3.963	3.816	3.551	3.320	2.852	2.498	2.221	2.000
22	19.660	17.658	14.451	12.042	10.201	8.772	7.645	6.743	6.359	6.011	5.410	4.909	4.488	4.130	3.970	3.822	3.556	3.323	2.853	2.498	2.222	2.000
23	20.456	18.292	14.857	12.303	10.371	8.883	7.718	6.792	6.399	6.044	5.432	4.925	4.499	4.137	3.976	3.827	3.559	3.325	2.854	2.499	2.222	2.000
24	21.243	18.914	15.247	12.550	10.529	8.985	7.784	6.835	6.434	6.073	5.451	4.937	4.507	4.143	3.981	3.831	3.562	3.327	2.855	2.499	2.222	2.000
25	22.023	19.523	15.622	12.783	10.675	9.077	7.843	6.873	6.464	6.097	5.467	4.948	4.514	4.147	3.985	3.834	3.564	3.329	2.856	2.499	2.222	2.000
26	22.795	20.121	15.983	13.003	10.810	9.161	7.896	6.906	6.491	6.118	5.480	4.956	4.520	4.151	3.988	3.837	3.566	3.330	2.856	2.500	2.222	2.000
27	23.560	20.707	16.330	13.211	10.935	9.237	7.943	6.935	6.514	6.136	5.492	4.964	4.524	4.154	3.990	3.839	3.567	3.331	2.856	2.500	2.222	2.000
28	24.316	21.281	16.663	13.406	11.051	9.307	7.984	6.961	6.534	6.152	5.502	4.970	4.528	4.157	3.992	3.840	3.568	3.331	2.857	2.500	2.222	2.000
29	25.066	21.844	16.984	13.591	11.158	9.370	8.022	6.983	6.551	6.166	5.510	4.975	4.531	4.159	3.994	3.841	3.569	3.332	2.857	2.500	2.222	2.000
30	25.808	22.396	17.292	13.765	11.258	9.427	8.055	7.003	6.566	6.177	5.517	4.979	4.534	4.160	3.995	3.842	3.569	3.332	2.857	2.500	2.222	2.000
40	32.835	27.355	19.793	15.046	11.925	9.779	8.244	7.105	6.642	6.234	5.548	4.997	4.544	4.166	3.999	3.846	3.571	3.333	2.857	2.500	2.222	2.000
50	39.196	31.424	21.482	15.762	12.234	9.915	8.304	7.133	6.661	6.246	5.554	4.999	4.545	4.167	4.000	3.846	3.571	3.333	2.857	2.500	2.222	2.000

Source: Management Accounting. Richard D. Irwin, Inc., Homewood, Ill., 1960. Reproduced by permission from Robert N. Anthony.

TABLE C Present Value of $1/12 Received Monthly for N Years

Years (N)	1%	2%	4%	6%	8%	10%	12%	14%	15%	16%	18%	20%	22%	24%	25%	26%	28%	30%	35%	40%	45%	50%
1	0.995	0.989	0.979	0.969	0.959	0.950	0.941	0.932	0.928	0.924	0.915	0.907	0.899	0.892	0.888	0.884	0.877	0.870	0.853	0.837	0.822	0.808
2	1.979	1.959	1.920	1.883	1.848	1.814	1.781	1.750	1.735	1.720	1.691	1.663	1.637	1.611	1.598	1.586	1.562	1.539	1.485	1.435	1.390	1.347
3	2.954	2.910	2.826	2.746	2.670	2.599	2.531	2.467	2.436	2.406	2.348	2.293	2.241	2.191	2.167	2.143	2.098	2.054	1.953	1.863	1.781	1.706
4	3.920	3.843	3.696	3.559	3.432	3.313	3.201	3.096	3.046	2.998	2.905	2.818	2.736	2.658	2.621	2.585	2.516	2.450	2.300	2.168	2.050	1.946
5	4.876	4.757	4.533	4.327	4.137	3.962	3.799	3.648	3.577	3.508	3.377	3.256	3.142	3.036	2.985	2.936	2.842	2.755	2.557	2.386	2.236	2.106
6	5.822	5.653	5.338	5.051	4.790	4.551	4.333	4.132	4.038	3.948	3.778	3.620	3.475	3.340	3.276	3.214	3.098	2.989	2.747	2.541	2.365	2.212
7	6.759	6.531	6.111	5.734	5.395	5.088	4.810	4.557	4.439	4.327	4.117	3.924	3.748	3.585	3.509	3.435	3.297	3.169	2.888	2.653	2.453	2.283
8	7.687	7.392	6.855	6.379	5.954	5.575	5.235	4.929	4.788	4.654	4.404	4.177	3.971	3.783	3.695	3.611	3.453	3.308	2.992	2.732	2.514	2.330
9	8.605	8.237	7.571	6.987	6.473	6.018	5.615	5.256	5.091	4.935	4.647	4.388	4.154	3.942	3.844	3.750	3.575	3.414	3.070	2.789	2.556	2.362
10	9.515	9.065	8.259	7.560	6.953	6.421	5.955	5.543	5.355	5.178	4.854	4.564	4.305	4.071	3.963	3.860	3.670	3.497	3.127	2.829	2.585	2.383
11	10.415	9.876	8.920	8.101	7.397	6.788	6.258	5.794	5.584	5.388	5.029	4.711	4.428	4.175	4.058	3.948	3.744	3.560	3.169	2.858	2.605	2.397
12	11.307	10.672	9.556	8.612	7.890	7.121	6.528	6.015	5.784	5.568	5.177	4.833	4.529	4.259	4.135	4.018	3.802	3.608	3.201	2.879	2.619	2.406
13	12.189	11.452	10.167	9.094	8.190	7.423	6.770	6.208	5.957	5.724	5.302	4.935	4.611	4.326	4.196	4.073	3.847	3.646	3.224	2.894	2.629	2.412
14	13.063	12.217	10.755	9.548	8.542	7.699	6.985	6.378	6.108	5.858	5.409	5.019	4.679	4.380	4.245	4.117	3.883	3.674	3.241	2.904	2.635	2.417
15	13.928	12.967	11.321	9.977	8.869	7.949	7.178	6.527	6.239	5.973	5.499	5.090	4.735	4.424	4.284	4.152	3.911	3.696	3.254	2.912	2.640	2.419
16	14.785	13.702	11.864	10.381	9.171	8.176	7.350	6.658	6.353	6.073	5.576	5.149	4.780	4.460	4.315	4.179	3.932	3.713	3.264	2.917	2.643	2.421
17	15.633	14.422	12.387	10.762	9.451	8.383	7.503	6.772	6.452	6.159	5.640	5.198	4.818	4.488	4.340	4.201	3.949	3.726	3.271	2.921	2.645	2.422
18	16.473	15.129	12.890	11.122	9.711	8.571	7.640	6.873	6.539	6.233	5.695	5.239	4.848	4.511	4.360	4.218	3.962	3.736	3.276	2.924	2.647	2.423
19	17.305	15.822	13.373	11.462	9.951	8.742	7.763	6.961	6.614	6.297	5.742	5.273	4.873	4.530	4.376	4.232	3.973	3.744	3.280	2.926	2.648	2.424
20	18.128	16.501	13.838	11.782	10.173	8.897	7.872	7.038	6.679	6.352	5.781	5.301	4.894	4.545	4.389	4.243	3.981	3.750	3.283	2.927	2.648	2.424
21	18.943	17.167	14.285	12.084	10.379	9.038	7.969	7.106	6.735	6.399	5.815	5.325	4.911	4.557	4.399	4.252	3.987	3.755	3.285	2.928	2.649	2.424
22	19.750	17.819	14.714	12.369	10.570	9.167	8.056	7.165	6.785	6.440	5.843	5.345	4.925	4.567	4.407	4.259	3.992	3.758	3.286	2.929	2.649	2.425
23	20.549	18.459	15.127	12.638	10.746	9.283	8.134	7.218	6.828	6.476	5.867	5.361	4.936	4.574	4.414	4.264	3.996	3.761	3.287	2.929	2.649	2.425
24	21.341	19.087	15.525	12.892	10.909	9.389	8.204	7.263	6.865	6.506	5.887	5.375	4.945	4.581	4.419	4.269	3.999	3.763	3.288	2.930	2.650	2.425
25	22.124	19.702	15.906	13.131	11.061	9.486	8.266	7.304	6.897	6.532	5.904	5.386	4.953	4.586	4.423	4.272	4.001	3.765	3.289	2.930	2.650	2.425
26	22.899	20.305	16.274	13.357	11.201	9.574	8.321	7.339	6.926	6.555	5.919	5.396	4.959	4.590	4.426	4.275	4.003	3.766	3.289	2.930	2.650	2.425
27	23.667	20.896	16.627	13.570	11.331	9.653	8.370	7.370	6.950	6.574	5.931	5.404	4.964	4.593	4.429	4.277	4.004	3.767	3.290	2.930	2.650	2.425
28	24.428	21.476	16.966	13.771	11.451	9.726	8.415	7.397	6.971	6.591	5.942	5.410	4.968	4.596	4.431	4.279	4.005	3.768	3.290	2.930	2.650	2.425
29	25.180	22.044	17.293	13.961	11.562	9.792	8.454	7.421	6.990	6.606	5.951	5.416	4.972	4.598	4.433	4.280	4.006	3.768	3.290	2.930	2.650	2.425
30	25.926	22.601	17.607	14.139	11.665	9.852	8.489	7.441	7.006	6.618	5.958	5.420	4.975	4.600	4.434	4.281	4.007	3.769	3.290	2.930	2.650	2.425
40	32.985	27.605	20.153	15.456	12.356	10.220	8.688	7.550	7.087	6.678	5.992	5.440	4.986	4.606	4.439	4.285	4.009	3.770	3.291	2.931	2.650	2.425
50	39.375	31.711	21.873	16.191	12.676	10.361	8.752	7.580	7.107	6.692	5.999	5.443	4.987	4.607	4.440	4.285	4.009	3.770	3.291	2.931	2.650	2.425

Note: It is assumed that monthly increments earn simple interest until the end of each year and that entire amount is discounted annually.

Formula: $\dfrac{1 - (1 + i)^{-n}}{12[(1 + i)^{1/12} - 1]}$

Source: Management Accounting, Richard D. Irwin, Inc. Homewood, Ill., 1960. Reproduced by permission from Robert N. Anthony.

Indexes

Name Index

Case Index

Subject Index